The Cricketer Who's Who 2014

Foreword by
PAUL COLLINGWOOD

Editor
JO HARMAN

Compiled by
JAMES BROWNE, HENRY COWEN, PHIL EDWARDS,
VITHUSHAN EHANTHARAJAH, ED KEMP, JOEL LAMY & PHIL WALKER

Design
JOE PROVIS & ROB WHITEHOUSE

The
Cricketers'
Who's Who
2014

This edition first published in the UK by All Out Cricket Ltd

© All Out Cricket Ltd 2014
www.alloutcricket.com

ISBN: 978-0-85719-403-9

Editor: *Jo Harman*
Research and editorial: *James Browne, Henry Cowen, Phil Edwards,*
Vithushan Ehantharajah, Ed Kemp, Joel Lamy, Phil Walker
Design: *Joe Provis, Rob Whitehouse*
Images: *Getty Images unless stated*
Print: *Jellyfish Print Solutions*

Acknowledgements
The publishers would like to thank the county clubs, the Professional Cricketers'
Association and the players for their assistance in helping to put together this book.
Additional information has been gathered from espncricinfo.com and cricketarchive.com.

CONTENTS

The **Cricketers'** Who's Who *2014*

Openers

FOREWORD

by Paul Collingwood

Welcome to the 2014 edition of the Cricketers' Who's Who. I'm thrilled to write the foreword to a publication that has been part of the cricketing summer for so many years now.

It's great that fans have the opportunity to learn a bit more about what makes county cricketers tick, both on and off the field, and it's always a good laugh seeing what my teammates have written – there's plenty of dressing room banter when the new edition arrives!

I still get butterflies in my stomach ahead of a new season, even as I enter my 19th campaign as a county cricketer. Last year I had the honour of captaining Durham to their third County Championship title and I can assure you that success ranks right up there with anything else I've achieved in my career.

When I retired from England duty after the 2010/11 Ashes win I seriously considered hanging up my boots altogether. I gave myself some time to get away from the game for a while and had a long, hard think about it. Having played at such a high intensity of international cricket for such a long period of time, I thought it might be hard to go back to county cricket. But I eventually decided I wanted to give something back to Durham for the 10 years or so I was away playing with England, and also to give something back to county cricket as a whole. It was, after all, my formative years in county cricket that equipped me with the game and the mentality to succeed at the top level.

I'm so glad that I did decide to continue playing. County cricket continues to thrive and to be part of that and to lead a young, homegrown side to the Championship title was immensely satisfying. Our match against Yorkshire at Scarborough towards the end of last season, which went a long way to deciding the destination of the title, was honestly like playing in a Test match. It was as close to Test level as anything I've ever experienced in domestic cricket and, in fact, better than some of the cricket I'd played for England. I knew once we won that game that we had the characters in the dressing room to go on and win the Championship.

Last year was unbelievable, it really was. For the club to come through the adversity that we did in terms of a tricky financial situation, Geoff Cook going down ill and the fact that we were missing a lot of major players throughout the season was an incredible achievement. To see the youngsters stick their hands up and produce match-winning spells and match-winning innings was actually unbelievable at times. Academy lads came in and guys who

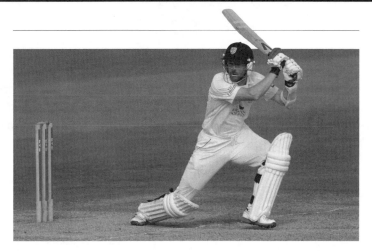

weren't household names were turning in incredible performances. I didn't see it coming, if I'm honest. But it just proves that if you have the belief in your ability and you produce the right environment in the dressing room, then anything can be achieved.

The upcoming season promises to be a particularly exciting one, with the visits of India and Sri Lanka, a fiercely competitive County Championship and two revamped limited-overs competitions to look forward to.

While England's Ashes whitewash over the winter was obviously hugely disappointing, it does add an extra bit of spice to the start of the county season. For the first time in a while there are several spots in the Test team up for grabs and there will be players up and down the country who fancy their chances of taking one of them if they can hit the ground running in 2014. It will be fascinating to see who can lay down an early signal of intent and force their way into the series against Sri Lanka and India – two opponents who both pose their own unique challenges.

Enjoy the summer. We've got a good one in store.

Paul Collingwood
Durham captain and 2013 County Championship winner

by Jo Harman

Welcome to The Cricketers' Who's Who 2014, the 35th edition of this publication. Many of you will have spent the off-season deprived of sleep, trying to come to terms with England's Ashes capitulation, but after a winter to forget we now have a tantalising summer to look forward to.

Last year's domestic campaign threw up more than its fair share of surprises, with Durham walking away with the County Championship title, Northamptonshire bouncing back from a miserable 2012 to win the Friends Life t20 as well as sealing promotion to the top tier of the Championship, and Nottinghamshire winning their first limited-overs silverware for 22 years by lifting the Yorkshire Bank 40. County cricket remains gloriously unpredictable and I certainly won't be making any pre-season predictions after tipping Durham for the drop in last year's pre-season issue of All Out Cricket magazine. I still haven't lived that one down…

On the international front, a torturous winter down under has left the England team in flux. But this brings its own excitement. Whereas for the last four or five years there have been perhaps one or two places up for grabs in England's Test side, this time round there are as many as five or six. Players across the country know that a few stand-out early season performances could see them walking out at Lord's on June 12 for the first Test of the summer against Sri Lanka. Prospective internationals will be under the microscope and that can only be a good thing for the profile of county cricket and its exposure to a wider audience.

I'd like to thank all of the players who took the time to fill out this year's questionnaire, as well as the clubs who helped facilitate this. Without their contribution this book wouldn't be possible. We were entertained as ever by the responses we received. For instance, who knew that Ashes-winning seamer Kate Cross was told at 15 years old that she'd be blind by the age of 18 due to a rare eye condition? Or that Joe Root has been spending his downtime learning to play the ukulele? It's heartening that so many of the players still appreciate the value of sharing a little bit of themselves with the supporters of county cricket.

We restored an old favourite to this year's questionnaire, asking players to tell us which rule or regulation they would change if they were in charge. We didn't print all the suggestions (neither one hand-one bounce nor first-ball grace seemed viable options!) but it was noticeable the number of players who feel that limited-overs cricket is now weighted too heavily in favour of the batsmen. And, tellingly, that feedback didn't just come from bowlers. The switch back from 40-over cricket to 50 overs for this year's domestic one-day competition was also an area of concern, with several players saying they felt 40 overs was more appealing for players and supporters alike.

For the past three years we've asked the players to tell us who they currently rate as the best player on the county circuit. In 2012 and 2013 Marcus Trescothick was the comfortable winner but this year has seen votes spread much more widely and evenly. Worcestershire's Moeen Ali takes it by a nose this time, but as you leaf through these pages you'll see that Durham seamer Graham Onions and Middlesex opener Sam Robson weren't too far behind after stellar campaigns in 2013.

County cricket has bid a fond farewell to Scotland, the Netherlands and the Unicorns this year, with the restructured Royal London One-Day Cup restricted to the 18 first-class counties. As a result you'll no longer find personal profiles for players of those teams in these pages, but the England Women's team make their second appearance in this publication, and many thanks to Charlotte Edwards and her squad for taking on the questionnaire with such enthusiasm. For several of the players we could have filled their profile page several times over!

Based on feedback from last year, you'll notice that we've added a transfers page (page 89) for the new edition, helping you get up to speed on the comings and goings at each county during the off-season. As ever, we'd appreciate any feedback on this year's edition so please drop me a line at cwweditor@alloutcricket.co.uk with any comments.

Enjoy the season.

Jo Harman
March 24, 2014

KEY

R – 1,000 or more first-class runs in an English season (the number next to 'R' denotes how many times the player has achieved this feat)

W – 50 or more first-class wickets in an English season (the number next to 'W' denotes how many times the player has achieved this feat)

MVP – Denotes a player's presence in the top 100 places of the 2013 Overall FTI MVP Rankings (the number next to 'MVP' denotes the player's specific placing)

---

* – Not out innings (e.g. 137*)

(s) – A competition has been shared between two or more winners

CB40 – Clydesdale Bank 40 (English domestic 40-over competition, 2010-2012)

CC1/CC2 – County Championship Division One/County Championship Division Two

FL t20 – Friends Life t20 (English domestic 20-over competition, 2010-2013)

LB – Leg-break bowler

LF – Left-arm fast bowler

LFM – Left-arm fast-medium bowler

LHB – Left-hand batsman

LM – Left-arm medium bowler

LMF – Left-arm medium-fast bowler

MCCU – Marylebone Cricket Club University

NWT20 – NatWest T20 Blast (English domestic 20-over competition, 2014)

OB – Off-break bowler

ODI – One-Day International

RF – Right-arm fast bowler

RFM – Right-arm fast-medium bowler

RHB – Right-hand batsman

RL50 – Royal London One-Day Cup (English domestic 50-over competition, 2014)

RM – Right-arm medium bowler

RMF – Right-arm medium-fast bowler

SLA – Slow left-arm orthodox bowler

SLC – Slow left-arm Chinaman bowler

T20/T20I – Twenty20/Twenty20 International

UCCE – University Centre of Cricketing Excellence

WK – Wicketkeeper

YB40 – Yorkshire Bank 40 (English domestic 40-over competition, 2013)

NOTES: The statistics given for a player's best batting and best bowling performance are limited to first-class cricket. If a field within a player's career statistics is left blank then the record for that particular statistic is incomplete, e.g. there is no record for how many balls a player has faced in first-class cricket. An '-' indicates that a particular statistic is inapplicable, e.g. a player has never bowled a ball in first-class cricket. All stats correct as of March 10, 2014

The
Teams

FORMED: 1870
HOME GROUND: The 3aaa County Ground, Derby
ONE-DAY NAME: Derbyshire Falcons
CAPTAIN: Wayne Madsen
2013 RESULTS: CC1: 8/9; YB40: 6/7 in Group B; FL t20: 5/6 in North Division
HONOURS: Championship: 1936; Gillette/NatWest/C&G/FP Trophy: 1981; Benson & Hedges Cup: 1993; Sunday League: 1990

THE LOWDOWN

Winless in their first 10 Championship games last year and unable to find solace in the shorter forms of the game, Derbyshire struggled from the off to retain their Division One status. Despite this, they came close to pulling off an incredible escape when, from game 13, they won three in four, against Sussex, Middlesex and fellow strugglers Somerset. Captain Wayne Madsen, disappointed with relegation a year after promotion, would have been buoyed by his form in 2013, becoming the first player of the season to pass 1,000 runs and earning himself the Cricket Writers' Club's Championship Player of the Year. He signed on for another three years at Derby last November and will be looking for more support from his fellow batsmen in 2014. However, Karl Krikken will not be continuing as head coach, after deciding against reapplying for his job after a drop to Division Two triggered a restructuring of the management set-up.

HEAD COACH: GRAEME WELCH

Following the departures of Krikken and batting coach Dave Houghton, the former Warwickshire assistant coach comes in at the top of a new structure at the club. As assistant coach at Edgbaston, Welch was credited for the development of the Warwickshire bowling attack, particularly Chris Wright and Keith Barker who led the club's wicket-taking charts as they finished 2012 as county champions. Welch is familiar with the set-up at Derby, having spent five seasons there at the end of his playing career and captaining the side in 2006 before moving to Essex for his first coaching role.

Batting

	Mat	Inns	NO	Runs	HS	Ave	SR	100	50	4s	6s
WL Madsen	16	30	2	1221	152	43.60	49.27	3	8	161	1
S Chanderpaul	15	27	4	884	129	38.43	47.88	1	7	108	2
CF Hughes	11	20	1	612	270*	32.21	55.48	1	2	80	7
RM Johnson	12	21	1	526	72	26.30	46.26	0	4	72	2
PM Borrington	4	8	0	209	75	26.12	32.96	0	1	27	0
T Poynton	12	22	2	443	63*	22.15	46.09	0	3	60	4
PI Burgoyne	4	7	1	132	62*	22.00	45.20	0	1	18	1
DJ Wainwright	9	16	4	241	54*	20.08	36.40	0	1	26	0
ML Turner	5	7	3	79	23*	19.75	47.87	0	0	11	0
BT Slater	10	18	1	335	66*	19.70	39.04	0	3	45	0
AP Palladino	8	14	1	233	68	17.92	49.26	0	1	33	1
BA Godleman	8	14	0	236	55	16.85	32.91	0	1	27	0
WJ Durston	9	16	1	245	50	16.33	45.88	0	1	38	0
DJ Redfern	7	13	0	184	61	14.15	47.66	0	1	28	0
AL Hughes	6	11	0	136	33	12.36	37.46	0	0	14	0
JL Clare	6	12	1	130	49	11.81	43.91	0	0	17	0
TD Groenewald	15	26	5	231	49	11.00	55.00	0	0	30	4
MHA Footitt	12	20	5	131	24	8.73	72.37	0	0	19	1
AC Evans	1	2	1	6	6*	6.00	31.57	0	0	0	0
RA Whiteley	3	5	0	26	12	5.20	17.93	0	0	2	0
M Higginbottom	3	5	1	18	9	4.50	19.78	0	0	4	0

Bowling

	Overs	Mdns	Runs	Wkts	BBI	BBM	Ave	Econ	SR	5w	10w
S Chanderpaul	18.4	4	40	3	2/32	2/32	13.33	2.14	37.3	0	0
CF Hughes	5.0	1	19	1	1/19	1/19	19.00	3.80	30.0	0	0
AP Palladino	214.5	43	644	23	6/90	7/91	28.00	2.99	56.0	2	0
DJ Redfern	32.1	2	119	4	3/33	3/43	29.75	3.69	48.2	0	0
TD Groenewald	437.5	86	1404	45	5/30	8/114	31.20	3.20	58.3	3	0
M Higginbottom	77.5	19	283	9	3/59	4/99	31.44	3.63	51.8	0	0
JL Clare	124.0	7	554	17	5/29	5/48	32.58	4.46	43.7	1	0
MHA Footitt	352.5	54	1293	36	6/53	7/134	35.91	3.66	58.8	2	0
AL Hughes	71.0	12	230	6	3/49	4/76	38.33	3.23	71.0	0	0
WL Madsen	43.0	10	121	3	2/9	2/9	40.33	2.81	86.0	0	0
WJ Durston	166.0	21	538	10	2/29	2/32	53.80	3.24	99.6	0	0
DJ Wainwright	296.0	42	924	17	3/46	5/118	54.35	3.12	104.4	0	0
ML Turner	91.4	9	407	6	3/51	3/69	67.83	4.44	91.6	0	0
RA Whiteley	15.0	1	71	1	1/43	1/43	71.00	4.73	90.0	0	0
PI Burgoyne	138.1	25	388	5	3/66	3/93	77.60	2.80	165.8	0	0
AC Evans	15.0	1	92	0	-	-	-	6.13	-	0	0

Catches/Stumpings:
30 Poynton (inc 3st), 9 Johnson, 11 Madsen, Clare, Durston, 7 C Hughes, Groenewald, 6 Redfern, 3 Whiteley, A Hughes, Godleman, Slater, Footitt, 2 Borrington, Burgoyne, 1 Palladino

YORKSHIRE BANK 40 AVERAGES 2013

Batting

	Mat	Inns	NO	Runs	HS	Ave	SR	100	50	4s	6s
DJ Redfern	3	1	0	53	53	53.00	110.41	0	1	5	0
S Chanderpaul	8	7	3	207	85*	51.75	86.25	0	2	15	2
BA Godleman	5	4	2	92	60	46.00	74.79	0	1	9	0
WL Madsen	10	7	1	225	78	37.50	84.58	0	1	14	4
CF Hughes	12	11	1	345	80	34.50	92.74	0	3	35	10
TD Groenewald	4	2	1	31	27*	31.00	155.00	0	0	1	2
PM Borrington	11	10	1	237	72	26.33	75.23	0	1	20	2
DJ Wainwright	10	6	2	103	40	25.75	87.28	0	0	7	0
AL Hughes	9	6	1	116	59*	23.20	93.54	0	1	8	4
WJ Durston	9	7	1	145	71	20.71	101.39	0	1	16	6
RM Johnson	10	6	1	89	58	17.80	89.00	0	1	9	0
AP Palladino	3	3	0	33	22	11.00	100.00	0	0	3	1
JL Clare	2	1	0	8	8	8.00	114.28	0	0	1	0
SL Elstone	2	2	0	13	12	6.50	61.90	0	0	1	0
TC Knight	4	4	2	13	10	6.50	56.52	0	0	0	0
BT Slater	2	2	0	11	6	5.50	55.00	0	0	0	0
T Poynton	3	3	0	14	13	4.66	53.84	0	0	1	0
PI Burgoyne	5	1	0	4	4	4.00	200.00	0	0	0	0
ML Turner	7	1	1	7	7*	-	77.77	0	0	0	0
AC Evans	3	2	2	0	0*	-	0.00	0	0	0	0
MHA Footitt	9	1	1	0	0*	-	-	0	0	0	0
RA Whiteley	1	-	-	-	-	-	-	-	-	-	-

Bowling

	Overs	Mdns	Runs	Wkts	BBI	Ave	Econ	SR	4w	5w
AP Palladino	21.0	1	89	2	2/27	44.50	4.23	63.0	0	0
DJ Redfern	8.0	0	35	0	-	-	4.37	-	0	0
WL Madsen	14.0	1	63	4	3/27	15.75	4.50	21.0	0	0
DJ Wainwright	51.4	1	283	10	4/11	28.30	5.47	31.0	1	0
TC Knight	28.0	2	154	3	3/36	51.33	5.50	56.0	0	0
WJ Durston	39.0	0	218	5	2/31	43.60	5.58	46.8	0	0
AC Evans	12.0	0	76	4	2/38	19.00	6.33	18.0	0	0
PI Burgoyne	25.0	0	162	2	1/5	81.00	6.48	75.0	0	0
TD Groenewald	23.0	2	157	6	3/53	26.16	6.82	23.0	0	0
MHA Footitt	36.0	0	248	11	5/28	22.54	6.88	19.6	0	1
AL Hughes	44.5	0	317	10	3/56	31.70	7.07	26.9	0	0
ML Turner	38.0	0	270	7	2/37	38.57	7.10	32.5	0	0
JL Clare	6.0	0	47	2	2/47	23.50	7.83	18.0	0	0

Catches/Stumpings:
8 Johnson, 7 Madsen, 5 Burgoyne, Durston, 4 Turner, 3 Godleman, C Hughes, 2 Groenewald, Wainwright, A Hughes, 1 Palladino, Knight, Chanderpaul, Footitt, Borrington

FRIENDS LIFE T20 AVERAGES 2013

Derbyshire
FALCONS

Batting

	Mat	Inns	NO	Runs	HS	Ave	SR	100	50	4s	6s
JL Clare	5	4	3	47	35*	47.00	97.91	0	0	4	1
S Chanderpaul	7	7	1	207	87*	34.50	111.89	0	1	20	3
WJ Durston	10	10	2	254	83	31.75	145.14	0	2	23	10
JA Morkel	7	7	3	111	51*	27.75	119.35	0	1	8	5
DJ Wainwright	6	2	1	22	15*	22.00	95.65	0	0	2	0
CF Hughes	10	10	0	208	46	20.80	116.85	0	0	27	7
WL Madsen	10	10	2	164	36	20.50	116.31	0	0	16	1
DJ Redfern	10	7	0	79	43	11.28	108.21	0	0	6	1
T Poynton	10	7	1	66	19	11.00	95.65	0	0	3	2
TD Groenewald	10	5	2	33	14	11.00	117.85	0	0	3	0
PI Burgoyne	4	3	2	10	4*	10.00	66.66	0	0	0	0
RM Johnson	4	3	0	25	12	8.33	92.59	0	0	2	0
BA Godleman	3	1	0	8	8	8.00	66.66	0	0	0	0
AL Hughes	3	2	0	13	7	6.50	81.25	0	0	0	0
MHA Footitt	5	2	1	2	2*	2.00	100.00	0	0	0	0
ML Turner	5	1	1	1	1*	-	33.33	0	0	0	0
TC Knight	1	-	-	-	-	-	-	-	-	-	-

Bowling

	Overs	Mdns	Runs	Wkts	BBI	Ave	Econ	SR	4w	5w
WL Madsen	2.0	0	12	0	-	-	6.00	-	0	0
JA Morkel	22.0	0	139	9	4/25	15.44	6.31	14.6	1	0
WJ Durston	23.0	0	152	5	2/25	30.40	6.60	27.6	0	0
TC Knight	3.0	0	21	1	1/21	21.00	7.00	18.0	0	0
DJ Wainwright	21.0	0	148	7	3/21	21.14	7.04	18.0	0	0
DJ Redfern	27.3	0	201	10	2/17	20.10	7.30	16.5	0	0
TD Groenewald	33.0	0	248	12	4/21	20.66	7.51	16.5	1	0
PI Burgoyne	13.0	0	100	4	2/13	25.00	7.69	19.5	0	0
JL Clare	4.0	0	31	1	1/13	31.00	7.75	24.0	0	0
AL Hughes	9.0	0	76	5	3/32	15.20	8.44	10.8	0	0
ML Turner	15.0	0	149	7	4/35	21.28	9.93	12.8	1	0
MHA Footitt	11.0	0	112	4	3/22	28.00	10.18	16.5	0	0

Catches/Stumpings:
10 Poynton (inc 4st), 7 C Hughes, 5 Groenewald, 4 Turner, Redfern, 3 Godleman, Durston, 2 Clare, Madsen, 1 A Hughes, Johnson, Burgoyne, Footitt, Wainwright, Chanderpaul, Morkel

FORMED: 1882
HOME GROUND: Emirates Durham International Cricket Ground
NWT20 NAME: Durham Jets
CAPTAIN: Paul Collingwood (Championship), Phil Mustard (RL50 and NWT20)
2013 RESULTS: CC1: Champions; YB40: 4/7 in Group B; FL t20: Quarter-finalists
HONOURS: Championship: (3) 2008, 2009, 2013; Gillette/NatWest/C&G/FP Trophy: 2007

THE LOWDOWN

In just 18 months Durham were transformed from relegation candidates to county champions. Paul Collingwood inherited the captaincy midway through the 2012 season, with the club winless at the foot of Division One, and set about a change in discipline and focus that carried through all of last summer. Stepping up following the loss of senior players, Mark Stoneman and Scott Borthwick both passed 1,000 first-class runs in 2013, while Ben Stokes' all-round displays across the three forms earned him the Young Player of the Year award from both the Cricket Writers' Club and the PCA. With the ball Graham Onions was typically effective, leading the way with 70 Championship wickets, ably supported by the unsung Chris Rushworth. In the close season a handful of influential players have moved on, most notably the ex-skippers Dale Benkenstein and Will Smith, both of whom have moved on to Hampshire – the former taking the reins as first-team coach – and the now-retired Steve Harmison. A lighter-looking squad in terms of experience has nonetheless been boosted by some frugal signings such as Irish wicketkeeper Stuart Poynter and Scotland's Calum MacLeod.

HEAD COACH: JON LEWIS

Geoff Cook decided to step away from first-team responsibilities after suffering a heart attack last June, returning at the end of the season to inspire his side to glory. He will stay on as director of cricket but focus more on the next generation, with Lewis, who took charge during Cook's absence last year, taking the job full-time. Lewis joined Durham as an opening batsman in 1997, captaining the side three years later. He retired in 2006 and began working with the club's academy and 2nd XI before becoming involved with the senior side.

COUNTY CHAMPIONSHIP AVERAGES 2013

	Mat	Inns	NO	Runs	HS	Ave	SR	100	50	4s	6s
SG Borthwick	16	28	2	1022	135	39.30	57.57	3	5	137	4
MD Stoneman	16	30	1	1011	122	34.86	69.77	3	6	146	6
P Mustard	16	26	4	763	77	34.68	54.50	0	6	107	5
MJ Richardson	10	15	0	501	129	33.40	57.91	2	2	56	5
WR Smith	16	28	2	786	153	30.23	38.83	1	2	101	1
PD Collingwood	15	25	3	646	88*	29.36	44.00	0	5	72	0
DM Benkenstein	5	10	2	233	74*	29.12	49.36	0	2	28	1
U Arshad	5	6	0	170	83	28.33	67.72	0	1	22	4
KK Jennings	14	26	1	707	127	28.28	38.54	2	1	71	1
BA Stokes	13	24	2	615	127	27.95	60.89	1	3	82	8
GR Breese	3	6	2	110	44	27.50	56.70	0	0	12	2
MA Wood	8	10	2	153	58*	19.12	53.31	0	1	16	1
CD Thorp	7	11	2	147	27	16.33	65.33	0	0	21	1
J Harrison	4	4	0	60	35	15.00	42.55	0	0	11	0
G Onions	12	17	5	148	27	12.33	49.66	0	0	22	1
C Rushworth	14	20	8	107	18*	8.91	58.79	0	0	17	0
RS Buckley	2	2	0	10	6	5.00	23.80	0	0	1	0
ME Claydon	1	2	2	30	18*	-	103.44	0	0	4	0

	Overs	Mdns	Runs	Wkts	BBI	BBM	Ave	Econ	SR	5w	10w
P Mustard	1.1	0	9	1	1/9	1/9	9.00	7.71	7.0	0	0
ME Claydon	18.5	2	56	6	3/25	6/56	9.33	2.97	18.8	0	0
U Arshad	73.1	16	249	16	3/16	6/34	15.56	3.40	27.4	0	0
G Onions	419.1	87	1292	70	7/62	9/85	18.45	3.08	35.9	5	0
C Rushworth	402.2	99	1202	54	6/58	10/103	22.25	2.98	44.7	3	1
CD Thorp	169.5	59	341	15	3/29	4/42	22.73	2.00	67.9	0	0
J Harrison	96.1	20	336	14	5/31	7/74	24.00	3.49	41.2	1	0
KK Jennings	11.2	0	48	2	1/5	1/5	24.00	4.23	34.0	0	0
MA Wood	209.4	38	650	27	5/44	6/79	24.07	3.10	46.5	1	0
BA Stokes	327.4	50	1116	42	4/49	7/91	26.57	3.40	46.8	0	0
GR Breese	53.0	18	117	4	2/40	3/106	29.25	2.20	79.5	0	0
WR Smith	34.2	5	137	4	1/4	1/4	34.25	3.99	51.5	0	0
RS Buckley	114.2	21	344	10	5/86	6/172	34.40	3.00	68.6	1	0
SG Borthwick	266.4	35	1064	28	6/70	8/92	38.00	3.99	57.1	1	0
PD Collingwood	35.4	14	73	1	1/14	1/22	73.00	2.04	214.0	0	0
DM Benkenstein	1.0	0	1	0	-	-	-	1.00	-	0	0

Catches/Stumpings:
65 Mustard (inc 1st), 29 Borthwick, 20 Collingwood, 13 Richardson, Smith, 10 Stokes, 7 Breese, Jennings, 6 Stoneman, 5 Benkenstein, 4 Rushworth, 2 Onions, 1 Claydon, Buckley, Arshad, Thorp, Wood

YORKSHIRE BANK 40 AVERAGES 2013

Batting

	Mat	Inns	NO	Runs	HS	Ave	SR	100	50	4s	6s
WR Smith	10	6	2	248	120*	62.00	111.71	1	2	22	6
GJ Muchall	12	10	5	242	57*	48.40	96.80	0	2	24	2
DM Benkenstein	3	2	1	33	17*	33.00	57.89	0	0	0	1
BA Stokes	12	11	2	290	87	32.22	97.31	0	2	27	7
MD Stoneman	12	11	1	302	85	30.20	95.87	0	2	46	1
P Mustard	12	11	0	329	92	29.90	100.61	0	3	41	5
PD Collingwood	12	10	2	239	79	29.87	80.20	0	1	20	2
GR Breese	7	4	1	89	41*	29.66	95.69	0	0	9	1
SG Borthwick	12	8	0	177	80	22.12	84.68	0	1	18	3
MA Wood	9	4	2	21	15*	10.50	100.00	0	0	1	0
RD Pringle	10	5	0	48	26	9.60	82.75	0	0	1	2
G Onions	6	2	1	2	2	2.00	100.00	0	0	0	0
C Rushworth	12	3	3	4	4*	-	100.00	0	0	1	0
U Arshad	1	-	-	-	-	-	-	-	-	-	-
CD Thorp	2	-	-	-	-	-	-	-	-	-	-

Bowling

	Overs	Mdns	Runs	Wkts	BBI	Ave	Econ	SR	4w	5w
G Onions	45.0	4	179	10	4/45	17.90	3.97	27.0	1	0
U Arshad	3.0	0	13	0	-	-	4.33	-	0	0
GR Breese	33.5	1	155	6	4/33	25.83	4.58	33.8	1	0
CD Thorp	11.0	1	51	1	1/28	51.00	4.63	66.0	0	0
RD Pringle	30.0	0	150	3	1/12	50.00	5.00	60.0	0	0
PD Collingwood	32.3	0	169	12	3/5	14.08	5.20	16.2	0	0
WR Smith	10.0	1	52	4	2/19	13.00	5.20	15.0	0	0
BA Stokes	60.1	6	330	11	3/50	30.00	5.48	32.8	0	0
MA Wood	57.0	1	314	12	3/23	26.16	5.50	28.5	0	0
C Rushworth	72.1	5	407	20	5/42	20.35	5.63	21.6	1	1
SG Borthwick	47.0	0	306	9	3/41	34.00	6.51	31.3	0	0

Catches/Stumpings:
13 Mustard (inc 3st), 9 Stokes, 5 Rushworth, Stoneman, 4 Breese, Borthwick, 3 Onions, Collingwood, 2 Benkenstein, Pringle, Muchall, 1 Wood, Smith

www.durhamccc.co.uk / tel: 0191 387 1717

Batting

	Mat	Inns	NO	Runs	HS	Ave	SR	100	50	4s	6s
BA Stokes	11	11	4	328	72*	46.85	153.27	0	2	15	22
GJ Muchall	11	11	5	274	66*	45.66	137.00	0	1	23	5
P Mustard	11	11	0	379	91	34.45	123.45	0	3	41	11
GR Breese	9	8	4	126	32	31.50	185.29	0	0	16	5
SG Borthwick	11	11	0	232	62	21.09	104.97	0	1	18	5
PD Collingwood	3	2	1	19	19	19.00	86.36	0	0	1	0
MD Stoneman	11	11	0	185	51	16.81	110.77	0	1	20	4
MJ Richardson	10	4	3	15	8*	15.00	107.14	0	0	2	0
WR Smith	10	8	1	73	14	10.42	115.87	0	0	6	1
RD Pringle	11	6	1	22	14	4.40	104.76	0	0	2	0
MA Wood	6	2	0	3	2	1.50	75.00	0	0	0	0
C Rushworth	11	2	2	1	1*	-	33.33	0	0	0	0
MG Morley	1	-	-	-	-	-	-	-	-	-	-
G Onions	5	-	-	-	-	-	-	-	-	-	-

Bowling

	Overs	Mdns	Runs	Wkts	BBI	Ave	Econ	SR	4w	5w
WR Smith	19.0	0	108	6	2/20	18.00	5.68	19.0	0	0
G Onions	19.0	0	122	4	2/23	30.50	6.42	28.5	0	0
GR Breese	30.0	0	221	8	2/31	27.62	7.36	22.5	0	0
C Rushworth	38.5	0	297	13	3/19	22.84	7.64	17.9	0	0
RD Pringle	32.0	0	245	10	2/13	24.50	7.65	19.2	0	0
BA Stokes	33.3	0	259	6	2/27	43.16	7.73	33.5	0	0
PD Collingwood	4.0	0	32	1	1/13	32.00	8.00	24.0	0	0
SG Borthwick	18.0	0	164	7	2/19	23.42	9.11	15.4	0	0
MG Morley	4.0	0	41	0	-	-	10.25	-	0	0
MA Wood	16.0	0	167	1	1/20	167.00	10.43	96.0	0	0

Catches/Stumpings:
5 Mustard (inc 3st), 7 Stoneman, 4 Richardson, Borthwick, Muchall, 2 Collingwood, Breese, Pringle, Stokes, 1 Onions, Smith

ESSEX

FORMED: 1876
HOME GROUND: The Essex County Ground, Chelmsford
ONE-DAY NAME: Essex Eagles
CAPTAIN: James Foster (Championship), Ryan ten Doeschate (RL50 and NWT20)
2013 RESULTS: CC2: 3/9; YB40: 2/7 in Group C; FL t20: Semi-finalists
HONOURS: Championship: (6) 1979, 1983, 1984, 1986, 1991, 1992; Gillette/NatWest/C&G/FP Trophy: (3) 1985, 1997, 2008; Benson & Hedges Cup: (2) 1979, 1998; Pro40/National League/CB40/YB40: (2) 2005, 2006; Sunday League: (3) 1981, 1984, 1985

THE LOWDOWN

Another ultimately disappointing season in 2013 given the talent they possessed in their squad. Essex pushed for promotion, taking matters into the final game of the season, and reached Twenty20 Finals Day, but went away empty-handed when the spoils were divvied up. The bowling unit was one to rival any in the country, with David Masters, the youthful left-armer Reece Topley and Graham Napier taking 147 Division Two wickets between them. Napier was also the star turn with the bat, digging his side out of many a hole. Along with Jaik Mickleburgh, Tom Westley and James Foster, Napier was one of only four batsmen to pass 700 first-class runs. Their batting woes were most evident in a chastening defeat to Lancashire at Chelmsford in which they were bowled out for 20 in their second innings, the lowest total by any side in the County Championship for 30 years. However, Monty Panesar's acquisition after a brief loan spell will enhance their chances and should they rediscover their touch with the bat, promotion should be well within their reach.

HEAD COACH: PAUL GRAYSON

As a Yorkshireman who made his home-county debut in 1990, Essex's coach enjoyed a steadily improving career before moving to Chelmsford, where as a one-day specialist left-arm spinner and flinty batsman he flourished over an eight-year period that culminated in two ODIs in 2000 and 2001. After retiring from the first-class game in 2005, he returned to Essex as coach in 2008.

COUNTY CHAMPIONSHIP AVERAGES 2013

	Mat	Inns	NO	Runs	HS	Ave	SR	100	50	4s	6s
GR Napier	16	22	6	796	102*	49.75	73.22	1	7	95	18
JC Mickleburgh	13	21	1	829	243	41.45	52.04	2	4	101	3
AN Cook	2	4	0	157	60	39.25	37.83	0	2	20	0
GM Smith	10	15	2	498	177	38.30	63.92	1	1	67	3
JS Foster	16	24	3	762	143	36.28	53.96	1	4	91	2
RS Bopara	7	11	0	397	145	36.09	60.88	1	2	46	5
RN ten Doeschate	9	13	2	391	103	35.54	63.88	1	1	40	4
G Gambhir	5	7	0	239	106	34.14	47.60	1	0	26	1
T Westley	10	18	0	583	163	32.38	46.94	1	2	86	0
OA Shah	7	11	1	307	120	30.70	51.94	1	1	37	3
BT Foakes	14	18	1	500	120	29.41	53.59	1	3	66	3
ML Pettini	8	14	3	319	72	29.00	42.59	0	1	35	0
TJ Phillips	3	3	1	47	40*	23.50	44.76	0	0	6	0
RJ Quiney	4	7	0	150	56	21.42	51.36	0	1	25	0
SI Mahmood	4	6	0	112	54	18.66	74.66	0	1	16	1
TS Mills	5	6	3	53	17	17.66	84.12	0	0	8	0
KS Velani	1	2	0	22	13	11.00	44.00	0	0	3	0
DD Masters	13	12	3	95	37*	10.55	33.45	0	0	12	0
HD Rutherford	2	3	0	29	24	9.66	37.17	0	0	4	0
MS Panesar	6	6	0	55	22	9.16	58.51	0	0	8	0
TR Craddock	3	3	0	24	20	8.00	41.37	0	0	3	1
NLJ Browne	3	5	1	26	22*	6.50	33.33	0	0	4	0
MA Chambers	2	2	0	4	3	2.00	4.81	0	0	0	0
RJW Topley	13	14	7	12	8*	1.71	9.52	0	0	1	0

Batting

	Overs	Mdns	Runs	Wkts	BBI	BBM	Ave	Econ	SR	5w	10w
TJ Phillips	39.4	10	98	6	3/20	3/20	16.33	2.47	39.6	0	0
DD Masters	467.4	122	1163	51	6/41	9/70	22.80	2.48	55.0	4	0
GM Smith	112.5	21	365	15	5/42	6/91	24.33	3.23	45.1	2	0
RS Bopara	129.5	24	378	14	3/41	5/64	27.00	2.91	55.6	0	0
RJW Topley	411.4	78	1364	48	6/29	11/85	28.41	3.31	51.4	3	1
GR Napier	459.1	80	1516	48	7/90	8/157	31.58	3.30	57.3	3	0
RN ten Doeschate	77.0	9	267	8	4/28	5/65	33.37	3.46	57.7	0	0
MS Panesar	189.4	50	504	14	4/49	4/57	36.00	2.65	81.2	0	0
TR Craddock	43.0	9	132	3	2/77	3/106	44.00	3.06	86.0	0	0
TS Mills	102.4	18	398	6	2/24	4/82	66.33	3.87	102.6	0	0
SI Mahmood	66.0	4	329	3	2/112	2/112	109.66	4.98	132.0	0	0
T Westley	41.0	4	142	1	1/7	1/7	142.00	3.46	246.0	0	0
MA Chambers	32.0	2	151	1	1/62	1/62	151.00	4.71	192.0	0	0
KS Velani	2.0	0	8	0	-	-	-	4.00	-	0	0
OA Shah	2.0	0	12	0	-	-	-	6.00	-	0	0
NLJ Browne	16.5	4	59	0	-	-	-	3.50	-	0	0

Bowling

Catches/Stumpings:
49 Foster (inc 1st), 11 Foakes, 10 Shah, 7 Pettini, 6 Topley, 5 Quiney, Bopara, Westley, Napier, 4 Gambhir, 3 Mahmood, ten Doeschate, Masters, Mickleburgh, 2 Cook, Smith, 1 Chambers, Rutherford, Browne, Phillips, Mills

YORKSHIRE BANK 40 AVERAGES 2013

Batting

	Mat	Inns	NO	Runs	HS	Ave	SR	100	50	4s	6s
RN ten Doeschate	9	9	3	382	180	63.66	131.72	1	1	23	23
RS Bopara	8	8	1	441	130	63.00	99.77	2	2	36	11
RJ Quiney	2	2	0	121	71	60.50	85.81	0	2	11	1
TJ Phillips	11	8	6	86	36	43.00	162.26	0	0	8	4
GM Smith	8	8	1	290	78	41.42	87.87	0	2	21	6
T Westley	7	7	0	227	71	32.42	94.97	0	2	29	0
OA Shah	5	5	0	155	68	31.00	88.57	0	1	7	7
HD Rutherford	7	7	0	214	110	30.57	114.43	1	1	19	11
ML Pettini	11	11	0	296	88	26.90	91.64	0	1	26	2
JS Foster	12	11	3	201	41	25.12	117.54	0	0	19	5
GR Napier	12	9	1	201	50	25.12	164.75	0	1	18	12
JC Mickleburgh	3	2	0	28	22	14.00	90.32	0	0	2	0
G Gambhir	2	2	0	23	21	11.50	60.52	0	0	2	0
SI Mahmood	6	4	2	23	20*	11.50	191.66	0	0	1	2
DD Masters	9	3	0	29	16	9.66	65.90	0	0	3	0
BT Foakes	2	1	0	6	6	6.00	75.00	0	0	0	0
RJW Topley	11	3	1	4	4*	2.00	33.33	0	0	1	0
TS Mills	7	1	1	1	1*	-	100.00	0	0	0	0

Bowling

	Overs	Mdns	Runs	Wkts	BBI	Ave	Econ	SR	4w	5w
DD Masters	65.5	2	305	9	2/27	33.88	4.63	43.8	0	0
RS Bopara	18.0	0	92	0	-	-	5.11	-	0	0
TS Mills	31.0	0	173	10	3/23	17.30	5.58	18.6	0	0
RJW Topley	77.4	1	435	17	4/26	25.58	5.60	27.4	1	0
GR Napier	80.4	6	461	21	7/32	21.95	5.71	23.0	0	2
RN ten Doeschate	34.0	0	196	8	3/38	24.50	5.76	25.5	0	0
TJ Phillips	53.4	1	311	12	5/42	25.91	5.79	26.8	0	1
GM Smith	22.0	0	138	1	1/16	138.00	6.27	132.0	0	0
T Westley	12.0	0	83	0	-	-	6.91	-	0	0
SI Mahmood	35.0	0	251	5	2/48	50.20	7.17	42.0	0	0

Catches/Stumpings:
11 Foster (inc 1st), 6 Pettini, 5 Bopara, 4 Smith, Napier, 3 Mills, ten Doeschate, 2 Shah, Mahmood, Masters, Topley, 1 Foakes, Gambhir, Mickleburgh, Phillips

FRIENDS LIFE T20 AVERAGES 2013

	Mat	Inns	NO	Runs	HS	Ave	SR	100	50	4s	6s	
OA Shah	9	8	2	311	68	51.83	118.25	0	2	21	16	
RN ten Doeschate	12	10	3	288	82	41.14	150.00	0	2	14	14	
HD Rutherford	12	12	1	304	84	27.63	169.83	0	1	29	18	
RS Bopara	11	10	2	201	39	25.12	113.55	0	0	16	5	
ML Pettini	6	6	1	120	37	24.00	139.53	0	0	15	4	
GR Napier	12	8	3	95	38*	19.00	163.79	0	0	9	5	Batting
GM Smith	11	11	0	189	62	17.18	119.62	0	1	18	4	
JS Foster	12	9	3	97	32*	16.16	116.86	0	0	10	2	
TJ Phillips	11	5	2	24	16	8.00	77.41	0	0	3	0	
DD Masters	6	1	0	7	7	7.00	87.50	0	0	1	0	
JC Mickleburgh	2	2	1	5	4*	5.00	125.00	0	0	1	0	
RJW Topley	12	2	1	5	4*	5.00	45.45	0	0	1	0	
SW Tait	12	4	2	2	1*	1.00	25.00	0	0	0	0	
T Westley	1	1	0	0	0	0.00	0.00	0	0	0	0	
TS Mills	3	1	1	8	8*	-	133.33	0	0	0	1	

	Overs	Mdns	Runs	Wkts	BBI	Ave	Econ	SR	4w	5w	
RS Bopara	9.4	0	58	5	3/12	11.60	6.00	11.6	0	0	
SW Tait	39.4	0	275	16	4/26	17.18	6.93	14.8	2	0	
DD Masters	24.0	1	170	7	3/26	24.28	7.08	20.5	0	0	
RJW Topley	37.0	0	278	21	4/26	13.23	7.51	10.5	2	0	Bowling
TJ Phillips	28.5	0	222	5	2/14	44.40	7.69	34.6	0	0	
GR Napier	35.5	1	314	12	4/18	26.16	8.76	17.9	1	0	
RN ten Doeschate	19.2	0	173	3	1/17	57.66	8.94	38.6	0	0	
TS Mills	2.0	0	20	0	-	-	10.00	-	0	0	
GM Smith	3.0	0	35	0	-	-	11.66	-	0	0	

Catches/Stumpings:
10 Foster (inc 1st), 8 Smith, 5 Bopara, Napier, Phillips, ten Doeschate, 3 Rutherford, Topley, 2 Masters, 1 Shah, Tait

GLAMORGAN

FORMED: 1888
HOME GROUND: SWALEC Stadium, Cardiff
CAPTAIN: Mark Wallace (Championship and RL50), Jim Allenby (NWT20)
2013 RESULTS: CC2: 8/9; YB40: Finalists; FL t20: 3/6 in Midlands/Wales/West Division
HONOURS: Championship: (3) 1948, 1969, 1997; Pro40/National League/CB40/YB40: (2) 2002, 2004; Sunday League: 1993

THE LOWDOWN

Disappointment in the County Championship in 2013 was eased by an impressive showing in the shorter forms, particularly the 40-over competition. After negotiating a tricky group, Glamorgan reached a Lord's final for the first time since 2000, eventually losing out to Nottinghamshire. Australian-born allrounder Jim Allenby was superb throughout with both bat and ball, averaging over 40 in all three forms and ably backing up frontline pacers Michael Hogan and Graham Wagg. Hogan in particular enjoyed a fine 2013, as did veteran batsman Murray Goodwin in his first season at the club, while Marcus North also shone with the bat in the one-day game. The acquisition of South African Jacques Rudolph – who misses the first Championship game to take part in the 'Iron Man South Africa' race – will help offset the departure of North but much will depend on local lads Mark Wallace and Gareth Rees to keep the ship steady as a crop of talented youngsters, including tall fast bowler Mike Reed and young off-spinner Andrew Salter, continue their development at first-team level.

HEAD COACH: TOBY RADFORD

Radford comes into the role under new chief executive Hugh Morris. He enjoyed domestic success with Middlesex, whom he coached to the 2008 Twenty20 Cup, before moving to Barbados to work at the High Performance Centre. From there he worked with the West Indies as batting coach, eventually being appointed assistant to Ottis Gibson. It was in this role that he experienced his career highlight, as the West Indies won the ICC World Twenty20 in 2012.

COUNTY CHAMPIONSHIP AVERAGES 2013

	Mat	Inns	NO	Runs	HS	Ave	SR	100	50	4s	6s
J Allenby	15	23	4	1116	138*	58.73	68.34	2	8	140	7
MW Goodwin	16	26	4	1263	194	57.40	48.13	4	7	167	1
NL McCullum	1	2	1	49	35*	49.00	35.50	0	0	4	0
GP Rees	8	14	1	524	112	40.30	51.02	2	3	67	3
CB Cooke	7	11	1	394	92	39.40	52.60	0	3	53	2
RAJ Smith	3	4	1	100	39	33.33	61.34	0	0	13	1
GG Wagg	10	12	1	308	58	28.00	58.00	0	2	42	4
MA Wallace	16	23	0	631	101	27.43	60.20	1	2	72	3
WD Bragg	14	24	2	535	71*	24.31	44.80	0	2	70	1
BJ Wright	13	23	2	499	63	23.76	46.20	0	2	68	0
MJ North	10	16	1	354	68	23.60	37.65	0	1	50	0
SJ Walters	9	15	0	343	98	22.86	45.61	0	2	35	0
MG Hogan	14	18	3	297	51	19.80	85.59	0	1	40	7
DA Cosker	15	21	6	281	44*	18.73	39.85	0	0	27	2
JC Glover	7	9	2	127	51*	18.14	45.68	0	1	14	0
DL Lloyd	1	1	0	16	16	16.00	39.02	0	0	2	0
WT Owen	2	3	0	45	40	15.00	60.00	0	0	7	0
MT Reed	11	15	7	71	27	8.87	29.09	0	0	11	0
AG Salter	3	4	0	29	16	7.25	20.42	0	0	4	0
Alex J Jones	1	1	1	5	5*	-	25.00	0	0	1	0

Batting

	Overs	Mdns	Runs	Wkts	BBI	BBM	Ave	Econ	SR	5w	10w
MJ North	48.2	6	143	7	5/30	5/43	20.42	2.95	41.4	1	0
MG Hogan	512.0	133	1376	67	7/92	7/92	20.53	2.68	45.8	4	0
AG Salter	55.0	14	182	7	3/66	5/100	26.00	3.30	47.1	0	0
RAJ Smith	61.0	6	274	10	3/50	5/87	27.40	4.49	36.6	0	0
DA Cosker	429.2	82	1261	37	5/120	6/121	34.08	2.93	69.6	1	0
MT Reed	309.5	58	1074	31	5/27	5/63	34.64	3.46	59.9	1	0
J Allenby	371.5	103	909	26	4/16	7/47	34.96	2.44	85.8	0	0
NL McCullum	47.4	6	191	5	5/191	5/191	38.20	4.00	57.2	1	0
JC Glover	147.1	26	498	13	4/51	6/70	38.30	3.38	67.9	0	0
GG Wagg	295.2	63	971	18	3/78	3/78	53.94	3.28	98.4	0	0
WD Bragg	22.0	2	111	2	2/10	2/10	55.50	5.04	66.0	0	0
WT Owen	47.0	8	170	1	1/51	1/51	170.00	3.61	282.0	0	0
GP Rees	1.0	0	2	0	-	-	-	2.00	-	0	0
BJ Wright	1.0	0	7	0	-	-	-	7.00	-	0	0
Alex J Jones	12.0	0	53	0	-	-	-	4.41	-	0	0

Bowling

Catches/Stumpings:
43 Wallace (inc 3st), 27 Allenby, 13 Walters, 10 Wright, 7 Cosker, Goodwin, 5 Rees, North, Hogan, 3 Bragg, 2 Owen, Cooke, Reed, 1 A Jones, Salter, Glover, Wagg

GLAMORGAN

	Mat	Inns	NO	Runs	HS	Ave	SR	100	50	4s	6s
BJ Wright	8	8	5	179	75*	59.66	122.60	0	1	17	3
CB Cooke	13	13	0	546	98	42.00	101.11	0	5	54	5
J Allenby	13	13	2	454	85	41.27	113.78	0	3	31	12
MJ North	11	11	1	381	137*	38.10	98.19	1	1	37	5
MA Wallace	13	13	1	437	118*	36.41	101.62	1	4	44	6
WD Bragg	6	6	0	203	62	33.83	87.12	0	2	25	1
GP Rees	7	7	0	218	83	31.14	67.28	0	1	17	1
MW Goodwin	13	12	1	333	49	30.27	122.42	0	0	37	4
GG Wagg	13	11	3	174	54	21.75	121.67	0	1	15	9
DA Cosker	13	7	2	56	37	11.20	107.69	0	0	4	2
MG Hogan	12	5	2	23	11*	7.66	88.46	0	0	1	1
AG Salter	4	2	1	3	2	3.00	75.00	0	0	0	0
WT Owen	4	3	3	25	13*	-	125.00	0	0	3	0
SP Jones	9	4	4	11	5*	-	100.00	0	0	2	0
Alex J Jones	1	-	-	-	-	-	-	-	-	-	-
MT Reed	3	-	-	-	-	-	-	-	-	-	-

Batting

	Overs	Mdns	Runs	Wkts	BBI	Ave	Econ	SR	4w	5w
AG Salter	29.0	1	138	3	2/41	46.00	4.75	58.0	0	0
J Allenby	86.0	5	439	12	3/37	36.58	5.10	43.0	0	0
DA Cosker	94.0	0	507	15	3/32	33.80	5.39	37.6	0	0
MG Hogan	87.2	9	488	28	4/34	17.42	5.58	18.7	2	0
SP Jones	56.0	2	329	10	2/17	32.90	5.87	33.6	0	0
MJ North	18.4	0	113	2	1/16	56.50	6.05	56.0	0	0
Alex J Jones	4.0	0	26	1	1/26	26.00	6.50	24.0	0	0
WT Owen	22.0	1	149	5	3/48	29.80	6.77	26.4	0	0
WD Bragg	3.2	1	23	1	1/11	23.00	6.90	20.0	0	0
MT Reed	11.0	0	78	0	-	-	7.09	-	0	0
GG Wagg	90.0	0	657	18	4/51	36.50	7.30	30.0	1	0

Bowling

Catches/Stumpings:
9 Wallace (inc 1st), Cooke, 7 Wagg, 6 Hogan, 5 Cosker, 4 Owen, Wright, Allenby, Goodwin, 2 A Jones, North, 1 Reed, Salter, Rees, S Jones

GLAMORGAN

	Mat	Inns	NO	Runs	HS	Ave	SR	100	50	4s	6s
J Allenby	9	9	2	355	85*	50.71	134.98	0	3	41	9
MJ North	9	7	1	145	37	24.16	86.82	0	0	8	2
CB Cooke	10	10	1	217	57	24.11	130.72	0	2	16	9
MA Wallace	10	9	1	188	69*	23.50	118.23	0	1	19	3
MW Goodwin	10	9	1	158	59	19.75	128.45	0	1	14	3
NA James	8	5	2	50	27	16.66	76.92	0	0	2	1
BJ Wright	8	6	2	52	22*	13.00	89.65	0	0	4	0
DA Cosker	10	3	1	25	15	12.50	89.28	0	0	0	1
NL McCullum	10	7	2	53	20	10.60	126.19	0	0	4	2
GG Wagg	10	6	2	30	14	7.50	103.44	0	0	2	1
MG Hogan	10	2	1	4	3*	4.00	100.00	0	0	0	0
Alex J Jones	4	2	1	0	0*	0.00	0.00	0	0	0	0
SP Jones	1	-	-	-	-	-	-	-	-	-	-
WT Owen	1	-	-	-	-	-	-	-	-	-	-

	Overs	Mdns	Runs	Wkts	BBI	Ave	Econ	SR	4w	5w
MG Hogan	35.0	0	197	8	3/11	24.62	5.62	26.2	0	0
MJ North	0.5	0	5	0	-	-	6.00	-	0	0
DA Cosker	35.0	0	232	7	2/18	33.14	6.62	30.0	0	0
GG Wagg	33.0	0	240	15	5/14	16.00	7.27	13.2	0	1
J Allenby	21.0	0	156	2	1/27	78.00	7.42	63.0	0	0
NL McCullum	31.0	1	252	10	2/20	25.20	8.12	18.6	0	0
Alex J Jones	4.0	0	35	1	1/12	35.00	8.75	24.0	0	0
NA James	17.0	0	154	3	1/19	51.33	9.05	34.0	0	0
SP Jones	4.0	0	44	0	-	-	11.00	-	0	0
WT Owen	1.0	0	14	0	-	-	14.00	-	0	0

Catches/Stumpings:
6 Cooke, 5 Hogan, 4 Wallace (inc 3st), 3 A Jones, James, Cosker, McCullum, Wagg, 2 Goodwin, 1 Wright, Allenby, North

Batting

Bowling

TEAM PROFILE

FORMED: 1871
HOME GROUND: County Ground, Bristol
ONE-DAY NAME: Gloucestershire Gladiators
CAPTAIN: Michael Klinger
2013 RESULTS: CC2: 6/9; YB40: 4/7 in Group C; FL t20: 6/6 in Midlands/Wales/West Division
HONOURS: Gillette/NatWest/C&G/FP Trophy: (5) 1973, 1999, 2000, 2003, 2004; Benson & Hedges Cup: (3) 1977, 1999, 2000; Pro40/National League/CB40/YB40: 2000

THE LOWDOWN

Having finished rock bottom of Division Two the previous year, 2013 showed signs of progress at Nevil Road. The acquisition of Michael Klinger proved inspired, as the South Australia batsman produced exceptional performances across the three competitions, leading Gloucestershire's run charts in each. Chris Dent enjoyed a breakthrough season with the bat, making it to four-figures in the Championship for the first time in his career, while Will Gidman led the way with the ball once again and became the fifth Gloucestershire player to take 10 wickets and score a century in a match. With development of their ground ongoing, the signings of Tom Smith from Middlesex and William Tavaré (nephew of Chris) represent frugal yet interesting additions for 2014.

DIRECTOR OF CRICKET: JOHN BRACEWELL

Bracewell's first stint as coach at Gloucestershire began in 1998 and ended in 2003 when he took charge of New Zealand, the land of his birth. In that five-year period he led the club to unprecedented success in one-day competitions, winning five trophies in the space of two seasons between 1999 and 2000. He returned to Bristol in 2009, charged with reviving the fortunes of a talented but inexperienced squad. That remains a work in progress, but with a youthful-looking group and an excellent skipper in Klinger, there are signs of life again down in the west country.

COUNTY CHAMPIONSHIP AVERAGES 2013

	Mat	Inns	NO	Runs	HS	Ave	SR	100	50	4s	6s
M Klinger	15	24	3	1105	163	52.61	52.51	4	4	132	11
APR Gidman	16	22	0	1125	211	51.13	60.41	3	5	137	13
HJH Marshall	16	21	1	1007	149	50.35	50.80	4	2	119	7
GH Roderick	12	17	4	625	152*	48.07	50.44	2	2	78	1
CDJ Dent	15	25	2	1049	153	45.60	56.21	2	6	153	5
JMR Taylor	4	5	1	178	61*	44.50	81.65	0	1	24	2
DM Housego	9	14	2	443	150	36.91	44.52	1	3	48	4
WRS Gidman	13	15	4	401	143	36.45	53.53	1	1	47	2
BAC Howell	16	22	4	561	60	31.16	48.74	0	4	54	9
MD Taylor	3	3	2	31	26*	31.00	67.39	0	0	5	0
TMJ Smith	8	9	2	181	50	25.85	39.00	0	1	26	0
CL Herring	5	5	0	105	43	21.00	41.33	0	0	17	0
JK Fuller	7	6	0	84	42	14.00	45.16	0	0	12	0
CN Miles	13	13	1	161	50*	13.41	52.10	0	1	24	0
GJ McCarter	4	6	1	51	20	10.20	20.64	0	0	6	0
DA Payne	10	9	2	42	16	6.00	31.57	0	0	5	0
LC Norwell	5	7	5	9	8*	4.50	15.78	0	0	2	0
MAH Hammond	2	2	0	4	4	2.00	28.57	0	0	1	0
IA Cockbain	1	2	0	2	2	1.00	40.00	0	0	0	0
TW Shrewsbury	1	1	1	2	2*	-	10.00	0	0	0	0
EGC Young	1	2	2	2	2*	-	6.66	0	0	0	0

	Overs	Mdns	Runs	Wkts	BBI	BBM	Ave	Econ	SR	5w	10w
WRS Gidman	384.1	85	1127	50	6/15	10/43	22.54	2.93	46.1	2	1
CN Miles	358.0	69	1315	43	6/88	7/135	30.58	3.67	49.9	3	0
BAC Howell	347.0	83	992	28	5/57	8/96	35.42	2.85	74.3	1	0
LC Norwell	119.0	16	491	13	3/80	5/160	37.76	4.12	54.9	0	0
JMR Taylor	89.1	17	247	6	2/39	2/39	41.16	2.77	89.1	0	0
JK Fuller	211.4	44	699	15	5/43	6/102	46.60	3.30	84.6	1	0
GJ McCarter	110.0	19	431	9	4/95	6/170	47.88	3.91	73.3	0	0
TMJ Smith	229.5	37	731	15	4/91	5/124	48.73	3.18	91.9	0	0
DA Payne	275.4	59	917	18	3/75	3/93	50.94	3.32	91.8	0	0
CDJ Dent	19.1	5	60	1	1/12	1/12	60.00	3.13	115.0	0	0
MD Taylor	75.0	19	246	4	3/108	3/128	61.50	3.28	112.5	0	0
APR Gidman	28.3	6	93	1	1/5	1/10	93.00	3.26	171.0	0	0
TW Shrewsbury	23.0	0	94	1	1/94	1/94	94.00	4.08	138.0	0	0
MAH Hammond	49.0	3	196	1	1/96	1/155	196.00	4.00	294.0	0	0
DM Housego	3.0	0	15	0	-	-	-	5.00	-	0	0
EGC Young	5.0	0	25	0	-	-	-	5.00	-	0	0

Catches/Stumpings:
41 Roderick, 19 Dent, 16 Klinger, 12 Herring, A Gidman, 7 Howell, 5 Housego, Marshall, 4 J Taylor, 3 W Gidman, 2 Fuller, Payne, 1 Cockbain, Hammond, Norwell, Smith, Miles

YORKSHIRE BANK 40 AVERAGES 2013

GLADIATORS

Batting

	Mat	Inns	NO	Runs	HS	Ave	SR	100	50	4s	6s
M Klinger	12	11	3	702	131*	87.75	90.46	1	5	62	11
CDJ Dent	12	10	2	384	151*	48.00	111.95	1	1	41	10
IA Cockbain	12	10	3	232	53	33.14	100.00	0	1	15	6
BAC Howell	12	9	1	246	75*	30.75	112.84	0	1	15	10
GH Roderick	12	8	3	139	63	27.80	89.10	0	1	9	1
DA Payne	11	3	2	26	18	26.00	96.29	0	0	3	0
HJH Marshall	12	11	0	277	67	25.18	109.48	0	2	34	4
APR Gidman	12	10	1	167	41	18.55	84.77	0	0	12	3
EGC Young	7	3	0	41	29	13.66	83.67	0	0	2	1
WRS Gidman	4	2	0	27	23	13.50	87.09	0	0	1	0
JK Fuller	10	8	2	71	16	11.83	133.96	0	0	8	2
TMJ Smith	4	2	1	1	1	1.00	50.00	0	0	0	0
GJ McCarter	5	1	1	18	18*	-	100.00	0	0	3	0
CN Miles	4	1	1	0	0*	-	0.00	0	0	0	0
MAH Hammond	2	-	-	-	-	-	-	-	-	-	-
LC Norwell	1	-	-	-	-	-	-	-	-	-	-

Bowling

	Overs	Mdns	Runs	Wkts	BBI	Ave	Econ	SR	4w	5w
GJ McCarter	27.0	0	127	4	2/36	31.75	4.70	40.5	0	0
APR Gidman	14.0	0	76	3	2/27	25.33	5.42	28.0	0	0
TMJ Smith	29.3	0	162	6	3/46	27.00	5.49	29.5	0	0
CDJ Dent	17.0	0	96	2	1/15	48.00	5.64	51.0	0	0
BAC Howell	80.0	0	461	10	2/59	46.10	5.76	48.0	0	0
LC Norwell	8.0	0	48	1	1/48	48.00	6.00	48.0	0	0
DA Payne	74.0	0	449	19	4/44	23.63	6.06	23.3	1	0
MAH Hammond	13.0	0	79	3	2/29	26.33	6.07	26.0	0	0
JK Fuller	64.3	4	401	12	3/42	33.41	6.21	32.2	0	0
EGC Young	35.0	0	219	4	2/31	54.75	6.25	52.5	0	0
WRS Gidman	24.0	3	156	3	2/21	52.00	6.50	48.0	0	0
CN Miles	27.2	0	186	7	2/49	26.57	6.80	23.4	0	0

Catches/Stumpings:
11 Roderick (inc 1st), 10 Klinger, 9 Cockbain, 6 A Gidman, 4 Dent, Howell, 3 Fuller, Payne, Marshall, 2 W Gidman, Young, 1 McCarter, Miles

www.gloscricket.co.uk / tel: 0117 910 8000

GLADIATORS

	Mat	Inns	NO	Runs	HS	Ave	SR	100	50	4s	6s
M Klinger	10	10	3	366	108*	52.28	129.32	1	2	33	11
BAC Howell	10	8	4	94	23*	23.50	127.02	0	0	8	2
IA Cockbain	10	8	0	184	63	23.00	115.00	0	2	16	4
CDJ Dent	10	10	1	182	63*	20.22	115.92	0	1	24	3
TMJ Smith	10	4	3	20	13*	20.00	100.00	0	0	1	0
APR Gidman	10	8	0	140	49	17.50	138.61	0	0	8	9
HJH Marshall	10	8	0	136	49	17.00	110.56	0	0	14	2
DT Christian	10	9	1	113	25*	14.12	108.65	0	0	11	1
DA Payne	9	4	3	13	8*	13.00	118.18	0	0	1	0
RG Coughtrie	1	1	0	11	11	11.00	84.61	0	0	1	0
GH Roderick	9	5	2	20	12	6.66	80.00	0	0	1	0
JK Fuller	5	3	0	9	4	3.00	64.28	0	0	0	0
CN Miles	2	1	0	2	2	2.00	50.00	0	0	0	0
EGC Young	2	1	0	0	0	0.00	0.00	0	0	0	0
MAH Hammond	1	-	-	-	-	-	-	-	-	-	-
TW Shrewsbury	1	-	-	-	-	-	-	-	-	-	-

Batting

	Overs	Mdns	Runs	Wkts	BBI	Ave	Econ	SR	4w	5w
TW Shrewsbury	1.0	0	3	0	-	-	3.00	-	0	0
TMJ Smith	36.0	0	223	11	2/14	20.27	6.19	19.6	0	0
JK Fuller	17.0	1	119	7	3/23	17.00	7.00	14.5	0	0
BAC Howell	32.1	0	233	10	2/15	23.30	7.24	19.3	0	0
CDJ Dent	12.0	0	98	2	1/16	49.00	8.16	36.0	0	0
DA Payne	28.0	0	231	9	3/17	25.66	8.25	18.6	0	0
MAH Hammond	2.0	0	17	0	-	-	8.50	-	0	0
EGC Young	7.0	0	60	3	3/21	20.00	8.57	14.0	0	0
DT Christian	30.4	0	264	4	1/15	66.00	8.60	46.0	0	0
CN Miles	8.0	0	78	0	-	-	9.75	-	0	0
APR Gidman	4.0	0	39	1	1/14	39.00	9.75	24.0	0	0

Bowling

Catches/Stumpings:
5 Cockbain, 4 Dent, A Gidman, 3 Roderick, Christian, 2 Fuller, Payne, Howell, Klinger, Smith, 1 Coughtrie (inc 1st), Miles

TEAM PROFILE

HAMPSHIRE
CRICKET

FORMED: 1863
HOME GROUND: The Ageas Bowl, Southampton
CAPTAIN: Jimmy Adams
2013 RESULTS: CC2: 4/9; YB40: Semi-finalists; FL t20: Semi-finalists
HONOURS: Championship: (2) 1961, 1973; Gillette/NatWest/C&G/FP Trophy: (2) 1991, 2005; Benson & Hedges Cup: (2) 1988, 1992; Pro40/National League/CB40/YB40: 2012; Sunday League: (3) 1975, 1978, 1986; Twenty20 Cup: (2) 2010, 2012

THE LOWDOWN

After doing the limited-overs double in 2012, Hampshire will be disappointed to have finished last season empty-handed, falling at the semi-final stage in both the YB40 and FL t20. Failure to gain promotion to Division One of the County Championship was also a setback but they will have been buoyed by the performances of homegrown talents James Vince and Liam Dawson, who both stepped up to pass 1,000 runs for the campaign. Given the extensive recruitment over the winter, Hampshire fans will be expecting to compete on all fronts in 2014. South African paceman Kyle Abbott looks a shrewd signing, while the returning Aussie Glenn Maxwell will bolster their T20 line-up. Matt Coles impressed on loan from Kent last year to secure a three-year deal, while the signings of Joe Gatting (Sussex) and Durham duo Ruel Brathwaite and Will Smith will add depth to the squad.

FIRST-TEAM COACH: DALE BENKENSTEIN

After hanging up his boots at the end of Durham's Championship-winning campaign last year, Benkenstein's role at Hampshire is his first crack at a head coach position. Over the winter, he worked as a batting coach for the South African side Sunfoil Dolphins, who won the domestic T20 competition. He has a wealth of first-class experience behind him, debuting for Durham back in 2005 and scoring 9,000 first-class runs in a hugely successful period for the club, which included three Championship titles.

COUNTY CHAMPIONSHIP AVERAGES 2013

	Mat	Inns	NO	Runs	HS	Ave	SR	100	50	4s	6s
JM Vince	15	22	4	1101	148	61.16	64.16	4	6	162	7
SP Terry	2	2	0	115	58	57.50	43.07	0	2	17	1
LA Dawson	16	24	3	1031	136*	49.09	46.99	1	8	131	2
ND McKenzie	6	10	1	433	146	48.11	50.58	1	2	66	0
MA Carberry	11	16	0	687	154	42.93	46.60	1	5	98	4
AD Mascarenhas	1	1	0	41	41	41.00	82.00	0	0	7	1
JHK Adams	16	24	3	833	219*	39.66	44.49	3	1	113	2
GJ Bailey	5	7	0	263	93	37.57	56.68	0	2	36	1
AJ Wheater	15	18	2	585	140	36.56	58.44	2	1	83	5
MT Coles	5	5	1	118	68	29.50	60.20	0	2	16	3
MD Bates	5	4	0	117	71	29.25	56.52	0	1	16	0
DR Briggs	12	12	3	244	54	27.11	49.69	0	1	28	2
Sohail Tanvir	4	5	0	133	38	26.60	59.90	0	0	15	3
SM Ervine	15	19	1	458	86	25.44	47.31	0	4	60	0
CP Wood	9	12	1	256	69	23.27	54.93	0	2	34	1
BJ Taylor	1	2	1	20	20	20.00	62.50	0	0	4	0
MDT Roberts	5	8	0	143	44	17.87	40.85	0	0	20	1
RMR Brathwaite	3	2	0	26	17	13.00	47.27	0	0	1	1
JA Tomlinson	15	15	8	72	30*	10.28	32.87	0	0	10	1
DJ Balcombe	12	13	2	106	30*	9.63	45.49	0	0	12	2
AP Rouse	1	1	0	9	9	9.00	23.68	0	0	0	0
DA Griffiths	2	2	0	15	14	7.50	41.66	0	0	0	2

	Overs	Mdns	Runs	Wkts	BBI	BBM	Ave	Econ	SR	5w	10w
AD Mascarenhas	25.0	7	61	4	4/61	4/61	15.25	2.44	37.5	0	0
ND McKenzie	10.0	4	17	1	1/10	1/17	17.00	1.70	60.0	0	0
MT Coles	127.0	27	504	21	6/71	10/154	24.00	3.96	36.2	2	1
JA Tomlinson	454.5	126	1281	53	5/44	6/72	24.16	2.81	51.4	1	0
BJ Taylor	22.0	3	106	4	4/64	4/106	26.50	4.81	33.0	0	0
SM Ervine	179.1	39	577	17	2/17	3/77	33.94	3.22	63.2	0	0
Sohail Tanvir	107.2	19	348	10	3/62	4/105	34.80	3.24	64.4	0	0
DR Briggs	270.0	59	798	22	3/33	5/51	36.27	2.95	73.6	0	0
RMR Brathwaite	58.0	13	222	6	3/112	3/126	37.00	3.82	58.0	0	0
CP Wood	231.3	65	659	15	3/30	4/48	43.93	2.84	92.6	0	0
JM Vince	102.4	11	396	9	2/2	2/30	44.00	3.85	68.4	0	0
DA Griffiths	53.3	7	237	5	2/70	3/134	47.40	4.42	64.2	0	0
DJ Balcombe	349.0	80	1101	22	5/104	6/165	50.04	3.15	95.1	1	0
JHK Adams	14.0	1	52	1	1/26	1/26	52.00	3.71	84.0	0	0
LA Dawson	196.5	49	602	9	2/77	3/147	66.88	3.05	131.2	0	0
MA Carberry	19.3	2	87	1	1/44	1/44	87.00	4.46	117.0	0	0
MDT Roberts	3.5	1	19	0	-	-	-	4.95	-	0	0

Catches/Stumpings:
23 Dawson, 21 Wheater (inc 2st), Ervine, 16 Bates, Vince, 7 Adams, 6 Wood, Briggs, 3 Bailey, Carberry, 2 Terry, Roberts, 1 Taylor, Brathwaite, Coles, McKenzie, Balcombe, Tomlinson

HAMPSHIRE
CRICKET

Batting

	Mat	Inns	NO	Runs	HS	Ave	SR	100	50	4s	6s
JHK Adams	13	13	3	519	67	51.90	85.08	0	5	41	4
MA Carberry	11	11	1	471	150*	47.10	114.32	1	3	57	10
LA Dawson	13	10	2	318	69	39.75	108.16	0	2	30	6
JM Vince	12	12	2	396	129*	39.60	101.02	1	2	56	1
SM Ervine	12	10	1	311	65*	34.55	95.39	0	3	31	2
SP Terry	1	1	0	33	33	33.00	70.21	0	0	2	0
AJ Wheater	12	10	3	195	70	27.85	110.79	0	1	18	3
ND McKenzie	8	7	0	168	65	24.00	73.04	0	1	12	0
MDT Roberts	3	2	0	48	25	24.00	65.75	0	0	6	0
CP Wood	13	8	4	90	41	22.50	128.57	0	0	13	1
AD Mascarenhas	10	7	1	112	31	18.66	105.66	0	0	11	2
GJ Bailey	5	3	0	46	24	15.33	73.01	0	0	4	0
H Riazuddin	3	1	0	15	15	15.00	125.00	0	0	2	0
Sohail Tanvir	6	3	2	14	11*	14.00	155.55	0	0	0	1
DR Briggs	12	3	2	7	6	7.00	100.00	0	0	0	0
JA Tomlinson	2	1	1	1	1*	-	100.00	0	0	0	0
DA Griffiths	4	1	1	0	0*	-	-	0	0	0	0
DJ Balcombe	1	-	-	-	-	-	-	-	-	-	-
MD Bates	1	-	-	-	-	-	-	-	-	-	-
BJ Taylor	1	-	-	-	-	-	-	-	-	-	-

Bowling

	Overs	Mdns	Runs	Wkts	BBI	Ave	Econ	SR	4w	5w
Sohail Tanvir	47.1	4	207	17	4/29	12.17	4.38	16.6	2	0
AD Mascarenhas	69.0	1	315	13	5/42	24.23	4.56	31.8	0	1
DJ Balcombe	6.0	0	28	2	2/28	14.00	4.66	18.0	0	0
MA Carberry	13.0	0	68	3	3/37	22.66	5.23	26.0	0	0
H Riazuddin	19.0	1	100	2	1/28	50.00	5.26	57.0	0	0
CP Wood	96.3	4	532	17	3/23	31.29	5.51	34.0	0	0
LA Dawson	76.0	2	430	10	2/26	43.00	5.65	45.6	0	0
SM Ervine	41.0	0	233	6	2/20	38.83	5.68	41.0	0	0
DR Briggs	84.0	2	510	10	2/35	51.00	6.07	50.4	0	0
BJ Taylor	8.0	0	50	2	2/50	25.00	6.25	24.0	0	0
JM Vince	6.0	0	38	0	-	-	6.33	-	0	0
JA Tomlinson	9.0	1	63	1	1/38	63.00	7.00	54.0	0	0
DA Griffiths	22.0	0	164	5	3/42	32.80	7.45	26.4	0	0

Catches/Stumpings:
10 Wheater (inc 4st), 8 Dawson, 7 Adams, Wood, 5 Vince, 4 Briggs, Ervine, 3 Mascarenhas, 2 Bailey, McKenzie, Carberry, 1 Bates, Balcombe, Terry, Riazuddin, Griffiths

FRIENDS LIFE T20 AVERAGES 2013

HAMPSHIRE
CRICKET

	Mat	Inns	NO	Runs	HS	Ave	SR	100	50	4s	6s
ND McKenzie	10	8	5	301	71*	100.33	129.18	0	1	33	2
MA Carberry	12	11	2	502	100*	55.77	142.61	1	4	59	16
SM Ervine	12	11	3	238	60*	29.75	127.27	0	1	19	9
JM Vince	12	11	0	269	84	24.45	138.65	0	2	35	7
JHK Adams	12	11	0	210	43	19.09	118.64	0	0	21	4
CP Wood	12	2	1	13	12	13.00	216.66	0	0	1	1
LA Dawson	12	10	4	63	24*	10.50	98.43	0	0	3	1
Sohail Tanvir	9	2	1	9	7*	9.00	100.00	0	0	1	0
AD Mascarenhas	11	4	1	24	15	8.00	104.34	0	0	2	0
AJ Wheater	11	5	2	22	12*	7.33	78.57	0	0	0	1
DR Briggs	12	1	1	5	5*	-	166.66	0	0	1	0
MD Bates	3	1	1	0	0*	-	-	0	0	0	0
DA Griffiths	4	-	-	-	-	-	-	-	-	-	-

Batting

	Overs	Mdns	Runs	Wkts	BBI	Ave	Econ	SR	4w	5w
JM Vince	6.0	0	30	1	1/5	30.00	5.00	36.0	0	0
DR Briggs	44.0	0	286	15	3/19	19.06	6.50	17.6	0	0
SM Ervine	1.0	0	7	0	-	-	7.00	-	0	0
DA Griffiths	16.0	0	116	4	2/23	29.00	7.25	24.0	0	0
LA Dawson	38.0	0	277	13	4/19	21.30	7.28	17.5	1	0
AD Mascarenhas	41.0	0	310	12	2/19	25.83	7.56	20.5	0	0
CP Wood	44.1	0	344	12	3/31	28.66	7.78	22.0	0	0
Sohail Tanvir	31.2	0	272	9	3/29	30.22	8.68	20.8	0	0

Bowling

Catches/Stumpings:
9 Dawson, 5 Ervine, Vince, Wheater (inc 2st), 4 Carberry, Wood, 3 McKenzie, Adams, 2 Bates, Mascarenhas, Briggs,
1 Griffiths, Tanvir

FORMED: 1870
HOME GROUND: The Spitfire Ground, Canterbury
ONE-DAY NAME: Kent Spitfires
CAPTAIN: Rob Key
2013 RESULTS: CC2: 7/9; YB40: 4/7 in Group A; FL t20: 5/6 in South Division
HONOURS: Championship: (7) 1906, 1909, 1910, 1913, 1970, 1977(s), 1978; Gillette/NatWest/C&G/FP Trophy: (2) 1967, 1974; Pro40/National League/CB40: 2001; Benson & Hedges Cup: (3) 1973, 1976, 1978; Sunday League: (4) 1972, 1973, 1976, 1995; Twenty20 Cup: 2007

THE LOWDOWN

Taking wickets proved difficult for Kent in 2013, as the club endured an indifferent season in all three competitions. Batting was no issue, particularly in the four-day game, with Rob Key, Darren Stevens and Brendan Nash all passing 1,000 runs in the Championship. Indeed, the star-turns were left to those three, particularly Nash, who hit a brilliant 199 before succumbing to heat exhaustion as he helped Kent chase down 411 against Gloucestershire in July. This year sees Key resume the captaincy with Sam Northeast acting as his deputy, after James Tredwell, newly awarded an incremental contract by England, stepping aside. The bowling has been strengthened with the signing of Australian left-arm seamer Doug Bollinger, who is expected to be available for the entire season as Kent's overseas player. The recruitment of former Hampshire quick David Griffiths will also bolster the pace department.

HEAD COACH: JIMMY ADAMS

The ex-West Indies captain begins his third season at the helm, having been appointed in January 2012. In his playing days, Adams made a stunning start to his Test career, averaging 87 after 12 matches. After retirement he moved into a role working with the West Indies under 19s before making the move to England to lead Kent. He will be supported this season by club legend Matt Walker as assistant coach.

Batting

	Mat	Inns	NO	Runs	HS	Ave	SR	100	50	4s	6s
DI Stevens	15	21	1	1268	205*	63.40	80.30	4	7	161	21
RWT Key	16	27	3	1168	180	48.66	52.51	5	3	139	4
BP Nash	16	26	4	1064	199*	48.36	62.55	5	5	135	4
BW Harmison	13	19	3	712	106	44.50	48.23	2	5	92	4
CJ Haggett	11	13	7	249	44*	41.50	42.56	0	0	31	0
AJ Ball	2	3	0	108	69	36.00	48.00	0	1	13	0
MJ Powell	6	9	3	203	70	33.83	38.01	0	2	25	0
SA Northeast	15	26	1	650	94	26.00	48.21	0	6	84	0
GO Jones	14	19	2	403	67	23.70	53.37	0	2	51	0
DJ Bell-Drummond	13	20	0	466	79	23.30	43.18	0	4	59	2
ME Claydon	3	4	0	93	40	23.25	62.00	0	0	13	0
MT Coles	7	9	1	136	59	17.00	51.71	0	1	17	1
JC Tredwell	11	14	1	197	48	15.15	53.97	0	0	25	0
AEN Riley	5	6	2	60	21*	15.00	24.39	0	0	9	0
SW Billings	2	3	0	45	24	15.00	41.66	0	0	5	0
M Davies	10	14	3	158	41	14.36	64.75	0	0	19	2
VD Philander	2	2	0	25	23	12.50	39.68	0	0	1	1
CE Shreck	14	15	8	82	19*	11.71	47.39	0	0	10	2
MD Hunn	1	1	0	0	0	0.00	0.00	0	0	0	0

Bowling

	Overs	Mdns	Runs	Wkts	BBI	BBM	Ave	Econ	SR	5w	10w
M Davies	266.3	74	629	25	4/36	7/67	25.16	2.36	63.9	0	0
AEN Riley	102.3	11	361	14	7/150	7/167	25.78	3.52	43.9	1	0
DI Stevens	403.4	111	1051	32	5/39	6/57	32.84	2.60	75.6	1	0
CJ Haggett	298.0	72	907	26	4/94	4/94	34.88	3.04	68.7	0	0
CE Shreck	429.2	98	1294	33	4/65	4/91	39.21	3.01	78.0	0	0
MD Hunn	31.4	6	118	3	2/51	3/118	39.33	3.72	63.3	0	0
MT Coles	162.0	28	549	13	5/31	5/35	42.23	3.38	74.7	1	0
BP Nash	9.0	0	43	1	1/9	1/9	43.00	4.77	54.0	0	0
ME Claydon	64.4	12	226	4	3/85	3/85	56.50	3.49	97.0	0	0
AJ Ball	37.0	4	170	3	2/42	2/100	56.66	4.59	74.0	0	0
JC Tredwell	331.3	67	965	17	5/51	6/170	56.76	2.91	117.0	1	0
SA Northeast	20.0	0	131	1	1/60	1/60	131.00	6.55	120.0	0	0
BW Harmison	37.0	1	161	1	1/21	1/21	161.00	4.35	222.0	0	0
DJ Bell-Drummond	6.5	0	54	0	-	-	-	7.90	-	0	0
RWT Key	9.2	0	86	0	-	-	-	9.21	-	0	0
VD Philander	64.0	9	170	0	-	-	-	2.65	-	0	0

Catches/Stumpings:

41 Jones (inc 1st), 13 Stevens, 11 Northeast, 9 Tredwell, 8 Harmison, 7 Bell-Drummond, 6 Coles, 5 Billings (inc 1st), 4 Nash, 3 Haggett, Key, 2 Riley, 1 Hunn, Claydon, Shreck

		Mat	Inns	NO	Runs	HS	Ave	SR	100	50	4s	6s
Batting	FK Cowdrey	4	4	2	110	52*	55.00	102.80	0	1	8	3
	RWT Key	11	11	1	505	144*	50.50	94.04	2	2	62	2
	BP Nash	12	12	3	436	98*	48.44	86.33	0	2	38	0
	SA Northeast	10	10	0	382	115	38.20	86.03	1	1	31	3
	DI Stevens	12	12	2	309	118	30.90	108.80	1	1	29	11
	AJ Blake	2	2	0	57	43	28.50	142.50	0	0	8	1
	JC Tredwell	10	6	3	81	42*	27.00	89.01	0	0	7	2
	MT Coles	10	7	4	74	21	24.66	132.14	0	0	8	3
	BW Harmison	7	6	2	96	42	24.00	75.59	0	0	9	1
	GO Jones	12	10	3	155	46*	22.14	92.81	0	0	14	2
	SW Billings	5	5	0	80	57	16.00	68.37	0	1	6	0
	AJ Ball	9	6	0	64	28	10.66	110.34	0	0	8	0
	ME Claydon	5	1	0	8	8	8.00	266.66	0	0	0	1
	AEN Riley	11	2	1	3	2	3.00	60.00	0	0	0	0
	CJ Haggett	3	2	0	2	2	1.00	33.33	0	0	0	0
	M Davies	8	2	1	1	1	1.00	25.00	0	0	0	0
	CE Shreck	1	-	-	-	-	-	-	-	-	-	-

		Overs	Mdns	Runs	Wkts	BBI	Ave	Econ	SR	4w	5w
Bowling	JC Tredwell	70.0	2	304	13	4/22	23.38	4.34	32.3	1	0
	FK Cowdrey	4.0	0	18	0	-	-	4.50	-	0	0
	BP Nash	3.0	0	15	1	1/15	15.00	5.00	18.0	0	0
	DI Stevens	83.1	1	421	13	3/19	32.38	5.06	38.3	0	0
	M Davies	51.2	5	280	8	2/14	35.00	5.45	38.5	0	0
	MT Coles	62.2	2	367	15	4/20	24.46	5.88	24.9	1	0
	AEN Riley	64.0	0	377	10	2/33	37.70	5.89	38.4	0	0
	AJ Ball	43.0	0	282	4	3/36	70.50	6.55	64.5	0	0
	ME Claydon	27.4	1	193	5	2/29	38.60	6.97	33.2	0	0
	CJ Haggett	20.0	0	161	4	2/97	40.25	8.05	30.0	0	0
	CE Shreck	3.0	0	27	0	-	-	9.00	-	0	0

Catches/Stumpings:
9 Jones (inc 1st), 8 Stevens, 5 Billings, Coles, Tredwell, 4 Riley, 3 Harmison, Northeast, Nash, 2 Davies, Ball, Key, 1 Blake, Haggett

	Mat	Inns	NO	Runs	HS	Ave	SR	100	50	4s	6s
DI Stevens	10	9	2	267	67*	38.14	160.84	0	1	20	15
FK Cowdrey	5	5	1	152	50	38.00	115.15	0	1	17	2
SA Northeast	5	5	0	119	61	23.80	112.26	0	1	8	3
VD Philander	7	6	3	71	15*	23.66	102.89	0	0	2	1
SW Billings	10	10	1	189	28	21.00	109.24	0	0	19	2
BW Harmison	7	5	2	51	19*	17.00	94.44	0	0	3	1
RWT Key	5	5	0	80	26	16.00	93.02	0	0	6	2
BP Nash	1	1	0	15	15	15.00	48.38	0	0	0	0
AJ Blake	10	9	2	98	37*	14.00	102.08	0	0	10	2
DJ Bell-Drummond	4	4	0	50	27	12.50	100.00	0	0	6	1
MT Coles	10	7	1	71	40	11.83	139.21	0	0	5	4
GO Jones	7	4	0	37	22	9.25	82.22	0	0	2	0
JC Tredwell	6	4	1	18	15*	6.00	112.50	0	0	2	0
ME Claydon	10	5	2	9	4*	3.00	33.33	0	0	0	0
AEN Riley	10	4	3	3	2	3.00	60.00	0	0	0	0
M Davies	2	1	0	0	0	0.00	-	0	0	0	0
CJ Haggett	1	-	-	-	-	-	-	-	-	-	-

Batting

	Overs	Mdns	Runs	Wkts	BBI	Ave	Econ	SR	4w	5w
JC Tredwell	20.0	0	115	7	3/19	16.42	5.75	17.1	0	0
AEN Riley	33.4	0	230	6	2/23	38.33	6.83	33.6	0	0
FK Cowdrey	6.0	0	48	1	1/30	48.00	8.00	36.0	0	0
VD Philander	26.0	1	211	9	4/8	23.44	8.11	17.3	1	0
DI Stevens	26.0	0	216	6	2/16	36.00	8.30	26.0	0	0
ME Claydon	35.1	0	294	13	3/22	22.61	8.36	16.2	0	0
MT Coles	31.4	0	272	8	3/14	34.00	8.58	23.7	0	0
M Davies	8.0	0	77	2	1/33	38.50	9.62	24.0	0	0

Bowling

Catches/Stumpings:
8 Billings, 7 Coles, 6 Blake, 4 Harmison, Claydon, Stevens, 2 Riley, 1 Jones, Haggett, Nash, Bell-Drummond, Northeast, Tredwell

TM

Lancashire County Cricket Club

FORMED: 1864
HOME GROUND: Emirates Old Trafford, Manchester
ONE-DAY NAME: Lancashire Lightning
CAPTAIN: Glen Chapple
2013 RESULTS: CC2: Winners; YB40: 3/7 in Group B; FL t20: Quarter-finalists
HONOURS: Championship: (9) 1897, 1904, 1926, 1927, 1928, 1930, 1950(s), 2011; Gillette/NatWest/C&G/FP Trophy: (7) 1970, 1971, 1972, 1985, 1990, 1996, 1998; Benson & Hedges Cup: (4) 1984, 1990, 1995, 1996; Pro40/National League/CB40/YB40: 1999; Sunday League: (4) 1969, 1970, 1989, 1998

THE LOWDOWN

For all of Lancashire's homegrown talent, it was the experience of Ashwell Prince, Simon Katich and the evergreen Glen Chapple that showed the way last season, as the Red Rose returned to the top table of county cricket with a comprehensive Division Two title win. Chapple passed the 50-wicket mark in first-class cricket once again and the Lancashire skipper was ably supported by seamer Kyle Hogg and spinner Simon Kerrigan, who shared 118 wickets between them. Young opener Luis Reece was also a notable performer, stringing together seven consecutive half-centuries at one stage and finishing the season with an average in excess of 50. Going into 2014, Lancashire have been hugely boosted by the signing of keeper-batsman Jos Buttler from Somerset. An exceptional player making waves on the international stage, he will add some flair and sparkle to the Lancs middle-order. Also well worth keeping an eye on will be Zimbabwean-born seamer Kyle Jarvis, who has signed for the club and plans to qualify for England.

HEAD COACH: PETER MOORES

The genial former England coach remains one of the world leaders in his field and in March 2013 he was one of only 10 people accepted on to an elite coaching programme run by UK Sport. In 2003 he made history by helping Sussex to their first Championship title and Lancashire's title win in 2011 further enhanced his reputation.

COUNTY CHAMPIONSHIP AVERAGES 2013

	Mat	Inns	NO	Runs	HS	Ave	SR	100	50	4s	6s
SM Katich	12	16	1	1097	200	73.13	66.08	4	6	142	7
LM Reece	10	16	3	722	97	55.53	51.79	0	8	103	3
AG Prince	16	26	2	1169	134	48.70	56.50	3	7	137	12
TC Smith	7	8	2	289	88	48.16	51.33	0	2	41	1
PJ Horton	10	16	0	645	156	40.31	47.25	3	3	86	2
SJ Croft	8	13	3	379	101*	37.90	57.68	1	2	41	7
AP Agathangelou	11	16	2	497	121	35.50	53.96	1	2	63	9
LA Procter	15	21	0	718	106	34.19	48.77	1	7	95	4
AL Davies	3	3	1	58	30*	29.00	53.21	0	0	6	1
KR Brown	10	16	0	428	87	26.75	44.31	0	3	59	4
SC Kerrigan	13	11	5	146	62*	24.33	40.00	0	1	11	2
GD Cross	13	17	0	409	100	24.05	51.38	1	2	47	3
G Chapple	14	16	3	308	63	23.69	62.34	0	3	35	4
WA White	6	9	3	133	61	22.16	63.94	0	1	15	1
KW Hogg	15	16	5	241	58	21.90	48.68	0	1	29	0
SC Moore	2	4	0	81	34	20.25	76.41	0	0	11	0
JM Anderson	2	3	1	37	26	18.50	32.74	0	0	6	0
SD Parry	3	3	1	37	20	18.50	39.78	0	0	6	0
OJ Newby	3	2	1	10	9*	10.00	25.00	0	0	1	0
AM Lilley	2	2	2	39	35*	-	108.33	0	0	5	0
KM Jarvis	1	1	1	3	3*	-	15.78	0	0	0	0

Batting

	Overs	Mdns	Runs	Wkts	BBI	BBM	Ave	Econ	SR	5w	10w
KW Hogg	436.0	105	1105	60	7/27	9/73	18.41	2.53	43.6	3	0
G Chapple	430.4	110	1099	53	5/9	8/56	20.73	2.55	48.7	2	0
SC Kerrigan	461.2	108	1191	57	7/63	12/252	20.89	2.58	48.5	5	1
OJ Newby	68.2	12	264	12	4/71	6/112	22.00	3.86	34.1	0	0
JM Anderson	72.1	20	180	8	4/57	4/86	22.50	2.49	54.1	0	0
TC Smith	150.5	35	498	22	4/49	5/88	22.63	3.30	41.1	0	0
SD Parry	65.3	5	197	5	3/51	3/136	39.40	3.00	78.6	0	0
AP Agathangelou	43.0	12	125	3	2/18	2/18	41.66	2.90	86.0	0	0
LA Procter	194.0	31	633	15	4/39	4/39	42.20	3.26	77.6	0	0
LM Reece	22.0	2	89	2	1/20	1/20	44.50	4.04	66.0	0	0
KM Jarvis	34.0	1	179	4	3/72	4/179	44.75	5.26	51.0	0	0
WA White	131.0	16	452	8	2/69	2/52	56.50	3.45	98.2	0	0
AM Lilley	69.0	9	212	2	1/41	2/83	106.00	3.07	207.0	0	0
SJ Croft	41.0	6	132	1	1/11	1/32	132.00	3.21	246.0	0	0

Bowling

Catches/Stumpings:
37 Cross (inc 2st), 24 Agathangelou, 16 Prince, 9 Smith, Chapple, 8 Brown, Reece, 7 Katich, 5 Procter, 4 Croft, 3 Davies, Kerrigan, 2 White, Hogg, 1 Jarvis, Anderson, Horton

Batting

	Mat	Inns	NO	Runs	HS	Ave	SR	100	50	4s	6s
AG Prince	12	11	2	506	100	56.22	101.81	1	3	49	7
TC Smith	6	6	2	204	97	51.00	84.64	0	1	20	0
J Clark	7	5	1	145	72	36.25	100.69	0	1	17	3
KR Brown	10	9	1	277	80	34.62	83.68	0	2	26	4
Kabir Ali	8	4	1	90	59	30.00	163.63	0	1	7	5
SC Moore	12	11	0	296	53	26.90	94.56	0	2	38	5
WA White	6	4	1	75	37	25.00	78.12	0	0	6	0
SM Katich	9	8	1	174	60	24.85	95.08	0	2	16	3
PJ Horton	2	2	0	48	45	24.00	73.84	0	0	2	0
GD Cross	12	8	1	148	36	21.14	111.27	0	0	18	2
SJ Croft	12	10	0	191	65	19.10	77.32	0	1	13	1
KW Hogg	8	4	1	16	12	5.33	39.02	0	0	0	1
AM Lilley	4	2	0	10	10	5.00	125.00	0	0	2	0
SC Kerrigan	6	3	2	5	4*	5.00	125.00	0	0	1	0
OJ Newby	4	2	0	8	8	4.00	40.00	0	0	0	0
SD Parry	8	4	4	51	23*	-	96.22	0	0	5	0
G Chapple	5	2	2	27	22*	-	180.00	0	0	4	0
AP Agathangelou	1	-	-	-	-	-	-	-	-	-	-

Bowling

	Overs	Mdns	Runs	Wkts	BBI	Ave	Econ	SR	4w	5w
SD Parry	52.0	4	216	11	5/17	19.63	4.15	28.3	0	1
G Chapple	39.0	3	164	8	3/33	20.50	4.20	29.2	0	0
TC Smith	41.0	0	213	6	2/22	35.50	5.19	41.0	0	0
AM Lilley	28.0	0	148	7	4/30	21.14	5.28	24.0	1	0
SC Kerrigan	41.0	2	241	2	1/45	120.50	5.87	123.0	0	0
KW Hogg	54.0	0	319	6	2/54	53.16	5.90	54.0	0	0
SJ Croft	38.0	1	238	5	1/11	47.60	6.26	45.6	0	0
Kabir Ali	60.1	2	378	18	4/37	21.00	6.28	20.0	1	0
WA White	30.0	1	209	10	4/35	20.90	6.96	18.0	2	0
OJ Newby	13.5	0	97	2	2/41	48.50	7.01	41.5	0	0
J Clark	24.0	0	172	3	2/45	57.33	7.16	48.0	0	0
AP Agathangelou	1.0	0	13	0	-	-	13.00	-	0	0

Catches/Stumpings:
17 Cross (inc 4st), 6 Croft, Prince, 5 Kerrigan, 4 Parry, Katich, 3 Lilley, Chapple, 2 Smith, Moore, 1 Newby, White, Clark, Ali, Hogg, Brown

FRIENDS LIFE T20 AVERAGES 2013

	Mat	Inns	NO	Runs	HS	Ave	SR	100	50	4s	6s	
SM Katich	10	9	3	265	62*	44.16	140.21	0	1	27	6	
SC Moore	11	11	1	338	75	33.80	143.22	0	3	39	8	
KR Brown	11	11	3	260	62	32.50	131.31	0	2	22	9	
SJ Croft	11	10	2	238	52	29.75	119.00	0	1	15	5	
GD Cross	11	8	2	139	32*	23.16	149.46	0	0	6	7	
TC Smith	10	9	0	200	42	22.22	133.33	0	0	16	10	Batting
AG Prince	9	9	1	136	32	17.00	113.33	0	0	10	2	
MJ McClenaghan	11	3	2	15	10*	15.00	150.00	0	0	2	0	
AM Lilley	8	3	1	24	18	12.00	150.00	0	0	4	0	
Kabir Ali	11	6	2	23	10	5.75	69.69	0	0	0	1	
G Chapple	7	3	0	7	6	2.33	87.50	0	0	1	0	
SC Kerrigan	5	2	2	5	4*	-	166.66	0	0	1	0	
J Clark	1	-	-	-	-	-	-	-	-	-	-	
SD Parry	5	-	-	-	-	-	-	-	-	-	-	

	Overs	Mdns	Runs	Wkts	BBI	Ave	Econ	SR	4w	5w	
AM Lilley	27.0	0	187	5	1/21	37.40	6.92	32.4	0	0	
SC Kerrigan	18.0	0	126	5	1/20	25.20	7.00	21.6	0	0	
SJ Croft	22.0	0	157	2	1/15	78.50	7.13	66.0	0	0	
G Chapple	26.0	0	191	6	2/22	31.83	7.34	26.0	0	0	Bowling
J Clark	2.0	0	15	0	-	-	7.50	-	0	0	
SD Parry	19.0	0	150	4	1/21	37.50	7.89	28.5	0	0	
MJ McClenaghan	43.0	1	355	17	5/29	20.88	8.25	15.1	0	1	
TC Smith	24.0	0	206	6	2/21	34.33	8.58	24.0	0	0	
Kabir Ali	36.1	0	316	14	3/23	22.57	8.73	15.5	0	0	

Catches/Stumpings:
9 Prince, 6 Cross, Croft, 5 Kerrigan, Smith, 4 Brown, 3 Lilley, Moore, 2 Chapple, Katich, Ali, 1 McClenaghan

LEICESTERSHIRE
COUNTY CRICKET CLUB

FORMED: 1879
HOME GROUND: County Ground, Grace Road, Leicester
ONE-DAY NAME: Leicestershire Foxes
CAPTAIN: Ramnaresh Sarwan (Championship), Josh Cobb (RL50 and NWT20)
2013 RESULTS: CC2: 9/9; YB40: 5/7 in Group C; FL t20: 4/6 in North Division
HONOURS: Championship: (3) 1975, 1996, 1998; Benson & Hedges Cup: (3) 1972, 1975, 1985; Sunday League: (2) 1974, 1977; Twenty20 Cup: (3) 2004, 2006, 2011

THE LOWDOWN

Finishing at the bottom of the pile for the second time in three years, Leicestershire could at least take solace from the fact that a handful of their younger players came forward as real talents in this period of flux for the club. Limited-overs captain Josh Cobb started the 40-over season in superb fashion with three back-to-back centuries but the brightest spark was Ned Eckersley, who finished as the club's leading run-scorer in the Championship, taking home no less than six awards at the club's end of season bash. Matthew Hoggard and Claude Henderson have retired and, while Charlie Shreck has been signed from Kent to add some experience to the seam attack and Ramnaresh Sarwan has been retained as overseas player and four-day skipper, it will be down to an exciting crop of youngsters to revitalise the county this summer. Former Derbyshire batsman Dan Redfern is an exciting but unfulfilled talent and he will be hoping to find some consistency after his switch to Grace Road.

DIRECTOR OF CRICKET: PHIL WHITTICASE

Whitticase is part of the furniture at Grace Road, having spent the duration of his playing career with Leicestershire before moving into a coaching role at the club. He replaced Tim Boon as head coach in 2010, combining the role with that of academy director. In October 2013 his role was changed to director of cricket, with the former Leicestershire batsman Ben Smith becoming first-team coach.

	Mat	Inns	NO	Runs	HS	Ave	SR	100	50	4s	6s
EJH Eckersley	16	27	3	1275	147	53.12	53.45	4	4	180	3
CW Henderson	1	2	1	38	33	38.00	80.85	0	0	7	0
NL Buck	4	3	2	37	16*	37.00	45.12	0	0	3	1
RR Sarwan	5	8	1	255	79	36.42	42.92	0	2	37	1
MAG Boyce	14	21	1	633	135	31.65	39.73	1	2	91	0
SJ Thakor	14	22	3	583	114	30.68	40.94	1	4	61	1
JA Burns	5	8	1	214	77	30.57	50.23	0	1	28	1
NJ O'Brien	14	23	0	695	67	30.21	50.28	0	6	93	0
BA Raine	5	8	1	190	72	27.14	38.15	0	1	25	1
GP Smith	12	21	1	487	70	24.35	53.28	0	4	82	1
TJ Wells	5	8	0	177	82	22.12	62.98	0	1	30	1
MA Thornely	10	15	0	269	53	17.93	37.56	0	1	37	3
AJ Robson	3	4	0	59	49	14.75	39.33	0	0	9	0
JJ Cobb	11	18	2	234	46*	14.62	43.73	0	0	31	3
AJ Ireland	2	3	1	28	15*	14.00	103.70	0	0	5	0
JS Sykes	7	12	2	139	34	13.90	35.91	0	0	14	0
JKH Naik	9	11	2	123	47*	13.66	28.27	0	0	7	0
ACF Wyatt	10	15	6	107	28	11.88	47.98	0	0	14	0
OH Freckingham	15	21	2	204	30	10.73	39.00	0	0	32	1
MJ Hoggard	7	11	3	75	24	9.37	40.76	0	0	12	0
RML Taylor	2	2	0	12	12	6.00	57.14	0	0	1	0
REM Williams	5	5	1	18	12	4.50	30.50	0	0	2	0

Batting

	Overs	Mdns	Runs	Wkts	BBI	BBM	Ave	Econ	SR	5w	10w
EJH Eckersley	8.1	1	42	2	2/29	2/29	21.00	5.14	24.5	0	0
MJ Hoggard	171.0	35	545	16	6/66	7/102	34.06	3.18	64.1	1	0
BA Raine	98.3	17	349	9	4/98	4/98	38.77	3.54	65.6	0	0
JKH Naik	286.3	53	844	21	5/98	6/118	40.19	2.94	81.8	1	0
OH Freckingham	399.0	61	1584	36	6/125	9/188	44.00	3.96	66.5	1	0
ACF Wyatt	287.4	65	904	20	3/35	6/115	45.20	3.14	86.3	0	0
REM Williams	122.1	20	436	8	4/69	4/94	54.50	3.56	91.6	0	0
NL Buck	94.3	19	365	6	3/83	3/83	60.83	3.86	94.5	0	0
JS Sykes	199.3	30	733	12	4/176	4/176	61.08	3.67	99.7	0	0
SJ Thakor	133.1	21	537	7	2/24	2/24	76.71	4.03	114.1	0	0
RML Taylor	48.1	11	156	2	1/53	1/57	78.00	3.23	144.5	0	0
MA Thornely	63.2	13	262	3	1/14	1/21	87.33	4.13	126.6	0	0
CW Henderson	30.0	5	93	1	1/57	1/93	93.00	3.10	180.0	0	0
AJ Ireland	54.0	7	192	2	1/83	1/83	96.00	3.55	162.0	0	0
TJ Wells	37.0	5	129	1	1/36	1/36	129.00	3.48	222.0	0	0
AJ Robson	1.0	0	11	0	-	-		11.00	-	0	0
RR Sarwan	2.0	0	11	0	-	-		5.50	-	0	0
JJ Cobb	58.1	5	202	0	-	-		3.47	-	0	0

Bowling

Catches/Stumpings:
28 O'Brien (inc 3st), 12 Smith, 8 Thornely, 7 Naik, Boyce, 4 Eckersley, Burns, Sarwan, Thakor, Freckingham, 3 Sykes, Cobb, 2 Wells, 1 Williams, Hoggard, Wyatt

Batting

	Mat	Inns	NO	Runs	HS	Ave	SR	100	50	4s	6s
JJ Cobb	12	12	1	578	130	52.54	113.77	3	1	68	12
NJ O'Brien	10	10	0	380	104	38.00	90.26	1	1	39	2
GP Smith	11	11	1	318	135*	31.80	97.84	1	2	35	5
EJH Eckersley	9	9	0	282	108	31.33	92.15	1	1	25	3
RML Taylor	11	9	4	150	48*	30.00	108.69	0	0	11	5
MA Thornely	12	10	1	245	68	27.22	106.98	0	1	18	8
MAG Boyce	10	10	0	223	53	22.30	85.76	0	1	17	2
JKH Naik	4	4	1	54	22*	18.00	73.97	0	0	2	1
JA Burns	5	5	0	82	71	16.40	67.21	0	1	7	2
SJ Thakor	12	12	2	151	64*	15.10	74.01	0	1	9	0
AJ Ireland	7	6	1	63	27	12.60	106.77	0	0	7	2
REM Williams	7	3	2	9	5	9.00	42.85	0	0	1	0
RR Sarwan	1	1	0	8	8	8.00	88.88	0	0	1	0
NL Buck	6	2	1	7	7*	7.00	116.66	0	0	1	0
BA Raine	2	1	0	7	7	7.00	175.00	0	0	0	1
JS Sykes	8	4	1	15	15	5.00	88.23	0	0	2	0
ACF Wyatt	2	2	0	0	0	0.00	0.00	0	0	0	0
TJ Wells	3	3	3	88	32*	-	204.65	0	0	9	6

Bowling

	Overs	Mdns	Runs	Wkts	BBI	Ave	Econ	SR	4w	5w
JJ Cobb	57.0	1	319	7	3/34	45.57	5.59	48.8	0	0
JKH Naik	25.2	0	142	4	2/34	35.50	5.60	38.0	0	0
ACF Wyatt	12.0	0	68	1	1/23	68.00	5.66	72.0	0	0
JS Sykes	45.0	0	270	4	2/37	67.50	6.00	67.5	0	0
AJ Ireland	46.0	1	284	5	2/41	56.80	6.17	55.2	0	0
REM Williams	50.1	1	316	6	3/34	52.66	6.29	50.1	0	0
RML Taylor	68.3	2	444	14	3/45	31.71	6.48	29.3	0	0
BA Raine	15.0	1	101	2	2/59	50.50	6.73	45.0	0	0
MA Thornely	20.0	0	136	1	1/25	136.00	6.80	120.0	0	0
NL Buck	44.2	1	324	10	3/25	32.40	7.30	26.6	0	0
SJ Thakor	51.2	1	390	9	3/39	43.33	7.59	34.2	0	0

Catches/Stumpings:
12 O'Brien (inc 1st), 4 Eckersley, Taylor, Thakor, 3 Burns, Boyce, Smith, Thornely, 1 Raine, Buck, Williams, Sykes

	Mat	Inns	NO	Runs	HS	Ave	SR	100	50	4s	6s
GP Smith	8	8	1	279	84	39.85	130.98	0	2	35	4
JJ Cobb	10	10	2	232	67*	29.00	122.10	0	2	22	8
JA Burns	8	8	1	197	81*	28.14	129.60	0	1	18	6
EJH Eckersley	9	7	3	104	42	26.00	114.28	0	0	7	2
RML Taylor	9	6	2	86	29	21.50	159.25	0	0	3	6
NJ O'Brien	7	6	0	123	47	20.50	104.23	0	0	11	0
Shakib Al Hasan	10	9	1	146	43*	18.25	130.35	0	0	15	4
AJ Ireland	10	4	2	36	23	18.00	138.46	0	0	1	4
SJ Thakor	8	6	1	62	42	12.40	98.41	0	0	2	1
MA Thornely	9	7	1	50	20	8.33	83.33	0	0	1	2
MAG Boyce	5	5	0	38	19	7.60	97.43	0	0	2	0
TJ Wells	2	1	0	4	4	4.00	66.66	0	0	0	0
REM Williams	3	1	0	0	0	0.00	-	0	0	0	0
NL Buck	3	1	1	8	8*	-	200.00	0	0	0	1
JKH Naik	3	1	1	6	6*	-	200.00	0	0	1	0
MJ Hoggard	3	1	1	3	3*	-	75.00	0	0	0	0
ACF Wyatt	2	1	1	0	0*	-	-	0	0	0	0
JS Sykes	1	-	-	-	-	-	-	-	-	-	-

Batting

	Overs	Mdns	Runs	Wkts	BBI	Ave	Econ	SR	4w	5w
JS Sykes	1.0	0	3	0	-	-	3.00	-	0	0
JKH Naik	9.3	0	61	2	2/25	30.50	6.42	28.5	0	0
Shakib Al Hasan	37.2	0	243	9	2/7	27.00	6.50	24.8	0	0
JJ Cobb	26.1	0	185	9	3/9	20.55	7.07	17.4	0	0
AJ Ireland	33.2	1	236	15	4/11	15.73	7.08	13.3	2	0
RML Taylor	27.0	0	196	14	4/11	14.00	7.25	11.5	2	0
REM Williams	10.0	0	74	1	1/32	74.00	7.40	60.0	0	0
MJ Hoggard	9.0	0	73	1	1/37	73.00	8.11	54.0	0	0
SJ Thakor	13.0	0	109	6	3/30	18.16	8.38	13.0	0	0
ACF Wyatt	6.0	0	56	0	-	-	9.33	-	0	0
MA Thornely	2.3	0	26	0	-	-	10.40	-	0	0
NL Buck	9.0	0	99	0	-	-	11.00	-	0	0

Bowling

Catches/Stumpings:
8 Cobb, 5 O'Brien, 4 Taylor, 3 Wells, Smith, Thornely, 2 Boyce, Burns, Thakor, Al Hasan, 1 Eckersley, Ireland

MIDDLESEX

FORMED: 1864
HOME GROUND: Lord's Cricket Ground
ONE-DAY NAME: Middlesex Panthers
CAPTAIN: Chris Rogers (Championship), Eoin Morgan (RL50 and NWT20)
2013 RESULTS: CC1: 5/9; YB40: 3/7 in Group C; FL t20: 4/6 in South Division
HONOURS: Championship: (12) 1903, 1920, 1921, 1947, 1949(s), 1976, 1977(s), 1980, 1982, 1985, 1990, 1993; Gillette/NatWest/C&G/FP Trophy: (4) 1977, 1980, 1984, 1988; Benson & Hedges Cup: (2) 1983, 1986; Sunday League: 1992; Twenty20 Cup: 2008

THE LOWDOWN

Middlesex looked like genuine Championship title contenders in the early stages of the 2013 campaign but the loss of Chris Rogers, their four-day captain and most prolific run-scorer, to Ashes duty eventually took its toll. With Rogers expected to be available for the duration of 2014 and his opening partner Sam Robson backing up an excellent 2013 with big runs for the England Lions over the winter, Middlesex fans will be hoping their opening pair can set the platform to end their 21-year wait for a Championship title. They'll need more support from the middle order though, with talented stroke-makers Joe Denly and Dawid Malan both averaging sub-30 in the last campaign. The bowling unit looks nicely balanced, with Tim Murtagh (60 Championship wickets last term), Steven Finn, James Harris and Toby Roland-Jones forming a potent seam attack and Ollie Rayner, who enjoyed a career-high in 2013, on spin duties. Middlesex will be hoping the appointment of Eoin Morgan as limited-overs skipper will revive their fortunes in white-ball cricket after middling performances in the YB40 and FL t20 last year.

HEAD COACH: RICHARD SCOTT

Scott had a six-year county career with Hampshire and Gloucestershire, as well as playing some 2nd XI matches for Middlesex. After a spell as Dorset's director of cricket he returned to Lord's in 2007 to take charge of the 2nd XI before being elevated to head coach midway through the 2009 season. He was given the role on a permanent basis after impressing in difficult circumstances and, alongside managing director of cricket Angus Fraser, he has helped take the club back to the top table of county cricket, with supporters hopeful that silverware is on the horizon.

	Mat	Inns	NO	Runs	HS	Ave	SR	100	50	4s	6s
CJL Rogers	12	22	3	1068	214	56.21	62.67	3	6	134	4
AC Voges	4	7	0	383	150	54.71	56.82	1	2	43	1
SD Robson	16	29	4	1180	215*	47.20	55.87	3	4	148	2
TMJ Smith	2	2	1	36	19	36.00	21.95	0	0	3	0
NJ Dexter	16	26	2	772	104	32.16	48.40	1	4	93	7
EJG Morgan	2	4	1	96	39*	32.00	45.07	0	0	14	0
JA Simpson	16	25	4	648	97*	30.85	45.31	0	5	87	3
JL Denly	16	28	3	652	77	26.08	59.48	0	4	89	2
GK Berg	15	23	2	501	71	23.85	59.43	0	2	68	1
DJ Malan	12	19	1	387	61	21.50	57.24	0	2	53	1
OP Rayner	13	18	3	293	52*	19.53	49.40	0	1	40	2
AB London	2	3	0	49	28	16.33	34.02	0	0	5	0
JAR Harris	9	12	3	146	37	16.22	34.92	0	0	20	0
RH Patel	3	6	2	47	26*	11.75	34.81	0	0	5	0
TS Roland-Jones	8	11	1	111	21	11.10	46.25	0	0	13	1
TG Helm	1	2	0	22	18	11.00	55.00	0	0	4	0
TJ Murtagh	13	15	4	112	29	10.18	45.02	0	0	13	1
CD Collymore	9	11	5	22	6*	3.66	25.88	0	0	1	0
ST Finn	6	7	1	15	8	2.50	20.54	0	0	2	0
PR Stirling	1	2	0	1	1	0.50	12.50	0	0	0	0
GS Sandhu	2	-	-	-	-	-	-	-	-	-	-

Batting

	Overs	Mdns	Runs	Wkts	BBI	BBM	Ave	Econ	SR	5w	10w
TG Helm	18.0	0	78	5	3/46	5/78	15.60	4.33	21.6	0	0
AC Voges	9.0	1	16	1	1/10	1/10	16.00	1.77	54.0	0	0
TJ Murtagh	444.1	113	1224	60	6/49	10/77	20.40	2.75	44.4	3	1
NJ Dexter	163.2	33	415	18	5/27	6/47	23.05	2.54	54.4	1	0
OP Rayner	356.1	74	958	41	8/46	15/118	23.36	2.68	52.1	4	0
PR Stirling	18.0	2	47	2	2/43	2/47	23.50	2.61	54.0	0	0
CD Collymore	229.2	49	613	25	4/61	5/63	24.52	2.67	55.0	0	0
ST Finn	160.5	38	503	17	4/46	7/102	29.58	3.12	56.7	0	0
TS Roland-Jones	219.2	39	694	21	6/63	8/138	33.04	3.16	62.6	1	0
GK Berg	324.4	71	942	25	3/49	4/71	37.68	2.90	77.9	0	0
JAR Harris	227.4	31	805	21	3/46	5/129	38.33	3.53	65.0	0	0
RH Patel	110.0	24	321	8	4/89	4/89	40.12	2.91	82.5	0	0
JL Denly	28.4	3	96	2	2/47	2/48	48.00	3.34	86.0	0	0
GS Sandhu	28.0	5	115	2	2/54	2/54	57.50	4.10	84.0	0	0
TMJ Smith	22.0	0	71	1	1/46	1/46	71.00	3.22	132.0	0	0
AB London	1.0	0	5	0	-	-	-	5.00	-	0	0
DJ Malan	15.5	0	58	0	-	-	-	3.66	-	0	0

Bowling

Catches/Stumpings:
60 Simpson (inc 5st), 22 Robson, 19 Malan, Rayner, 11 Rogers, Dexter, 8 Berg, 6 Voges, Denly, 4 Roland-Jones, Murtagh, 3 Collymore, 2 Morgan, Finn, Harris, 1 London, Smith

Batting

	Mat	Inns	NO	Runs	HS	Ave	SR	100	50	4s	6s
JA Simpson	6	5	3	149	58*	74.50	120.16	0	2	18	2
DJ Malan	12	11	3	552	113*	69.00	91.84	1	4	58	6
AM Rossington	6	4	1	139	79*	46.33	96.52	0	1	13	0
JL Denly	12	10	1	365	99*	40.55	91.70	0	3	37	6
NJ Dexter	11	8	2	215	54	35.83	90.33	0	1	16	2
PR Stirling	12	11	1	334	132*	33.40	115.57	1	0	48	3
GK Berg	10	6	0	155	75	25.83	105.44	0	1	12	2
EJG Morgan	5	5	0	124	90	24.80	98.41	0	1	9	5
OP Rayner	8	4	2	45	22*	22.50	84.90	0	0	4	0
O Wilkin	1	1	0	20	20	20.00	100.00	0	0	2	0
AC Voges	3	2	0	38	37	19.00	73.07	0	0	1	0
CJL Rogers	5	3	0	52	29	17.33	100.00	0	0	8	0
JAR Harris	8	4	2	21	13*	10.50	67.74	0	0	1	0
TS Roland-Jones	10	4	0	27	13	6.75	58.69	0	0	1	0
JH Davey	1	1	0	5	5	5.00	55.55	0	0	0	0
TJ Murtagh	7	2	1	3	3*	3.00	33.33	0	0	0	0
SD Robson	1	1	0	1	1	1.00	25.00	0	0	0	0
TMJ Smith	3	2	2	22	17*	-	129.41	0	0	1	0
ST Finn	4	2	2	4	3*	-	30.76	0	0	0	0
CD Collymore	3	2	2	1	1*	-	25.00	0	0	0	0
TG Helm	2	-	-	-	-	-	-	-	-	-	-
RH Patel	2	-	-	-	-	-	-	-	-	-	-

Bowling

	Overs	Mdns	Runs	Wkts	BBI	Ave	Econ	SR	4w	5w
TG Helm	8.0	0	27	3	3/27	9.00	3.37	16.0	0	0
OP Rayner	45.0	1	194	6	3/31	32.33	4.31	45.0	0	0
ST Finn	29.0	3	132	5	2/32	26.40	4.55	34.8	0	0
O Wilkin	8.0	0	44	2	2/44	22.00	5.50	24.0	0	0
GK Berg	44.2	1	244	5	2/38	48.80	5.50	53.2	0	0
TJ Murtagh	41.0	1	233	7	3/35	33.28	5.68	35.1	0	0
TS Roland-Jones	69.3	2	412	18	4/44	22.88	5.92	23.1	1	0
PR Stirling	20.0	0	119	4	2/18	29.75	5.95	30.0	0	0
NJ Dexter	22.0	0	132	0	-	-	6.00	-	0	0
JAR Harris	58.5	2	374	15	3/30	24.93	6.35	23.5	0	0
RH Patel	14.0	0	90	4	2/41	22.50	6.42	21.0	0	0
JH Davey	8.0	0	55	1	1/55	55.00	6.87	48.0	0	0
TMJ Smith	12.0	0	84	1	1/47	84.00	7.00	72.0	0	0
CD Collymore	11.0	0	91	0	-	-	8.27	-	0	0
DJ Malan	2.0	0	20	0	-	-	10.00	-	0	0

Catches/Stumpings:
8 Rossington (inc 1st), 7 Morgan, Dexter, 5 Denly, Stirling, 4 Simpson (inc 1st), Rayner, Malan, 3 Finn, Berg, 2 Smith, Voges, Rogers, Harris, Roland-Jones, 1 Wilkin

FRIENDS LIFE T20 AVERAGES 2013

Batting

	Mat	Inns	NO	Runs	HS	Ave	SR	100	50	4s	6s
DJ Malan	10	10	1	351	86	39.00	118.98	0	3	42	6
JL Denly	10	10	3	261	67	37.28	125.48	0	3	22	10
AM Rossington	10	9	2	182	74	26.00	155.55	0	1	21	9
NJ Dexter	10	7	2	108	40	21.60	142.10	0	0	7	7
EJG Morgan	2	2	0	38	29	19.00	118.75	0	0	4	1
GK Berg	10	5	1	64	33	16.00	120.75	0	0	5	1
PR Stirling	8	8	0	118	33	14.75	129.67	0	0	17	4
AC Voges	10	9	2	98	28	14.00	111.36	0	0	10	1
JH Davey	5	3	1	27	14	13.50	122.72	0	0	2	1
KD Mills	10	3	1	25	12	12.50	119.04	0	0	2	1
RH Patel	8	1	0	1	1	1.00		0	0	0	0
OP Rayner	8	3	3	17	11*	-	121.42	0	0	2	0
GS Sandhu	4	1	1	2	2*	-	25.00	0	0	0	0
TS Roland-Jones	3	1	1	0	0*	-	-	0	0	0	0
TJ Murtagh	2	-	-	-	-	-	-	-	-	-	-

Bowling

	Overs	Mdns	Runs	Wkts	BBI	Ave	Econ	SR	4w	5w
AC Voges	18.0	0	119	7	2/21	17.00	6.61	15.4	0	0
RH Patel	28.0	0	186	10	4/18	18.60	6.64	16.8	1	0
OP Rayner	24.0	0	177	5	2/24	35.40	7.37	28.8	0	0
NJ Dexter	23.0	0	187	5	2/18	37.40	8.13	27.6	0	0
TS Roland-Jones	8.0	0	66	3	2/19	22.00	8.25	16.0	0	0
KD Mills	34.0	1	291	11	3/4	26.45	8.55	18.5	0	0
GK Berg	29.0	0	249	8	3/19	31.12	8.58	21.7	0	0
PR Stirling	4.0	0	35	0	-	-	8.75	-	0	0
DJ Malan	2.0	0	19	1	1/19	19.00	9.50	12.0	0	0
JH Davey	3.0	0	33	1	1/9	33.00	11.00	18.0	0	0
GS Sandhu	8.0	0	93	4	2/15	23.25	11.62	12.0	0	0
TJ Murtagh	6.0	0	76	1	1/46	76.00	12.66	36.0	0	0

Catches/Stumpings:

11 Rossington (inc 3st), 5 Davey, Dexter, Malan, 3 Mills, Voges, 2 Roland-Jones, Stirling, Denly, 1 Rayner

FORMED: 1878

HOME GROUND: County Ground, Northampton

ONE-DAY NAME: Northamptonshire Steelbacks

CAPTAIN: Stephen Peters (Championship), TBC (RL50 and NWT20)

2013 RESULTS: CC2: 2/9; YB40: 2/7 in Group A; FL t20: Winners

HONOURS: Gillette/NatWest/C&G/FP Trophy: (2) 1976, 1992; Benson & Hedges Cup: 1980; Twenty20 Cup: 2013

THE LOWDOWN

From a disastrous 2012 to an imperious 2013, Northamptonshire supplemented promotion to Division One of the County Championship last term with a fantastic FL t20 win. They also came within a whisker of reaching the semi-finals of the YB40 in a season that will live long in the memory for Northants fans. Andrew Hall, David Sales and skipper Stephen Peters led the way with the bat in the Championship, while Trent Copeland, David Willey and Steven Crook did the job with the ball. Alex Wakely led the T20 team superbly, backed up by a brains trust that included hard-hitting Australian batsman Cameron White. Big-hitting South African Richard Levi proved an inspired short-format signing, scoring the team's only T20 century, and he will return for white-ball cricket in 2014. The club have bolstered their already formidable seam attack with the signings of Maurice Chambers from Essex and Aussie quick Jackson Bird, who will play six Championship matches for them. The only setback of the close season has been a ruptured Achilles tendon injury to Wakely. He is expected to be unavailable for most of the season, meaning that Northants will need to find a new limited-overs stand-in skipper.

HEAD COACH: DAVID RIPLEY

Ripley has been a loyal servant of Northamptonshire both as a player and coach. He represented Northants in 307 first-class matches and 281 one-day matches, scoring over 10,000 runs and affecting over 1,000 dismissals as a wicketkeeper during his 17-year career. Ripley moved up from 2nd XI coach to take charge of the first team in July 2012 and led the club back to the big-time a year later.

COUNTY CHAMPIONSHIP AVERAGES 2013

	Mat	Inns	NO	Runs	HS	Ave	SR	100	50	4s	6s
AJ Hall	16	21	4	936	130*	55.05	49.57	3	5	120	1
SD Peters	10	15	1	735	106	52.50	53.72	2	5	107	0
DJG Sales	16	23	3	919	255*	45.95	57.54	3	1	128	6
RI Keogh	8	12	2	458	221	45.80	46.87	1	1	66	0
RI Newton	6	8	2	251	81	41.83	50.91	0	1	31	3
SP Crook	14	15	3	482	88*	40.16	84.71	0	5	56	9
KJ Coetzer	10	15	1	527	219	37.64	49.53	2	1	79	3
CL White	2	3	0	107	90	35.66	42.29	0	1	13	0
JD Middlebrook	16	21	1	711	109	35.55	52.35	1	6	101	3
TA Copeland	10	10	3	247	70	35.28	79.67	0	2	37	1
BM Duckett	4	6	1	145	53*	29.00	65.61	0	1	21	0
D Murphy	14	14	3	293	81	26.63	44.06	0	2	27	4
DJ Willey	13	15	1	346	81	24.71	93.51	0	3	39	14
AG Wakely	15	21	1	457	88	22.85	48.15	0	2	57	10
MNW Spriegel	8	12	2	134	76	13.40	39.18	0	1	15	0
JN Batty	1	1	0	12	12	12.00	25.00	0	0	1	0
LM Daggett	3	2	0	12	11	6.00	15.58	0	0	2	0
Azharullah	9	10	6	12	8	3.00	16.00	0	0	1	0
GG White	1	2	0	0	0	0.00	0.00	0	0	0	0

Batting

	Overs	Mdns	Runs	Wkts	BBI	BBM	Ave	Econ	SR	5w	10w
TA Copeland	394.4	139	822	45	7/63	10/113	18.26	2.08	52.6	4	1
DJ Willey	361.3	66	1122	45	5/67	8/110	24.93	3.10	48.2	2	0
AJ Hall	325.3	85	937	37	5/30	7/75	25.32	2.87	52.7	1	0
SP Crook	326.0	46	1139	43	4/30	7/95	26.48	3.49	45.4	0	0
Azharullah	225.4	51	717	25	4/42	4/51	28.68	3.17	54.1	0	0
MNW Spriegel	48.0	7	183	5	3/75	3/75	36.60	3.81	57.6	0	0
JD Middlebrook	249.1	53	775	21	6/78	6/78	36.90	3.11	71.1	1	0
CL White	25.2	4	99	2	1/18	1/45	49.50	3.90	76.0	0	0
LM Daggett	59.3	13	203	2	1/34	1/34	101.50	3.41	178.5	0	0
AG Wakely	1.0	0	3	0	-	-	-	3.00	-	0	0
RI Keogh	4.0	1	9	0	-	-	-	2.25	-	0	0
GG White	4.0	1	14	0	-	-	-	3.50	-	0	0
KJ Coetzer	7.0	1	16	0	-	-	-	2.28	-	0	0

Bowling

Catches/Stumpings:
55 Murphy (inc 4st), 13 Hall, 11 Copeland, Sales, 5 Wakely, Middlebrook, 4 Duckett, Peters, 3 Azharullah, Coetzer, Crook, Willey, 2 Spriegel, 1 Daggett, Duckett, Newton, Keogh

YORKSHIRE BANK 40 AVERAGES 2013

Batting

	Mat	Inns	NO	Runs	HS	Ave	SR	100	50	4s	6s
RI Newton	3	3	1	132	88*	66.00	80.98	0	1	14	2
CL White	4	4	1	181	65	60.33	70.98	0	2	15	2
AJ Hall	6	5	3	99	58*	49.50	83.19	0	1	10	0
KJ Coetzer	10	10	1	361	105*	40.11	79.86	1	1	42	3
RI Keogh	2	2	0	75	61	37.50	113.63	0	1	10	1
AG Wakely	11	11	1	366	102	36.60	96.82	1	2	29	6
BM Duckett	5	4	1	94	47*	31.33	85.45	0	0	11	0
DJ Willey	8	8	0	246	167	30.75	132.25	1	0	18	15
JD Middlebrook	10	8	4	123	43	30.75	82.00	0	0	13	1
SP Crook	9	9	1	171	61*	21.37	111.76	0	1	17	5
SD Peters	2	2	0	41	21	20.50	73.21	0	0	5	0
DJG Sales	9	9	0	156	31	17.33	69.33	0	0	17	0
MNW Spriegel	10	9	2	92	35	13.14	58.59	0	0	8	0
TA Copeland	6	3	2	13	12*	13.00	162.50	0	0	2	0
LM Daggett	8	2	1	13	10*	13.00	130.00	0	0	1	0
D Murphy	9	2	2	8	7*	-	61.53	0	0	0	0
CAL Davis	1	1	1	3	3*	-	150.00	0	0	0	0
Azharullah	7	-	-	-	-	-	-	-	-	-	-
OP Stone	1	-	-	-	-	-	-	-	-	-	-

Bowling

	Overs	Mdns	Runs	Wkts	BBI	Ave	Econ	SR	4w	5w
KJ Coetzer	1.0	0	2	1	1/2	2.00	2.00	6.0	0	0
LM Daggett	55.0	4	225	7	2/28	32.14	4.09	47.1	0	0
AJ Hall	39.3	2	183	6	2/32	30.50	4.63	39.5	0	0
CL White	5.0	0	25	2	2/18	12.50	5.00	15.0	0	0
MNW Spriegel	57.0	1	290	8	3/29	36.25	5.08	42.7	0	0
TA Copeland	44.4	0	229	15	5/32	15.26	5.12	17.8	1	1
DJ Willey	48.4	2	253	9	3/28	28.11	5.19	32.4	0	0
JD Middlebrook	53.0	0	290	4	1/29	72.50	5.47	79.5	0	0
SP Crook	57.0	2	314	17	5/36	18.47	5.50	20.1	1	1
Azharullah	46.0	0	258	15	4/20	17.20	5.60	18.4	2	0
RI Keogh	1.0	0	6	0	-	-	6.00	-	0	0
OP Stone	5.0	0	44	0	-	-	8.80	-	0	0

Catches/Stumpings:
8 Murphy (inc 4st), 5 Spriegel, 4 Willey, 3 Copeland, Coetzer, Wakely, Duckett, 2 Hall, Crook, 1 Keogh, Peters, Newton, C White, Daggett, Middlebrook

FRIENDS LIFE T20 AVERAGES 2013

	Mat	Inns	NO	Runs	HS	Ave	SR	100	50	4s	6s
CL White	13	13	4	417	71*	46.33	125.60	0	4	29	18
JD Middlebrook	10	4	3	36	13*	36.00	163.63	0	0	1	2
DJ Willey	12	8	2	198	60	33.00	163.63	0	1	16	12
RE Levi	12	12	1	360	110*	32.72	145.74	1	2	39	18
SP Crook	10	9	3	195	63	32.50	159.83	0	1	13	10
KJ Coetzer	12	12	1	337	71*	30.63	107.32	0	1	46	1
AG Wakely	13	13	3	293	59*	29.30	134.40	0	2	23	10
MNW Spriegel	13	5	1	54	22	13.50	91.52	0	0	2	1
LM Daggett	13	2	1	3	2*	3.00	37.50	0	0	0	0
D Murphy	13	3	0	7	6	2.33	58.33	0	0	1	0
AJ Hall	3	1	1	16	16*	-	94.11	0	0	1	0
BM Duckett	3	2	2	15	15*	-	250.00	0	0	1	1
Azharullah	12	1	1	1	1*	-	100.00	0	0	0	0
GG White	3	1	1	1	1*	-	100.00	0	0	0	0
OP Stone	1	-	-	-	-	-	-	-	-	-	-

Batting

	Overs	Mdns	Runs	Wkts	BBI	Ave	Econ	SR	4w	5w
GG White	11.0	0	60	7	4/14	8.57	5.45	9.4	1	0
KJ Coetzer	3.0	0	19	1	1/4	19.00	6.33	18.0	0	0
DJ Willey	42.3	1	280	21	4/9	13.33	6.58	12.1	2	0
LM Daggett	45.0	0	304	6	2/22	50.66	6.75	45.0	0	0
SP Crook	32.0	0	238	9	2/26	26.44	7.43	21.3	0	0
Azharullah	45.5	1	341	27	4/14	12.62	7.44	10.1	3	0
JD Middlebrook	25.0	0	192	7	2/21	27.42	7.68	21.4	0	0
OP Stone	4.0	0	31	2	2/31	15.50	7.75	12.0	0	0
CL White	6.0	0	48	0	-	-	8.00	-	0	0
MNW Spriegel	25.3	0	213	5	2/22	42.60	8.35	30.6	0	0
AJ Hall	4.0	0	34	0	-	-	8.50	-	0	0

Bowling

Catches/Stumpings:
9 Murphy (inc 1st), Spriegel, 6 Middlebrook, 5 Willey, Wakely, C White, 3 Levi, Daggett, 2 Coetzer, 1 Duckett, G White, Crook, Azharullah

NOTTINGHAMSHIRE
COUNTY CRICKET CLUB

FORMED: 1841
HOME GROUND: Trent Bridge, Nottingham
ONE-DAY NAME: Nottinghamshire Outlaws
CAPTAIN: Chris Read (Championship), James Taylor (RL50 and NWT20)
2013 RESULTS: CC1: 7/9; YB40: Winners; FL t20: Quarter-finalists
HONOURS: County Championship: (6) 1907, 1929, 1981, 1987, 2005, 2010; Gillette/NatWest/C&G/FP Trophy: 1987; Pro40/National League/CB40/YB40: 2013; Benson & Hedges Cup: 1989; Sunday League: 1991

THE LOWDOWN

In winning the YB40 to claim their first piece of limited-overs silverware in more than two decades, Nottinghamshire got their just rewards for excellent white-ball performances throughout the season. Theirs was a batting card packed full of talent: James Taylor and Samit Patel were superb throughout the 40-over tournament, while skipper Chris Read scored a pivotal fifty in the final against Glamorgan. However, their four-day form left a lot to be desired and they were dragged into a relegation scrap at one stage. A lack of runs was the main issue, with Michael Lumb the only batsman to pass 1,000 for the season. Luke Fletcher yet again proved himself to be a very fine Championship bowler, while left-armer Harry Gurney produced his most profitable campaign to date with 48 first-class wickets and a season average below 30 for the first time in his career. Notts have strengthened both their batting and bowling in the off-season with the acquisition of experienced Australians Phil Jaques and Peter Siddle.

DIRECTOR OF CRICKET: MICK NEWELL

Newell spent eight years with Nottinghamshire as a player, opening the batting between 1984 and 1992. Ten years later he took control of team affairs and since then he has guided Notts to two Championship titles and two second-placed finishes. One of the most highly regarded coaches on the county circuit, he has made no secret of the fact that he would like to lead an international team at some stage in the future.

COUNTY CHAMPIONSHIP AVERAGES 2013

	Mat	Inns	NO	Runs	HS	Ave	SR	100	50	4s	6s
GP Swann	1	2	1	65	57	65.00	65.00	0	1	11	0
BA Hutton	1	2	1	62	42	62.00	81.57	0	0	12	0
MJ Lumb	15	25	3	1037	221*	47.13	50.02	4	2	132	3
JWA Taylor	15	21	1	925	204*	46.25	44.59	2	5	100	2
EJM Cowan	7	13	2	478	81	43.45	48.87	0	4	64	1
SJ Mullaney	14	21	0	834	125	39.71	53.98	2	6	112	8
DJ Hussey	9	13	0	478	125	36.76	73.99	1	3	66	6
SR Patel	16	24	0	830	157	34.58	60.27	3	0	108	3
SCJ Broad	2	3	0	97	46	32.33	74.04	0	0	11	4
AR Adams	11	15	2	354	80	27.23	113.82	0	2	30	17
A Shahzad	11	17	2	363	77	24.20	35.55	0	2	33	7
PJ Franks	8	11	0	257	78	23.36	56.98	0	2	33	2
CMW Read	15	22	2	452	58	22.60	48.81	0	2	62	0
MH Wessels	11	16	1	316	77	21.06	49.14	0	1	42	0
LJ Fletcher	15	22	3	368	64	19.36	50.34	0	2	47	5
AD Hales	10	18	0	251	58	13.94	38.79	0	2	30	1
HF Gurney	14	18	11	61	22*	8.71	34.85	0	0	7	0
GG White	1	1	0	0	0	0.00	0.00	0	0	0	0
A Carter	1	2	2	0	0*	-	0.00	0	0	0	0

Batting

	Overs	Mdns	Runs	Wkts	BBI	BBM	Ave	Econ	SR	5w	10w
SCJ Broad	80.0	21	213	12	4/34	8/91	17.75	2.66	40.0	0	0
LJ Fletcher	460.1	133	1288	43	5/52	9/108	29.95	2.79	64.2	2	0
AR Adams	302.5	55	929	31	4/69	5/156	29.96	3.06	58.6	0	0
HF Gurney	396.3	65	1334	44	5/81	7/148	30.31	3.36	54.0	1	0
GP Swann	41.0	7	146	4	4/56	4/146	36.50	3.56	61.5	0	0
PJ Franks	128.0	26	449	11	3/16	5/49	40.81	3.50	69.8	0	0
GG White	35.0	7	85	2	2/24	2/85	42.50	2.42	105.0	0	0
A Shahzad	324.1	60	1083	22	3/43	6/128	49.22	3.34	88.4	0	0
SR Patel	446.2	120	1293	26	3/40	5/169	49.73	2.89	103.0	0	0
SJ Mullaney	75.3	12	254	5	3/22	3/22	50.80	3.36	90.6	0	0
A Carter	28.0	5	113	2	2/87	2/113	56.50	4.03	84.0	0	0
BA Hutton	22.0	4	109	1	1/31	1/109	109.00	4.95	132.0	0	0
EJM Cowan	1.0	0	3	0	-	-	-	3.00	-	0	0
MH Wessels	2.0	0	11	0	-	-	-	5.50	-	0	0
DJ Hussey	4.0	1	25	0	-	-	-	6.25	-	0	0
JWA Taylor	2.0	0	16	0	-	-	-	8.00	-	0	0

Bowling

Catches/Stumpings:
55 Read (inc 2st), 17 Patel, 14 Wessels (inc 1st), 10 Hales, 8 Mullaney, Taylor, 5 Fletcher, 4 Cowan, Gurney, Lumb, 3 Franks, Adams, 2 Broad, Hussey, 1 Shahzad

OUTLAWS

Batting

	Mat	Inns	NO	Runs	HS	Ave	SR	100	50	4s	6s
JWA Taylor	13	13	5	585	108	73.12	85.02	1	4	47	3
DJ Hussey	7	6	3	187	82*	62.33	103.31	0	1	13	4
SR Patel	14	14	2	566	129*	47.16	97.92	1	3	59	7
CMW Read	14	10	6	146	53	36.50	108.14	0	1	15	3
AD Hales	14	14	0	491	101	35.07	101.65	1	4	52	6
SJ Mullaney	14	6	3	98	26	32.66	142.02	0	0	10	2
MH Wessels	11	10	4	172	37*	28.66	124.63	0	0	10	9
MJ Lumb	14	14	0	345	57	24.64	113.48	0	2	53	5
EJM Cowan	3	3	0	38	18	12.66	70.37	0	0	3	1
A Shahzad	11	2	0	12	10	6.00	85.71	0	0	1	0
JT Ball	12	2	0	2	1	1.00	40.00	0	0	0	0
HF Gurney	13	2	0	1	1	0.50	7.69	0	0	0	0
SCJ Broad	1	1	0	0	0	0.00	0.00	0	0	0	0
GP Swann	3	1	1	29	29*	-	152.63	0	0	4	0
GG White	5	1	1	0	0*	-	-	0	0	0	0
A Carter	3	-	-	-	-	-	-	-	-	-	-
LJ Fletcher	1	-	-	-	-	-	-	-	-	-	-
SKW Wood	1	-	-	-	-	-	-	-	-	-	-

Bowling

	Overs	Mdns	Runs	Wkts	BBI	Ave	Econ	SR	4w	5w
SKW Wood	6.0	1	19	1	1/19	19.00	3.16	36.0	0	0
GP Swann	21.0	1	75	1	1/15	75.00	3.57	126.0	0	0
SCJ Broad	7.0	0	29	3	3/29	9.66	4.14	14.0	0	0
SJ Mullaney	78.0	3	377	17	4/29	22.17	4.83	27.5	1	0
LJ Fletcher	6.0	0	29	1	1/29	29.00	4.83	36.0	0	0
GG White	24.0	0	127	4	2/30	31.75	5.29	36.0	0	0
SR Patel	91.1	4	492	15	3/21	32.80	5.39	36.4	0	0
A Shahzad	71.4	3	402	22	3/26	18.27	5.60	19.5	0	0
JT Ball	75.3	0	430	19	4/25	22.63	5.69	23.8	1	0
HF Gurney	85.0	4	496	18	5/48	27.55	5.83	28.3	0	1
DJ Hussey	19.0	0	115	2	1/15	57.50	6.05	57.0	0	0
A Carter	14.0	1	116	2	1/27	58.00	8.28	42.0	0	0

Catches/Stumpings:
17 Read (inc 4st), 13 Mullaney, 11 Patel, 7 Wessels, 4 Hussey, Lumb, 3 Taylor, 2 Shahzad, Gurney, 1 Carter, Cowan, White, Ball, Hales

OUTLAWS

	Mat	Inns	NO	Runs	HS	Ave	SR	100	50	4s	6s
DJ Hussey	11	11	4	298	61	42.57	143.96	0	3	24	7
AD Hales	11	11	0	365	82	33.18	146.58	0	2	32	17
JWA Taylor	9	9	3	196	54	32.66	104.81	0	1	13	2
MJ Lumb	11	11	0	330	96	30.00	165.00	0	2	40	16
SR Patel	11	9	2	169	50	24.14	129.00	0	1	20	5
MH Wessels	7	6	1	90	22	18.00	128.57	0	0	6	3
IG Butler	10	5	2	41	18	13.66	164.00	0	0	1	4
SJ Mullaney	10	6	2	40	16	10.00	125.00	0	0	3	0
CMW Read	11	8	2	46	19	7.66	104.54	0	0	3	1
GG White	7	3	1	2	2*	1.00	66.66	0	0	0	0
HF Gurney	9	1	0	0	0	0.00	0.00	0	0	0	0
JT Ball	8	1	1	1	1*	-	100.00	0	0	0	0
LJ Fletcher	1	-	-	-	-	-	-	-	-	-	-
A Shahzad	5	-	-	-	-	-	-	-	-	-	-

Batting

	Overs	Mdns	Runs	Wkts	BBI	Ave	Econ	SR	4w	5w
HF Gurney	33.0	0	211	8	3/26	26.37	6.39	24.7	0	0
GG White	21.0	0	143	10	5/22	14.30	6.80	12.6	0	1
DJ Hussey	11.0	0	79	5	2/5	15.80	7.18	13.2	0	0
SR Patel	38.5	0	297	14	3/16	21.21	7.64	16.6	0	0
IG Butler	36.4	0	301	12	3/23	25.08	8.20	18.3	0	0
JT Ball	27.0	0	224	8	2/20	28.00	8.29	20.2	0	0
SJ Mullaney	17.0	0	151	2	1/6	75.50	8.88	51.0	0	0
LJ Fletcher	4.0	0	37	1	1/37	37.00	9.25	24.0	0	0
A Shahzad	15.0	0	141	3	1/30	47.00	9.40	30.0	0	0

Bowling

Catches/Stumpings:
9 Read (inc 3st), 7 Mullaney, 5 White, Taylor, Patel, 3 Butler, Lumb, 2 Ball, Hales, Hussey, 1 Wessels

TEAM PROFILE

SOMERSET
CRICKET CLUB

FORMED: 1875
HOME GROUND: County Ground, Taunton
CAPTAIN: Marcus Trescothick
2013 RESULTS: CC1: 6/9; YB40: Semi-finalists; FL t20: Quarter-finalists
HONOURS: Gillette/NatWest/ C&G/FP Trophy: (3) 1979, 1983, 2001; Benson & Hedges Cup: (2) 1981, 1982; Sunday League: 1979; Twenty20 Cup: 2005

THE LOWDOWN

Despite reaching the latter stages of both the YB40 and FL t20, the Somerset faithful would have been left frustrated by a disappointing 2013. Their Championship form was poor by their standards and their skipper Marcus Trescothick was uncharacteristically short of runs, ending the English summer without a first-class century to his name for the first time since 1998. Nick Compton was the only player to pass the 1,000-run mark in the County Championship and Alfonso Thomas led from the front with the ball, with only intermittent support from their teammates. Peter Trego and Craig Kieswetter carried the run-scoring burden in the YB40 and FL t20 respectively – finishing as top-scorers in those competitions. However, despite the relative gloom after the loss of Jos Buttler to Lancashire, there looks to be a bright future at Somerset, with the highly-regarded young quick Jamie Overton and Craig Meschede enjoying breakthrough seasons with the ball. Jamie's twin brother Craig will be looking to have a bigger impact on 2014 after he missed the vast majority of the last campaign through injury.

FIRST-TEAM COACH: ANDY HURRY

An ex-Royal Marine, Hurry worked for free when he first linked up with Somerset's youth system before being given the top job in 2006. He has lifted the team from the foot of the County Championship's second tier to regular contenders across all formats but fans are impatiently waiting for silverware after several near misses since their last trophy nine years ago. In 2012, Hurry took charge of England at the Hong Kong Sixes.

Batting

	Mat	Inns	NO	Runs	HS	Ave	SR	100	50	4s	6s
NRD Compton	12	23	3	1001	166	50.05	49.80	2	7	128	4
AN Petersen	6	12	0	562	167	46.83	66.66	2	2	61	4
PP Chawla	4	6	0	231	112	38.50	66.37	1	0	29	5
JC Buttler	9	15	1	508	119*	36.28	62.33	1	2	69	5
C Kieswetter	11	19	2	584	148	34.35	56.92	1	3	71	10
JC Hildreth	16	29	2	867	161	32.11	65.33	2	2	124	2
ME Trescothick	16	30	1	804	74	27.72	52.75	0	6	135	2
AWR Barrow	9	15	1	370	83*	26.42	46.95	0	2	45	0
D Elgar	3	5	0	123	33	24.60	46.06	0	0	17	0
L Gregory	6	8	1	141	52	20.14	51.27	0	1	17	1
CR Jones	6	11	1	198	58	19.80	41.94	0	2	27	2
PD Trego	14	23	1	374	82	17.00	57.98	0	1	48	0
CAJ Meschede	9	13	1	192	59	16.00	46.71	0	1	27	2
AC Thomas	13	21	5	239	54*	14.93	39.43	0	1	31	0
GH Dockrell	7	10	2	106	31	13.25	25.85	0	0	13	1
AV Suppiah	6	11	0	130	36	11.81	46.42	0	0	22	0
J Overton	12	18	6	125	24	10.41	71.83	0	0	17	2
MJ Leach	5	9	2	66	21	9.42	31.42	0	0	8	0
SP Kirby	10	15	6	75	15	8.33	22.52	0	0	9	0
C Overton	1	1	0	8	8	8.00	29.62	0	0	0	0
GM Hussain	2	2	2	2	2*	-	18.18	0	0	0	0

Bowling

	Overs	Mdns	Runs	Wkts	BBI	BBM	Ave	Econ	SR	5w	10w
MJ Leach	149.4	51	324	13	5/63	7/106	24.92	2.16	69.0	1	0
L Gregory	119.4	25	358	14	5/38	7/52	25.57	2.99	51.2	1	0
AC Thomas	386.4	108	1077	42	5/69	7/147	25.64	2.78	55.2	1	0
CAJ Meschede	177.1	33	639	24	4/43	7/80	26.62	3.60	44.2	0	0
PP Chawla	122.4	13	453	17	5/97	10/208	26.64	3.69	43.2	2	1
PD Trego	340.2	80	1029	31	4/69	6/83	33.19	3.02	65.8	0	0
J Overton	284.5	48	1121	33	6/95	7/134	33.96	3.93	51.7	1	0
SP Kirby	277.5	54	913	26	4/18	6/79	35.11	3.28	64.1	0	0
GH Dockrell	210.4	54	568	14	4/96	6/112	40.57	2.69	90.2	1	0
GM Hussain	55.5	4	224	5	3/99	3/99	44.80	4.01	67.0	0	0
AN Petersen	14.0	4	48	1	1/27	1/27	48.00	3.42	84.0	0	0
D Elgar	19.0	4	55	1	1/26	1/26	55.00	2.89	114.0	0	0
C Overton	23.0	6	67	1	1/7	1/67	67.00	2.91	138.0	0	0
AV Suppiah	6.0	1	19	0	-	-	-	3.16	-	0	0
C Kieswetter	6.0	0	26	0	-	-	-	4.33	-	0	0

Catches/Stumpings:

44 Kieswetter (inc 3st), 30 Trescothick, 16 Buttler, Hildreth, 9 Barrow, 6 Meschede, Compton, 4 Thomas, Trego, 3 Petersen, Gregory, Kirby, 2 Elgar, Suppiah, Dockrell, Jones, 1 Hussain, Chawla

SOMERSET
CRICKET CLUB

Batting

	Mat	Inns	NO	Runs	HS	Ave	SR	100	50	4s	6s
PD Trego	12	12	3	745	140*	82.77	124.37	2	5	90	17
JC Buttler	8	7	3	301	89	75.25	146.11	0	4	31	10
JC Hildreth	11	8	3	294	102*	58.80	97.35	1	1	22	4
C Kieswetter	7	6	1	284	126*	56.80	108.81	1	1	26	13
AN Petersen	7	6	1	191	63*	38.20	93.62	0	2	12	4
ME Trescothick	13	13	1	393	87	32.75	127.18	0	3	46	17
D Elgar	4	3	0	75	51	25.00	70.75	0	1	5	0
NRD Compton	9	8	3	124	50	24.80	76.07	0	1	12	1
CAJ Meschede	13	6	2	88	40*	22.00	122.22	0	0	6	3
AV Suppiah	5	5	0	100	60	20.00	111.11	0	1	9	1
AWR Barrow	4	3	1	36	15	18.00	64.28	0	0	3	0
AJ Dibble	3	2	1	15	15	15.00	136.36	0	0	3	0
J Overton	9	3	1	23	14	11.50	153.33	0	0	4	0
L Gregory	5	3	1	13	12	6.50	54.16	0	0	0	0
AC Thomas	8	3	0	13	12	4.33	41.93	0	0	1	0
PP Chawla	2	2	0	4	3	2.00	66.66	0	0	0	0
SP Kirby	12	2	1	0	0*	0.00	0.00	0	0	0	0
MTC Waller	9	3	3	28	25*	-	116.66	0	0	5	0
GH Dockrell	2	-	-	-	-	-	-	-	-	-	-

Bowling

	Overs	Mdns	Runs	Wkts	BBI	Ave	Econ	SR	4w	5w
AV Suppiah	12.5	0	66	0	-	-	5.14	-	0	0
PP Chawla	8.0	0	43	1	1/43	43.00	5.37	48.0	0	0
CAJ Meschede	85.2	4	478	22	4/5	21.72	5.60	23.2	2	0
AJ Dibble	22.0	0	125	6	4/52	20.83	5.68	22.0	1	0
PD Trego	60.0	1	344	6	2/22	57.33	5.73	60.0	0	0
D Elgar	13.1	0	77	3	2/35	25.66	5.84	26.3	0	0
SP Kirby	82.2	2	495	17	4/52	29.11	6.01	29.0	1	0
MTC Waller	52.0	0	325	8	3/39	40.62	6.25	39.0	0	0
AC Thomas	46.3	0	291	16	4/41	18.18	6.25	17.4	1	0
L Gregory	19.1	0	133	2	1/35	66.50	6.93	57.5	0	0
J Overton	54.0	0	377	12	3/45	31.41	6.98	27.0	0	0
AN Petersen	3.0	0	22	1	1/13	22.00	7.33	18.0	0	0
GH Dockrell	10.0	0	77	0	-	-	7.70	-	0	0

Catches/Stumpings:
10 Buttler, 9 Hildreth, 7 Barrow, 6 Kieswetter, Waller, Trego, 4 Gregory, Petersen, 3 Dockrell, Elgar, Thomas, J Overton, 2 Trescothick, 1 Chawla, Dibble, Meschede

 www.somersetcountycc.co.uk / tel: 0845 337 1875

SOMERSET
CRICKET CLUB

	Mat	Inns	NO	Runs	HS	Ave	SR	100	50	4s	6s
C Kieswetter	11	11	3	517	89*	64.62	137.13	0	5	46	19
PD Trego	11	10	2	289	62	36.12	117.95	0	1	31	8
CR Jones	6	6	2	125	53*	31.25	108.69	0	1	14	2
AN Petersen	4	4	1	91	64*	30.33	142.18	0	1	8	3
JC Buttler	11	9	2	185	48	26.42	160.86	0	0	10	11
CAJ Meschede	11	8	3	99	30	19.80	132.00	0	0	3	7
NRD Compton	8	5	0	89	32	17.80	120.27	0	0	8	1
ME Trescothick	5	5	0	78	49	15.60	118.18	0	0	11	1
JC Hildreth	10	8	1	75	29	10.71	101.35	0	0	5	1
AC Thomas	11	2	0	8	7	4.00	133.33	0	0	0	1
Yasir Arafat	11	5	5	28	12*	-	164.70	0	0	4	0
MTC Waller	10	2	2	1	1*	-	100.00	0	0	0	0
GH Dockrell	3	-	-	-	-	-	-	-	-	-	-
SP Kirby	9	-	-	-	-	-	-	-	-	-	-

Batting

	Overs	Mdns	Runs	Wkts	BBI	Ave	Econ	SR	4w	5w
PD Trego	23.0	0	135	4	2/16	33.75	5.86	34.5	0	0
SP Kirby	35.0	1	245	8	2/22	30.62	7.00	26.2	0	0
Yasir Arafat	41.1	1	292	20	4/5	14.60	7.09	12.3	1	0
MTC Waller	36.0	0	282	11	4/27	25.63	7.83	19.6	1	0
AC Thomas	40.0	1	325	15	4/35	21.66	8.12	16.0	1	0
CAJ Meschede	27.4	0	251	10	3/36	25.10	9.07	16.6	0	0
GH Dockrell	6.2	0	65	1	1/15	65.00	10.26	38.0	0	0

Bowling

Catches/Stumpings:
11 Kieswetter (inc 1st), 10 Buttler, 7 Hildreth, 5 Compton, 4 Waller, 3 Thomas, Trego, 2 Jones, 1 Dockrell, Trescothick, Meschede

FORMED: 1845
GROUND: The Kia Oval, London
CAPTAIN: Graeme Smith
2013 RESULTS: CC1: 9/9; YB40: 5/7 in Group B; FL t20: Finalists
HONOURS: Championship: (19) 1890, 1891, 1892, 1894, 1895, 1899, 1914, 1950, 1952, 1953, 1954, 1955, 1956, 1957, 1958, 1971, 1999, 2000, 2002; Gillette/NatWest/C&G/FP Trophy: 1982; Benson & Hedges Cup: (3) 1974, 1997, 2001; Pro40/National League/CB40/YB40: (2) 2003, 2011; Sunday League: 1996; Twenty20 Cup: 2003

THE LOWDOWN

Surrey suffered relegation in the County Championship after a season marked by a brace of high-profile departures. One of which was temporary, as Graeme Smith succumbed to a troublesome ankle to miss most of his debut season as skipper, and then team director Chris Adams was shown the door in June. Things didn't get much better with Alec Stewart at the helm, with Surrey managing just one Championship win all season as they struggled to bowl teams out to turn draws in to wins. T20 cricket was a much happier affair, with the experienced duo of Vikram Solanki and Azhar Mahmood helping to steer Surrey to Finals Day, only to miss out to Northants in the final. With the continued development of youngsters like Rory Burns, Dom Sibley and George Edwards, together with the signing-on of Kevin Pietersen for the T20 Blast and potentially a handful of Championship and 50-over games, Surrey will be expecting an immediate return to the top tier in 2014.

HEAD COACH: GRAHAM FORD

Ford, who has previous experience in county cricket as coach of Kent, took charge of Surrey in February, with Alec Stewart moving upstairs to become director of cricket. He built his reputation in South Africa, coaching domestically with Natal and then moving on to South Africa A. He acted as Bob Woolmer's assistant with the full side before taking on the top job after the 1999 World Cup. His last role was as coach of Sri Lanka before he put pen to paper on a three-year deal at Surrey.

COUNTY CHAMPIONSHIP AVERAGES 2013

	Mat	Inns	NO	Runs	HS	Ave	SR	100	50	4s	6s
RT Ponting	4	6	2	493	192	123.25	56.66	2	1	51	1
DP Sibley	3	4	0	264	242	66.00	42.71	1	0	28	2
HM Amla	6	10	0	545	151	54.50	61.09	1	4	63	2
SM Davies	15	23	4	867	147	45.63	58.22	2	3	112	1
VS Solanki	16	25	0	995	162	39.80	56.50	2	5	141	9
RJ Burns	16	27	1	917	115	35.26	41.38	2	4	122	1
GC Wilson	12	17	4	447	124	34.38	49.61	1	1	51	1
A Harinath	12	21	2	584	154	30.73	39.03	1	4	73	3
GC Smith	3	5	1	120	67	30.00	68.18	0	1	11	0
Z de Bruyn	14	23	0	571	111	24.82	38.92	1	1	62	2
ZS Ansari	6	8	3	114	27	22.80	25.73	0	0	9	0
GJ Batty	13	18	2	313	41	19.56	57.53	0	0	42	4
SC Meaker	8	11	4	80	30*	11.42	32.65	0	0	10	1
CT Tremlett	11	12	1	110	54	10.00	48.03	0	1	10	5
JJ Roy	4	7	1	49	17	8.16	49.49	0	0	5	0
TE Linley	12	14	1	84	22*	6.46	39.25	0	0	11	1
JW Dernbach	10	14	5	58	22	6.44	34.31	0	0	6	2
G Keedy	6	6	4	2	2*	1.00	5.71	0	0	0	0
GA Edwards	1	1	0	0	0	0.00	0.00	0	0	0	0
KP Pietersen	1	1	1	177	177*	-	94.14	1	0	17	7
J Lewis	2	1	1	2	2*	-	20.00	0	0	0	0
MP Dunn	1	-	-	-	-	-	-	-	-	-	-
TM Jewell	1	-	-	-	-	-	-	-	-	-	-

Batting

	Overs	Mdns	Runs	Wkts	BBI	BBM	Ave	Econ	SR	5w	10w
A Harinath	3.0	0	6	1	1/2	1/2	6.00	2.00	18.0	0	0
JJ Roy	5.4	0	35	3	3/35	3/35	11.66	6.17	11.3	0	0
GA Edwards	37.0	14	80	3	3/29	3/80	26.66	2.16	74.0	0	0
JW Dernbach	315.0	57	1043	34	5/57	6/136	30.67	3.31	55.5	1	0
ZS Ansari	164.1	30	468	15	4/70	5/149	31.20	2.85	65.6	0	0
CT Tremlett	349.1	66	1057	32	8/96	8/96	33.03	3.02	65.4	2	0
MP Dunn	35.0	2	133	4	3/97	4/133	33.25	3.80	52.5	0	0
TE Linley	438.1	106	1268	37	4/59	6/92	34.27	2.89	71.0	0	0
SC Meaker	195.4	33	840	24	5/60	8/134	35.00	4.29	48.9	1	0
G Keedy	269.0	51	796	22	7/99	9/162	36.18	2.95	73.3	2	0
GJ Batty	395.4	68	1141	27	5/71	6/104	42.25	2.88	87.9	2	0
VS Solanki	15.0	0	90	2	2/46	2/46	45.00	6.00	45.0	0	0
TM Jewell	33.0	5	147	3	3/100	3/147	49.00	4.45	66.0	0	0
J Lewis	60.0	14	154	3	3/80	3/114	51.33	2.56	120.0	0	0
Z de Bruyn	253.2	52	824	13	3/28	4/105	63.38	3.25	116.9	0	0
RJ Burns	15.0	0	90	1	1/18	1/18	90.00	6.00	90.0	0	0
DP Sibley	1.0	0	4	0	-	-	-	4.00	-	0	0
KP Pietersen	4.0	1	13	0	-	-	-	3.25	-	0	0
HM Amla	5.0	0	22	0	-	-	-	4.40	-	0	0
GC Wilson	7.0	0	43	0	-	-	-	6.14	-	0	0

Bowling

Catches/Stumpings:
27 Davies (inc 3st), 18 Solanki, 16 de Bruyn, 13 Burns, 12 Wilson, 6 Linley, Batty, 4 Smith, Ponting, Harinath, 3 Roy, Ansari, Tremlett, 2 Keedy, 1 Pietersen, Sibley, Amla

YORKSHIRE BANK 40 AVERAGES 2013

SURREY
COUNTY CRICKET CLUB

Batting

	Mat	Inns	NO	Runs	HS	Ave	SR	100	50	4s	6s
GC Smith	1	1	0	74	74	74.00	134.54	0	1	10	1
SM Davies	9	9	1	387	127*	48.37	130.74	1	3	47	9
JJ Roy	12	11	1	432	117	43.20	105.62	2	1	56	3
VS Solanki	12	11	2	379	109*	42.11	84.03	1	2	32	6
DP Sibley	2	2	1	39	37	39.00	88.63	0	0	4	0
RJ Burns	6	6	1	136	49	27.20	106.25	0	0	5	5
GC Wilson	11	9	1	217	85	27.12	87.50	0	1	19	5
A Harinath	2	2	0	53	52	26.50	88.33	0	1	5	1
ZS Ansari	7	6	0	152	62	25.33	85.87	0	1	10	2
Z de Bruyn	10	8	1	174	60	24.85	70.44	0	1	12	2
Azhar Mahmood	4	4	1	73	36	24.33	87.95	0	0	6	1
TE Linley	4	4	2	36	15	18.00	97.29	0	0	4	1
J Lewis	10	8	3	82	25	16.40	118.84	0	0	11	1
CT Tremlett	6	5	3	29	15*	14.50	120.83	0	0	1	2
RT Ponting	3	2	0	19	17	9.50	70.37	0	0	1	1
GJ Batty	7	4	0	31	12	7.75	52.54	0	0	2	1
TM Jewell	6	5	0	30	13	6.00	83.33	0	0	4	0
JW Dernbach	6	2	0	11	11	5.50	68.75	0	0	1	0
G Keedy	7	3	1	11	8	5.50	44.00	0	0	1	0
SC Meaker	1	1	0	3	3	3.00	75.00	0	0	0	0
TK Curran	5	4	1	3	1*	1.00	18.75	0	0	0	0
GA Edwards	1	1	1	0	0*	-	-	0	0	0	0

Bowling

	Overs	Mdns	Runs	Wkts	BBI	Ave	Econ	SR	4w	5w
GJ Batty	33.0	1	150	6	3/35	25.00	4.54	33.0	0	0
SC Meaker	8.0	0	39	1	1/39	39.00	4.87	48.0	0	0
CT Tremlett	40.0	2	201	5	2/23	40.20	5.02	48.0	0	0
G Keedy	39.0	0	215	5	2/26	43.00	5.51	46.8	0	0
J Lewis	58.0	4	323	13	3/57	24.84	5.56	26.7	0	0
JW Dernbach	30.0	1	185	4	1/40	46.25	6.16	45.0	0	0
ZS Ansari	35.0	0	218	8	4/42	27.25	6.22	26.2	2	0
TK Curran	32.1	1	202	9	5/34	22.44	6.27	21.4	0	1
TE Linley	27.5	0	187	5	2/59	37.40	6.71	33.4	0	0
Azhar Mahmood	20.3	0	147	3	2/51	49.00	7.17	41.0	0	0
GA Edwards	6.0	0	44	1	1/44	44.00	7.33	36.0	0	0
Z de Bruyn	44.0	1	341	8	4/72	42.62	7.75	33.0	1	0
TM Jewell	13.0	0	102	1	1/20	102.00	7.84	78.0	0	0

Catches/Stumpings:
10 Davies (inc 2st), 7 Solanki, 4 Wilson, de Bruyn, 3 Jewell, 2 Burns, Smith, Batty, Curran, Ansari, Lewis, Roy, 1 Meaker, Harinath, Tremlett

SURREY
COUNTY CRICKET CLUB

	Mat	Inns	NO	Runs	HS	Ave	SR	100	50	4s	6s
Z de Bruyn	11	7	4	138	41*	46.00	107.81	0	0	10	2
KJ O'Brien	3	3	1	72	54	36.00	167.44	0	1	7	4
SM Davies	12	12	1	280	95*	25.45	139.30	0	2	36	5
ZS Ansari	13	12	5	173	30*	24.71	94.53	0	0	6	3
GC Wilson	12	11	1	240	44*	24.00	121.82	0	0	15	7
JJ Roy	13	13	0	290	52	22.30	125.00	0	1	34	8
RT Ponting	5	5	0	103	65	20.60	101.98	0	1	6	2
GJ Maxwell	8	8	0	142	32	17.75	124.56	0	0	10	6
VS Solanki	9	9	0	147	38	16.33	114.84	0	0	11	5
Azhar Mahmood	13	13	3	154	47*	15.40	128.33	0	0	13	5
RJ Burns	2	2	0	28	27	14.00	87.50	0	0	3	0
J Lewis	12	5	1	24	12	6.00	126.31	0	0	3	0
GJ Batty	11	3	1	12	8	6.00	171.42	0	0	1	0
CT Tremlett	6	3	2	4	3*	4.00	100.00	0	0	0	0
JW Dernbach	12	3	3	1	1*	-	100.00	0	0	0	0
MP Dunn	1	-	-	-	-	-	-	-	-	-	-

Batting

	Overs	Mdns	Runs	Wkts	BBI	Ave	Econ	SR	4w	5w
GJ Batty	31.0	0	201	9	2/14	22.33	6.48	20.6	0	0
J Lewis	35.0	0	228	8	2/15	28.50	6.51	26.2	0	0
JW Dernbach	44.1	0	296	18	3/15	16.44	6.70	14.7	0	0
GJ Maxwell	8.0	0	57	1	1/13	57.00	7.12	48.0	0	0
ZS Ansari	29.0	0	208	5	2/7	41.60	7.17	34.8	0	0
Azhar Mahmood	48.0	1	346	16	2/9	21.62	7.20	18.0	0	0
Z de Bruyn	28.2	0	239	13	4/19	18.38	8.43	13.0	1	0
CT Tremlett	17.2	0	153	4	2/20	38.25	8.82	26.0	0	0
MP Dunn	2.0	0	21	0	-	-	10.50	-	0	0
JJ Roy	2.0	0	23	1	1/23	23.00	11.50	12.0	0	0

Bowling

Catches/Stumpings:
10 Davies (inc 3st), 6 Wilson, Roy, 4 Dernbach, 3 O'Brien, Ponting, Maxwell, Solanki, Lewis, 2 Ansari, 1 Dunn, Batty, de Bruyn, Mahmood

TEAM PROFILE

FORMED: 1839
HOME GROUND: The BrightonandHoveJobs.com County Ground, Hove
ONE-DAY NAME: Sussex Sharks
CAPTAIN: Ed Joyce
2013 RESULTS: CC1: 3/9; YB40: 3/7 in Group A; FL t20: 6/6 in South Division
HONOURS: Championship: (3) 2003, 2006, 2007; Gillette/NatWest/C&G/FP Trophy: (5) 1963, 1964, 1978, 1986, 2006; Pro40/National League/CB40: (2) 2008, 2009; Sunday League: 1982; Twenty20 Cup: 2009

THE LOWDOWN

With Ed Joyce's serene run-making and the impressive new-ball partnership of Steve Magoffin and Chris Jordan sharing 126 first-class wickets between them, Sussex were able to put together a persuasive bid for the Championship, even occupying top spot for a portion of the season. Chris Nash also enjoyed a good season with the bat, while young top-order southpaw Luke Wells came within six runs of reaching 1,000 for the season. The most disappointing aspect of the campaign for Sussex was their limited-overs' performances, as they lost nine of their 10 group games in the FL t20. The signing of Yasir Arafat, the leading wicket-taker in domestic English T20 cricket, will certainly bolster their short-form bowling attack, while former Warwickshire seamer Steffan Piolet and ex-England man Jon Lewis look like canny signings.

HEAD COACH: MARK ROBINSON

Robinson is a highly-regarded coach who has been in charge at Hove since October 2005, leading the club to two County Championship titles in that time. His links with Sussex were already well established, having spent the latter part of his 15-year career with the south coast club, following profitable spells at Northants and the county of his birth, Yorkshire. Further recognition of his coaching credentials came in the close season, when he was given the chance to guide England Lions on their recent winter tours.

COUNTY CHAMPIONSHIP AVERAGES 2013

	Mat	Inns	NO	Runs	HS	Ave	SR	100	50	4s	6s
EC Joyce	14	21	4	1118	204*	65.76	59.12	2	6	139	5
LJ Wright	7	12	0	676	187	56.33	70.85	2	2	101	2
MW Machan	4	5	1	193	103	48.25	60.88	1	0	27	2
CD Nash	16	27	3	1072	167*	44.66	59.88	3	3	148	5
BC Brown	15	22	6	620	93	38.75	54.00	0	5	76	0
LWP Wells	16	27	1	982	208	37.76	45.63	2	5	132	2
MH Yardy	16	26	2	834	156	34.75	54.97	2	1	122	0
RJ Hamilton-Brown	13	19	1	576	126*	32.00	74.70	2	2	79	11
Ashar Zaidi	2	2	0	62	45	31.00	82.66	0	0	10	1
MJ Prior	7	9	0	245	62	27.22	74.92	0	1	38	1
CJ Jordan	14	18	1	408	92	24.00	52.44	0	2	47	0
WAT Beer	3	6	0	106	39	17.66	25.85	0	0	12	0
JE Anyon	13	16	6	134	24*	13.40	34.01	0	0	10	1
JS Gatting	4	5	0	58	20	11.60	50.87	0	0	5	1
SJ Magoffin	15	19	2	187	32	11.00	50.95	0	0	29	0
MS Panesar	11	11	7	40	17*	10.00	35.39	0	0	6	0
HZ Finch	1	2	0	14	11	7.00	21.53	0	0	1	0
LJ Hatchett	4	5	0	27	21	5.40	40.29	0	0	4	0
CJ Liddle	1	2	2	10	7*	-	31.25	0	0	1	0
AS Miller	1	-	-	-	-	-	-	-	-	-	-

	Overs	Mdns	Runs	Wkts	BBI	BBM	Ave	Econ	SR	5w	10w
Ashar Zaidi	39.3	6	129	7	4/57	5/81	18.42	3.26	33.8	0	0
SJ Magoffin	496.0	128	1354	63	8/20	12/31	21.49	2.72	47.2	3	1
CJ Jordan	435.3	78	1577	59	6/48	9/155	26.72	3.62	44.2	4	0
JE Anyon	386.4	71	1432	50	5/44	8/166	28.64	3.70	46.4	1	0
CJ Liddle	25.0	4	98	3	2/24	3/98	32.66	3.92	50.0	0	0
MS Panesar	329.4	72	929	23	5/95	5/95	40.39	2.81	86.0	2	0
LJ Wright	77.3	15	256	6	2/36	2/36	42.66	3.30	77.5	0	0
WAT Beer	72.0	8	215	4	3/89	3/89	53.75	2.98	108.0	0	0
CD Nash	188.3	30	551	9	2/51	2/51	61.22	2.92	125.6	0	0
LJ Hatchett	116.0	15	423	6	3/56	4/147	70.50	3.64	116.0	0	0
LWP Wells	45.0	4	164	2	2/44	2/44	82.00	3.64	135.0	0	0
JS Gatting	5.0	0	14	0	-	-	-	2.80	-	0	0
HZ Finch	4.0	0	15	0	-	-	-	3.75	-	0	0
MH Yardy	7.0	0	27	0	-	-	-	3.85	-	0	0
RJ Hamilton-Brown	7.0	1	28	0	-	-	-	4.00	-	0	0
AS Miller	28.0	6	102	0	-	-	-	3.64	-	0	0

Catches/Stumpings:
60 Brown (inc 2st), 22 Jordan, 15 Prior, 14 Joyce, 10 Nash, 9 Yardy, 7 Wells, 4 Machan, Magoffin, 3 Gatting, Hamilton-Brown, 2 Beer, Panesar, 1 Finch, Zaidi, Wright, Anyon

SUSSEX
SHARKS

Batting

	Mat	Inns	NO	Runs	HS	Ave	SR	100	50	4s	6s
MW Machan	6	6	2	257	79	64.25	129.79	0	3	32	5
LJ Wright	8	8	0	502	115	62.75	148.52	3	1	55	20
EC Joyce	10	9	2	403	123*	57.57	95.72	1	3	39	3
WAT Beer	6	3	2	44	20*	44.00	97.77	0	0	4	1
MH Yardy	10	8	2	248	52	41.33	95.75	0	1	26	3
CD Nash	11	9	1	286	95	35.75	98.28	0	2	31	1
CJ Jordan	6	5	2	57	37*	19.00	95.00	0	0	6	1
JS Gatting	4	3	1	31	24*	15.50	72.09	0	0	2	0
RJ Hamilton-Brown	11	8	0	103	40	12.87	67.32	0	0	11	0
BC Brown	8	7	1	70	40	11.66	67.30	0	0	1	1
MJ Prior	2	2	0	20	17	10.00	68.96	0	0	2	0
MJG Rippon	3	2	1	10	10*	10.00	90.90	0	0	1	0
CJ Liddle	11	4	1	14	11*	4.66	63.63	0	0	1	0
JE Anyon	5	3	1	9	8*	4.50	52.94	0	0	1	0
ME Hobden	1	1	0	2	2	2.00	28.57	0	0	0	0
LWP Wells	5	4	0	7	5	1.75	36.84	0	0	1	0
LJ Hatchett	7	1	0	1	1	1.00	25.00	0	0	0	0
HZ Finch	1	-	-	-	-	-	-	-	-	-	-
CF Jackson	3	-	-	-	-	-	-	-	-	-	-
AS Miller	3	-	-	-	-	-	-	-	-	-	-

Bowling

	Overs	Mdns	Runs	Wkts	BBI	Ave	Econ	SR	4w	5w
HZ Finch	1.0	0	2	0	-	-	2.00	-	0	0
ME Hobden	8.0	0	39	1	1/39	39.00	4.87	48.0	0	0
CD Nash	44.0	0	221	8	2/13	27.62	5.02	33.0	0	0
AS Miller	11.5	0	63	2	2/24	31.50	5.32	35.5	0	0
WAT Beer	46.0	1	250	11	3/49	22.72	5.43	25.0	0	0
MJG Rippon	12.0	0	66	1	1/43	66.00	5.50	72.0	0	0
CJ Liddle	68.2	2	390	19	3/21	20.52	5.70	21.5	0	0
LJ Hatchett	41.4	2	239	10	3/65	23.90	5.73	25.0	0	0
MH Yardy	49.0	0	286	6	1/22	47.66	5.83	49.0	0	0
JE Anyon	30.2	2	182	6	2/14	30.33	6.00	30.3	0	0
CJ Jordan	40.3	0	244	11	3/20	22.18	6.02	22.0	0	0
LJ Wright	9.3	0	91	1	1/13	91.00	9.57	57.0	0	0
RJ Hamilton-Brown	4.0	0	47	0	-	-	11.75	-	0	0

Catches/Stumpings:
9 Hamilton-Brown, 7 Brown (inc 3st), 6 Jordan, 5 Nash, 4 Gatting, 3 Jackson (inc 2st), Beer, Wright, Liddle, 2 Hatchett, 1 Prior, Rippon, Anyon, Machan, Yardy

FRIENDS LIFE T20 AVERAGES 2013

SUSSEX
SHARKS

Batting

	Mat	Inns	NO	Runs	HS	Ave	SR	100	50	4s	6s
MW Machan	8	8	1	219	67	31.28	133.53	0	2	23	7
CD Nash	10	10	1	244	61*	27.11	125.12	0	1	29	7
SB Styris	10	10	2	209	46	26.12	122.22	0	0	12	7
RJ Hamilton-Brown	10	10	0	233	47	23.30	114.77	0	0	24	5
CJ Jordan	7	5	4	23	10*	23.00	121.05	0	0	2	0
LJ Wright	6	6	0	130	81	21.66	130.00	0	1	15	4
EC Joyce	3	3	0	57	26	19.00	98.27	0	0	3	1
MH Yardy	9	7	1	109	44	18.16	99.09	0	0	10	0
DR Smith	9	9	1	110	26	13.75	119.56	0	0	9	7
BC Brown	7	6	2	32	13	8.00	84.21	0	0	1	0
JS Gatting	4	3	0	18	11	6.00	56.25	0	0	1	0
WAT Beer	10	6	2	15	6*	3.75	107.14	0	0	1	0
CF Jackson	3	1	0	3	3	3.00	75.00	0	0	0	0
JE Anyon	1	1	0	2	2	2.00	66.66	0	0	0	0
CJ Liddle	10	1	1	0	0*	-	-	0	0	0	0
LJ Hatchett	2	-	-	-	-	-	-	-	-	-	-
AS Miller	1	-	-	-	-	-	-	-	-	-	-

Bowling

	Overs	Mdns	Runs	Wkts	BBI	Ave	Econ	SR	4w	5w
CD Nash	23.1	0	141	5	2/12	28.20	6.08	27.8	0	0
SB Styris	26.1	0	181	2	1/19	90.50	6.91	78.5	0	0
WAT Beer	32.0	0	224	6	2/20	37.33	7.00	32.0	0	0
AS Miller	3.0	0	21	1	1/21	21.00	7.00	18.0	0	0
MH Yardy	31.0	1	219	10	3/30	21.90	7.06	18.6	0	0
CJ Jordan	23.5	0	201	8	2/28	25.12	8.43	17.8	0	0
DR Smith	11.4	0	105	3	2/11	35.00	9.00	23.3	0	0
CJ Liddle	32.0	0	291	11	3/43	26.45	9.09	17.4	0	0
JE Anyon	2.0	0	22	1	1/22	22.00	11.00	12.0	0	0
LJ Wright	1.0	0	11	0	-	-	11.00	-	0	0
LJ Hatchett	3.0	0	55	0	-	-	18.33	-	0	0

Catches/Stumpings:
6 Brown (inc 2st), Smith, 5 Jordan, 4 Hamilton-Brown, 3 Jackson (inc 3st), Wright, Machan, 2 Gatting, Yardy, Liddle, 1 Nash

W

FORMED: 1882
HOME GROUND: Edgbaston Stadium
ONE-DAY NAME: Birmingham Bears
CAPTAIN: Jim Troughton
2013 RESULTS: CC1: 4/9; YB40: 7/7 in Group A;
FL t20: 4/6 in Midlands/Wales/West Division
HONOURS: Championship: (7) 1911, 1951, 1972,
1994, 1995, 2004, 2012; Gillette/NatWest/C&G/
FP Trophy: (5) 1966, 1968, 1989, 1993, 1995;
Benson & Hedges Cup: (2) 1994, 2002; Pro40/
National League/CB40/YB40: 2010; Sunday
League: (3) 1980, 1994, 1997

THE LOWDOWN

Recreating the glories of 2012 was always going to be difficult and Warwickshire weren't
helped by injuries to key figures that curtailed any chance of a successful Championship title
defence. Chris Wright, an integral part of the title-winning side with 61 wickets in 2012, suffered
a stress fracture of his back in July to end his participation for the season. Chris Woakes,
Keith Barker and Varun Chopra were consistent throughout in all forms of the game, but often
when they didn't fire, Warwickshire were caught short. Darren Maddy, in his final season of
professional cricket, shone for one last time in the FL t20 as the club's top-scorer. While they
will lose a stalwart, the signing of Laurie Evans in 2010 now looks to be bearing fruit. His 943
Championship runs (which included three centuries), as well as the form of academy product
Ateeq Javid, are both promising signs for the season ahead. Warwickshire also welcome
Alan Richardson onto their coaching team as bowling coach, and then there is Jonathan Trott,
available for the start of the season, and possibly, England depending, the whole of it. A back
injury to captain Jim Troughton, which puts his fitness for the start of the season in question, is
the only major worry.

DIRECTOR OF CRICKET: DOUGIE BROWN

The Edgbaston faithful will have fond memories of Ashley Giles and
Brown combining on the pitch and they will know too that, after Giles'
departure to England, Brown is now perfectly placed to deliver continuity.
An allrounder of underrated ability, Brown played for both England and
Scotland, representing the latter at the 2007 World Cup, and also coached
Namibia at the 2003 World Cup.

Batting

	Mat	Inns	NO	Runs	HS	Ave	SR	100	50	4s	6s
IJL Trott	2	2	0	161	96	80.50	49.08	0	2	22	1
IR Bell	2	2	0	118	62	59.00	50.42	0	2	15	0
CR Woakes	10	16	5	640	152*	58.18	58.12	1	4	87	4
LJ Evans	13	19	2	943	178	55.47	47.86	3	4	131	4
V Chopra	15	25	4	1069	228*	50.90	53.26	3	5	131	1
A Javid	11	17	3	619	133	44.21	37.51	2	2	63	0
DL Maddy	3	5	1	157	65	39.25	50.32	0	1	23	0
TR Ambrose	13	20	2	685	105	38.05	64.07	1	5	102	0
PJ McKay	1	2	1	36	33	36.00	25.35	0	0	2	1
JO Troughton	7	11	1	322	84	32.20	43.39	0	2	46	0
R Clarke	13	18	4	449	92	32.07	65.83	0	4	58	6
KHD Barker	11	12	1	350	125	31.81	51.47	1	0	37	1
JS Patel	16	18	4	438	78*	31.28	76.70	0	5	61	3
IJ Westwood	12	20	2	481	71	26.72	45.76	0	4	68	0
TP Milnes	7	7	0	160	48	22.85	42.44	0	0	20	2
MA Chambers	4	4	0	80	58	20.00	31.87	0	1	8	0
SA Piolet	1	2	0	31	30	15.50	37.80	0	0	2	0
OJ Hannon-Dalby	2	2	1	15	10*	15.00	16.66	0	0	2	0
WTS Porterfield	11	16	0	235	36	14.68	39.56	0	0	35	0
RO Gordon	3	2	0	23	13	11.50	23.95	0	0	1	0
WB Rankin	9	9	6	32	12*	10.66	41.55	0	0	4	0
CJC Wright	8	8	1	30	11	4.28	37.97	0	0	5	0
TW Allin	1	1	0	0	0	0.00	0.00	0	0	0	0
SW Poynter	1	1	0	0	0	0.00	0.00	0	0	0	0
JJ Atkinson	1	-				-					

Bowling

	Overs	Mdns	Runs	Wkts	BBI	BBM	Ave	Econ	SR	5w	10w
IJ Westwood	6.5	1	11	1	1/11	1/11	11.00	1.60	41.0	0	0
WB Rankin	216.4	20	709	31	4/29	6/99	22.87	3.27	41.9	0	0
KHD Barker	345.0	83	1055	46	5/55	6/74	22.93	3.05	45.0	1	0
CR Woakes	245.4	46	711	31	5/42	8/105	22.93	2.89	47.5	1	0
MA Chambers	103.2	16	383	14	5/68	5/142	27.35	3.70	44.2	1	0
JS Patel	576.1	139	1561	52	5/56	8/128	30.01	2.70	66.4	2	0
R Clarke	229.3	61	642	19	4/70	5/54	33.78	2.79	72.4	0	0
CJC Wright	209.0	43	689	19	6/31	7/96	36.26	3.29	66.0	1	0
RO Gordon	70.0	9	220	4	2/45	3/90	55.00	3.14	105.0	0	0
SA Piolet	12.0	0	59	1	1/59	1/59	59.00	4.91	72.0	0	0
DL Maddy	26.0	5	71	1	1/50	1/50	71.00	2.73	156.0	0	0
A Javid	49.0	10	154	2	1/27	1/29	77.00	3.14	147.0	0	0
TP Milnes	89.1	9	382	4	2/64	2/82	95.50	4.28	133.7	0	0
OJ Hannon-Dalby	33.0	4	164	1	1/57	1/57	164.00	4.96	198.0	0	0
V Chopra	2.0	0	2	0	-	-	-	1.00	-	0	0
LJ Evans	14.0	2	37	0	-	-	-	2.64	-	0	0
IJL Trott	16.0	2	47	0	-	-	-	2.93	-	0	0
TW Allin	17.0	3	65	0	-	-	-	3.82	-	0	0

Catches/Stumpings:
40 Ambrose (inc 1st), 26 Chopra, 19 Clarke, 14 Patel, 8 Westwood, 7 Porterfield, 6 Poynter, Evans, 5 Troughton, Javid, 4 Barker, 3 Milnes, 2 Woakes, 1 Piolet, Trott, Maddy, Gordon, Chambers

Batting

	Mat	Inns	NO	Runs	HS	Ave	SR	100	50	4s	6s
A Javid	9	9	4	194	43	38.80	101.04	0	0	15	3
V Chopra	10	10	0	352	111	35.20	76.35	1	1	33	1
IR Bell	1	1	0	35	35	35.00	152.17	0	0	4	2
R Clarke	6	6	0	208	65	34.66	99.04	0	2	22	3
WTS Porterfield	9	9	0	290	62	32.22	80.55	0	2	27	5
LJ Evans	5	5	2	90	47*	30.00	93.75	0	0	7	1
FRJ Coleman	2	2	0	57	34	28.50	67.85	0	0	6	0
TR Ambrose	5	5	0	125	55	25.00	86.80	0	1	7	1
DL Maddy	10	10	0	152	56	15.20	103.40	0	1	15	4
JO Troughton	8	8	0	111	36	13.87	83.45	0	0	12	0
PJ McKay	5	4	2	26	17*	13.00	104.00	0	0	3	1
JS Patel	10	9	3	75	50	12.50	129.31	0	1	8	2
IJ Westwood	1	1	0	12	12	12.00	92.30	0	0	2	0
TP Milnes	3	3	1	22	16	11.00	64.70	0	0	0	0
SA Piolet	9	9	0	95	30	10.55	97.93	0	0	9	3
CR Woakes	2	2	0	13	8	6.50	72.22	0	0	1	0
IJL Trott	1	1	0	3	3	3.00	37.50	0	0	0	0
CJC Wright	5	3	1	4	3*	2.00	40.00	0	0	0	0
RO Gordon	2	1	0	1	1	1.00	50.00	0	0	0	0
SR Hain	1	1	0	1	1	1.00	33.33	0	0	0	0
WB Rankin	5	1	1	18	18*	-	150.00	0	0	2	1
OJ Hannon-Dalby	1	-	-	-	-	-	-	-	-	-	-

Bowling

	Overs	Mdns	Runs	Wkts	BBI	Ave	Econ	SR	4w	5w
WB Rankin	24.3	2	111	5	2/45	22.20	4.53	29.4	0	0
JS Patel	67.0	1	363	16	4/43	22.68	5.41	25.1	1	0
DL Maddy	43.0	1	235	8	2/27	29.37	5.46	32.2	0	0
R Clarke	22.3	0	126	2	1/28	63.00	5.60	67.5	0	0
IJ Westwood	2.0	0	12	0	-	-	6.00	-	0	0
SA Piolet	55.0	1	352	10	3/74	35.20	6.40	33.0	0	0
A Javid	45.0	0	292	5	2/34	58.40	6.48	54.0	0	0
CR Woakes	11.0	0	75	2	2/46	37.50	6.81	33.0	0	0
CJC Wright	27.0	0	199	7	3/27	28.42	7.37	23.1	0	0
TP Milnes	23.0	1	177	3	2/73	59.00	7.69	46.0	0	0
LJ Evans	5.0	0	41	0	-	-	8.20	-	0	0
OJ Hannon-Dalby	5.1	0	45	1	1/45	45.00	8.70	31.0	0	0
RO Gordon	14.0	0	122	2	1/46	61.00	8.71	42.0	0	0

Catches/Stumpings:
7 Porterfield, 5 McKay (inc 1st), Patel, 4 Maddy, 3 Troughton, Javid, 2 Ambrose, Chopra, 1 Trott, Westwood, Evans, Wright, Clarke

www.edgbaston.com / tel: 0844 847 1902

	Mat	Inns	NO	Runs	HS	Ave	SR	100	50	4s	6s
DL Maddy	10	10	3	296	84*	42.28	129.25	0	2	25	8
V Chopra	10	10	1	282	75*	31.33	99.29	0	2	22	4
R Clarke	10	9	2	216	42	30.85	118.68	0	0	14	12
CR Woakes	10	7	2	90	28*	18.00	121.62	0	0	11	1
WTS Porterfield	8	8	0	124	34	15.50	102.47	0	0	15	1
SA Piolet	10	5	2	43	20	14.33	119.44	0	0	1	1
LJ Evans	10	8	2	80	51*	13.33	91.95	0	1	6	2
A Javid	10	5	0	64	41	12.80	98.46	0	0	3	1
KHD Barker	3	3	1	21	12*	10.50	72.41	0	0	1	0
JS Patel	10	5	1	15	8*	3.75	125.00	0	0	1	1
PJ McKay	10	4	3	3	2*	3.00	42.85	0	0	0	0
WB Rankin	3	1	0	3	3	3.00	42.85	0	0	0	0
CJC Wright	3	1	1	1	1*	-	100.00	0	0	0	0
FRJ Coleman	3	-	-	-	-	-	-	-	-	-	-

Batting

	Overs	Mdns	Runs	Wkts	BBI	Ave	Econ	SR	4w	5w
WB Rankin	8.0	0	45	4	2/9	11.25	5.62	12.0	0	0
JS Patel	32.4	0	199	10	2/13	19.90	6.09	19.6	0	0
R Clarke	25.0	0	174	7	2/15	24.85	6.96	21.4	0	0
CJC Wright	10.1	0	74	1	1/26	74.00	7.27	61.0	0	0
CR Woakes	31.2	0	233	10	3/28	23.30	7.43	18.8	0	0
A Javid	28.0	0	215	11	4/17	19.54	7.67	15.2	1	0
SA Piolet	34.3	0	268	6	3/24	44.66	7.76	34.5	0	0
DL Maddy	12.0	0	99	3	1/6	33.00	8.25	24.0	0	0
LJ Evans	1.4	0	15	1	1/5	15.00	9.00	10.0	0	0

Bowling

Catches/Stumpings:
6 McKay (inc 2st), 5 Porterfield, 4 Woakes, 3 Chopra, Clarke, Evans, 2 Patel, 1 Barker, Coleman, Rankin, Wright, Maddy, Piolet

WORCESTERSHIRE

FORMED: 1865
HOME GROUND: County Ground, New Road, Worcester
NWT20 NAME: Worcestershire Rapids
CAPTAIN: Daryl Mitchell
2013 RESULTS: CC2: 5/9; YB40: 5/7 in Group A; FL t20: 5/6 in Midland/Wales/West Division
HONOURS: Championship: (5) 1964, 1965, 1974, 1988, 1989; Gillette/NatWest/C&G/FP Trophy: 1994; Benson & Hedges Cup: 1991; Pro40/National League/CB40/YB40: 2007; Sunday League: (3) 1971, 1987, 1988

THE LOWDOWN

Last year was a middling season for Worcestershire, who competed ably in all three competitions but did not have quite enough bite to finish the season with any accolades. They did, however, record a surplus for the fourth successive season. Moeen Ali was the star of the show across the board, as he was voted the PCA Player of the Year, along with being rated the most valuable player in the country according to the FTI MVP rankings. He was the leading run-scorer in the Championship and also became the first player since 2005 to score more than 2,000 runs and take 40 wickets in all formats. Worcestershire's seam attack has been depleted by the loss of Alan Richardson and Richard Jones to Warwickshire – the former as bowling coach – and David Lucas who has retired. That is in part negated by the signing of Pakistan's world-class spinner Saeed Ajmal, who is set for his second spell at the club.

DIRECTOR OF CRICKET: STEVE RHODES

Rhodes began his career with his home county Yorkshire before making the move to New Road in 1985, where he became a Worcestershire institution. A talented wicketkeeper and nuggety batsman, Rhodes was named as one of Wisden's five Cricketers of the Year in 1995 having made his Test debut the previous year against New Zealand at Trent Bridge. He went on to represent England a further 10 times in Test matches and played in nine one-day internationals. He has been director of cricket at Worcester since 2006.

COUNTY CHAMPIONSHIP AVERAGES 2013

	Mat	Inns	NO	Runs	HS	Ave	SR	100	50	4s	6s
MM Ali	16	27	5	1375	250	62.50	56.32	4	8	178	15
TT Samaraweera	15	22	4	702	144*	39.00	47.33	2	4	89	0
J Leach	6	9	2	260	114	37.14	56.03	1	1	38	0
TC Fell	7	10	1	333	94*	37.00	50.07	0	2	51	0
DKH Mitchell	16	29	4	824	156	32.96	43.18	1	4	96	0
MG Pardoe	16	29	3	794	102	30.53	36.28	1	5	105	4
OB Cox	6	9	2	180	65	25.71	60.40	0	1	29	1
RA Whiteley	4	7	0	162	56	23.14	47.36	0	1	24	3
JD Shantry	12	14	1	294	55*	22.61	54.14	0	2	42	4
SH Choudhry	6	9	2	146	61*	20.85	40.78	0	1	23	0
GM Andrew	10	14	0	287	66	20.50	53.04	0	3	42	2
ND Pinner	7	9	0	131	29	14.55	29.11	0	0	17	1
MA Johnson	10	14	1	184	44	14.15	34.26	0	0	22	0
A Richardson	16	18	10	109	21	13.62	65.66	0	0	16	1
G Cessford	5	6	2	45	20	11.25	35.43	0	0	8	0
AN Kervezee	10	14	0	148	35	10.57	53.62	0	0	24	0
DS Lucas	3	5	0	34	12	6.80	40.47	0	0	6	0
RA Jones	1	2	0	11	7	5.50	28.20	0	0	2	0
CJ Russell	9	11	2	42	10	4.66	29.16	0	0	5	0
A Kapil	1	2	0	8	4	4.00	114.28	0	0	0	0

	Overs	Mdns	Runs	Wkts	BBI	BBM	Ave	Econ	SR	5w	10w
A Richardson	541.4	157	1368	69	8/37	12/63	19.82	2.52	47.1	5	2
JD Shantry	323.5	88	949	34	7/69	8/142	27.91	2.93	57.1	1	0
GM Andrew	219.0	57	698	21	4/79	6/58	33.23	3.18	62.5	0	0
MM Ali	284.4	38	944	28	6/77	9/107	33.71	3.31	61.0	1	0
G Cessford	118.0	13	524	15	4/73	5/112	34.93	4.44	47.2	0	0
DKH Mitchell	26.2	6	70	2	1/1	1/3	35.00	2.65	79.0	0	0
SH Choudhry	156.4	21	443	12	4/111	4/111	36.91	2.82	78.3	0	0
RA Whiteley	8.0	0	42	1	1/23	1/23	42.00	5.25	48.0	0	0
CJ Russell	181.4	32	710	16	3/47	4/112	44.37	3.90	68.1	0	0
J Leach	65.0	6	293	5	2/36	3/89	58.60	4.50	78.0	0	0
DS Lucas	55.1	13	183	3	1/40	1/47	61.00	3.31	110.3	0	0
RA Jones	15.0	3	78	1	1/78	1/78	78.00	5.20	90.0	0	0
A Kapil	2.0	0	14	0	-	-	-	7.00	-	0	0
ND Pinner	3.0	0	15	0	-	-	-	5.00	-	0	0

Catches/Stumpings:
22 Ali, 21 Mitchell, 17 Cox (inc 1st), 14 Johnson, 9 Pinner, 6 Samaraweera, 5 Andrew, 4 Richardson, 3 Fell, Kervezee, Shantry, Pardoe, 2 Whiteley, C Russell, 1 Lucas, Leach

YORKSHIRE BANK 40 AVERAGES 2013

Batting

	Mat	Inns	NO	Runs	HS	Ave	SR	100	50	4s	6s
DKH Mitchell	12	12	0	530	107	44.16	92.17	1	5	48	2
TT Samaraweera	12	12	3	344	78	38.22	90.52	0	2	29	1
MM Ali	12	12	0	368	114	30.66	116.45	1	2	42	8
GM Andrew	8	8	1	194	62*	27.71	115.47	0	1	15	9
AN Kervezee	12	12	0	279	81	23.25	86.37	0	2	24	2
BL D'Oliveira	12	10	4	108	28	18.00	99.08	0	0	8	2
A Kapil	5	4	0	71	42	17.75	69.60	0	0	5	1
TC Fell	6	6	0	100	55	16.66	74.62	0	1	7	0
OB Cox	12	11	2	139	34*	15.44	102.20	0	0	12	4
RA Whiteley	4	4	0	50	34	12.50	74.62	0	0	5	1
MA Johnson	6	5	2	32	17*	10.66	68.08	0	0	3	0
ND Pinner	3	3	0	25	14	8.33	50.00	0	0	0	0
JD Shantry	12	8	3	40	14	8.00	65.57	0	0	3	0
G Cessford	3	2	1	0	0*	0.00	0.00	0	0	0	0
DS Lucas	3	2	2	8	7*	-	160.00	0	0	1	0
CAJ Morris	4	2	2	7	6*	-	77.77	0	0	1	0
A Richardson	2	1	1	2	2*	-	200.00	0	0	0	0
CJ Russell	4	1	1	1	1*	-	33.33	0	0	0	0

Bowling

	Overs	Mdns	Runs	Wkts	BBI	Ave	Econ	SR	4w	5w
A Richardson	9.0	1	41	3	2/31	13.66	4.55	18.0	0	0
DKH Mitchell	58.0	1	292	11	3/27	26.54	5.03	31.6	0	0
CJ Russell	20.0	1	102	4	4/32	25.50	5.10	30.0	1	0
JD Shantry	70.3	4	388	16	3/11	24.25	5.50	26.4	0	0
MM Ali	73.3	1	428	15	3/28	28.53	5.82	29.4	0	0
CAJ Morris	23.2	0	139	4	2/25	34.75	5.95	35.0	0	0
TT Samaraweera	1.0	0	6	0	-	-	6.00	-	0	0
BL D'Oliveira	40.0	0	247	9	3/35	27.44	6.17	26.6	0	0
GM Andrew	35.2	0	222	5	2/20	44.40	6.28	42.4	0	0
G Cessford	19.5	1	128	5	4/24	25.60	6.45	23.8	1	0
DS Lucas	11.0	0	77	2	1/13	38.50	7.00	33.0	0	0
RA Whiteley	8.0	0	60	2	1/25	30.00	7.50	24.0	0	0
A Kapil	4.0	0	39	1	1/20	39.00	9.75	24.0	0	0

Catches/Stumpings:
6 Cox, Shantry, 5 Mitchell, 4 Johnson (inc 2st), Whiteley, Samaraweera, 3 C Russell, Ali, Kervezee, 2 Andrew, D'Oliveira, 1 Morris, Fell

www.wccc.co.uk / tel: 01905 748474

	Mat	Inns	NO	Runs	HS	Ave	SR	100	50	4s	6s	
AD Russell	9	9	2	240	77*	34.28	158.94	0	1	19	15	
AN Kervezee	10	10	1	267	53	29.66	114.10	0	1	20	5	
RA Whiteley	2	2	0	55	43	27.50	134.14	0	0	3	3	
MM Ali	10	10	0	273	85	27.30	155.11	0	2	30	11	
OB Cox	10	9	2	139	37	19.85	124.10	0	0	15	4	
TT Samaraweera	8	8	0	155	65	19.37	142.20	0	1	23	1	Batting
DKH Mitchell	10	10	2	139	38*	17.37	102.20	0	0	13	0	
JD Shantry	10	2	1	17	9*	17.00	94.44	0	0	2	0	
J Leach	8	6	3	50	14*	16.66	125.00	0	0	3	1	
SH Choudhry	10	2	0	18	10	9.00	85.71	0	0	1	0	
GM Andrew	10	10	2	62	19	7.75	84.93	0	0	3	3	
A Kapil	2	2	0	3	3	1.50	75.00	0	0	0	0	
BL D'Oliveira	8	3	3	24	9*	-	184.61	0	0	3	0	
CJ Russell	2	2	2	6	3*	-	66.66	0	0	0	0	
CAJ Morris	1	-	-	-	-	-	-	-	-	-	-	

	Overs	Mdns	Runs	Wkts	BBI	Ave	Econ	SR	4w	5w	
SH Choudhry	27.0	0	185	4	2/21	46.25	6.85	40.5	0	0	
CAJ Morris	2.0	0	14	0	-	-	7.00	-	0	0	
MM Ali	28.3	0	201	9	5/34	22.33	7.05	19.0	0	1	
BL D'Oliveira	12.0	0	91	2	1/20	45.50	7.58	36.0	0	0	Bowling
JD Shantry	39.0	1	311	12	3/34	25.91	7.97	19.5	0	0	
GM Andrew	25.3	0	216	6	3/27	36.00	8.47	25.5	0	0	
DKH Mitchell	15.0	0	133	4	3/21	33.25	8.86	22.5	0	0	
AD Russell	24.0	0	219	9	2/26	24.33	9.12	16.0	0	0	
J Leach	12.1	0	123	4	3/20	30.75	10.10	18.2	0	0	
CJ Russell	4.3	0	62	0	-	-	13.77	-	0	0	

Catches/Stumpings:
6 Cox (inc 1st), Kervezee, 5 A Russell, Mitchell, 4 Andrew, 3 Choudhry, 2 Shantry, 1 Morris, Whiteley, Ali

FORMED: 1863
HOME GROUND: Headingley Cricket Ground
ONE-DAY NAME: Yorkshire Vikings
CAPTAIN: Andrew Gale
2013 RESULTS: CC1: 2/9; YB40: 6/7 in Group C;
FL t20: 6/6 in North Division
HONOURS: County Championship: (31) 1893,
1896, 1898, 1900, 1901, 1902, 1905, 1908, 1912,
1919, 1922, 1923, 1924, 1925, 1931, 1932, 1933,
1935, 1937, 1938, 1939, 1946, 1949, 1959, 1960,
1962, 1963, 1966, 1967, 1968, 2001; Gillette/
NatWest/C&G/FP Trophy: (3) 1965, 1969, 2002;
Benson & Hedges Cup: 1987; Sunday League: 1983

THE YORKSHIRE
COUNTY CRICKET CLUB

THE LOWDOWN

Yorkshire looked favourites to win the County Championship title in their 150th year until Durham defeated them at Scarborough and completed a late run to the summit. The White Rose eventually finished second and they will fancy their chances of going one better this year. Flush with young English batting talent, Yorkshire weren't unduly affected by the international commitments of Joe Root and Jonny Bairstow, as Gary Ballance and young opener Alex Lees rose to the challenge. Ballance ended the season as Division One's leading run-scorer and their batting has been further strengthened in the off-season with the signings of Kiwi vice-captain Kane Williamson and, for T20 cricket, the hard-hitting Aaron Finch. While last season's limited-overs fixtures took a backseat to four-day cricket, with Finch on board Yorkshire will be looking to make an impact this time round.

FIRST-TEAM COACH: JASON GILLESPIE

The pressure was on when former Australian Test bowler Gillespie was appointed at the beginning of the 2012 season after several years of underachievement from one of the country's proudest counties. He has surpassed expectations though, nearly taking home the Championship title in his second season with the club, having achieved promotion at the first time of asking in his first year at the helm. Gillespie enjoyed an illustrious international career, taking 402 international wickets for his country and playing a key role in an all-conquering side.

Batting

	Mat	Inns	NO	Runs	HS	Ave	SR	100	50	4s	6s
JE Root	2	3	0	467	236	155.66	66.71	2	0	55	0
GS Ballance	14	21	1	1251	148	62.55	54.67	5	6	153	10
AU Rashid	15	22	6	825	180	51.56	60.97	3	3	110	3
KS Williamson	5	9	1	403	97	50.37	41.54	0	5	52	0
AZ Lees	8	14	3	500	275*	45.45	48.07	2	1	67	1
AW Gale	16	24	0	1067	272	44.45	52.90	3	3	114	7
JM Bairstow	8	13	0	528	186	40.61	65.42	1	2	76	4
PA Jaques	14	21	0	770	152	36.66	56.65	2	3	111	5
RM Pyrah	5	3	1	70	55	35.00	84.33	0	1	9	1
A Lyth	16	27	4	730	105	31.73	47.37	1	4	108	0
AJ Hodd	9	9	2	217	68*	31.00	42.71	0	1	27	0
LE Plunkett	12	17	2	394	68	26.26	55.02	0	2	48	1
TT Bresnan	4	5	1	66	38	16.50	63.46	0	0	10	0
SA Patterson	16	17	8	147	40	16.33	35.00	0	0	15	1
Azeem Rafiq	2	4	0	55	28	13.75	43.65	0	0	8	0
JA Brooks	11	13	6	79	33*	11.28	45.40	0	0	4	2
RJ Sidebottom	14	16	0	155	48	9.68	32.76	0	0	17	2
JJ Sayers	5	7	0	57	24	8.14	22.98	0	0	4	0
JA Leaning	1	1	0	0	0	0.00	0.00	0	0	0	0
MA Ashraf	2	-	-	-	-	-	-	-	-	-	-

Bowling

	Overs	Mdns	Runs	Wkts	BBI	BBM	Ave	Econ	SR	5w	10w
RJ Sidebottom	369.1	100	995	49	4/27	7/73	20.30	2.69	45.2	0	0
TT Bresnan	130.2	31	393	16	4/41	6/111	24.56	3.01	48.8	0	0
SA Patterson	413.5	119	1153	46	5/43	6/65	25.06	2.78	53.9	1	0
JA Brooks	241.0	49	859	34	5/40	7/67	25.26	3.56	42.5	1	0
LE Plunkett	258.5	42	1020	36	5/32	6/85	28.33	3.94	43.1	1	0
MA Ashraf	38.3	13	119	4	3/60	3/60	29.75	3.09	57.7	0	0
A Lyth	36.0	4	155	4	2/15	2/15	38.75	4.30	54.0	0	0
AU Rashid	359.5	39	1358	29	5/78	5/78	46.82	3.77	74.4	1	0
KS Williamson	65.4	13	247	4	2/44	2/48	61.75	3.76	98.5	0	0
Azeem Rafiq	16.0	1	74	1	1/70	1/70	74.00	4.62	96.0	0	0
PA Jaques	6.0	0	75	1	1/75	1/75	75.00	12.50	36.0	0	0
RM Pyrah	77.0	19	244	2	1/45	1/45	122.00	3.16	231.0	0	0
AZ Lees	1.0	0	14	0	-	-	-	14.00	-	0	0
JE Root	9.0	4	14	0	-	-	-	1.55	-	0	0
JA Leaning	4.0	0	22	0	-	-	-	5.50	-	0	0
AW Gale	9.0	0	94	0	-	-	-	10.44	-	0	0
GS Ballance	14.0	0	98	0	-	-	-	7.00	-	0	0

Catches/Stumpings:
27 Bairstow, 25 Lyth, 18 Hodd (inc 1st), 13 Ballance, 9 Plunkett, 7 Rashid, 5 Pyrah, Brooks, Jaques, 4 Sayers, Williamson, Gale, 3 Root, Sidebottom, 2 Patterson, 1 Bresnan, Lees

YORKSHIRE BANK 40 AVERAGES 2013

Batting

	Mat	Inns	NO	Runs	HS	Ave	SR	100	50	4s	6s
GS Ballance	8	7	0	426	139	60.85	97.93	1	3	40	9
JM Bairstow	1	1	0	53	53	53.00	147.22	0	1	7	1
AU Rashid	8	7	3	183	46*	45.75	116.56	0	0	17	1
KS Williamson	1	1	0	45	45	45.00	65.21	0	0	2	2
A Lyth	11	11	2	397	58*	44.11	92.75	0	2	35	8
JA Leaning	3	3	1	85	60	42.50	118.05	0	1	7	2
DM Hodgson	6	5	0	197	90	39.40	103.68	0	2	23	3
JJ Sayers	3	2	0	78	58	39.00	84.78	0	1	7	0
AZ Lees	4	4	0	155	63	38.75	81.15	0	2	11	1
PA Jaques	6	6	0	211	81	35.16	84.06	0	2	24	0
LE Plunkett	5	4	1	89	53	29.66	185.41	0	1	9	5
AW Gale	11	11	1	272	65	27.20	82.42	0	1	34	3
Azeem Rafiq	2	2	0	30	18	15.00	150.00	0	0	2	2
I Wardlaw	8	4	2	27	17*	13.50	135.00	0	0	3	1
RM Pyrah	11	9	2	83	34	11.85	112.16	0	0	7	2
AJ Hodd	7	6	1	56	21	11.20	100.00	0	0	6	0
WMH Rhodes	7	6	1	53	19*	10.60	80.30	0	0	4	0
MD Fisher	2	1	0	10	10	10.00	250.00	0	0	2	0
R Gibson	3	2	1	10	6	10.00	83.33	0	0	1	0
RJ Sidebottom	2	1	0	10	10	10.00	125.00	0	0	1	0
SA Patterson	3	2	0	17	12	8.50	106.25	0	0	3	0
MA Ashraf	8	2	1	0	0*	0.00	0.00	0	0	0	0
TT Bresnan	1	1	0	0	0	0.00	0.00	0	0	0	0
JE Root	1	1	0	0	0	0.00	0.00	0	0	0	0
JA Tattersall	1	1	0	0	0	0.00	0.00	0	0	0	0
OE Robinson	3	2	2	16	12*	-	100.00	0	0	0	0
BO Coad	6	2	2	1	1*	-	50.00	0	0	0	0

Bowling

	Overs	Mdns	Runs	Wkts	BBI	Ave	Econ	SR	4w	5w
KS Williamson	8.0	0	42	1	1/42	42.00	5.25	48.0	0	0
JA Leaning	11.0	0	60	6	5/22	10.00	5.45	11.0	0	1
AU Rashid	57.0	1	328	5	2/27	65.60	5.75	68.4	0	0
LE Plunkett	38.0	3	221	7	2/38	31.57	5.81	32.5	0	0
RM Pyrah	75.0	3	446	15	4/43	29.73	5.94	30.0	1	0
SA Patterson	24.0	0	145	4	2/35	36.25	6.04	36.0	0	0
MD Fisher	14.0	0	85	1	1/40	85.00	6.07	84.0	0	0
I Wardlaw	52.4	1	333	14	3/39	23.78	6.32	22.5	0	0
TT Bresnan	7.0	0	45	1	1/45	45.00	6.42	42.0	0	0
OE Robinson	10.0	0	66	0	-	-	6.60	-	0	0
A Lyth	13.0	0	86	1	1/6	86.00	6.61	78.0	0	0
MA Ashraf	55.1	1	366	10	3/38	36.60	6.63	33.1	0	0
WMH Rhodes	20.0	0	133	4	2/26	33.25	6.65	30.0	0	0
BO Coad	35.2	1	244	3	1/34	81.33	6.90	70.6	0	0
R Gibson	14.0	0	98	3	1/21	32.66	7.00	28.0	0	0
RJ Sidebottom	16.0	0	114	3	2/77	38.00	7.12	32.0	0	0
Azeem Rafiq	4.0	0	36	1	1/36	36.00	9.00	24.0	0	0
JE Root	2.0	0	18	0	-	-	9.00	-	0	0

Catches/Stumpings:
9 Hodd (inc 1st), 6 Lyth, 5 Hodgson, 4 Robinson, 3 Leaning, Plunkett, Coad, 2 Patterson, Rhodes, Ballance, Wardlaw, Gale, Pyrah, 1 Root, Lees, Ashraf, Rashid

	Mat	Inns	NO	Runs	HS	Ave	SR	100	50	4s	6s
PA Jaques	4	4	1	99	66*	33.00	104.21	0	1	11	1
GS Ballance	10	10	1	269	68	29.88	116.45	0	1	24	8
Azeem Rafiq	10	7	5	47	15*	23.50	117.50	0	0	5	0
DM Hodgson	10	10	1	177	52*	19.66	102.90	0	1	19	3
AW Gale	3	3	0	57	34	19.00	118.75	0	0	10	1
A Lyth	6	6	0	101	32	16.83	108.60	0	0	13	2
AZ Lees	2	2	0	33	32	16.50	97.05	0	0	5	0
JJ Sayers	5	5	0	81	38	16.20	96.42	0	0	11	1
RM Pyrah	10	9	2	104	42	14.85	119.54	0	0	8	2
RJ Sidebottom	8	4	3	14	5*	14.00	77.77	0	0	1	0
LE Plunkett	10	9	1	101	30	12.62	107.44	0	0	7	3
JM Bairstow	1	1	0	12	12	12.00	80.00	0	0	1	0
AU Rashid	8	8	1	76	19	10.85	104.10	0	0	5	2
AJ Hodd	6	5	2	29	11	9.66	90.62	0	0	3	0
WMH Rhodes	2	2	0	13	13	6.50	65.00	0	0	0	0
JA Leaning	3	3	0	14	8	4.66	56.00	0	0	0	0
MA Ashraf	1	1	0	4	4	4.00	66.66	0	0	1	0
I Wardlaw	3	1	1	1	1*	-	100.00	0	0	0	0
JA Brooks	8	-	-	-	-	-	-	-	-	-	-

Batting

	Overs	Mdns	Runs	Wkts	BBI	Ave	Econ	SR	4w	5w
RM Pyrah	32.0	1	192	9	3/15	21.33	6.00	21.3	0	0
RJ Sidebottom	27.5	0	200	3	1/29	66.66	7.18	55.6	0	0
JA Brooks	25.0	1	189	13	5/21	14.53	7.56	11.5	1	1
Azeem Rafiq	31.0	0	247	13	3/22	19.00	7.96	14.3	0	0
A Lyth	2.0	0	16	1	1/16	16.00	8.00	12.0	0	0
AU Rashid	19.0	0	156	1	1/24	156.00	8.21	114.0	0	0
LE Plunkett	33.3	0	277	8	2/20	34.62	8.26	25.1	0	0
I Wardlaw	4.1	0	46	0	-	-	11.04	-	0	0
WMH Rhodes	1.1	0	14	0	-	-	12.00	-	0	0
MA Ashraf	2.0	0	28	0	-	-	14.00	-	0	0
JA Leaning	1.0	0	18	0	-	-	18.00	-	0	0

Bowling

Catches/Stumpings:
6 Hodgson (inc 1st), 5 Pyrah, 4 Ballance 3 Hodd (inc 1st), Sayers, Brooks, Plunkett, 2 Bairstow, Lyth, Rashid, Rafiq, 1 Jaques, Sidebottom

County
Ins and Outs

DERBYSHIRE

▶IN: Scott Elstone (Nottinghamshire), Stephen Moore (Lancashire)

◀OUT: Alasdair Evans (released), Dan Redfern (Leicestershire), Ross Whiteley (Worcestershire)

DURHAM

▶IN: John Hastings (Australia), Calum MacLeod (Scotland), Stuart Poynter (Ireland)

◀OUT: Dale Benkenstein (retired), Ruel Brathwaite (Hampshire), Mitchell Claydon (Kent), Steve Harmison (retired), Will Smith (Hampshire), Callum Thorp (released)

ESSEX

▶IN: Monty Panesar (Essex)

◀OUT: Maurice Chambers (Northamptonshire), Owais Shah (released)

GLAMORGAN

▶IN: Jacques Rudolph (South Africa)

◀OUT: Nick James (released), Alex Jones (released), Simon Jones (released), Marcus North (Australia)

GLOUCESTERSHIRE

▶IN: Tom Smith (Middlesex), William Tavaré

◀OUT: Richard Coughtrie (released), Paul Muchall (released), Ed Young (released)

HAMPSHIRE

▶IN: Kyle Abbott (South Africa), Ruel Brathwaite (Durham), Matt Coles (Kent), Joe Gatting (Sussex), Glenn Maxwell (Australia), Will Smith (Durham)

◀OUT: Jake George (released), David Griffiths (Kent), Dimitri Mascarenhas (retired), Neil McKenzie (South Africa), Hamza Riazuddin (released), Michael Roberts (released), Adam Rouse (released), Jack Sheppard (released)

KENT

▶IN: Doug Bollinger (Australia), Mitchell Claydon (Durham), David Griffiths (Hampshire)

◀OUT: Matt Coles (Hampshire), Ben Kemp (released), Michael Powell (retired), Ashley Shaw (released), Charlie Shreck (Leicestershire)

LANCASHIRE

▶IN: Jos Buttler (Somerset), Kyle Jarvis (Zimbabwe)

◀OUT: Gareth Cross (released), Simon Katich (retired), Stephen Moore (Derbyshire)

LEICESTERSHIRE

▶IN: Ben Raine (Durham), Dan Redfern (Derbyshire), Charlie Shreck (Kent)

◀OUT: Claude Henderson (retired), Matthew Hoggard (retired), Robbie Williams (released)

COUNTY INS AND OUTS 2013/14

MIDDLESEX
▶IN: Cameron Steel (Somerset)
◀OUT: Corey Collymore (released), Josh Davey (released), Adam London (released), Tom Smith (Gloucestershire)

NORTHAMPTONSHIRE
▶IN: Jackson Bird (Australia), Maurice Chambers (Northamptonshire), Richard Levi (South Africa), Graeme White (Nottinghamshire)
◀OUT: Lee Daggett (retired), Christian Davis (released), Con de Lange (released), Luke Evans (released), Sam Sweeney (released)

NOTTINGHAMSHIRE
▶IN: Phil Jaques (Yorkshire), Gary Keedy (Surrey), Peter Siddle (Australia)
◀OUT: Scott Elstone (Derbyshire), David Hussey (Australia), Ben Phillips (released), Graeme Swann (retired), Graeme White (Northamptonshire)

SOMERSET
▶IN: Johann Myburgh (South Africa)
◀OUT: Jos Buttler (Lancashire), Gemaal Hussain (released), Arul Suppiah (retired)

SURREY
▶IN:
◀OUT: Zander de Bruyn (released), Gary Keedy (Nottinghamshire), Jon Lewis (Sussex)

SUSSEX
▶IN: Yasir Arafat (Pakistan), Jon Lewis (Surrey), Steffan Piolet (Warwickshire), Ashar Zaidi (Pakistan)
◀OUT: Joe Gatting (Hampshire), Amjad Khan (released), Andrew Miller (released), Monty Panesar (Essex)

WARWICKSHIRE
▶IN: Richard Jones (Warwickshire), Shoaib Malik (Pakistan)
◀OUT: Tom Allin (released), Darren Maddy (retired), Chris Metters (released), Steffan Piolet (Sussex)

WORCESTERSHIRE
▶IN: Saeed Ajmal (Pakistan), Ross Whiteley (Derbyshire)
◀OUT: Michael Johnson (released), Richard Jones (Warwickshire), Aneesh Kapil (released), Steve Leach (released), David Lucas (retired), Neil Pinner (released), Alan Richardson (retired), Thilan Samaraweera (Sri Lanka)

YORKSHIRE
▶IN: Aaron Finch (Australia), Oliver Robinson (Kent), Kane Williamson (New Zealand)
◀OUT: Phil Jaques (Nottinghamshire), Gurman Randhawa (Shropshire), Joe Sayers (retired), Iain Wardlaw (released)

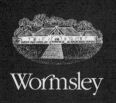

Wormsley

"Quintessentially English"

Cricket at Wormsley
www.wormsleycricket.co.uk

The
Players

HAMPSHIRE

FULL NAME: Kyle John Abbott
BORN: June 18, 1987, Empangeni, KwaZulu-Natal, South Africa
SQUAD NO: 87
TEAMS: South Africa, Dolphins, Hampshire, KwaZulu-Natal, Somerset 2nd XI, South Africa A
CAREER: Test: 2013; ODI: 2013; T20I: 2013; First-class: 2009; List A: 2009; T20: 2011

BEST BATTING: 80 Dolphins vs Titans, Benoni, 2011
BEST BOWLING: 8-45 Dolphins vs Cape Cobras, Cape Town, 2013

TWITTER FEED: @Kyle_Abbott87
NOTES: South African seamer Abbott will be Hampshire's overseas player for 2014. On Test debut, against Pakistan in February last year, he claimed match-figures of 9-68 to take the Man of the Match award, including a second-innings haul of 7-29. He had to wait more than a year for his second opportunity though, when he was recalled for the third Test against Australia at Cape Town in March, taking three second-innings wickets and batting for 89 balls as South Africa tried but failed to save the match and the series. The 2012/13 South African domestic season was his best to date, as he took 65 first-class wickets at 14.29. Abbott is expected to be available for the entirety of the 2014 campaign

Batting	Mat	Inns	NO	Runs	HS	Ave	SR	100	50	Ct	St
Tests	2	3	0	23	13	7.66	16.19	0	0	1	0
ODIs	2	1	0	5	5	5.00	125.00	0	0	2	0
T20Is	1	1	0	2	2	2.00	100.00	0	0	0	0
First-class	48	71	13	1042	80	17.96	41.94	0	4	13	0
List A	59	29	13	320	45*	20.00	100.31	0	0	17	0
Twenty20	32	11	8	38	15*	12.66	100.00	0	0	7	0

Bowling	Mat	Balls	Runs	Wkts	BBI	BBM	Ave	Econ	SR	5w	10
Tests	2	424	197	12	7/29	9/68	16.41	2.78	35.3	1	0
ODIs	2	86	66	1	1/35	1/35	66.00	4.60	86.0	0	0
T20Is	1	24	41	1	1/41	1/41	41.00	10.25	24.0	0	0
First-class	48	8697	3930	182	8/45	12/96	21.59	2.71	47.7	11	2
List A	59	2506	2157	77	4/36	4/36	28.01	5.16	32.5	0	0
Twenty20	32	655	756	33	3/13	3/13	22.90	6.92	19.8	0	0

TOM ABELL   RHB RM

FULL NAME: Thomas Benjamin Abell
BORN: March 5, 1994, Taunton, Somerset
SQUAD NO: 28
HEIGHT: 5ft 11in
NICKNAME: Tabez
EDUCATION: Taunton School; Exeter University
TEAMS: Somerset 2nd XI
CAREER: Yet to make first-team debut

SOMERSET

WHO WOULD PLAY YOU IN A FILM OF YOUR LIFE? Russell Crowe
CAREER HIGHLIGHTS? Scoring 246* for Somerset U17 vs Sussex U17. Scoring over 1,000 runs for my school 1st XI. Being 12th man for Somerset 1st XI
SUPERSTITIONS? I am quite superstitious when I bat. I have to make sure all my kit feels right, so I adjust everything after each ball: pads, gloves, etc
MOST MARKED CHARACTERISTIC? Probably my dodgy-looking hair
BEST PLAYER IN COUNTY CRICKET? James Hildreth
TIPS FOR THE TOP? Jos Buttler, hopefully myself
IF YOU WEREN'T A CRICKETER? I am currently at university, so hopefully something in the sport/sports science field
DESERT ISLAND DISC? The Kooks – Naive
FAVOURITE TV? Geordie Shore
BIGGEST DRESSING DOWN YOU'VE RECEIVED? After our school team was bowled out for 54 – that was a major reality check
CRICKETING HEROES? Brian Lara, Andrew Flintoff, Marcus Trescothick
NON-CRICKETING HEROES? Sonny Bill Williams, David Haye, Jonny Wilkinson
ACCOMPLISHMENTS? Hockey success with my school team (four national finals). I was runner-up in the Aviva/Telegraph School Sport Matters Awards
SURPRISING FACT? I was Somerset U8 tennis champion
FANTASY SLIP CORDON? Keeper: James Corden, 1st: Lee Mack, 2nd: Jimmy Carr, 3rd: Jonny Wilkinson, Gully: Yohan Blake
TWITTER FEED: @tomabell1

ANDRE ADAMS   RHB RFM W3

FULL NAME: Andre Ryan Adams
BORN: July 17, 1975, Auckland, New Zealand
SQUAD NO: 41
HEIGHT: 5ft 11in
NICKNAME: Dre, Doctor, Dizzy
EDUCATION: West Lake Boys' High School, Auckland
TEAMS: New Zealand, Auckland, Essex, Herefordshire, Kolkata Tigers, Nottinghamshire
CAREER: Test: 2002; ODI: 2001; T20I: 2005; First-class: 1998; List A: 1997; T20: 2004

BEST BATTING: 124 Essex vs Leicestershire, Leicester, 2004
BEST BOWLING: 7-32 Nottinghamshire vs Lancashire, Manchester, 2012
COUNTY CAPS: 2004 (Essex); 2007 (Nottinghamshire)

CAREER HIGHLIGHTS? Winning the County Championship, playing in a World Cup and playing a Test match
CRICKETING HEROES? Michael Holding, Viv Richards
TIPS FOR THE TOP? Alex Hales, Jos Buttler
IF YOU WEREN'T A CRICKETER? I'd be running a hunting lodge
FAVOURITE FILM? The Usual Suspects
DREAM HOLIDAY? Rarotonga
GUILTY PLEASURES? BBQ food and chocolate
SURPRISING FACTS? My grandfather is Corsican and my grandmother is Scottish. I like classical music
TWITTER FEED: @AndreAdams

Batting	Mat	Inns	NO	Runs	HS	Ave	SR	100	50	Ct	St
Tests	1	2	0	18	11	9.00	90.00	0	0	1	0
ODIs	42	34	10	419	45	17.45	100.47	0	0	8	0
T20Is	4	2	1	13	7	13.00	108.33	0	0	1	0
First-class	160	220	23	4421	124	22.44		3	20	102	0
List A	165	119	29	1504	90*	16.71		0	1	40	0
Twenty20	71	42	14	417	54*	14.89	131.96	0	1	21	0

Bowling	Mat	Balls	Runs	Wkts	BBI	BBM	Ave	Econ	SR	5w	10
Tests	1	190	105	6	3/44	6/105	17.50	3.31	31.6	0	0
ODIs	42	1885	1643	53	5/22	5/22	31.00	5.22	35.5	1	0
T20Is	4	77	105	3	2/20	2/20	35.00	8.18	25.6	0	0
First-class	160	30742	15144	645	7/32		23.47	2.95	47.6	31	6
List A	165	7561	5957	209	5/7	5/7	28.50	4.72	36.1	4	0
Twenty20	71	1498	1914	87	5/20	5/20	22.00	7.66	17.2	1	0

JIMMY ADAMS

LHB LM R4 MVP75

FULL NAME: James Henry Kenneth Adams
BORN: September 23, 1980, Winchester, Hampshire
SQUAD NO: 4
HEIGHT: 6ft
NICKNAME: Bison
EDUCATION: Twyford School; Sherborne School; Loughborough University
TEAMS: Auckland, British Universities, England Lions, Hampshire, Hampshire 2nd XI, Loughborough UCCE
CAREER: First-class: 2002; List A: 2002; T20: 2005

BEST BATTING: 262* Hampshire vs Nottinghamshire, Nottingham, 2006
BEST BOWLING: 2-16 Hampshire vs Durham, Chester-le-Street, 2004
COUNTY CAP: 2006

FAMILY TIES? My dad played a bit for Kent Schoolboys and my brothers played Hampshire age-group cricket until they decided to pursue other things
WHO WOULD PLAY YOU IN A FILM OF YOUR LIFE? Wishful thinking would say Christian Bale but it'd probably be best done on the radio
MOST MARKED CHARACTERISTIC? Indecisiveness and an over-sized big toe
TIPS FOR THE TOP? Most of the guys are already on the England radar with the EPP and Lions. However, of Hampshire's next batch of young players Tom Barber looks very exciting
FAVOURITE TV? Most detective series
BIGGEST DRESSING DOWN YOU'VE RECEIVED? I've been fairly fortunate really. I remember Jimmy Cook not seeing the funny side of my 12th man efforts and you were never late twice for a session with Graham Dilley
CRICKETING HEROES? Robin Smith, Jimmy Adams
NON-CRICKETING HEROES? Jimmy Page, Keith Moon
ACCOMPLISHMENTS? Getting married, renovating our house and beating a certain friend at squash
WHEN YOU RETIRE? I'd ideally stay in the game. Coaching hopefully

Batting	Mat	Inns	NO	Runs	HS	Ave	SR	100	50	Ct	St
First-class	159	279	26	9811	262*	38.77			19	49	134	0
List A	83	79	10	2720	131	39.42	86.15	2	21	35	0
Twenty20	103	93	12	1997	101*	24.65	118.93	2	4	25	0

Bowling	Mat	Balls	Runs	Wkts	BBI	BBM	Ave	Econ	SR	5w	10
First-class	159	1063	718	13	2/16		55.23	4.05	81.7	0	0
List A	83	79	105	1	1/34	1/34	105.00	7.97	79.0	0	0
Twenty20	103	36	60	0	-	-	-	10.00	-	0	0

LANCASHIRE

FULL NAME: Andrea Peter Agathangelou
BORN: November 16, 1989, Rustenberg, South Africa
SQUAD NO: 11
HEIGHT: 6ft 3in
NICKNAME: Aggers, Greek, Swaggers, China
EDUCATION: Fields College; University of South Africa; University of Cape Town
TEAMS: Lancashire, Lancashire 2nd XI, North West, North West Under-19s, South Africa Under-19s
CAREER: First-class: 2008; List A: 2008

BEST BATTING: 158 North West vs KwaZulu-Natal, Potchefstroom, 2010
BEST BOWLING: 2-18 Lancashire vs Gloucestershire, Liverpool, 2013

WHO WOULD PLAY YOU IN A FILM OF YOUR LIFE? I would try and select someone good-looking and witty to boost my rep a little

CAREER HIGHLIGHTS? Representing Lancashire in the 2013 season and winning Division Two. Representing South Africa U19

SUPERSTITIONS? Only preventing Simon Kerrigan from coming over to my side of the changing room!

MOST MARKED CHARACTERISTIC? Probably dedication or tenacity

TIPS FOR THE TOP? Simon Kerrigan, Alex Davies, Luis Reece, Arron Lilley, Liam Livingstone

IF YOU WEREN'T A CRICKETER? I would have studied Mechanical Engineering and started a business which allowed me to play golf every day

DESERT ISLAND DISC? Linkin Park – Minutes To Midnight

CRICKETING HEROES? Jacques Kallis, Master Sachin, Steve Waugh

ACCOMPLISHMENTS? Starting my own company and completing numerous courses in my chosen fields. Landing my current girlfriend, Caylene Marais (hopefully this earns me some brownie points)

SURPRISING FACT? I was head boy in both primary and high school. I'm studying Property Investment and Import and Export. I'll shortly be launching my first product in the UK…

TWITTER FEED: @Agathangelou11

Batting	Mat	Inns	NO	Runs	HS	Ave	SR	100	50	Ct	St
First-class	41	72	4	2364	158	34.76	53.14	5	13	66	0
List A	25	23	3	679	94	33.95	77.86	0	5	9	1

Bowling	Mat	Balls	Runs	Wkts	BBI	BBM	Ave	Econ	SR	5w	10
First-class	41	723	436	9	2/18	3/66	48.44	3.61	80.3	0	0
List A	25	36	48	0	-	-	-	8.00	-	0	0

SAEED AJMAL

RHB OB

FULL NAME: Saeed Ajmal
BORN: October 14, 1977, Faisalabad, Pakistan
SQUAD NO: 50
HEIGHT: 5ft 8in
TEAMS: Pakistan, Dhaka Gladiators,
Faisalabad, Faisalabad Wolves, Islamabad
Cricket Association, Khan Research Labs,
Water and Power Development Authority,
Worcestershire, Zarai Taraqiati Bank Limited
CAREER: Test: 2009; ODI: 2008; T20I: 2009;
First-class: 1996; List A: 1995; T20: 2005

WORCESTERSHIRE

BEST BATTING: 53 Faisalabad vs Quetta, Sargodha, 2004
BEST BOWLING: 7-55 Pakistan vs England, Dubai, 2012

NOTES: Ajmal returns for his second spell at Worcestershire, having previously played
for the club in 2011 when he took 17 first-class wickets at 27.70. He was due to play for
Hampshire last year but international commitments eventually prevented him from doing
so. The Pakistani spinner came late into international cricket – he was 32 before he played
a Test – but he made up for lost time, taking five wickets on debut against Sri Lanka in Galle.
In 2011, he was the leading wicket-taker in Tests, with 50 in eight matches, and he took 24
wickets in three matches against England during the 2012 Test series whitewash in UAE

Batting	Mat	Inns	NO	Runs	HS	Ave	SR	100	50	Ct	St
Tests	33	49	11	428	50	11.26	42.08	0	1	11	0
ODIs	110	68	24	318	33	7.22	61.62	0	0	25	0
T20Is	59	22	12	90	21*	9.00	108.43	0	0	9	0
First-class	123	168	47	1432	53	11.83		0	3	40	0
List A	216	120	49	515	33	7.25		0	0	51	0
Twenty20	131	42	21	164	21*	7.80	102.50	0	0	20	0

Bowling	Mat	Balls	Runs	Wkts	BBI	BBM	Ave	Econ	SR	5w	10
Tests	33	10727	4642	169	7/55	11/111	27.46	2.59	63.4	9	4
ODIs	110	5861	4049	182	5/24	5/24	22.24	4.14	32.2	2	0
T20Is	59	1320	1379	81	4/19	4/19	17.02	6.26	16.2	0	0
First-class	123	28370	12748	474	7/55		26.89	2.69	59.8	30	5
List A	216	11366	8229	336	5/18	5/18	24.49	4.34	33.8	3	0
Twenty20	131	2912	3022	191	4/14	4/14	15.82	6.22	15.2	0	0

KABIR ALI RHB RMF W5

FULL NAME: Kabir Ali
BORN: November 24, 1980, Moseley, Birmingham, Warwickshire
SQUAD NO: 23
HEIGHT: 6ft
NICKNAME: Kabby, Taxi
EDUCATION: Moseley School; Wolverhampton University
TEAMS: England, Barisal Burners, England A, Hampshire, Lancashire, Lancashire 2nd XI, Rajasthan, Worcestershire
CAREER: Test: 2003; ODI: 2003; First-class: 1999; List A: 2000; T20: 2004

BEST BATTING: 84* Worcestershire vs Durham, Stockton-on-Tees, 2003
BEST BOWLING: 8-50 Worcestershire vs Lancashire, Manchester, 2007

FAMILY TIES? My father played club cricket, my cousin Moeen plays for Worcestershire and another cousin Kadeer played for Gloucestershire
CRICKETING HEROES? Wasim Akram, Glenn McGrath
CAREER HIGHLIGHTS? Playing for England
TIP FOR THE TOP? Moeen Ali
TWITTER FEED: @Imkabirali

Batting	Mat	Inns	NO	Runs	HS	Ave	SR	100	50	Ct	St
Tests	1	2	0	10	9	5.00	35.71	0	0	0	0
ODIs	14	9	3	93	39*	15.50	86.11	0	0	1	0
First-class	130	182	28	2621	84*	17.01		0	7	33	0
List A	172	106	28	1240	92	15.89		0	4	31	0
Twenty20	57	40	14	458	50	17.61	134.70	0	1	14	0

Bowling	Mat	Balls	Runs	Wkts	BBI	BBM	Ave	Econ	SR	5w	10
Tests	1	216	136	5	3/80	5/136	27.20	3.77	43.2	0	0
ODIs	14	673	682	20	4/45	4/45	34.10	6.08	33.6	0	0
First-class	130	22125	13214	483	8/50		27.35	3.58	45.8	23	4
List A	172	7284	6386	255	5/36	5/36	25.04	5.26	28.5	2	0
Twenty20	57	1124	1612	62	4/44	4/44	26.00	8.60	18.1	0	0

FULL NAME: Moeen Munir Ali
BORN: June 18, 1987, Birmingham
SQUAD NO: 8
HEIGHT: 6ft
NICKNAME: Moe, Brother Mo
EDUCATION: Moseley School
TEAMS: England, Duronto Rajshahi, England Lions, England Performance Programme, England Under-19s, Matabeleland Tuskers, Moors Sports Club, Warwickshire, Worcestershire
CAREER: ODI: 2014; T20I: 2014; First-class: 2005; List A: 2006; T20: 2007

WORCESTERSHIRE

BEST BATTING: 250 Worcestershire vs Glamorgan, Worcester, 2013
BEST BOWLING: 6-29 Worcestershire vs Lancashire, Manchester, 2012
COUNTY CAP: 2007 (Worcestershire)

FAMILY TIES? My dad is a cricket coach. Kadeer Ali [former Leicestershire, Worcestershire, Gloucestershire batsman] is my brother and Kabir Ali [Lancashire] is my cousin
CAREER HIGHLIGHTS? Captaining Worcestershire. Being promoted twice with Worcestershire. Winning the CB40. Scoring 136 against Sri Lanka
CRICKETING HEROES? Brian Lara, Saeed Anwar, Marcus Trescothick, Saeed Ajmal
IF YOU WEREN'T A CRICKETER? I'd own and run a chippy called Big Mo's
WHEN RAIN STOPS PLAY? I'm usually playing changing room cricket or sleeping
FAVOURITE FILM? The Message
DREAM HOLIDAY? Saudi Arabia or Palestine
ACCOMPLISHMENTS? Performing the fifth pillar of Islam, the Hajj
SURPRISING FACT? I wear my trousers above my ankles. My grandmother is a white English woman
FANTASY SLIP CORDON? Keeper: Superman, 1st: Spider-Man, 2nd: Batman, 3rd: Me, Gully: Iron Man

Batting	Mat	Inns	NO	Runs	HS	Ave	SR	100	50	Ct	St
ODIs	3	3	0	109	55	36.33	81.34	0	1	3	0
First-class	109	190	17	6522	250	37.69	53.96	12	40	69	0
List A	103	98	2	2903	158	30.23	99.34	7	13	30	0
Twenty20	74	71	3	1539	85	22.63	125.02	0	8	20	0

Bowling	Mat	Balls	Runs	Wkts	BBI	BBM	Ave	Econ	SR	5w	10
ODIs	3	60	41	3	1/5	1/5	13.66	4.10	20.0	0	0
First-class	109	9142	5416	132	6/29	12/96	41.03	3.55	69.2	4	1
List A	103	2235	2131	54	3/28	3/28	39.46	5.72	41.3	0	0
Twenty20	74	902	1095	43	5/34	5/34	25.46	7.28	20.9	1	0

JIM ALLENBY · RHB RM R1 MVP4

GLAMORGAN

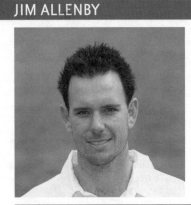

FULL NAME: James Allenby
BORN: September 12, 1982, Perth, Australia
SQUAD NO: 5
HEIGHT: 6ft
NICKNAME: Hank
EDUCATION: Christ Church Grammar School, Perth
TEAMS: Durham Cricket Board, Glamorgan, Leicestershire, Western Australia, Western Australia Under-19s
CAREER: First-class: 2006; List A: 2003; T20: 2005

BEST BATTING: 138* Leicestershire vs Bangladesh A, Leicester, 2008
BEST BOWLING: 5-44 Glamorgan vs Derbyshire, Cardiff, 2011
COUNTY CAP: 2010 (Glamorgan)

WHO WOULD PLAY YOU IN A FILM OF YOUR LIFE? Jim Carrey
CAREER HIGHLIGHTS? Signing my first pro contract in 2005 after three years trialling all over the country. Winning the T20 with Leicestershire in 2006 and playing Finals Day in 2005. Scoring a century on my County Championship debut. Scoring a T20 century for Leicestershire
SUPERSTITIONS? I prepare for each ball in the same way and walk out on the left-hand side
MOST MARKED CHARACTERISTIC? Too many to even begin!
IF YOU WEREN'T A CRICKETER? Lawn mowing
DESERT ISLAND DISC? Triple J Hottest 100
FAVOURITE TV? The Simpsons
BIGGEST DRESSING DOWN YOU'VE RECEIVED? Once again, far too many to mention!
CRICKETING HEROES? Dean Jones, Steve Waugh, Matt and Tom Maynard
TWITTER FEED: @jimallenby

Batting	Mat	Inns	NO	Runs	HS	Ave	SR	100	50	Ct	St
First-class	104	162	26	5687	138*	41.81	59.01	9	41	106	0
List A	88	83	10	1942	91*	26.60	87.79	0	9	27	0
Twenty20	82	76	13	1859	110	29.50	121.18	1	12	23	0

Bowling	Mat	Balls	Runs	Wkts	BBI	BBM	Ave	Econ	SR	5w	10
First-class	104	12075	5432	200	5/44	7/47	27.16	2.69	60.3	3	0
List A	88	2778	2325	78	5/43	5/43	29.80	5.02	35.6	1	0
Twenty20	82	1038	1364	45	5/21	5/21	30.31	7.88	23.0	2	0

TIM AMBROSE   RHB WK

FULL NAME: Timothy Raymond Ambrose
BORN: December 1, 1982, Newcastle, New South Wales, Australia
SQUAD NO: 11
HEIGHT: 5ft 7in
NICKNAME: Freak
EDUCATION: Merewether Selective High, New South Wales
TEAMS: England, Sussex, Warwickshire
CAREER: Test: 2008; ODI: 2008; T20I: 2008; First-class: 2001; List A: 2001; T20: 2003

BEST BATTING: 251* Warwickshire vs Worcestershire, Worcester, 2007
COUNTY CAPS: 2003 (Sussex); 2007 (Warwickshire)

CAREER HIGHLIGHTS? Winning the Championship with Sussex in 2003 and any time I've played for England
SUPERSTITIONS? I put my left pad on before my right
CRICKETING HEROES? Steve Waugh, Adam Gilchrist, Mushtaq Ahmed
NON-CRICKETING HEROES? Peter Griffin, Eric Cantona
BEST PLAYER IN COUNTY CRICKET? Marcus Trescothick
TIP FOR THE TOP? Laurie Evans
WHEN RAIN STOPS PLAY? Debating random topics – North vs South is always fun!
FAVOURITE TV? Dexter, Family Guy
FAVOURITE FILM? Cool Hand Luke
FAVOURITE BOOK? Bravo Two Zero
ACCOMPLISHMENTS? Learning to play guitar

Batting	Mat	Inns	NO	Runs	HS	Ave	SR	100	50	Ct	St
Tests	11	16	1	447	102	29.80	46.41	1	3	31	0
ODIs	5	5	1	10	6	2.50	29.41	0	0	3	0
T20Is	1	-	-	-	-	-	-	-	-	1	1
First-class	165	249	24	7715	251*	34.28	52.87	11	48	406	23
List A	136	113	17	2797	135	29.13	75.18	3	12	130	23
Twenty20	55	43	13	800	77	26.66	114.77	0	2	32	17

Bowling	Mat	Balls	Runs	Wkts	BBI	BBM	Ave	Econ	SR	5w	10
Tests	11	-	-	-	-	-	-	-	-	-	-
ODIs	5	-	-	-	-	-	-	-	-	-	-
T20Is	1	-	-	-	-	-	-	-	-	-	-
First-class	165	6	1	0	-	-	-	1.00	-	0	0
List A	136	-	-	-	-	-	-	-	-	-	-
Twenty20	55	-	-	-	-	-	-	-	-	-	-

LANCASHIRE

FULL NAME: James Michael Anderson
BORN: July 30, 1982, Burnley, Lancashire
SQUAD NO: 9
HEIGHT: 6ft 2in
NICKNAME: Jimmy, Jimbo, Jimbob
EDUCATION: St Theodore's RC High School;
St Theodore's RC Sixth Form Centre, Burnley
TEAMS: England, Auckland, England Under-19s, Lancashire, Lancashire Cricket Board
CAREER: Test: 2003; ODI: 2002; T20I: 2007;
First-class: 2002; List A: 2000; T20: 2004

BEST BATTING: 37* Lancashire vs Durham, Manchester, 2005
BEST BOWLING: 7-43 England vs New Zealand, Nottingham, 2008
COUNTY CAP: 2003; BENEFIT YEAR: 2012

WHO WOULD PLAY YOU IN A FILM OF YOUR LIFE? Jim Carrey
CAREER HIGHLIGHTS? Three Ashes wins and my County Championship winners' medal
DESERT ISLAND DISC? James – Runaground
CRICKETING HEROES? Allan Donald, Peter Martin, Glen Chapple
BEST PLAYER IN COUNTY CRICKET? Marcus Trescothick
TIP FOR THE TOP? Simon Kerrigan
FAVOURITE FILM? Les Enfants Terribles (1950)
FAVOURITE BOOK? Birdsong
SURPRISING SKILL? I can peel a potato in 2.4 seconds
FANTASY SLIP CORDON? Keeper: Inspector Gadget, Gully: Me
TWITTER FEED: @jimmy9

Batting	Mat	Inns	NO	Runs	HS	Ave	SR	100	50	Ct	St
Tests	92	127	47	828	34	10.35	39.07	0	0	55	0
ODIs	174	69	37	237	28	7.40	46.37	0	0	47	0
T20Is	19	4	3	1	1*	1.00	50.00	0	0	3	0
First-class	163	201	75	1238	37*	9.82		0	0	90	0
List A	227	90	54	330	28	9.16		0	0	56	0
Twenty20	40	9	6	23	16	7.66	92.00	0	0	8	0

Bowling	Mat	Balls	Runs	Wkts	BBI	BBM	Ave	Econ	SR	5w	10
Tests	92	20350	10522	343	7/43	11/71	30.67	3.10	59.3	15	2
ODIs	174	8609	7132	245	5/23	5/23	29.11	4.97	35.1	2	0
T20Is	19	422	552	18	3/23	3/23	30.66	7.84	23.4	0	0
First-class	163	32420	16822	606	7/43		27.75	3.11	53.4	28	4
List A	227	11019	8928	319	5/23	5/23	27.98	4.86	34.5	2	0
Twenty20	40	855	1190	37	3/23	3/23	32.16	8.35	23.1	0	0

GARETH ANDREW LHB RMF W1

FULL NAME: Gareth Mark Andrew
BORN: December 27, 1983, Yeovil, Somerset
SQUAD NO: 14
HEIGHT: 6ft
NICKNAME: Gaz, Brad, Golden Gary
EDUCATION: Ansford Communtity School;
Richard Huish College, Taunton
TEAMS: Canterbury, Somerset, Somerset
Cricket Board, Worcestershire,
Worcestershire 2nd XI
CAREER: First-class: 2003; List A: 2000; T20:
2003

BEST BATTING: 180* Canterbury vs Auckland, Auckland, 2012
BEST BOWLING: 5-58 Worcestershire vs Middlesex, Kidderminster, 2008

CAREER HIGHLIGHTS? Winning the 2005 T20 Cup with Somerset, getting promoted to Division One with Worcestershire in 2008 and 2010 and helping Worcestershire avoid relegation in 2011
MOST MARKED CHARACTERISTIC? I'm laid-back, organised and wanting to improve
TIP FOR THE TOP? Brett D'Oliveira
IF YOU WEREN'T A CRICKETER? I'd be an archaeologist, like Indiana Jones
DESERT ISLAND DISC? Kings Of Leon – Only By The Night
FAVOURITE TV? Strike Back
BIGGEST DRESSING DOWN YOU'VE RECEIVED? A massive angry spray by our captain at the time Vikram Solanki after a one-day defeat to Glamorgan at the SWALEC
CRICKETING HEROES? Ian Botham, Keith Parsons, Ivan Short
ACCOMPLISHMENTS? I've got a few qualifications and I like to do my bit for charities
WHEN YOU RETIRE? I'd like to set up my own business and play lots of golf
SURPRISING FACT? I'm seriously colourblind
FANTASY SLIP CORDON? Keeper: Angelina Jolie, 1st: John Bishop, 2nd: Myself, 3rd: Keith Lemon, Gully: Dynamo
TWITTER FEED? @GAndrew14

Batting	Mat	Inns	NO	Runs	HS	Ave	SR	100	50	Ct	St
First-class	83	126	16	2649	180*	24.08	55.25	1	15	30	0
List A	110	78	15	1167	104	18.52		1	2	37	0
Twenty20	102	71	22	787	65*	16.06	135.68	0	4	27	0

Bowling	Mat	Balls	Runs	Wkts	BBI	BBM	Ave	Econ	SR	5w	10
First-class	83	11151	7163	201	5/58		35.63	3.85	55.4	4	0
List A	110	3524	3667	104	5/31	5/31	35.25	6.24	33.8	1	0
Twenty20	102	1751	2492	87	4/22	4/22	28.64	8.53	20.1	0	0

ZAFAR ANSARI — LHB SLA

FULL NAME: Zafar Shahaan Ansari
BORN: December 10, 1991, Ascot, Berkshire
SQUAD NO: 22
HEIGHT: 5ft 11in
NICKNAME: Zaf, PM
EDUCATION: Hampton School; University of Cambridge
TEAMS: Cambridge MCCU, England Under-19s, Surrey, Surrey 2nd XI, Surrey Under-13s, Surrey Under-15s, Surrey Under-17s, Surrey Under-19s
CAREER: First-class: 2011; List A: 2010; T20: 2011

BEST BATTING: 83* Surrey vs Warwickshire, Birmingham, 2012
BEST BOWLING: 5-33 Cambridge MCCU vs Surrey, Cambridge, 2011

FAMILY TIES? My dad played three first-class matches in Pakistan. My brother [Akbar] has played a lot of county 2nd XI cricket [Surrey, Worcestershire, Nottinghamshire, Hampshire] and captained Cambridge Blues for two years
CAREER HIGHLIGHTS? My T20 debut and winning the CB40 at Lord's
CRICKETING HEROES? Garry Sobers, Graham Thorpe, Wasim Akram, Chris Scott
NON-CRICKETING HEROES? Akbar Ansari, Costas Douzinas
BEST PLAYER IN COUNTY CRICKET? Steve Davies
TIPS FOR THE TOP? Jason Roy, Chris Jones
IF YOU WEREN'T A CRICKETER? I'd be an American footballer or studying Law
WHEN RAIN STOPS PLAY? Reading, drinking tea
FAVOURITE TV? The West Wing
FAVOURITE BOOK? Half Of A Yellow Sun by Chimamanda Ngozi Adichie
DREAM HOLIDAY? Barcelona
ACCOMPLISHMENTS? Starred 1st in my first-year Cambridge exams
GUILTY PLEASURES? Juicy Drop Pops, Mario Kart and I love Nando's
FANTASY SLIP CORDON? Keeper: Malcolm X, 1st: Michael Vick, 2nd: Leon Trotsky, 3rd: Me, Gully: Mike Hussey

Batting	Mat	Inns	NO	Runs	HS	Ave	SR	100	50	Ct	St
First-class	23	37	5	630	83*	19.68	35.19	0	3	11	0
List A	23	19	6	388	62	29.84	91.50	0	2	12	0
Twenty20	33	27	11	425	38*	26.56	107.05	0	0	4	0

Bowling	Mat	Balls	Runs	Wkts	BBI	BBM	Ave	Econ	SR	5w	10
First-class	23	2236	1154	29	5/33	5/39	39.79	3.09	77.1	1	0
List A	23	612	591	20	4/42	4/42	29.55	5.79	30.6	0	0
Twenty20	33	480	600	15	2/7	2/7	40.00	7.50	32.0	0	0

JAMES ANYON

LHB RFM W2 MVP91

FULL NAME: James Edward Anyon
BORN: May 5, 1983, Lancaster
SQUAD NO: 30
HEIGHT: 6ft 2in
NICKNAME: Jimmy
EDUCATION: Garstang High School; Preston College; Loughborough University
TEAMS: Cumberland, Loughborough MCCU, Surrey, Sussex, Warwickshire
CAREER: First-class: 2003; List A: 2004; T20: 2005

SUSSEX

BEST BATTING: 64* Sussex vs Surrey, Horsham, 2012
BEST BOWLING: 6-82 Warwickshire vs Glamorgan, Cardiff, 2008
COUNTY CAP: 2011 (Sussex)

CAREER HIGHLIGHTS? My T20 hat-trick vs Somerset in 2005. My Man of the Match performance against Nottinghamshire in 2011
MOST MARKED CHARACTERISTIC? Grumpiness
CRICKETING HEROES? Curtly Ambrose, Glenn McGrath, Darren Gough, Michael Atherton
NON-CRICKETING HEROES? Fred Dibnah
ACCOMPLISHMENTS? Getting married
SURPRISING FACT? I represented the North-West in a cow-judging competition
TIP FOR THE TOP? Matthew Hobden
IF YOU WEREN'T A CRICKETER? I'd be a fitness instructor
FAVOURITE TV? Anything on the History or Discovery Channel
FAVOURITE FILM? The Godfather
DREAM HOLIDAY? Rome
ACCOMPLISHMENTS? Getting a degree
GUILTY PLEASURES? Basshunter – shocking!
FANTASY SLIP CORDON? I wouldn't have any. Spread the field and let's have some quiet, no?
CRICKET RULE YOU'D CHANGE? Back-foot no balls

Batting	Mat	Inns	NO	Runs	HS	Ave	SR	100	50	Ct	St
First-class	102	132	42	1282	64*	14.24	37.29	0	4	30	0
List A	43	14	6	43	12	5.37	72.88	0	0	9	0
Twenty20	23	5	3	18	8*	9.00	69.23	0	0	3	0

Bowling	Mat	Balls	Runs	Wkts	BBI	BBM	Ave	Econ	SR	5w	10
First-class	102	16405	10161	290	6/82		35.03	3.71	56.5	6	0
List A	43	1557	1436	47	3/6	3/6	30.55	5.53	33.1	0	0
Twenty20	23	363	520	26	3/6	3/6	20.00	8.59	13.9	0	0

SUSSEX

FULL NAME: Yasir Arafat Satti
BORN: March 12, 1982, Rawalpindi, Pakistan
SQUAD NO: 7
NICKNAME: Yas
TEAMS: Pakistan, Scotland, Barisal Burners, Canterbury, Dolphins, Kent, Khan Research Labs, Lancashire, Otago, Pakistan Reserves, Rawalpindi, Redco Pakistan Ltd, Somerset, Surrey, Sussex
CAREER: Test: 2007; ODI: 2000; T20I: 2007; First-class: 1997; List A: 1997; T20: 2006

BEST BATTING: 170 Khan Research Laboratories vs Multan, Multan, 2011
BEST BOWLING: 9-35 Khan Research Laboratories vs Sui Southern Gas Company, Rawalpindi, 2009
COUNTY CAPS: 2006 (Sussex); 2007 (Kent)

NOTES: Arafat has a wealth of experience in county cricket having represented Sussex, Surrey, Kent, Somerset and Lancashire. He is set for his fourth spell at Sussex this summer, having signed up to play in the NatWest T20 Blast. He is fifth on the all-time list of T20 wicket-takers with 219 scalps and the leading wicket-taker in the history of domestic T20 in England. He represented Pakistan as recently as 2012 but has only ever featured sporadically for his country. He took five wickets in the space of six balls in a Pakistani domestic game in 2004, a feat only matched by three other bowlers in the history of the game

Batting	Mat	Inns	NO	Runs	HS	Ave	SR	100	50	Ct	St
Tests	3	3	1	94	50*	47.00	46.76	0	1	0	0
ODIs	11	8	3	74	27	14.80	67.27	0	0	2	0
T20Is	13	11	4	92	17	13.14	116.45	0	0	1	0
First-class	197	287	41	6708	170	27.26		5	35	53	0
List A	237	171	48	2596	110*	21.10		1	8	50	0
Twenty20	171	107	36	1027	49	14.46	118.45	0	0	28	0

Bowling	Mat	Balls	Runs	Wkts	BBI	BBM	Ave	Econ	SR	5w	10
Tests	3	627	438	9	5/161	7/210	48.66	4.19	69.6	1	0
ODIs	11	414	373	4	1/28	1/28	93.25	5.40	103.5	0	0
T20Is	13	236	316	16	3/18	3/18	19.75	8.03	14.7	0	0
First-class	197	32379	18550	767	9/35		24.18	3.43	42.2	43	5
List A	237	11212	9290	376	6/24	6/24	24.70	4.97	29.8	7	0
Twenty20	171	3499	4595	219	4/5	4/5	20.98	7.87	15.9	0	0

USMAN ARSHAD
RHB RFM

FULL NAME: Usman Arshad
BORN: January 9, 1993, Bradford, Yorkshire
SQUAD NO: 78
HEIGHT: 5ft 11in
NICKNAME: Benny
EDUCATION: Beckfoot Grammar School, Bingley, Bradford
TEAMS: Durham, Durham 2nd XI, Durham Academy, Durham Under-17s, Northumberland
CAREER: First-class: 2013; List A: 2013

DURHAM

BEST BATTING: 83 Durham vs Sussex, Hove, 2013
BEST BOWLING: 3-16 Durham vs Sussex, Chester-le-Street, 2013

WHO WOULD PLAY YOU IN A FILM OF YOUR LIFE? Mr Bean
CAREER HIGHLIGHTS? Making my first-class debut
SUPERSTITIONS? I always put my right pad on first
BEST PLAYER IN COUNTY CRICKET? Ryan Buckley
TIPS FOR THE TOP? Graham Clark, Rammy Singh
IF YOU WEREN'T A CRICKETER? I'd be studying
DESERT ISLAND DISC? J. Cole – Born Sinner
FAVOURITE TV? EastEnders
CRICKETING HEROES? Wasim Akram
NON-CRICKETING HEROES? My dad
ACCOMPLISHMENTS? Raised £1,455 for charity
WHEN YOU RETIRE? I'd like to own a business
SURPRISING FACT? I played for Yorkshire when I was 14
FANTASY SLIP CORDON? Keeper: Brother Waj, 1st: Brother Omar, 2nd: Had to be Brother Barry, 3rd: Myself, Gully: Rammy Singh
TWITTER FEED: @usman_arshad65

Batting	Mat	Inns	NO	Runs	HS	Ave	SR	100	50	Ct	St
First-class	5	6	0	170	83	28.33	67.72	0	1	1	0
List A	1	-	-	-	-	-	-	-	-	0	0

Bowling	Mat	Balls	Runs	Wkts	BBI	BBM	Ave	Econ	SR	5w	10
First-class	5	439	249	16	3/16	6/34	15.56	3.40	27.4	0	0
List A	1	18	13	0	-	-	-	4.33	-	0	0

MOIN ASHRAF

RHB RFM

YORKSHIRE

FULL NAME: Moin Aqeeb Ashraf
BORN: January 5, 1992, Bradford, Yorkshire
SQUAD NO: 23
HEIGHT: 6ft 3in
NICKNAME: MoJo, Mo, The Official
EDUCATION: Dixons City Academy; Leeds Metropolitan University
TEAMS: Yorkshire, Yorkshire 2nd XI, Yorkshire Academy, Yorkshire Under-17s
CAREER: First-class: 2010; List A: 2011; T20: 2012

BEST BATTING: 10 Yorkshire vs Kent, Leeds, 2010
BEST BOWLING: 5-32 Yorkshire vs Kent, Leeds, 2010

FAMILY TIES? My brothers and two of my uncles played club cricket in the Bradford League. They were the ones who got me playing. My dad has always been a keen cricketer but he's never been any good!
WHO WOULD PLAY YOU IN A FILM OF YOUR LIFE? Jamie Foxx
CAREER HIGHLIGHTS? Taking 5-32 vs Kent at Headingley on my home debut, 4-16 against Derbyshire in the T20 and playing in the Champions League in South Africa
SUPERSTITIONS? It's not a superstition but I pray to God for the health and well-being of everyone in attendance at the game I am taking part in
MOST MARKED CHARACTERISTIC? My hair
BEST PLAYER IN COUNTY CRICKET? Graham Onions
TIPS FOR THE TOP? Alex Lees, Matthew Fisher
DESERT ISLAND DISC? Aloe Blacc – The Man
CRICKETING HEROES? Imran Khan
NON-CRICKETING HEROES? Muhammad Ali, Cristiano Ronaldo
CRICKET RULE YOU'D CHANGE? The lbw rule. If it's going on to hit the wickets it should be out, regardless of where it pitches
TWITTER FEED: @MoinA23

Batting	Mat	Inns	NO	Runs	HS	Ave	SR	100	50	Ct	St
First-class	21	19	5	56	10	4.00	18.66	0	0	2	0
List A	23	6	4	3	3*	1.50	50.00	0	0	4	0
Twenty20	17	1	0	4	4	4.00	66.66	0	0	1	0

Bowling	Mat	Balls	Runs	Wkts	BBI	BBM	Ave	Econ	SR	5w	10
First-class	21	2336	1268	43	5/32	6/45	29.48	3.25	54.3	1	0
List A	23	930	920	25	3/38	3/38	36.80	5.93	37.2	0	0
Twenty20	17	345	462	17	4/18	4/18	27.17	8.03	20.2	0	0

MUHAMMAD AZHARULLAH   RHB RFM MVP97

FULL NAME: Muhammad Azharullah
BORN: December 25, 1983, Burewala, Pakistan
SQUAD NO: 92
TEAMS: Multan Region, Multan Tigers, Northamptonshire, Northamptonshire 2nd XI, Quetta Bears, Water and Power Development Authority
CAREER: First-class: 2004; List A: 2005; T20: 2005

BEST BATTING: 41 Water and Power Development Authority vs Kerachi Whites, Kerachi, 2007
BEST BOWLING: 7-74 Quetta vs Lahore Ravi, Quetta, 2005

TWITTER FEED: @Azhar_ullah
NOTES: The Pakistan-born seamer signed for Northamptonshire on a one-year deal ahead of the 2013 season and finished the campaign as the leading wicket-taker in the FL t20 with a haul of 27, helping his side to the trophy. He also took 25 first-class wickets at 28.68 as Northants won promotion to Division One of the County Championship, earning himself a new two-year deal. Azharullah played first-class cricket in Pakistan before moving to England in 2010 and had to wait three years to gain UK citizenship and in turn qualification for a county side. Married to Emma Taylor, the scorer at his Bradford League club Pudsey Congs

Batting	Mat	Inns	NO	Runs	HS	Ave	SR	100	50	Ct	St
First-class	62	80	44	497	41	13.80		0	0	17	0
List A	34	14	8	57	9	9.50	58.76	0	0	9	0
Twenty20	20	6	5	7	5*	7.00	63.63	0	0	2	0

Bowling	Mat	Balls	Runs	Wkts	BBI	BBM	Ave	Econ	SR	5w	10
First-class	62	9846	5754	215	7/74		26.76	3.50	45.7	11	1
List A	34	1540	1369	55	5/56	5/56	24.89	5.33	28.0	1	0
Twenty20	20	427	534	28	4/14	4/14	19.07	7.50	15.2	0	0

TOM BAILEY RHB RFM

LANCASHIRE

FULL NAME: Tom Ernest Bailey
BORN: April 21, 1991, Preston, Lancashire
SQUAD NO: TBC
HEIGHT: 6ft 4in
NICKNAME: Space
EDUCATION: Myerscough College
TEAMS: Lancashire, Lancashire 2nd XI
CAREER: First-class: 2012

BEST BOWLING: 1-67 Lancashire vs Surrey, Liverpool, 2012

FAMILY TIES? My dad introduced me to the game. He played for his local side Withnell Fold CC for 25 years
WHO WOULD PLAY YOU IN A FILM OF YOUR LIFE? The Rock
CAREER HIGHLIGHTS? Making my first-class debut for Lancashire
MOST MARKED CHARACTERISTIC? My big ears
BEST PLAYER IN COUNTY CRICKET? Glen Chapple
TIPS FOR THE TOP? Luis Reece and Alex Davies
IF YOU WEREN'T A CRICKETER? I'd be on the dole
DESERT ISLAND DISC? Any album by The Fugees
FAVOURITE TV? Underbelly
CRICKETING HEROES? Brett Lee and Steve Harmison
NON-CRICKETING HEROES? My old man
FANTASY SLIP CORDON? Keeper: Karl Pilkington, 1st: Chris Eubank, 2nd: Mike Skinner, 3rd: Leonardo DiCaprio, Gully: Lee Evans
TWITTER FEED: @TomBaildog

Batting	Mat	Inns	NO	Runs	HS	Ave	SR	100	50	Ct	St
First-class	1	-	-	-	-	-	-	-	-	0	0

Bowling	Mat	Balls	Runs	Wkts	BBI	BBM	Ave	Econ	SR	5w	10
First-class	1	102	67	1	1/67	1/67	67.00	3.94	102.0	0	0

JONNY BAIRSTOW

RHB WK R1

FULL NAME: Jonathan Marc Bairstow
BORN: September 26, 1989, Bradford, Yorkshire
SQUAD NO: 21
HEIGHT: 6ft
NICKNAME: Bluey
EDUCATION: St. Peter's School, York; Leeds Metropolitan University
TEAMS: England, England Lions, England Performance Programme, Yorkshire, Yorkshire 2nd XI
CAREER: Test: 2012; ODI: 2011; T20I: 2011; First-class: 2009; List A: 2009; T20: 2010

YORKSHIRE

BEST BATTING: 205 Yorkshire vs Nottinghamshire, Nottingham, 2011
COUNTY CAP: 2011

FAMILY TIES? My father David played for Yorkshire and England
WHO WOULD PLAY YOU IN A FILM OF YOUR LIFE? Ed Sheeran
CAREER HIGHLIGHTS? Making my Test debut and being named Man of the Match on my ODI debut
MOST MARKED CHARACTERISTIC? Blue eyes
TIP FOR THE TOP? Joe Root
IF YOU WEREN'T A CRICKETER? I'd be a rugby player
FAVOURITE TV? Entourage
CRICKETING HEROES? Sachin Tendulkar
NON-CRICKETING HEROES? Jonny Wilkinson and Steve Irwin
SURPRISING FACT? I played football for the Leeds United Academy for seven years
TWITTER FEED: @jbairstow21

Batting	Mat	Inns	NO	Runs	HS	Ave	SR	100	50	Ct	St
Tests	14	24	2	593	95	26.95	48.36	0	4	16	0
ODIs	7	6	1	119	41*	23.80	76.77	0	0	3	0
T20Is	18	14	4	194	60*	19.40	108.37	0	1	21	0
First-class	87	145	20	5249	205	41.99		9	31	193	5
List A	50	45	5	1099	114	27.47	98.21	1	5	31	3
Twenty20	61	50	9	733	68*	17.87	114.53	0	2	35	4

Bowling	Mat	Balls	Runs	Wkts	BBI	BBM	Ave	Econ	SR	5w	10
Tests	14	-	-	-	-	-	-	-	-	-	-
ODIs	7	-	-	-	-	-	-	-	-	-	-
T20Is	18	-	-	-	-	-	-	-	-	-	-
First-class	87	-	-	-	-	-	-	-	-	-	-
List A	50	-	-	-	-	-	-	-	-	-	-
Twenty20	61	-	-	-	-	-	-	-	-	-	-

ANDREW BALBIRNIE

RHB OB WK

FULL NAME: Andrew Balbirnie
BORN: December 28, 1990, Dublin, Ireland
SQUAD NO: 15
HEIGHT: 6ft 1in
NICKNAME: Balbo
EDUCATION: St Andrew's College, Dublin
TEAMS: Ireland, Cardiff MCCU, Ireland
Under-13s, Ireland Under-15s, Ireland
Under-17s, Ireland Under-19s, Middlesex,
Middlesex 2nd XI
CAREER: ODI: 2010; First-class: 2012; List A:
2010

BEST BATTING: 38 Ireland vs Scotland, Dublin, 2013
BEST BOWLING: 1-5 Ireland vs Netherlands, Deventer, 2013

FAMILY TIES? My grandfather played club cricket in Dublin and my younger brothers Harry
and Jack play for Pembroke CC in Dublin
WHO WOULD PLAY YOU IN A FILM OF YOUR LIFE? Ben Affleck
CAREER HIGHLIGHTS? My Ireland debut in 2010 and my Middlesex debut in 2012
SUPERSTITIONS? I put my left shoe and pad on first
MOST MARKED CHARACTERISTIC? Probably the size of my head
BEST PLAYER IN COUNTY CRICKET? Chris Rogers, Ed Joyce
TIP FOR THE TOP? Stuart Poynter
IF YOU WEREN'T A CRICKETER? I'm interested in photography so maybe something to do
with that
DESERT ISLAND DISC? Mumford And Sons – Babel
FAVOURITE TV? Cake Boss
CRICKETING HEROES? Michael Vaughan
ACCOMPLISHMENTS? Graduating from university in 2013 with a degree in Sports Coaching
WHEN YOU RETIRE? I'd like to travel
CRICKET RULE YOU'D CHANGE? The tea break should last for 30 minutes
TWITTER FEED: @balbo90

Batting	Mat	Inns	NO	Runs	HS	Ave	SR	100	50	Ct	St
ODIs	4	4	0	29	17	7.25	33.72	0	0	1	0
First-class	9	13	1	181	38	15.08	52.76	0	0	6	0
List A	6	5	0	30	17	6.00	31.57	0	0	3	0
Bowling	Mat	Balls	Runs	Wkts	BBI	BBM	Ave	Econ	SR	5w	10
ODIs	4	-	-	-	-	-	-	-	-	-	-
First-class	9	168	95	2	1/5	2/25	47.50	3.39	84.0	0	0
List A	6	24	27	0	-	-	-	6.75	-	0	0

DAVID BALCOMBE

RHB RMF W1

FULL NAME: David John Balcombe
BORN: December 24, 1984, London
SQUAD NO: 84
HEIGHT: 6ft 3in
NICKNAME: Balcs, Snowman, Polar
EDUCATION: St John's School, Leatherhead; Durham University
TEAMS: Durham MCCU, Hampshire, Kent, Surrey 2nd XI
CAREER: First-class: 2005; List A: 2007; T20: 2006

HAMPSHIRE

BEST BATTING: 73 Hampshire vs Leicestershire, Leicester, 2012
BEST BOWLING: 8-71 Hampshire vs Gloucestershire, Southampton, 2012
COUNTY CAP: 2013 (Hampshire)

WHO WOULD PLAY YOU IN A FILM OF YOUR LIFE? Bradley Cooper
CAREER HIGHLIGHTS? My maiden County Championship five-wicket haul for Kent against Surrey at The Oval, taking 5-63. My best first-class bowling figures of 8-71 vs Gloucestershire at the Ageas Bowl, which was a ground record. Making my highest first-class score of 73, which was the highest score by a Hampshire No.11
TIPS FOR THE TOP? Daniel Bell-Drummond, Sam Billings
DESERT ISLAND DISC? Oasis
FAVOURITE TV? Downton Abbey
CRICKETING HEROES? Shane Warne, Glenn McGrath, Alec Stewart
ACCOMPLISHMENTS? My degree and my Durham Palatinate for achievements in, and contributions to, university sport
FANTASY SLIP CORDON? Keeper: Michael McIntyre, 1st: Jack Whitehall (they'd both add some humour to the field of play and the changing room), 2nd: Berenice Marlohe, 3rd: Jessica Ennis (Olympic champion, enough said), Gully: Dave Brailsford (brilliant strategist)
TWITTER FEED: @DavidBalcombe1

Batting	Mat	Inns	NO	Runs	HS	Ave	SR	100	50	Ct	St
First-class	63	79	18	867	73	14.21	52.54	0	2	14	0
List A	13	5	0	10	6	2.00	32.25	0	0	5	0
Twenty20	3	2	1	3	3	3.00	60.00	0	0	0	0

Bowling	Mat	Balls	Runs	Wkts	BBI	BBM	Ave	Econ	SR	5w	10
First-class	63	10900	6192	191	8/71		32.41	3.40	57.0	9	2
List A	13	519	492	18	4/38	4/38	27.33	5.68	28.8	0	0
Twenty20	3	49	61	1	1/23	1/23	61.00	7.46	49.0	0	0

ADAM BALL

RHB LMF

KENT

FULL NAME: Adam James Ball
BORN: March 1, 1993, Greenwich, London
SQUAD NO: 24
HEIGHT: 6ft 2in
NICKNAME: Bally
EDUCATION: Beths Grammar School, Bexley
TEAMS: England Under-19s, Kent, Kent 2nd XI, Kent Academy XI, Kent Under-13s, Kent Under-15s, Kent Under-17s
CAREER: First-class: 2011; List A: 2010; T20: 2011

BEST BATTING: 69 Kent vs Lancashire, Canterbury, 2013
BEST BOWLING: 3-36 Kent vs Leicestershire, Leicester, 2011

CRICKETING HEROES? Andrew Flintoff
FAVOURITE MUSICIAN? Taio Cruz
FAVOURITE FOOD? Nando's
FAVOURITE FILM? Ali G Indahouse
CAREER HIGHLIGHTS? Signing my first professional contract with Kent and being named as England U19 captain. Playing in the T20 quarter-finals
TWITTER FEED: @AdamBall2
NOTES: Left-arm seamer Ball was handed his Kent List A debut in 2010 and was called up to the England U19 squad in the same year. He made nine Championship appearances in 2011, taking 15 wickets including career-best figures of 3-36 vs Leicestershire at Leicester. In 2012 he captained the England U19 side and was Kent's leading T20 wicket-taker with 12 at an average of 18. He was plagued by injury last year and only made two County Championship appearances. He made his highest first-class score in one of these, hitting 69 in the final game of the season against Lancashire at Canterbury

Batting	Mat	Inns	NO	Runs	HS	Ave	SR	100	50	Ct	St
First-class	11	18	1	292	69	17.17	39.08	0	1	5	0
List A	24	16	6	132	28	13.20	98.50	0	0	3	0
Twenty20	22	9	2	61	18	8.71	115.09	0	0	12	0

Bowling	Mat	Balls	Runs	Wkts	BBI	BBM	Ave	Econ	SR	5w	10
First-class	11	1080	730	18	3/36	3/45	40.55	4.05	60.0	0	0
List A	24	765	723	21	3/36	3/36	34.42	5.67	36.4	0	0
Twenty20	22	399	497	22	2/18	2/18	22.59	7.47	18.1	0	0

FULL NAME: Jacob Timothy Ball
BORN: March 14, 1991, Mansfield, Nottinghamshire
SQUAD NO: 28
HEIGHT: 6ft 3in
EDUCATION: Meden School, Mansfield
TEAMS: England Under-19s, Nottinghamshire, Nottinghamshire 2nd XI
CAREER: First-class: 2011; List A: 2009; T20: 2011

NOTTINGHAMSHIRE

BEST BATTING: 15 Nottinghamshire vs Durham MCCU, Nottingham, 2013
BEST BOWLING: 3-18 Nottinghamshire vs Durham MCCU, Nottingham, 2013

FAMILY TIES? My mum's side of the family are cricket-mad and my uncle, Bruce French, played for England and is now the England wicketkeeping coach
CAREER HIGHLIGHTS? Probably taking four wickets in the semi-final of the YB40 last year and getting Man of the Match. Going on to lift the trophy made it even better
SUPERSTITIONS? I walk back to my mark on the same side every time and a weird one is that I have to bowl in Calvin Klein boxers
MOST MARKED CHARACTERISTIC? I would like it to be my hair but I think it's my long, gangly, twig-like legs
BEST PLAYER IN COUNTY CRICKET? I'm not sure we will see him much this year but I think it's Ben Stokes
DESERT ISLAND DISC? Difficult one but I'm a big Beatles fan so probably the 1 album
FAVOURITE TV? It has to be Suits, closely followed by Strictly Come Dancing
CRICKETING HEROES? My uncle Bruce French and Dale Steyn
NON-CRICKETING HEROES? My mum, dad and brother – they would literally do anything for me
SURPRISING FACT? I have mild dyslexia
TWITTER FEED: @JakeBall30

Batting	Mat	Inns	NO	Runs	HS	Ave	SR	100	50	Ct	St
First-class	2	3	1	19	15	9.50	57.57	0	0	0	0
List A	27	10	3	62	19*	8.85	96.87	0	0	1	0
Twenty20	10	1	1	1	1*	-	100.00	0	0	3	0

Bowling	Mat	Balls	Runs	Wkts	BBI	BBM	Ave	Econ	SR	5w	10
First-class	2	210	145	6	3/18	3/39	24.16	4.14	35.0	0	0
List A	27	895	840	30	4/25	4/25	28.00	5.63	29.8	0	0
Twenty20	10	186	268	8	2/20	2/20	33.50	8.64	23.2	0	0

YORKSHIRE

FULL NAME: Gary Simon Ballance
BORN: November 22, 1989, Harare, Zimbabwe
SQUAD NO: 19
HEIGHT: 6ft
NICKNAME: Gazza, GB
EDUCATION: Peterhouse School, Zimbabwe; Harrow School
TEAMS: England, Derbyshire, Derbyshire 2nd XI, England Lions, Mid West Rhinos, Yorkshire, Zimbabwe Under-19s
CAREER: Test: 2014; ODI: 2013; First-class: 2008; List A: 2006; T20: 2010

BEST BATTING: 210 Mid West Rhinos vs Southern Rocks, Masvingo, 2011
COUNTY CAP: 2012 (Yorkshire)

NOTES: A close family friend of former Zimbabwe skipper David Houghton, Ballance signed for Derbyshire at 16 before joining the Yorkshire Academy in 2008. He played for Zimbabwe U19 at the World Cup in 2006 before qualifying to play for England. Toured Australia with the England Lions squad in February 2013 and made his ODI debut against Ireland last summer before being selected in England's Ashes tour party, making his Test bow at Sydney in January. Ballance played for the Mid West Rhinos in Zimbabwe under current Yorkshire coach Jason Gillespie during the winters of 2010/11 and 2011/12, and scored four first-class hundreds for them before his first for Yorkshire in 2011. In 2012 he scored an undefeated 121 to help Yorkshire chase down 400 against Gloucestershire at Bristol. Last year he scored 1,363 first-class runs at an average of 64.90, including six centuries

Batting	Mat	Inns	NO	Runs	HS	Ave	SR	100	50	Ct	St
Tests	1	2	0	25	18	12.50	32.05	0	0	0	0
ODIs	5	5	0	132	79	26.40	69.84	0	1	5	0
First-class	68	105	14	4772	210	52.43	52.18	18	22	63	0
List A	61	58	10	2601	139	54.18	91.00	6	15	29	0
Twenty20	56	51	8	1158	68	26.93	120.49	0	5	29	0

Bowling	Mat	Balls	Runs	Wkts	BBI	BBM	Ave	Econ	SR	5w	10
Tests	1	-	-	-	-	-	-	-	-	-	-
ODIs	5	-	-	-	-	-	-	-	-	-	-
First-class	68	144	138	0	-	-	-	5.75	-	0	0
List A	61	-	-	-	-	-	-	-	-	-	-
Twenty20	56	-	-	-	-	-	-	-	-	-	-

TOM BARBER

RHB LFM

FULL NAME: Thomas Barber
BORN: May 31, 1994, Bournemouth
SQUAD NO: 20
HEIGHT: 6ft 3in
NICKNAME: Barbs, Rocket Man
EDUCATION: Bournemouth Grammar School
TEAMS: England Under-19s, Hampshire 2nd XI, Hampshire Cricket Academy, Hampshire Under-17s
CAREER: Yet to make first-team debut

HAMPSHIRE

FAMILY TIES? My dad, uncle, brothers and cousins all play/played cricket to a high level. They encouraged me to play at a young age

WHO WOULD PLAY YOU IN A FILM OF YOUR LIFE? Morgan Freeman

CAREER HIGHLIGHTS? Gaining a full professional contract in 2013 for Hampshire. Representing England U19 in South Africa in February 2013 and in the Tri-Series with Pakistan and Bangladesh last summer

SUPERSTITIONS? I always have to re-tuck my shirt at the end of every over and scrape my bowling mark at the start of every over

MOST MARKED CHARACTERISTIC? Probably my height

TIPS FOR THE TOP? Dom Sibley, Ben Duckett, Matt Fisher

IF YOU WEREN'T A CRICKETER? I'd be at university doing a degree in Chemistry or Physics

FAVOURITE TV? Top Gear or The Big Bang Theory

CRICKETING HEROES? Dale Steyn, Andrew Flintoff, Steven Finn, Brett Lee

NON-CRICKETING HEROES? Richard Feynman, Brian Cox, Frankie Boyle, Karl Pilkington, Ricky Gervais

ACCOMPLISHMENTS? Gaining seven A*'s in my GCSEs. I got AAB in Biology, Chemistry and Physics in my A-Levels

WHEN YOU RETIRE? I'll most likely go to university to do a degree or become a coach

SURPRISING FACT? I represented my school in a Chemistry Olympiad

CRICKET RULE YOU'D CHANGE? The number of fielders allowed outside the inner ring in ODI cricket

FANTASY SLIP CORDON? Keeper: Karl Pilkington, 1st: Frankie Boyle, 2nd: Warwick Davis, 3rd: Myself, Gully: Jonty Rhodes

TWITTER FEED: @Tom_Barber20

KEITH BARKER

LHB LFM W1 MVP90

WARWICKSHIRE

FULL NAME: Keith Hubert Douglas Barker
BORN: October 21, 1986, Manchester, Lancashire
SQUAD NO: 13
HEIGHT: 6ft 2in
NICKNAME: Barksy
EDUCATION: Moorhead High School
TEAMS: Warwickshire, Warwickshire 2nd XI
CAREER: First-class: 2009; List A: 2009; T20: 2009

BEST BATTING: 125 Warwickshire vs Surrey, Guildford, 2013
BEST BOWLING: 6-40 Warwickshire vs Somerset, Taunton, 2012

FAMILY TIES? My father Keith Barker played for British Guinea and my godfather Clive Lloyd is a West Indies legend
NON-CRICKETING HEROES? Lewis Hamilton
BEST PLAYER IN COUNTY CRICKET? Marcus Trescothick
TIP FOR THE TOP? Chris Woakes
IF YOU WEREN'T A CRICKETER? I'd be a cricket coach
WHEN RAIN STOPS PLAY? Resting or playing cricket inside with a tennis ball
FAVOURITE TV? Family Guy, Man vs Food
FAVOURITE FILM? The Dark Knight
DREAM HOLIDAY? Barbados
ACCOMPLISHMENTS? Playing international football at age-group level
GUILTY PLEASURES? Everything that tastes good
SURPRISING FACTS? My heart stopped beating during an operation when I was 15 and I was brought back to life. I played football in the UEFA Cup for Blackburn Rovers
FANTASY SLIP CORDON? Keeper: James Corden, 1st: Karl Pilkington, 2nd: Keith Barker Jr, 3rd: Keith Barker Sr, Gully: Chris Tucker
TWITTER FEED? @KBarks13

Batting	Mat	Inns	NO	Runs	HS	Ave	SR	100	50	Ct	St
First-class	43	50	7	1212	125	28.18	55.95	3	2	15	0
List A	43	30	7	397	56	17.26	89.01	0	1	8	0
Twenty20	51	26	5	306	46	14.57	105.88	0	0	13	0

Bowling	Mat	Balls	Runs	Wkts	BBI	BBM	Ave	Econ	SR	5w	10
First-class	43	6458	3334	130	6/40	10/70	25.64	3.09	49.6	7	1
List A	43	1498	1468	48	4/33	4/33	30.58	5.87	31.2	0	0
Twenty20	51	919	1178	55	4/19	4/19	21.41	7.69	16.7	0	0

ED BARNARD

RHB RMF

FULL NAME: Edward George Barnard
BORN: November 20, 1995, Shrewsbury
SQUAD NO: 17
HEIGHT: 6ft 1in
NICKNAME: Barn
EDUCATION: Meole Brace School;
Shrewsbury School
TEAMS: England Under-19s, Shropshire,
Worcestershire Under-19s
CAREER: Yet to make first-team debut

FAMILY TIES? My dad Andy played minor counties cricket at Shropshire for many years. My brother Mike plays for Shropshire and played first-class cricket at university
WHO WOULD PLAY YOU IN A FILM OF YOUR LIFE? Channing Tatum
CAREER HIGHLIGHTS? Scoring 114 on my England U19 Test match debut vs South Africa at Newlands
MOST MARKED CHARACTERISTIC? Positivity
BEST PLAYER IN COUNTY CRICKET? Moeen Ali
TIPS FOR THE TOP? Ben Duckett, Matthew Fisher, Joe Clarke
IF YOU WEREN'T A CRICKETER? I'd be a footballer
DESERT ISLAND DISC? Mac Miller – Best Day Ever
FAVOURITE TV? Match Of The Day
CRICKETING HEROES? Andrew Flintoff, Jacques Kallis
NON-CRICKETING HEROES? Nelson Mandela, Alan Shearer
ACCOMPLISHMENTS? I've never broken a bone in my body
WHEN YOU RETIRE? I'd like to be a PE teacher or travel the world
SURPRISING FACT? I used to be in the Shropshire Boys Choir
CRICKET RULE YOU'D CHANGE? Batsmen should get 10 runs for hitting the ball out of the ground
FANTASY SLIP CORDON? Keeper: Sir Bobby Robson, 1st: Mila Kunis, 2nd: Tim Vine, 3rd: Me, Gully: David Beckham
TWITTER FEED: @EdBarn95

ALEX BARROW
RHB OB

SOMERSET

FULL NAME: Alexander William Rodgerson Barrow
BORN: May 6, 1992, Bath, Somerset
SQUAD NO: 18
HEIGHT: 5ft 7in
NICKNAME: Baz, Wheels, Pocket Rocket
EDUCATION: King's College, Taunton
TEAMS: England Under-19s, Somerset, Somerset 2nd XI, Somerset Under-17s
CAREER: First-class: 2011; List A: 2012

BEST BATTING: 83* Somerset vs Durham, Taunton, 2013
BEST BOWLING: 1-4 Somerset vs Hampshire, Southampton, 2011

FAMILY TIES? My dad played first-class cricket
WHO WOULD PLAY YOU IN A FILM OF YOUR LIFE? Patrick J Adams
CAREER HIGHLIGHTS? Playing in the Champions League and my first-class and List A debuts
SUPERSTITIONS? Just the order that I pad up. It's not really a superstition, just a routine
BEST PLAYER IN COUNTY CRICKET? Marcus Trescothick
TIPS FOR THE TOP? Joe Root, Jos Buttler
IF YOU WEREN'T A CRICKETER? Anything but working in an office!
DESERT ISLAND DISC? The Verve – Bitter Sweet Symphony
FAVOURITE TV? Suits
CRICKETING HEROES? Jonty Rhodes, Ian Bell, Michael Clarke
NON-CRICKETING HEROES? Jonny Wilkinson
SURPRISING FACT? My mum is half Maltese
FANTASY SLIP CORDON? Keeper: Meghan Markle, 1st: Jonny Wilkinson, 2nd: James Corden, 3rd: Rihanna, Gully: George Dockrell
TWITTER FEED: @Alex_Barrow5

Batting	Mat	Inns	NO	Runs	HS	Ave	SR	100	50	Ct	St
First-class	26	43	1	782	83*	18.61	44.89	0	3	30	0
List A	9	6	2	144	72	36.00	80.00	0	1	9	0

Bowling	Mat	Balls	Runs	Wkts	BBI	BBM	Ave	Econ	SR	5w	10
First-class	26	42	36	1	1/4	1/4	36.00	5.14	42.0	0	0
List A	9	-	-	-	-	-	-	-	-	-	-

MICHAEL BATES

RHB WK

FULL NAME: Michael David Bates
BORN: October 10, 1990, Frimley
SQUAD NO: 16
HEIGHT: 5ft 8in
NICKNAME: Batesy
EDUCATION: Yateley Manor; Lord Wandsworth College
TEAMS: England Under-19s, Hampshire, Hampshire 2nd XI
CAREER: First-class: 2010; List A: 2010; T20: 2010

BEST BATTING: 103 Hampshire vs Yorkshire, Leeds, 2012

CAREER HIGHLIGHTS? Winning at T20 Finals Day in 2010
CRICKETING HEROES? Alec Stewart
TIPS FOR THE TOP? Jos Buttler, James Vince, Danny Briggs, Ben Stokes
IF YOU WEREN'T A CRICKETER? I don't know!
FAVOURITE TV? Scrubs
FAVOURITE FILM? Blood Diamond
DREAM HOLIDAY? Greece
TWITTER FEED: @batesy10_16

Batting	Mat	Inns	NO	Runs	HS	Ave	SR	100	50	Ct	St
First-class	39	50	4	943	103	20.50	45.95	1	4	120	5
List A	32	13	4	73	24*	8.11	62.93	0	0	21	4
Twenty20	32	5	2	25	10	8.33	80.64	0	0	14	6

Bowling	Mat	Balls	Runs	Wkts	BBI	BBM	Ave	Econ	SR	5w	10
First-class	39	-	-	-	-	-	-	-	-	-	-
List A	32	-	-	-	-	-	-	-	-	-	-
Twenty20	32	-	-	-	-	-	-	-	-	-	-

GARETH BATTY

RHB OB W2 MVP83

SURREY

FULL NAME: Gareth Jon Batty
BORN: October 13, 1977, Bradford, Yorkshire
SQUAD NO: 13
HEIGHT: 5ft 11in
NICKNAME: Bats, Mick, Boom Boom, Jack
EDUCATION: Bingley Grammar School
TEAMS: England, Surrey, Surrey Cricket
Board, Worcestershire, Yorkshire
CAREER: Test: 2003; ODI: 2002; T20I: 2009;
First-class: 1997; List A: 1998; T20: 2003

BEST BATTING: 133 Worcestershire vs Surrey, The Oval, 2004
BEST BOWLING: 7-52 Worcestershire vs Northamptonshire, Northampton, 2004
COUNTY CAP: 2011 (Surrey)

FAMILY TIES? My dad played for and coached at Yorkshire Academy and my brother Jeremy
played for Yorkshire and Somerset
CAREER HIGHLIGHTS? Playing for England and receiving my Surrey county cap
MOST MARKED CHARACTERISTIC? Competitiveness
BEST PLAYER IN COUNTY CRICKET? Too many to mention but from 2014 there's a very good
chance it will be Kevin Pietersen
TIPS FOR THE TOP? Roy Burns, Jason Roy, George Edwards, Zafar Ansari
FAVOURITE TV? Only Fools And Horses, 24, Luther
CRICKETING HEROES? Viv Richards, Richie Richardson, Robin Smith
NON-CRICKETING HEROES? Jack Bauer, Idris Elba, James Bond, Steve McQueen
CRICKET RULE YOU'D CHANGE? No heavy roller from the start of the game

Batting	Mat	Inns	NO	Runs	HS	Ave	SR	100	50	Ct	St
Tests	7	8	1	144	38	20.57	27.01	0	0	3	0
ODIs	10	8	2	30	17	5.00	41.09	0	0	4	0
T20Is	1	1	0	4	4	4.00	57.14	0	0	0	0
First-class	194	296	46	5990	133	23.96		2	28	145	0
List A	223	171	35	2203	83*	16.19		0	5	76	0
Twenty20	93	63	17	533	87	11.58	106.38	0	1	31	0

Bowling	Mat	Balls	Runs	Wkts	BBI	BBM	Ave	Econ	SR	5w	10
Tests	7	1394	733	11	3/55	5/153	66.63	3.15	126.7	0	0
ODIs	10	440	366	5	2/40	2/40	73.20	4.99	88.0	0	0
T20Is	1	18	17	0	-	-		5.66	-	0	0
First-class	194	35115	17271	505	7/52		34.20	2.95	69.5	21	2
List A	223	8513	6489	205	5/35	5/35	31.65	4.57	41.5	1	0
Twenty20	93	1626	1959	76	4/13	4/13	25.77	7.22	21.3	0	0

WILL BEER RHB LB

FULL NAME: William Andrew Thomas Beer
BORN: October 8, 1988, Crawley, Sussex
SQUAD NO: 18
HEIGHT: 5ft 10in
NICKNAME: Beery
EDUCATION: Reigate Grammar School
TEAMS: Sussex, Sussex 2nd XI
CAREER: First-class: 2008; List A: 2009; T20: 2008

SUSSEX

BEST BATTING: 39 Sussex vs Middlesex, Lord's, 2013
BEST BOWLING: 3-31 Sussex vs Worcestershire, Worcester, 2010

FAMILY TIES? My dad played for Sussex 2nd XI
CAREER HIGHLIGHTS? Winning the T20 domestic tournament in 2009 and going to the Champions League
CRICKETING HEROES? Shane Warne, Michael Yardy
NON-CRICKETING HEROES? David Beckham, Joey Essex
BEST PLAYER IN COUNTY CRICKET? Marcus Trescothick
TIPS FOR THE TOP? Matt Machan, Luke Wells
IF YOU WEREN'T A CRICKETER? I'd like to be a professional golfer
WHEN RAIN STOPS PLAY? Play Monopoly with teammates on my iPad – it can get very competitive! Dressing room golf is another option
FAVOURITE FILM? Snakes On A Plane
FAVOURITE TV? The Only Way Is Essex
FAVOURITE BOOK? The Harry Potter series
DREAM HOLIDAY? New York
ACCOMPLISHMENTS? My 25m swimming badge. Orange belt in judo
GUILTY PLEASURES? Dairy Milk Buttons
TWITTER FEED: @willbeer18

Batting	Mat	Inns	NO	Runs	HS	Ave	SR	100	50	Ct	St
First-class	8	10	2	182	39	22.75	30.08	0	0	3	0
List A	29	14	6	137	27*	17.12	83.03	0	0	8	0
Twenty20	51	25	9	121	22	7.56	116.34	0	0	7	0

Bowling	Mat	Balls	Runs	Wkts	BBI	BBM	Ave	Econ	SR	5w	10
First-class	8	820	443	13	3/31	3/36	34.07	3.24	63.0	0	0
List A	29	1170	979	28	3/27	3/27	34.96	5.02	41.7	0	0
Twenty20	51	936	1121	37	3/19	3/19	30.29	7.18	25.2	0	0

IAN BELL

WARWICKSHIRE

FULL NAME: Ian Ronald Bell
BORN: April 11, 1982, Walsgrave, Coventry, Warwickshire
SQUAD NO: 4
HEIGHT: 5ft 10in
NICKNAME: Belly
EDUCATION: Princethorpe College, Rugby
TEAMS: England, England Lions, England Under-19s, Marylebone Cricket Club, Warwickshire, Warwickshire Cricket Board
CAREER: Test: 2004; ODI: 2004; T20I: 2006; First-class: 1999; List A: 1999; T20: 2003

BEST BATTING: 262* Warwickshire vs Sussex, Horsham, 2004
BEST BOWLING: 4-4 Warwickshire vs Middlesex, Lord's, 2004
COUNTY CAP: 2001; BENEFIT YEAR: 2011

CAREER HIGHLIGHTS? Winning the County Championship with Warwickshire and the Ashes victories
CRICKETING HEROES? Ricky Ponting, Dominic Ostler, Jeetan Patel
NON-CRICKETING HEROES? Gary Shaw, Gordon Cowans
BEST PLAYER IN COUNTY CRICKET? Marcus Trescothick
TIP FOR THE TOP? Chris Woakes
IF YOU WEREN'T A CRICKETER? I'd be sitting at the Holte End watching the Villa
DREAM HOLIDAY? Maldives
ACCOMPLISHMENTS? Honorary doctorate at Coventry University
TWITTER FEED: @Ian_Bell

Batting	Mat	Inns	NO	Runs	HS	Ave	SR	100	50	Ct	St
Tests	98	170	22	6722	235	45.41	49.29	20	39	78	0
ODIs	140	136	11	4635	126*	37.08	75.19	3	29	45	0
T20Is	7	7	1	175	60*	29.16	119.86	0	1	4	0
First-class	235	396	45	15998	262*	45.57		45	82	170	0
List A	269	258	24	9335	158	39.89		10	66	93	0
Twenty20	44	43	6	926	85	25.02	114.60	0	4	16	0

Bowling	Mat	Balls	Runs	Wkts	BBI	BBM	Ave	Econ	SR	5w	10
Tests	98	108	76	1	1/33	1/33	76.00	4.22	108.0	0	0
ODIs	140	88	88	6	3/9	3/9	14.66	6.00	14.6	0	0
T20Is	7	-	-	-	-	-	-	-	-	-	-
First-class	235	2827	1598	47	4/4		34.00	3.39	60.1	0	0
List A	269	1290	1138	33	5/41	5/41	34.48	5.29	39.0	1	0
Twenty20	44	132	186	3	1/12	1/12	62.00	8.45	44.0	0	0

DANIEL BELL-DRUMMOND

RHB RM

FULL NAME: Daniel James Bell-Drummond
BORN: August 4, 1993, Lewisham, London
SQUAD NO: 23
HEIGHT: 5ft 11in
NICKNAME: DBD, Deebs
EDUCATION: Millfield School
TEAMS: England Under-19s, Kent, Kent 2nd XI
CAREER: First-class: 2011; List A: 2011; T20: 2011

BEST BATTING: 102* Kent vs Cardiff MCCU, Canterbury, 2013

WHY CRICKET? My father got me into the game and I've always really enjoyed spending time at my local club Catford Wanderers CC
CAREER HIGHLIGHTS? Making my first-class debut
CRICKETING HEROES? Brian Lara, Kevin Pietersen, Chris Gayle
NON-CRICKETING HEROES? Nelson Mandela, Muhammad Ali
BEST PLAYER IN COUNTY CRICKET? Marcus Trescothick
TIPS FOR THE TOP? Adam Ball, Ben Foakes, Sam Northeast
IF YOU WEREN'T A CRICKETER? I'd be a musician
WHEN RAIN STOPS PLAY? I listen to my iPod, read magazines or watch TV
FAVOURITE TV? EastEnders
FAVOURITE FILM? Coach Carter
FAVOURITE BOOK? Animal Farm
DREAM HOLIDAY? The Caribbean
FANTASY SLIP CORDON? Keeper: Floyd Mayweather Jr, 1st: Me, 2nd: Robin van Persie, 3rd: Lee Evans, Gully: Brian Lara
TWITTER FEED: @deebzz23

Batting	Mat	Inns	NO	Runs	HS	Ave	SR	100	50	Ct	St
First-class	20	32	2	838	102*	27.93	48.83	1	5	11	0
List A	5	5	0	111	42	22.20	98.23	0	0	0	0
Twenty20	6	6	0	92	31	15.33	108.23	0	0	1	0

Bowling	Mat	Balls	Runs	Wkts	BBI	BBM	Ave	Econ	SR	5w	10
First-class	20	41	54	0	-	-	-	7.90	-	0	0
List A	5	-	-	-	-	-	-	-	-	-	-
Twenty20	6	-	-	-	-	-	-	-	-	-	-

MIDDLESEX

FULL NAME: Gareth Kyle Berg
BORN: January 18, 1981, Cape Town, Cape Province, South Africa
SQUAD NO: 8
HEIGHT: 6ft
NICKNAME: Ice, Bergy, Ford
EDUCATION: South African College School
TEAMS: Italy, Middlesex, Western Province
CAREER: First-class: 2008; List A: 2008; T20: 2009

BEST BATTING: 130* Middlesex vs Leicestershire, Leicester, 2011
BEST BOWLING: 6-58 Middlesex vs Glamorgan, Cardiff, 2011
COUNTY CAP: 2010

WHO WOULD PLAY YOU IN A FILM OF YOUR LIFE? Some might say I live a boring life, but far from it. People know very little of who I actually am and what I enjoy doing. Perhaps someone like Matt Damon – he's a great actor and seems to be quite a genuine down-to-earth guy who lives life outside of the limelight
CAREER HIGHLIGHTS? Winning promotion to Division One in 2011, my first five-fer and maiden hundred both coming at the Home of Cricket, and getting capped by Middlesex
MOST MARKED CHARACTERISTIC? Being friendly and polite to everyone I meet in life
TIP FOR THE TOP? Tom Helm
IF YOU WEREN'T A CRICKETER? I coached cricket for 10 years before becoming a pro-cricketer so it's something I have a passion for, seeing young kids develop and reach their goals and dreams. I like to help them achieve that if possible
DESERT ISLAND DISC? Probably Roy Orbison or Johnny Cash
FAVOURITE TV? The Middle or Friends
CRICKETING HEROES? I've never really had a hero but Brian McMillan was someone I enjoyed watching
TWITTER FEED: @Bergy646

Batting	Mat	Inns	NO	Runs	HS	Ave	SR	100	50	Ct	St
First-class	70	112	12	2980	130*	29.80	64.14	2	17	45	0
List A	59	45	6	999	75	25.61	91.31	0	5	19	0
Twenty20	55	43	11	860	90	26.87	129.32	0	3	14	0
Bowling	Mat	Balls	Runs	Wkts	BBI	BBM	Ave	Econ	SR	5w	10
First-class	70	8198	4454	140	6/58	7/90	31.81	3.25	58.5	3	0
List A	59	1515	1407	40	4/24	4/24	35.17	5.57	37.8	0	0
Twenty20	55	977	1207	44	4/20	4/20	27.43	7.41	22.2	0	0

PAUL BEST   LHB SLA

FULL NAME: Paul Merwood Best
BORN: March 8, 1991, Nuneaton
SQUAD NO: 15
HEIGHT: 5ft 11in
NICKNAME: Besty
EDUCATION: Bablake School, Coventry;
Cambridge University
TEAMS: Cambridge MCCU, Cambridge
University, England Under-19s,
Northamptonshire, Warwickshire,
Warwickshire 2nd XI
CAREER: First-class: 2011; List A: 2011; T20:
2012

WARWICKSHIRE

BEST BATTING: 150 Cambridge MCCU vs Warwickshire, Cambridge, 2011
BEST BOWLING: 6-86 Cambridge University vs Oxford University, Cambridge, 2011

FAMILY TIES? My dad played club cricket and my younger brother Mark is in the Warwickshire Academy
CAREER HIGHLIGHTS? Captaining the England U19 side in 2009 and 2010. Scoring 150* for Cambridge MCCU vs Surrey in 2011 and winning the game. Getting a six-fer vs Middlesex for Cambridge MCCU in 2011. Making my Warwickshire Championship debut. Being in the Cambridge team that won the treble vs Oxford in 2011
CRICKETING HEROES? Daniel Vettori
NON-CRICKETING HEROES? Hugh Laurie
BEST PLAYER IN COUNTY CRICKET? Marcus Trescothick
TIPS FOR THE TOP? Mark Best, Zafar Ansari, Charlie Taylor
IF YOU WEREN'T A CRICKETER? Either working in the City or owning a set of delicatessens
WHEN RAIN STOPS PLAY? I read or play cards
FAVOURITE TV? The Wire
FAVOURITE FILM? The Shawshank Redemption
DREAM HOLIDAY? Tanzania
ACCOMPLISHMENTS? Getting to Cambridge University
SURPRISING FACT? The subjects I studied at university are Anglo Saxon, Norse and Celtic

Batting	Mat	Inns	NO	Runs	HS	Ave	SR	100	50	Ct	St
First-class	10	12	2	378	150	37.80	49.15	1	1	5	0
List A	13	9	4	57	16*	11.40	75.00	0	0	3	0
Twenty20	3	-	-	-	-	-	-	-	-	1	0

Bowling	Mat	Balls	Runs	Wkts	BBI	BBM	Ave	Econ	SR	5w	10
First-class	10	2413	1415	32	6/86	9/131	44.21	3.51	75.4	2	0
List A	13	443	463	11	3/43	3/43	42.09	6.27	40.2	0	0
Twenty20	3	60	61	4	3/19	3/19	15.25	6.10	15.0	0	0

SAM BILLINGS   RHB WK

FULL NAME: Samuel William Billings
BORN: June 15, 1991, Pembury, Kent
SQUAD NO: 20
HEIGHT: 5ft 11in
NICKNAME: Bilbo, Doug
EDUCATION: Haileybury College
TEAMS: England Under-19s, Kent, Kent 2nd XI, Loughborough MCCU
CAREER: First-class: 2011; List A: 2011; T20: 2011

BEST BATTING: 131 Loughborough MCCU vs Northamptonshire, Loughborough, 2011

FAVOURITE MUSICIAN? Tinie Tempah
FAVOURITE FOOD? Roast lamb or steak and chips
FAVOURITE FILM? The Blindside
BEST CRICKETING MEMORY? Seeing England win the Ashes in Australia in 2010/11
CAREER HIGHLIGHTS? Making my debuts for Kent and England U19
WORST HABIT? Playing too much FIFA
LOOKALIKE? Alex Pettyfer
TWITTER FEED: @sambillings
NOTES: Billings was Kent's leading run-scorer in limited-overs cricket in 2012. The wicketkeeper-batsman's 143 from 113 balls in a CB40 game against Derbyshire that season was the highest ever one-day score by a Kent player at Canterbury. A mainstay in the T20 side, he remained second-choice to veteran wicketkeeper Geraint Jones for the 2013 County Championship season

Batting	Mat	Inns	NO	Runs	HS	Ave	SR	100	50	Ct	St
First-class	8	12	0	398	131	33.16	51.15	1	1	10	1
List A	19	19	4	449	143	29.93	92.38	1	2	11	2
Twenty20	24	22	1	417	59	19.85	103.99	0	1	15	0

Bowling	Mat	Balls	Runs	Wkts	BBI	BBM	Ave	Econ	SR	5w	10
First-class	8	-	-	-	-	-	-	-	-	-	-
List A	19	-	-	-	-	-	-	-	-	-	-
Twenty20	24	-	-	-	-	-	-	-	-	-	-

JACKSON BIRD RHB RFM

FULL NAME: Jackson Munro Bird
BORN: December 11, 1986, Sydney, New South Wales, Australia
SQUAD NO: 22
HEIGHT: 6ft 4in
NICKNAME: Squid
EDUCATION: St Pius X College, Chatswood, Sydney; St Ignatius College, Riverview
TEAMS: Australia, Australia A, Australia Under-19s, Melbourne Stars, Northamptonshire, Tasmania
CAREER: Test: 2012; First-class: 2011; List A: 2011; T20: 2012

BEST BATTING: 26 Tasmania vs Western Australia, Hobart, 2012
BEST BOWLING: 6-25 Tasmania vs Western Australia, Hobart, 2012

NOTES: The Australian fast bowler signed a deal with Northamptonshire in October 2013 which will see him play six Championship matches for the county this season, replacing his compatriot Trent Copeland as their overseas player in red-ball cricket. Having made his Test debut in the 2012 Boxing Day Test against Sri Lanka, Bird played in the Chester-le-Street Test during last summer's Ashes before he was forced to leave the tour early following the recurrence of a back injury. He took 53 first-class wickets at 16 in his first season of professional cricket in 2011/12, finishing the campaign as Sheffield Shield Player of the Year, and took 38 at 19.28 in 2012/13. Outside of cricket, Bird has studied a Bachelor of Business, specialising in Marketing

Batting	Mat	Inns	NO	Runs	HS	Ave	SR	100	50	Ct	St
Tests	3	4	3	7	6*	7.00	13.20	0	0	1	0
First-class	23	22	11	87	26	7.90	28.15	0	0	10	0
List A	7	2	1	7	5*	7.00	175.00	0	0	3	0
Twenty20	15	1	1	0	0*	-	0.00	0	0	5	0

Bowling	Mat	Balls	Runs	Wkts	BBI	BBM	Ave	Econ	SR	5w	10
Tests	3	633	303	13	4/41	7/117	23.30	2.87	48.6	0	0
First-class	23	4614	2264	109	6/25	11/95	20.77	2.94	42.3	6	2
List A	7	382	277	8	3/39	3/39	34.62	4.35	47.7	0	0
Twenty20	15	339	409	20	4/31	4/31	20.45	7.23	16.9	0	0

ALEX BLAKE

LHB RM

KENT

FULL NAME: Alexander James Blake
BORN: January 25, 1989, Farnborough, Kent
SQUAD NO: 18
HEIGHT: 6ft 2in
NICKNAME: Blakey, Butler, TS
EDUCATION: Hayes Secondary School;
Leeds Metropolitan University
TEAMS: Kent, Kent 2nd XI, Leeds/Bradford
MCCU
CAREER: First-class: 2008; List A: 2007; T20:
2010

BEST BATTING: 105* Kent vs Yorkshire, Leeds, 2010
BEST BOWLING: 2-9 Kent vs Pakistanis, Canterbury, 2010

CAREER HIGHLIGHTS? My maiden first-class century and representing England U19
CRICKETING HEROES? Graham Thorpe, Freddie Flintoff
NON-CRICKETING HEROES? David Beckham
BEST PLAYER IN COUNTY CRICKET? Marcus Trescothick
TIPS FOR THE TOP? Ben Stokes, Matt Coles, Jonny Bairstow
WHEN RAIN STOPS PLAY? I'll be winding up Fabian Cowdrey
FAVOURITE FILM? Moulin Rouge
FAVOURITE BOOK? The Game
DREAM HOLIDAY? Magaluf
ACCOMPLISHMENTS? A second-class Honours degree
GUILTY PLEASURES? Domino's pizza
SURPRISING FACTS? I lived with Jonny Bairstow at university, I can name all the countries of
the world and I have a pet budgie
FANTASY SLIP CORDON? Keeper: Calvin Harris (to bust out some beats), 1st: Karl Pilkington
(to entertain us all day by not having a clue), 2nd: Me, 3rd: Joey Barton (chief sledger), Gully:
Joey Essex
TWITTER FEED: @aj_blake10

Batting	Mat	Inns	NO	Runs	HS	Ave	SR	100	50	Ct	St
First-class	28	47	2	993	105*	22.06	56.80	1	4	17	0
List A	35	27	6	491	81*	23.38	95.89	0	2	16	0
Twenty20	36	29	4	307	37*	12.28	114.98	0	0	20	0

Bowling	Mat	Balls	Runs	Wkts	BBI	BBM	Ave	Econ	SR	5w	10
First-class	28	204	129	3	2/9	2/9	43.00	3.79	68.0	0	0
List A	35	84	74	3	2/13	2/13	24.66	5.28	28.0	0	0
Twenty20	36	-	-	-	-	-	-	-	-	-	-

FULL NAME: Douglas Erwin Bollinger
BORN: July 24, 1981, Baulkham Hills, Sydney, New South Wales, Australia
SQUAD NO: 6
HEIGHT: 6ft 3in
NICKNAME: Eagle
TEAMS: Australia, Australia A, Chennai Super Kings, Kent, New South Wales, Sydney Thunder, Worcestershire
CAREER: Test: 2009; ODI: 2009; T20I: 2011; First-class: 2002; List A: 2003; T20: 2006

KENT

BEST BATTING: 31* New South Wales vs Queensland, Brisbane, 2006
BEST BOWLING: 6-47 New South Wales vs South Australia, Sydney, 2008
COUNTY CAP: 2007 (Worcestershire)

NOTES: Kent have signed Australian seamer Bollinger as their overseas player for 2014. It is his second spell in county cricket, having played for Worcestershire in 2007. In 12 Tests, between January 2009 and December 2010, he took 50 wickets at an average of 25.92 and his form in the 2013/14 season earned him a recall to the Australian squad as a stand-by player during the Ashes series. He hasn't played Test cricket since 2010 but he has continued to be a regular wicket-taker for Victoria, taking 25 first-class wickets at 26.40 in the 2013/14 season to go with 28 and 27.32 the previous year. His Test-best figures of 5-28 came against New Zealand at Wellington in 2010

Batting	Mat	Inns	NO	Runs	HS	Ave	SR	100	50	Ct	St
Tests	12	14	7	54	21	7.71	33.96	0	0	2	0
ODIs	39	8	2	50	30	8.33	92.59	0	0	12	0
T20Is	2	-	-	-	-	-	-	-	-	0	0
First-class	87	98	42	397	31*	7.08		0	0	32	0
List A	110	33	17	125	30	7.81	69.83	0	0	24	0
Twenty20	84	8	4	49	17	12.25	113.95	0	0	18	0

Bowling	Mat	Balls	Runs	Wkts	BBI	BBM	Ave	Econ	SR	5w	10
Tests	12	2401	1296	50	5/28	8/141	25.92	3.23	48.0	2	0
ODIs	39	1942	1482	62	5/35	5/35	23.90	4.57	31.3	2	0
T20Is	2	48	59	2	1/23	1/23	29.50	7.37	24.0	0	0
First-class	87	15492	8374	298	6/47		28.10	3.24	51.9	13	2
List A	110	5600	4401	158	5/35	5/35	27.85	4.71	35.4	2	0
Twenty20	84	1783	2263	87	4/13	4/13	26.01	7.61	20.4	0	0

RAVI BOPARA

RHB RM R1 MVP69

ESSEX

FULL NAME: Ravinder Singh Bopara
BORN: May 4, 1985, Forest Gate, London
SQUAD NO: 25
HEIGHT: 5ft 10in
NICKNAME: Puppy
EDUCATION: Brampton Manor School
TEAMS: England, Chittagong Kings, Dolphins, England Lions, England Under-19s, Essex, Essex Cricket Board, Gloucestershire, Kings XI Punjab, Marylebone Cricket Club, Prime Bank Cricket Club, Sydney Sixers
CAREER: Test: 2007; ODI: 2007; T20I: 2008; First-class: 2002; List A: 2002; T20: 2003

BEST BATTING: 229 Essex vs Northamptonshire, Chelmsford, 2007
BEST BOWLING: 5-75 Essex vs Surrey, Colchester, 2006
COUNTY CAP: 2005 (Essex)

FAMILY TIES? My brother played Essex age-group cricket
WHO WOULD PLAY YOU IN A FILM OF YOUR LIFE? Anyone from The Godfather
CAREER HIGHLIGHTS? Playing for England, playing for Essex, scoring 201* vs Leicestershire in a one-day match, playing in the IPL and BPL, and scoring three centuries in a row for England
MOST MARKED CHARACTERISTIC? I'm chilled out
FAVOURITE TV? Mock The Week, Dragons' Den
NON-CRICKETING HEROES? My dad, my son, my family
WHEN YOU RETIRE? I'd like to be a commentator
SURPRISING FACT? I have a fast-food business
TWITTER FEED: @ravibopara

Batting	Mat	Inns	NO	Runs	HS	Ave	SR	100	50	Ct	St
Tests	13	19	1	575	143	31.94	52.89	3	0	6	0
ODIs	102	94	21	2372	101*	32.49	78.59	1	11	30	0
T20Is	30	27	5	558	65*	25.36	114.34	0	3	6	0
First-class	138	229	28	8338	229	41.48	53.50	23	32	80	0
List A	253	237	49	7684	201*	40.87		12	43	80	0
Twenty20	158	145	21	3035	105*	24.47	115.13	1	14	50	0

Bowling	Mat	Balls	Runs	Wkts	BBI	BBM	Ave	Econ	SR	5w	10
Tests	13	434	290	1	1/39	1/39	290.00	4.00	434.0	0	0
ODIs	102	1547	1232	34	4/38	4/38	36.23	4.77	45.5	0	0
T20Is	30	220	283	12	4/10	4/10	23.58	7.71	18.3	0	0
First-class	138	9976	6263	150	5/75		41.75	3.76	66.5	1	0
List A	253	5820	5054	190	5/63	5/63	26.60	5.21	30.6	1	0
Twenty20	158	1887	2384	93	4/10	4/10	25.63	7.58	20.2	0	0

PAUL BORRINGTON   RHB RM

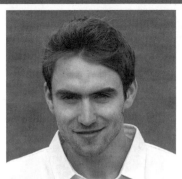

FULL NAME: Paul Michael Borrington
BORN: May 24, 1988, Nottingham
SQUAD NO: 17
HEIGHT: 5ft 11in
NICKNAME: Bozza, Boz
EDUCATION: Chellaston School; Repton
School; Loughborough University
TEAMS: Derbyshire, Loughborough UCCE
CAREER: First-class: 2005; List A: 2009

BEST BATTING: 105 Loughborough UCCE vs Hampshire, Southampton, 2005

FAMILY TIES? My father [Tony] played for Derbyshire (1970-82)
CAREER HIGHLIGHTS? Captaining the Midlands to victory at the Bunbury Festival in 2003.
My first-class debut against Leicestershire at Grace Road in 2005. Winning the County
Championship Division Two title in 2012
BEST PLAYER IN COUNTY CRICKET? Graham Onions
DESERT ISLAND DISC? Coldplay – Paradise
FAVOURITE TV? An Idiot Abroad, 24, The X Factor
CRICKETING HEROES? Michael Vaughan
NON-CRICKETING HEROES? Dario Gradi, Jack Bauer
CRICKET RULE YOU'D CHANGE? Make lunch and tea the same length of time!
FANTASY SLIP CORDON? Keeper: Karl Pilkington, 1st: Me, 2nd: Nick Powell, 3rd: Jack Bauer,
Gully: David Beckham
TWITTER FEED: @pborrington

Batting	Mat	Inns	NO	Runs	HS	Ave	SR	100	50	Ct	St
First-class	42	72	8	1753	105	27.39	35.30	2	8	24	0
List A	13	11	1	262	72	26.20	74.43	0	1	1	0

Bowling	Mat	Balls	Runs	Wkts	BBI	BBM	Ave	Econ	SR	5w	10
First-class	42	12	7	0	-	-	-	3.50	-	0	0
List A	13	-	-	-	-	-	-	-	-	-	-

SCOTT BORTHWICK

LHB LB R1 MVP9

DURHAM

FULL NAME: Scott George Borthwick
BORN: April 19, 1990, Sunderland, Co Durham
SQUAD NO: 16
HEIGHT: 5ft 10in
EDUCATION: Farringdon Community Sports College, Sunderland
TEAMS: England, Durham, Durham 2nd XI, England Lions, England Under-19s
CAREER: Test: 2014; ODI: 2011; T20I: 2011; First-class 2009; List A: 2009; T20: 2008

BEST BATTING: 135 Durham vs Surrey, Chester-le-Street, 2013
BEST BOWLING: 6-70 Durham vs Surrey, The Oval, 2013

FAMILY TIES? My uncle [David] played for Northumberland
NOTES: Toured South Africa with England U19 in 2009, following selection for the Elite England Player Development XI in 2008. He was awarded the NBC Denis Compton Award as Durham's most promising young player in 2009. In the course of taking 35 first-class wickets in 2011, he made his ODI debut for England against Ireland in August, his T20I bow in September at The Oval vs the West Indies and his overseas senior debut in India in October 2011. He spent the 2011/12 winter with the England Lions in Bangladesh and toured Australia with the Lions in early 2013 before making his Test debut in the Ashes Test at Sydney in January 2014, taking four wickets

Batting	Mat	Inns	NO	Runs	HS	Ave	SR	100	50	Ct	St
Tests	1	2	0	5	4	2.50	26.31	0	0	2	0
ODIs	2	2	0	18	15	9.00	112.50	0	0	0	0
T20Is	1	1	0	14	14	14.00	87.50	0	0	1	0
First-class	65	101	16	2653	135	31.21	54.93	4	15	82	0
List A	52	33	7	386	80	14.84	75.53	0	1	16	0
Twenty20	38	23	7	346	62	21.62	101.76	0	1	9	0

Bowling	Mat	Balls	Runs	Wkts	BBI	BBM	Ave	Econ	SR	5w	10
Tests	1	78	82	4	3/33	4/82	20.50	6.30	19.5	0	0
ODIs	2	54	72	0	-	-	-	8.00	-	0	0
T20Is	1	24	15	1	1/15	1/15	15.00	3.75	24.0	0	0
First-class	65	6071	3879	122	6/70	8/84	31.79	3.83	49.7	2	0
List A	52	1548	1523	40	4/51	4/51	38.07	5.90	38.7	0	0
Twenty20	38	476	646	29	3/19	3/19	22.27	8.14	16.4	0	0

MATT BOYCE   LHB RM

FULL NAME: Matthew Andrew Golding Boyce
BORN: August 13, 1985, Cheltenham
SQUAD NO: 11
HEIGHT: 5ft 9in
NICKNAME: Boycey, Weasel
EDUCATION: Oakham School; Nottingham University
TEAMS: Leicestershire, Leicestershire 2nd XI
CAREER: First-class: 2006; List A: 2007; T20: 2008

LEICESTERSHIRE

BEST BATTING: 135 Leicestershire vs Kent, Leicester, 2013

WHO WOULD PLAY YOU IN A FILM OF YOUR LIFE? Leonardo DiCaprio
CAREER HIGHLIGHTS? Winning the T20 in 2011 and my maiden first-class century in 2008
BEST PLAYER IN COUNTY CRICKET? James Taylor
TIPS FOR THE TOP? Shiv Thakor, Tom Wells
IF YOU WEREN'T A CRICKETER? I'd be working in the City pretending I knew something about stocks and shares!
DESERT ISLAND DISC? Nirvana – Sam Smith
FAVOURITE TV? Game Of Thrones
CRICKETING HEROES? Brian Lara, Graham Thorpe
NON-CRICKETING HEROES? Jonny Wilkinson
ACCOMPLISHMENTS? My university degree and walking from John O'Groats to Land's End in 2012, raising £18,000 in the process
TWITTER FEED: @boycey85

Batting	Mat	Inns	NO	Runs	HS	Ave	SR	100	50	Ct	St
First-class	93	163	9	4413	135	28.65	40.83	6	21	56	0
List A	61	56	3	1339	80	25.26	83.32	0	8	16	0
Twenty20	40	29	6	464	63*	20.17	111.53	0	1	7	0

Bowling	Mat	Balls	Runs	Wkts	BBI	BBM	Ave	Econ	SR	5w	10
First-class	93	54	72	0	-	-	-	8.00	-	0	0
List A	61	-	-	-	-	-	-	-	-	-	-
Twenty20	40	-	-	-	-	-	-	-	-	-	-

WILL BRAGG LHB WK R1

GLAMORGAN

FULL NAME: William David Bragg
BORN: October 24, 1986, Newport, Wales
SQUAD NO: 22
HEIGHT: 5ft 10in
NICKNAME: BPOT, Shelf
EDUCATION: Rougemont School, Newport; University of Wales Institute, Cardiff
TEAMS: Glamorgan, Glamorgan 2nd XI, Wales Minor Counties
CAREER: First-class 2007; List A: 2005; T20: 2010

BEST BATTING: 110 Glamorgan vs Leicestershire, Colwyn Bay, 2011
BEST BOWLING: 2-10 Glamorgan vs Worcestershire, Cardiff, 2013

FAMILY TIES? My dad played club cricket in the South Wales League
CAREER HIGHLIGHTS? Scoring 1,000 runs in my first full season in 2011
SUPERSTITIONS? Always go to the toilet before batting!
CRICKETING HEROES? Herschelle Gibbs, Brian Lara, Daryll Cullinan
NON-CRICKETING HEROES? Kenny Powers, Ricky Gervais
BEST PLAYER IN COUNTY CRICKET? Marcus Trescothick
TIPS FOR THE TOP? James Harris, Scott Murphy
IF YOU WEREN'T A CRICKETER? I'd be working abroad in some kind of financial role
WHEN RAIN STOPS PLAY? Coffee and a book or magazine
FAVOURITE TV? The Office
FAVOURITE FILM? See No Evil, Hear No Evil
FAVOURITE BOOK? Financial Times
DREAM HOLIDAY? Thailand
ACCOMPLISHMENTS? Getting a BSc degree in Civil Engineering
SURPRISING SKILL? I play acoustic guitar
GUILTY PLEASURES? Feeding the ducks whilst eating chocolate
TWITTER FEED: @WDBragg22

Batting	Mat	Inns	NO	Runs	HS	Ave	SR	100	50	Ct	St
First-class	60	103	2	2815	110	27.87	51.90	1	19	25	1
List A	20	19	1	486	78	27.00	76.65	0	3	2	0
Twenty20	1	1	0	15	15	15.00	68.18	0	0	0	0

Bowling	Mat	Balls	Runs	Wkts	BBI	BBM	Ave	Econ	SR	5w	10
First-class	60	379	268	4	2/10	2/10	67.00	4.24	94.7	0	0
List A	20	32	40	1	1/11	1/11	40.00	7.50	32.0	0	0
Twenty20	1	-	-	-	-	-	-	-	-	-	-

RUEL BRATHWAITE
RHB RFM

FULL NAME: Ruel Marlon Ricardo Brathwaite
BORN: September 6, 1985, Barbados
SQUAD NO: 16
HEIGHT: 6ft 3in
NICKNAME: Brath
EDUCATION: Dulwich College; Loughborough University; Cambridge University
TEAMS: Cambridge MCCU, Combined Campuses and Colleges, Durham, Hampshire, Loughborough MCCU
CAREER: First-class: 2006; List A: 2007; T20: 2010

HAMPSHIRE

BEST BATTING: 76* Loughborough UCCE vs Worcestershire, Worcester, 2007
BEST BOWLING: 5-54 Cambridge University vs Oxford University, Cambridge, 2009

CAREER HIGHLIGHTS? Taking five wickets in an innings in the first two Championship matches I played as a professional cricketer. Playing for a West Indies A team, captained by Chris Gayle, in a warm-up match against the England Lions. Scoring 75* to see an MCC Universities team to victory over Ireland A in Ireland
CRICKETING HEROES? Malcolm Marshall, Michael Holding, Courtney Walsh, Curtly Ambrose, Brian Lara, Sir Vivian Richards, George Headley, Andrew Flintoff
NON-CRICKETING HEROES? The late Stephen Alleyne
IF YOU WEREN'T A CRICKETER? I have two degrees in Engineering and I am interested in investment management so I would pursue a career in one of those fields
WHEN RAIN STOPS PLAY? A number of things from watching TV, reading, looking over footage of the game so far and talking to my teammates
FAVOURITE FILM? Taken
FAVOURITE BOOK? Angels And Demons by Dan Brown
DREAM HOLIDAY? I was born in Barbados so I think I'm a little bit biased
ACCOMPLISHMENTS? Outside of cricket my greatest achievement was graduating from Cambridge University with a Masters
SURPRISING FACT? I love beaches but I can't swim

Batting	Mat	Inns	NO	Runs	HS	Ave	SR	100	50	Ct	St
First-class	26	28	10	226	76*	12.55	54.19	0	1	3	0
List A	2	-	-	-	-	-	-	-	-	0	0
Twenty20	1	1	0	0	0	0.00	0.00	0	0	0	0

Bowling	Mat	Balls	Runs	Wkts	BBI	BBM	Ave	Econ	SR	5w	10
First-class	26	3778	2309	71	5/54	8/130	32.52	3.66	53.2	3	0
List A	2	54	68	1	1/19	1/19	68.00	7.55	54.0	0	0
Twenty20	1	18	33	1	1/33	1/33	33.00	11.00	18.0	0	0

GARETH BREESE

RHB OB

FULL NAME: Gareth Rohan Breese
BORN: January 9, 1976, Montego Bay, St James, Jamaica
SQUAD NO: 70
HEIGHT: 5ft 7in
NICKNAME: Briggy
EDUCATION: Wolmer's Boys' School, Kingston; University of Technology, Jamaica
TEAMS: West Indies, Durham, Jamaica
CAREER: Test: 2002; First-class: 1995; List A: 1996; T20: 2004

BEST BATTING: 165* Durham vs Somerset, Taunton, 2004
BEST BOWLING: 7-60 Jamaica vs Barbados, Bridgetown, 2004
BENEFIT YEAR: 2014

FAMILY TIES? My father played league cricket and is a cricket administrator
WHO WOULD PLAY YOU IN A FILM OF YOUR LIFE? Me – film stars make a lot of money!
CAREER HIGHLIGHTS? Winning the FP Trophy with Durham in the Lord's final, being part of Durham's back-to-back County Championship titles and playing Test cricket
SUPERSTITIONS? No, I just love to fiddle with my kit
MOST MARKED CHARACTERISTIC? Being easy to talk to
BEST PLAYER IN COUNTY CRICKET? As a batsman Marcus Trescothick has to be up there
TIP FOR THE TOP? I've been really impressed with Joe Root. I think he will be a fantastic player for England
DESERT ISLAND DISC? You can't get better island music than Bob Marley
FAVOURITE TV? Cricket, Arrow, Chicago Fire, Suits, Last Resort
CRICKETING HEROES? Jimmy Adams, Courtney Walsh
WHEN YOU RETIRE? Coaching if possible
SURPRISING FACT? I loved to spear fish as a hobby when I lived in Jamaica

Batting	Mat	Inns	NO	Runs	HS	Ave	SR	100	50	Ct	St
Tests	1	2	0	5	5	2.50	19.23	0	0	1	0
First-class	120	193	22	4511	165*	26.38		4	27	106	0
List A	176	132	34	2048	68*	20.89		0	3	69	0
Twenty20	93	64	18	698	37	15.17	125.99	0	0	38	0

Bowling	Mat	Balls	Runs	Wkts	BBI	BBM	Ave	Econ	SR	5w	10
Tests	1	188	135	2	2/108	2/135	67.50	4.30	94.0	0	0
First-class	120	18483	8507	285	7/60		29.84	2.76	64.8	12	3
List A	176	6518	5105	184	5/41	5/41	27.74	4.69	35.4	2	0
Twenty20	93	1566	1787	81	4/14	4/14	22.06	6.84	19.3	0	0

TIM BRESNAN   RHB RFM

FULL NAME: Timothy Thomas Bresnan
BORN: February 28, 1985, Pontefract, Yorkshire
SQUAD NO: 16
HEIGHT: 6ft 1in
NICKNAME: Brez
EDUCATION: Castleford High School; Pontefract New College
TEAMS: England, England Lions, England Under-19s, Marylebone Cricket Club, Yorkshire
CAREER: Test: 2009; ODI: 2006; T20I: 2006; First-class: 2003; List A: 2001; T20: 2003

BEST BATTING: 126* England Lions vs Indians, Chelmsford, 2007
BEST BOWLING: 5-42 Yorkshire vs Worcestershire, Worcester, 2005
COUNTY CAP: 2006; BENEFIT YEAR: 2014

WHO WOULD PLAY YOU IN A FILM OF YOUR LIFE? Jimmy Anderson
CAREER HIGHLIGHTS? The Ashes in 2010/11
MOST MARKED CHARACTERISTIC? My curly hair
TIP FOR THE TOP? Joe Root
IF YOU WEREN'T A CRICKETER? I'd be a secret agent
BIGGEST DRESSING DOWN YOU'VE RECEIVED? Too many to pick just one!
CRICKETING HEROES? Jacques Kallis
SURPRISING FACT? I'm very handy around the house: shelves, flooring, etc
FANTASY SLIP CORDON? Keeper: Roy Chubby Brown, 1st: Myself, 2nd: Michael McIntyre, 3rd: Sean Lock, Gully: Keith Lemon. Should be a good laugh
TWITTER FEED: @timbresnan

Batting	Mat	Inns	NO	Runs	HS	Ave	SR	100	50	Ct	St
Tests	23	26	4	575	91	26.13	39.43	0	3	8	0
ODIs	84	64	20	871	80	19.79	90.25	0	1	20	0
T20Is	29	18	7	170	47*	15.45	114.09	0	0	9	0
First-class	130	170	29	3765	126*	26.70	47.02	3	17	51	0
List A	224	160	47	2104	80	18.61	90.33	0	4	56	0
Twenty20	81	55	20	600	47*	17.14	116.27	0	0	24	0

Bowling	Mat	Balls	Runs	Wkts	BBI	BBM	Ave	Econ	SR	5w	10
Tests	23	4674	2357	72	5/48	8/141	32.73	3.02	64.9	1	0
ODIs	84	4185	3802	108	5/48	5/48	35.20	5.45	38.7	1	0
T20Is	29	580	739	21	3/10	3/10	35.19	7.64	27.6	0	0
First-class	130	22463	11501	368	5/42		31.25	3.07	61.0	6	0
List A	224	9983	8649	254	5/48	5/48	34.05	5.19	39.3	1	0
Twenty20	81	1623	2012	72	3/10	3/10	27.94	7.43	22.5	0	0

DANNY BRIGGS

RHB SLA

FULL NAME: Danny Richard Briggs
BORN: April 30, 1991, Newport, Isle of Wight
SQUAD NO: 19
HEIGHT: 6ft 2in
NICKNAME: Briggsy
EDUCATION: Carisbrooke High School
TEAMS: England, Berkshire, England Lions, England Under-19s, Hampshire, Hampshire 2nd XI
CAREER: ODI: 2012; T20I: 2012; First-class: 2009; List A: 2009; T20: 2010

BEST BATTING: 54 Hampshire vs Gloucestershire, Bristol, 2011
BEST BOWLING: 6-45 England Lions vs Windward Islands, Roseau, 2011
COUNTY CAP: 2012

CAREER HIGHLIGHTS? Winning the T20 Cup in 2010
CRICKETING HEROES? Daniel Vettori
BEST PLAYER IN COUNTY CRICKET? James Tomlinson
TIP FOR THE TOP? Jos Buttler
IF YOU WEREN'T A CRICKETER? Anything to do with sport
WHEN RAIN STOPS PLAY? I'm either very bored, sleeping or listening to music
FAVOURITE TV? Any comedy
FAVOURITE FILM? The Shawshank Redemption
DREAM HOLIDAY? Caribbean
GUILTY PLEASURES? 80s music
FANTASY SLIP CORDON? Keeper: Happy Gilmore, 1st: Viv Richards, 2nd: James Tomlinson, 3rd: Pelé
TWITTER FEED: @DannyBriggs19

Batting	Mat	Inns	NO	Runs	HS	Ave	SR	100	50	Ct	St
ODIs	1	-	-	-	-	-	-	-	-	0	0
T20Is	7	1	1	0	0*	-	-	0	0	1	0
First-class	50	58	12	615	54	13.36		0	1	17	0
List A	57	22	7	145	25	9.66	85.79	0	0	17	0
Twenty20	72	12	7	32	10	6.40	110.34	0	0	14	0

Bowling	Mat	Balls	Runs	Wkts	BBI	BBM	Ave	Econ	SR	5w	10
ODIs	1	60	39	2	2/39	2/39	19.50	3.90	30.0	0	0
T20Is	7	108	199	5	2/25	2/25	39.80	11.05	21.6	0	0
First-class	50	9132	4711	143	6/45	9/96	32.94	3.09	63.8	5	0
List A	57	2610	2163	65	4/32	4/32	33.27	4.97	40.1	0	0
Twenty20	72	1465	1708	87	5/19	5/19	19.63	6.99	16.8	1	0

STUART BROAD · LHB RFM

FULL NAME: Stuart Christopher John Broad
BORN: June 24, 1986, Nottingham
SQUAD NO: 16
HEIGHT: 6ft 5in
NICKNAME: Broady
EDUCATION: Oakham School
TEAMS: England, Leicestershire, Nottinghamshire
CAREER: Test: 2007; ODI: 2006; T20I: 2006; First-class: 2005; List A: 2005; T20: 2006

NOTTINGHAMSHIRE

BEST BATTING: 169 England vs Pakistan, Lord's, 2010
BEST BOWLING: 8-52 Nottinghamshire vs Warwickshire, Birmingham, 2010
COUNTY CAP: 2007 (Leicestershire)

FAMILY TIES? My father [Chris] played for England, Nottinghamshire and Gloucestershire and is now an ICC match official
SUPERSTITIONS? Three warm-up balls before I bowl a new spell
TIP FOR THE TOP? Joe Root
BIGGEST DRESSING DOWN YOU'VE RECEIVED? I've upset most international referees
CRICKETING HEROES? Glenn McGrath, Shaun Pollock
ACCOMPLISHMENTS? Setting up the Broad Appeal
WHEN YOU RETIRE? I'd like to be a racing-car driver
FANTASY SLIP CORDON? Keeper: Mark Crossley, 1st: Des Lyttle, 2nd: Steve Chettle, 3rd: Des Walker, 4th: Stuart Pearce
TWITTER FEED: @StuartBroad8

Batting	Mat	Inns	NO	Runs	HS	Ave	SR	100	50	Ct	St
Tests	67	95	12	2010	169	24.21	64.40	1	10	20	0
ODIs	108	58	21	470	45*	12.70	74.13	0	0	25	0
T20Is	52	24	9	113	18*	7.53	100.89	0	0	21	0
First-class	122	165	27	3212	169	23.27	60.10	1	17	40	0
List A	126	65	22	516	45*	12.00	72.77	0	0	27	0
Twenty20	70	26	10	122	18*	7.62	97.60	0	0	24	0

Bowling	Mat	Balls	Runs	Wkts	BBI	BBM	Ave	Econ	SR	5w	10
Tests	67	13896	7215	238	7/44	11/121	30.31	3.11	58.3	11	2
ODIs	108	5472	4767	168	5/23	5/23	28.37	5.22	32.5	1	0
T20Is	52	1101	1389	61	4/24	4/24	22.77	7.56	18.0	0	0
First-class	122	23331	12611	447	8/52		28.21	3.24	52.1	21	3
List A	126	6296	5484	196	5/23	5/23	27.97	5.22	32.1	1	0
Twenty20	70	1503	1761	87	4/24	4/24	20.24	7.02	17.2	0	0

JACK BROOKS   RHB RFM

YORKSHIRE

FULL NAME: Jack Alexander Brooks
BORN: June 4, 1984, Oxford
SQUAD NO: 70
HEIGHT: 6ft 2in
NICKNAME: Brooksy, Ferret, Animal, Gianluigi Von Burgernips, Scrumpy, Subo, Headband Warrior
EDUCATION: Wheatley Park School, Oxford
TEAMS: England Lions, Northamptonshire, Northamptonshire 2nd XI, Oxfordshire, Yorkshire
CAREER: First-class: 2009; List A: 2009; T20: 2010

BEST BATTING: 53 Northamptonshire vs Gloucestershire, Bristol, 2010
BEST BOWLING: 5-23 Northamptonshire vs Leicestershire, Leicester, 2011
COUNTY CAP: 2012 (Northamptonshire)

FAMILY TIES? My father Don played for and captained local village side Tiddington for 100 years and my brother Nathan also plays for Tiddington and has represented Oxfordshire Development XI
SUPERSTITIONS? I always scratch my bowling marker with a J and change the headband now and then
CRICKETING HEROES? Dennis Lillee, Curtly Ambrose, Colin Milburn
NON-CRICKETING HEROES? Vincent Chase, John Malkovich and Rambo
BEST PLAYER IN COUNTY CRICKET? Batsman: Marcus Trescothick. Bowler: David Masters is an annoyingly good English seamer who is never injured!
FAVOURITE TV? Entourage
FAVOURITE FILM? Rambo or The Goonies
DREAM HOLIDAY? Oxfordshire
FANTASY SLIP CORDON? Keeper: Liam Gallagher (must be decent at sledging!), 1st: Me (for mature conversation and catching prowess), 2nd: Mila Kunis (my future ex-girlfriend), 3rd: Micky Flanagan (hilarious comedian), Gully: Ashton Kutcher (for Hollywood stories)
TWITTER FEED: @BrooksyFerret

Batting	Mat	Inns	NO	Runs	HS	Ave	SR	100	50	Ct	St
First-class	49	56	21	427	53	12.20	48.19	0	1	14	0
List A	23	10	4	34	10	5.66	64.15	0	0	0	0
Twenty20	41	10	6	59	33*	14.75	134.09	0	0	8	0

Bowling	Mat	Balls	Runs	Wkts	BBI	BBM	Ave	Econ	SR	5w	10
First-class	49	7803	4325	155	5/23	7/67	27.90	3.32	50.3	5	0
List A	23	918	760	19	3/35	3/35	40.00	4.96	48.3	0	0
Twenty20	41	744	889	38	5/21	5/21	23.39	7.16	19.5	1	0

BEN BROWN   RHB WK

FULL NAME: Ben Christopher Brown
BORN: November 23, 1988, Crawley, Sussex
SQUAD NO: 26
HEIGHT: 5ft 8in
NICKNAME: Brownie
EDUCATION: Balcombe Primary; Ardingly College
TEAMS: England Under-19s, Sussex, Sussex 2nd XI
CAREER: First-class: 2007; List A: 2007; T20: 2008

BEST BATTING: 112 Sussex vs Derbyshire, Horsham, 2010

CAREER HIGHLIGHTS? Scoring my maiden Championship century and Sussex winning the T20 in 2009
CRICKETING HEROES? Alec Stewart and Adam Gilchrist
BEST PLAYER IN COUNTY CRICKET? Chris Nash
TIPS FOR THE TOP? Luke Wells, Will Beer and Matt Machan
WHEN RAIN STOPS PLAY? Talking rubbish in the dressing room and trying to irritate anybody attempting to do a crossword or Sudoku!
FAVOURITE TV? Match Of The Day
FAVOURITE FILM? Gladiator
FAVOURITE BOOK? One Day by David Nicholls
DREAM HOLIDAY? Rome
ACCOMPLISHMENTS? School exam results
GUILTY PLEASURES? Ben and Jerry's Chocolate Fudge Brownie (preferably the whole tub)
FANTASY SLIP CORDON? Keeper: Me, 1st: Julius Caesar (commanding leader), 2nd: Jesus (must be a good fielder), 3rd: Russell Brand, Gully: David Beckham
TWITTER FEED: @Ben_Brown26

Batting	Mat	Inns	NO	Runs	HS	Ave	SR	100	50	Ct	St
First-class	51	79	13	2291	112	34.71	58.04	4	15	122	10
List A	38	28	9	421	60	22.15	97.67	0	3	34	9
Twenty20	34	28	4	314	68	13.08	100.96	0	1	15	5

Bowling	Mat	Balls	Runs	Wkts	BBI	BBM	Ave	Econ	SR	5w	10
First-class	51	-	-	-	-	-	-	-	-	-	-
List A	38	-	-	-	-	-	-	-	-	-	-
Twenty20	34	-	-	-	-	-	-	-	-	-	-

KARL BROWN   RHB RM

LANCASHIRE

FULL NAME: Karl Robert Brown
BORN: May 17, 1988, Bolton, Lancashire
SQUAD NO: 14
HEIGHT: 5ft 10in
NICKNAME: Browny, Charlie
EDUCATION: Hesketh Fletcher CofE High School, Atherton, Lancashire
TEAMS: Lancashire, Lancashire 2nd XI, Moors Sports Club
CAREER: First-class: 2006; List A: 2007; T20: 2011

BEST BATTING: 114 Lancashire vs Sussex, Liverpool, 2011
BEST BOWLING: 2-30 Lancashire vs Nottinghamshire, Nottingham, 2009

FAMILY TIES? My dad played league cricket for Atherton CC and was the professional for Clifton CC
CAREER HIGHLIGHTS? Scoring my maiden first-class and one-day hundreds and playing for England U19
CRICKETING HEROES? Andrew Flintoff, Stuart Law
NON-CRICKETING HEROES? Kevin Davies, Lionel Messi, Ronnie O'Sullivan, Phil Taylor, Sergio Garcia
BEST PLAYER IN COUNTY CRICKET? Marcus Trescothick
TIP FOR THE TOP? Simon Kerrigan
WHEN RAIN STOPS PLAY? Playing cards or watching TV
FAVOURITE TV? Celebrity Juice
FAVOURITE FILM? Snatch, Layer Cake
DREAM HOLIDAY? Anywhere with a golf course
ACCOMPLISHMENTS? Playing football for Wigan Athletic
GUILTY PLEASURES? Sweets
TWITTER FEED: @karlos173

Batting	Mat	Inns	NO	Runs	HS	Ave	SR	100	50	Ct	St
First-class	55	92	5	2290	114	26.32	47.22	1	13	28	0
List A	46	43	8	1283	101*	36.65	84.51	1	7	8	0
Twenty20	30	28	6	645	62	29.31	127.21	0	4	8	0

Bowling	Mat	Balls	Runs	Wkts	BBI	BBM	Ave	Econ	SR	5w	10
First-class	55	84	49	2	2/30	2/37	24.50	3.50	42.0	0	0
List A	46	-	-	-	-	-	-	-	-	-	-
Twenty20	30	-	-	-	-	-	-	-	-	-	-

FULL NAME: Nathan Liam Buck
BORN: April 26, 1991, Leicester
SQUAD NO: 9
HEIGHT: 6ft 3in
EDUCATION: Ashby Grammar School
TEAMS: England Lions, England Under-17s, England Under-19s, Leicestershire, Leicestershire 2nd XI
CAREER: First-class: 2009; List A: 2009; T20: 2010

LEICESTERSHIRE

BEST BATTING: 27 Leicestershire vs Kent, Canterbury, 2012
BEST BOWLING: 5-99 Leicestershire vs Gloucestershire, Bristol, 2011
COUNTY CAP: 2011

FAMILY TIES? My brother Mitchell plays in the local Leicestershire league
WHO WOULD PLAY YOU IN A FILM OF YOUR LIFE? Peter Griffin
CAREER HIGHLIGHTS? England Lions tours – West Indies then Bangladesh/Sri Lanka. Receiving my county cap
BEST PLAYER IN COUNTY CRICKET? Graham Onions
TIPS FOR THE TOP? Rob Sayer and Harry Bow
IF YOU WEREN'T A CRICKETER? I'd be struggling…
FAVOURITE TV? Victoria's Secret Fashion Show
NON-CRICKETING HEROES? Batman and Robin
ACCOMPLISHMENTS? I once cooked one-minute noodles in 58 seconds
TWITTER FEED: @NathanBuck17

Batting	Mat	Inns	NO	Runs	HS	Ave	SR	100	50	Ct	St
First-class	51	67	18	421	27	8.59		0	0	6	0
List A	34	14	6	78	21	9.75	66.66	0	0	7	0
Twenty20	18	4	3	16	8*	16.00	100.00	0	0	4	0

Bowling	Mat	Balls	Runs	Wkts	BBI	BBM	Ave	Econ	SR	5w	10
First-class	51	7696	4377	108	5/99	7/79	40.52	3.41	71.2	1	0
List A	34	1425	1448	42	4/39	4/39	34.47	6.09	33.9	0	0
Twenty20	18	362	505	20	3/16	3/16	25.25	8.37	18.1	0	0

RYAN BUCKLEY RHB OB

DURHAM

FULL NAME: Ryan Sean Buckley
BORN: April 2, 1994, Darlington, County Durham
SQUAD NO: 4
NICKNAME: Buckers
EDUCATION: Hummersknott Academy, Darlington; Darlington Queen Elizabeth Sixth Form College
TEAMS: Durham, Durham 2nd XI, Durham Under-17s
CAREER: First-class: 2013

BEST BATTING: 6 Durham vs Surrey, The Oval, 2013
BEST BOWLING: 5-86 Durham vs Surrey, The Oval, 2013

TWITTER FEED: @buckers02
NOTES: Buckley made a memorable debut for Durham last year, the young off-spinner taking 5-86 in the first innings of the County Championship fixture against Surrey at The Oval, including the wickets of Vikram Solanki and Zander de Bruyn. He took four more wickets in his second appearance for the county, against Somerset at Taunton in June, including the scalps of Nick Compton, Peter Trego and James Hildreth

Batting	Mat	Inns	NO	Runs	HS	Ave	SR	100	50	Ct	St
First-class	2	2	0	10	6	5.00	23.80	0	0	1	0

Bowling	Mat	Balls	Runs	Wkts	BBI	BBM	Ave	Econ	SR	5w	10
First-class	2	686	344	10	5/86	6/172	34.40	3.00	68.6	1	0

KIERAN BULL   RHB OB

FULL NAME: Kieran Andrew Bull
BORN: April 5, 1995, Haverfordwest, Pembrokeshire, Wales
SQUAD NO: 11
HEIGHT: 6ft 2in
NICKNAME: Bully
EDUCATION: Queen Elizabeth High School; Cardiff Metropolitan University
TEAMS: Glamorgan 2nd XI, Wales Minor Counties
CAREER: Yet to make first-team debut

GLAMORGAN

FAMILY TIES? My father played club cricket
WHO WOULD PLAY YOU IN A FILM OF YOUR LIFE? Will Ferrell
CAREER HIGHLIGHTS? A successful season with Wales Minor Counties, making my Glamorgan 2nd XI debut and receiving the Glamorgan Academy Most Promising Player Award
MOST MARKED CHARACTERISTIC? My bucket hands
BEST PLAYER IN COUNTY CRICKET? Kevin Pietersen
TIPS FOR THE TOP? Aneurin Donald (Glamorgan) and my five-year-old nephew Luke
IF YOU WEREN'T A CRICKETER? I'd be studying at university
DESERT ISLAND DISC? Arctic Monkeys – AM
FAVOURITE TV? Two And A Half Men
CRICKETING HEROES? Darren Gough and Andrew Flintoff
NON-CRICKETING HEROES? Steven Gerrard and Muhammad Ali
ACCOMPLISHMENTS? Being a Cardiff City Junior Academy football player and passing my driving test at the third attempt
WHEN YOU RETIRE? I'd like to move on to a career coaching cricket
SURPRISING FACT? I moved to Spain aged 10 to take up a place in a tennis academy and lived there for two years, representing Spain at age-group level vs Qatar. I was also a ball boy for Rafael Nadal
FANTASY SLIP CORDON? Keeper: James Corden, 1st: Myself, 2nd: John Bishop, 3rd: Dynamo, Gully: Bruce Grobbelaar
TWITTER FEED: @Kieran_Bull89

PETER BURGOYNE

RHB OB

FULL NAME: Peter Ian Burgoyne
BORN: November 11, 1993, Nottingham
SQUAD NO: 32
HEIGHT: 6ft 2in
NICKNAME: Pie Man, Burgy, Stench
EDUCATION: St John Houghton School, Ilkeston; Derby Sixth Form College
TEAMS: Derbyshire, Derbyshire 2nd XI, Derbyshire Under-19s, England Under-19s, Southern Rocks
CAREER: First-class: 2012; List A: 2011; T20: 2012

BEST BATTING: 104 Southern Rocks vs Mid West Rhinos, Kwekwe, 2013
BEST BOWLING: 3-27 Southern Rocks vs Mid West Rhinos, Kwekwe, 2013

FAMILY TIES? My dad and brother play club cricket, but that's about it
WHO WOULD PLAY YOU IN A FILM OF YOUR LIFE? Alan from The Hangover because he is an absolute legend
CAREER HIGHLIGHTS? Making my Derbyshire 1st XI debut, playing for England U19 and making my first-class debut in Zimbabwe and getting my maiden first-class hundred
SUPERSTITIONS? Just that I make sure I have some toast before playing
BEST PLAYER IN COUNTY CRICKET? Wes Durston, easily
TIPS FOR THE TOP? Matt Pardoe, Dan Redfern
DESERT ISLAND DISC? Right Said Fred – You're My Mate. Unreal song!
FAVOURITE TV? Premier League Darts, Two And A Half Men, The Powerpuff Girls
CRICKETING HEROES? My dad and Dave Houghton
ACCOMPLISHMENTS? I won a few competitions playing golf for Derbyshire and I used to play in goal for Notts County FC
WHEN YOU RETIRE? I'd like to be an umpire in Zimbabwe
FANTASY SLIP CORDON? Keeper: Roy Cropper, 1st: Alan from The Hangover, 2nd: Peter Kay, 3rd: Scarlett Johansson, Gully: Me
TWITTER FEED: @PeterBurgoyne1

Batting	Mat	Inns	NO	Runs	HS	Ave	SR	100	50	Ct	St
First-class	12	21	2	538	104	28.31	38.53	2	1	9	0
List A	16	10	2	129	43	16.12	71.66	0	0	9	0
Twenty20	10	8	2	108	38	18.00	109.09	0	0	1	0

Bowling	Mat	Balls	Runs	Wkts	BBI	BBM	Ave	Econ	SR	5w	10
First-class	12	1473	814	16	3/27	6/113	50.87	3.31	92.0	0	0
List A	16	567	513	13	3/31	3/31	39.46	5.42	43.6	0	0
Twenty20	10	174	189	6	2/13	2/13	31.50	6.51	29.0	0	0

RORY BURNS

LHB RM WK

FULL NAME: Rory Joseph Burns
BORN: August 26, 1990, Epsom, Surrey
SQUAD NO: 17
HEIGHT: 5ft 9in
NICKNAME: Biebs, Fong, Chinese
EDUCATION: City of London Freemen's School; Cardiff Metropolitan University
TEAMS: Cardiff MCCU, Hampshire 2nd XI, Surrey, Surrey 2nd XI, Surrey Under-19s
CAREER: First-class: 2011; List A: 2012; T20: 2012

SURREY

BEST BATTING: 121 Surrey vs Middlesex, The Oval, 2012
BEST BOWLING: 1-18 Surrey vs Middlesex, Lord's, 2013

WHO WOULD PLAY YOU IN A FILM OF YOUR LIFE? Leonardo DiCaprio
CAREER HIGHLIGHTS? My first-class, List A, and T20 debuts and my first-class hundreds. Winning the Walter Lawrence Trophy. Becoming a professional cricketer
SUPERSTITIONS? I always walk out on the left of the other batter and I love taking the first ball
BEST PLAYER IN COUNTY CRICKET? Marcus Trescothick
TIPS FOR THE TOP? Jason Roy, Matthew Dunn
IF YOU WEREN'T A CRICKETER? I'd be a student
DESERT ISLAND DISC? Justin Bieber or maybe Skrillex. Depends on my mood!
FAVOURITE TV? Any teen drama
CRICKETING HEROES? Alec Stewart, Graham Thorpe, Kumar Sangakkara, Brian Lara
NON-CRICKETING HEROES? Jonny Wilkinson
ACCOMPLISHMENTS? Being able to play the saxophone and getting a place at university
SURPRISING FACT? I'm an outstanding dancer
FANTASY SLIP CORDON? Keeper: Alec Stewart, 1st: Brian Lara, 2nd: Me, 3rd: Superman, 4th: Hayden Panettiere, Gully: Russell Howard
TWITTER FEED: @roryburns17

Batting	Mat	Inns	NO	Runs	HS	Ave	SR	100	50	Ct	St
First-class	27	46	3	1693	121	39.37	44.90	4	8	22	0
List A	8	8	1	171	49	24.42	97.71	0	0	3	0
Twenty20	5	5	0	69	27	13.80	92.00	0	0	2	0

Bowling	Mat	Balls	Runs	Wkts	BBI	BBM	Ave	Econ	SR	5w	10
First-class	27	90	90	1	1/18	1/18	90.00	6.00	90.0	0	0
List A	8	-	-	-	-	-	-	-	-	-	-
Twenty20	5	-	-	-	-	-	-	-	-	-	-

JOS BUTTLER   RHB WK

FULL NAME: Joseph Charles Buttler
BORN: September 8, 1990, Taunton, Somerset
SQUAD NO: 6
HEIGHT: 6ft
EDUCATION: King's College, Taunton
TEAMS: England, England Lions, England Under-19s, Lancashire, Somerset, Somerset 2nd XI
CAREER: ODI: 2012; T20I: 2011; First-class: 2009; List A: 2009; T20: 2009

BEST BATTING: 144 Somerset vs Hampshire, Southampton, 2013

NOTES: Signed for Lancashire in September 2013 to pursue more opportunities as a keeper after sharing duties with Craig Kieswetter at Somerset. Came to prominence after scoring 55 from just 25 balls in the 2010 FP t20 semi-final between Somerset and Notts. Scored 440 runs at 55 in the 2010 CB40 and 411 runs at 137 in 2011, including 86 from 72 balls in the final. A successful tour with England Lions to Sri Lanka in early 2012 (262 runs at 87.33) led to a call-up for England's limited-overs squads for the series against Pakistan in UAE. Now established as a regular behind the stumps in England's limited-overs sides, Buttler made a career-best ODI score of 99 against West Indies at Antigua in March

Batting	Mat	Inns	NO	Runs	HS	Ave	SR	100	50	Ct	St
ODIs	27	22	3	572	99	30.10	124.89	0	4	41	3
T20Is	29	23	7	336	54	21.00	137.14	0	1	8	0
First-class	48	70	6	2031	144	31.73	60.41	3	9	82	2
List A	88	75	23	2570	119	49.42	123.26	2	19	85	8
Twenty20	104	86	22	1612	72*	25.18	141.52	0	7	59	10

Bowling	Mat	Balls	Runs	Wkts	BBI	BBM	Ave	Econ	SR	5w	10
ODIs	27	-	-	-	-	-	-	-	-	-	-
T20Is	29	-	-	-	-	-	-	-	-	-	-
First-class	48	12	11	0	-	-	-	5.50	-	0	0
List A	88	-	-	-	-	-	-	-	-	-	-
Twenty20	104	-	-	-	-	-	-	-	-	-	-

MICHAEL CARBERRY — LHB OB R3 MVP27

FULL NAME: Michael Alexander Carberry
BORN: September 29, 1980, Croydon, Surrey
SQUAD NO: 15
HEIGHT: 5ft 11in
NICKNAME: Carbs
EDUCATION: St John Rigby College
TEAMS: England, England Lions, Hampshire, Kent, Marylebone Cricket Club, Surrey, Surrey Cricket Board
CAREER: Test: 2010; ODI: 2013; First-class: 2001; List A: 1999; T20: 2003

BEST BATTING: 300* Hampshire vs Yorkshire, Southampton, 2011
BEST BOWLING: 2-85 Hampshire vs Durham, Chester-le-Street, 2006
COUNTY CAP: 2006 (Hampshire)

FAMILY TIES? My dad played club cricket
CAREER HIGHLIGHTS? Every day is a highlight
CRICKETERS PARTICULARLY ADMIRED? Ricky Ponting, Brian Lara
RELAXATIONS? Sleeping
TWITTER FEED: @carbs646
NOTES: A powerful opening batsman, Carberry made his Test debut against Bangladesh in 2010, scoring 30 and 34. It was three years until his next chance, when he was drafted in for the doomed tour of Australia in 2013/14. He was England's second-highest run-scorer in the series with 281. Scored 300* against Yorkshire in Southampton 2011. Helped Hampshire to two titles, the FL t20 and CB40, in 2012. In 13 first-class appearances last season he scored 889 runs at 46.78

Batting	Mat	Inns	NO	Runs	HS	Ave	SR	100	50	Ct	St
Tests	6	12	0	345	60	28.75	41.31	0	1	7	0
ODIs	5	5	0	108	63	21.60	62.79	0	1	2	0
First-class	154	268	22	10652	300*	43.30	51.65	29	50	77	0
List A	153	143	14	4289	150*	33.24		6	30	58	0
Twenty20	85	79	11	2102	100*	30.91	118.28	1	15	35	0

Bowling	Mat	Balls	Runs	Wkts	BBI	BBM	Ave	Econ	SR	5w	10
Tests	6	-	-	-	-	-	-	-	-	-	-
ODIs	5	6	12	0	-	-	-	12.00	-	0	0
First-class	154	1429	1010	16	2/85		63.12	4.24	89.3	0	0
List A	153	322	297	11	3/37	3/37	27.00	5.53	29.2	0	0
Twenty20	85	18	19	1	1/16	1/16	19.00	6.33	18.0	0	0

ANDY CARTER · RHB RFM

FULL NAME: Andrew Carter
BORN: August 27, 1988, Lincoln
SQUAD NO: 37
HEIGHT: 6ft 5in
NICKNAME: Carts
EDUCATION: Lincoln College
TEAMS: Essex, Essex 2nd XI, Lincolnshire, Nottinghamshire, Nottinghamshire 2nd XI
CAREER: First-class: 2009; List A: 2009; T20: 2010

BEST BATTING: 17* Nottinghamshire vs Sussex, Hove, 2012
BEST BOWLING: 5-40 Essex vs Kent, Canterbury, 2010

WHO WOULD PLAY YOU IN A FILM OF YOUR LIFE? Keith Lemon
CAREER HIGHLIGHTS? Staying fit
SUPERSTITIONS? I always carry a rabbit's foot
MOST MARKED CHARACTERISTIC? I'm ginger
TIPS FOR THE TOP? Brett Hutton, Sam Kelsall
IF YOU WEREN'T A CRICKETER? I'd be a plumber
DESERT ISLAND DISC? Iron Maiden – The Number Of The Beast
FAVOURITE TV? Jimmy's Farm
CRICKETING HEROES? Mike Hendrick, Luke Fletcher, Matthew Hoggard
NON-CRICKETING HEROES? Ted Nugent, butchers
ACCOMPLISHMENTS? My charity work
WHEN YOU RETIRE? I'll be a farmer or butcher
SURPRISING FACT? I was Lincolnshire trampoline junior champion
FANTASY SLIP CORDON? Keeper: My dog, 1st: Luke Fletcher, 2nd and 3rd: The Hairy Bikers, 4th: Lisa Riley, Gully: Nigel Dennis
TWITTER FEED: @andy_carter2011

Batting	Mat	Inns	NO	Runs	HS	Ave	SR	100	50	Ct	St
First-class	18	19	7	107	17*	8.91		0	0	4	0
List A	20	8	2	35	12	5.83	52.23	0	0	7	0
Twenty20	18	-	-	-	-	-	-	-	-	4	0

Bowling	Mat	Balls	Runs	Wkts	BBI	BBM	Ave	Econ	SR	5w	10
First-class	18	2905	1622	49	5/40	7/121	33.10	3.35	59.2	1	0
List A	20	657	702	26	4/45	4/45	27.00	6.41	25.2	0	0
Twenty20	18	341	471	18	4/20	4/20	26.16	8.28	18.9	0	0

KARL CARVER

LHB SLA

FULL NAME: Karl Carver
BORN: March 26, 1996, Northallerton, Yorkshire
SQUAD NO: TBC
HEIGHT: 5ft 10in
NICKNAME: Keith, Curley, Karvs, Karlos
EDUCATION: Thirsk School and Sixth Form College
TEAMS: England Development Programme Under-19s, England Under-19s, Yorkshire 2nd XI, Yorkshire Academy
CAREER: Yet to make first-team debut

FAMILY TIES? Cricket has always run in the family. Most of my family are involved with Sessay and South Kilvington CC

WHO WOULD PLAY YOU IN A FILM OF YOUR LIFE? Matt LeBlanc

CAREER HIGHLIGHTS? Being selected for a County Championship squad at The Oval, playing for England U19 and taking personal-best figures of 6-43 in the 2nd XI to earn a 1st XI call-up

SUPERSTITIONS? If I wear something one game (for example, a sweat band or long sleeve shirt), I will wear it again if I do well and scrap it if not

MOST MARKED CHARACTERISTIC? Happiness, calmness and my smile

BEST PLAYER IN COUNTY CRICKET? Gary Ballance

TIPS FOR THE TOP? Alex Lees, Ben Duckett, Matthew Fisher, Will Rhodes and Ryan Higgins

IF YOU WEREN'T A CRICKETER? I'd be an apprentice somewhere

DESERT ISLAND DISC? Status Quo – Rocking All Over The World

FAVOURITE TV? Friends

CRICKETING HEROES? Brian Lara, Robin Peterson and Graeme Swann

NON-CRICKETING HEROES? My family and friends

ACCOMPLISHMENTS? Gaining half-decent qualifications and attempting other sports

WHEN YOU RETIRE? I'll relax, chill and have connections to sporting clubs

SURPRISING FACT? I gained the nickname Keith Curle and Curley when I went to Sri Lanka. Sachin, who helped arrange the trip, struggled with my name and called me Curley; so the lads then called me Keith after the footballer Keith Curle. I came back with many nicknames

CRICKET RULE YOU'D CHANGE? You should be out lbw even if the ball pitches outside leg

FANTASY SLIP CORDON? Keeper: Jack Whitehall, 1st: Peter Kay, 2nd: Me, 3rd: Andrew Flintoff, Gully: Bumble

TWITTER FEED: @Carver_Karl

GRAEME CESSFORD

RHB RFM

WORCESTERSHIRE

FULL NAME: Graeme Cessford
BORN: October 4, 1983, Hexham, Northumberland
SQUAD NO: 16
HEIGHT: 6ft 2in
NICKNAME: Cess, Smallface
EDUCATION: Queen Elizabeth High School, Hexham; Newcastle College
TEAMS: Northumberland, Worcestershire, Worcestershire 2nd XI
CAREER: First-class: 2013; List A: 2013

BEST BATTING: 20 Worcestershire vs Gloucestershire, Cheltenham, 2013
BEST BOWLING: 4-73 Worcestershire vs Lancashire, Worcester, 2013

WHO WOULD PLAY YOU IN A FILM OF YOUR LIFE? Gordon Ramsey, because apparently I look like him
CAREER HIGHLIGHTS? Signing my first professional contract, making my County Championship debut vs Gloucestershire and taking my first Championship wicket (Hamish Marshall)
MOST MARKED CHARACTERISTIC? I'm a member of the Royal Air Force and I work in Air Traffic Control
BEST PLAYER IN COUNTY CRICKET? Moeen Ali
TIPS FOR THE TOP? Tom Kohler-Cadmore, Tom Fell, Charlie Morris
IF YOU WEREN'T A CRICKETER? I'd be landing aircraft somewhere in the British Isles
DESERT ISLAND DISC? I would take a DIY boat-building disc so I could sail off the island
FAVOURITE TV? I like watching Formula 1
CRICKETING HEROES? Allan Donald, Brett Lee
NON-CRICKETING HEROES? My family and members of the armed forces
ACCOMPLISHMENTS? Joining the Royal Air Force
CRICKET RULE YOU'D CHANGE? We should have uncovered pitches. Batsmen get it too easy
WHEN YOU RETIRE? Very little if possible. I'll look for somewhere warm to live
TWITTER FEED: @GCessford

Batting	Mat	Inns	NO	Runs	HS	Ave	SR	100	50	Ct	St
First-class	6	6	2	45	20	11.25	35.43	0	0	1	0
List A	4	2	1	0	0*	0.00	0.00	0	0	0	0

Bowling	Mat	Balls	Runs	Wkts	BBI	BBM	Ave	Econ	SR	5w	10
First-class	6	874	591	17	4/73	5/112	34.76	4.05	51.4	0	0
List A	4	167	176	6	4/24	4/24	29.33	6.32	27.8	0	0

MAURICE CHAMBERS   RHB RFM

FULL NAME: Maurice Anthony Chambers
BORN: September 14, 1987, Port Antonio, Portland, Jamaica
SQUAD NO: 29
HEIGHT: 6ft 3in
NICKNAME: Moza
EDUCATION: Homerton College of Technology; George Monoux College
TEAMS: England Lions, Essex, Essex 2nd XI, Northamptonshire, Warwickshire
CAREER: First-class: 2005; List A: 2008; T20: 2010

BEST BATTING: 58 Warwickshire vs Derbyshire, Derby, 2013
BEST BOWLING: 6-68 Essex vs Nottinghamshire, Chelmsford, 2010

WHO WOULD PLAY YOU IN A FILM OF YOUR LIFE? Will Smith
CAREER HIGHLIGHTS? Getting selected for the England Lions tour to Australia in 2010 and the tour to the West Indies in 2011
SUPERSTITIONS? No sexy time before cricket
MOST MARKED CHARACTERISTIC? I'm calm and steadfast in the face of adversity
BEST PLAYER IN COUNTY CRICKET? Ravi Bopara
TIPS FOR THE TOP? Reece Topley, Tymal Mills, Kishen Velani
DESERT ISLAND DISC? Ne-Yo – Year Of The Gentleman
FAVOURITE TV? The Big Bang Theory
CRICKETING HEROES? Courtney Walsh and Curtly Ambrose
NON-CRICKETING HEROES? Usain Bolt
ACCOMPLISHMENTS? Getting through college and passing my driving test
WHEN YOU RETIRE? I'd like to be a fast-bowling coach, carpenter or electrician
FANTASY SLIP CORDON? Keeper: James Foster (a fantastic man and the best keeper in the country), 1st: Usain Bolt, 2nd: Will Smith, 3rd: Chris Gayle (Will and him will make me laugh until my belly hurts), Gully: Me
TWITTER FEED: @Maurice29chamb

Batting	Mat	Inns	NO	Runs	HS	Ave	SR	100	50	Ct	St
First-class	50	62	21	281	58	6.85		0	1	14	0
List A	6	2	1	3	2	3.00	42.85	0	0	2	0
Twenty20	18	8	5	28	10*	9.33	96.55	0	0	6	0

Bowling	Mat	Balls	Runs	Wkts	BBI	BBM	Ave	Econ	SR	5w	10
First-class	50	6911	4154	128	6/68		32.45	3.60	53.9	3	1
List A	6	180	179	5	1/21	1/21	35.80	5.96	36.0	0	0
Twenty20	18	312	461	17	3/31	3/31	27.11	8.86	18.3	0	0

SHIVNARINE CHANDERPAUL   LHB LB R1 MVP78

FULL NAME: Shivnarine Chanderpaul
BORN: August 16, 1974, Unity Village, East Coast, Demerara, Guyana
SQUAD NO: 11
HEIGHT: 5ft 8in
TEAMS: West Indies, Derbyshire, Durham, Guyana, Khulna Royal Bengals, Lancashire, Royal Challengers Bangalore, Stanford Superstars, Uva Next, Warwickshire, Warwickshire 2nd XI
CAREER: Test: 1994; ODI: 1994; T20I: 2006; First-class: 1992; List A: 1992; T20: 2006

BEST BATTING: 303* Guyana vs Jamaica, Kingston, 1996
BEST BOWLING: 4-48 Guyana vs Leeward Islands, Basseterre, 1993
COUNTY CAP: 2010 (Lancashire)

NOTES: Chanderpaul signed a two-year deal with Derbyshire in January 2013, with the club retaining the option for a third season for 2015. He will be available across all formats in 2014. At the time of writing he sits seventh on the list of all-time leading run-scorers in Test cricket and is only the second West Indian to score in excess of 10,000 Test runs. Chanderpaul has a wealth of experience in county cricket, having previously represented Durham, Lancashire and Warwickshire. Named one of Wisden's five Cricketers of the Year in 2008 and won the ICC Player of the Year award in the same year

Batting	Mat	Inns	NO	Runs	HS	Ave	SR	100	50	Ct	St
Tests	153	261	45	11219	203*	51.93	43.30	29	62	64	0
ODIs	268	251	40	8778	150	41.60	70.74	11	59	73	0
T20Is	22	22	5	343	41	20.17	98.84	0	0	7	0
First-class	316	516	96	23321	303*	55.52		69	116	176	0
List A	396	368	66	12646	150	41.87		12	92	111	0
Twenty20	78	75	11	1565	87*	24.45	106.75	0	8	23	0

Bowling	Mat	Balls	Runs	Wkts	BBI	BBM	Ave	Econ	SR	5w	10
Tests	153	1740	883	9	1/2	1/2	98.11	3.04	193.3	0	0
ODIs	268	740	636	14	3/18	3/18	45.42	5.15	52.8	0	0
T20Is	22	-	-	-	-		-	-	-	-	-
First-class	316	4812	2532	60	4/48		42.20	3.15	80.2	0	0
List A	396	1681	1388	56	4/22	4/22	24.78	4.95	30.0	0	0
Twenty20	78	-	-	-	-		-	-	-	-	-

FULL NAME: Glen Chapple
BORN: January 23, 1974, Skipton, Yorkshire
SQUAD NO: 3
HEIGHT: 6ft 2in
NICKNAME: Chappie, Boris
EDUCATION: West Craven High School;
Nelson and Colne College
TEAMS: England, Lancashire
CAREER: ODI: 2006; First-class: 1992; List A:
1993; T20: 2003

LANCASHIRE

BEST BATTING: 155 Lancashire vs Somerset, Manchester, 2001
BEST BOWLING: 7-53 Lancashire vs Durham, Blackpool, 2007
COUNTY CAP: 1994; **BENEFIT YEAR:** 2004

FAMILY TIES? My father played in the Lancashire League for Nelson CC and was a professional for Darwen and Earby
CRICKETING HEROES? Dennis Lillee, Robin Smith
FAVOURITE BAND? U2, Oasis, Stone Roses
RELAXATIONS? Golf
OTHER SPORTS FOLLOWED? Football (Liverpool)
TWITTER FEED: @chappie03

Batting	Mat	Inns	NO	Runs	HS	Ave	SR	100	50	Ct	St
ODIs	1	1	0	14	14	14.00	200.00	0	0	0	0
First-class	295	408	70	8215	155	24.30		6	37	98	0
List A	283	160	44	2062	81*	17.77		0	9	66	0
Twenty20	66	36	13	301	55*	13.08	110.25	0	1	16	0

Bowling	Mat	Balls	Runs	Wkts	BBI	BBM	Ave	Econ	SR	5w	10
ODIs	1	24	14	0	-	-	-	3.50	-	0	0
First-class	295	50449	24410	936	7/53		26.07	2.90	53.8	38	3
List A	283	12165	9138	320	6/18	6/18	28.55	4.50	38.0	5	0
Twenty20	66	1300	1586	68	3/36	3/36	23.32	7.32	19.1	0	0

VARUN CHOPRA

RHB OB R3 MVP26

WARWICKSHIRE

FULL NAME: Varun Chopra
BORN: June 21, 1987, Barking, Essex
SQUAD NO: 3
HEIGHT: 6ft 1in
NICKNAME: Tidz, Chops
EDUCATION: Ilford County High School
TEAMS: England Lions, England Performance Programme, England Under-19s, Essex, Essex 2nd XI, Tamil Union Cricket and Athletic Club, Warwickshire
CAREER: First-class: 2006; List A: 2006; T20: 2006

BEST BATTING: 233* Tamil Union vs Sinhalese Sports Club, Colombo, 2012
COUNTY CAP: 2012 (Warwickshire)

WHO WOULD PLAY YOU IN A FILM OF YOUR LIFE? Will Smith
CAREER HIGHLIGHTS? Winning the County Championship in 2012, scoring a hundred on my Championship debut and back-to-back double hundreds in 2011
MOST MARKED CHARACTERISTIC? My laugh and my two tattoos
BEST PLAYER IN COUNTY CRICKET? Chris Woakes
TIPS FOR THE TOP? Tymal Mills, Sam Hain
IF YOU WEREN'T A CRICKETER? Maybe a broker, working in the City
DESERT ISLAND DISC? A mixtape from DJ Carberry
FAVOURITE TV? Suits, Homeland, 24, Entourage
CRICKETING HEROES? Sachin Tendulkar, Shane Warne
NON-CRICKETING HEROES? My parents
ACCOMPLISHMENTS? 10 A/A*'s at GCSE and brown belt at karate
WHEN YOU RETIRE? I'd like to run my own business
SURPRISING FACT? I'm allergic to cats
FANTASY SLIP CORDON? Keeper: Mark Zuckerburg, 1st: Me, 2nd: Shane Warne, 3rd: Scarlett Johansson, Gully: Charlie Sheen
TWITTER FEED: @vchops3

Batting	Mat	Inns	NO	Runs	HS	Ave	SR	100	50	Ct	St
First-class	119	198	14	6959	233*	37.82	51.11	14	34	135	0
List A	76	74	3	2818	115	39.69	75.99	6	19	22	0
Twenty20	48	46	7	874	75*	22.41	102.34	0	5	7	0

Bowling	Mat	Balls	Runs	Wkts	BBI	BBM	Ave	Econ	SR	5w	10
First-class	119	186	115	0	-	-	-	3.70	-	0	0
List A	76	18	18	0	-	-	-	6.00	-	0	0
Twenty20	48	-	-	-	-	-	-	-	-	-	-

SHAAIQ CHOUDHRY　　　　　　　　　　RHB SLA

FULL NAME: Shaaiq Hussain Choudhry
BORN: November 3, 1985, Rotherham, Yorkshire
SQUAD NO: 28
HEIGHT: 5ft 11in
NICKNAME: Shak, Chouds
EDUCATION: Fire Vale School; Rotherham College of Arts and Technology; University of Bradford
TEAMS: Leeds-Bradford UCCE, Marylebone Cricket Club, Warwickshire, Worcestershire
CAREER: First-class: 2007; List A: 2010; T20: 2010

WORCESTERSHIRE

BEST BATTING: 75 Warwickshire vs Durham UCCE, Durham University, 2009
BEST BOWLING: 4-38 Worcestershire vs Lancashire, Manchester, 2012

CAREER HIGHLIGHTS? My first-class debut against West Indies, scoring 54*. My Championship debut for Worcestershire against Sussex, scoring 63 and taking 1-30. Taking 4-54 in a CB40 game against Surrey
SUPERSTITIONS? I tend to blink four times before facing each ball
CRICKETING HEROES? Muttiah Muralitharan, Jacques Kallis, Sachin Tendulkar
BEST PLAYER IN COUNTY CRICKET? Marcus Trescothick
IF YOU WEREN'T A CRICKETER? I would be working in graphics and photography
WHEN RAIN STOPS PLAY? I play games on my iPhone and eat
FAVOURITE FILM? Scarface
FANTASY SLIP CORDON? Keeper: Charlie Sheen, 1st: Mario Balotelli, 2nd: Rihanna, 3rd: Me, Gully: Muhammad Ali
TWITTER FEED: @ShaaiqChoudhry

Batting	Mat	Inns	NO	Runs	HS	Ave	SR	100	50	Ct	St
First-class	16	25	6	420	75	22.10	36.33	0	4	6	0
List A	23	16	7	163	39	18.11	87.16	0	0	7	0
Twenty20	21	12	8	79	26*	19.75	105.33	0	0	3	0

Bowling	Mat	Balls	Runs	Wkts	BBI	BBM	Ave	Econ	SR	5w	10
First-class	16	1670	805	25	4/38	6/54	32.20	2.89	66.8	0	0
List A	23	678	681	17	4/54	4/54	40.05	6.02	39.8	0	0
Twenty20	21	318	367	10	2/21	2/21	36.70	6.92	31.8	0	0

JONATHAN CLARE

RHB RMF

FULL NAME: Jonathan Luke Clare
BORN: June 14, 1986, Burnley, Lancashire
SQUAD NO: 13
HEIGHT: 6ft 3in
NICKNAME: JC, Sidewinder, Scream
EDUCATION: St Theodore's RC High School and Sixth Form
TEAMS: Derbyshire, Derbyshire 2nd XI, Lancashire 2nd XI, Surrey 2nd XI
CAREER: First-class: 2007; List A: 2007; T20: 2008

BEST BATTING: 130 Derbyshire vs Glamorgan, Derby, 2011
BEST BOWLING: 7-74 Derbyshire vs Northamptonshire, Northampton, 2008
COUNTY CAP: 2012 (Derbyshire)

CAREER HIGHLIGHTS? Taking 5-90 on debut vs Nottinghamshire. Taking 7-79 and scoring 130* in the same game vs Northamptonshire. Taking 11 wickets in the match vs Glamorgan. Winning Division Two in 2012
WHO WOULD PLAY YOU IN A FILM OF YOUR LIFE? Alan Partridge
SUPERSTITIONS? Nope, I wear the number 13 so I don't worry about things like that. Whatever will be will be!
BEST PLAYER IN COUNTY CRICKET? Graham Onions
TIPS FOR THE TOP? Ben Stokes and James Taylor
IF YOU WEREN'T A CRICKETER? I'd be running a coffee shop somewhere
CRICKETING HEROES? Andrew Flintoff, Glenn McGrath and Allan Donald
WHEN YOU RETIRE? I'd like to be a Premier League referee
SURPRISING FACT? I'm a Burnley FC season-ticket holder and I have a single-figure handicap at golf
CRICKET RULE YOU'D CHANGE? There should be 90 overs in a Championship day with half-an-hour for tea
TWITTER FEED: @jcfalcons13

Batting	Mat	Inns	NO	Runs	HS	Ave	SR	100	50	Ct	St
First-class	55	80	9	1720	130	24.22	66.58	2	8	27	0
List A	41	31	3	321	57	11.46	96.39	0	1	11	0
Twenty20	36	24	9	210	35*	14.00	112.90	0	0	14	0
Bowling	Mat	Balls	Runs	Wkts	BBI	BBM	Ave	Econ	SR	5w	10
First-class	55	6874	4166	152	7/74	11/57	27.40	3.63	45.2	6	1
List A	41	1292	1204	30	3/39	3/39	40.13	5.59	43.0	0	0
Twenty20	36	322	457	8	2/20	2/20	57.12	8.51	40.2	0	0

GRAHAM CLARK

RHB LB

FULL NAME: Graham Clark
BORN: March 16, 1993, Whitehaven, Cumbria
SQUAD NO: 7
HEIGHT: 6ft 2in
NICKNAME: Clarky, Snoz, Sparky
EDUCATION: St Benedict's Catholic High School, Whitehaven
TEAMS: Durham 2nd XI, Durham Academy, Durham Under-17s, England Under-17s, Marylebone Cricket Club Young Cricketers
CAREER: Yet to make first-team debut

DURHAM

FAMILY TIES? My dad is a Level 3 qualified coach and is coach of the Cumbrian U15 side. My brother Jordan plays for Lancashire CCC

WHO WOULD PLAY YOU IN A FILM OF YOUR LIFE? Anyone who would be desperate enough to take the role

CAREER HIGHLIGHTS? Representing England at U17 level. Helping win the Middlesex Premier League with Hampstead CC

SUPERSTITIONS? A rain dance can go a long way

MOST MARKED CHARACTERISTIC? My 'snoz' (big nose) or massive ears… I wasn't blessed with looks

BEST PLAYER IN COUNTY CRICKET? Graham Onions

TIP FOR THE TOP? Josh Bousefield

IF YOU WEREN'T A CRICKETER? I'd probably be at university

DESERT ISLAND DISC? Hardwell – Revealed Recordings

FAVOURITE TV? Friends

CRICKETING HEROES? Sachin Tendulkar, Shane Warne, Jamie Harrison

NON-CRICKETING HEROES? Whoever invented Tinder

ACCOMPLISHMENTS? I haven't really achieved anything worth noting

WHEN YOU RETIRE? I'd like to lower my handicap to single figures

SURPRISING FACT? I was a wicketkeeper until I was 14. I kept wicket in an ECB U17 Development Squad match when a mistake I made injured the first-choice keeper

FANTASY SLIP CORDON? Keeper: Peter Kay (he can make anything funny), 1st: Me, 2nd: Kelly Brook (no explanation needed), 3rd: Karl Pilkington (funniest man on the planet and I wouldn't be the thickest in the cordon!), Gully: Ricky Gervais (he'd make Karl funnier)

TWITTER FEED: @GrahamClark16

LANCASHIRE

FULL NAME: Jordan Clark
BORN: October 14, 1990, Whitehaven, Cumbria
SQUAD NO: 16
HEIGHT: 6ft 4in
NICKNAME: Clarky
EDUCATION: Sedbergh School
TEAMS: Cumberland, England Under-15s, Lancashire, Lancashire 2nd XI
CAREER: List A: 2010; T20: 2011

FAMILY TIES? My dad plays cricket so me and my two brothers followed. My younger brother [Graham] has a scholarship at Durham CCC
CAREER HIGHLIGHTS? Hitting six sixes in an over for Lancashire 2nd XI and being involved in the one-day format at Lancashire
SUPERSTITIONS? I have to bat in a jumper
BEST PLAYER IN COUNTY CRICKET? Glen Chapple
TIPS FOR THE TOP? Alex Davies, Luis Reece
IF YOU WEREN'T A CRICKETER? I'd write books and poetry or be a newsreader
DESERT ISLAND DISC? Anything by Drake
FAVOURITE TV? Breaking Bad, Entourage, Geordie Shore
CRICKETING HEROES? Adam Gilchrist, Andrew Flintoff
NON-CRICKETING HEROES? Jeremy Piven
CRICKET RULE YOU'D CHANGE? You can't be out slogging
WHEN YOU RETIRE? I want to open up a business
SURPRISING FACT? I have an arm of tattoos
TWITTER FEED: @Clarksy16

Batting	Mat	Inns	NO	Runs	HS	Ave	SR	100	50	Ct	St
List A	13	7	1	185	72	30.83	93.90	0	1	1	0
Twenty20	10	8	2	127	38	21.16	138.04	0	0	4	0

Bowling	Mat	Balls	Runs	Wkts	BBI	BBM	Ave	Econ	SR	5w	10
List A	13	168	193	3	2/45	2/45	64.33	6.89	56.0	0	0
Twenty20	10	12	15	0	-	-	-	7.50	-	0	0

RIKKI CLARKE   RHB RFM R1 MVP37

FULL NAME: Rikki Clarke
BORN: September 29, 1981, Orsett, Essex
SQUAD NO: 81
HEIGHT: 6ft 4in
NICKNAME: Clarkey, Bad Lad
EDUCATION: Broadwater Secondary;
Godalming College
TEAMS: England, Derbyshire, Marylebone
Cricket Club, Surrey, Warwickshire
CAREER: Test: 2003; ODI: 2003; First-class:
2002; List A: 2001; T20: 2003

WARWICKSHIRE

BEST BATTING: 214 Surrey vs Somerset, Guildford, 2006
BEST BOWLING: 6-63 Warwickshire vs Kent, Canterbury, 2010
COUNTY CAPS: 2005 (Surrey); 2011 (Warwickshire)

CAREER HIGHLIGHTS? My England Test and ODI debuts, winning the County Championship with Surrey and Warwickshire, winning the first ever T20 Cup with Surrey, taking a wicket with my first ball in international cricket, becoming joint world-record holder for catches taken by an outfielder in a first-class innings, being named Cricket Writers' Young Player of the Year in 2002 and winning the CB40 with Warwickshire in 2010
BEST PLAYER IN COUNTY CRICKET? Samit Patel. He's always up there every season in the PCA MVP ratings. Also, Marcus Trescothick is still the godfather of the county game!
TIPS FOR THE TOP? Laurie Evans has international potential
CRICKETING HEROES? Darren Gough and Freddie Flintoff – both good characters of the game and they always gave 110 per cent
SURPRISING FACT? I was named after Ricky Villa, FA Cup winner with Spurs in 1981, who scored that amazing goal in the final
TWITTER FEED: @rikkiclarke81

Batting	Mat	Inns	NO	Runs	HS	Ave	SR	100	50	Ct	St
Tests	2	3	0	96	55	32.00	37.94	0	1	1	0
ODIs	20	13	0	144	39	11.07	62.06	0	0	11	0
First-class	164	251	29	7880	214	35.49		16	37	251	0
List A	186	155	21	3505	98*	26.15		0	18	87	0
Twenty20	97	90	25	1385	79*	21.30	121.17	0	3	45	0

Bowling	Mat	Balls	Runs	Wkts	BBI	BBM	Ave	Econ	SR	5w	10
Tests	2	174	60	4	2/7	3/11	15.00	2.06	43.5	0	0
ODIs	20	469	415	11	2/28	2/28	37.72	5.30	42.6	0	0
First-class	164	15068	9090	264	6/63		34.43	3.61	57.0	2	0
List A	186	4310	4039	103	4/28	4/28	39.21	5.62	41.8	0	0
Twenty20	97	972	1301	49	3/11	3/11	26.55	8.03	19.8	0	0

MITCHELL CLAYDON   LHB RMF

KENT

FULL NAME: Mitchell Eric Claydon
BORN: November 25, 1982, Fairfield, New South Wales, Australia
SQUAD NO: 8
HEIGHT: 6ft 4in
NICKNAME: Lips, Ellen, Precious, Big Fella
EDUCATION: Robert Townson Primary School; West Field Sports High School, Sydney
TEAMS: Canterbury, Durham, Durham 2nd XI, Kent, Yorkshire, Yorkshire 2nd XI
CAREER: First-class: 2005; List A: 2006; T20: 2006

BEST BATTING: 55 Durham vs Nottinghamshire, Chester-le-Street, 2012
BEST BOWLING: 6-104 Durham vs Somerset, Taunton, 2011
COUNTY CAP: 2012 (Durham)

FAMILY TIES? My father played Yorkshire league cricket
CAREER HIGHLIGHTS? Being part of two Championship-winning teams. Playing T20 cricket in New Zealand for the Canterbury Wizards as their overseas player
BEST PLAYER IN COUNTY CRICKET? Graham Onions
TIPS FOR THE TOP? Ben Stokes, Scott Borthwick
IF YOU WEREN'T A CRICKETER? I'd be working in a factory
DESERT ISLAND DISC? Powderfinger – Happiness
FAVOURITE TV? Mrs Brown's Boys
CRICKETING HEROES? Ricky Ponting
SURPRISING FACT? I am a part-time magician
FANTASY SLIP CORDON? Keeper: Shane Warne, 1st: Tiger Woods, 2nd: Me, 3rd: Michael Jordan
TWITTER FEED: @mitchellclaydon

Batting	Mat	Inns	NO	Runs	HS	Ave	SR	100	50	Ct	St
First-class	53	67	14	816	55	15.39	58.41	0	1	8	0
List A	67	32	9	187	19	8.13	84.23	0	0	3	0
Twenty20	77	23	13	100	19	10.00	100.00	0	0	19	0

Bowling	Mat	Balls	Runs	Wkts	BBI	BBM	Ave	Econ	SR	5w	10
First-class	53	6888	4149	130	6/104		31.91	3.61	52.9	2	0
List A	67	2794	2520	83	4/39	4/39	30.36	5.41	33.6	0	0
Twenty20	77	1524	2035	85	5/26	5/26	23.94	8.01	17.9	2	0

BEN COAD

RHB RFM

FULL NAME: Benjamin Oliver Coad
BORN: January 10, 1994, Harrogate, Yorkshire
SQUAD NO: 10
HEIGHT: 6ft 2in
NICKNAME: Coady
EDUCATION: Thirsk School and Sixth Form College
TEAMS: Yorkshire, Yorkshire 2nd XI, Yorkshire Academy, Yorkshire Under-15s, Yorkshire Under-17s
CAREER: List A: 2013

YORKSHIRE

FAMILY TIES? Cricket runs through the family. My brothers play for, and my dad is chairman of, Studley Royal CC. My mum helps with coaching and finances at the club
WHO WOULD PLAY YOU IN A FILM OF YOUR LIFE? Bradley Cooper
CAREER HIGHLIGHTS? My debut and first wicket vs Gloucester last year was a massive highlight. Getting a professional contract this October
MOST MARKED CHARACTERISTIC? I'm a pretty relaxed and laid-back person
BEST PLAYER IN COUNTY CRICKET? I'd have to say Graham Onions. He just always seems to get wickets and go for next-to no runs
TIP FOR THE TOP? Matt Fisher. He's a special talent and only 16 years of age
IF YOU WEREN'T A CRICKETER? I'd probably be at university right now but I'm not sure what I'd be studying
DESERT ISLAND DISC? Arctic Monkeys – Whatever People Say I Am, That's What I'm Not
FAVOURITE TV? Friends
CRICKETING HEROES? Glenn McGrath. I believe he was the most skilled bowler I ever watched
NON-CRICKETING HEROES? Will Smith. He's just a great actor and I would love to meet him
WHEN YOU RETIRE? Maybe coaching but it's a long way away hopefully
SURPRISING FACT? I'm a big Newcastle FC fan and I try to watch them as much as I can
CRICKET RULE YOU'D CHANGE? You should be out lbw no matter where the ball hits you (outside the line of off-stump or otherwise)
TWITTER FEED: @BenCoad10

Batting	Mat	Inns	NO	Runs	HS	Ave	SR	100	50	Ct	St
List A	6	2	2	1	1*	-	50.00	0	0	3	0

Bowling	Mat	Balls	Runs	Wkts	BBI	BBM	Ave	Econ	SR	5w	10
List A	6	212	244	3	1/34	1/34	81.33	6.90	70.6	0	0

JOSH COBB RHB OB MVP62

LEICESTERSHIRE

FULL NAME: Joshua James Cobb
BORN: August 17, 1990, Leicester
SQUAD NO: 5
HEIGHT: 6ft
NICKNAME: Cobby
EDUCATION: Oakham School; Bosworth College
TEAMS: Central Districts, Dhaka Gladiators, England Under-19s, Leicestershire, Leicestershire 2nd XI, Prime Doleshwar Sporting Club
CAREER: First-class: 2007; List A: 2008; T20: 2008

BEST BATTING: 148* Leicestershire vs Middlesex, Lord's, 2008
BEST BOWLING: 2-11 Leicestershire vs Gloucestershire, Leicester, 2011

FAMILY TIES? My dad [Russell] is a former Leicestershire CCC player and current Loughborough University MCCU head coach. My uncle is a former minor counties player
WHO WOULD PLAY YOU IN A FILM OF YOUR LIFE? Leonardo DiCaprio
CAREER HIGHLIGHTS? Scoring 148* at Lords in my fourth first-class game aged 17, winning two T20 titles (for Dhaka Gladiators in 2013 and Leicestershire in 2011) and being Man of the Match for Leicestershire in the final, scoring three hundreds in the first three YB40 games of 2013
SUPERSTITIONS? I put my left pad on before my right
MOST MARKED CHARACTERISTIC? I'm laid-back
BEST PLAYER IN COUNTY CRICKET? James Taylor
TIPS FOR THE TOP? Ned Eckersley
IF YOU WEREN'T A CRICKETER? I'd be a scientist
FAVOURITE TV? Homeland and Breaking Bad
CRICKETING HEROES? AB de Villiers
WHEN YOU RETIRE? Coach or umpire
CRICKET RULE YOU'D CHANGE? No balls should be free hits across all formats of cricket
TWITTER FEED: @cobby24

Batting	Mat	Inns	NO	Runs	HS	Ave	SR	100	50	Ct	St
First-class	63	109	8	2330	148*	23.06	46.42	2	12	30	0
List A	58	55	4	1843	137	36.13	101.20	5	8	17	0
Twenty20	66	61	8	1041	67*	19.64	137.15	0	4	32	0

Bowling	Mat	Balls	Runs	Wkts	BBI	BBM	Ave	Econ	SR	5w	10
First-class	63	1165	732	9	2/11	2/11	81.33	3.76	129.4	0	0
List A	58	1122	1093	22	3/34	3/34	49.68	5.84	51.0	0	0
Twenty20	66	517	717	26	4/22	4/22	27.57	8.32	19.8	0	0

IAN COCKBAIN RHB RM

FULL NAME: Ian Andrew Cockbain
BORN: February 17, 1987, Liverpool, Lancashire
SQUAD NO: 28
HEIGHT: 6ft
NICKNAME: Coey, Mini
EDUCATION: Maghull High School; Liverpool John Moores University
TEAMS: Gloucestershire, Gloucestershire 2nd XI, Lancashire 2nd XI, Marylebone Cricket Club Young Cricketers
CAREER: First-class: 2011; List A: 2011; T20: 2011

BEST BATTING: 127 Gloucestershire vs Middlesex, Uxbridge, 2011
COUNTY CAP: 2011

FAMILY TIES? My father played for Lancashire back in the day
WHO WOULD PLAY YOU IN A FILM OF YOUR LIFE? Probably Channing Tatum, as the girls seem to like him a lot
CAREER HIGHLIGHTS? Scoring my maiden first-class hundred vs Middlesex
MOST MARKED CHARACTERISTIC? Id like to say my sense of humour but a few of the lads may disagree and say it's how I wind them all up
BEST PLAYER IN COUNTY CRICKET? I think Michael Klinger would be a fair shout on his performances last year
TIP FOR THE TOP? Chris Dent is starting to score some big runs so it will be exciting to see how he goes this season
DESERT ISLAND DISC? I'm loving the Bruno Mars album at the minute
CRICKETING HEROES? Shane Warne, Ricky Ponting and AB de Villiers
CRICKET RULE YOU'D CHANGE? We should have double plays like baseball. That would keep everyone on their toes
WHEN YOU RETIRE? Hopefully I'll be able to work with my old man
SURPRISING FACT? I'm a massive Everton fan
TWITTER FEED: @IanCoey

Batting	Mat	Inns	NO	Runs	HS	Ave	SR	100	50	Ct	St
First-class	28	47	3	1308	127	29.72	45.04	2	8	23	0
List A	36	32	7	781	79	31.24	95.47	0	6	25	0
Twenty20	29	26	3	529	78	23.00	112.55	0	3	13	0

Bowling	Mat	Balls	Runs	Wkts	BBI	BBM	Ave	Econ	SR	5w	10
First-class	28	-	-	-	-	-	-	-	-	-	-
List A	36	-	-	-	-	-	-	-	-	-	-
Twenty20	29	-	-	-	-	-	-	-	-	-	-

KYLE COETZER

RHB RM MVP96

FULL NAME: Kyle James Coetzer
BORN: April 14, 1984, Aberdeen, Scotland
SQUAD NO: 30
HEIGHT: 5ft 11in
NICKNAME: Costa, Meerkat, Shortbread
EDUCATION: Aberdeen Grammar School
TEAMS: Scotland, Durham, Northamptonshire, Scotland Under-19s, Western Province
CAREER: ODI: 2008; T20I: 2008; First-class: 2004; List A: 2003; T20: 2007

BEST BATTING: 219 Northamptonshire vs Leicestershire, Leicester, 2013
BEST BOWLING: 2-16 Scotland vs Kenya, Nairobi, 2009

FAMILY TIES? My elder brothers Shaun and Stuart both played some level of cricket for Scotland. My grandfather Sid Dugmore played for Eastern Province and so did my uncle Grant Dugmore, who has coached and played for Argentina. He is now the development officer for the Americas
WHO WOULD PLAY YOU IN A FILM OF YOUR LIFE? Will Ferrell
SUPERSTITIONS? I touch my bat in the crease after each ball
BEST PLAYER IN COUNTY CRICKET? Graham Onions
TIP FOR THE TOP? Olly Stone
CRICKETING HEROES? Brian McMillan, Allan Donald, Jacques Kallis, Robin Smith, Jack Brooks
WHEN YOU RETIRE? I'd like to get involved in coaching in some way
SURPRISING FACT? I was given a Meerkat toy by my ex-teammate Paul Wiseman who claimed I looked like it. It has never left my kitbag since, hence the nickname
TWITTER FEED: @MeerGoose11

Batting	Mat	Inns	NO	Runs	HS	Ave	SR	100	50	Ct	St
ODIs	15	15	1	670	133	47.85	81.50	1	5	8	0
T20Is	20	20	1	442	62	23.26	101.14	0	1	10	0
First-class	74	124	11	3833	219	33.92	48.20	8	16	36	0
List A	104	102	12	3169	133	35.21	79.42	5	19	38	0
Twenty20	66	63	7	1395	71*	24.91	104.33	0	3	22	0

Bowling	Mat	Balls	Runs	Wkts	BBI	BBM	Ave	Econ	SR	5w	10
ODIs	15	114	125	1	1/35	1/35	125.00	6.57	114.0	0	0
T20Is	20	66	71	5	3/25	3/25	14.20	6.45	13.2	0	0
First-class	74	414	247	4	2/16	2/16	61.75	3.57	103.5	0	0
List A	104	312	303	4	1/2	1/2	75.75	5.82	78.0	0	0
Twenty20	66	120	135	7	3/25	3/25	19.28	6.75	17.1	0	0

FREDDIE COLEMAN   RHB OB

FULL NAME: Freddie Robert John Coleman
BORN: December 15, 1991, Edinburgh, Midlothian, Scotland
SQUAD NO: 21
HEIGHT: 6ft
EDUCATION: Strathallan School; Oxford Brookes University
TEAMS: Scotland, Scotland Under-19s, Oxford MCCU, Warwickshire, Warwickshire 2nd XI
CAREER: ODI: 2013; T20I: 2013; First-class: 2012; List A: 2010; T20: 2013

BEST BATTING: 110 Oxford MCCU vs Worcestershire, Oxford, 2012

WHO WOULD PLAY YOU IN A FILM OF YOUR LIFE? Brad Pitt or Christian Bale
CAREER HIGHLIGHTS? My maiden first-class century and qualifying for the 2015 World Cup with Scotland
SUPERSTITIONS? I have a pair of lucky socks
MOST MARKED CHARACTERISTIC? The fact I'm a Scot without an accent
TIPS FOR THE TOP? Jonny Webb and Sam Hain
IF YOU WEREN'T A CRICKETER? I'd be working in business
DESERT ISLAND DISC? Red Hot Chili Peppers – By the Way
FAVOURITE TV? The Mentalist
CRICKETING HEROES? AB de Villiers
NON-CRICKETING HEROES? Ray Lewis
WHEN YOU RETIRE? I'd like to work in business
SURPRISING FACT? I played the bagpipes when I was 12
TWITTER FEED: @FRJcoleman

Batting	Mat	Inns	NO	Runs	HS	Ave	SR	100	50	Ct	St
ODIs	8	8	0	102	40	12.75	56.35	0	0	3	0
T20Is	1	1	0	9	9	9.00	69.23	0	0	0	0
First-class	7	12	0	219	110	18.25	49.32	1	0	4	0
List A	30	27	1	604	64*	23.23	72.94	0	4	7	0
Twenty20	4	1	0	9	9	9.00	69.23	0	0	1	0

Bowling	Mat	Balls	Runs	Wkts	BBI	BBM	Ave	Econ	SR	5w	10
ODIs	8	-	-	-	-	-	-	-	-	-	-
T20Is	1	-	-	-	-	-	-	-	-	-	-
First-class	7	-	-	-	-	-	-	-	-	-	-
List A	30	-	-	-	-	-	-	-	-	-	-
Twenty20	4	-	-	-	-	-	-	-	-	-	-

MATT COLES   LHB RFM W1 MVP54

HAMPSHIRE

FULL NAME: Matthew Thomas Coles
BORN: May 26, 1990, Maidstone, Kent
SQUAD NO: 26
HEIGHT: 6ft 3in
NICKNAME: Colesy
EDUCATION: Maplesden Noakes Secondary School
TEAMS: England Lions, Hampshire, Kent, Kent 2nd XI
CAREER: First-class: 2009; List A: 2009; T20: 2010

BEST BATTING: 103* Kent vs Yorkshire, Leeds, 2012
BEST BOWLING: 6-51 Kent vs Northamptonshire, Northampton, 2012
COUNTY CAP: 2012 (Kent)

CRICKETING HEROES? Andrew Flintoff
FAVOURITE BAND? Red Hot Chili Peppers
FAVOURITE FOOD? Roast lamb
FAVOURITE FILM? Anchorman
BEST CRICKETING MEMORY? Watching the 2005 Ashes
WORST HABIT? Talking when I shouldn't
TWITTER FEED: @MattColes_90

Batting	Mat	Inns	NO	Runs	HS	Ave	SR	100	50	Ct	St
First-class	55	74	13	1296	103*	21.24	64.63	1	6	18	0
List A	36	17	4	157	47	12.07	106.80	0	0	12	0
Twenty20	34	23	4	174	40	9.15	129.85	0	0	16	0

Bowling	Mat	Balls	Runs	Wkts	BBI	BBM	Ave	Econ	SR	5w	10
First-class	55	7628	4584	154	6/51	10/154	29.76	3.60	49.5	7	1
List A	36	1225	1240	55	6/32	6/32	22.54	6.07	22.2	1	0
Twenty20	34	582	883	28	3/14	3/14	31.53	9.10	20.7	0	0

PAUL COLLINGWOOD — RHB RM R2

FULL NAME: Paul David Collingwood
BORN: May 26, 1976, Shotley Bridge, Co Durham
SQUAD NO: 5
HEIGHT: 5ft 11in
NICKNAME: Colly, Weed, Wobbles
EDUCATION: Blackfyne Comprehensive School; Derwentside College
TEAMS: England, Delhi Daredevils, Durham, Impi, Perth Scorchers, Rajasthan Royals
CAREER: Test: 2003; ODI: 2001; T20I: 2005; First-class: 1996; List A: 1995; T20: 2005

DURHAM

BEST BATTING: 206 England vs Australia, Adelaide, 2006
BEST BOWLING: 5-52 Durham vs Somerset, Stockton-on-Tees, 2005
BENEFIT YEAR: 2007

FAMILY TIES? My dad and brother played for Shotley Bridge and my mother was and still is their biggest fan
CAREER HIGHLIGHTS? Playing for England, winning the World T20 and the three Ashes wins
SUPERSTITIONS? Putting my left pad on first and doing a little jig as I walk out to bat, but it's getting harder as it involves squatting three times!
MOST MARKED CHARACTERISTIC? Tenacity
TIPS FOR THE TOP? Ben Stokes, Joe Root, Scott Borthwick
BIGGEST DRESSING DOWN YOU'VE RECEIVED? Michael Roseberry at Hove in 1997
NON-CRICKETING HEROES? Luke Donald
WHEN YOU RETIRE? I'd like to coach, commentate or play golf every day if I win the lottery
TWITTER FEED: @Colly622

Batting	Mat	Inns	NO	Runs	HS	Ave	SR	100	50	Ct	St
Tests	68	115	10	4259	206	40.56	46.44	10	20	96	0
ODIs	197	181	37	5092	120*	35.36	76.98	5	26	108	0
T20Is	35	33	2	583	79	18.80	127.01	0	3	14	0
First-class	233	400	34	13139	206	35.89		26	69	271	0
List A	394	368	65	10189	120*	33.62		8	57	198	0
Twenty20	92	79	7	1349	79	18.73	120.98	0	6	26	0

Bowling	Mat	Balls	Runs	Wkts	BBI	BBM	Ave	Econ	SR	5w	10
Tests	68	1905	1018	17	3/23	3/35	59.88	3.20	112.0	0	0
ODIs	197	5186	4294	111	6/31	6/31	38.68	4.96	46.7	1	0
T20Is	35	222	329	16	4/22	4/22	20.56	8.89	13.8	0	0
First-class	233	10574	5317	134	5/52		39.67	3.01	78.9	1	0
List A	394	10191	8256	242	6/31	6/31	34.11	4.86	42.1	1	0
Twenty20	92	823	1007	59	5/6	5/6	17.06	7.34	13.9	2	0

NICK COMPTON

RHB OB R4

FULL NAME: Nicholas Richard Denis Compton
BORN: June 26, 1983, Durban, South Africa
SQUAD NO: 3
HEIGHT: 6ft 2in
NICKNAME: Compo, Ledge, Cheser
EDUCATION: Hilton College, South Africa; Harrow School; Durham University
TEAMS: England, England Lions, Mashonaland Eagles, Middlesex, Somerset, Worcestershire
CAREER: Test: 2012; First-class: 2004; List A: 2001; T20: 2004

BEST BATTING: 254* Somerset vs Durham, Chester-le-Street, 2011
BEST BOWLING: 1-1 Somerset vs Hampshire, Southampton, 2010
COUNTY CAPS: 2006 (Middlesex); 2011 (Somerset)

FAMILY TIES? My grandfather Denis played cricket for Middlesex and England, my great-uncle Leslie played cricket for Middlesex, my father Richard played first-class cricket in South Africa and my uncle Patrick played a few games too
CAREER HIGHLIGHTS? My maiden first-class century at Lord's – getting there with a six! My Somerset county cap and being selected for the England Lions tour to Bangladesh 2007. My career best 254* vs Durham
SUPERSTITIONS? I only walk over the white line after my batting partner – I like to feel like I've given them the respect
CRICKETING HEROES? Jacques Kallis, Rahul Dravid and Brian Lara
BEST PLAYER IN COUNTY CRICKET? Marcus Trescothick
TIPS FOR THE TOP? Jos Buttler, Craig Meschede and James Vince
IF YOU WEREN'T A CRICKETER? Trying my hand at radio – I was told I had a face for it!
FAVOURITE FILM? The Matrix, Gladiator, Lock Stock And Two Smoking Barrels
TWITTER FEED: @thecompdog

Batting	Mat	Inns	NO	Runs	HS	Ave	SR	100	50	Ct	St
Tests	9	17	2	479	117	31.93	34.68	2	1	4	0
First-class	122	213	28	8129	254*	43.94	47.37	20	39	61	0
List A	101	92	20	2802	131	38.91	80.21	6	17	42	0
Twenty20	72	60	6	1055	74	19.53	109.89	0	5	28	0

Bowling	Mat	Balls	Runs	Wkts	BBI	BBM	Ave	Econ	SR	5w	10
Tests	9	-	-	-	-	-	-	-	-	-	-
First-class	122	164	215	3	1/1	1/1	71.66	7.86	54.6	0	0
List A	101	61	53	1	1/0	1/0	53.00	5.21	61.0	0	0
Twenty20	72	-	-	-	-	-	-	-	-	-	-

ALASTAIR COOK — LHB OB R5

FULL NAME: Alastair Nathan Cook
BORN: December 25, 1984, Gloucester
SQUAD NO: 26
HEIGHT: 6ft 2in
NICKNAME: Cookie, Chef
EDUCATION: Bedford School
TEAMS: England, Bedfordshire, England Lions, England Under-19s, Essex, Marylebone Cricket Club
CAREER: Test: 2006; ODI: 2006; T20I: 2007; First-class: 2003; List A: 2003; T20: 2005

BEST BATTING: 294 England vs India, Birmingham, 2011
BEST BOWLING: 3-13 Essex vs Northamptonshire, Chelmsford, 2005
COUNTY CAP: 2005; **BENEFIT YEAR:** 2014

FAMILY TIES? My dad played for the local club side and was a very good opening bat, while my mum made the teas. My brothers played for Maldon Cricket Club
CAREER HIGHLIGHTS? The Ashes wins home and away, becoming the world's No.1 Test team, Essex winning the 50-over competition and making my England debut
CRICKETING HEROES? Graham Gooch – I watched him playing for Essex at the County Ground as a kid
BEST PLAYER IN COUNTY CRICKET? Ryan ten Doeschate and James Foster
TIP FOR THE TOP? Ben Foakes
WHEN RAIN STOPS PLAY? Watching the rain!
FAVOURITE TV? Gavin And Stacey
DREAM HOLIDAY? Maldives or skiing

Batting	Mat	Inns	NO	Runs	HS	Ave	SR	100	50	Ct	St
Tests	102	183	10	8047	294	46.51	46.99	25	35	96	0
ODIs	77	77	3	2825	137	38.17	78.58	5	18	28	0
T20Is	4	4	0	61	26	15.25	112.96	0	0	1	0
First-class	198	353	26	15401	294	47.09	51.45	45	75	187	0
List A	133	131	9	4700	137	38.52	79.37	9	28	53	0
Twenty20	30	28	2	862	100*	33.15	128.84	1	5	12	0

Bowling	Mat	Balls	Runs	Wkts	BBI	BBM	Ave	Econ	SR	5w	10
Tests	102	6	1	0	-	-	-	1.00	-	0	0
ODIs	77	-	-	-	-	-	-	-	-	-	-
T20Is	4	-	-	-	-	-	-	-	-	-	-
First-class	198	270	205	6	3/13	-	34.16	4.55	45.0	0	0
List A	133	18	10	0	-	-	-	3.33	-	0	0
Twenty20	30	-	-	-	-	-	-	-	-	-	-

CHRIS COOKE
RHB WK

FULL NAME: Christopher Barry Cooke
BORN: May 30, 1986, Johannesburg, Gauteng, South Africa
SQUAD NO: 24
HEIGHT: 5ft 11in
NICKNAME: Minty, Shapeless, Cookie
EDUCATION: Bishops; University of Cape Town (UCT)
TEAMS: Glamorgan, Glamorgan 2nd XI, Hampshire 2nd XI, Western Province
CAREER: First-class: 2009; List A: 2009; T20: 2011

BEST BATTING: 92 Glamorgan vs Hampshire, Southampton, 2013

WHO WOULD PLAY YOU IN A FILM OF YOUR LIFE? Christian Bale
CAREER HIGHLIGHTS? Scoring my maiden List A hundred at Newlands. Hitting my second, third and fourth balls for six on my Glamorgan T20 debut. Scoring my first hundred for the county in a 40-over match at Taunton, which was also the fourth highest one-day score for Glamorgan
SUPERSTITIONS? Batting: left pad on first. Keeping: right pad on first
MOST MARKED CHARACTERISTIC? My back-lift probably!
BEST PLAYER IN COUNTY CRICKET? Matt Prior
TIPS FOR THE TOP? Aneurin Donald, Rory Smith, Andrew Salter, Dave Lloyd
IF YOU WEREN'T A CRICKETER? I'd be an international DJ
CRICKETING HEROES? Kevin Pietersen, Hylton Ackerman
ACCOMPLISHMENTS? A degree in Psychology and Media from UCT
WHEN YOU RETIRE? I'd like to have apartments in Camps Bay and Spain and play lots of golf
SURPRISING FACTS? I'm allergic to shellfish, I'm a massive Chelsea fan and I have to have the volume on an even number
FANTASY SLIP CORDON? Keeper: Shane Warne, 1st: José Mourinho, 2nd: Georgie Thompson, 3rd: Myself, Gully: Jimmy Carr
TWITTER FEED: @Cooky_24

Batting	Mat	Inns	NO	Runs	HS	Ave	SR	100	50	Ct	St
First-class	13	22	2	580	92	29.00	46.32	0	3	14	1
List A	45	42	5	1336	137*	36.10	101.21	2	7	20	2
Twenty20	31	28	3	483	57	19.32	137.60	0	2	15	0

Bowling	Mat	Balls	Runs	Wkts	BBI	BBM	Ave	Econ	SR	5w	10
First-class	13	-	-	-	-	-	-	-	-	-	-
List A	45	-	-	-	-	-	-	-	-	-	-
Twenty20	31	-	-	-	-	-	-	-	-	-	-

GREG CORK — RHB LMF

FULL NAME: Gregory Teodor Gerald Cork
BORN: September 29, 1994, Derby
SQUAD NO: 14
HEIGHT: 6ft 1in
NICKNAME: Corky
EDUCATION: Denstone College; Leeds Metropolitan University
TEAMS: Derbyshire, Derbyshire 2nd XI, Derbyshire Under-13s, Derbyshire Under-14s, Derbyshire Under-15s, Derbyshire Under-17s
CAREER: Yet to make first-team debut

DERBYSHIRE

FAMILY TIES? My father is [former England allrounder] Dominic Cork
WHO WOULD PLAY YOU IN A FILM OF YOUR LIFE? Leonardo DiCaprio
CAREER HIGHLIGHTS? Signing my first professional cricket contract in 2013 and playing at Lord's for MCC
SUPERSTITIONS? I remove all the bowling machine marks off my bat
MOST MARKED CHARACTERISTIC? Voicing my opinions
BEST PLAYER IN COUNTY CRICKET? Wayne Madsen
TIP FOR THE TOP? Ben Slater
IF YOU WEREN'T A CRICKETER? I'm currently studying Physical Education at university
DESERT ISLAND DISC? Destiny's Child – Survivor
FAVOURITE TV? Made In Chelsea
CRICKETING HEROES? AB de Villiers
NON-CRICKETING HEROES? Thierry Henry and Muhammad Ali
ACCOMPLISHMENTS? Achieving ABC in my A-Levels
WHEN YOU RETIRE? I'd like to become a sports pundit or live abroad
SURPRISING FACT? I am one quarter Italian and one quarter Polish
FANTASY SLIP CORDON? Keeper – Joey Essex (his banter would always crack the cordon up), 1st: Ron Burgundy (TV legend), 2nd: Lee Evans (he could cheer the cordon up in the last session), 3rd: Justin Timberlake (I would love to just speak to him and ask him to sing me a few of his classics), Gully: Me
TWITTER FEED: @Greg_Cork

DEAN COSKER

RHB SLA W1 MVP63

FULL NAME: Dean Andrew Cosker
BORN: January 7, 1978, Weymouth, Dorset
SQUAD NO: 23
HEIGHT: 5ft 11in
NICKNAME: Lurks
EDUCATION: Millfield School
TEAMS: England A, Glamorgan
CAREER: First-class: 1996; List A: 1996; T20: 2003

BEST BATTING: 52 Glamorgan vs Gloucestershire, Bristol, 2005
BEST BOWLING: 6-91 Glamorgan vs Essex, Cardiff, 2009
COUNTY CAP: 2000; **BENEFIT YEAR:** 2010

CAREER HIGHLIGHTS? My debut at Glamorgan in 1997, my Championship medal in 1997, my England A caps and winning trophies with Glamorgan
CRICKET MOMENTS TO FORGET? Every time I bowl from the Taff End at the SWALEC Stadium in T20 when the wind is with the batsman
FAVOURITE BAND? Bananarama
CRICKETERS PARTICULARLY ADMIRED? Mike Kasprowicz, Matt Elliott, Matt Maynard, Robert Croft, Steve Watkin, Graham Thorpe
NOTES: Leading wicket-taker on the England A tour of Zimbabwe and South Africa in 1998/99. Third youngest Glamorgan player to receive his county cap. Passed 500 first-class wickets in 2012
TWITTER FEED: @DCosker23

Batting	Mat	Inns	NO	Runs	HS	Ave	SR	100	50	Ct	St
First-class	225	295	85	3017	52	14.36		0	1	133	0
List A	235	126	55	804	50*	11.32		0	1	89	0
Twenty20	90	29	20	143	21*	15.88	89.93	0	0	26	0

Bowling	Mat	Balls	Runs	Wkts	BBI	BBM	Ave	Econ	SR	5w	10
First-class	225	41739	19849	547	6/91		36.28	2.85	76.3	9	1
List A	235	9847	7900	240	5/54	5/54	32.91	4.81	41.0	1	0
Twenty20	90	1595	2048	68	3/11	3/11	30.11	7.70	23.4	0	0

BEN COTTON   RHB RMF

FULL NAME: Benjamin David Cotton
BORN: September 13, 1993, Stoke-on-Trent, Staffordshire
SQUAD NO: 36
HEIGHT: 6ft 6in
NICKNAME: Cotts, Lurchio
EDUCATION: Clayton Hall Business and Language College, Newcastle-under-Lyme; Stoke-on-Trent Sixth Form College
TEAMS: Derbyshire 2nd XI, Staffordshire Under-17s
CAREER: Yet to make first-team debut

FAMILY TIES? Both of my grandads played cricket and my dad still plays now

WHO WOULD PLAY YOU IN A FILM OF YOUR LIFE? Liam Neeson, for how he played his character in the film Taken

CAREER HIGHLIGHTS? Getting my summer contract with Derbyshire would be the highlight so far but hopefully there are many more to come

SUPERSTITIONS? Things that go on the left-side first: left boot, left pad, etc

MOST MARKED CHARACTERISTIC? Being rather large, and my big feet

BEST PLAYER IN COUNTY CRICKET? I would say that Graham Onions is the best bowler on the circuit at the moment. He takes wickets for fun

TIP FOR THE TOP? Ben Stokes. He has just shown us what he can do at Test-match level and I think he can become a very good player for England

IF YOU WEREN'T A CRICKETER? Sports coaching or PE teaching

DESERT ISLAND DISC? Arctic Monkeys – Whatever People Say I Am, That's What I'm Not

FAVOURITE TV? The Inbetweeners

CRICKET RULE YOU'D CHANGE? I'd make tea breaks longer

CRICKETING HEROES? I would say Andrew Flintoff because he was a great player but also because he had great passion for the game. And Glenn McGrath, one of the greatest seam bowlers I've seen

NON-CRICKETING HEROES? Ian Poulter – he shows great passion for the game

WHEN YOU RETIRE? I'd like to become a groundsman

FANTASY SLIP CORDON? Keeper: James Corden, 1st: Peter Kay, 2nd: Myself, 3rd: Noel Gallagher, Gully: Keith Lemon

TWITTER FEED: @Cotts1993

PAUL COUGHLIN

RHB RM

FULL NAME: Paul Coughlin
BORN: October 23, 1992, Sunderland, Co Durham
SQUAD NO: 29
EDUCATION: St Robert of Newminster Catholic Comprehensive School, Washington, Co Durham
TEAMS: Durham, Durham 2nd XI, Durham Academy, Durham Under-17s
CAREER: First-class: 2012; List A: 2012

BEST BATTING: 29* Durham vs Australia A, Chester-le-Street, 2012
BEST BOWLING: 1-26 Durham vs Australia A, Chester-le-Street, 2012

TWITTER FEED: @Coughlin92
NOTES: A bowling allrounder who graduated from the Durham Academy to make his first-class debut against Australia A in August 2012, Coughlin has also appeared for Northumberland in the Minor Counties Championship and turns out for South Northumberland in the North East Premier League. He made his List A debut for Durham against Hampshire in 2012 but did not feature in the first-team in 2013

Batting	Mat	Inns	NO	Runs	HS	Ave	SR	100	50	Ct	St
First-class	1	2	1	32	29*	32.00	58.18	0	0	1	0
List A	1	-	-	-	-	-	-	-	-	0	0

Bowling	Mat	Balls	Runs	Wkts	BBI	BBM	Ave	Econ	SR	5w	10
First-class	1	60	46	1	1/26	1/46	46.00	4.60	60.0	0	0
List A	1	6	15	0	-	-	-	15.00	-	0	0

FABIAN COWDREY

RHB SLA

FULL NAME: Fabian Kruuse Cowdrey
BORN: January 30, 1993, Canterbury, Kent
SQUAD NO: 30
HEIGHT: 6ft
NICKNAME: Cow, Fabs, Fabes, Calf
EDUCATION: Tonbridge School; Cardiff
Metropolitan University
TEAMS: Cardiff MCCU, Kent, Kent 2nd XI
CAREER: First-class: 2013; List A: 2013; T20:
2013

KENT

BEST BATTING: 62 Cardiff MCCU vs Glamorgan, Cardiff, 2013

FAMILY TIES? My grandfather [Colin], father [Chris] and uncle [Graham] all played for Kent,
with my grandfather and father both captaining England
CAREER HIGHLIGHTS? Winning the 2nd XI Championship by one wicket at Grace Road and
becoming a professional in late 2011
BEST PLAYER IN COUNTY CRICKET? Nick Compton
TIPS FOR THE TOP? I'll stick with the Kent boys! Daniel Bell-Drummond and Adam Ball
IF YOU WEREN'T A CRICKETER? I'd be writing songs, cleaning the dishes and probably
studying harder
CRICKETING HEROES? Sir Vivian Richards, Kevin Pietersen
NON-CRICKETING HEROES? Will Smith, Mike Tyson
ACCOMPLISHMENTS? Getting into university and playing first-team hockey and rackets at
school
WHEN YOU RETIRE? I'd like to be a motivator, own a business and be a renowned
songwriter
SURPRISING FACT? I am unbelievably scared of heights!
FANTASY SLIP CORDON? Keeper: Bugs Bunny, 1st: Charlie Sheen, 2nd: David Lloyd, 3rd: Me,
Gully: Forrest Gump
TWITTER FEED: @fkcowdrey

Batting	Mat	Inns	NO	Runs	HS	Ave	SR	100	50	Ct	St
First-class	2	3	1	100	62	50.00	60.24	0	1	0	0
List A	4	4	2	110	52*	55.00	102.80	0	1	0	0
Twenty20	6	6	2	173	50	43.25	118.49	0	1	0	0

Bowling	Mat	Balls	Runs	Wkts	BBI	BBM	Ave	Econ	SR	5w	10
First-class	2	96	70	0	-	-	-	4.37	-	0	0
List A	4	24	18	0	-	-	-	4.50	-	0	0
Twenty20	6	48	67	1	1/30	1/30	67.00	8.37	48.0	0	0

BEN COX

RHB WK

FULL NAME: Oliver Benjamin Cox
BORN: February 2, 1992, Wordsley, Stourbridge, Worcestershire
SQUAD NO: 10
HEIGHT: 5ft 10in
EDUCATION: Bromsgrove School, Bromsgrove
TEAMS: Worcestershire, Worcestershire 2nd XI
CAREER: First-class: 2009; List A: 2010; T20: 2010

BEST BATTING: 65 Worcestershire vs Hampshire, Worcester, 2013

CAREER HIGHLIGHTS? My debut vs Somerset whilst I was still at school in 2009
SUPERSTITIONS? I put my left pad on first and I don't wash my keeping inners!
CRICKETING HEROES? Steve Rhodes and Steve Davies
NON-CRICKETING HEROES? Jonny Wilkinson for his determination to succeed
BEST PLAYER IN COUNTY CRICKET? Marcus Trescothick
TIPS FOR THE TOP? Christian Davies, Ross Whiteley
IF YOU WEREN'T A CRICKETER? I'd hopefully be playing rugby for Worcester Warriors after a couple of hard years in the gym!
WHEN RAIN STOPS PLAY? Sleep, Football Manager, iPad, receiving abuse about my hairline
FAVOURITE TV? Friday Night Lights
FAVOURITE FILM? The Blind Side, Transformers
DREAM HOLIDAY? Cape Town
ACCOMPLISHMENTS? England U18 rugby trials and beating Millfield School 25-20
SURPRISING FACTS? I was close to quitting cricket to play rugby. I was once on the books at West Bromwich Albion. I trialled with Manu Tuilagi
FANTASY SLIP CORDON? Keeper: Owen Farrell, 1st: David Beckham, 2nd: Will Beer, 3rd: Lee Evans, Gully: Mila Kunis
TWITTER FEED? @BenCox10

Batting	Mat	Inns	NO	Runs	HS	Ave	SR	100	50	Ct	St
First-class	25	44	11	719	65	21.78	53.97	0	4	67	3
List A	26	17	5	164	34*	13.66	93.18	0	0	18	3
Twenty20	18	14	5	152	37	16.88	122.58	0	0	7	3

Bowling	Mat	Balls	Runs	Wkts	BBI	BBM	Ave	Econ	SR	5w	10
First-class	25	-	-	-	-	-	-	-	-	-	-
List A	26	-	-	-	-	-	-	-	-	-	-
Twenty20	18	-	-	-	-	-	-	-	-	-	-

TOM CRADDOCK

RHB LB

FULL NAME: Thomas Richard Craddock
BORN: July 13, 1989, Huddersfield
SQUAD NO: 20
HEIGHT: 5ft 9in
NICKNAME: Crads
EDUCATION: Holmfith High School; Huddersfield New College; Leeds Metropolitan University
TEAMS: Essex, Essex 2nd XI, Gloucestershire 2nd XI, Leeds/Bradford MCCU, Marylebone Cricket Club Universities, Unicorns
CAREER: First-class: 2011; List A: 2011; T20: 2011

ESSEX

BEST BATTING: 21 Essex vs Leicestershire, Southend, 2011
BEST BOWLING: 5-96 Essex vs Derbyshire, Chelmsford, 2012

FAMILY TIES? My mother's side of the family all played and my grandfather was a league umpire and my mum's cousin played for Yorkshire
CAREER HIGHLIGHTS? Making my first-class debut against Sri Lanka, my County Championship debut against Northamptonshire and taking my first first-class five-fer against Derbyshire
BEST PLAYER IN COUNTY CRICKET? Chris Woakes
TIP FOR THE TOP? Ben Foakes
IF YOU WEREN'T A CRICKETER? I completed a degree at university so I'd probably be looking for a nine-to-five job
BIGGEST DRESSING DOWN YOU'VE RECEIVED? For getting out on a hat-trick ball against Sri Lanka on my first-class debut
CRICKETING HEROES? Shane Warne, Ricky Ponting
SURPRISING FACT? I didn't start playing cricket until I was 15
FANTASY SLIP CORDON? Keeper: Mila Kunis (speaks for itself), 1st: Denzel Washington (favourite actor), 2nd: Karl Pilkington (favourite comedian), 3rd: Shane Warne (cricket idol)
TWITTER FEED: @tcradd20

Batting	Mat	Inns	NO	Runs	HS	Ave	SR	100	50	Ct	St
First-class	17	22	7	135	21	9.00	29.41	0	0	3	0
List A	7	5	5	13	5*	-	32.50	0	0	2	0
Twenty20	2	-	-	-	-	-	-	-	-	3	0

Bowling	Mat	Balls	Runs	Wkts	BBI	BBM	Ave	Econ	SR	5w	10
First-class	17	2239	1198	40	5/96	6/71	29.95	3.21	55.9	1	0
List A	7	282	220	5	2/38	2/38	44.00	4.68	56.4	0	0
Twenty20	2	12	23	0	-	-	-	11.50	-	0	0

STEVEN CROFT RHB RMF/OB

FULL NAME: Steven John Croft
BORN: October 11, 1984, Blackpool, Lancashire
SQUAD NO: 15
HEIGHT: 5ft 11in
NICKNAME: Crofty
EDUCATION: Highfield High School, Blackpool; Myerscough College
TEAMS: Auckland, Lancashire, Lancashire Cricket Board, Northern Districts
CAREER: First-class: 2005; List A: 2003; T20: 2006

BEST BATTING: 154* Lancashire vs Surrey, Guildford, 2012
BEST BOWLING: 6-41 Lancashire vs Worcestershire, Manchester, 2012
COUNTY CAP: 2010

FAMILY TIES? My family moved to Sri Lanka was I was seven years old for three years and I played nothing but cricket out there. My father was a bad leg-spinner
CAREER HIGHLIGHTS? Winning the County Championship with Lancashire in 2011 and hitting the winning runs. Being included in the 2012 provisional World T20 squad
SUPERSTITIONS? Putting my left pad on first
MOST MARKED CHARACTERISTIC? I'm competitive in everything I do
BEST PLAYER IN COUNTY CRICKET? Graham Onions and Simon Kerrigan
TIPS FOR THE TOP? Liam Livingstone and Arron Lilley
CRICKETING HEROES? Andrew Flintoff, Jacques Kallis and Stuart Law
ACCOMPLISHMENTS? Finding someone to marry me. Qualifying as a personal trainer
WHEN YOU RETIRE? I'll help coach and train other players
SURPRISING FACT? I run a personal training business with ex-Lancashire player Steven Cheetham – www.ProSportPT.co.uk
CRICKET RULE YOU'D CHANGE? The Duckworth-Lewis method. I don't know how though – tough one…
TWITTER FEED: @Stevenjcroft

Batting	Mat	Inns	NO	Runs	HS	Ave	SR	100	50	Ct	St
First-class	102	159	15	4507	154*	31.29	52.01	6	27	88	0
List A	114	103	20	2888	107	34.79		1	21	55	0
Twenty20	104	96	17	2431	88	30.77	122.96	0	14	61	0

Bowling	Mat	Balls	Runs	Wkts	BBI	BBM	Ave	Econ	SR	5w	10
First-class	102	3491	2047	51	6/41	9/105	40.13	3.51	68.4	1	0
List A	114	1960	1783	51	4/24	4/24	34.96	5.45	38.4	0	0
Twenty20	104	675	928	29	3/6	3/6	32.00	8.24	23.2	0	0

FULL NAME: Steven Paul Crook
BORN: May 28, 1983, Adelaide, Australia
SQUAD NO: 25
HEIGHT: 5ft 11in
NICKNAME: Crookster, Crooky, Weirdo
EDUCATION: Rostrevor College
TEAMS: Lancashire, Middlesex, Northamptonshire, South Australia Under-17s, South Australia Under-19s
CAREER: First-class: 2003; List A: 2003; T20: 2004

NORTHAMPTONSHIRE

BEST BATTING: 97 Northamptonshire vs Yorkshire, Northampton, 2005
BEST BOWLING: 5-48 Middlesex vs Lancashire, Lord's, 2012

FAMILY TIES? My brother [Andrew] played for South Australia, Lancashire and Northants
CRICKETING HEROES? Chris Rogers
NON-CRICKETING HEROES? Chris Martin from Coldplay
BEST PLAYER IN COUNTY CRICKET? Jack Brooks
TIP FOR THE TOP? Adam Rossington
IF YOU WEREN'T A CRICKETER? I'd be a bin man
WHEN RAIN STOPS PLAY? I'd be sleeping
FAVOURITE TV? CSI
FAVOURITE FILM? Point Break
FAVOURITE BOOK? Where's Wally?
DREAM HOLIDAY? Phuket
ACCOMPLISHMENTS? Starting my own business
SURPRISING SKILL? I sing opera
GUILTY PLEASURES? Rick Astley
SURPRISING FACT? My dad had a No.1 hit in Australia

Batting	Mat	Inns	NO	Runs	HS	Ave	SR	100	50	Ct	St
First-class	66	81	11	2092	97	29.88	73.55	0	16	21	0
List A	62	44	4	755	100	18.87	99.60	1	4	15	0
Twenty20	66	44	9	565	63	16.14	136.47	0	1	12	0

Bowling	Mat	Balls	Runs	Wkts	BBI	BBM	Ave	Econ	SR	5w	10
First-class	66	8247	5327	146	5/48		36.48	3.87	56.4	3	0
List A	62	2260	2158	66	5/36	5/36	32.69	5.72	34.2	1	0
Twenty20	66	811	1123	42	3/21	3/21	26.73	8.30	19.3	0	0

TOM CURRAN

RHB RFM

SURREY

FULL NAME: Thomas Kevin Curran
BORN: March 12, 1995, Cape Town, South Africa
SQUAD NO: 59
HEIGHT: 6ft
NICKNAME: TC
EDUCATION: Hilton College, Durban
TEAMS: KwaZulu-Natal Inland Under-19s, Surrey, Surrey 2nd XI
CAREER: List A: 2013

FAMILY TIES? My dad [Kevin Jr] and grandad [Kevin Sr] both played for Zimbabwe
WHO WOULD PLAY YOU IN A FILM OF YOUR LIFE? Leonardo DiCaprio
CAREER HIGHLIGHTS? My five wickets against Scotland for Surrey in last year's YB40
MOST MARKED CHARACTERISTIC? My lid
BEST PLAYER IN COUNTY CRICKET? Graeme Smith
TIPS FOR THE TOP? Jack Winslade and Dom Sibley
IF YOU WEREN'T A CRICKETER? I'd be a lifeguard
DESERT ISLAND DISC? Every Eminem album. I wouldn't be able to choose just one so I'd take them all
FAVOURITE TV? Ross Kemp On Gangs
CRICKETING HEROES? Kevin Pietersen, Brett Lee
NON-CRICKETING HEROES? James Hunt
ACCOMPLISHMENTS? Passing my AS Level exams
WHEN YOU RETIRE? I'd like to become a professional fisherman
SURPRISING FACT? I'm not very good at filling out questionnaires. As you can see
FANTASY SLIP CORDON? Keeper: Snoop Dogg, 1st: Me, 2nd: Blake Lively, 3rd: Jack Winslade, Gully: Ricky Fowler
TWITTER FEED? @TommyCurran159

Batting	Mat	Inns	NO	Runs	HS	Ave	SR	100	50	Ct	St
List A	5	4	1	3	1*	1.00	18.75	0	0	2	0

Bowling	Mat	Balls	Runs	Wkts	BBI	BBM	Ave	Econ	SR	5w	10
List A	5	193	202	9	5/34	5/34	22.44	6.27	21.4	1	0

BRETT D'OLIVEIRA   RHB LB

FULL NAME: Brett Louis D'Oliveira
BORN: February 28, 1992, Worcester
SQUAD NO: 15
HEIGHT: 5ft 8in
NICKNAME: Dolly, Bdoll
EDUCATION: Blessed Edwards High School; Worcestershire Sixth Form College
TEAMS: Worcestershire, Worcestershire 2nd XI, Worcestershire Under-13s, Worcestershire Under-14s, Worcestershire Under-15s, Worcestershire Under-17s
CAREER: First-class: 2012; List A: 2011; T20: 2012

BEST BATTING: 19 Worcestershire vs Warwickshire, Birmingham, 2012

FAMILY TIES? My dad Damian played for Worcestershire and is the current Academy and 2nd XI director. My grandfather Basil played for Worcestershire and England
WHO WOULD PLAY YOU IN A FILM OF YOUR LIFE? Denzel Washington (no chance!)
CAREER HIGHLIGHTS? Signing a professional contract with Worcestershire, making my debut in all forms for Worcestershire and playing in the T20 quarter-finals
SUPERSTITIONS? I always put my left pad on first and I always look to the sky and say a few words on my way out to bat
MOST MARKED CHARACTERISTIC? Enthusiasm
BEST PLAYER IN COUNTY CRICKET? Marcus Trescothick
IF YOU WEREN'T A CRICKETER? I'd be trying to get involved in the coaching side of things
DESERT ISLAND DISC? Drake – Take Care
FAVOURITE TV? The Fresh Prince Of Bel-Air
CRICKETING HEROES? Shane Warne, Sachin Tendulkar
NON-CRICKETING HEROES? Nelson Mandela
ACCOMPLISHMENTS? My national diploma in Sport and Exercise Science
WHEN YOU RETIRE? I'll play a lot of golf
TWITTER FEED: @Bdolly09

Batting	Mat	Inns	NO	Runs	HS	Ave	SR	100	50	Ct	St
First-class	3	6	0	62	19	10.33	42.46	0	0	0	0
List A	20	14	7	149	28	21.28	103.47	0	0	6	0
Twenty20	16	6	6	32	9*	-	160.00	0	0	1	0

Bowling	Mat	Balls	Runs	Wkts	BBI	BBM	Ave	Econ	SR	5w	10
First-class	3	258	198	0	-	-	-	4.60	-	0	0
List A	20	582	537	15	3/35	3/35	35.80	5.53	38.8	0	0
Twenty20	16	144	195	5	3/20	3/20	39.00	8.12	28.8	0	0

ALEX DAVIES   RHB WK

FULL NAME: Alexander Luke Davies
BORN: August 23, 1994, Darwen, Lancashire
SQUAD NO: 17
HEIGHT: 5ft 8in
NICKNAME: AD, Davo
EDUCATION: Queen Elizabeth's Grammar
School, Blackburn
TEAMS: England Under-19s, Lancashire,
Lancashire 2nd XI, Lancashire Cricket
Academy, Lancashire Under-13s, Lancashire
Under-14s, Lancashire Under-15s,
Lancashire Under-17s
CAREER: First-class: 2012; List A: 2011

BEST BATTING: 30* Lancashire vs Leicestershire, Manchester, 2013

FAMILY TIES? My dad played club cricket. I watched him from a very young age
WHO WOULD PLAY YOU IN A FILM OF YOUR LIFE? Leonardo DiCaprio or Adam Sandler
CAREER HIGHLIGHTS? My Lancashire List A debut at 16. My first-class debut, representing
England U19 in a World Cup and my first professional contract (all when I was 17)
SUPERSTITIONS? Everything left goes on first: shoe, pad, foot on field, etc
MOST MARKED CHARACTERISTIC? Lack of height!
BEST PLAYER IN COUNTY CRICKET? Simon Kerrigan
TIPS FOR THE TOP? Gavin Griffiths, Arron Lilley, Liam Livingstone, Luis Reece
IF YOU WEREN'T A CRICKETER? I'd be at university
DESERT ISLAND DISC? Avicii – True
FAVOURITE TV? Prison Break, Breaking Bad
CRICKETING HEROES? Sachin Tendulkar, Adam Gilchrist, AB de Villiers
NON-CRICKETING HEROES? Tiger Woods, Jonny Wilkinson
ACCOMPLISHMENTS? Playing football for Blackburn Rovers
WHEN YOU RETIRE? I'll play golf and travel
SURPRISING FACT? I can bowl with both arms
FANTASY SLIP CORDON? Keeper: Myself, 1st: Brian Potter (Peter Kay), 2nd: Mario Balotelli,
3rd: David Beckham, Gully: Happy Gilmore
TWITTER FEED: @aldavies23

Batting	Mat	Inns	NO	Runs	HS	Ave	SR	100	50	Ct	St
First-class	4	3	1	58	30*	29.00	53.21	0	0	5	0
List A	2	2	1	19	13	19.00	70.37	0	0	2	0

Bowling	Mat	Balls	Runs	Wkts	BBI	BBM	Ave	Econ	SR	5w	10
First-class	4	-	-	-	-	-	-	-	-	-	-
List A	2	-	-	-	-	-	-	-	-	-	-

MARK DAVIES
RHB RMF W1

FULL NAME: Anthony Mark Davies
BORN: October 4, 1980, Stockton-on-Tees, Co Durham
SQUAD NO: 31
HEIGHT: 6ft 2in
NICKNAME: Davo, Bob
EDUCATION: Northfield School, Billingham; Stockton Sixth Form College
TEAMS: Durham, Durham 2nd XI, Durham Cricket Board, England Lions, Kent
CAREER: First-class: 2002; List A: 1998; T20: 2003

BEST BATTING: 62 Durham vs Somerset, Stockton-on-Tees, 2005
BEST BOWLING: 8-24 Durham vs Hampshire, Basingstoke, 2008
COUNTY CAP: 2005 (Durham)

FAMILY TIES? My uncle Paul played for Yorkshire's 2nd XI
CAREER HIGHLIGHTS? Winning back-to-back Championships with Durham. Being picked for the England Lions tour to New Zealand was also a special time for me
CRICKETING HEROES? My uncle Paul in the early years and then Glenn McGrath
NON-CRICKETING HEROES? Oasis
BEST PLAYER IN COUNTY CRICKET? Marcus Trescothick
TIP FOR THE TOP? Ben Stokes
IF YOU WEREN'T A CRICKETER? Anything to do with sport
FAVOURITE TV? This Is England
FAVOURITE FILM? Wedding Crashers
FAVOURITE BOOK? Racing Through The Dark by David Millar
DREAM HOLIDAY? Marbella
ACCOMPLISHMENTS? Becoming a dad in 2008
GUILTY PLEASURES? Curries and lager
FANTASY SLIP CORDON? Keeper: Noel Gallagher, 1st: Liam Gallagher, 2nd: Gazza, 3rd: Myself, Gully: Floyd Mayweather Jr

Batting	Mat	Inns	NO	Runs	HS	Ave	SR	100	50	Ct	St
First-class	109	138	49	1118	62	12.56	37.97	0	2	21	0
List A	90	39	16	170	31*	7.39		0	0	14	0
Twenty20	20	9	4	26	13	5.20	81.25	0	0	4	0

Bowling	Mat	Balls	Runs	Wkts	BBI	BBM	Ave	Econ	SR	5w	10
First-class	109	16386	7064	315	8/24		22.42	2.58	52.0	13	2
List A	90	3704	2622	86	4/13	4/13	30.48	4.24	43.0	0	0
Twenty20	20	468	524	17	2/14	2/14	30.82	6.71	27.5	0	0

STEVEN DAVIES · LHB WK R4 MVP20

SURREY

FULL NAME: Steven Michael Davies
BORN: June 17, 1986, Bromsgrove, Worcestershire
SQUAD NO: 9
HEIGHT: 5ft 11in
NICKNAME: Davo
EDUCATION: King Charles High School, Kidderminster
TEAMS: England, England Lions, Marylebone Cricket Club, Surrey, Worcestershire, Worcestershire Cricket Board
CAREER: ODI: 2009; T20I: 2009; First-class: 2005; List A: 2003; T20: 2006

BEST BATTING: 192 Worcestershire vs Gloucestershire, Bristol, 2006
COUNTY CAP: 2011 (Surrey)

CAREER HIGHLIGHTS? Getting my first professional contract, my debuts for Worcestershire, Surrey and England. Winning the CB40 with both Worcestershire and Surrey and being part of the Ashes squad that won in Australia in 2010/11
BEST PLAYER IN COUNTY CRICKET? Graham Onions
TIPS FOR THE TOP? Arun Harinath, Rory Burns, Matthew Dunn, George Edwards
IF YOU WEREN'T A CRICKETER? I'd be a tennis player
DESERT ISLAND DISC? Elton John's Greatest Hits
FAVOURITE TV? An Idiot Abroad
CRICKETING HEROES? Adam Gilchrist, Brian Lara
NON-CRICKETING HEROES? Roger Federer
ACCOMPLISHMENTS? Playing tennis on the grass at Wimbledon
WHEN YOU RETIRE? I'd like to run a successful business
SURPRISING FACT? I can serve both left- and right-handed at tennis
TWITTER FEED: @SteveDavies43

Batting	Mat	Inns	NO	Runs	HS	Ave	SR	100	50	Ct	St
ODIs	8	8	0	244	87	30.50	105.62	0	1	8	0
T20Is	5	5	0	102	33	20.40	124.39	0	0	2	1
First-class	137	227	24	7872	192	38.77	62.00	13	38	384	20
List A	143	132	13	4267	127*	35.85		6	26	126	41
Twenty20	92	85	8	1851	99*	24.03	142.93	0	10	50	18

Bowling	Mat	Balls	Runs	Wkts	BBI	BBM	Ave	Econ	SR	5w	10
ODIs	8	-	-	-	-	-	-	-	-	-	-
T20Is	5	-	-	-	-	-	-	-	-	-	-
First-class	137	-	-	-	-	-	-	-	-	-	-
List A	143	-	-	-	-	-	-	-	-	-	-
Twenty20	92	-	-	-	-	-	-	-	-	-	-

LIAM DAWSON   RHB SLA R1 MVP21

FULL NAME: Liam Andrew Dawson
BORN: March 1, 1990, Swindon, Wiltshire
SQUAD NO: 8
HEIGHT: 5ft 10in
NICKNAME: Daws, Leemo, Stomper
EDUCATION: John Bentley School
TEAMS: England Lions, England Under-19s, Hampshire, Hampshire 2nd XI, Mountaineers, Prime Bank Cricket Club
CAREER: First-class: 2007; List A: 2007; T20: 2008

HAMPSHIRE

BEST BATTING: 169 Hampshire vs Somerset, Southampton, 2011
BEST BOWLING: 7-51 Mountaineers vs Mashonaland Eagles, Mutare, 2011
COUNTY CAP: 2013

FAMILY TIES? My dad and brother play for Goatacre CC
WHO WOULD PLAY YOU IN A FILM OF YOUR LIFE? Adam Sandler
CAREER HIGHLIGHTS? Winning a Lord's final and two T20 finals. Winning Man of the Match at Lord's in the CB40
MOST MARKED CHARACTERISTIC? My stomping around the outfield
BEST PLAYER IN COUNTY CRICKET? Michael Carberry
TIP FOR THE TOP? Sean Terry
DESERT ISLAND DISC? Wiley – Heatwave
FAVOURITE TV? Crimewatch
CRICKETING HEROES? Shane Warne, Shaun Udal, Simon Katich
WHEN YOU RETIRE? I'll sit and watch my kids play sport professionally
SURPRISING FACT? I turned down a career in football
FANTASY SLIP CORDON? Keeper: Alan Garner, 1st: Rihanna, 2nd: Me, 3rd: David Beckham, Gully: Cheryl Cole
TWITTER FEED: @daws128

Batting	Mat	Inns	NO	Runs	HS	Ave	SR	100	50	Ct	St
First-class	79	125	14	3889	169	35.03	48.55	6	22	96	0
List A	84	67	13	1522	97	28.18	95.12	0	6	46	0
Twenty20	59	39	12	330	30	12.22	104.10	0	0	30	0

Bowling	Mat	Balls	Runs	Wkts	BBI	BBM	Ave	Econ	SR	5w	10
First-class	79	4537	2540	64	7/51	7/84	39.68	3.35	70.8	2	0
List A	84	2497	2108	54	4/45	4/45	39.03	5.06	46.2	0	0
Twenty20	59	694	878	31	4/19	4/19	28.32	7.59	22.3	0	0

JOE DENLY — RHB LB R2 MVP72

FULL NAME: Joseph Liam Denly
BORN: March 16, 1986, Canterbury, Kent
SQUAD NO: 10
HEIGHT: 6ft
NICKNAME: JD, Denners
EDUCATION: Chaucer Technology College
TEAMS: England, England Lions, England Performance Programme, England Under-19s, Kent, Kent 2nd XI, Marylebone Cricket Club, Middlesex
CAREER: ODI: 2009; T20I: 2009; First-class: 2004; List A: 2004; T20: 2004

BEST BATTING: 199 Kent vs Derbyshire, Derby, 2011
BEST BOWLING: 3-43 Kent vs Surrey, The Oval, 2011
COUNTY CAPS: 2008 (Kent); 2012 (Middlesex)

WHO WOULD PLAY YOU IN A FILM OF YOUR LIFE? Channing Tatum (wife's favourite)
CAREER HIGHLIGHTS? Playing for England, winning the T20 and getting capped for both Kent and Middlesex
SUPERSTITIONS? I put my left pad on first
MOST MARKED CHARACTERISTIC? Bandy legs
BEST PLAYER IN COUNTY CRICKET? Sam Robson or Tim Murtagh
TIPS FOR THE TOP? Max Holden, Jaydn Denly
IF YOU WEREN'T A CRICKETER? I'd be a footballer
DESERT ISLAND DISC? Westlife – Unbreakable
SURPRISING FACT? I cut my own hair
FANTASY SLIP CORDON? Keeper: Ricky Gervais, 1st: Me, 2nd: Angelina Jolie, 3rd: Jennifer Aniston, Gully: Will Ferrell
TWITTER FEED: @joed1986

Batting	Mat	Inns	NO	Runs	HS	Ave	SR	100	50	Ct	St
ODIs	9	9	0	268	67	29.77	65.52	0	2	5	0
T20Is	5	5	0	20	14	4.00	68.96	0	0	1	0
First-class	118	209	13	6625	199	33.80	57.70	15	32	50	0
List A	103	99	9	3051	115	33.90	74.87	4	16	32	0
Twenty20	103	100	9	2344	100	25.75	112.42	1	15	37	0

Bowling	Mat	Balls	Runs	Wkts	BBI	BBM	Ave	Econ	SR	5w	10
ODIs	9	-	-	-	-	-	-	-	-	-	-
T20Is	5	6	9	1	1/9	1/9	9.00	9.00	6.0	0	0
First-class	118	2081	1167	23	3/43	6/114	50.73	3.36	90.4	0	0
List A	103	128	132	5	3/42	3/42	26.40	6.18	25.6	0	0
Twenty20	103	48	76	1	1/9	1/9	76.00	9.50	48.0	0	0

CHRIS DENT   LHB SLA WK R1 MVP33

FULL NAME: Christopher David James Dent
BORN: January 20, 1991, Bristol
SQUAD NO: 15
HEIGHT: 5ft 10in
NICKNAME: Denty, Maggot, Weezle, Harry
EDUCATION: Filton College
TEAMS: England Under-19s, Gloucestershire, Gloucestershire 2nd XI
CAREER: First-class: 2010; List A: 2009; T20: 2010

GLOUCESTERSHIRE

BEST BATTING: 153 Gloucestershire vs Kent, Cheltenham, 2013
BEST BOWLING: 1-12 Gloucestershire vs Hampshire, Bristol, 2013
COUNTY CAP: 2010

CAREER HIGHLIGHTS? My maiden first-class hundred
CRICKETING HEROES? Brian Lara, Chris Taylor, Jack Russell
NON-CRICKETING HEROES? Tiger Woods
BEST PLAYER IN COUNTY CRICKET? Marcus Trescothick
TIP FOR THE TOP? Jos Buttler
IF YOU WEREN'T A CRICKETER? I'd be working in Mbargos in Bristol
WHEN RAIN STOPS PLAY? I'm on my phone or sleeping
FAVOURITE TV? The Joy Of Teen Sex
FAVOURITE FILM? The Girl With The Dragon Tattoo
FAVOURITE BOOK? The Game
DREAM HOLIDAY? Las Vegas
ACCOMPLISHMENTS? Getting through college
GUILTY PLEASURES? A night out and bubble bath in the changing rooms
FANTASY SLIP CORDON? Keeper: Rihanna, 1st: Megan Fox, 2nd: Me, 3rd: Tiger Woods, Gully: Jessica Alba
TWITTER FEED: @Cdent15

Batting	Mat	Inns	NO	Runs	HS	Ave	SR	100	50	Ct	St
First-class	52	94	8	2926	153	34.02	52.94	4	16	72	0
List A	24	19	2	509	151*	29.94	103.24	1	1	7	0
Twenty20	18	17	1	351	63*	21.93	117.00	0	2	4	0

Bowling	Mat	Balls	Runs	Wkts	BBI	BBM	Ave	Econ	SR	5w	10
First-class	52	259	143	1	1/12	1/12	143.00	3.31	259.0	0	0
List A	24	276	245	9	4/43	4/43	27.22	5.32	30.6	0	0
Twenty20	18	72	98	2	1/16	1/16	49.00	8.16	36.0	0	0

JADE DERNBACH

RHB RFM W1 MVP89

SURREY

FULL NAME: Jade Winston Dernbach
BORN: April 3, 1986, Johannesburg, South
Africa
SQUAD NO: 16
HEIGHT: 6ft 2in
NICKNAME: Dirtbag
EDUCATION: St John The Baptist,
Johannesburg
TEAMS: England, England Lions, Surrey,
Surrey 2nd XI
CAREER: ODI: 2011; T20I: 2011; First-class:
2003; List A: 2005; T20: 2005

BEST BATTING: 56* Surrey vs Northamptonshire, Northampton, 2011
BEST BOWLING: 6-47 Surrey vs Leicestershire, Leicester, 2010
COUNTY CAP: 2011

NOTES: Leading wicket-taker in the 2008 Pro40, with 24 wickets at 13.08. Took 51 first-class
wickets at 27.75 in 2010. Replaced the injured Ajmal Shahzad for the knockout stages of
the 2011 World Cup. Made his ODI and T20I debuts against Sri Lanka in 2011. Impressed in
the 2012 T20I series against Pakistan, claiming four wickets at 17 with an economy of 6.18.
Named in England's squad for the 2014 World T20 in Bangladesh

Batting	Mat	Inns	NO	Runs	HS	Ave	SR	100	50	Ct	St
ODIs	24	8	1	19	5	2.71	48.71	0	0	5	0
T20Is	29	7	2	24	12	4.80	114.28	0	0	8	0
First-class	83	107	39	619	56*	9.10		0	1	10	0
List A	114	42	15	197	31	7.29	79.43	0	0	22	0
Twenty20	88	22	9	66	12	5.07	90.41	0	0	20	0

Bowling	Mat	Balls	Runs	Wkts	BBI	BBM	Ave	Econ	SR	5w	10
ODIs	24	1234	1308	31	4/45	4/45	42.19	6.35	39.8	0	0
T20Is	29	606	853	34	4/22	4/22	25.08	8.44	17.8	0	0
First-class	83	13427	7581	237	6/47		31.98	3.38	56.6	10	0
List A	114	4823	4917	172	5/31	5/31	28.58	6.11	28.0	2	0
Twenty20	88	1732	2389	94	4/22	4/22	25.41	8.27	18.4	0	0

FULL NAME: Neil John Dexter
BORN: August 21, 1984, Johannesburg, South Africa
SQUAD NO: 8
HEIGHT: 6ft
NICKNAME: Ted
EDUCATION: Northwood School, Durban; UNISA
TEAMS: Essex, Essex 2nd XI, Kent, Kent 2nd XI, Middlesex
CAREER: First-class: 2005; List A: 2005; T20: 2006

MIDDLESEX

BEST BATTING: 146 Middlesex vs Kent, Uxbridge, 2009
BEST BOWLING: 5-27 Middlesex vs Nottinghamshire, Nottingham, 2013
COUNTY CAP: 2010 (Middlesex)

WHO WOULD PLAY YOU IN A FILM OF YOUR LIFE? Jude Law
CAREER HIGHLIGHTS? Captaining Middlesex
MOST MARKED CHARACTERISTIC? My receding hairline
BEST PLAYER IN COUNTY CRICKET? Graham Onions for bowling and Sam Robson for batting
TIP FOR THE TOP? Sam Robson
IF YOU WEREN'T A CRICKETER? I'd be begging
DESERT ISLAND DISC? Alphaville – Forever Young
FAVOURITE TV? Take Me Out
CRICKETING HEROES? Brett Lee
WHEN YOU RETIRE? I'll work for Turbofluid
SURPRISING FACT? I have two Pekingese dogs and I'm not related to Ted Dexter
FANTASY SLIP CORDON? Keeper: Borat, 1st: Graham Dexter, 2nd: AB de Villiers, 3rd: Myself, Gully: Sachin Tendulkar
TWITTER FEED: @dexy214

Batting	Mat	Inns	NO	Runs	HS	Ave	SR	100	50	Ct	St
First-class	94	154	19	5024	146	37.21	53.32	11	26	77	0
List A	84	71	15	1785	135*	31.87	82.79	2	8	23	0
Twenty20	87	74	9	1369	73	21.06	111.66	0	2	36	0

Bowling	Mat	Balls	Runs	Wkts	BBI	BBM	Ave	Econ	SR	5w	10
First-class	94	4521	2355	67	5/27		35.14	3.12	67.4	1	0
List A	84	1751	1627	30	3/17	3/17	54.23	5.57	58.3	0	0
Twenty20	87	941	1218	43	4/21	4/21	28.32	7.76	21.8	0	0

SOMERSET

FULL NAME: Adam John Dibble
BORN: March 9, 1991, Exeter, Devon
SQUAD NO: 23
HEIGHT: 6ft 4in
NICKNAME: Dibbs, Officer
EDUCATION: St John's School, Sidmouth;
Taunton School
TEAMS: Devon, Somerset, Somerset 2nd XI
CAREER: First-class: 2011; List A: 2011; T20:
2011

BEST BATTING: 43 Somerset vs Warwickshire, Birmingham, 2012
BEST BOWLING: 3-42 Somerset vs Warwickshire, Birmingham, 2012

FAMILY TIES? My dad played cricket for Sidmouth CC. My sister [Jodie] plays for England
Women
WHO WOULD PLAY YOU IN A FILM OF YOUR LIFE? Ryan Reynolds
CAREER HIGHLIGHTS? My Somerset debut and the Champions League T20 semi-final in 2011
BEST PLAYER IN COUNTY CRICKET? James Hildreth
TIP FOR THE TOP? Tom Abell
DESERT ISLAND DISC? Coldplay – Viva La Vida
FAVOURITE TV? Sherlock
CRICKETING HEROES? Chris Gayle
NON-CRICKETING HEROES? David Beckham, Jonny Wilkinson, Will Smith, Jay-Z, Eminem
WHEN YOU RETIRE? I'd like to travel
FANTASY SLIP CORDON? Keeper: David Beckham, 1st: Ricky Gervais, 2nd: Will Smith, 3rd:
Jay-Z, Gully: Steve Jobs
TWITTER FEED: @adam_dibble

Batting	Mat	Inns	NO	Runs	HS	Ave	SR	100	50	Ct	St
First-class	3	6	2	84	43	21.00	72.41	0	0	0	0
List A	7	2	1	15	15	15.00	136.36	0	0	1	0
Twenty20	2	-	-	-	-	-	-	0	0	0	0

Bowling	Mat	Balls	Runs	Wkts	BBI	BBM	Ave	Econ	SR	5w	10
First-class	3	294	184	5	3/42	3/42	36.80	3.75	58.8	0	0
List A	7	288	295	11	4/52	4/52	26.81	6.14	26.1	0	0
Twenty20	2	48	44	2	1/20	1/20	22.00	5.50	24.0	0	0

FULL NAME: George Henry Dockrell
BORN: July 22, 1992, Dublin, Ireland
SQUAD NO: 20
HEIGHT: 6ft 4in
NICKNAME: Doc
EDUCATION: Gonzaga College, Dublin; Trinity College, Dublin
TEAMS: Ireland, Ireland Under-13s, Ireland Under-15s, Ireland Under-19s, Somerset, Somerset 2nd XI
CAREER: ODI: 2010; T20I: 2010; First-class: 2010; List A: 2010; T20: 2010

SOMERSET

BEST BATTING: 53 Ireland vs Namibia, Belfast, 2011
BEST BOWLING: 6-27 Somerset vs Middlesex, Taunton, 2012

FAMILY TIES? My dad played cricket in school and continued playing for YMCA in Dublin after that. He still plays a bit and umpires too
CAREER HIGHLIGHTS? Beating England in the 2011 World Cup with Ireland and taking six wickets vs Middlesex and Durham at Taunton in 2012
MOST MARKED CHARACTERISTIC? I'm a thinker
BEST PLAYER IN COUNTY CRICKET? Kevin Pietersen – he's impossible to bowl to
TIP FOR THE TOP? Lewis Gregory
CRICKETING HEROES? Daniel Vettori – consistent performances at the top level year after year
ACCOMPLISHMENTS? Making the Irish U16 hockey squad
SURPRISING FACT? I've never had a cup of tea or coffee in my life
FANTASY SLIP CORDON? Keeper: Michael McIntyre, 1st: Brian O'Driscoll, 2nd: Myself, 3rd: Mila Kunis, 4th: Daniel Vettori
TWITTER FEED: @georgedockrell

Batting	Mat	Inns	NO	Runs	HS	Ave	SR	100	50	Ct	St
ODIs	38	20	11	89	19	9.88	67.42	0	0	16	0
T20Is	23	3	2	2	2*	2.00	25.00	0	0	5	0
First-class	30	36	11	313	53	12.52	28.04	0	1	12	0
List A	60	30	17	163	22*	12.53	70.56	0	0	27	0
Twenty20	57	8	6	4	2*	2.00	21.05	0	0	32	0

Bowling	Mat	Balls	Runs	Wkts	BBI	BBM	Ave	Econ	SR	5w	10
ODIs	38	1807	1265	45	4/24	4/24	28.11	4.20	40.1	0	0
T20Is	23	472	468	30	4/20	4/20	15.60	5.94	15.7	0	0
First-class	30	5523	2671	98	6/27	9/71	27.25	2.90	56.3	6	0
List A	60	2641	1918	62	4/24	4/24	30.93	4.35	42.5	0	0
Twenty20	57	1097	1180	65	4/20	4/20	18.15	6.45	16.8	0	0

ANEURIN DONALD

RHB OB

GLAMORGAN

FULL NAME: Aneurin Henry Thomas Donald
BORN: December 20, 1996, Swansea, Glamorgan, Wales
SQUAD NO: 12
HEIGHT: 6ft 3in
NICKNAME: Sir Don, The Don
EDUCATION: Pontarddulais Comprehensive School
TEAMS: Glamorgan 2nd XI, Wales Minor Counties
CAREER: Yet to make first-team debut

FAMILY TIES? My recently late grand-uncle, Bernard Hedges, scored the first one-day century for Glamorgan. My brother Gafyn played for the Wales age groups and now plays in the Welsh Premier League for Pontarddulais CC
WHO WOULD PLAY YOU IN A FILM OF YOUR LIFE? Leonardo DiCaprio
CAREER HIGHLIGHTS? Captaining England Development Programme U17 vs Sri Lanka U17, Bangaladesh U19 and Pakistan U19, and making my 2nd XI debut for Glamorgan at 15
MOST MARKED CHARACTERISTIC? My remarkable resemblance to Jackson Bird, the Australian fast bowler
BEST PLAYER IN COUNTY CRICKET? Graham Onions, Jim Allenby
TIPS FOR THE TOP? Andrew Salter, Haseeb Hameed, Brad Taylor
DESERT ISLAND DISC? Bastille – Bad Blood
FAVOURITE TV? Suits
CRICKETING HEROES? Kevin Pietersen, Jos Buttler
NON-CRICKETING HEROES? My dad
ACCOMPLISHMENTS? Playing regional age-grade rugby and not failing my GCSEs!
WHEN YOU RETIRE? I'll relax and move somewhere hot
SURPRISING FACT? When I used to go and net with my brother and father on a Saturday morning, Leigh Halfpenny would be there every week practising his goal-kicking. I could never get the courage to ask him to feed the bowling machine…
FANTASY SLIP CORDON? Keeper: Matt Taylor (Northamptonshire Academy – for general amusement and to make me feel better about myself), 1st: Me, 2nd: Leigh Halfpenny (to run after the ball as it goes through the rest of the cordon), 3rd: Piers Morgan (to add some controversy and to listen to his opinions on just about everything), Gully: To keep the peace, anyone who feels they should have been mentioned…
TWITTER FEED: @aneurindonald12

BEN DUCKETT
LHB OB WK

FULL NAME: Ben Matthew Duckett
BORN: October 17, 1994, Farnborough, Kent
SQUAD NO: 24
HEIGHT: 5ft 9in
NICKNAME: Ducky
EDUCATION: Stowe School
TEAMS: England Under-19s, Northamptonshire, Northamptonshire 2nd XI, Northamptonshire Under-13s, Northamptonshire Under-14s, Northamptonshire Under-15s
CAREER: First-class: 2013; List A: 2013; T20: 2012

BEST BATTING: 53* Northamptonshire vs Leicestershire, Northampton, 2013

FAMILY TIES? My dad was on the Surrey staff for a few years. My grandfather Tom Duckett played and was then a successful umpire
WHO WOULD PLAY YOU IN A FILM OF YOUR LIFE? Adam Sandler
CAREER HIGHLIGHTS? Winning the 2nd XI T20 competition with England U19 and getting Man of the Match in the final with 73*. Getting picked for the U19 World Cup in Australia two years later. Making my debut for Northants in 2012 in a T20 game
SUPERSTITIONS? I always put my left pad on first
MOST MARKED CHARACTERISTIC? My hair
BEST PLAYER IN COUNTY CRICKET? Kevin Pietersen
TIPS FOR THE TOP? Dom Sibley, Shiv Thakor, Olly Stone, Ben Collins
DESERT ISLAND DISC? Mac Miller
FAVOURITE TV? The Only Way Is Essex
CRICKETING HEROES? Chris Gayle, Brian Lara
NON-CRICKETING HEROES? Jonny Wilkinson, Joey Essex
ACCOMPLISHMENTS? I came second in the tennis nationals when I was 13
WHEN YOU RETIRE? I'll do something that involves cricket, maybe coaching
TWITTER FEED? @benduckett1

Batting	Mat	Inns	NO	Runs	HS	Ave	SR	100	50	Ct	St
First-class	4	6	1	145	53*	29.00	65.61	0	1	4	0
List A	5	4	1	94	47*	31.33	85.45	0	0	3	0
Twenty20	4	3	3	20	15*	-	111.11	0	0	1	0

Bowling	Mat	Balls	Runs	Wkts	BBI	BBM	Ave	Econ	SR	5w	10
First-class	4	-	-	-	-	-	-	-	-	-	-
List A	5	-	-	-	-	-	-	-	-	-	-
Twenty20	4	-	-	-	-	-	-	-	-	-	-

MATT DUNN

LHB RFM

SURREY

FULL NAME: Matthew Peter Dunn
BORN: May 5, 1992, Egham, Surrey
SQUAD NO: 4
HEIGHT: 6ft 1in
NICKNAME: Dunny
EDUCATION: Bishopsgate School; Bearwood College
TEAMS: England Under-15s, England Under-19s, Surrey, Surrey Under-15s, Surrey Under-17s, Surrey Under-19s
CAREER: First-class: 2010; List A: 2011; T20: 2013

BEST BATTING: 2* Surrey vs Cambridge MCCU, Cambridge, 2011
BEST BOWLING: 5-56 Surrey vs Derbyshire, Derby, 2011

WHO WOULD PLAY YOU IN A FILM OF YOUR LIFE? Tom Hardy
CAREER HIGHLIGHTS? Taking five wickets on debut for Surrey against Derbyshire and having the chance to represent my country at U19 level
MOST MARKED CHARACTERISTIC? My smile
BEST PLAYER IN COUNTY CRICKET? Steve Davies
TIP FOR THE TOP? Dominic Sibley
IF YOU WEREN'T A CRICKETER? I'd be at university
DESERT ISLAND DISC? Drake – Take Care
FAVOURITE TV? The Office
BIGGEST DRESSING DOWN YOU'VE RECEIVED? Getting told off by the umpire for cursing all the way from finishing my over to my position at fine-leg!
CRICKETING HEROES? Brett Lee, Dale Steyn, Dirk Nannes
NON-CRICKETING HEROES? Tom Hardy, Mario Balotelli, Channing Tatum, David Beckham
ACCOMPLISHMENTS? Completing my A-Levels
WHEN YOU RETIRE? I'll travel the world with a backpack!
SURPRISING FACT? I lived in Norway for a bit of my childhood
TWITTER FEED: @MatthewDunn05

Batting	Mat	Inns	NO	Runs	HS	Ave	SR	100	50	Ct	St
First-class	7	6	6	3	2*	-	8.57	0	0	0	0
List A	1	-	-	-	-	-	-	-	-	1	0
Twenty20	1	-	-	-	-	-	-	-	-	1	0

Bowling	Mat	Balls	Runs	Wkts	BBI	BBM	Ave	Econ	SR	5w	10
First-class	7	679	510	17	5/56	5/68	30.00	4.50	39.9	1	0
List A	1	36	32	2	2/32	2/32	16.00	5.33	18.0	0	0
Twenty20	1	12	21	0	-	-	-	10.50	-	0	0

WES DURSTON RHB OB R1 MVP99

FULL NAME: Wesley John Durston
BORN: October 6, 1980, Taunton, Somerset
SQUAD NO: 3
HEIGHT: 5ft 9in
NICKNAME: Ace, Pringles, Bestie, Durst
EDUCATION: Millfield School, Glastonbury;
University of Worcester
TEAMS: Derbyshire, Somerset, Somerset
Cricket Board, Unicorns
CAREER: First-class: 2002; List A: 2000; T20:
2003

DERBYSHIRE

BEST BATTING: 151 Derbyshire vs Gloucestershire, Derby, 2011
BEST BOWLING: 5-34 Derbyshire vs Yorkshire, Leeds, 2012
COUNTY CAP: 2012 (Derbyshire)

FAMILY TIES? My dad was a good club cricketer, as are both my brothers. We used to all play in the same side a few years back which was always a bit of fun
WHO WOULD PLAY YOU IN A FILM OF YOUR LIFE? Is Harrison Ford any good at cricket?
CAREER HIGHLIGHTS? Winning trophies as a team will always leave me with very fond memories: the T20 Cup in 2005 with Somerset, County Championship Division Two title in 2007 with Somerset and Division Two title with Derbyshire in 2012. Besides that, scoring 117 for the Unicorns in the CB40 and 111 in T20 for Derbyshire were two of my more dynamic and exciting innings to date
SUPERSTITIONS? I always salute magpies, cross the lines with my right foot first and tap my forehead with my index finger before every ball I face!
BEST PLAYER IN COUNTY CRICKET? Marcus Trescothick is still the best player in county cricket but Kevin Pietersen possesses the x-factor and I love watching them both bat
CRICKETING HEROES? Viv Richards, Graham Gooch, Shane Warne, Keith Parsons
ACCOMPLISHMENTS? Being a dad to Daisy and Joseph
WHEN YOU RETIRE? I'd like to become a teacher and director of coaching in a nice school
TWITTER FEED: @wjdurston3

Batting	Mat	Inns	NO	Runs	HS	Ave	SR	100	50	Ct	St
First-class	83	144	19	4299	151	34.39	58.65	6	25	84	0
List A	101	87	18	2266	120*	32.84		2	13	34	0
Twenty20	86	77	13	1568	111	24.50	124.64	1	9	34	0

Bowling	Mat	Balls	Runs	Wkts	BBI	BBM	Ave	Econ	SR	5w	10
First-class	83	4982	3001	65	5/34		46.16	3.61	76.6	1	0
List A	101	1767	1650	45	3/7	3/7	36.66	5.60	39.2	0	0
Twenty20	86	696	903	40	3/25	3/25	22.57	7.78	17.4	0	0

NED ECKERSLEY   RHB WK R1 MVP56

LEICESTERSHIRE

FULL NAME: Edmund James Holden Eckersley
BORN: August 9, 1989, Oxford
SQUAD NO: 33
HEIGHT: 5ft 11in
NICKNAME: Eckers
EDUCATION: St Benedict's School, Ealing
TEAMS: Leicestershire, Leicestershire 2nd XI, Marylebone Cricket Club, Marylebone Cricket Club Young Cricketers, Middlesex 2nd XI, Mountaineers
CAREER: First-class: 2011; List A: 2008; T20: 2011

BEST BATTING: 147 Leicestershire vs Essex, Chelmsford, 2013
BEST BOWLING: 2-29 Leicestershire vs Lancashire, Manchester, 2013

WHO WOULD PLAY YOU IN A FILM OF YOUR LIFE? Bradley Cooper
CAREER HIGHLIGHTS? My two first-class wickets!
SUPERSTITIONS? I always crouch down when entering the field before batting
MOST MARKED CHARACTERISTIC? My newly grown beard!
BEST PLAYER IN COUNTY CRICKET? James Taylor
TIP FOR THE TOP? Tymal Mills
IF YOU WEREN'T A CRICKETER? I'd be a pilot
DESERT ISLAND DISC? Coldplay – X&Y
FAVOURITE TV? Friends
CRICKETING HEROES? Alec Stewart
NON-CRICKETING HEROES? David Beckham
ACCOMPLISHMENTS? Playing the piano badly
FANTASY SLIP CORDON? Keeper: Jack Bauer, 1st: Jay-Z, 2nd: Lee Evans, 3rd: Myself, Gully: Jonah Hill
TWITTER FEED: @nedeckersley

Batting	Mat	Inns	NO	Runs	HS	Ave	SR	100	50	Ct	St
First-class	41	71	7	2495	147	38.98	49.36	6	10	80	3
List A	21	20	3	493	108	29.00	101.64	1	2	17	1
Twenty20	23	19	8	171	42	15.54	99.41	0	0	4	2

Bowling	Mat	Balls	Runs	Wkts	BBI	BBM	Ave	Econ	SR	5w	10
First-class	41	49	42	2	2/29	2/29	21.00	5.14	24.5	0	0
List A	21	-	-	-	-	-	-	-	-	-	-
Twenty20	23	-	-	-	-	-	-	-	-	-	-

GEORGE EDWARDS   RHB RFM

FULL NAME: George Alexander Edwards
BORN: July 29, 1992, King's College Hospital, Lambeth, London
SQUAD NO: 56
HEIGHT: 6ft 4in
NICKNAME: Chicken
EDUCATION: St Joseph's College, Upper Norwood
TEAMS: Surrey, Surrey 2nd XI
CAREER: First-class: 2011; List A: 2013

BEST BATTING: 19 Surrey vs Cambridge MCCU, Cambridge, 2011
BEST BOWLING: 4-44 Surrey vs Worcestershire, Worcester, 2012

WHO WOULD PLAY YOU IN A FILM OF YOUR LIFE? Will Smith
CAREER HIGHLIGHTS? My Championship debut against Worcestershire
MOST MARKED CHARACTERISTIC? My height
BEST PLAYER IN COUNTY CRICKET? Marcus Trescothick
TIPS FOR THE TOP? Rory Burns, Matthew Dunn, Dominic Sibley
IF YOU WEREN'T A CRICKETER? I'd be working on Dave Chappelle's Show
DESERT ISLAND DISC? Kid Cudi – Man On The Moon Part II
FAVOURITE TV? Breaking Bad
CRICKETING HEROES? The West Indies team
FANTASY SLIP CORDON? Keeper: Kevin Garnett, 1st: Myself, 2nd: Alicia Keys, 3rd: Carmelo Anthony, Gully: Eva Mendes
TWITTER FEED: @GEdwards29

Batting	Mat	Inns	NO	Runs	HS	Ave	SR	100	50	Ct	St
First-class	4	5	1	56	19	14.00	38.35	0	0	1	0
List A	1	1	1	0	0*	-	-	0	0	0	0

Bowling	Mat	Balls	Runs	Wkts	BBI	BBM	Ave	Econ	SR	5w	10
First-class	4	602	346	8	4/44	5/92	43.25	3.44	75.2	0	0
List A	1	36	44	1	1/44	1/44	44.00	7.33	36.0	0	0

SCOTT ELSTONE

RHB OB

FULL NAME: Scott Liam Elstone
BORN: June 10, 1990, Burton-on-Trent, Staffordshire
SQUAD NO: 10
HEIGHT: 5ft 8in
EDUCATION: Friary School, Lichfield; Cathedral School
TEAMS: Derbyshire, Derbyshire 2nd XI, Nottinghamshire, Nottinghamshire 2nd XI
CAREER: List A: 2010; T20: 2010

WHO WOULD PLAY YOU IN A FILM OF YOUR LIFE? Denzel Washington or Leonardo DiCaprio
BEST PLAYER IN COUNTY CRICKET? Shivnarine Chanderpaul
TIP FOR THE TOP? Alex Hughes
IF YOU WEREN'T A CRICKETER? I'd be at university
DESERT ISLAND DISC? Jay-Z – Watch The Throne
FAVOURITE TV? Entourage, Prison Break, The Walking Dead
CRICKETING HEROES? AB de Villiers and Chris Read
NON-CRICKETING HEROES? Steven Gerrard
FANTASY SLIP CORDON? Keeper: Tiger Woods, 1st: Jay-Z, 2nd: Steven Gerrard, 3rd: Mark Francis, Gully: Kevin Bridges
TWITTER FEED: @scottelstone

Batting	Mat	Inns	NO	Runs	HS	Ave	SR	100	50	Ct	St
List A	25	25	4	512	75*	24.38	91.42	0	1	5	0
Twenty20	18	13	8	91	21*	18.20	135.82	0	0	8	0

Bowling	Mat	Balls	Runs	Wkts	BBI	BBM	Ave	Econ	SR	5w	10
List A	25	34	32	1	1/22	1/22	32.00	5.64	34.0	0	0
Twenty20	18	-	-	-	-	-	-	-	-	-	-

SEAN ERVINE LHB RM MVP76

FULL NAME: Sean Michael Ervine
BORN: December 6, 1982, Harare, Zimbabwe
SQUAD NO: 7
HEIGHT: 6ft 2in
NICKNAME: Slug, Lion
EDUCATION: Lomagundi College
TEAMS: Zimbabwe, Brothers Union, Duronto Rajshahi, Hampshire, Midlands, Southern Rocks, Western Australia
CAREER: Test: 2003; ODI: 2001; First-class: 2001; List A: 2001; T20: 2005

BEST BATTING: 237* Hampshire vs Somerset, Southampton, 2010
BEST BOWLING: 6-82 Midlands vs Mashonaland, Kwekwe, 2003
COUNTY CAP: 2005

FAMILY TIES? My father Rory played first-class cricket in Zimbabwe, my brother Craig plays for the current Zimbabwe team, my brother Ryan plays for the franchise Southern Rocks in Zimbabwe and my uncle Neil played first-class cricket in Zimbabwe
CAREER HIGHLIGHTS? Scoring 100 vs India at Adelaide Oval in the 2004/05 VB series. My hundreds and Man of the Match in both the semi-final and final of the C&G Trophy in 2005. Four wickets vs Australia in the first Test match at Perth in 2003 for Zimbabwe. Scoring 208 and 160 in the same game for the Southern Rocks in 2010. Playing in the 2003 World Cup in South Africa. Playing with Shane Warne at Hampshire
CRICKETING HEROES? Andy Flower, Shane Warne, Neil McKenzie
TIPS FOR THE TOP? James Vince, Chris Wood, Ben Stokes
IF YOU WEREN'T A CRICKETER? I'd be a golfer, fisherman or African wildlife conservationist
FAVOURITE BOOK? Mukiwa – a story about a white boy growing up in Africa
TWITTER FEED: @Slug_7

Batting	Mat	Inns	NO	Runs	HS	Ave	SR	100	50	Ct	St
Tests	5	8	0	261	86	32.62	55.41	0	3	7	0
ODIs	42	34	7	698	100	25.85	85.53	1	2	5	0
First-class	168	262	29	8139	237*	34.93		14	43	141	0
List A	218	192	29	5103	167*	31.30		7	23	61	0
Twenty20	135	123	29	2404	82	25.57	128.14	0	9	47	0

Bowling	Mat	Balls	Runs	Wkts	BBI	BBM	Ave	Econ	SR	5w	10
Tests	5	570	388	9	4/146	4/146	43.11	4.08	63.3	0	0
ODIs	42	1649	1561	41	3/29	3/29	38.07	5.67	40.2	0	0
First-class	168	17074	10121	243	6/82		41.65	3.55	70.2	5	0
List A	218	7243	6749	202	5/50	5/50	33.41	5.59	35.8	2	0
Twenty20	135	1302	1884	65	4/12	4/12	28.98	8.68	20.0	0	0

STEVIE ESKINAZI — RHB WK

FULL NAME: Stephen Eskinazi
BORN: March 28, 1994, Johannesburg, Transvaal, South Africa
SQUAD NO: 28
HEIGHT: 6ft 2in
NICKNAME: Eski, Esk
EDUCATION: Christ Church Grammar School, Western Australia; University of Western Australia
TEAMS: Middlesex 2nd XI, Western Australia Under-17s, Western Australia Under-19s
CAREER: Yet to make first-team debut

FAMILY TIES? My family has always played. My dad played grade cricket in South Africa and my brother and I have played since we were very young

WHO WOULD PLAY YOU IN A FILM OF YOUR LIFE? Leonardo DiCaprio

CAREER HIGHLIGHTS? Being part of Middlesex CCC since 2013, winning the 2nd XI County Championship and being selected for the Australian U19 team in 2013

SUPERSTITIONS? Never again will I keep the rubber duck that came in my Christmas cracker in my room! My pads always go on first

MOST MARKED CHARACTERISTIC? Resilience and patience

BEST PLAYER IN COUNTY CRICKET? Sam Robson

TIPS FOR THE TOP? Sam Robson, James Taylor

IF YOU WEREN'T A CRICKETER? I'd be at university studying Commerce and playing hockey

DESERT ISLAND DISC? Macklemore & Ryan Lewis – The Heist

FAVOURITE TV? Anything in Shark Week!

CRICKETING HEROES? Jacques Kallis, Chris Smith, Robin Smith, Mike Hussey

NON-CRICKETING HEROES? My parents Rob and Gen and my brother Greg

ACCOMPLISHMENTS? Making the Australian U16 and Western Australia U21 men's hockey teams at the age of 15 and 18 respectively. Getting in the top four per cent of academic results in my state

WHEN YOU RETIRE? First option: move to the Caribbean and live on the beach. Second option: own my own business

SURPRISING FACT? I played for Hampshire U10 before moving to Australia for 10 years before returning to Middlesex. I'm an English cricketer, raised in Australia, born in South Africa!

FANTASY SLIP CORDON? Keeper: Myself, 1st: Greg Eskinazi, 2nd: Sachin Tendulkar, 3rd: Nelson Mandela, Gully: Usain Bolt

TWITTER FEED: @seskinazi

LAURIE EVANS

RHB RM

FULL NAME: Laurie John Evans
BORN: October 12, 1987, Lambeth, London
SQUAD NO: 32
HEIGHT: 6ft 1in
NICKNAME: LJ, Loz
EDUCATION: Whitgift School; The John Fisher School; Durham University
TEAMS: Durham UCCE, ECB Development of Excellence XI, Malden Wanderers, Marylebone Cricket Club, Surrey, Surrey 2nd XI, Warwickshire
CAREER: First-class: 2007; List A: 2009; T20: 2009

BEST BATTING: 178 Warwickshire vs Nottinghamshire, Birmingham, 2013
BEST BOWLING: 1-30 Surrey vs Bangladeshis, The Oval, 2010

WHO WOULD PLAY YOU IN A FILM OF YOUR LIFE? Jamie Foxx
CAREER HIGHLIGHTS? My maiden first-class hundred
BEST PLAYER IN COUNTY CRICKET? Kevin Pietersen
IF YOU WEREN'T A CRICKETER? I'd be playing rugby
DESERT ISLAND DISC? Jay-Z – Magna Carta Holy Grail
FAVOURITE TV? Top Gear
CRICKETING HEROES? Brian Lara
NON-CRICKETING HEROES? Ray Lewis
ACCOMPLISHMENTS? Going round a golf course level par
CRICKET RULE YOU'D CHANGE? You shouldn't be allowed to get out first ball
WHEN YOU RETIRE? I'll become The Wolf of Wall Street
TWITTER FEED: @laurieevans32

Batting	Mat	Inns	NO	Runs	HS	Ave	SR	100	50	Ct	St
First-class	28	46	3	1702	178	39.58	46.22	4	9	16	0
List A	10	10	3	164	47*	23.42	80.78	0	0	5	0
Twenty20	19	15	6	233	68*	25.88	129.44	0	2	5	0

Bowling	Mat	Balls	Runs	Wkts	BBI	BBM	Ave	Econ	SR	5w	10
First-class	28	318	213	1	1/30	1/30	213.00	4.01	318.0	0	0
List A	10	30	41	0	-	-	-	8.20	-	0	0
Twenty20	19	10	15	1	1/5	1/5	15.00	9.00	10.0	0	0

TOM FELL

RHB WK

FULL NAME: Thomas Charles Fell
BORN: October 17, 1993, Hillingdon, Middlesex
SQUAD NO: 29
HEIGHT: 6ft 1in
NICKNAME: Felly
EDUCATION: Oakham School
TEAMS: Oxford MCCU, Staffordshire Under-13s, Staffordshire Under-14s, Staffordshire Under-15s, Staffordshire Under-17s, Worcestershire, Worcestershire 2nd XI, Worcestershire Academy
CAREER: First-class: 2013; List A: 2013

BEST BATTING: 94* Worcestershire vs Kent, Worcester, 2013

CAREER HIGHLIGHTS? Playing for the MCC Schools at Lord's. Breaking the school record for most runs scored in a season. Scoring a double-century for Staffs U17
SUPERSTITIONS? I tread on the rope as I go out to bat
CRICKETING HEROES? Sachin Tendulkar
NON-CRICKETING HEROES? Lionel Messi, Gareth Bale, Matt Hampson
BEST PLAYER IN COUNTY CRICKET? Marcus Trescothick
TIP FOR THE TOP? Shiv Thakor from Leicestershire
WHEN RAIN STOPS PLAY? I'm listening to music or playing one hand-one bounce in the changing room
FAVOURITE TV? Sky Sports News and Top Gear
FAVOURITE FILM? Gladiator
FAVOURITE BOOK? Holes by Louis Sachar
DREAM HOLIDAY? Anywhere hot where they play cricket – the Caribbean probably
FANTASY SLIP CORDON? Keeper: Me, 1st: Jeff Stelling, 2nd: Jeremy Clarkson, 3rd: Harry Redknapp, Gully: David Lloyd (Bumble)

Batting	Mat	Inns	NO	Runs	HS	Ave	SR	100	50	Ct	St
First-class	10	16	2	477	94*	34.07	48.82	0	3	3	0
List A	7	7	1	142	55	23.66	75.53	0	1	1	0

Bowling	Mat	Balls	Runs	Wkts	BBI	BBM	Ave	Econ	SR	5w	10
First-class	10	-	-	-	-	-	-	-	-	-	-
List A	7	-	-	-	-	-	-	-	-	-	-

AARON FINCH

RHB LM

FULL NAME: Aaron James Finch
BORN: November 17, 1986, Colac, Victoria, Australia
SQUAD NO: 20
HEIGHT: 5ft 9in
NICKNAME: Finchy
TEAMS: Australia, Auckland, Australia A, Australia Under-19s, Delhi Daredevils, Melbourne Renegades, Pune Warriors, Rajasthan Royals, Victoria, Victoria Under-19s, Yorkshire
CAREER: ODI: 2013; T20I: 2013; First-class: 2007; List A: 2007; T20: 2009

BEST BATTING: 122 Australia A vs Zimbabwe XI, Harare, 2011
BEST BOWLING: 1-0 Victoria vs Western Australia, Perth, 2013

TWITTER FEED: @AaronFinch5
NOTES: Australian batsman Finch will share Yorkshire's overseas players duties for 2014 with Kane Williamson, playing predominantly limited-overs cricket depending on Williamson's availability. He will join up with the White Rose after the completion of the IPL, in which he will be representing Sunrisers Hyderabad. He holds the record for the highest score in a T20I, hitting 156 from from 63 balls against England at Southampton last August. He was Man of the Series in Australia's T20 series win over England in January 2014. He captains Melbourne Renegades in the Big Bash League and has previously played for Pune Warriors and Delhi Daredevils in the IPL

Batting	Mat	Inns	NO	Runs	HS	Ave	SR	100	50	Ct	St
ODIs	23	22	0	772	148	35.09	92.34	3	2	12	0
T20Is	12	12	2	458	156	45.80	170.89	1	3	2	0
First-class	39	70	1	1896	122	27.47	52.27	2	13	35	0
List A	83	82	4	3116	154	39.94	87.30	7	16	34	0
Twenty20	84	81	9	2759	156	38.31	138.08	2	19	25	0

Bowling	Mat	Balls	Runs	Wkts	BBI	BBM	Ave	Econ	SR	5w	10
ODIs	23	40	26	2	1/2	1/2	13.00	3.90	20.0	0	0
T20Is	12	6	9	0	-	-	-	9.00	-	0	0
First-class	39	230	207	3	1/0	1/0	69.00	5.40	76.6	0	0
List A	83	229	191	7	2/44	2/44	27.28	5.00	32.7	0	0
Twenty20	84	145	233	5	1/11	1/11	46.60	9.64	29.0	0	0

HARRY FINCH

RHB RM

SUSSEX

FULL NAME: Harry Zacariah Finch
BORN: February 10, 1995, Hastings, Sussex
SQUAD NO: 6
HEIGHT: 5ft 9in
NICKNAME: Finchkins, Finchy, Chozza
EDUCATION: St Richard's Catholic College, Bexhill; Eastbourne College
TEAMS: England Under-19s, Sussex, Sussex 2nd XI, Sussex Under-13s, Sussex Under-14s, Sussex Under-15s, Sussex Under-17s
CAREER: First-class: 2013; List A: 2013

BEST BATTING: 11 Durham vs Sussex, Chester-le-Street, 2013

FAMILY TIES? My dad played for Sussex 2nd XI and for Sussex Cricket Board
WHO WOULD PLAY YOU IN A FILM OF YOUR LIFE? Leonardo DiCaprio or Gerard Butler
CAREER HIGHLIGHTS? My first-class debut, making a hundred for England U19, playing a Test match for them at Newlands and making the World Cup squad
BEST PLAYER IN COUNTY CRICKET? Ed Joyce or Graham Onions
TIPS FOR THE TOP? Matt Fisher from Yorkshire has ability well beyond his years. The same goes for Tom Haynes – he's got a wise head on young shoulders
IF YOU WEREN'T A CRICKETER? I'd be at university or giving football a go
DESERT ISLAND DISC? Bastille – Bad Blood
FAVOURITE TV? How Not To Live Your Life and Friends
CRICKETING HEROES? Ricky Ponting, Andrew Flintoff and Michael Yardy
NON-CRICKETING HEROES? My dad, Tim Sherwood and Leonardo DiCaprio
ACCOMPLISHMENTS? Completing my A-Levels at college
WHEN YOU RETIRE? I'd like to become a coach and play a lot of golf
CRICKET RULE YOU'D CHANGE? The backing up rule
FANTASY SLIP CORDON? Keeper: Alan from The Hangover, 1st: Megan Fox, 2nd: Me, 3rd: Shakira, Gully: Gareth Bale
TWITTER FEED: @hfinch72

Batting	Mat	Inns	NO	Runs	HS	Ave	SR	100	50	Ct	St
First-class	1	2	0	14	11	7.00	21.53	0	0	1	0
List A	1	-	-	-	-	-	-	-	-	0	0

Bowling	Mat	Balls	Runs	Wkts	BBI	BBM	Ave	Econ	SR	5w	10
First-class	1	24	15	0	-	-	-	3.75	-	0	0
List A	1	6	2	0	-	-	-	2.00	-	0	0

FULL NAME: Steven Thomas Finn
BORN: April 4, 1989, Watford, Hertfordshire
SQUAD NO: 9
HEIGHT: 6ft 7in
NICKNAME: Finny, Gonzo, Cyril
EDUCATION: Parmiter's School, Watford
TEAMS: England, England Lions, England Under-19s, Middlesex, Middlesex 2nd XI, Otago
CAREER: Test: 2010; ODI: 2011; T20I: 2011; First-class: 2005; List A: 2007; T20: 2008

MIDDLESEX

BEST BATTING: 56 England vs New Zealand, Dunedin, 2013
BEST BOWLING: 9-37 Middlesex vs Worcestershire, Worcester, 2010
COUNTY CAP: 2009

WHO WOULD PLAY YOU IN A FILM OF YOUR LIFE? Blake Harrison
CAREER HIGHLIGHTS? My Test debut, winning the Ashes and the 2012 Test series win in India
BEST PLAYER IN COUNTY CRICKET? Tim Murtagh
TIPS FOR THE TOP? Sam Robson (Middlesex), Joe Root (Yorkshire), Jos Buttler (Lancashire)
IF YOU WEREN'T A CRICKETER? I'd be jobless after completing a pointless university course
FAVOURITE TV? Come Dine With Me
CRICKETING HEROES? Glenn McGrath
WHEN YOU RETIRE? I'd like to coach
TWITTER FEED: @finnysteve

Batting	Mat	Inns	NO	Runs	HS	Ave	SR	100	50	Ct	St
Tests	23	29	14	169	56	11.26	28.98	0	1	6	0
ODIs	39	13	6	96	35	13.71	85.71	0	0	8	0
T20Is	18	3	3	14	8*	-	73.68	0	0	4	0
First-class	93	112	34	567	56	7.26	30.76	0	1	29	0
List A	87	28	10	170	35	9.44	68.27	0	0	15	0
Twenty20	45	8	6	32	8*	16.00	82.05	0	0	8	0

Bowling	Mat	Balls	Runs	Wkts	BBI	BBM	Ave	Econ	SR	5w	10
Tests	23	4348	2646	90	6/125	9/187	29.40	3.65	48.3	4	0
ODIs	39	2084	1637	59	4/34	4/34	27.74	4.71	35.3	0	0
T20Is	18	408	487	25	3/16	3/16	19.48	7.16	16.3	0	0
First-class	93	16530	9535	337	9/37		28.29	3.46	49.0	9	1
List A	87	4034	3285	119	5/33	5/33	27.60	4.88	33.8	1	0
Twenty20	45	950	1174	48	3/16	3/16	24.45	7.41	19.7	0	0

YORKSHIRE

FULL NAME: Matthew David Fisher
BORN: November 9, 1997, York
SQUAD NO: TBC
HEIGHT: 6ft 2in
EDUCATION: Easingwold School
TEAMS: England Under-19s, Yorkshire,
Yorkshire 2nd XI, Yorkshire Academy,
Yorkshire Under-13s, Yorkshire Under-14s,
Yorkshire Under-15s, Yorkshire Under-17s
CAREER: List A: 2013

TWITTER FEED: @mfisher97
NOTES: Fisher became the youngest cricketer to play in a competitive county game when he made his debut for Yorkshire aged 15 years and 212 days in a YB40 match last year against Leicestershire. He returned figures of 1-40, taking the wicket of Shiv Thakor. He has played 15 ODIs for England U19 and featured in the 2014 U19 World Cup in UAE, taking 10 wickets at 19.70 and earning the Man of the Match award against New Zealand for his spell of 3-18. He took three more wickets, for 55 runs, in the quarter-final win over India. Made a senior league century in 2011, aged only 13

Batting	Mat	Inns	NO	Runs	HS	Ave	SR	100	50	Ct	St
List A	2	1	0	10	10	10.00	250.00	0	0	0	0

Bowling	Mat	Balls	Runs	Wkts	BBI	BBM	Ave	Econ	SR	5w	10
List A	2	84	85	1	1/40	1/40	85.00	6.07	84.0	0	0

LUKE FLETCHER · RHB RFM MVP87

FULL NAME: Luke Jack Fletcher
BORN: September 18, 1988, Nottingham
SQUAD NO: 19
HEIGHT: 6ft 6in
NICKNAME: Fletch
EDUCATION: Henry Mellish Comprehensive School
TEAMS: England Under-19s, Nottinghamshire, Nottinghamshire 2nd XI
CAREER: First-class: 2008; List A: 2008; T20: 2009

BEST BATTING: 92 Nottinghamshire vs Hampshire, Southampton, 2009
BEST BOWLING: 5-52 Nottinghamshire vs Warwickshire, Nottingham, 2013

WHO WOULD PLAY YOU IN A FILM OF YOUR LIFE? Tom Hanks
CAREER HIGHLIGHTS? Winning the County Championship in 2010
SUPERSTITIONS? I always tap my bat down twice in the crease when the umpire calls over
BEST PLAYER IN COUNTY CRICKET? Graham Onions
TIP FOR THE TOP? Luke Wood
IF YOU WEREN'T A CRICKETER? Maybe a policeman
DESERT ISLAND DISC? Anything by Deadmau5
FAVOURITE TV? Match Of The Day
CRICKETING HEROES? Freddie Flintoff
ACCOMPLISHMENTS? I played football at Wembley and Old Trafford as a youngster
WHEN YOU RETIRE? I'd like to be a bowling coach
TWITTER FEED: @fletcherluke

Batting	Mat	Inns	NO	Runs	HS	Ave	SR	100	50	Ct	St
First-class	53	76	19	890	92	15.61	53.80	0	3	12	0
List A	32	16	5	99	40*	9.00	86.08	0	0	3	0
Twenty20	25	5	3	7	5	3.50	46.66	0	0	7	0

Bowling	Mat	Balls	Runs	Wkts	BBI	BBM	Ave	Econ	SR	5w	10
First-class	53	9707	4807	161	5/52	9/108	29.85	2.97	60.2	3	0
List A	32	1268	1157	29	3/27	3/27	39.89	5.47	43.7	0	0
Twenty20	25	522	675	27	4/30	4/30	25.00	7.75	19.3	0	0

BEN FOAKES

RHB WK

ESSEX

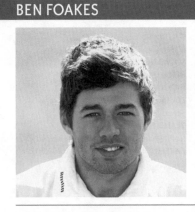

FULL NAME: Benjamin Thomas Foakes
BORN: February 15, 1993, Colchester, Essex
SQUAD NO: 4
HEIGHT: 6ft 1in
NICKNAME: Brad, Scarface
EDUCATION: Tendring Technology College
TEAMS: England Lions, England Under-17s,
England Under-19s, Essex, Essex 2nd XI
CAREER: First-class: 2011; List A: 2013

BEST BATTING: 120 Essex vs Leicestershire, Chelmsford, 2013

FAMILY TIES? My father played for Clacton Cricket Club and my brother still plays for my local club Frinton-on-Sea

CAREER HIGHLIGHTS? Making 93 on debut in the Championship against Leicestershire. Scoring 111 in the third U19 ODI in Chittagong. Being named Man of the Tournament in an U19 quadrangular tournament against Australia, India and New Zealand

SUPERSTITIONS? I have to touch my lip and my belly button whilst waiting to face the next delivery

BEST PLAYER IN COUNTY CRICKET? Nick Compton

TIPS FOR THE TOP? Tymal Mills, Reece Topley, Sam Wood, Daniel Bell-Drummond

IF YOU WEREN'T A CRICKETER? I would be studying Sports Science at Loughborough University

BIGGEST DRESSING DOWN YOU'VE RECEIVED? I haven't really had a big one but there was a little telling off for us when we played Derby and lost in three days

CRICKETING HEROES? James Foster was unbelievable to watch when I was a youngster, especially with the gloves

ACCOMPLISHMENTS? Nothing significant but I banged in a few goals for Ipswich Town when I played in their Elite Squad as a kid

WHEN YOU RETIRE? It would be good to work for Gray-Nicolls as a kit designer

SURPRISING FACT? When I was young my two front teeth were both completely black for three years after my brother pushed me and I hit my face on the bathtub

Batting	Mat	Inns	NO	Runs	HS	Ave	SR	100	50	Ct	St
First-class	21	27	3	802	120	33.41	56.67	2	4	18	0
List A	8	7	0	86	56	12.28	86.00	0	1	2	1

Bowling	Mat	Balls	Runs	Wkts	BBI	BBM	Ave	Econ	SR	5w	10
First-class	21	-	-	-	-	-	-	-	-	-	-
List A	8	-	-	-	-	-	-	-	-	-	-

FULL NAME: Mark Harold Alan Footitt
BORN: November 25, 1985, Nottingham
SQUAD NO: 4
HEIGHT: 6ft 2in
NICKNAME: Footy
EDUCATION: Carlton Le Willows School
TEAMS: Derbyshire, England Under-19s, Marylebone Cricket Club, Nottinghamshire, Nottinghamshire Cricket Board
CAREER: First-class: 2005; List A: 2002; T20: 2005

DERBYSHIRE

BEST BATTING: 30 Derbyshire vs Surrey, The Oval, 2010
BEST BOWLING: 6-53 Derbyshire vs Durham, Chester-le-Street, 2013

FAMILY TIES? Both my dad and grandad played local cricket
WHO WOULD PLAY YOU IN A FILM OF YOUR LIFE? Adam Sandler
CAREER HIGHLIGHTS? Winning Division Two of the County Championship with Derbyshire in 2012
BEST PLAYER IN COUNTY CRICKET? Jos Buttler
TIPS FOR THE TOP? Ben Slater
IF YOU WEREN'T A CRICKETER? Not too sure. A plumber perhaps
DESERT ISLAND DISC? Anything from the 80s
FAVOURITE TV? Boardwalk Empire
CRICKETING HEROES? Brett Lee
NON-CRICKETING HEROES? Adam Sandler and Sir Alex Ferguson
ACCOMPLISHMENTS? Becoming a dad to Heidi Footitt
WHEN YOU RETIRE? I'd like to be a film critic
SURPRISING FACT? I'm studying Film Studies
FANTASY SLIP CORDON? Keeper: Adam Sandler, 1st: Kevin James, 2nd: David Beckham 3rd: 'Stone Cold' Steve Austin, Gully: Hulk Hogan

Batting	Mat	Inns	NO	Runs	HS	Ave	SR	100	50	Ct	St
First-class	40	54	17	318	30	8.59	57.29	0	0	12	0
List A	20	4	2	5	4	2.50	83.33	0	0	2	0
Twenty20	7	2	1	2	2*	2.00	100.00	0	0	1	0

Bowling	Mat	Balls	Runs	Wkts	BBI	BBM	Ave	Econ	SR	5w	10
First-class	40	5877	3611	114	6/53		31.67	3.68	51.5	5	0
List A	20	564	611	21	5/28	5/28	29.09	6.50	26.8	1	0
Twenty20	7	90	168	4	3/22	3/22	42.00	11.20	22.5	0	0

JAMES FOSTER

RHB WK R1 MVP79

ESSEX

FULL NAME: James Savin Foster
BORN: April 15, 1980, Whipps Cross, Leytonstone, Essex
SQUAD NO: 7
HEIGHT: 6ft
NICKNAME: Fozzy, Chief
EDUCATION: Forest School; Durham University
TEAMS: England, Durham UCCE, Essex, Marylebone Cricket Club, Northern Districts
CAREER: Test: 2001; ODI: 2001; T20I: 2009; First-class: 2000; List A: 2000; T20: 2003

BEST BATTING: 212 Essex vs Leicestershire, Chelmsford, 2004
BEST BOWLING: 1-122 Essex vs Northamptonshire, Northampton, 2008
COUNTY CAP: 2001; BENEFIT YEAR: 2011

FAMILY TIES? My dad played for Essex Amateurs
CAREER HIGHLIGHTS? Playing for my country
CRICKETERS PARTICULARLY ADMIRED? Nasser Hussain, Stuart Law, Robert Rollins, Ian Healy, Jack Russell, Alec Stewart, Adam Gilchrist
OTHER SPORTS PLAYED? Hockey (Essex U21), tennis (I played for GB U14 vs Sweden U14)
OTHER SPORTS FOLLOWED? Football
NOTES: Current Essex captain in four-day cricket. Achieved the 'double' of 1,037 runs and 51 dismissals in 2004. In a Pro40 match against Durham in September 2009, he hit five sixes in consecutive balls from Scott Borthwick

Batting	Mat	Inns	NO	Runs	HS	Ave	SR	100	50	Ct	St
Tests	7	12	3	226	48	25.11	34.55	0	0	17	1
ODIs	11	6	3	41	13	13.66	57.74	0	0	13	7
T20Is	5	5	2	37	14*	12.33	115.62	0	0	3	3
First-class	223	336	44	10829	212	37.08		19	55	624	52
List A	193	145	38	3044	83*	28.44		0	15	216	56
Twenty20	120	101	28	1686	65*	23.09	139.10	0	6	55	40

Bowling	Mat	Balls	Runs	Wkts	BBI	BBM	Ave	Econ	SR	5w	10
Tests	7	-	-	-	-	-	-	-	-	-	-
ODIs	11	-	-	-	-	-	-	-	-	-	-
T20Is	5	-	-	-	-	-	-	-	-	-	-
First-class	223	84	128	1	1/122	1/122	128.00	9.14	84.0	0	0
List A	193	-	-	-	-	-	-	-	-	-	-
Twenty20	120	-	-	-	-	-	-	-	-	-	-

PAUL FRANKS   LHB RMF W2

FULL NAME: Paul John Franks
BORN: February 3, 1979, Mansfield, Nottinghamshire
SQUAD NO: 8
HEIGHT: 6ft 2in
NICKNAME: Franksie, Pike, The General
EDUCATION: Minster School, Southwell
TEAMS: England, Mid West Rhinos, Nottinghamshire
CAREER: ODI: 2000; First-class: 1996; List A: 1997; T20: 2003

NOTTINGHAMSHIRE

BEST BATTING: 123* Nottinghamshire vs Leicestershire, Leicester, 2003
BEST BOWLING: 7-56 Nottinghamshire vs Middlesex, Lord's, 2000
COUNTY CAP: 1999; BENEFIT YEAR: 2007

CAREER HIGHLIGHTS? My England debut, the County Championship wins in 2005 and 2010 and T20 Finals Day
CRICKETING HEROES? Ian Botham, Andrew Flintoff, Graeme Swann
NON-CRICKETING HEROES? Eric Cantona, Seve Ballesteros
BEST PLAYER IN COUNTY CRICKET? Marcus Trescothick
TIPS FOR THE TOP? Alex Hales, Jos Buttler
WHEN RAIN STOPS PLAY? Changing-room banter or catching up on sleep
FAVOURITE FILM? Top Gun, Major League
DREAM HOLIDAY? Bali
FANTASY SLIP CORDON? Keeper: Paul Gascoigne, 1st: Me, 2nd: Elle Macpherson, 3rd: David Beckham, Gully: Luke Fletcher
TWITTER FEED: @thegeneral_8

Batting	Mat	Inns	NO	Runs	HS	Ave	SR	100	50	Ct	St
ODIs	1	1	0	4	4	4.00	23.52	0	0	1	0
First-class	215	313	56	7185	123*	27.95		4	41	69	0
List A	184	135	41	2039	84*	21.69		0	7	28	0
Twenty20	50	30	13	287	29*	16.88	117.62	0	0	8	0

Bowling	Mat	Balls	Runs	Wkts	BBI	BBM	Ave	Econ	SR	5w	10
ODIs	1	54	48	0	-	-	-	5.33	-	0	0
First-class	215	31587	17322	524	7/56		33.05	3.29	60.2	11	0
List A	184	6757	5701	198	6/27	6/27	28.79	5.06	34.1	3	0
Twenty20	50	479	687	20	2/12	2/12	34.35	8.60	23.9	0	0

OLLIE FRECKINGHAM RHB RFM

FULL NAME: Oliver Henry Freckingham
BORN: November 12, 1988, Oakham, Rutland
SQUAD NO: 24
HEIGHT: 6ft 1in
NICKNAME: Frecko
EDUCATION: King Edward School, Melton Mowbray
TEAMS: Leicestershire, Leicestershire 2nd XI
CAREER: First-class: 2013

BEST BATTING: 30 Leicestershire vs Gloucestershire, Bristol, 2013
BEST BOWLING: 6-125 Leicestershire vs Northamptonshire, Northampton, 2013

FAMILY TIES? My dad and uncle played huge amounts of village cricket
WHO WOULD PLAY YOU IN A FILM OF YOUR LIFE? Liam Neeson
CAREER HIGHLIGHTS? Taking my first five-wicket haul against Northamptonshire in the 2013 season
SUPERSTITIONS? I always put my left boot on first and when batting my left pad has to be strapped before the right
MOST MARKED CHARACTERISTIC? My increasingly balding hair
BEST PLAYER IN COUNTY CRICKET? From what I saw in the 2013 season, Will Gidman was the toughest opponent
TIPS FOR THE TOP? Shiv Thakor, Tymal Mills and James Taylor
IF YOU WEREN'T A CRICKETER? I'd be cutting fairways at Rutland County Golf Club
DESERT ISLAND DISC? Westlife – Coast To Coast
CRICKETING HEROES? Andrew Flintoff, Brett Lee and Dale Steyn
NON-CRICKETING HEROES? Tiger Woods – I'm a huge golf fan and he single-handedly took the game to another level. David Beckham – he's been a hero of mine ever since he scored that goal against Greece
ACCOMPLISHMENTS? I would love to write about a degree or A-Levels in here but I have none so my six Rutland Count Golf Club Championships will have to do
WHEN YOU RETIRE? I'd like to run a coffee shop/bar/night club abroad somewhere hot
TWITTER FEED: @olliefreck

Batting	Mat	Inns	NO	Runs	HS	Ave	SR	100	50	Ct	St
First-class	15	21	2	204	30	10.73	39.00	0	0	4	0

Bowling	Mat	Balls	Runs	Wkts	BBI	BBM	Ave	Econ	SR	5w	10
First-class	15	2394	1584	36	6/125	9/188	44.00	3.96	66.5	1	0

JAMES FULLER

RHB RFM

FULL NAME: James Kerr Fuller
BORN: January 24, 1990, Cape Town, Cape Province, South Africa
SQUAD NO: 26
HEIGHT: 6ft 3in
NICKNAME: Foz, Fozza, Fuller
EDUCATION: Westlake Boys' High School; Otago University
TEAMS: Gloucestershire, Gloucestershire 2nd XI, New Zealand Under-19s, Otago, Otago Under-19s
CAREER: First-class: 2010; List A: 2011; T20: 2011

BEST BATTING: 57 Gloucestershire vs Leicestershire, Cheltenham, 2012
BEST BOWLING: 6-24 Otago vs Wellington, Dunedin, 2013
COUNTY CAP: 2011

WHO WOULD PLAY YOU IN A FILM OF YOUR LIFE? Hugh Jackman – close enough to the Kiwi accent
CAREER HIGHLIGHTS? Playing as an overseas player for Otago and winning the New Zealand T20 competition. Taking six wickets in the CB40 vs the Netherlands. Taking my first 10-wicket haul in a first-class match vs Wellington
SUPERSTITIONS? I always put my left pad on first before going out to bat
MOST MARKED CHARACTERISTIC? I'm tall with a big fast bowler's bum
BEST PLAYER IN COUNTY CRICKET? Darren Stevens
IF YOU WEREN'T A CRICKETER? I'd be an engineer or a professional golfer
FAVOURITE TV? The Crowd Goes Wild, South Park
CRICKETING HEROES? Glenn McGrath, Brett Lee, Chris Cairns
SURPRISING FACT? I studied Neuroscience at university
FANTASY SLIP CORDON? Keeper: Muhammad Ali, 1st: Glenn McGrath, 2nd: Lance Armstrong (because he would convince the umpires the ball had carried), 3rd: Stephen Fleming, 4th: Jono Anderson, 5th: Richard Branson, Gully: Myself
TWITTER FEED? @james_fuller246

Batting	Mat	Inns	NO	Runs	HS	Ave	SR	100	50	Ct	St
First-class	20	25	2	299	57	13.00	60.16	0	1	7	0
List A	26	21	7	295	43	21.07	104.98	0	0	7	0
Twenty20	30	17	7	208	36	20.80	155.22	0	0	12	0

Bowling	Mat	Balls	Runs	Wkts	BBI	BBM	Ave	Econ	SR	5w	10
First-class	20	3071	1818	53	6/24	10/79	34.30	3.55	57.9	3	1
List A	26	1048	1012	43	6/35	6/35	23.53	5.79	24.3	1	0
Twenty20	30	636	895	42	4/24	4/24	21.30	8.44	15.1	0	0

ANDREW GALE
LHB LB R1 MVP94

FULL NAME: Andrew William Gale
BORN: November 28, 1983, Dewsbury, Yorkshire
SQUAD NO: 26
HEIGHT: 6ft 2in
NICKNAME: Galey, Bobby
EDUCATION: Heckmondwike Grammar
TEAMS: England Lions, England Under-19s, Yorkshire, Yorkshire Cricket Board
CAREER: First-class: 2004; List A: 2002; T20: 2004

BEST BATTING: 272 Yorkshire vs Nottinghamshire, Scarborough, 2013
BEST BOWLING: 1-33 Yorkshire vs Loughborough UCCE, Leeds, 2007
COUNTY CAP: 2008

CAREER HIGHLIGHTS? Being capped for Yorkshire, being appointed captain of Yorkshire, captaining England Lions, scoring 272 vs Nottinghamshire and leading Yorkshire in the Champions League
SUPERSTITIONS? I don't like odd numbers and I always chew gum in the field
MOST MARKED CHARACTERISTIC? Determination
BEST PLAYER IN COUNTY CRICKET? Gary Ballance
TIPS FOR THE TOP? Matthew Fisher, Will Rhodes, the Overton brothers
IF YOU WEREN'T A CRICKETER? I'd be running my own company, Pro Coach Cricket Academy
DESERT ISLAND DISC? A Simply Red album
FAVOURITE TV? Breaking Bad, Entourage
CRICKETING HEROES? Marcus Trescothick, Ricky Ponting, Michael Vaughan, Graeme Smith
NON-CRICKETING HEROES? David Beckham, Andy Booth, Ronnie Jepson
CRICKET RULE YOU'D CHANGE? You should be allowed to play in the rain!
SURPRISING FACT? I've reached Grade 2 at piano
TWITTER FEED? @GaleyLad

Batting	Mat	Inns	NO	Runs	HS	Ave	SR	100	50	Ct	St
First-class	111	175	14	6039	272	37.50		15	25	42	0
List A	123	115	11	3270	125*	31.44		2	18	25	0
Twenty20	86	78	9	1879	91	27.23	123.21	0	14	28	0

Bowling	Mat	Balls	Runs	Wkts	BBI	BBM	Ave	Econ	SR	5w	10
First-class	111	115	238	1	1/33	1/33	238.00	12.41	115.0	0	0
List A	123	-	-	-	-	-	-	-	-	-	-
Twenty20	86	-	-	-	-	-	-	-	-	-	-

JOE GATTING RHB OB

FULL NAME: Joe Stephen Gatting
BORN: November 25, 1987, Brighton, Sussex
SQUAD NO: 6
HEIGHT: 5ft 11in
EDUCATION: Brighton College
TEAMS: Hampshire, Sussex, Sussex 2nd XI
CAREER: First-class: 2009; List A: 2009; T20: 2009

HAMPSHIRE

BEST BATTING: 152 Sussex vs Cambridge UCCE, Cambridge, 2009
BEST BOWLING: 1-8 Sussex vs Nottinghamshire, Nottingham, 2011

FAMILY TIES? My uncle [Mike of England and Middlesex] and dad [Steve of Middlesex 2nd XI] both played
CAREER HIGHLIGHTS? Playing in the Champions League in India and my first centuries in first-class and List A cricket
SUPERSTITIONS? I put my left pad on first
CRICKETING HEROES? My uncle, Brian Lara and Andrew Symonds
NON-CRICKETING HEROES? Tiger Woods
BEST PLAYER IN COUNTY CRICKET? Marcus Trescothick
TIP FOR THE TOP? Luke Wells
IF YOU WEREN'T A CRICKETER? I'd be a footballer
FAVOURITE BOOK? Bounce by Matthew Syed
DREAM HOLIDAY? Barbados
ACCOMPLISHMENTS? Playing Championship football for Brighton and Hove Albion
SURPRISING FACT? I'm colour blind (green and red)
FANTASY SLIP CORDON? Keeper: John Bishop (good for sledging), 1st: James Corden (funny banter and would have a supply of sweets), 2nd: Me, 3rd: Eric Cantona (arrogant and skillful), Gully: Mike Tyson (to scare the batsmen)

Batting	Mat	Inns	NO	Runs	HS	Ave	SR	100	50	Ct	St
First-class	35	50	4	1376	152	29.91	60.53	3	6	17	0
List A	43	40	5	975	122	27.85	86.20	1	4	15	0
Twenty20	52	41	8	486	45*	14.72	111.72	0	0	22	0

Bowling	Mat	Balls	Runs	Wkts	BBI	BBM	Ave	Econ	SR	5w	10
First-class	35	210	130	2	1/8	1/8	65.00	3.71	105.0	0	0
List A	43	20	22	0	-	-	-	6.60	-	0	0
Twenty20	52	10	14	1	1/12	1/12	14.00	8.40	10.0	0	0

ALEX GIDMAN

RHB RM R5 MVP93

FULL NAME: Alexander Peter Richard Gidman
BORN: June 22, 1981, High Wycombe, Buckinghamshire
SQUAD NO: 5
HEIGHT: 6ft 2in
NICKNAME: Giddo
EDUCATION: Wycliffe College
TEAMS: England A, England Lions, Gloucestershire, Gloucestershire 2nd XI, Marylebone Cricket Club, Otago
CAREER: First-class: 2002; List A: 2001; T20: 2003

BEST BATTING: 211 Gloucestershire vs Kent, Cheltenham, 2013
BEST BOWLING: 4-47 Gloucestershire vs Glamorgan, Cardiff, 2009
BENEFIT YEAR: 2012

FAMILY TIES? I play with my brother Will at Gloucestershire
WHO WOULD PLAY YOU IN A FILM OF YOUR LIFE? Gerard Butler
CAREER HIGHLIGHTS? Winning the 2003 and 2004 one-day trophies. Representing England A on three tours
MOST MARKED CHARACTERISTIC? My ears
BEST PLAYER IN COUNTY CRICKET? Marcus Trescothick
TIP FOR THE TOP? Dan Housego
DESERT ISLAND DISC? Kings Of Leon – Only By The Night
FAVOURITE TV? MasterChef
BIGGEST DRESSING DOWN YOU'VE RECEIVED? Our coach John Bracewell has given us plenty of dressing downs. All deserved!
CRICKETING HEROES? Steve Waugh
NON-CRICKETING HEROES? Jonny Wilkinson, Michael Jordan
ACCOMPLISHMENTS? Bringing up children is pretty challenging!
WHEN YOU RETIRE? I'd like to run my own business
TWITTER FEED: @agiddo

Batting	Mat	Inns	NO	Runs	HS	Ave	SR	100	50	Ct	St
First-class	174	298	24	9904	211	36.14	57.64	20	54	114	0
List A	190	178	19	4367	116	27.46		5	21	65	0
Twenty20	81	70	11	1212	64	20.54	120.47	0	3	16	0

Bowling	Mat	Balls	Runs	Wkts	BBI	BBM	Ave	Econ	SR	5w	10
First-class	174	7304	4521	102	4/47		44.32	3.71	71.6	0	0
List A	190	3256	2786	71	5/42	5/42	39.23	5.13	45.8	1	0
Twenty20	81	292	410	9	2/24	2/24	45.55	8.42	32.4	0	0

WILL GIDMAN

LHB RMF R1 W2 MVP88

FULL NAME: William Robert Simon Gidman
BORN: February 14, 1985, High Wycombe, Buckinghamshire
SQUAD NO: 23
HEIGHT: 6ft 2in
NICKNAME: Gidders, Giddo, Wilbur, PT
EDUCATION: Wycliffe College, Stonehouse; Berkshire College of Agriculture
TEAMS: Durham, Durham 2nd XI, Gloucestershire, Gloucestershire 2nd XI, Marylebone Cricket Club Young Cricketers
CAREER: First-class: 2007; List A: 2003; T20: 2011

BEST BATTING: 143 Gloucestershire vs Leicestershire, Bristol, 2013
BEST BOWLING: 6-15 Gloucestershire vs Leicestershire, Bristol, 2013
COUNTY CAP: 2011 (Gloucestershire)

FAMILY TIES? My brother Alex plays for Gloucestershire
WHO WOULD PLAY YOU IN A FILM OF YOUR LIFE? Will Poulter
CAREER HIGHLIGHTS? Any hundreds or five-fer. Getting 10 wickets and a hundred in the same match was really special
TIPS FOR THE TOP? Chris Dent, Craig Miles, Mark Wood
IF YOU WEREN'T A CRICKETER? I'd be doing sports coaching. Or I'd be an astronaut!
DESERT ISLAND DISC? Meatloaf's Greatest Hits
FAVOURITE TV? Breaking Bad
CRICKETING HEROES? Garry Sobers
NON-CRICKETING HEROES? Jonny Wilkinson, Muhammad Ali
ACCOMPLISHMENTS? Getting married and bringing up our daughter
WHEN YOU RETIRE? I'll work for NASA!
SURPRISING FACT? I am king of the Gloucestershire CCC table-tennis table
FANTASY SLIP CORDON? Keeper: Jack Whitehall, 1st: Andrew Flintoff, 2nd: James Corden, 3rd: Jamie Redknapp, Gully: John Bishop
TWITTER FEED: @wgiddo

Batting	Mat	Inns	NO	Runs	HS	Ave	SR	100	50	Ct	St
First-class	42	64	11	1900	143	35.84	49.72	2	12	9	0
List A	38	23	4	379	76	19.94		0	1	12	0
Twenty20	8	7	1	78	40*	13.00	86.66	0	0	2	0

Bowling	Mat	Balls	Runs	Wkts	BBI	BBM	Ave	Econ	SR	5w	10
First-class	42	6742	3326	154	6/15	10/43	21.59	2.95	43.7	7	1
List A	38	1266	1044	30	4/36	4/36	34.80	4.94	42.2	0	0
Twenty20	8	48	76	1	1/18	1/18	76.00	9.50	48.0	0	0

JOHN GLOVER
RHB RMF

FULL NAME: John Charles Glover
BORN: August 29, 1989, Cardiff
SQUAD NO: 36
HEIGHT: 6ft 4in
NICKNAME: Gloves, Glovebox, MC
EDUCATION: Llantarnam Comprehensive School; Durham University
TEAMS: Durham MCCU, Durham UCCE, Glamorgan, Wales Minor Counties
CAREER: First-class: 2008; List A: 2012

BEST BATTING: 55 Glamorgan vs Kent, Cardiff, 2012
BEST BOWLING: 5-38 Durham UCCE vs Durham, Durham University, 2009

WHY CRICKET? My father played for Panteg Cricket Club so I grew up watching and playing
CAREER HIGHLIGHTS? My Glamorgan debut in 2011 and playing in the first County Championship game under floodlights
SUPERSTITIONS? I always put my left pad on first
CRICKETING HEROES? Courtney Walsh
NON-CRICKETING HEROES? Graeme McDowell, Martyn Williams, Kevin McNaughton
IF YOU WEREN'T A CRICKETER? I would probably be trying to find a job in sport development
WHEN RAIN STOPS PLAY? Either reading books or watching films
FAVOURITE TV? Friends
FAVOURITE FILM? Pulp Fiction, Gladiator, Inception
FAVOURITE BOOK? 1984 by George Orwell
ACCOMPLISHMENTS? Getting a 2:1 from Durham University
GUILTY PLEASURES? Standing on the terraces at Cardiff City FC and football accumulators on a Saturday afternoon
FANTASY SLIP CORDON? Keeper: Dave Grohl, 1st: Jimi Hendrix, 2nd: Flea from Red Hot Chili Peppers, 3rd: Eric Clapton, Gully: James Brown – the jam session after the game would be amazing
TWITTER FEED: @John_Gloves

Batting	Mat	Inns	NO	Runs	HS	Ave	SR	100	50	Ct	St
First-class	26	34	9	328	55	13.12	37.48	0	2	7	0
List A	5	3	1	16	10	8.00	94.11	0	0	1	0

Bowling	Mat	Balls	Runs	Wkts	BBI	BBM	Ave	Econ	SR	5w	10
First-class	26	3441	1945	53	5/38	7/121	36.69	3.39	64.9	1	0
List A	5	216	230	7	3/34	3/34	32.85	6.38	30.8	0	0

BILLY GODLEMAN   LHB LB

FULL NAME: Billy Ashley Godleman
BORN: February 11, 1989, Camden, London
SQUAD NO: 1
HEIGHT: 6ft 3in
EDUCATION: Islington Green School
TEAMS: Derbyshire, England Under-19s,
Essex, Middlesex, Middlesex 2nd XI
CAREER: First-class: 2005; List A: 2007; T20:
2006

DERBYSHIRE

BEST BATTING: 130 Essex vs Leicestershire, Leicester, 2011

NOTES: At 17, left-hander Godleman became the second-youngest debutant ever for Middlesex when he turned out for them against Cambridge UCCE at Fenner's in 2005. The first-youngest was Steven Finn, playing in the same game. He was called up for England U19 in 2007 for whom he made 149* against Pakistan at Grace Road. Joined Essex in 2009 where he hit his highest first-class score of 130 vs Leicestershire at Leicester two years later. After mixed success, he was released and joined Derbyshire in 2012. He did not feature heavily in the 2013 season but returned to the first team for the last two YB40 games, scoring 60 against Essex at Colchester

Batting	Mat	Inns	NO	Runs	HS	Ave	SR	100	50	Ct	St
First-class	78	134	4	3722	130	28.63	40.70	5	18	55	0
List A	22	21	3	434	82	24.11	71.61	0	2	7	0
Twenty20	27	24	0	427	69	17.79	106.21	0	3	14	0
Bowling	Mat	Balls	Runs	Wkts	BBI	BBM	Ave	Econ	SR	5w	10
First-class	78	30	35	0	-	-	-	7.00	-	0	0
List A	22	-	-	-	-	-	-	-	-	-	-
Twenty20	27	-	-	-	-	-	-	-	-	-	-

GLAMORGAN

FULL NAME: Murray William Goodwin
BORN: December 11, 1972, Harare, Zimbabwe
SQUAD NO: 40
HEIGHT: 5ft 9in
NICKNAME: Muzza, Fuzz, Goodie
EDUCATION: St John's, Zimbabwe; Newtonmoore Senior High, Australia
TEAMS: Netherlands, Zimbabwe, Glamorgan, Mashonaland, Subiaco-Floreat, Sussex, Warriors, Western Australia
CAREER: Test: 1998; ODI: 1998; First-class: 1994; List A: 1994; T20: 2003

BEST BATTING: 344* Sussex vs Somerset, Taunton, 2009
BEST BOWLING: 2-23 Zimbabweans vs Lahore City, Lahore, 1998
COUNTY CAP: 2001 (Sussex); BENEFIT YEAR: 2009 (Sussex)

FAMILY TIES? My dad is a coach and my eldest brother [Darrell] played for Zimbabwe
CAREER HIGHLIGHTS? Becoming the highest individual scorer in Sussex's history – 335* vs Leicestershire, September 2003 at Hove. I broke Duleepsinhji's record of 333 from 1930
CRICKETING HEROES? Allan Border, Steve Waugh, Curtly Ambrose, Sachin Tendulkar
OTHER SPORTS PLAYED? Hockey, golf, tennis
NOTES: Goodwin scored over 24,000 runs in all competitions during a 12-year stay at Sussex after calling time on his international career in 2000. Moved to Glamorgan ahead of the 2013 season and scored 1,263 first-class runs at 57.40 in his first year with the club, as well as playing a lead role in their progress to the YB40 final

Batting	Mat	Inns	NO	Runs	HS	Ave	SR	100	50	Ct	St
Tests	19	37	4	1414	166*	42.84	46.31	3	8	10	0
ODIs	71	70	3	1818	112*	27.13	68.50	2	8	20	0
First-class	312	539	46	23376	344*	47.41		71	97	162	0
List A	375	356	42	11170	167	35.57		14	67	112	0
Twenty20	108	100	13	2423	102*	27.85	122.80	2	13	21	0

Bowling	Mat	Balls	Runs	Wkts	BBI	BBM	Ave	Econ	SR	5w	10
Tests	19	119	69	0	-	-	-	3.47	-	0	0
ODIs	71	248	210	4	1/12	1/12	52.50	5.08	62.0	0	0
First-class	312	713	376	7	2/23		53.71	3.16	101.8	0	0
List A	375	351	306	7	1/9	1/9	43.71	5.23	50.1	0	0
Twenty20	108	-	-	-	-	-	-	-	-	-	-

RECORDO GORDON

RHB RFM

FULL NAME: Recordo Olton Gordon
BORN: October 12, 1991, St Elizabeth's, Jamaica
SQUAD NO: 44
HEIGHT: 6ft
NICKNAME: Ricky, Flash
EDUCATION: Aston Manor Academy; Hamstead Hall Sixth Form
TEAMS: Herefordshire, Warwickshire, Warwickshire 2nd XI, Warwickshire Under-15s, Warwickshire Under-17s
CAREER: First-class: 2013; List A: 2013

BEST BATTING: 13 Warwickshire vs Somerset, Birmingham, 2013
BEST BOWLING: 2-45 Warwickshire vs Sussex, Birmingham, 2013

CAREER HIGHLIGHTS? Taking 4-4 in a T20 game and gaining a contract with Warwickshire
CRICKETING HEROES? Courtney Walsh and Curtly Ambrose
NON-CRICKETING HEROES? My father
BEST PLAYER IN COUNTY CRICKET? There are a lot of good players but I really rate Alfonso Thomas as a bowler
TIPS FOR THE TOP? Jos Buttler, Ben Stokes
IF YOU WEREN'T A CRICKETER? I'd be at universiy
WHEN RAIN STOPS PLAY? I'm putting my feet up and getting them out of my bowling boots
FAVOURITE TV? The Big Bang Theory
FAVOURITE BOOK? The Tomb
DREAM HOLIDAY? Jamaica
ACCOMPLISHMENTS? Being head boy of my school
SURPRISING SKILL? I'm a good cook and baker
TWITTER FEED: @recordogordon

Batting	Mat	Inns	NO	Runs	HS	Ave	SR	100	50	Ct	St
First-class	4	4	1	38	13	12.66	25.85	0	0	2	0
List A	2	1	0	1	1	1.00	50.00	0	0	0	0

Bowling	Mat	Balls	Runs	Wkts	BBI	BBM	Ave	Econ	SR	5w	10
First-class	4	570	288	7	2/45	3/68	41.14	3.03	81.4	0	0
List A	2	84	122	2	1/46	1/46	61.00	8.71	42.0	0	0

LEWIS GREGORY · RHB RMF

SOMERSET

FULL NAME: Lewis Gregory
BORN: May 24, 1992, Plymouth, Devon
SQUAD NO: 24
EDUCATION: Hele's School, Plymouth
TEAMS: Devon, England Under-19s, Somerset, Somerset 2nd XI
CAREER: First-class: 2011; List A: 2010; T20: 2011

BEST BATTING: 52 Somerset vs Derbyshire, Taunton, 2013
BEST BOWLING: 5-38 Somerset vs Middlesex, Lord's, 2013

TWITTER FEED: @lewisgregory23
NOTES: A former England U19 skipper. Took a hat-trick for Somerset's 2nd XI against Essex in 2010. Claimed 4-49 on his List A debut in 2010 against the touring Pakistanis. The leading wicket-taker in the 2011 FL t20, claiming 18 wickets at 17. Returned figures of 4-39 in Somerset's 2012 FL t20 quarter-final win against Essex. In 2013 he played six first-class matches, taking 14 wickets at 25.57, including a career-best 5-38 against Middlesex at Lord's. Scored a maiden half-century against Derbyshire at Taunton last September

Batting	Mat	Inns	NO	Runs	HS	Ave	SR	100	50	Ct	St
First-class	16	22	3	282	52	14.84	47.07	0	1	3	0
List A	23	12	1	128	39	11.63	68.44	0	0	9	0
Twenty20	22	10	3	110	22	15.71	105.76	0	0	7	0

Bowling	Mat	Balls	Runs	Wkts	BBI	BBM	Ave	Econ	SR	5w	10
First-class	16	1240	770	25	5/38	7/52	30.80	3.72	49.6	1	0
List A	23	539	566	25	4/27	4/27	22.64	6.30	21.5	0	0
Twenty20	22	345	444	26	4/15	4/15	17.07	7.72	13.2	0	0

DAVID GRIFFITHS   LHB RFM

FULL NAME: David Andrew Griffiths
BORN: September 10, 1985, Newport, Isle of Wight
SQUAD NO: 18
HEIGHT: 6ft 1in
NICKNAME: Griff
EDUCATION: Sandown High School
TEAMS: Hampshire, Hampshire 2nd XI, Kent
CAREER: First-class: 2006; List A: 2008; T20: 2007

KENT

BEST BATTING: 31* Hampshire vs Surrey, Southampton, 2007
BEST BOWLING: 6-85 Hampshire vs Nottinghamshire, Nottingham, 2011

FAMILY TIES? My dad captained Wales and my step-dad and all my uncles have played for the Isle Of Wight
WHO WOULD PLAY YOU IN A FILM OF YOUR LIFE? Mark Wahlberg
CAREER HIGHLIGHTS? Winning the Pro40 final at Lord's with Hampshire on the last ball
SUPERSTITIONS? I always put my left ankle brace on first and always turn right at the end of my run-up
MOST MARKED CHARACTERISTIC? I'm always happy and will talk to anyone
BEST PLAYER IN COUNTY CRICKET? Michael Carberry
TIPS FOR THE TOP? My little brother Kieran Griffiths and Lewis McManus
IF YOU WEREN'T A CRICKETER? I'd be working on a farm on the Isle of Wight or in Wales
DESERT ISLAND DISC? Any Carribean music. I love it!
CRICKETING HEROES? Darren Gough, Brett Lee, Graham Thorpe
NON-CRICKETING HEROES? David Beckham, Michael Schumacher
ACCOMPLISHMENTS? Renovating my whole house
FANTASY SLIP CORDON? Keeper: David Beckham, 1st: Michael Schumacher, 2nd: Steve Irwin, 3rd: Scarlett Johansson, Gully: Eva Mendes
TWITTER FEED: @griffta18

Batting	Mat	Inns	NO	Runs	HS	Ave	SR	100	50	Ct	St
First-class	36	50	19	202	31*	6.51	25.76	0	0	4	0
List A	22	6	5	15	7	15.00	50.00	0	0	4	0
Twenty20	9	1	1	4	4*	-	36.36	0	0	1	0

Bowling	Mat	Balls	Runs	Wkts	BBI	BBM	Ave	Econ	SR	5w	10
First-class	36	5716	3654	105	6/85	7/102	34.80	3.83	54.4	3	0
List A	22	780	795	27	4/29	4/29	29.44	6.11	28.8	0	0
Twenty20	9	186	237	9	3/13	3/13	26.33	7.64	20.6	0	0

GAVIN GRIFFITHS   RHB RFM

LANCASHIRE

FULL NAME: Gavin Timothy Griffiths
BORN: November 19, 1993, Ormskirk, Lancashire
SQUAD NO: 18
HEIGHT: 6ft 2in
NICKNAME: Gavlar
EDUCATION: St Michael's Church of England High School, Chorley; St Mary's College, Crosby
TEAMS: England Under-19s, Lancashire 2nd XI, Lancashire Under-17s
CAREER: Yet to make first-team debut

WHO WOULD PLAY YOU IN A FILM OF YOUR LIFE? Liam Neeson
CAREER HIGHLIGHTS? Representing England U19, being 12th man for England at Old Trafford and signing for Lancashire at 17
MOST MARKED CHARACTERISTIC? My brick head
BEST PLAYER IN COUNTY CRICKET? Moeen Ali
TIP FOR THE TOP? Haseeb Hameed
IF YOU WEREN'T A CRICKETER? I'd be a chess grandmaster
DESERT ISLAND DISC? Eminem
FAVOURITE TV? The Inbetweeners
CRICKETING HEROES? Allan Donald, Freddie Flintoff, Glen Chapple
SURPRISING FACT? I once played chess for my country
CRICKET RULE YOU'D CHANGE? There should be smaller bats and bigger stumps
FANTASY SLIP CORDON? Keeper: Jay Cartwright, 1st: Russell Howard, 2nd: Myself, 3rd: Andrew Flintoff, Gully: Jimmy Bullard
TWITTER FEED: @gavvlar

TIM GROENEWALD — RHB RFM MVP32

FULL NAME: Timothy Duncan Groenewald
BORN: January 10, 1984, Pietermaritzburg, South Africa
SQUAD NO: 12
HEIGHT: 6ft 2in
NICKNAME: TG, Groeners
EDUCATION: Maritzburg College, Natal; University of South Africa
TEAMS: Derbyshire, Warwickshire, Warwickshire 2nd XI
CAREER: First-class: 2006; List A: 2006; T20: 2006

DERBYSHIRE

BEST BATTING: 78 Warwickshire vs Bangladesh A, Birmingham, 2008
BEST BOWLING: 6-50 Derbyshire vs Surrey, Croydon, 2009
COUNTY CAP: 2011 (Derbyshire)

WHO WOULD PLAY YOU IN A FILM OF YOUR LIFE? Tony Palladino – he knows how to imitate a South African accent pretty well. He's a great impersonator!
CAREER HIGHLIGHTS? Winning Division Two of the Championship with Derbyshire in 2012
SUPERSTITIONS? It's not really a superstition but I don't really eat on match days. I'll have a bit of breakfast but that's about it till dinner time
MOST MARKED CHARACTERISTIC? I talk a lot when I'm nervous or excited
BEST PLAYER IN COUNTY CRICKET? Joe Root
TIP FOR THE TOP? Mark Wood at Durham
IF YOU WEREN'T A CRICKETER? I'd run a coffee shop/deli and do a bit of coaching
DESERT ISLAND DISC? Any house music by Mark Turner
CRICKETING HEROES? Allan Donald and Jonty Rhodes
WHEN YOU RETIRE? I'd like to own a coffee shop/deli
SURPRISING FACT? I'm a big fan of deep-sea fishing
CRICKET RULE YOU'D CHANGE? No heavy roller after the start of play on day one of first-class cricket
TWITTER FEED: @timmyg12

Batting	Mat	Inns	NO	Runs	HS	Ave	SR	100	50	Ct	St
First-class	82	113	31	1515	78	18.47	48.85	0	4	29	0
List A	69	40	12	391	36	13.96	97.75	0	0	17	0
Twenty20	73	29	13	298	41	18.62	124.68	0	0	20	0

Bowling	Mat	Balls	Runs	Wkts	BBI	BBM	Ave	Econ	SR	5w	10
First-class	82	14011	7257	233	6/50	8/97	31.14	3.10	60.1	9	0
List A	69	2480	2259	71	4/22	4/22	31.81	5.46	34.9	0	0
Twenty20	73	1295	1720	65	4/21	4/21	26.46	7.96	19.9	0	0

NICK GUBBINS

LHB LB

MIDDLESEX

FULL NAME: Nicholas Richard Trail Gubbins
BORN: December 31, 1993, Richmond, Surrey
SQUAD NO: 18
HEIGHT: 6ft
NICKNAME: Gubbs, Gubbo
EDUCATION: Radley College; Leeds University
TEAMS: Leeds/Bradford MCCU, Middlesex, Middlesex 2nd XI, Middlesex Under-15s, Middlesex Under-17s
CAREER: First-class: 2013

BEST BATTING: 14 Middlesex vs Yorkshire, Leeds, 2013

FAMILY TIES? My dad played a high level of club cricket in the Surrey Premier Division when he was younger. My brother plays in the Sussex League for Stirlands CC
WHO WOULD PLAY YOU IN A FILM OF YOUR LIFE? Probably someone like Tom Hardy – we're both absolute beasts in the gym
CAREER HIGHLIGHTS? Making my first-class debut for Leeds/Bradford MCCU against Yorkshire at Headingley last season
MOST MARKED CHARACTERISTIC? I get called "posh boy" a lot in the cricketing world. Imagine what I think of them…
BEST PLAYER IN COUNTY CRICKET? Graham Onions. His record last season speaks for itself!
TIPS FOR THE TOP? My MCCU captain last season, Luis Reece of Lancashire CCC, is absolute quality and his work-rate is as high as I've seen. He could go very far
IF YOU WEREN'T A CRICKETER? Anything I can do to become a millionaire fairly quickly would be nice. I fancy that kind of lifestyle and not having to work for it…
DESERT ISLAND DISC? Earth, Wind And Fire – September
FAVOURITE TV? Friends
CRICKETING HEROES? Andrew Strauss has always been a role model of mine. Still is!
NON-CRICKETING HEROES? All of my family and my girlfriend. They keep my feet on the ground when I've done well and boost my morale when I'm down
ACCOMPLISHMENTS? I'm currently sitting on a 2:1 degree from the University of Leeds which is a nice back-up
TWITTER FEED: @ngubbins18

Batting	Mat	Inns	NO	Runs	HS	Ave	SR	100	50	Ct	St
First-class	2	4	0	40	14	10.00	40.40	0	0	1	0

Bowling	Mat	Balls	Runs	Wkts	BBI	BBM	Ave	Econ	SR	5w	10
First-class	2	-	-	-	-	-	-	-	-	-	-

HARRY GURNEY RHB LFM MVP53

FULL NAME: Harry Frederick Gurney
BORN: October 25, 1986, Nottingham
SQUAD NO: 11
HEIGHT: 6ft 1in
NICKNAME: Gurns, Sicknote, Contract, Chicken Legs
EDUCATION: Garendon High School; Loughborough Grammar School; University of Leeds
TEAMS: Leeds/Bradford MCCU, Leicestershire, Nottinghamshire
CAREER: First-class: 2007; List A: 2009; T20: 2009

BEST BATTING: 24* Leicestershire vs Middlesex, Leicester, 2009
BEST BOWLING: 5-81 Nottinghamshire vs Somerset, Nottingham, 2013

CAREER HIGHLIGHTS? Signing my first professional contract and my Championship and Pro40 five-wicket hauls
CRICKETING HEROES? Ryan Sidebottom, Dale Steyn
NON-CRICKETING HEROES? Peter Jones, Richard Branson, Alan Sugar
BEST PLAYER IN COUNTY CRICKET? Marcus Trescothick
TIP FOR THE TOP? Joe Root
IF YOU WEREN'T A CRICKETER? I'd probably be doing something in the financial sector
WHEN RAIN STOPS PLAY? Poker, reading, and drinking coffee
FAVOURITE TV? Frozen Planet
FAVOURITE FILM? Crash
FAVOURITE BOOK? Bounce by Matthew Syed
DREAM HOLIDAY? St Anton, Austria
SURPRISING SKILL? I play the piano and speak pretty good French
SURPRISING FACTS? I was once a sponsored poker player
FANTASY SLIP CORDON? Keeper: Ricky Gervais, 1st: Alan Sugar, 2nd: Natalie Portman, 3rd: Me, Gully: Harry Redknapp
TWITTER FEED? @gurneyhf

Batting	Mat	Inns	NO	Runs	HS	Ave	SR	100	50	Ct	St
First-class	42	46	20	135	24*	5.19	29.73	0	0	6	0
List A	39	9	2	25	13*	3.57	54.34	0	0	3	0
Twenty20	47	3	2	5	5*	5.00	83.33	0	0	5	0

Bowling	Mat	Balls	Runs	Wkts	BBI	BBM	Ave	Econ	SR	5w	10
First-class	42	6260	3536	100	5/81	7/148	35.36	3.38	62.6	2	0
List A	39	1483	1355	40	5/24	5/24	33.87	5.48	37.0	2	0
Twenty20	47	941	1131	52	3/21	3/21	21.75	7.21	18.0	0	0

CALUM HAGGETT

LHB RM

KENT

FULL NAME: Calum John Haggett
BORN: October 30, 1990, Taunton, Somerset
SQUAD NO: 25
HEIGHT: 6ft 3in
NICKNAME: Haggs
EDUCATION: Crispin School, Street; Millfield School
TEAMS: England Under-19s, Kent, Kent 2nd XI, Somerset, Somerset 2nd XI
CAREER: First-class: 2013; List A: 2013; T20: 2011

BEST BATTING: 44* Kent vs Gloucestershire, Canterbury, 2013
BEST BOWLING: 4-94 Kent vs Glamorgan, Canterbury, 2013

FAMILY TIES? My dad played village cricket
WHO WOULD PLAY YOU IN A FILM OF YOUR LIFE? Peter Kay
CAREER HIGHLIGHTS? Making my Championship debut
BEST PLAYER IN COUNTY CRICKET? Rob Key
TIP FOR THE TOP? Daniel Bell-Drummond
IF YOU WEREN'T A CRICKETER? I'd be struggling
DESERT ISLAND DISC? Baha Men – Who Let The Dogs Out?
FAVOURITE TV? The Inbetweeners.
CRICKETING HEROES? Mark Davies
NON-CRICKETING HEROES? The Dalai Lama, Nelson Mandela and the Queen
CRICKET RULE YOU'D CHANGE? Batsmen should use smaller bats!

Batting	Mat	Inns	NO	Runs	HS	Ave	SR	100	50	Ct	St
First-class	12	14	7	249	44*	35.57	42.13	0	0	3	0
List A	3	2	0	2	2	1.00	33.33	0	0	1	0
Twenty20	5	3	1	4	2	2.00	80.00	0	0	1	0

Bowling	Mat	Balls	Runs	Wkts	BBI	BBM	Ave	Econ	SR	5w	10
First-class	12	1788	907	26	4/94	4/94	34.88	3.04	68.7	0	0
List A	3	120	161	4	2/97	2/97	40.25	8.05	30.0	0	0
Twenty20	5	48	71	1	1/15	1/15	71.00	8.87	48.0	0	0

SAM HAIN

RHB LB

FULL NAME: Samuel Robert Hain
BORN: July 16, 1995, Hong Kong
SQUAD NO: 16
HEIGHT: 6ft 1in
NICKNAME: Hainy
EDUCATION: The Southport School, Gold Coast, Queensland
TEAMS: Australia Under-19s, Queensland Under-17s, Queensland Under-19s, Warwickshire, Warwickshire 2nd XI
CAREER: List A: 2013

FAMILY TIES? I have no real family ties to cricket. My mum was into her hockey and running and my dad was into his rugby. I started playing at about six or seven with my two brothers in the backyard and it just went from there

WHO WOULD PLAY YOU IN A FILM OF YOUR LIFE? I'm thinking Leonardo DiCaprio

CAREER HIGHLIGHTS? It's only my second year here at Warwickshire but I really enjoyed settling in around the group. No particular highlights as of yet but if I had to pick one it would be my making my debut last year against Worcestershire

SUPERSTITIONS? I don't have any. I am bit of a neat freak though!

MOST MARKED CHARACTERISTIC? Going round picking up all the lads' bats

BEST PLAYER IN COUNTY CRICKET? It's hard to pick just one but I'm thinking Moeen Ali, who had a great season across all formats

TIP FOR THE TOP? Varun Chopra is in for big things in the future I reckon

IF YOU WEREN'T A CRICKETER? I'd most likely be back at home in Australia, just coming out of school and going to university

CRICKETING HEROES? Michael Clarke and Freddie Flintoff back in the day were the ones I loved to watch

NON-CRICKETING HEROES? Kelly Slater

ACCOMPLISHMENTS? I've finished school and got my driver's license. Exciting stuff…

WHEN YOU RETIRE? I'm hoping to go to university after cricket to become a paramedic

CRICKET RULE YOU'D CHANGE? Starting up day/night Test matches somewhere down the line would be exciting I think

TWITTER FEED: @SammieHain

Batting	Mat	Inns	NO	Runs	HS	Ave	SR	100	50	Ct	St
List A	1	1	0	1	1	1.00	33.33	0	0	0	0

Bowling	Mat	Balls	Runs	Wkts	BBI	BBM	Ave	Econ	SR	5w	10
List A	1	-	-	-	-	-	-	-	-	-	-

ALEX HALES   RHB RM R1 MVP92

NOTTINGHAMSHIRE

FULL NAME: Alexander Daniel Hales
BORN: January 3, 1989, Hillingdon, Middlesex
SQUAD NO: 10
HEIGHT: 6ft 5in
NICKNAME: Baz, Halesy, Trigg
EDUCATION: Chesham High School
TEAMS: England, Buckinghamshire, Duronto Rajshahi, England Lions, Melbourne Renegades, Nottinghamshire, Nottinghamshire 2nd XI
CAREER: T20I: 2011; First-class: 2008; List A: 2008; T20: 2009

BEST BATTING: 184 Nottinghamshire vs Somerset, Nottingham, 2011
BEST BOWLING: 2-63 Nottinghamshire vs Yorkshire, Nottingham, 2009
COUNTY CAP: 2011

WHO WOULD PLAY YOU IN A FILM OF YOUR LIFE? Daniel Radcliffe
CAREER HIGHLIGHTS? My England debut
MOST MARKED CHARACTERISTIC? Patience
BEST PLAYER IN COUNTY CRICKET? Jonny Bairstow
TIPS FOR THE TOP? Jake Ball, George Bacon
IF YOU WEREN'T A CRICKETER? I'd be a groundsman
FAVOURITE TV? Keeping Up With The Kardashians
CRICKETING HEROES? Ian Bell, Nick Lines, Vinnie Fazio
NON-CRICKETING HEROES? Steve Jobs, Paul Merson
ACCOMPLISHMENTS? I rowed across the English Channel in an old tin bath
WHEN YOU RETIRE? I'd like to be a professional poker player
FANTASY SLIP CORDON? Keeper: Bilal Shafayat, 1st: Maria Sharapova, 2nd: Arsene Wenger, 3rd: Kirstie Edwards, Gully: Jimmy Carr
TWITTER FEED: @AlexHales1

Batting	Mat	Inns	NO	Runs	HS	Ave	SR	100	50	Ct	St
T20Is	25	25	4	712	99	33.90	134.59	0	6	11	0
First-class	61	104	5	3367	184	34.01	56.37	6	22	57	0
List A	72	70	2	2262	150*	33.26	99.38	4	13	21	0
Twenty20	96	95	6	2565	99	28.82	139.62	0	19	33	0

Bowling	Mat	Balls	Runs	Wkts	BBI	BBM	Ave	Econ	SR	5w	10
T20Is	25	-	-	-	-	-	-	-	-	-	-
First-class	61	281	167	3	2/63	2/63	55.66	3.56	93.6	0	0
List A	72	4	10	0	-	-	-	15.00	-	0	0
Twenty20	96	3	7	0	-	-	-	14.00	-	0	0

ANDREW HALL

RHB RMF R1 MVP49

FULL NAME: Andrew James Hall
BORN: July 31, 1975, Johannesburg, Transvaal, South Africa
SQUAD NO: 1
HEIGHT: 6ft
NICKNAME: HB, HBomb, Hancock
EDUCATION: Hoerskool Alberton
TEAMS: South Africa, Chandigarh Lions, Dolphins, Easterns, Gauteng, Kent, Mashonaland Eagles, Northamptonshire, Transvaal, Worcestershire
CAREER: Test: 2002; ODI: 1999; T20I: 2006; First-class: 1995; List A: 1995; T20: 2003

BEST BATTING: 163 South Africa vs India, Kanpur, 2004
BEST BOWLING: 6-77 Easterns vs Western Province, Benoni, 2002
COUNTY CAPS: 2003 (Worcestershire); 2005 (Kent); 2009 (Northamptonshire)

CAREER HIGHLIGHTS? The ODI against Australia when we chased down 438 to win, scoring 163 vs India in Kanpur and taking 5-18 vs England in the 2007 World Cup
SUPERSTITIONS? They're more like habits but I always pad up the same way and like to keep whites for batting and bowling if I've done well in them. I always cross the boundary with my left foot first
TIPS FOR THE TOP? Olly Stone and David Willey
CRICKETING HEROES? Ray Jennings, Clive Rice, Jimmy Cook
FANTASY SLIP CORDON? Keeper: Tom Daley (a good diver), 1st: Me, 2nd: Peter Schmeichel (steady hands), 3rd: Lee Evans (you've got to have a laugh), Gully: Usain Bolt (he can sprint to field balls that beat the cordon)
TWITTER FEED: @AndrewHall99

Batting	Mat	Inns	NO	Runs	HS	Ave	SR	100	50	Ct	St
Tests	21	33	4	760	163	26.20	46.06	1	3	16	0
ODIs	88	56	13	905	81	21.04	75.04	0	3	29	0
T20Is	2	1	0	11	11	11.00	110.00	0	0	0	0
First-class	226	332	44	10379	163	36.03		15	62	213	0
List A	314	248	49	5932	129*	29.80		6	33	92	1
Twenty20	101	86	21	1420	66*	21.84	118.62	0	4	27	0

Bowling	Mat	Balls	Runs	Wkts	BBI	BBM	Ave	Econ	SR	5w	10
Tests	21	3001	1617	45	3/1	5/20	35.93	3.23	66.6	0	0
ODIs	88	3341	2515	95	5/18	5/18	26.47	4.51	35.1	1	0
T20Is	2	48	60	3	3/22	3/22	20.00	7.50	16.0	0	0
First-class	226	33648	16337	604	6/77		27.04	2.91	55.7	17	1
List A	314	12448	9905	360	5/18	5/18	27.51	4.77	34.5	2	0
Twenty20	101	1918	2432	118	6/21	6/21	20.61	7.60	16.2	2	0

RORY HAMILTON-BROWN

RHB OB R1

FULL NAME: Rory James Hamilton-Brown
BORN: September 3, 1987, Wellington Hospital, London
SQUAD NO: 27
HEIGHT: 6ft
NICKNAME: Razza
EDUCATION: Millfield School
TEAMS: England Under-19s, Mashonaland Eagles, Surrey, Surrey 2nd XI, Sussex, Sussex 2nd XI
CAREER: First-class: 2005; List A: 2005; T20: 2008

BEST BATTING: 171* Sussex vs Yorkshire, Hove, 2009
BEST BOWLING: 2-49 Sussex vs Yorkshire, Hove, 2009
COUNTY CAP: 2011 (Surrey)

CAREER HIGHLIGHTS? Being appointed Surrey captain and winning the CB40 in 2011
CRICKETING HEROES? Jacques Kallis and Herschelle Gibbs
NON-CRICKETING HEROES? Joel Stransky and Mark Wright
BEST PLAYER IN COUNTY CRICKET? Marcus Trescothick
TIPS FOR THE TOP? Daniel Bell-Drummond, Billy Godleman
IF YOU WEREN'T A CRICKETER? I would like to be working in the City
FAVOURITE TV? An Idiot Abroad
FAVOURITE FILM? The Other Guys
FAVOURITE BOOK? The Innocent Man by John Grisham
DREAM HOLIDAY? Las Vegas
GUILTY PLEASURES? A love of the commentary-style of Bob Willis

Batting	Mat	Inns	NO	Runs	HS	Ave	SR	100	50	Ct	St
First-class	66	112	7	3576	171*	34.05	74.63	8	16	39	0
List A	83	72	3	1720	115	24.92	108.44	2	7	32	0
Twenty20	83	77	3	1340	87*	18.10	117.54	0	4	26	0

Bowling	Mat	Balls	Runs	Wkts	BBI	BBM	Ave	Econ	SR	5w	10
First-class	66	961	594	9	2/49	3/85	66.00	3.70	106.7	0	0
List A	83	1266	1211	32	3/28	3/28	37.84	5.73	39.5	0	0
Twenty20	83	526	667	36	4/15	4/15	18.52	7.60	14.6	0	0

MILES HAMMOND

LHB OB

FULL NAME: Miles Arthur Halhead Hammond
BORN: January 11, 1996, Cheltenham, Gloucestershire
SQUAD NO: 88
EDUCATION: St Edward's School, Oxford
TEAMS: England Under-19s, Gloucestershire, Gloucestershire 2nd XI
CAREER: First-class: 2013; List A: 2013; T20: 2013

BEST BATTING: 4 Gloucestershire vs Worcestershire, Cheltenham, 2013
BEST BOWLING: 1-96 Gloucestershire vs Glamorgan, Bristol, 2013

NOTES: Young off-spinner Hammond debuted across all formats for Gloucestershire last year and featured in the 2014 U19 World Cup in February, as England finished in third place in UAE. He made his only appearance of the tournament in the third-place play-off against Australia, taking 1-41 from eight overs. He made his first-class debut against Glamorgan last June and took three wickets in two matches against Yorkshire in last year's YB40. He has played two U19 Tests for England, both against South Africa last year, and 11 U19 ODIs

Batting	Mat	Inns	NO	Runs	HS	Ave	SR	100	50	Ct	St
First-class	2	2	0	4	4	2.00	28.57	0	0	1	0
List A	2	-	-	-	-	-	-	-	-	0	0
Twenty20	1	-	-	-	-	-	-	-	-	0	0

Bowling	Mat	Balls	Runs	Wkts	BBI	BBM	Ave	Econ	SR	5w	10
First-class	2	294	196	1	1/96	1/155	196.00	4.00	294.0	0	0
List A	2	78	79	3	2/29	2/29	26.33	6.07	26.0	0	0
Twenty20	1	12	17	0	-	-	-	8.50	-	0	0

OLIVER HANNON-DALBY

LHB RMF

FULL NAME: Oliver James Hannon-Dalby
BORN: June 20, 1989, Halifax, Yorkshire
SQUAD NO: 20
HEIGHT: 6ft 8in
NICKNAME: Bunse, Dave, OHD, Shaggy
EDUCATION: Brooksbank School, Elland
TEAMS: Warwickshire, Warwickshire 2nd XI,
Yorkshire, Yorkshire 2nd XI
CAREER: First-class: 2008; List A: 2011; T20: 2012

BEST BATTING: 13 Warwickshire vs Oxford MCCU, Oxford, 2013
BEST BOWLING: 5-68 Yorkshire vs Somerset, Leeds, 2010

CAREER HIGHLIGHTS? My professional debut and first five-fer
CRICKETING HEROES? Glenn McGrath, Brett Lee
BEST PLAYER IN COUNTY CRICKET? Marcus Trescothick
TIPS FOR THE TOP? Jonny Bairstow, Azeem Rafiq
IF YOU WEREN'T A CRICKETER? I'd be a teacher
WHEN RAIN STOPS PLAY? Eating or crosswords
FAVOURITE TV? Top Gear, Family Guy
FAVOURITE FILM? Blades Of Glory
FAVOURITE BOOK? The Guinness Book Of World Records
DREAM HOLIDAY? Barbados
ACCOMPLISHMENTS? Buying my first house
SURPRISING SKILL? I can juggle
SURPRISING FACTS? I was local high jump champion aged 12, Yorkshire CCC Scrabble champion in 2011 and I'm a Cyril Sneer impressionist
TWITTER FEED: @OHD_20

Batting	Mat	Inns	NO	Runs	HS	Ave	SR	100	50	Ct	St
First-class	28	29	12	82	13	4.82	15.27	0	0	3	0
List A	6	1	1	21	21*	-	210.00	0	0	3	0
Twenty20	2	-	-	-	-	-	-	-	-	0	0

Bowling	Mat	Balls	Runs	Wkts	BBI	BBM	Ave	Econ	SR	5w	10
First-class	28	4011	2328	55	5/68	7/122	42.32	3.48	72.9	2	0
List A	6	197	247	6	2/22	2/22	41.16	7.52	32.8	0	0
Twenty20	2	48	58	3	2/23	2/23	19.33	7.25	16.0	0	0

ARUN HARINATH LHB OB

FULL NAME: Arun Harinath
BORN: April 3, 1987, Sutton, Surrey
SQUAD NO: 10
HEIGHT: 5ft 10in
NICKNAME: The Baron
EDUCATION: Tiffin Boys' Grammar School; Loughborough University
TEAMS: Loughborough UCCE, Marylebone Cricket Club, Surrey, Surrey 2nd XI
CAREER: First-class: 2007; List A: 2009

SURREY

BEST BATTING: 154 Surrey vs Derbyshire, Derby, 2013
BEST BOWLING: 1-2 Surrey vs Middlesex, Lord's, 2013

FAMILY TIES? My father played cricket in Sri Lanka and my brother Muhunthan Harinath was on the staff at Surrey
WHO WOULD PLAY YOU IN A FILM OF YOUR LIFE? My brother – he would do a very good impression of me!
CAREER HIGHLIGHTS? Making my Surrey debut and getting my maiden first-class hundred in 2012
BEST PLAYER IN COUNTY CRICKET? Chris Rogers, Marcus Trescothick
TIP FOR THE TOP? Dom Sibley
DESERT ISLAND DISC? The Strokes – Is This It?
FAVOURITE TV? The West Wing
BIGGEST DRESSING DOWN YOU'VE RECEIVED? From Dil [Graham Dilley] after losing one of our UCCE games!
CRICKETING HEROES? Brian Lara, Graham Thorpe, Mark Ramprakash
NON-CRICKETING HEROES? Tom Hanks, Roger Federer
ACCOMPLISHMENTS? Obtaining my degree
FANTASY SLIP CORDON? Keeper: Frank Sinatra, 1st: Russell Brand, 2nd: Barack Obama, 3rd: Me, 4th: Roger Federer, Gully: Spider-Man

Batting	Mat	Inns	NO	Runs	HS	Ave	SR	100	50	Ct	St
First-class	44	76	4	2081	154	28.90	40.52	3	12	11	0
List A	3	3	1	74	52	37.00	86.04	0	1	1	0

Bowling	Mat	Balls	Runs	Wkts	BBI	BBM	Ave	Econ	SR	5w	10
First-class	44	54	36	1	1/2	1/2	36.00	4.00	54.0	0	0
List A	3	-	-	-	-	-	-	-	-	-	-

BEN HARMISON

LHB RM

KENT

FULL NAME: Ben William Harmison
BORN: January 9, 1986, Ashington, Northumberland
SQUAD NO: 21
HEIGHT: 6ft 5in
NICKNAME: Harmy
EDUCATION: Ashington High School
TEAMS: Durham, Durham 2nd XI, Kent, Northumberland
CAREER: First-class: 2006; List A: 2005; T20: 2006

BEST BATTING: 110 Durham vs Oxford UCCE, The Parks, 2006
BEST BOWLING: 4-27 Durham vs Surrey, Guildford, 2008

CAREER HIGHLIGHTS? Signing my first professional contract at the age of 18. Consecutive hundreds in my first two first-class games for Durham
CRICKET MOMENT TO FORGET? Getting a first-baller vs Bangladesh in a one-dayer
CRICKETERS PARTICULARLY ADMIRED? Andrew Flintoff
FAVOURITE FILM? Armageddon
FAVOURITE BAND? Take That
OTHER SPORTS PLAYED? Golf, fishing, football
OTHER SPORTS FOLLOWED? Football (Newcastle United)
RELAXATIONS? Fishing and listening to music
FAMILY TIES? My brother Steve played for Durham and England. My father Jim and brother James play league cricket for Ashington CC
TWITTER FEED: @harmy14

Batting	Mat	Inns	NO	Runs	HS	Ave	SR	100	50	Ct	St
First-class	62	98	9	2525	110	28.37	44.91	5	12	34	0
List A	61	50	7	1049	67	24.39	71.99	0	3	21	0
Twenty20	38	23	9	177	24	12.64	103.50	0	0	14	0

Bowling	Mat	Balls	Runs	Wkts	BBI	BBM	Ave	Econ	SR	5w	10
First-class	62	1893	1371	34	4/27	6/98	40.32	4.34	55.6	0	0
List A	61	865	855	24	3/43	3/43	35.62	5.93	36.0	0	0
Twenty20	38	348	471	23	3/20	3/20	20.47	8.12	15.1	0	0

JAMES HARRIS — RHB RMF W1

FULL NAME: James Alexander Russell Harris
BORN: May 16, 1990, Morriston, Swansea, Glamorgan, Wales
SQUAD NO: 5
HEIGHT: 6ft 1in
NICKNAME: Rolf, Bones, Lloyd Christmas, LC
EDUCATION: Pontarddulais Comprehensive; Gorseinon College
TEAMS: England Lions, England Performance Programme, England Under-19s, Glamorgan, Middlesex, Wales Minor Counties
CAREER: First-class: 2007; List A: 2007; T20: 2008

BEST BATTING: 87* Glamorgan vs Nottinghamshire, Swansea, 2007
BEST BOWLING: 7-66 Glamorgan vs Gloucestershire, Bristol, 2007
COUNTY CAP: 2010 (Glamorgan)

FAMILY TIES? My father played for British Universities
CAREER HIGHLIGHTS? Taking 12 wickets in my second first-class game on my 17th birthday. Receiving my county cap in 2010. The England Lions tour to the West Indies in 2011
SUPERSTITIONS? I put my left pad on before my right
CRICKETING HEROES? Glenn McGrath, Jacques Kallis
NON-CRICKETING HEROES? Tiger Woods
BEST PLAYER IN COUNTY CRICKET? Marcus Trescothick
TIPS FOR THE TOP? James Taylor, Ben Stokes, Jos Buttler
IF YOU WEREN'T A CRICKETER? Attempting to play golf most probably
WHEN RAIN STOPS PLAY? I'm on the iPad
FAVOURITE TV? Entourage
FAVOURITE FILM? The Shawshank Redemption, Anchorman
FAVOURITE BOOK? The Da Vinci Code, Angels And Demons
DREAM HOLIDAY? Barbados
TWITTER FEED: @James_Harris9

Batting	Mat	Inns	NO	Runs	HS	Ave	SR	100	50	Ct	St
First-class	76	102	21	1721	87*	21.24		0	7	19	0
List A	43	27	7	200	29	10.00	70.67	0	0	10	0
Twenty20	28	16	8	100	18	12.50	114.94	0	0	3	0

Bowling	Mat	Balls	Runs	Wkts	BBI	BBM	Ave	Econ	SR	5w	10
First-class	76	13441	7199	255	7/66	12/118	28.23	3.21	52.7	9	1
List A	43	1691	1596	59	4/48	4/48	27.05	5.66	28.6	0	0
Twenty20	28	494	723	24	4/23	4/23	30.12	8.78	20.5	0	0

JAMIE HARRISON

RHB LFM

DURHAM

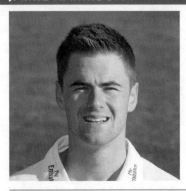

FULL NAME: Jamie Harrison
BORN: November 19, 1990, Whiston, Knowsley, Lancashire
SQUAD NO: 13
HEIGHT: 6ft 1in
NICKNAME: Bieber, Jay
EDUCATION: Sedbergh School
TEAMS: Durham, Durham 2nd XI, Durham Academy, Gloucestershire 2nd XI, Sedbergh School
CAREER: First-class: 2012; List A: 2012

BEST BATTING: 35 Durham vs Yorkshire, Scarborough, 2013
BEST BOWLING: 5-31 Durham vs Surrey, Chester-le-Street, 2013

FAMILY TIES? My step-dad played in the local Cumbria leagues
WHO WOULD PLAY YOU IN A FILM OF YOUR LIFE? Jack O'Connell
CAREER HIGHLIGHTS? Being part of the Championship-winning side last season
SUPERSTITIONS? I always neatly lay out the clothes I'm going to wear to the ground on a chair the night before. I pack my bag with warm-up gear on the left and whites to the right. I swim and stretch the night and morning before play
MOST MARKED CHARACTERISTIC? Unnecessary aggression, stuttering start to my run-up and my taste in music (good or bad)
BEST PLAYER IN COUNTY CRICKET? Graham Onions
TIPS FOR THE TOP? Paul Coughlin, Rammy Singh, Graham Clark
IF YOU WEREN'T A CRICKETER? Who knows! Probably travelling the world blagging a living
DESERT ISLAND DISC? Dirty Vegas – Greatest Hits
FAVOURITE TV? Shameless
CRICKETING HEROES? Wasim Akram
NON-CRICKETING HEROES? Sean Long, Keiron Cunningham, my dad
ACCOMPLISHMENTS? My life has been/is nothing other than cricket
WHEN YOU RETIRE? I'd like to work in social care
SURPRISING FACT? I own two budgies – Boris and Beryl!
TWITTER FEED: @jayharrison13

Batting	Mat	Inns	NO	Runs	HS	Ave	SR	100	50	Ct	St
First-class	7	10	1	120	35	13.33	42.85	0	0	0	0
List A	2	1	1	7	7*	-	140.00	0	0	0	0

Bowling	Mat	Balls	Runs	Wkts	BBI	BBM	Ave	Econ	SR	5w	10
First-class	7	985	596	24	5/31	7/74	24.83	3.63	41.0	1	0
List A	2	72	83	2	2/51	2/51	41.50	6.91	36.0	0	0

NICK HARRISON

RHB RMF

FULL NAME: Nicholas Luke Harrison
BORN: February 3, 1992, Bath, Somerset
SQUAD NO: 12
HEIGHT: 6ft 4in
NICKNAME: Gink, Ninky
EDUCATION: Hardenhuish School, Chippenham
TEAMS: Wiltshire, Worcestershire, Worcestershire 2nd XI
CAREER: First-class: 2012; List A: 2011

BEST BATTING: 10 Worcestershire vs Somerset, Taunton, 2012
BEST BOWLING: 2-78 Worcestershire vs Oxford MCCU, Oxford, 2012

WHO WOULD PLAY YOU IN A FILM OF YOUR LIFE? It'd be rock, paper, scissors between Matt Damon, Ben Affleck and Christian Bale
CAREER HIGHLIGHTS? My first-class and Pro40 debuts
MOST MARKED CHARACTERISTIC? I'm very laid-back
BEST PLAYER IN COUNTY CRICKET? Moeen Ali
TIPS FOR THE TOP? Tom Fell, Tom Kohler-Cadmore
DESERT ISLAND DISC? Lorde – Pure Heroin
FAVOURITE TV? Two And A Half Men, Breaking Bad, Rules Of Engagement
CRICKETING HEROES? Glenn McGrath
NON-CRICKETING HEROES? Floyd Mayweather, Usain Bolt, Ronnie O'Sullivan
ACCOMPLISHMENTS? I represented my county for basketball age groups and in a golf competition aged 15
CRICKET RULE YOU'D CHANGE? Teams should get the new ball earlier – quick games are good games
WHEN YOU RETIRE? I'll hopefully retire to a 170-foot yacht and travel the world
FANTASY SLIP CORDON? Keeper: Jimmy Carr, 1st: Myself, 2nd: Joey Essex, 3rd: Usain Bolt, Gully: Rihanna
TWITTER FEED: @NickHarro10

Batting	Mat	Inns	NO	Runs	HS	Ave	SR	100	50	Ct	St
First-class	3	4	0	12	10	3.00	20.68	0	0	1	0
List A	7	2	2	7	5*	-	100.00	0	0	0	0

Bowling	Mat	Balls	Runs	Wkts	BBI	BBM	Ave	Econ	SR	5w	10
First-class	3	276	176	3	2/78	2/78	58.66	3.82	92.0	0	0
List A	7	306	364	8	2/43	2/43	45.50	7.13	38.2	0	0

CHARLIE HARTLEY RHB RMF

FULL NAME: Charles Frederick Hartley
BORN: January 4, 1994, Bromsgrove, Worcestershire
SQUAD NO: 22
HEIGHT: 6ft 2in
NICKNAME: Chappers, Chaps
EDUCATION: Millfield School
TEAMS: Kent 2nd XI
CAREER: Yet to make first-team debut

WHO WOULD PLAY YOU IN A FILM OF YOUR LIFE? Adam Sandler
CAREER HIGHLIGHTS? Signing a contract with Kent, closely followed by winning the National Club T20 with Millfield
MOST MARKED CHARACTERISTIC? Over-thinking... actually, maybe not
BEST PLAYER IN COUNTY CRICKET? Jos Buttler
TIP FOR THE TOP? Daniel Bell-Drummond
IF YOU WEREN'T A CRICKETER? I'd be in events hospitality or working hard to get into property
DESERT ISLAND DISC? The Beach Boys – Pet Sounds
FAVOURITE TV? NCIS, Top Gear and 8 Out Of 10 Cats
CRICKETING HEROES? Andrew Flintoff
NON-CRICKETING HEROES? Johnny Wilkinson and Maximus Decimus Meridius from Gladiator
WHEN YOU RETIRE? Events hospitality, management, property and something on TV
SURPRISING FACT? I spent a lot of my time during school cricket being dropped from first teams and having my character tested. Keep pursuing your dreams and you will make it
FANTASY SLIP CORDON? Keeper: James Corden, 1st: Chris Stark, 2nd: Mila Kunis, 3rd: Will Smith, Gully: Jack Whitehall. I'd be listening over the stump mic

JOHN HASTINGS   RHB RFM

FULL NAME: John Wayne Hastings
BORN: November 4, 1985, Penrith, New
South Wales, Australia
SQUAD NO: 2
HEIGHT: 6ft 4in
NICKNAME: The Duke
TEAMS: Australia, Australia A, Durham,
Kochi Tuskers Kerala, New South Wales 2nd
XI, New South Wales U17, New South Wales
U19, Victoria
CAREER: Test: 2012; ODI: 2010; T20I: 2010;
First-class: 2007; List A: 2007; T20: 2007

DURHAM

BEST BATTING: 93 Victoria vs Tasmania, Hobart, 2010
BEST BOWLING: 5-30 Victoria vs Western Australia, Perth, 2012

NOTES: Hastings has been announced as Durham's overseas player for the 2014 season and
will be available in all forms of cricket. He signed as a T20 player for Sussex ahead of the
2013 season but an ankle injury prevented him playing a game. The muscular allrounder
built his reputation in Australian domestic cricket when in 2009/10 he was Victoria's highest
wicket-taker across all three formats, including 446 runs at 37.16 and 36 wickets at 26.13 in
the Sheffield Shield. He was subsequently named Bradman Young Cricketer of the Year.
Played a solitary Test in 2012, against South Africa at Perth

Batting	Mat	Inns	NO	Runs	HS	Ave	SR	100	50	Ct	St
Tests	1	2	0	52	32	26.00	59.09	0	0	1	0
ODIs	11	9	4	82	21*	16.40	105.12	0	0	2	0
T20Is	3	3	2	32	15	32.00	177.77	0	0	0	0
First-class	38	54	4	1109	93	22.18	46.89	0	4	18	0
List A	55	41	12	614	69*	21.17	101.15	0	1	18	0
Twenty20	39	27	7	179	23*	8.95	117.76	0	0	11	0

Bowling	Mat	Balls	Runs	Wkts	BBI	BBM	Ave	Econ	SR	5w	10
Tests	1	234	153	1	1/51	1/153	153.00	3.92	234.0	0	0
ODIs	11	546	410	8	2/35	2/35	51.25	4.50	68.2	0	0
T20Is	3	60	66	3	3/14	3/14	22.00	6.60	20.0	0	0
First-class	38	6638	3094	119	5/30	7/87	26.00	2.79	55.7	4	0
List A	55	2882	2363	83	4/28	4/28	28.46	4.91	34.7	0	0
Twenty20	39	783	962	38	3/14	3/14	25.31	7.37	20.6	0	0

LEWIS HATCHETT

LHB LMF

SUSSEX

FULL NAME: Lewis James Hatchett
BORN: January 21, 1990, Shoreham-by-Sea, Sussex
SQUAD NO: 5
HEIGHT: 6ft 3in
NICKNAME: Hatch
EDUCATION: Steyning Grammar School
TEAMS: Sussex, Sussex 2nd XI
CAREER: First-class: 2010; List A: 2013; T20: 2013

BEST BATTING: 21 Sussex vs Yorkshire, Hove, 2013
BEST BOWLING: 5-47 Sussex vs Leicestershire, Leicester, 2010

CAREER HIGHLIGHTS? My first-class debut, my maiden first-class five-fer and signing a contract with my home county Sussex. All of these happening in the same year!
SUPERSTITIONS? I try not to move places when the team are doing well and I sometimes shave my head before games. I always turn left at the top of my run-up
CRICKETING HEROES? I grew up watching the old West Indian bowlers such as Courtney Walsh and Curtly Ambrose. I watched a lot of Jason Lewry at Sussex, which is probably where I learnt my action from
NON-CRICKETING HEROES? My family and our country's servicemen, past and present
BEST PLAYER IN COUNTY CRICKET? Batting: Marcus Trescothick. Bowling: Glen Chapple
TIPS FOR THE TOP? Jos Buttler and Alex Hales look super-talented, those are two who stand out for me. I'd also back my mate Luke Wells to push on to higher things
IF YOU WEREN'T A CRICKETER? I would love to have been a Marine
DREAM HOLIDAY? Barbados – just to go and chill with friends out there
GUILTY PLEASURES? Chocolate fudge cake is my Achilles heel!
SURPRISING FACTS? I suffer from Poland Syndrome and I have my Sussex cap number tattooed under my left arm
TWITTER FEED: @lewis_hatchett

Batting	Mat	Inns	NO	Runs	HS	Ave	SR	100	50	Ct	St
First-class	13	16	4	104	21	8.66	31.23	0	0	2	0
List A	7	1	0	1	1	1.00	25.00	0	0	2	0
Twenty20	2	-	-	-	-	-	-	-	-	0	0

Bowling	Mat	Balls	Runs	Wkts	BBI	BBM	Ave	Econ	SR	5w	10
First-class	13	1759	1070	32	5/47	6/92	33.43	3.64	54.9	1	0
List A	7	250	239	10	3/65	3/65	23.90	5.73	25.0	0	0
Twenty20	2	18	55	0	-	-	-	18.33	-	0	0

FULL NAME: Thomas George Helm
BORN: May 7, 1994, Stoke Mandeville Hospital, Buckinghamshire
SQUAD NO: 14
HEIGHT: 6ft 4in
NICKNAME: Ched, Helmy
EDUCATION: Misbourne School
TEAMS: Buckinghamshire, Buckinghamshire Under-13s, Buckinghamshire Under-14s, Buckinghamshire Under-15s, Buckinghamshire Under-17s, England Under-19s, Middlesex, Middlesex 2nd XI
CAREER: First-class: 2013; List A: 2013

MIDDLESEX

BEST BATTING: 18 Middlesex vs Yorkshire, Leeds, 2013
BEST BOWLING: 3-46 Middlesex vs Yorkshire, Leeds, 2013

FAMILY TIES? My brother played minor counties cricket for Buckinghamshire
WHO WOULD PLAY YOU IN A FILM OF YOUR LIFE? Justin Timberlake
CAREER HIGHLIGHTS? Making my List A debut vs the Unicorns and my County Championship debut vs Yorkshire
MOST MARKED CHARACTERISTIC? Long limbs
BEST PLAYER IN COUNTY CRICKET? Ben Stokes
TIPS FOR THE TOP? Craig Miles and Harry Podmore
IF YOU WEREN'T A CRICKETER? I'd be studying at university
DESERT ISLAND DISC? Anything by Michael Bublé
FAVOURITE TV? Rules Of Engagement
CRICKETING HEROES? James Anderson
NON-CRICKETING HEROES? David Beckham, Ian Poulter, José Mourinho
ACCOMPLISHMENTS? Passing my A-Levels
WHEN YOU RETIRE? I'd like to become a coach in a hot country
FANTASY SLIP CORDON? Keeper: Lee Mack, 1st: Myself, 2nd: Jamie Foxx, 3rd: José Mourinho, Gully: Robert Downey Jr
TWITTER FEED: @TomHelm14

Batting	Mat	Inns	NO	Runs	HS	Ave	SR	100	50	Ct	St
First-class	1	2	0	22	18	11.00	55.00	0	0	0	0
List A	2	-	-	-	-	-	-	-	-	0	0

Bowling	Mat	Balls	Runs	Wkts	BBI	BBM	Ave	Econ	SR	5w	10
First-class	1	108	78	5	3/46	5/78	15.60	4.33	21.6	0	0
List A	2	48	27	3	3/27	3/27	9.00	3.37	16.0	0	0

H

CAMERON HERRING   RHB WK

GLOUCESTERSHIRE

FULL NAME: Cameron Lee Herring
BORN: July 15, 1994, Abergavenny,
Monmouthshire, Wales
SQUAD NO: 29
HEIGHT: 5ft 5in
EDUCATION: Tredegar Comprehensive
TEAMS: Glamorgan Under-15s,
Gloucestershire, Gloucestershire 2nd XI
CAREER: First-class: 2013

BEST BATTING: 43 Gloucestershire vs Northamptonshire, Bristol , 2013

FAMILY TIES? I'm the first in my family to play county cricket but my dad is an ECB elite coach and my sister has played for the Wales Ladies' team
CAREER HIGHLIGHTS? Making my first-class debut against Essex at the start of the 2013 season and playing against Australia A later that year
SUPERSTITIONS? If two batsmen have been batting a while, I like to sit in the same spot until a wicket falls
MOST MARKED CHARACTERISTIC? My height (or lack of it)
BEST PLAYER IN COUNTY CRICKET? Kevin Pietersen
TIPS FOR THE TOP? Miles Hammond and Tom Shrewsbury have both already made their first-class debuts and I believe both will have very successful careers
IF YOU WEREN'T A CRICKETER? I'd probably be studying Sports Coaching at university to become a PE teacher
CRICKETING HEROES? Marcus Trescothick and AB de Villiers
NON-CRICKETING HEROES? Steven Gerrard
ACCOMPLISHMENTS? Playing for Newport County Football Academy and passing all my A-Levels while at school
WHEN YOU RETIRE? I'll go on a skiing holiday and spend weeks travelling around the big cities in America
CRICKET RULE YOU'D CHANGE? If the ball goes straight over the keeper's head from a delivery it shouldn't be given as byes
TWITTER FEED: @Camlee_196

Batting	Mat	Inns	NO	Runs	HS	Ave	SR	100	50	Ct	St
First-class	6	7	0	122	43	17.42	36.96	0	0	14	0
Bowling	Mat	Balls	Runs	Wkts	BBI	BBM	Ave	Econ	SR	5w	10
First-class	6	-	-	-	-	-	-	-	-	-	-

250

FULL NAME: Matthew Higginbottom
BORN: October 20, 1990, Stockport, Cheshire
SQUAD NO: 20
HEIGHT: 6ft 3in
NICKNAME: Higgy, Arthur, Higuain
EDUCATION: New Mills School; Leeds Metropolitan University
TEAMS: Bradford/Leeds UCCE, Derbyshire, Derbyshire 2nd XI, Leeds/Bradford MCCU
CAREER: First-class: 2012; List A: 2012

DERBYSHIRE

BEST BATTING: 31* Leeds/Bradford MCCU vs Yorkshire, Leeds, 2012
BEST BOWLING: 3-59 Derbyshire vs Middlesex, Derby, 2013

FAMILY TIES? My family has always played for the local village side
WHO WOULD PLAY YOU IN A FILM OF YOUR LIFE? Bradley Cooper
CAREER HIGHLIGHTS? Making my first-team debut against Australia in a tour game
BEST PLAYER IN COUNTY CRICKET? Shivnarine Chanderpaul
TIPS FOR THE TOP? Alex Hughes and Ben Cotton
IF YOU WEREN'T A CRICKETER? I'd still be at university
DESERT ISLAND DISC? Bastille – Bad Blood
FAVOURITE TV? Prison Break, Family Guy, How I Met Your Mother
CRICKETING HEROES? Darren Gough, Brian Lara
ACCOMPLISHMENTS? Getting a degree
WHEN YOU RETIRE? I'll play golf
FANTASY SLIP CORDON? Keeper: Jack Whitehall, 1st: Mila Kunis, 2nd: Dwayne 'The Rock' Johnson, 3rd: Jay-Z, Gully: Me
TWITTER FEED: @matthigg12

Batting	Mat	Inns	NO	Runs	HS	Ave	SR	100	50	Ct	St
First-class	6	11	4	108	31*	15.42	36.12	0	0	0	0
List A	1	-	-	-	-	-	-	-	-	0	0

Bowling	Mat	Balls	Runs	Wkts	BBI	BBM	Ave	Econ	SR	5w	10
First-class	6	731	484	14	3/59	4/99	34.57	3.97	52.2	0	0
List A	1	30	43	0	-	-	-	8.60	-	0	0

RYAN HIGGINS RHB OB

FULL NAME: Ryan F Higgins
BORN: April 3, 1995, Harare, Zimbabwe
SQUAD NO: 11
HEIGHT: 5ft 10in
NICKNAME: Higgo
EDUCATION: Bradfield College
TEAMS: Berkshire Under-14s, Berkshire Under-15s, Berkshire Under-17s, England Under-19s, Middlesex 2nd XI, Middlesex Under-17s, Middlesex Under-19s
CAREER: Yet to make first-team debut

FAMILY TIES? I'm related to Lesley Ames, an English wicketkeeper-batsman
WHO WOULD PLAY YOU IN A FILM OF YOUR LIFE? Probably Taylor Kitsch – he's an absolute legend in Friday Night Lights
CAREER HIGHLIGHTS? Playing for England U19 at the World Cup
MOST MARKED CHARACTERISTIC? Aggression
BEST PLAYER IN COUNTY CRICKET? Chris Rogers
TIPS FOR THE TOP? Matthew Fisher, Joe Clarke
IF YOU WEREN'T A CRICKETER? I'd be on a beach in Australia on my gap year
DESERT ISLAND DISC? Tyga – Careless World
FAVOURITE TV? Friday Night Lights
CRICKETING HEROES? Kevin Pietersen and Ricky Ponting
NON-CRICKETING HEROES? Rafael Nadal and my dad
ACCOMPLISHMENTS? Passing my A-Levels was a decent day
WHEN YOU RETIRE? I'll go back and live in Zimbabwe
SURPRISING FACT? I have a skull and roses tattoo
FANTASY SLIP CORDON? Keeper: Muhammad Ali, 1st: Rafael Nadal, 2nd: Miley Cyrus, 3rd: Me, Gully: Elvis Presley
TWITTER FEED: @ryanhiggins21

JAMES HILDRETH

RHB RM R4 MVP86

FULL NAME: James Charles Hildreth
BORN: September 9, 1984, Milton Keynes
SQUAD NO: 25
HEIGHT: 5ft 10in
NICKNAME: Hildy, Hildz
EDUCATION: Millfield School, Glastonbury
TEAMS: England Lions, Somerset, Somerset Cricket Board
CAREER: First-class: 2003; List A: 2003; T20: 2004

SOMERSET

BEST BATTING: 303* Somerset vs Warwickshire, Taunton, 2009
BEST BOWLING: 2-39 Somerset vs Hampshire, Taunton, 2009
COUNTY CAP: 2007

CAREER HIGHLIGHTS? Winning the T20 in 2005, captaining England Lions and captaining Somerset
BEST PLAYER IN COUNTY CRICKET? Marcus Trescothick
TIPS FOR THE TOP? Jamie and Craig Overton
IF YOU WEREN'T A CRICKETER? I'd be travelling or be on a beach somewhere
FAVOURITE TV? The Big Bang Theory
CRICKETING HEROES? Ricky Ponting
WHEN YOU RETIRE? I'd like to work in Sport Psychology
SURPRISING FACT? I'm a big MK Dons fan
TWITTER FEED? @dreth25

Batting	Mat	Inns	NO	Runs	HS	Ave	SR	100	50	Ct	St
First-class	168	273	21	10874	303*	43.15		29	50	145	0
List A	160	149	26	3996	151	32.48		5	16	59	0
Twenty20	119	111	18	2131	107*	22.91	118.58	1	9	51	0

Bowling	Mat	Balls	Runs	Wkts	BBI	BBM	Ave	Econ	SR	5w	10
First-class	168	492	444	5	2/39		88.80	5.41	98.4	0	0
List A	160	150	185	6	2/26	2/26	30.83	7.40	25.0	0	0
Twenty20	119	169	247	10	3/24	3/24	24.70	8.76	16.9	0	0

MATT HOBDEN · RHB RFM

FULL NAME: Matthew Edward Hobden
BORN: March 27, 1993, Eastbourne, Sussex
SQUAD NO: 19
HEIGHT: 6ft 4in
NICKNAME: Hobbo
EDUCATION: Millfield School; Eastbourne College; Cardiff Metropolitan University
TEAMS: Cardiff MCCU, Sussex, Sussex 2nd XI, Sussex Under-14s, Sussex Under-17s
CAREER: First-class: 2012; List A: 2013

BEST BATTING: 18 Cardiff MCCU vs Glamorgan, Cardiff, 2013
BEST BOWLING: 5-62 Cardiff MCCU vs Warwickshire, Birmingham, 2012

WHO WOULD PLAY YOU IN A FILM OF YOUR LIFE? Andy Samberg
CAREER HIGHLIGHTS? Playing at Trent Bridge last year in the YB40
MOST MARKED CHARACTERISTIC? Clumsiness
IF YOU WEREN'T A CRICKETER? I'd be travelling
DESERT ISLAND DISC? Moby – Play: The B Sides
FAVOURITE TV? Entourage
CRICKETING HEROES? Andrew Flintoff
ACCOMPLISHMENTS? I'm expecting to graduate from university in July
WHEN YOU RETIRE? I'd like to be a film critic
SURPRISING FACT? I hold many javelin records at age-group levels
TWITTER FEED: @Hobs19

Batting	Mat	Inns	NO	Runs	HS	Ave	SR	100	50	Ct	St
First-class	4	2	1	33	18	33.00	32.35	0	0	0	0
List A	1	1	0	2	2	2.00	28.57	0	0	0	0

Bowling	Mat	Balls	Runs	Wkts	BBI	BBM	Ave	Econ	SR	5w	10
First-class	4	633	433	13	5/62	5/62	33.30	4.10	48.6	2	0
List A	1	48	39	1	1/39	1/39	39.00	4.87	48.0	0	0

ANDY HODD RHB WK

FULL NAME: Andrew John Hodd
BORN: January 12, 1984, Chichester, West Sussex
SQUAD NO: 4
HEIGHT: 5ft 9in
NICKNAME: Hoddy
EDUCATION: Bexhill High School; Bexhill College; Loughborough University
TEAMS: England Under-19s, Surrey, Sussex, Sussex Cricket Board, Yorkshire
CAREER: First-class: 2003; List A: 2002: T20: 2005

BEST BATTING: 123 Sussex vs Yorkshire, Hove, 2007

TWITTER FEED: @Hoddfather
NOTES: Hodd began his career at Sussex before moving on to Surrey, but he returned to the south coast in 2006 to act as Matt Prior's deputy. He performed well for Sussex, including a career-best 123 against Yorkshire at Hove, but the emergence of Ben Brown meant Hodd's chances became fewer and he joined Yorkshire in August 2012 on a temporary contract after Jonny Bairstow's call up for England. His performances earned him a two-year deal, which he signed at the end of 2012. He made nine first-class appearances for the White Rose in 2013, scoring 217 runs at 31. Toured Australia with England at U17 and U19 level

Batting	Mat	Inns	NO	Runs	HS	Ave	SR	100	50	Ct	St
First-class	70	98	17	2314	123	28.56	43.52	4	11	148	13
List A	49	39	10	622	91	21.44		0	1	42	9
Twenty20	53	30	6	282	26	11.75	101.80	0	0	24	11
Bowling	Mat	Balls	Runs	Wkts	BBI	BBM	Ave	Econ	SR	5w	10
First-class	70	10	7	0	-	-	-	4.20	-	0	0
List A	49	-	-	-	-	-	-	-	-	-	-
Twenty20	53	-	-	-	-	-	-	-	-	-	-

DAN HODGSON RHB WK

FULL NAME: Daniel Mark Hodgson
BORN: February 26, 1990, Northallerton, Yorkshire
SQUAD NO: 18
HEIGHT: 5ft 7in
NICKNAME: Hodgy
EDUCATION: Richmond School; Leeds University
TEAMS: Leeds/Bradford MCCU, Mountaineers, Yorkshire, Yorkshire 2nd XI
CAREER: First-class: 2012; List A: 2012; T20: 2012

BEST BATTING: 94* Mountaineers vs Southern Rocks, Mutare, 2013

CAREER HIGHLIGHTS? Signing for Yorkshire
CRICKETING HEROES? Shane Warne, Kumar Sangakkara
NON-CRICKETING HEROES? My parents, Alan Shearer, The Rock, Jay-Z
BEST PLAYER IN COUNTY CRICKET? Marcus Trescothick
TIPS FOR THE TOP? Ben Slater, Tom Craddock
FAVOURITE TV? Match Of The Day, One Tree Hill, House
FAVOURITE FILM? Man On Fire, Role Models, Inception
FAVOURITE BOOK? The Da Vinci Code
DREAM HOLIDAY? Anywhere with snow for skiing, or hot with a beach for windsurfing
SURPRISING SKILL? I can do fire juggling
FANTASY SLIP CORDON? Keeper: Me, 1st: Sonny Bill Williams, 2nd: P Diddy, 3rd: Peter Griffin, Gully: David Attenborough

Batting	Mat	Inns	NO	Runs	HS	Ave	SR	100	50	Ct	St
First-class	10	19	2	431	94*	25.35	48.48	0	4	31	2
List A	13	10	1	245	90	27.22	98.00	0	2	12	3
Twenty20	17	15	2	225	52*	17.30	96.15	0	1	10	1

Bowling	Mat	Balls	Runs	Wkts	BBI	BBM	Ave	Econ	SR	5w	10
First-class	10	-	-	-	-	-	-	-	-	-	-
List A	13	-	-	-	-	-	-	-	-	-	-
Twenty20	17	-	-	-	-	-	-	-	-	-	-

MICHAEL HOGAN   RHB RFM W1 MVP8

FULL NAME: Michael Garry Hogan
BORN: May 31, 1981, Newcastle, New South Wales, Australia
SQUAD NO: 31
HEIGHT: 6ft 5in
NICKNAME: Hulk, Hoges
TEAMS: Glamorgan, New South Wales Country, New South Wales Second XI, Western Australia
CAREER: First-class: 2009; List A: 2009; T20: 2010

BEST BATTING: 51 Glamorgan vs Gloucestershire, Bristol, 2013
BEST BOWLING: 7-92 Glamorgan vs Gloucestershire, Bristol, 2013

WHO WOULD PLAY YOU IN A FILM OF YOUR LIFE? Kevin Bacon – apparently we look similar
CAREER HIGHLIGHTS? Breaking the 100-wicket mark last season for Glamorgan was a nice personal achievement. Unfortunately I haven't been involved in team success as yet but hopefully that'll change soon
BEST PLAYER IN COUNTY CRICKET? I'm not sure, I haven't played all of them yet. I found it hard to bowl to Jos Buttler though
TIPS FOR THE TOP? Mike Reed has all the attributes to go to the next level and I think Ruaidhri Smith has shown enough promise with bat and ball to be one to look out for
IF YOU WEREN'T A CRICKETER? Probably a career in horticulture
DESERT ISLAND DISC? Jack Johnson – Sitting, Waiting, Wishing
FAVOURITE TV? The Simpsons
CRICKETING HEROES? Glenn McGrath
ACCOMPLISHMENTS? My two children
WHEN YOU RETIRE? Maybe some coaching and a few business interests
SURPRISING FACT? No, there's nothing surprising about me
TWITTER FEED: @Hoges31

Batting	Mat	Inns	NO	Runs	HS	Ave	SR	100	50	Ct	St
First-class	58	84	27	971	51	17.03	88.43	0	1	25	0
List A	37	13	5	90	27	11.25	81.81	0	0	14	0
Twenty20	24	6	3	17	5*	5.66	77.27	0	0	9	0

Bowling	Mat	Balls	Runs	Wkts	BBI	BBM	Ave	Econ	SR	5w	10
First-class	58	12614	5750	229	7/92	9/86	25.10	2.73	55.0	10	0
List A	37	1974	1618	63	5/44	5/44	25.68	4.91	31.3	1	0
Twenty20	24	510	591	19	4/26	4/26	31.10	6.95	26.8	0	0

KYLE HOGG   LHB RFM W2 MVP71

LANCASHIRE

FULL NAME: Kyle William Hogg
BORN: July 2, 1983, Birmingham, Warwickshire
SQUAD NO: 22
HEIGHT: 6ft 4in
NICKNAME: Hoggy, Boss
EDUCATION: Saddleworth High School
TEAMS: England Under-19s, Lancashire, Otago, Worcestershire
CAREER: First-class: 2001; List A: 2001; T20: 2003

BEST BATTING: 88 Lancashire vs Yorkshire, Manchester, 2010
BEST BOWLING: 7-27 Lancashire vs Northamptonshire, Manchester, 2013
COUNTY CAPS: 2007 (Worcestershire); 2010 (Lancashire)

FAMILY TIES? My dad [Willie Hogg of Lancashire and Warwickshire] and grandad [Sonny Ramadhin of West Indies, Lancashire and Trinidad] played professionally
WHO WOULD PLAY YOU IN A FILM OF YOUR LIFE? Denzel Washington
CAREER HIGHLIGHTS? County Championship win in 2011
MOST MARKED CHARACTERISTIC? I'm laid-back
BEST PLAYER IN COUNTY CRICKET? Marcus Trescothick
TIP FOR THE TOP? Simon Kerrigan
IF YOU WEREN'T A CRICKETER? Asking: "Would you like fries with that, sir?"
DESERT ISLAND DISC? Impossible to pick. Maybe The Smiths
CRICKETING HEROES? Andrew Flintoff, Curtly Ambrose, Brian Lara
NON-CRICKETING HEROES? Too many musicians to mention
ACCOMPLISHMENTS? Having a milk-round for five years at school
WHEN YOU RETIRE? I'd like to work in the music industry as a rep
FANTASY SLIP CORDON? Keeper: Kurt Cobain, 1st: Jimi Hendrix, 3rd: Morrissey, 4th: Alex Turner, Gully: Ian Curtis
TWITTER FEED: @kylehogg22

Batting	Mat	Inns	NO	Runs	HS	Ave	SR	100	50	Ct	St
First-class	105	132	26	2596	88	24.49	57.11	0	16	21	0
List A	139	84	24	966	66*	16.10	68.55	0	1	24	0
Twenty20	28	18	4	226	44	16.14	137.80	0	0	5	0

Bowling	Mat	Balls	Runs	Wkts	BBI	BBM	Ave	Econ	SR	5w	10
First-class	105	14524	7259	253	7/27		28.69	2.99	57.4	7	1
List A	139	5286	4288	141	4/20	4/20	30.41	4.86	37.4	0	0
Twenty20	28	378	564	16	2/10	2/10	35.25	8.95	23.6	0	0

PAUL HORTON RHB RM R3

FULL NAME: Paul James Horton
BORN: September 20, 1982, Sydney, New South Wales, Australia
SQUAD NO: 20
HEIGHT: 5ft 10in
NICKNAME: Horts, Lefty, Aussie
EDUCATION: Colo High School, Sydney; Broadgreen Comp Liverpool; St Margaret's High School
TEAMS: Lancashire, Lancashire 2nd XI, Matabeleland Tuskers
CAREER: First-class: 2003; List A: 2003; T20: 2005

LANCASHIRE

BEST BATTING: 209 Matabeleland Tuskers vs Southern Rocks, Masvingo, 2011
COUNTY CAP: 2007

CAREER HIGHLIGHTS? Nothing can top winning the County Championship in 2011 with Lancashire but every time I score a first-class hundred is pretty special. Back-to-back Logan Cup trophies with Matabeleland Tuskers in 2010/11 and 2011/12 too
CRICKETING HEROES? Mark Waugh, Dean Jones, Brian Lara
NON-CRICKETING HEROES? Roger Federer, Robbie Fowler
BEST PLAYER IN COUNTY CRICKET? Marcus Trescothick
TIPS FOR THE TOP? Simon Kerrigan, Ben Stokes
IF YOU WEREN'T A CRICKETER? I'd be doing something in a suit
WHEN RAIN STOPS PLAY? It ranges from hitting balls to talking rubbish in the dressing room
FAVOURITE FILM? Notting Hill
DREAM HOLIDAY? New York
ACCOMPLISHMENTS? Finishing school in one piece!
SURPRISING FACT? I once stacked shelves in Sainsbury's and I was once held as an illegal immigrant!
FANTASY SLIP CORDON? Keeper: Tiger Woods, 1st: Myself, 2nd: Robbie Fowler, 3rd: Nelson Mandela, Gully: Wonder Woman
TWITTER FEED: @PJHorton20

Batting	Mat	Inns	NO	Runs	HS	Ave	SR	100	50	Ct	St
First-class	136	227	19	8020	209	38.55	48.43	18	43	136	1
List A	92	83	11	2239	111*	31.09		2	12	32	0
Twenty20	60	56	11	1037	71	23.04	105.06	0	2	22	0

Bowling	Mat	Balls	Runs	Wkts	BBI	BBM	Ave	Econ	SR	5w	10
First-class	136	18	16	0	-	-	-	5.33	-	0	0
List A	92	-	-	-	-	-	-	-	-	-	-
Twenty20	60	-	-	-	-	-	-	-	-	-	-

DAN HOUSEGO RHB LB

FULL NAME: Daniel Mark Housego
BORN: October 12, 1988, Windsor, Berkshire
SQUAD NO: 3
HEIGHT: 5ft 9in
NICKNAME: Housey
EDUCATION: The Oratory School, Reading;
Moulsford Prep School
TEAMS: Berkshire, Gloucestershire,
Gloucestershire 2nd XI, Khelaghar Samaj
Kallyan Samity, Middlesex, Middlesex 2nd XI
CAREER: First-class: 2008; List A: 2012; T20:
2008

BEST BATTING: 217* Mountaineers vs Southern Rocks, Masvingo, 2014
COUNTY CAP: 2012 (Gloucestershire)

WHO WOULD PLAY YOU IN A FILM OF YOUR LIFE? Denzel Washington
CAREER HIGHLIGHTS? Scoring 132 against South Africa in August 2012. Scoring a hundred
against Sri Lanka in July 2011. The T20 victory over Somerset at Taunton in June 2012
SUPERSTITIONS? I have to drink a pint of water as soon as I wake up on game day
BEST PLAYER IN COUNTY CRICKET? Marcus Trescothick
TIPS FOR THE TOP? James Fuller, Chris Dent
IF YOU WEREN'T A CRICKETER? I'd be a personal trainer or cricket coach
DESERT ISLAND DISC? Emeli Sandé – Clown
FAVOURITE TV? Only Fools And Horses
CRICKETING HEROES? Graeme Smith
NON-CRICKETING HEROES? It was Lance Armstrong but not anymore! José Mourinho, as
he's fearless
ACCOMPLISHMENTS? My carp fishing record is 22lb 6oz
WHEN YOU RETIRE? Lots of fishing and golf
SURPRISING FACT? I don't drink fizzy or juice drinks, just water
FANTASY SLIP CORDON? Keeper: Peter Kay, 1st: Cheryl Cole, 2nd: Mila Kunis, 3rd: Alan Carr

Batting	Mat	Inns	NO	Runs	HS	Ave	SR	100	50	Ct	St
First-class	37	63	6	1866	217*	32.73	46.14	4	7	19	0
List A	12	12	1	448	132	40.72	78.04	1	3	4	0
Twenty20	9	8	2	164	59*	27.33	114.68	0	1	2	0

Bowling	Mat	Balls	Runs	Wkts	BBI	BBM	Ave	Econ	SR	5w	10
First-class	37	58	58	1	1/5	1/5	58.00	6.00	58.0	0	0
List A	12	75	64	1	1/16	1/16	64.00	5.12	75.0	0	0
Twenty20	9	-	-	-	-	-	-	-	-	-	-

BENNY HOWELL · RHB RMF MVP36

FULL NAME: Benny Alexander Cameron Howell
BORN: October 5, 1988, Bordeaux, France
SQUAD NO: 13
HEIGHT: 5ft 11in
NICKNAME: Trowell, Max George
EDUCATION: Oratory School, Reading
TEAMS: Gloucestershire, Gloucestershire 2nd XI, Hampshire, Hampshire 2nd XI, Unicorns
CAREER: First-class: 2011; List A: 2010; T20: 2011

BEST BATTING: 83* Gloucestershire vs Yorkshire, Scarborough, 2012
BEST BOWLING: 5-57 Gloucestershire vs Leicestershire, Leicester, 2013
COUNTY CAP: 2012 (Gloucestershire)

FAMILY TIES? My dad John played for Lancashire age groups and Warwickshire 2nd XI
WHO WOULD PLAY YOU IN A FILM OF YOUR LIFE? Leonardo DiCaprio
CAREER HIGHLIGHTS? Scoring 122 vs Surrey in the Pro40 in 2011. My first-class debuts for Hampshire and Gloucestershire
BEST PLAYER IN COUNTY CRICKET? Michael Carberry
TIPS FOR THE TOP? James Fuller, Jack and Matt Taylor
IF YOU WEREN'T A CRICKETER? I'd be working in property investment
DESERT ISLAND DISC? Anything by U2
FAVOURITE TV? Modern Family
CRICKETING HEROES? Sachin Tendulkar, Brian Lara, Brett Lee
NON-CRICKETING HEROES? Nicky Howell
ACCOMPLISHMENTS? Getting three A's at A-Level. Passing my driving test at the fifth attempt – they say only the best drivers do that
CRICKET RULE YOU'D CHANGE? In T20 there should be numerous replacement balls ready when a ball lands in the crowd. That would make for a quicker game
SURPRISING FACT? I'm currently writing a novel

Batting	Mat	Inns	NO	Runs	HS	Ave	SR	100	50	Ct	St
First-class	31	50	7	1164	83*	27.06	49.93	0	8	13	0
List A	36	29	5	889	122	37.04	94.17	1	5	12	0
Twenty20	29	24	12	294	55*	24.50	116.20	0	1	6	0

Bowling	Mat	Balls	Runs	Wkts	BBI	BBM	Ave	Econ	SR	5w	10
First-class	31	2692	1295	36	5/57	8/96	35.97	2.88	74.7	1	0
List A	36	732	678	16	2/26	2/26	42.37	5.55	45.7	0	0
Twenty20	29	246	313	13	2/14	2/14	24.07	7.63	18.9	0	0

ALEX HUGHES

RHB RM

FULL NAME: Alex Lloyd Hughes
BORN: September 29, 1991, Wordsley, Staffordshire
SQUAD NO: 18
HEIGHT: 5ft 10in
NICKNAME: Yozza
EDUCATION: Ounsdale High School; Worcester University
TEAMS: Derbyshire, Derbyshire 2nd XI, Staffordshire
CAREER: First-class: 2013; List A: 2012; T20: 2011

BEST BATTING: 33 Derbyshire vs Middlesex, Derby, 2013
BEST BOWLING: 3-49 Derbyshire vs Sussex, Hove, 2013

FAMILY TIES? My brother Liam played for Derbyshire
WHO WOULD PLAY YOU IN A FILM OF YOUR LIFE? Dwayne Johnson
CAREER HIGHLIGHTS? Scoring 59* v Essex, winning on my first-class debut for Derbyshire vs Sussex and taking 3-49 in the first innings
MOST MARKED CHARACTERISTIC? My legs
BEST PLAYER IN COUNTY CRICKET? Graham Onions, Wayne Madsen
TIP FOR THE TOP? Ben Cotton
IF YOU WEREN'T A CRICKETER? I'd be a professional wrestler
DESERT ISLAND DISC? Nelly – Country Grammar
CRICKETING HEROES? Andrew Flintoff, Jacques Kallis
NON-CRICKETING HEROES? Leonardo DiCaprio, Dwayne Johnson
ACCOMPLISHMENTS? Getting a degree at Worcester University
SURPRISING FACT? I enjoy Russian history
CRICKET RULE YOU'D CHANGE? Back to four fielders inside the circle
FANTASY SLIP CORDON? Keeper: Leonardo DiCaprio, 1st: Scarlett Johansson, 2nd: Jimmy Carr, 3rd: Peter Griffin, Gully: Vladimir Lenin
TWITTER FEED: @yozza18

Batting	Mat	Inns	NO	Runs	HS	Ave	SR	100	50	Ct	St
First-class	6	11	0	136	33	12.36	37.46	0	0	3	0
List A	16	10	3	168	59*	24.00	90.81	0	1	3	0
Twenty20	7	5	1	26	11*	6.50	78.78	0	0	2	0

Bowling	Mat	Balls	Runs	Wkts	BBI	BBM	Ave	Econ	SR	5w	10
First-class	6	426	230	6	3/49	4/76	38.33	3.23	71.0	0	0
List A	16	467	468	13	3/56	3/56	36.00	6.01	35.9	0	0
Twenty20	7	114	166	5	3/32	3/32	33.20	8.73	22.8	0	0

CHESNEY HUGHES

LHB SLA MVP80

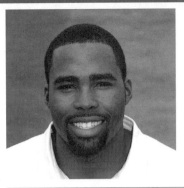

FULL NAME: Chesney Francis Hughes
BORN: January 20, 1991, Anguilla
SQUAD NO: 22
TEAMS: Anguilla, Derbyshire, Leeward Islands, West Indies Under-19s
CAREER: First-class: 2010; List A: 2007; T20: 2006

DERBYSHIRE

BEST BATTING: 270* Derbyshire vs Yorkshire, Leeds, 2013
BEST BOWLING: 2-9 Derbyshire vs Middlesex, Derby, 2011

TWITTER FEED: @ChesneyH22
NOTES: The Anguillan batsman made an immediate impact in his debut County Championship season in 2010, amassing 784 runs and averaging 41.26. His highest score came against Northamptonshire, when he hit 156 at Chesterfield. He was left out of Derbyshire's four-day side for the majority of 2012, playing just one game. Recorded career-best bowling figures in the YB40 vs Unicorns in the same season. Returned to the Championship side for 2013 and scored 270* against Yorkshire at Headingley, with 40 fours and three sixes. Derbyshire's top-scorer in the YB40 in 2013 with 271 runs

Batting	Mat	Inns	NO	Runs	HS	Ave	SR	100	50	Ct	St
First-class	39	71	3	2189	270*	32.19	54.97	5	8	32	0
List A	64	60	2	1435	81	24.74		0	12	12	0
Twenty20	58	55	2	1045	65	19.71	109.88	0	3	18	0

Bowling	Mat	Balls	Runs	Wkts	BBI	BBM	Ave	Econ	SR	5w	10
First-class	39	744	470	11	2/9	2/17	42.72	3.79	67.6	0	0
List A	64	877	754	22	5/29	5/29	34.27	5.15	39.8	1	0
Twenty20	58	528	642	23	4/23	4/23	27.91	7.29	22.9	0	0

MATT HUNN

RHB RFM

FULL NAME: Matthew David Hunn
BORN: March 22, 1994, Colchester
SQUAD NO: 14
HEIGHT: 6ft 5in
NICKNAME: Hunny
EDUCATION: St Joseph's College, Ipswich
TEAMS: Essex 2nd XI, Kent, Kent 2nd XI, Suffolk, Suffolk Under-13s, Suffolk Under-15s, Suffolk Under-17s
CAREER: First-class: 2013

BEST BATTING: 0 Kent vs Lancashire, Canterbury, 2013
BEST BOWLING: 2-51 Kent vs Lancashire, Canterbury, 2013

WHO WOULD PLAY YOU IN A FILM OF YOUR LIFE? Will Smith, because he's a legend
CAREER HIGHLIGHTS? Signing my first professional contract and making my debut
MOST MARKED CHARACTERISTIC? My height
BEST PLAYER IN COUNTY CRICKET? Darren Stevens
TIP FOR THE TOP? Ben Foakes
IF YOU WEREN'T A CRICKETER? I'd probably be at university studying something
DESERT ISLAND DISC? Bastille
FAVOURITE TV? The Big Bang Theory or Top Gear
CRICKETING HEROES? Andrew Flintoff, Morne Morkel
NON-CRICKETING HEROES? Nelson Mandela
ACCOMPLISHMENTS? Holding a 24-hour, indoor rowing Guinness world record with my school
CRICKET RULE YOU'D CHANGE? I'd make the game more bowler-friendly
WHEN YOU RETIRE? Something that will hopefully make me rich!
TWITTER FEED: @MattHunn10

Batting	Mat	Inns	NO	Runs	HS	Ave	SR	100	50	Ct	St
First-class	1	1	0	0	0	0.00	0.00	0	0	1	0

Bowling	Mat	Balls	Runs	Wkts	BBI	BBM	Ave	Econ	SR	5w	10
First-class	1	190	118	3	2/51	3/118	39.33	3.72	63.3	0	0

LIAM HURT   RHB RFM

FULL NAME: Liam Jack Hurt
BORN: March 15, Preston, Lancashire
SQUAD NO: TBC
HEIGHT: 6ft 3in
NICKNAME: Hurty
EDUCATION: Balshaw's CofE High School, Leyland
TEAMS: Lancashire 2nd XI
CAREER: Yet to make first-team debut

CAREER HIGHLIGHTS? Getting a scholarship contract with Lancashire. Playing in the National Club T20 at The Kia Oval
IF YOU WEREN'T A CRICKETER? I'd be a plumber
DESERT ISLAND DISC? Something by 50 Cent
FAVOURITE TV? Pawn Stars
CRICKETING HEROES? Andrew Flintoff
TWITTER FEED: @LiamHurt

BRETT HUTTON

RHB RM

NOTTINGHAMSHIRE

FULL NAME: Brett Alan Hutton
BORN: February 6, 1993, Doncaster, Yorkshire
SQUAD NO: 26
HEIGHT: 6ft
NICKNAME: Hutts
EDUCATION: Worksop College
TEAMS: England Under-19s, Nottinghamshire, Nottinghamshire 2nd XI
CAREER: First-class: 2011; List A: 2011

BEST BATTING: 42 Nottinghamshire vs Somerset, Nottingham, 2013
BEST BOWLING: 1-31 Nottinghamshire vs Somerset. Nottingham, 2013

WHO WOULD PLAY YOU IN A FILM OF YOUR LIFE? James McAvoy
CAREER HIGHLIGHTS? Playing for England U19 and my Notts debut vs MCC in Abu Dhabi
MOST MARKED CHARACTERISTIC? Stubble
BEST PLAYER IN COUNTY CRICKET? Andre Adams
TIPS FOR THE TOP? Sam Wood, Sam Kelsall
IF YOU WEREN'T A CRICKETER? I'd be a window cleaner
DESERT ISLAND DISC? Nicki Minaj – Pink Friday
FAVOURITE TV? Emmerdale
CRICKETING HEROES? Chris Tolley, Harold Larwood
NON-CRICKETING HEROES? Lee Westwood
SURPRISING FACT? I've got my own window cleaning round
FANTASY SLIP CORDON? Keeper: George Formby, 1st: Scarlett Johansson, 2nd: Tommy Johnson, 3rd: Stevie Wonder, 4th: Holly Willoughby

Batting	Mat	Inns	NO	Runs	HS	Ave	SR	100	50	Ct	St
First-class	2	4	1	71	42	23.66	75.53	0	0	1	0
List A	3	3	2	24	17*	24.00	126.31	0	0	2	0

Bowling	Mat	Balls	Runs	Wkts	BBI	BBM	Ave	Econ	SR	5w	10
First-class	2	240	178	1	1/31	1/109	178.00	4.45	240.0	0	0
List A	3	144	169	2	1/60	1/60	84.50	7.04	72.0	0	0

ANTHONY IRELAND

RHB RM

FULL NAME: Anthony John Ireland
BORN: August 30, 1984, Masvingo, Zimbabwe
SQUAD NO: 88
HEIGHT: 6ft 5in
NICKNAME: Mvuu
EDUCATION: Plumtree High School, Matabeleland
TEAMS: Zimbabwe, Gloucestershire, Gloucestershire 2nd XI, Leicestershire, Middlesex, Midlands, Southern Rocks
CAREER: ODI: 2005; T20I: 2006; First-class: 2002; List A: 2004; T20: 2006

BEST BATTING: 29 Middlesex vs Essex, Chelmsford, 2011
BEST BOWLING: 7-36 Zimbabwe A vs Bangladesh A, Mirpur, 2006
COUNTY CAP: 2007 (Gloucestershire)

WHO WOULD PLAY YOU IN A FILM OF YOUR LIFE? Sean Penn
CAREER HIGHLIGHTS? Playing for Zimbabwe in the 2007 World Cup
MOST MARKED CHARACTERISTIC? My broken nose
BEST PLAYER IN COUNTY CRICKET? Sam Robson
TIP FOR THE TOP? Craig Miles
IF YOU WEREN'T A CRICKETER? I'd be a lion tamer
DESERT ISLAND DISC? Bob Marley
FAVOURITE TV? Anything with David Attenborough
CRICKETING HEROES? Joe Burns
WHEN YOU RETIRE? I'd like to own a coffee shop
CRICKET RULE YOU'D CHANGE? There should be unlimited bouncers per over
SURPRISING FACT? I competed in the World Karate Championships
TWITTER FEED: @antireland88

Batting	Mat	Inns	NO	Runs	HS	Ave	SR	100	50	Ct	St
ODIs	26	13	5	30	8*	3.75	29.70	0	0	2	0
T20Is	1	1	1	2	2*	-	66.66	0	0	0	0
First-class	43	64	18	285	29	6.19	32.09	0	0	10	0
List A	78	40	17	179	27	7.78	54.57	0	0	9	0
Twenty20	50	18	9	76	23	8.44	87.35	0	0	11	0

Bowling	Mat	Balls	Runs	Wkts	BBI	BBM	Ave	Econ	SR	5w	10
ODIs	26	1326	1115	38	3/41	3/41	29.34	5.04	34.8	0	0
T20Is	1	18	33	1	1/33	1/33	33.00	11.00	18.0	0	0
First-class	43	6354	3907	124	7/36		31.50	3.68	51.2	4	1
List A	78	3271	3008	95	4/16	4/16	31.66	5.51	34.4	0	0
Twenty20	50	919	1311	57	4/11	4/11	23.00	8.55	16.1	0	0

CALLUM JACKSON

RHB WK

FULL NAME: Callum Frederick Jackson
BORN: September 7, 1994, Eastbourne, Sussex
SQUAD NO: 16
HEIGHT: 5ft 11in
NICKNAME: Jacko
EDUCATION: St Bede's School, Upper Dicker, Hailsham
TEAMS: England Under-19s, Sussex, Sussex 2nd XI, Sussex Under-13s, Sussex Under-14s, Sussex Under-15s, Sussex Under-17s
CAREER: First-class: 2013; List A: 2013; T20: 2013

BEST BATTING: 26 Sussex vs Australians, Hove, 2013

WHO WOULD PLAY YOU IN A FILM OF YOUR LIFE? Leonardo DiCaprio because he is just the coolest man ever
CAREER HIGHLIGHTS? Making my first-team debut in all three formats of the game last year and making my first-class debut against Australia
SUPERSTITIONS? I always have to bat with a sweat band on my left arm
MOST MARKED CHARACTERISTIC? Probably my nose
TIPS FOR THE TOP? I think Luke Wells and Matt Machan will go on to big things
IF YOU WEREN'T A CRICKETER? I'd be a business man. I have no idea what business though!
DESERT ISLAND DISC? Anything by Mumford And Sons
FAVOURITE TV? Made In Chelsea
CRICKETING HEROES? Ian Bell and Matt Prior
NON-CRICKETING HEROES? I'd probably say my brother is up there
ACCOMPLISHMENTS? Getting decent A-Levels despite my cricketing commitments
WHEN YOU RETIRE? I'd like to retire to somewhere hot, but still be involved in cricket in some way
SURPRISING FACT? I was diagnosed with type 1 diabetes when I was 14 years old
TWITTER FEED: @callumjackson99

Batting	Mat	Inns	NO	Runs	HS	Ave	SR	100	50	Ct	St
First-class	1	1	0	26	26	26.00	52.00	0	0	1	0
List A	3	-	-	-	-	-	-	-	-	1	2
Twenty20	3	1	0	3	3	3.00	75.00	0	0	0	3

Bowling	Mat	Balls	Runs	Wkts	BBI	BBM	Ave	Econ	SR	5w	10
First-class	1	-	-	-	-	-	-	-	-	-	-
List A	3	-	-	-	-	-	-	-	-	-	-
Twenty20	3	-	-	-	-	-	-	-	-	-	-

PHIL JAQUES

LHB LM R4

FULL NAME: Philip Anthony Jaques
BORN: May 3, 1979, Wollongong, New South Wales, Australia
SQUAD NO: 2
HEIGHT: 6ft 1in
NICKNAME: Pro, Wingers
TEAMS: Australia, New South Wales, Northamptonshire, Nottinghamshire, Worcestershire, Yorkshire
CAREER: Test: 2005; ODI: 2006; First-class: 2000; List A: 2000; T20: 2003

BEST BATTING: 244 Worcestershire vs Essex, Chelmsford, 2006
BEST BOWLING: 1-75 Yorkshire vs Sussex, Hove, 2013
COUNTY CAPS: 2003 (Northamptonshire); 2005 (Yorkshire)

FAMILY TIES? My dad used to play league cricket in the UK
CAREER HIGHLIGHTS? Making my Test debut on Boxing Day at the MCG. Being part of record-breaking side for the most Test match wins in a row
SUPERSTITIONS? I always put my gear on in a particular order and dislike people touching my bat before I go out to bat
BEST PLAYER IN COUNTY CRICKET? Chris Rogers
TIP FOR THE TOP? Gary Ballance
CRICKETING HEROES? Mike Hussey and Steve Waugh
WHEN YOU RETIRE? I'd like to stay in cricket and coach
FANTASY SLIP CORDON? I need humour either side of me to keep me going so: Keeper: Eddie Murphy, 1st: Me, 2nd: Ricky Gervais, 3rd: Warnie, Gully: The Incredible Hulk (try getting a cut shot past him)
TWITTER FEED: @philjaques

Batting	Mat	Inns	NO	Runs	HS	Ave	SR	100	50	Ct	St
Tests	11	19	0	902	150	47.47	54.23	3	6	7	0
ODIs	6	6	0	125	94	20.83	71.02	0	1	3	0
First-class	189	326	12	15141	244	48.21		42	70	146	0
List A	165	162	10	6180	171*	40.65	89.79	14	33	43	0
Twenty20	81	78	9	2028	92	29.39	123.96	0	13	18	0

Bowling	Mat	Balls	Runs	Wkts	BBI	BBM	Ave	Econ	SR	5w	10
Tests	11	-	-	-	-	-	-	-	-	-	-
ODIs	6	-	-	-	-	-	-	-	-	-	-
First-class	189	104	162	1	1/75	1/75	162.00	9.34	104.0	0	0
List A	165	18	19	0	-	-	-	6.33	-	0	0
Twenty20	81	6	15	0	-	-	-	15.00	-	0	0

KYLE JARVIS　　　　　　　　　　　RHB LFM

FULL NAME: Kyle Malcolm Jarvis
BORN: February 16, 1989, Harare, Zimbabwe
SQUAD NO: 27
HEIGHT: 6ft 2in
NICKNAME: Jarv
EDUCATION: St. John's College, Harare;
University of Pretoria
TEAMS: Zimbabwe, Central Districts,
Lancashire, Mashonaland Eagles, Zimbabwe
Under-19s, Zimbabwe XI
CAREER: Test: 2011; ODI: 2009; T20I: 2011;
First-class: 2009; List A: 2009; T20: 2011

BEST BATTING: 48 Mashonaland Eagles vs Mid West Rhinos, Harare, 2012
BEST BOWLING: 7-35 Mashonaland Eagles vs Matabeleland Tuskers, Bulawayo, 2012

FAMILY TIES? My father [Malcolm] played Test cricket for Zimbabwe
WHO WOULD PLAY YOU IN A FILM OF YOUR LIFE? Leonardo DiCaprio
CAREER HIGHLIGHTS? Two Test five-wicket hauls against New Zealand and West Indies
SUPERSTITIONS? Not really, more routines than superstitions
BEST PLAYER IN COUNTY CRICKET? Arron Lilley
TIPS FOR THE TOP? Haseeb Hameed – one of the youngsters at Lancashire
DESERT ISLAND DISC? Bob Marley
CRICKETING HEROES? Glenn McGrath, Brett Lee
NON-CRICKETING HEROES? Nelson Mandela
SURPRISING FACT? I'm a spearfisherman extraordinaire but a shockingly bad footballer
CRICKET RULE YOU'D CHANGE? Stop making every rule in favour of the batsman
TWITTER FEED: @kylejarv89

Batting	Mat	Inns	NO	Runs	HS	Ave	SR	100	50	Ct	St
Tests	8	14	6	58	25*	7.25	29.74	0	0	3	0
ODIs	24	15	5	52	13	5.20	40.62	0	0	6	0
T20Is	9	5	2	9	9*	3.00	52.94	0	0	0	0
First-class	30	42	15	355	48	13.14	46.34	0	0	10	0
List A	34	21	9	57	13	4.75	35.84	0	0	10	0
Twenty20	34	10	4	28	10	4.66	68.29	0	0	10	0

Bowling	Mat	Balls	Runs	Wkts	BBI	BBM	Ave	Econ	SR	5w	10
Tests	8	1569	952	30	5/54	7/115	31.73	3.64	52.3	2	0
ODIs	24	1217	1221	27	3/36	3/36	45.22	6.01	45.0	0	0
T20Is	9	193	270	10	3/15	3/15	27.00	8.39	19.3	0	0
First-class	30	5279	3080	127	7/35	10/53	24.25	3.50	41.5	8	1
List A	34	1607	1525	42	4/35	4/35	36.30	5.69	38.2	0	0
Twenty20	34	709	999	30	3/15	3/15	33.30	8.45	23.6	0	0

ATEEQ JAVID   RHB RM/OB

FULL NAME: Ateeq Javid
BORN: October 15, 1991, Birmingham, Warwickshire
SQUAD NO: 17
HEIGHT: 5ft 10in
EDUCATION: Aston Manor School, Birmingham
TEAMS: England Under-19s, Warwickshire, Warwickshire 2nd XI
CAREER: First-class: 2009; List A: 2011; T20: 2013

BEST BATTING: 133 Warwickshire vs Somerset, Birmingham, 2013
BEST BOWLING: 1-27 Warwickshire vs Sussex, Birmingham, 2013

CAREER HIGHLIGHTS? Playing against England for Warwickshire ahead of the 2009 Ashes
CRICKETING HEROES? Sachin Tendulkar
DREAM HOLIDAY? Las Vegas
GUILTY PLEASURES? Coca-Cola
TWITTER FEED: @ateeqjavid2000
NOTES: Javid scored his maiden first-class century last year, against Somerset at Edgbaston in the County Championship, and followed it up with another against Surrey in September to finish the season with 619 runs at an average of 44.21. A former England U19 player, he featured in four U19 Tests and 23 U19 ODIs between 2009 and 2011, scoring five half-centuries

Batting	Mat	Inns	NO	Runs	HS	Ave	SR	100	50	Ct	St
First-class	20	32	4	821	133	29.32	36.07	2	2	11	0
List A	12	12	4	256	43	32.00	87.97	0	0	3	0
Twenty20	10	5	0	64	41	12.80	98.46	0	0	0	0

Bowling	Mat	Balls	Runs	Wkts	BBI	BBM	Ave	Econ	SR	5w	10
First-class	20	378	233	2	1/27	1/29	116.50	3.69	189.0	0	0
List A	12	294	319	5	2/34	2/34	63.80	6.51	58.8	0	0
Twenty20	10	168	215	11	4/17	4/17	19.54	7.67	15.2	0	0

KEATON JENNINGS

LHB RM

DURHAM

FULL NAME: Keaton Kent Jennings
BORN: June 19, 1992, Johannesburg, Transvaal, South Africa
SQUAD NO: 1
HEIGHT: 6ft 3in
NICKNAME: Jet
EDUCATION: King Edward VII School; University Of South Africa
TEAMS: Durham, Durham 2nd XI, Gauteng, Gauteng Under-19s, South Africa Under-19s
CAREER: First-class: 2011; List A: 2012

BEST BATTING: 127 Durham vs Sussex, Hove, 2013
BEST BOWLING: 2-8 Gauteng vs Western Province, Cape Town, 2012

FAMILY TIES? My father, brother and uncle have all played at first-class level
WHO WOULD PLAY YOU IN A FILM OF YOUR LIFE? Bruce Willis
CAREER HIGHLIGHTS? Making my Durham debut, winning the County Championship with Durham and scoring my maiden first-class century
SUPERSTITIONS? None as such, but I do have a few routines like always padding up the same way
MOST MARKED CHARACTERISTIC? My self-discipline and determination
IF YOU WEREN'T A CRICKETER? I'd be finishing my Accountancy degree and trying to qualify as a chartered accountant
DESERT ISLAND DISC? U2 – Joshua Tree
FAVOURITE TV? Suits
CRICKETING HEROES? Michael Hussey and Jacques Kallis
NON-CRICKETING HEROES? My family
WHEN YOU RETIRE? I'll play a lot of golf
CRICKET RULE YOU'D CHANGE? First-ball grace at the Riverside would be great!
SURPRISING FACT? I eat a surprising amount for a skinny guy!
TWITTER FEED: @JetJennings

Batting	Mat	Inns	NO	Runs	HS	Ave	SR	100	50	Ct	St
First-class	26	46	2	1263	127	28.70	41.64	3	5	10	0
List A	6	6	1	286	71*	57.20	67.77	0	4	0	0

Bowling	Mat	Balls	Runs	Wkts	BBI	BBM	Ave	Econ	SR	5w	10
First-class	26	134	84	4	2/8	2/8	21.00	3.76	33.5	0	0
List A	6	18	11	0	-	-	-	3.66	-	0	0

FULL NAME: Thomas Melvin Jewell
BORN: January 13, 1991, Reading, Berkshire
SQUAD NO: 8
HEIGHT: 6ft 5in
NICKNAME: TJ, Jeweller, Jewellpig
EDUCATION: Bradfield College
TEAMS: Surrey, Surrey 2nd XI
CAREER: First-class: 2008; List A: 2009

SURREY

BEST BATTING: 70 Surrey vs Lancashire, Liverpool, 2012
BEST BOWLING: 5-49 Surrey vs Cambridge MCCU, Cambridge, 2011

WHO WOULD PLAY YOU IN A FILM OF YOUR LIFE? Javier Bardem
CAREER HIGHLIGHTS? My first-class debut in 2007, fielding for England in Test cricket and
the 2012 County Championship game against Lancashire [70 and 1-24]
MOST MARKED CHARACTERISTIC? My nose
BEST PLAYER IN COUNTY CRICKET? Nick Compton
TIPS FOR THE TOP? Jason Roy, Rory Burns and Matt Dunn
IF YOU WEREN'T A CRICKETER? I would be finishing up a degree
DESERT ISLAND DISC? Macklemore & Ryan Lewis – The Heist
FAVOURITE TV? Homes Under The Hammer
BIGGEST DRESSING DOWN YOU'VE RECEIVED? From Mick Powell in a Surrey U17 game. He
never held back
CRICKETING HEROES? Viv Richards
NON-CRICKETING HEROES? Steve Jobs
WHEN YOU RETIRE? I'd like to work in commercial property or property development
FANTASY SLIP CORDON? Keeper: Micky Flanagan, 1st: Sean Lock, 2nd: Jimmy Carr, 3rd: Jon
Richardson
TWITTER FEED: @TOMJEWELL8

Batting	Mat	Inns	NO	Runs	HS	Ave	SR	100	50	Ct	St
First-class	9	7	1	185	70	30.83	49.33	0	2	2	0
List A	8	7	1	31	13	5.16	68.88	0	0	3	0

Bowling	Mat	Balls	Runs	Wkts	BBI	BBM	Ave	Econ	SR	5w	10
First-class	9	898	521	19	5/49	5/49	27.42	3.48	47.2	1	0
List A	8	114	158	1	1/20	1/20	158.00	8.31	114.0	0	0

RICHARD JOHNSON

RHB WK

FULL NAME: Richard Matthew Johnson
BORN: September 1, 1988, Solihull, West Midlands
SQUAD NO: 25
HEIGHT: 5ft 10in
NICKNAME: Johnno, RJ
EDUCATION: Solihull School
TEAMS: Derbyshire, Herefordshire, Warwickshire, Warwickshire 2nd XI
CAREER: First-class: 2008; List A: 2008; T20: 2009

BEST BATTING: 72 Warwickshire vs Cambridge UCCE, Cambridge, 2008

FAMILY TIES? My dad played club cricket in the Birmingham League
WHO WOULD PLAY YOU IN A FILM OF YOUR LIFE? Ashton Kutcher
CAREER HIGHLIGHTS? My first-class debut, winning the 2010 CB40 Final at Lord's and 2012 County Championship Division One with Warwickshire, and winning the 2012 County Championship Division Two title with Derbyshire
BEST PLAYER IN COUNTY CRICKET? Wayne Madsen
TIPS FOR THE TOP? Ben Cotton, Laurie Evans
IF YOU WEREN'T A CRICKETER? I'd be a strength and conditioning coach
DESERT ISLAND DISC? Any album by The Twang
FAVOURITE TV? Made In Chelsea
CRICKETING HEROES? Keith Piper, Brendon McCullum, MS Dhoni
NON-CRICKETING HEROES? David Beckham and my dad
ACCOMPLISHMENTS? A-Levels and Personal Training diploma
WHEN YOU RETIRE? I'll live abroad and be a strength and conditioning coach
CRICKET RULE YOU'D CHANGE? Look after wicketkeepers. Ridiculous 'byes' should go into a different extras column called sundries!
FANTASY SLIP CORDON? Keeper: Me 1st: Mila Kunis, 2nd: MS Dhoni, 3rd: David Beckham, Gully: Vincent Kompany

Batting	Mat	Inns	NO	Runs	HS	Ave	SR	100	50	Ct	St
First-class	26	43	3	881	72	22.02	45.79	0	5	48	2
List A	26	14	4	215	79	21.50	92.27	0	2	19	4
Twenty20	22	8	3	46	14	9.20	95.83	0	0	6	3

Bowling	Mat	Balls	Runs	Wkts	BBI	BBM	Ave	Econ	SR	5w	10
First-class	26	-	-	-	-	-	-	-	-	-	-
List A	26	-	-	-	-	-	-	-	-	-	-
Twenty20	22	-	-	-	-	-	-	-	-	-	-

CHRIS JONES RHB OB

FULL NAME: Christopher Robert Jones
BORN: November 5, 1990, Harold Wood, Essex
SQUAD NO: 14
HEIGHT: 6ft 2in
NICKNAME: Jonesy, Nan
EDUCATION: Poole Grammar; Richard Huish College; Durham University
TEAMS: Dorset, Durham MCCU, Somerset, Somerset 2nd XI, Somerset Under-15s, Somerset Under-17s
CAREER: First-class: 2010; List A: 2011; T20: 2011

BEST BATTING: 130 Somerset vs Australians, Taunton, 2013
BEST BOWLING: 1-17 Somerset vs Surrey, Taunton, 2012

WHO WOULD PLAY YOU IN A FILM OF YOUR LIFE? Ryan Gosling
CAREER HIGHLIGHTS? Playing in the Champions League in India and winning the universities competition at Lord's
MOST MARKED CHARACTERISTIC? My nose
BEST PLAYER IN COUNTY CRICKET? Marcus Trescothick
TIPS FOR THE TOP? Craig Overton, Daniel Bell-Drummond
IF YOU WEREN'T A CRICKETER? I'd be a lifelong student
DESERT ISLAND DISC? Ben Howard – Every Kingdom
FAVOURITE TV? QI
BIGGEST DRESSING DOWN YOU'VE RECEIVED? When we lost the U15 national semi-final the coach gave us a pretty hefty spray!
CRICKETING HEROES? Jacques Kallis and Ricky Ponting
NON-CRICKETING HEROES? John Maynard Keynes, Stephen Fry
ACCOMPLISHMENTS? My academic performances, including four A's at A-Level
SURPRISING FACT? I am an avid supporter of the San Francisco 49ers NFL team
FANTASY SLIP CORDON? Keeper: Peter Schmeichel, 1st: Will Ferrell, 2nd: Jimmy Carr, 3rd: Colin Kaepernick, Gully: Jim Harbaugh

Batting	Mat	Inns	NO	Runs	HS	Ave	SR	100	50	Ct	St
First-class	28	46	2	883	130	20.06	40.37	1	6	14	0
List A	5	4	1	126	45*	42.00	78.75	0	0	0	0
Twenty20	9	9	2	161	53*	23.00	114.18	0	1	3	0

Bowling	Mat	Balls	Runs	Wkts	BBI	BBM	Ave	Econ	SR	5w	10
First-class	28	12	17	1	1/17	1/17	17.00	8.50	12.0	0	0
List A	5	-	-	-	-	-	-	-	-	-	-
Twenty20	9	-	-	-	-	-	-	-	-	-	-

GERAINT JONES

RHB WK R2

KENT

FULL NAME: Geraint Owen Jones
BORN: July 14, 1976, Kundiawa, Papua New Guinea
SQUAD NO: 9
HEIGHT: 5ft 10in
NICKNAME: Jonesy, Jonah, G
EDUCATION: Harristown State, Queensland
TEAMS: England, Papua New Guinea, Kent, Kent 2nd XI
CAREER: Test: 2004; ODI: 2004; T20I: 2005; First-class: 2001; List A: 2001; T20: 2003

BEST BATTING: 178 Kent vs Somerset, Canterbury, 2010
COUNTY CAP: 2003; BENEFIT YEAR: 2012

FAMILY TIES? James Tredwell is my brother-in-law, my father bowled off-spin once for his region in North Wales and my sister bowls right-arm rapid (I'm still recovering from a blow to the family jewels aged 11!)
CAREER HIGHLIGHTS? My hundred against New Zealand in 2004, the 2005 Ashes, winning the T20 Cup and scoring 105 for Ash CC vs Walmer CC
SUPERSTITIONS? I use the same shower and toilet during a match. Left-sided dressing first
BIGGEST DRESSING DOWN YOU'VE RECEIVED? For being bowled out twice in a day for Kent 2nd XI against Notts after being out the night before celebrating Alex Loudon's 21st birthday. I was out lbw leaving a ball I thought was down the leg-side!
CRICKETING HEROES? Ian Healy, Jack Russell, Steve Waugh
SURPRISING FACT? I'm a qualified sheep shearer
TWITTER FEED: @Gojones623

Batting	Mat	Inns	NO	Runs	HS	Ave	SR	100	50	Ct	St
Tests	34	53	4	1172	100	23.91	54.13	1	6	128	5
ODIs	49	41	8	815	80	24.69	78.21	0	4	68	4
T20Is	2	2	1	33	19	33.00	132.00	0	0	2	0
First-class	190	289	27	8479	178	32.36		15	45	580	36
List A	200	165	32	3288	86	24.72	81.24	0	13	207	42
Twenty20	111	87	16	1262	56	17.77	109.45	0	3	50	20

Bowling	Mat	Balls	Runs	Wkts	BBI	BBM	Ave	Econ	SR	5w	10
Tests	34	-	-	-	-	-	-	-	-	-	-
ODIs	49	-	-	-	-	-	-	-	-	-	-
T20Is	2	-	-	-	-	-	-	-	-	-	-
First-class	190	24	26	0	-	-	-	6.50	-	0	0
List A	200	-	-	-	-	-	-	-	-	-	-
Twenty20	111	-	-	-	-	-	-	-	-	-	-

RICHARD JONES

RHB RFM

FULL NAME: Richard Alan Jones
BORN: November 6, 1986, Stourbridge
SQUAD NO: 25
HEIGHT: 6ft 2in
NICKNAME: Jonah, Dick
EDUCATION: Grange School, Stourbridge;
King Edward VI College, Stourbridge;
Loughborough University
TEAMS: England Under-19s, Loughborough
MCCU, Matabeleland Tuskers,
Warwickshire, Worcestershire
CAREER: First-class: 2007; List A: 2008; T20:
2010

BEST BATTING: 62 Matabeleland Tuskers vs Southern Rocks, Bulawayo, 2012
BEST BOWLING: 7-115 Worcestershire vs Sussex, Hove, 2010
COUNTY CAP: 2007 (Worcestershire)

CAREER HIGHLIGHTS? Signing my first professional contract with Worcestershire,
representing my country at U19 level and on an Elite Performance Squad tour to South
Africa, taking seven wickets in an innings against Sussex and making the move up the M5 to
join Warwickshire
SUPERSTITIONS? I always turn up to the ground in my whites on the first day of a County
Championship game. A weirder one is Matt Pardoe of Worcestershire – he takes his playing
cap home from the ground every day in a Sainsbury's carrier bag
MOST MARKED CHARACTERISTIC? Either my immaculate hairline or my goatee
BEST PLAYER IN COUNTY CRICKET? The correct answer is Moeen Ali. Look it up
CRICKETING HEROES? Jacques Kallis is the best cricketer ever, but I'm going to say Alan
Richardson. Long live the windmill!
SURPRISING FACT? I think I'm the only player in the world to dismiss KP twice in a day –
sorry about that one
CRICKET RULE YOU'D CHANGE? In one-day cricket you should have one 'double-play' per
innings where both current batsmen can be dismissed with the same delivery
TWITTER FEED: @richardjones441

Batting	Mat	Inns	NO	Runs	HS	Ave	SR	100	50	Ct	St
First-class	44	67	12	633	62	11.50	40.47	0	2	18	0
List A	10	5	2	23	11*	7.66	69.69	0	0	1	0
Twenty20	6	2	1	14	9	14.00	77.77	0	0	7	0

Bowling	Mat	Balls	Runs	Wkts	BBI	BBM	Ave	Econ	SR	5w	10
First-class	44	5978	4153	133	7/115	8/105	31.22	4.16	44.9	5	0
List A	10	333	380	3	1/25	1/25	126.66	6.84	111.0	0	0
Twenty20	6	66	119	2	1/17	1/17	59.50	10.81	33.0	0	0

CHRIS JORDAN

RHB RFM W1 MVP15

SUSSEX

FULL NAME: Christopher James Jordan
BORN: October 4, 1988, Barbados
SQUAD NO: 8
HEIGHT: 6ft 2in
NICKNAME: CJ
EDUCATION: Dulwich College
TEAMS: England, Barbados, England Lions, Surrey, Surrey 2nd XI, Sussex
CAREER: ODI: 2013; T20I: 2014; First-class: 2007; List A: 2007; T20: 2008

BEST BATTING: 92 Sussex vs Derbyshire, Derby, 2013
BEST BOWLING: 7-43 Barbados vs Combined Campuses and Colleges, Bridgetown, 2013

TWITTER FEED: @ChrisJordan94
NOTES: Born in Barbados, Jordan is eligible to represent England through his grandmother and made his ODI debut in September 2013 against Australia at Southampton. He took 3-51 in the match. His T20I debut came in February 2014 against Australia at Sydney. Took four wickets on first-class debut against Kent. Claimed career-best figures of 7-43 for Barbados in the 2013 close season and began last year's County Championship with 6-48 against Yorkshire, finishing the campaign with 61 first-class wickets

Batting	Mat	Inns	NO	Runs	HS	Ave	SR	100	50	Ct	St
ODIs	7	5	3	30	14	15.00	63.82	0	0	2	0
T20Is	1	1	1	10	10*	-	83.33	0	0	0	0
First-class	59	78	12	1473	92	22.31		0	6	53	0
List A	38	25	7	233	38	12.94		0	0	17	0
Twenty20	20	16	7	144	31	16.00	105.10	0	0	9	0

Bowling	Mat	Balls	Runs	Wkts	BBI	BBM	Ave	Econ	SR	5w	10
ODIs	7	396	371	9	3/51	3/51	41.22	5.62	44.0	0	0
T20Is	1	24	23	1	1/23	1/23	23.00	5.75	24.0	0	0
First-class	59	8752	5194	161	7/43	9/58	32.26	3.56	54.3	6	0
List A	38	1684	1551	56	4/38	4/38	27.69	5.52	30.0	0	0
Twenty20	20	347	497	14	2/28	2/28	35.50	8.59	24.7	0	0

ED JOYCE

LHB RM R7 MVP59

FULL NAME: Edmund Christopher Joyce
BORN: September 22, 1978, Dublin, Ireland
SQUAD NO: 24
HEIGHT: 5ft 10in
NICKNAME: Joycey, Spud, Piece
EDUCATION: Presentation College, Bray;
Trinity College, Dublin
TEAMS: England, Ireland, England Lions,
Marylebone Cricket Club, Middlesex, Sussex
CAREER: ODI: 2006; T20I: 2006; First-class:
1997; List A: 1998; T20: 2003

SUSSEX

BEST BATTING: 211 Middlesex vs Warwickshire, Birmingham, 2006
BEST BOWLING: 2-34 Middlesex vs Cambridge UCCE, Cambridge, 2004
COUNTY CAP: 2002 (Middlesex)

TWITTER FEED: @edjoyce24
NOTES: Passed 1,000 first-class runs five English summers in a row between 2002-2006, also achieving the feat in 2011 and 2013. Has represented both Ireland and England in ODI cricket. Scored his one ODI century for England against Australia in the 2007 Commonwealth Bank Series. Appointed Sussex club captain ahead of the 2013 season. His brother, Dom, and sisters, Cecelia and Isobel, have all played international cricket for Ireland. Across 14 games at the ICC Trophies of 2001 and 2005 he averaged 84. Averaged 64 in first-class cricket in 2013, including a season-best 204* against Nottinghamshire at Trent Bridge. In 2014 he was named as the No.1 cricketer from non-Test playing nations by All Out Cricket

Batting	Mat	Inns	NO	Runs	HS	Ave	SR	100	50	Ct	St
ODIs	40	40	3	1277	116*	34.51	67.88	2	8	11	0
T20Is	15	12	3	312	78*	34.66	91.76	0	1	1	0
First-class	200	332	30	13918	211	46.08		31	78	175	0
List A	249	237	26	8072	146	38.25		13	48	83	0
Twenty20	81	75	13	1174	78*	18.93	93.76	0	1	21	0

Bowling	Mat	Balls	Runs	Wkts	BBI	BBM	Ave	Econ	SR	5w	10
ODIs	40	-	-	-	-	-	-	-	-	-	-
T20Is	15	-	-	-	-	-	-	-	-	-	-
First-class	200	1287	1025	11	2/34		93.18	4.77	117.0	0	0
List A	249	264	309	6	2/10	2/10	51.50	7.02	44.0	0	0
Twenty20	81	6	12	0	-	-	-	12.00	-	0	0

GARY KEEDY

NOTTINGHAMSHIRE

FULL NAME: Gary Keedy
BORN: November 27, 1974, Sandal, Wakefield, Yorkshire
SQUAD NO: 3
HEIGHT: 5ft 11in
NICKNAME: Keeds
EDUCATION: Garforth Comprehensive; University of Salford
TEAMS: England Lions, Lancashire, Marylebone Cricket Club, Nottinghamshire, Yorkshire
CAREER: First-class: 1994; List A: 1995; T20: 2004

BEST BATTING: 64 Lancashire vs Sussex, Hove, 2008
BEST BOWLING: 7-68 Lancashire vs Durham, Manchester, 2010
COUNTY CAP: 2000 (Lancashire); BENEFIT YEAR: 2009 (Lancashire)

WHO WOULD PLAY YOU IN A FILM OF YOUR LIFE? My twin brother
CAREER HIGHLIGHTS? Winning the Championship in 2011 with Lancashire, getting capped by Lancashire, playing for England Lions against Australia and T20 Finals Days
MOST MARKED CHARACTERISTIC? My baldness
BEST PLAYER IN COUNTY CRICKET? Marcus Trescothick
TIPS FOR THE TOP? Arron Lilley and George Edwards
DESERT ISLAND DISC? The Beatles – Help!
FAVOURITE TV? MasterChef
CRICKETING HEROES? Shane Warne and Graham Gooch
NON-CRICKETING HEROES? Jimmy Page
ACCOMPLISHMENTS? My degree
WHEN YOU RETIRE? I'd like to be a physiotherapist
SURPRISING FACT? I'm exceptionally good at playing the triangle
FANTASY SLIP CORDON? Keeper: Slash from Guns N' Roses, 1st: Gordon Ramsay, 2nd: Myself, 3rd: Karl Pilkington, Gully: Robert De Niro
TWITTER FEED: @keeds23

Batting	Mat	Inns	NO	Runs	HS	Ave	SR	100	50	Ct	St
First-class	223	256	125	1429	64	10.90		0	2	54	0
List A	97	35	17	161	33	8.94		0	0	14	0
Twenty20	71	11	6	27	9*	5.40	79.41	0	0	10	0

Bowling	Mat	Balls	Runs	Wkts	BBI	BBM	Ave	Econ	SR	5w	10
First-class	223	45469	21279	678	7/68		31.38	2.80	67.0	34	7
List A	97	3936	3150	119	5/30	5/30	26.47	4.80	33.0	2	0
Twenty20	71	1414	1541	72	4/15	4/15	21.40	6.53	19.6	0	0

FULL NAME: Samuel Kelsall
BORN: March 14, 1993, Stoke-on-Trent, Staffordshire
SQUAD NO: 18
HEIGHT: 5ft 7in
NICKNAME: Kels, Rugrat, Mouse
EDUCATION: Priory Primary School; Trentham High School; South Nottingham College
TEAMS: England Under-17s, England Under-19s, Nottinghamshire, Nottinghamshire 2nd XI
CAREER: First-class: 2011; List A: 2011

BEST BATTING: 35 Nottinghamshire vs Warwickshire, Nottingham, 2012

CAREER HIGHLIGHTS? Representing England at U15 and U19 level. Earning my first professional contract with Notts, having been a member since the age of 11
CRICKETING HEROES? Ian Bell has always been a role model to me
NON-CRICKETING HEROES? Phil Taylor
BEST PLAYER IN COUNTY CRICKET? Andre Adams and Marcus Trescothick
TIP FOR THE TOP? Thomas Rowe from Nottinghamshire
IF YOU WEREN'T A CRICKETER? I'd hopefully be a PE teacher or coach of some sort
WHEN RAIN STOPS PLAY? Listening to music, resting, playing Doodle Jump
FAVOURITE TV? EastEnders, Emmerdale, MasterChef, TOWIE
FAVOURITE FILM? Billy Elliot
FAVOURITE BOOK? Andre Agassi – Open
DREAM HOLIDAY? Barbados
ACCOMPLISHMENTS? Completing my Level 2 coaching badge and my BTEC course
GUILTY PLEASURES? Watching Loose Women or crying at The Lion King
FANTASY SLIP CORDON? Keeper: Shaka Hislop, 1st: Rihanna, 2nd: Chris Kelsall, 3rd: James Corden, Gully: David English
TWITTER FEED? @Kelsall93

Batting	Mat	Inns	NO	Runs	HS	Ave	SR	100	50	Ct	St
First-class	2	4	0	50	35	12.50	44.64	0	0	1	0
List A	2	2	0	49	40	24.50	64.47	0	0	1	0

Bowling	Mat	Balls	Runs	Wkts	BBI	BBM	Ave	Econ	SR	5w	10
First-class	2	-	-	-	-	-	-	-	-	-	-
List A	2	-	-	-	-	-	-	-	-	-	-

ROB KEOGH — RHB OB

NORTHAMPTONSHIRE

FULL NAME: Robert Ian Keogh
BORN: October 21, 1991, Dunstable
SQUAD NO: 14
HEIGHT: 6ft 2in
NICKNAME: Keezy, Chav, Kellogs
EDUCATION: Queensbury School; Dunstable College
TEAMS: Bedfordshire, Northamptonshire, Northamptonshire 2nd XI
CAREER: First-class: 2012; List A: 2010; T20: 2011

BEST BATTING: 221 Northamptonshire vs Hampshire, Southampton, 2013
BEST BOWLING: 1-69 Northamptonshire vs Glamorgan, Cardiff, 2012

FAMILY TIES? My dad was a gun cricketer for Dunstable Town CC
WHO WOULD PLAY YOU IN A FILM OF YOUR LIFE? Seann William Scott or Vincent Chase
CAREER HIGHLIGHTS? Signing my first pro deal and making my debut in all formats for Northants
SUPERSTITIONS? I put my kit on in a certain way before batting. I can't take the first ball when opening. My bag has to be packed in a specific way
MOST MARKED CHARACTERISTIC? I'm hard-working
BEST PLAYER IN COUNTY CRICKET? Peter Trego
TIPS FOR THE TOP? Ben Duckett, Olly Stone, Christian Davis, James Kettleborough
IF YOU WEREN'T A CRICKETER? I'd be a fireman
DESERT ISLAND DISC? Wiz Khalifa – Rolling Papers
CRICKETING HEROES? Michael Clarke, AB de Villiers, Viv Richards
NON-CRICKETING HEROES? David Beckham, Muhammad Ali
ACCOMPLISHMENTS? I played for Luton Town FC as a junior between the ages of seven and 15
WHEN YOU RETIRE? I'd like to run my own bar, restaurant or nightclub
TWITTER FEED: @RobKeogh91

Batting	Mat	Inns	NO	Runs	HS	Ave	SR	100	50	Ct	St
First-class	9	13	2	464	221	42.18	46.16	1	1	1	0
List A	9	8	1	168	61	24.00	75.67	0	1	2	0
Twenty20	8	2	0	2	1	1.00	22.22	0	0	5	0

Bowling	Mat	Balls	Runs	Wkts	BBI	BBM	Ave	Econ	SR	5w	10
First-class	9	144	78	1	1/69	1/69	78.00	3.25	144.0	0	0
List A	9	114	115	0	-	-	-	6.05	-	0	0
Twenty20	8	36	45	0	-	-	-	7.50	-	0	0

SIMON KERRIGAN

RHB SLA W2 MVP81

FULL NAME: Simon Christopher Kerrigan
BORN: May 10, 1989, Preston, Lancashire
SQUAD NO: 10
HEIGHT: 5ft 9in
NICKNAME: Kegs, Kegsy, Kegger, Bish
EDUCATION: Corpus Christi High School;
Preston College; Edge Hill University
TEAMS: England, England Lions, Lancashire,
Lancashire 2nd XI, Marylebone Cricket Club
CAREER: Test: 2013; First-class: 2010; List A:
2011; T20: 2010

LANCASHIRE

BEST BATTING: 62* Lancashire vs Hampshire, Southport, 2013
BEST BOWLING: 9-51 Lancashire vs Hampshire, Liverpool, 2011
COUNTY CAP: 2013

CAREER HIGHLIGHTS? Winning the Championship in 2011
SUPERSTITIONS? Not really, they come and go
CRICKETING HEROES? Andrew Flintoff, Darren Gough
NON-CRICKETING HEROES? Phil Ivey
BEST PLAYER IN COUNTY CRICKET? Marcus Trescothick
TIP FOR THE TOP? Karl Brown
IF YOU WEREN'T A CRICKETER? I'd be jobless
WHEN RAIN STOPS PLAY? I sleep or make tea for everyone
FAVOURITE TV? Modern Family
FAVOURITE FILM? The Other Guys
DREAM HOLIDAY? Blackpool
GUILTY PLEASURES? All bad foods
TWITTER FEED: @Kegs10

Batting	Mat	Inns	NO	Runs	HS	Ave	SR	100	50	Ct	St
Tests	1	1	1	1	1*	-	8.33	0	0	0	0
First-class	55	58	22	390	62*	10.83	31.45	0	1	16	0
List A	30	14	5	28	10	3.11	49.12	0	0	9	0
Twenty20	24	4	4	9	4*	-	180.00	0	0	11	0

Bowling	Mat	Balls	Runs	Wkts	BBI	BBM	Ave	Econ	SR	5w	10
Tests	1	48	53	0	-	-	-	6.62	-	0	0
First-class	55	10488	4965	185	9/51	12/192	26.83	2.84	56.6	11	2
List A	30	1226	1082	21	3/21	3/21	51.52	5.29	58.3	0	0
Twenty20	24	516	595	20	3/17	3/17	29.75	6.91	25.8	0	0

ALEXEI KERVEZEE
RHB RM R1

FULL NAME: Alexei Nicolaas Kervezee
BORN: September 11, 1989, Walvis Bay, Namibia
SQUAD NO: 5
HEIGHT: 5ft 9in
NICKNAME: Cub, Rowdy, Jason Bourne, Crazy
EDUCATION: Duneside High, Namibia; Segbroek College, Netherlands
TEAMS: Netherlands, Netherlands Under-19s, Worcestershire, Worcestershire 2nd XI
CAREER: ODI: 2006; T20I: 2009; First-class: 2005; List A: 2006; T20: 2009

BEST BATTING: 155 Worcestershire vs Derbyshire, Derby, 2010
BEST BOWLING: 1-14 Netherlands vs Namibia, Windhoek, 2008

FAMILY TIES? My uncle represented the Netherlands cricket team when he was younger
WHO WOULD PLAY YOU IN A FILM OF YOUR LIFE? Chris Hemsworth
CAREER HIGHLIGHTS? Playing in World Cups for the Netherlands (50-over and T20) and scoring 1,200 runs in a season for Worcestershire CCC
MOST MARKED CHARACTERISTIC? My tattooed right arm
BEST PLAYER IN COUNTY CRICKET? Marcus Trescothick
TIP FOR THE TOP? Tom Kohler-Cadmore
IF YOU WEREN'T A CRICKETER? Formula 1
DESERT ISLAND DISC? Any Bon Jovi or Eminem album
FAVOURITE TV? Two And A Half Men
CRICKETING HEROES? Jacques Kallis, Ricky Ponting
WHEN YOU RETIRE? I'll go into some form of coaching
SURPRISING FACT? I have four nationalities
TWITTER FEED: @cubbo455

Batting	Mat	Inns	NO	Runs	HS	Ave	SR	100	50	Ct	St
ODIs	39	36	3	924	92	28.00	73.15	0	4	18	0
T20Is	10	10	1	289	58*	32.11	110.30	0	2	4	0
First-class	71	121	7	3413	155	29.93		4	20	37	0
List A	91	85	6	2294	121*	29.03	78.10	2	10	34	0
Twenty20	68	64	9	1104	58*	20.07	111.40	0	4	27	0

Bowling	Mat	Balls	Runs	Wkts	BBI	BBM	Ave	Econ	SR	5w	10
ODIs	39	24	34	0	-	-	-	8.50	-	0	0
T20Is	10	-	-	-	-	-	-	-	-	-	-
First-class	71	183	145	2	1/14	1/14	72.50	4.75	91.5	0	0
List A	91	48	73	0	-	-	-	9.12	-	0	0
Twenty20	68	12	13	0	-	-	-	6.50	-	0	0

JAMES KETTLEBOROUGH RHB OB

FULL NAME: James Michael Kettleborough
BORN: October 22, 1992, Huntingdon
SQUAD NO: 3
HEIGHT: 6ft
NICKNAME: Ketts, JK
EDUCATION: Bedford School
TEAMS: Bedfordshire, Northamptonshire 2nd XI
CAREER: Yet to make first-team debut

FAMILY TIES? My dad played for Bedfordshire and MCC
WHO WOULD PLAY YOU IN A FILM OF YOUR LIFE? Henry Caville or Tom Hardy
CAREER HIGHLIGHTS? Signing a professional contract and being part of a T20-winning squad
SUPERSTITIONS? I always touch my bat over the rope when I go out to bat – no idea why!
MOST MARKED CHARACTERISTIC? Patience
BEST PLAYER IN COUNTY CRICKET? Sam Robson
TIP FOR THE TOP? Max Holden (Middlesex Academy)
IF YOU WEREN'T A CRICKETER? I'd probably just be a full-time triallist somewhere. I also quite like the idea of personal training
DESERT ISLAND DISC? Either David Guetta or Avicii's album
FAVOURITE TV? Modern Family
CRICKETING HEROES? Stephen Peters, Dan Housego, my dad
NON-CRICKETING HEROES? Sonny Bill Williams, my dad
ACCOMPLISHMENTS? I once won £20 at a casino
WHEN YOU RETIRE? I'd like to commentate for Sky Sports
SURPRISING FACT? I'm addicted to tattoos
FANTASY SLIP CORDON? Keeper: Lee Evans, 1st: Ricky Gervais, 2nd: Myself, 3rd: Tim Vine, Gully: Kelly Brook
TWITTER FEED: @JKetts1305

ROBERT KEY

RHB OB R7 MVP58

FULL NAME: Robert William Trevor Key
BORN: May 12, 1979, East Dulwich, London
SQUAD NO: 4
HEIGHT: 6ft 1in
NICKNAME: Keysy
EDUCATION: Colfe's School
TEAMS: England, Kent, Marylebone Cricket Club
CAREER: Test: 2002; ODI: 2003; T20I: 2009; First-class: 1998; List A: 1998; T20: 2004

BEST BATTING: 270* Kent vs Glamorgan, Cardiff, 2009
BEST BOWLING: 2-31 Kent vs Somerset, Canterbury, 2010
COUNTY CAP: 2001; BENEFIT YEAR: 2011

WHO WOULD PLAY YOU IN A FILM OF YOUR LIFE? Russell Crowe
CAREER HIGHLIGHTS? Scoring 221 vs West Indies for England at Lord's
BEST PLAYER IN COUNTY CRICKET? Marcus Trescothick
TIP FOR THE TOP? Sam Northeast
DESERT ISLAND DISC? John Mayer – Free Fallin'
CRICKETING HEROES? Philip Fussell
NON-CRICKETING HEROES? Will Ashby, George Digweed
ACCOMPLISHMENTS? Putting together a kids' trampoline
FANTASY SLIP CORDON? Keeper: George Digweed, 1st: Will Ashby, 2nd: James Fielding, 3rd: Glucka Wijesuriya, Gully: Andy Fussell
TWITTER FEED: @robkey612

Batting	Mat	Inns	NO	Runs	HS	Ave	SR	100	50	Ct	St
Tests	15	26	1	775	221	31.00	47.28	1	3	11	0
ODIs	5	5	0	54	19	10.80	40.00	0	0	0	0
T20Is	1	1	1	10	10*	-	125.00	0	0	1	0
First-class	270	466	36	17900	270*	41.62		51	69	149	0
List A	221	214	17	6381	144*	32.39		8	37	45	0
Twenty20	86	86	10	1855	98*	24.40	119.98	0	10	23	0

Bowling	Mat	Balls	Runs	Wkts	BBI	BBM	Ave	Econ	SR	5w	10
Tests	15	-	-	-	-	-	-	-	-	-	-
ODIs	5	-	-	-	-	-	-	-	-	-	-
T20Is	1	-	-	-	-	-	-	-	-	-	-
First-class	270	472	319	3	2/31	2/31	106.33	4.05	157.3	0	0
List A	221	-	-	-	-	-	-	-	-	-	-
Twenty20	86	-	-	-	-	-	-	-	-	-	-

CRAIG KIESWETTER   RHB OB WK R1 MVP22

FULL NAME: Craig Kieswetter
BORN: November 28, 1987, Johannesburg, Transvaal, South Africa
SQUAD NO: 22
HEIGHT: 6ft
NICKNAME: Hobnob
EDUCATION: Bishops Diocesan College; Millfield School
TEAMS: England, England Lions, Somerset, South Africa Under-19s
CAREER: ODI: 2010; T20I: 2010; First-class: 2007; List A: 2007; T20: 2007

BEST BATTING: 164 Somerset vs Nottinghamshire, Nottingham, 2011
BEST BOWLING: 2-3 Somerset vs Worcestershire, Worcester, 2012
COUNTY CAP: 2009

CAREER HIGHLIGHTS? Being awarded my cap for Somerset in 2009, being a World T20 winner in 2010 and being named Man of the Match in the final, becoming the second-youngest ODI centurion for England in 2010
CRICKETING HEROES? Jonty Rhodes, Adam Gilchrist, Justin Langer
NON-CRICKETING HEROES? Ayrton Senna, José Mourinho
BEST PLAYER IN COUNTY CRICKET? Nick Compton
TIP FOR THE TOP? Tom Abell
IF YOU WEREN'T A CRICKETER? I'd be studying Law
FAVOURITE FILM? Sherlock Holmes
ACCOMPLISHMENTS? Helping charities with donations of cricket equipment
FANTASY SLIP CORDON? Keeper: Myself, 1st: José Mourinho, 2nd: Johnny Depp, 3rd: Muhammad Ali, Gully: Natalie Portman
TWITTER FEED? @kiesy_22

Batting	Mat	Inns	NO	Runs	HS	Ave	SR	100	50	Ct	St
ODIs	46	40	5	1054	107	30.11	89.93	1	5	53	12
T20Is	25	25	1	526	63	21.91	111.91	0	3	17	3
First-class	101	152	21	5219	164	39.83		11	26	292	8
List A	134	124	16	4254	143	39.38	95.18	11	17	136	26
Twenty20	103	101	14	2671	89*	30.70	123.14	0	21	67	19

Bowling	Mat	Balls	Runs	Wkts	BBI	BBM	Ave	Econ	SR	5w	10
ODIs	46	-	-	-	-	-	-	-	-	-	-
T20Is	25	-	-	-	-	-	-	-	-	-	-
First-class	101	54	29	2	2/3	2/3	14.50	3.22	27.0	0	0
List A	134	12	19	1	1/19	1/19	19.00	9.50	12.0	0	0
Twenty20	103	-	-	-	-	-	-	-	-	-	-

STEVE KIRBY RHB RFM W3

SOMERSET

FULL NAME: Steven Paul Kirby
BORN: October 4, 1977, Bury, Lancashire
SQUAD NO: 9
HEIGHT: 6ft 3in
NICKNAME: Tango
EDUCATION: Elton High School; Bury College
TEAMS: England Lions, Gloucestershire, Leicestershire, Marylebone Cricket Club, Somerset, Yorkshire
CAREER: First-class: 2001; List A: 2001; T20: 2004

BEST BATTING: 57 Yorkshire vs Hampshire, Leeds, 2002
BEST BOWLING: 8-80 Yorkshire vs Somerset, Taunton, 2003
COUNTY CAPS: 2003 (Yorkshire); 2005 (Gloucestershire)

NOTES: Originally signed with Leicestershire but left for Yorkshire in 2001 before making a first-class appearance. Took 7-50 on debut for the White Rose. Claimed match figures of 12-72 against his old club in just his third match. His best return in a first-class season came in 2003, when he claimed 67 wickets. Moved to Gloucestershire in 2005 – taking 264 first-class wickets at 28.18 for the club – before switching to Somerset ahead of the 2011 season. Took 53 first-class wickets in his first year at Taunton and has taken a further 50 over the last two seasons. Dismissed Mike Atherton in both innings of the former England skipper's final Championship match. Represented England Lions in 2008, taking the wickets of Hashim Amla and Albie Morkel in a 50-over match at Grace Road

Batting	Mat	Inns	NO	Runs	HS	Ave	SR	100	50	Ct	St
First-class	167	234	72	1320	57	8.14	28.22	0	1	37	0
List A	104	36	14	88	15	4.00	41.90	0	0	16	0
Twenty20	77	24	8	70	25	4.37	74.46	0	0	12	0

Bowling	Mat	Balls	Runs	Wkts	BBI	BBM	Ave	Econ	SR	5w	10
First-class	167	29166	16442	572	8/80		28.74	3.38	50.9	17	4
List A	104	4222	3962	142	5/36	5/36	27.90	5.63	29.7	1	0
Twenty20	77	1499	1891	83	3/17	3/17	22.78	7.56	18.0	0	0

MICHAEL KLINGER

RHB R1 MVP10

FULL NAME: Michael Klinger
BORN: July 4, 1980, Kew, Melbourne, Victoria, Australia
SQUAD NO: 2
HEIGHT: 5ft 9in
NICKNAME: Maxy
TEAMS: Adelaide Strikers, Australia A, Gloucestershire, Gloucestershire 2nd XI, Kochi Tuskers Kerala, South Australia, Victoria, Worcestershire
CAREER: First-class: 1999; List A: 1999; T20: 2006

GLOUCESTERSHIRE

BEST BATTING: 255 South Australia vs Western Australia, Adelaide, 2008
COUNTY CAP: 2012 (Worcestershire)

TWITTER FEED: @maxyklinger
NOTES: An experienced Australian opening batsman, Klinger is set for his second season at Gloucestershire after a very productive campaign last year in which he scored 2,208 runs across all competitions. He will continue as the club's skipper and overseas player in 2014. He had previously played seven first-class matches for Worcestershire in 2012, scoring 413 runs at an average of 37.54. He continued his impressive form from last year in Australian domestic cricket over the winter, hitting 214 for South Australia vs Victoria at Adelaide in February

Batting	Mat	Inns	NO	Runs	HS	Ave	SR	100	50	Ct	St
First-class	127	224	22	7669	255	37.96	44.61	17	34	119	0
List A	122	121	15	4923	140*	46.44		11	32	47	0
Twenty20	66	64	10	1780	108*	32.96	123.43	1	11	22	0

Bowling	Mat	Balls	Runs	Wkts	BBI	BBM	Ave	Econ	SR	5w	10
First-class	127	6	3	0	-	-	-	3.00	-	0	0
List A	122	-	-	-	-	-	-	-	-	-	-
Twenty20	66	-	-	-	-	-	-	-	-	-	-

FULL NAME: Thomas Craig Knight
BORN: June 28, 1993, Sheffield, Yorkshire
SQUAD NO: 27
HEIGHT: 6ft 2in
NICKNAME: Knighty, Kizzle
EDUCATION: Eckington School
TEAMS: Derbyshire, Derbyshire 2nd XI, Derbyshire Under-15s, Derbyshire Under-17s, England Under-19s
CAREER: First-class: 2011; List A: 2011; T20: 2011

BEST BATTING: 14 Derbyshire vs Surrey, The Oval, 2011
BEST BOWLING: 2-32 Derbyshire vs Glamorgan, Cardiff, 2011

FAMILY TIES? My dad played local league cricket
WHO WOULD PLAY YOU IN A FILM OF YOUR LIFE? Tom Hardy
CAREER HIGHLIGHTS? Making my debut in T20 for Derbyshire vs Nottinghamshire at Trent Bridge. Playing for England U19 at the World Cup
SUPERSTITIONS? I always bowl in a long-sleeved shirt
MOST MARKED CHARACTERISTIC? My forehead
BEST PLAYER IN COUNTY CRICKET? Wayne Madsen
TIPS FOR THE TOP? Wes Durston, Alex Hughes
IF YOU WEREN'T A CRICKETER? I'd be at university
DESERT ISLAND DISC? Arctic Monkeys – AM
FAVOURITE TV? Criminal Minds
CRICKETING HEROES? Daniel Vettori, David Wainwright
NON-CRICKETING HEROES? David Beckham, Justin Timberlake
WHEN YOU RETIRE? I'd like to be a fisherman
SURPRISING FACT? I was born with webbed fingers
TWITTER FEED: @tomknight28

Batting	Mat	Inns	NO	Runs	HS	Ave	SR	100	50	Ct	St
First-class	2	3	1	15	14	7.50	39.47	0	0	1	0
List A	8	6	4	16	10	8.00	39.02	0	0	1	0
Twenty20	14	2	2	3	2*	-	60.00	0	0	5	0

Bowling	Mat	Balls	Runs	Wkts	BBI	BBM	Ave	Econ	SR	5w	10
First-class	2	288	143	2	2/32	2/59	71.50	2.97	144.0	0	0
List A	8	360	321	9	3/36	3/36	35.66	5.35	40.0	0	0
Twenty20	14	246	291	13	3/16	3/16	22.38	7.09	18.9	0	0

TOM KOHLER-CADMORE   RHB OB

FULL NAME: Tom Kohler-Cadmore
BORN: August 19, 1994, Chatham, Kent
SQUAD NO: 32
HEIGHT: 6ft 2in
NICKNAME: Pepsi
EDUCATION: Malvern College
TEAMS: Worcestershire, Worcestershire 2nd XI
CAREER: List A: 2013

FAMILY TIES? My dad played club cricket
CAREER HIGHLIGHTS? Playing against Bangladesh A last summer
BEST PLAYER IN COUNTY CRICKET? Moeen Ali
TIP FOR THE TOP? Ben Twohig
DESERT ISLAND DISC? Drake – Take Care
FAVOURITE TV? Family Guy
WHEN YOU RETIRE? I'd like to start my own business
FANTASY SLIP CORDON? Keeper: Peter Griffin, 1st: Dave Lucas, 2nd: Myself, 3rd: Will Ferrell, Gully: Winston Churchill
TWITTER FEED? @TomKohlerCadmor

Batting	Mat	Inns	NO	Runs	HS	Ave	SR	100	50	Ct	St
List A	1	1	0	47	47	47.00	90.38	0	0	0	0

Bowling	Mat	Balls	Runs	Wkts	BBI	BBM	Ave	Econ	SR	5w	10
List A	1	-	-	-	-	-	-	-	-	-	-

DANIEL LAWRENCE

RHB LB

FULL NAME: Daniel William Lawrence
BORN: July 12, 1997, Whipps Cross, Essex
SQUAD NO: 11
HEIGHT: 6ft 1in
EDUCATION: Trinity Catholic High School
TEAMS: Essex 2nd XI, Essex Under-13s,
Essex Under-14s, Essex Under-15s, Essex
Under-17s
CAREER: Yet to make first-team debut

FAMILY TIES? My dad is the groundsman at Chingford Cricket Club. My great-uncle played for England

WHO WOULD PLAY YOU IN A FILM OF YOUR LIFE? Leonardo DiCaprio

CAREER HIGHLIGHTS? Playing a season for Essex 2nd XI and scoring a hundred for them

MOST MARKED CHARACTERISTIC? Self-belief and being sure of what I want to do when I get older

BEST PLAYER IN COUNTY CRICKET? Moeen Ali

TIPS FOR THE TOP? Daniel Bell-Drummond, James Vince

IF YOU WEREN'T A CRICKETER? I'd still be at school and working towards going to university

DESERT ISLAND DISC? Red Hot Chili Peppers – Dani California

FAVOURITE TV? Hustle

CRICKETING HEROES? Ricky Ponting, Graeme Smith, AB de Villiers

NON-CRICKETING HEROES? Martin Luther King, David Beckham

ACCOMPLISHMENTS? My school grades from last year

WHEN YOU RETIRE? I will travel around and play lots of golf

CRICKET RULE YOU'D CHANGE? You should be allowed to bowl as many overs as you want when you are young – no restrictions

SURPRISING FACT? I've got Grade 3 on the saxophone but had to stop because of cricket

FANTASY SLIP CORDON? Keeper: Dr Sheldon Cooper, 1st: The Rock, 2nd: Rafael Nadal, 3rd: Myself, Gully: Viv Richards

FULL NAME: Matthew Jack Leach
BORN: June 22, 1991, Taunton, Somerset
SQUAD NO: 17
HEIGHT: 6ft
NICKNAME: Leachy, Donkey, Snoz
EDUCATION: Trinity Primary School; Bishop Fox's Community School; Richard Huish College; Cardiff Metropolitan University
TEAMS: Cardiff MCCU, Dorset, Somerset, Somerset 2nd XI, Somerset Under-17s, Valley District Cricket Club
CAREER: First-class: 2012; List A: 2012

SOMERSET

BEST BATTING: 21 Somerset vs Middlesex, Taunton, 2013
BEST BOWLING: 5-63 Somerset vs Warwickshire, Taunton, 2013

WHO WOULD PLAY YOU IN A FILM OF YOUR LIFE? Will Ferrell... the film would be a comedy!
CAREER HIGHLIGHTS? Making my Championship debut against Lancashire. Playing the tour match against South Africa (and claiming the prize wicket of Hashim Amla). Representing England at U15 level
BEST PLAYER IN COUNTY CRICKET? Graham Onions or Banger [Marcus Trescothick]
TIPS FOR THE TOP? The Overton brothers [Craig and Jamie], Chris Jones
DESERT ISLAND DISC? Project X Soundtrack
FAVOURITE TV? The Big Bang Theory
CRICKETING HEROES? Marcus Trescothick, Jacques Kallis, Steve Waugh
ACCOMPLISHMENTS? Achieving an Honours degree in Sports Psychology
WHEN YOU RETIRE? I'd like to become a sports psychologist in an elite sports team
SURPRISING FACT? I bowl with my left arm but throw with my right arm
FANTASY SLIP CORDON? Keeper: Dr Sheldon Cooper, 1st: Myself, 2nd: Karl Pilkington, 3rd: Jimmy Carr, Gully: Jack Whitehall
TWITTER FEED: @jackleach1991

Batting	Mat	Inns	NO	Runs	HS	Ave	SR	100	50	Ct	St
First-class	8	10	3	66	21	9.42	28.82	0	0	0	0
List A	3	1	0	2	2	2.00	20.00	0	0	0	0

Bowling	Mat	Balls	Runs	Wkts	BBI	BBM	Ave	Econ	SR	5w	10
First-class	8	1264	518	15	5/63	7/106	34.53	2.45	84.2	1	0
List A	3	114	90	1	1/30	1/30	90.00	4.73	114.0	0	0

JOE LEACH

RHB RFM

FULL NAME: Joseph Leach
BORN: October 30, 1990, Stafford, Staffordshire
SQUAD NO: 23
HEIGHT: 6ft 1in
NICKNAME: Hugh Jed
EDUCATION: Shrewsbury School; Leeds University
TEAMS: Leeds/Bradford MCCU, Shropshire, Staffordshire, Worcestershire, Worcestershire 2nd XI
CAREER: First-class: 2012; List A: 2012; T20: 2013

BEST BATTING: 114 Worcestershire vs Gloucestershire, Cheltenham, 2013
BEST BOWLING: 4-73 Leeds/Bradford MCCU vs Surrey, The Oval, 2012
COUNTY CAP: 2012

CAREER HIGHLIGHTS? Playing for Worcestershire and winning the National Knockout with Shrewsbury CC
CRICKETING HEROES? Jacques Kallis, Andrew Flintoff
TIPS FOR THE TOP? Ben Slater and Luis Reece
WHEN RAIN STOPS PLAY? Taking the mickey out of Chris Russell or traipsing through Twitter
FAVOURITE TV? An Idiot Abroad
FAVOURITE FILM? The Hangover 2
DREAM HOLIDAY? Somewhere in the Caribbean
ACCOMPLISHMENTS? I can speak French (fairly well)
SURPRISING SKILL? I study Philosophy at Leeds University
FANTASY SLIP CORDON? Keeper: Ricky Gervais, 1st: Al Murray, 2nd: Karl Pilkington, 3rd: Me
TWITTER FEED: @joeleach23

Batting	Mat	Inns	NO	Runs	HS	Ave	SR	100	50	Ct	St
First-class	14	23	3	474	114	23.70	49.32	1	3	3	0
List A	2	1	1	21	21*	-	75.00	0	0	0	0
Twenty20	8	6	3	50	14*	16.66	125.00	0	0	0	0

Bowling	Mat	Balls	Runs	Wkts	BBI	BBM	Ave	Econ	SR	5w	10
First-class	14	826	532	18	4/73	4/21	29.55	3.86	45.8	0	0
List A	2	66	92	1	1/45	1/45	92.00	8.36	66.0	0	0
Twenty20	8	73	123	4	3/20	3/20	30.75	10.10	18.2	0	0

FULL NAME: Jack Andrew Leaning
BORN: October 18, 1993, Bristol
SQUAD NO: 34
HEIGHT: 6ft
EDUCATION: Archbishop Holgate's School, York; York College
TEAMS: England Under-19s, Yorkshire, Yorkshire 2nd XI, Yorkshire Academy, Yorkshire Under-15s, Yorkshire Under-17s
CAREER: First-class: 2013; List A: 2012; T20: 2013

YORKSHIRE

BEST BATTING: 0 Yorkshire vs Surrey, Leeds, 2013

TWITTER FEED: @JackLeaning1
NOTES: Son of former York City goalkeeper Andy, Leaning wrote himself into the Yorkshire record-books as a 14-year-old, when he hit an unbeaten 164 during the U14 squad's clash with Cheshire. He won Yorkshire's Academy Player of the Year award in 2012 and made his List A debut in the same season, scoring 11 against Warwickshire. He made four more List A appearances last year, with a top score of 60 against Somerset in the YB40. He made his first-class debut in 2013 against Surrey at Headingley

Batting	Mat	Inns	NO	Runs	HS	Ave	SR	100	50	Ct	St
First-class	1	1	0	0	0	0.00	0.00	0	0	0	0
List A	5	5	1	114	60	28.50	92.68	0	1	3	0
Twenty20	3	3	0	14	8	4.66	56.00	0	0	0	0

Bowling	Mat	Balls	Runs	Wkts	BBI	BBM	Ave	Econ	SR	5w	10
First-class	1	24	22	0	-	-	-	5.50	-	0	0
List A	5	78	76	6	5/22	5/22	12.66	5.84	13.0	1	0
Twenty20	3	6	18	0	-	-	-	18.00	-	0	0

YORKSHIRE

FULL NAME: Alexander Zak Lees
BORN: April 14, 1993, Halifax, Yorkshire
SQUAD NO: 14
HEIGHT: 6ft 3in
NICKNAME: Leesy
EDUCATION: Holy Trinity Senior School
TEAMS: England Lions, England Performance Programme, Yorkshire, Yorkshire 2nd XI, Yorkshire Academy, Yorkshire Under-17s
CAREER: First-class: 2010; List A: 2011; T20: 2013

BEST BATTING: 275* Yorkshire vs Derbyshire, Chesterfield, 2013

WHO WOULD PLAY YOU IN A FILM OF YOUR LIFE? Will Ferrell
CAREER HIGHLIGHTS? My first hundred at Lord's
BEST PLAYER IN COUNTY CRICKET? Moeen Ali
TIP FOR THE TOP? Matt Fisher
IF YOU WEREN'T A CRICKETER? I'd be a policeman
DESERT ISLAND DISC? Something by Drake
FAVOURITE TV? Band Of Brothers
CRICKETING HEROES? Matthew Hayden, Brian Lara
WHEN YOU RETIRE? I'd like to own a casino
SURPRISING FACT? I do a bit of magic on the side
FANTASY SLIP CORDON? Keeper: Steve Carell, 1st: Will Ferrell, 2nd: Sean Lock, 3rd: Jessica Alba, Gully: Disclosure
TWITTER FEED: @aleesy14

Batting	Mat	Inns	NO	Runs	HS	Ave	SR	100	50	Ct	St
First-class	15	25	4	863	275*	41.09	46.37	4	1	2	0
List A	7	7	1	229	63	38.16	78.15	0	2	1	0
Twenty20	2	2	0	33	32	16.50	97.05	0	0	0	0

Bowling	Mat	Balls	Runs	Wkts	BBI	BBM	Ave	Econ	SR	5w	10
First-class	15	6	14	0	-	-	-	14.00	-	0	0
List A	7	-	-	-	-	-	-	-	-	-	-
Twenty20	2	-	-	-	-	-	-	-	-	-	-

RICHARD LEVI

RHB RM

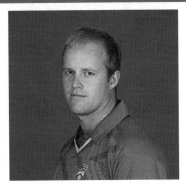

FULL NAME: Richard Ernst Levi
BORN: January 14, 1988, Johannesburg, South Africa
SQUAD NO: TBC
TEAMS: South Africa, Cape Cobras, Mumbai Indians, Northamptonshire; Somerset, Somerset 2nd XI, South Africa A, South Africa Academy, South Africa Under-19s, Western Province
CAREER: T20I: 2012; First-class: 2006; List A: 2005; T20: 2008

BEST BATTING: 150* Western Province vs Eastern Province, Cape Town, 2007

NOTES: A South African T20 international, aggressive opener Levi achieved global recognition when he posted 117* in a T20I game against New Zealand in 2012. The 45 balls it took to reach his century and the 13 sixes he struck were both a record for the format at the time. He was subsequently named South African Annual Cricketer of the Year but has not featured for the Proteas since December 2012. He has re-signed for Northamptonshire as a white-ball specialist, having played a key role in the club's FL t20 triumph last year. He will be available for all Northamptonshire's NatWest T20 Blast group games and eight Royal London One-Day Cup fixtures this season

Batting	Mat	Inns	NO	Runs	HS	Ave	SR	100	50	Ct	St
T20Is	13	13	2	236	117*	21.45	141.31	1	1	4	0
First-class	41	66	9	2326	150*	40.80	65.61	5	15	33	0
List A	74	69	5	2354	166	36.78	106.56	5	10	24	0
Twenty20	100	97	9	2273	117*	25.82	141.26	3	13	30	0

Bowling	Mat	Balls	Runs	Wkts	BBI	BBM	Ave	Econ	SR	5w	10
T20Is	13	-	-	-	-	-	-	-	-	-	-
First-class	41	-	-	-	-	-	-	-	-	-	-
List A	74	-	-	-	-	-	-	-	-	-	-
Twenty20	100	-	-	-	-	-	-	-	-	-	-

JON LEWIS

RHB RM W9

SUSSEX

FULL NAME: Jonathan Lewis
BORN: August 26, 1975, Aylesbury, Buckinghamshire
SQUAD NO: 4
HEIGHT: 6ft 3in
NICKNAME: Lewy
EDUCATION: Churchfields School, Swindon
TEAMS: England, Gloucestershire, Surrey, Sussex
CAREER: Test: 2006; ODI: 2005; T20I: 2005; First-class: 1995; List A: 1995; T20: 2003

BEST BATTING: 71 Gloucestershire vs Middlesex, Uxbridge, 2011
BEST BOWLING: 8-95 Gloucestershire vs Zimbabweans, Gloucester, 2000
COUNTY CAP: 1998 (Gloucestershire); BENEFIT YEAR: 2007 (Gloucestershire)

CAREER HIGHLIGHTS? Every time I played for England and all my one-day trophies with Gloucestershire
MOST MARKED CHARACTERISTIC? My calmness
BEST PLAYER IN COUNTY CRICKET? Marcus Trescothick
TIPS FOR THE TOP? Stuart Meaker, Rory Burns
DESERT ISLAND DISC? Roberta Flack – The First Time Ever I Saw Your Face
CRICKETING HEROES? Courtney Walsh, Richard Hadlee, Jack Russell
WHEN YOU RETIRE? I'd like to sit on the beach with an ice-cold beer
FANTASY SLIP CORDON? Keeper: Mick Jagger, 1st: Tiger Woods, 2nd: Rory McIlroy, 3rd: Paolo Di Canio
TWITTER FEED: @jonlew800

Batting	Mat	Inns	NO	Runs	HS	Ave	SR	100	50	Ct	St
Tests	1	2	0	27	20	13.50	60.00	0	0	0	0
ODIs	13	8	2	50	17	8.33	79.36	0	0	0	0
T20Is	2	2	1	1	1	1.00	25.00	0	0	1	0
First-class	243	347	70	4519	71	16.31		0	13	61	0
List A	232	135	48	1000	54	11.49		0	1	43	0
Twenty20	68	42	10	377	43	11.78	125.66	0	0	13	0

Bowling	Mat	Balls	Runs	Wkts	BBI	BBM	Ave	Econ	SR	5w	10
Tests	1	246	122	3	3/68	3/122	40.66	2.97	82.0	0	0
ODIs	13	716	500	18	4/36	4/36	27.77	4.18	39.7	0	0
T20Is	2	42	55	4	4/24	4/24	13.75	7.85	10.5	0	0
First-class	243	43648	21757	832	8/95		26.15	2.99	52.4	35	5
List A	232	10372	7990	302	5/19	5/19	26.45	4.62	34.3	2	0
Twenty20	68	1356	1828	62	4/24	4/24	29.48	8.08	21.8	0	0

TOM LEWIS

LHB RM

FULL NAME: Thomas Peter Lewis
BORN: March 7, 1991, Coventry, Warwickshire
SQUAD NO: 7
HEIGHT: 6ft 1in
NICKNAME: Lewy
EDUCATION: Princethorpe College
TEAMS: Marylebone Cricket Club Young Cricketers, Warwickshire 2nd XI
CAREER: Yet to make first-team debut

FAMILY TIES? My brother [Mark] played for Oxford UCCE and Warwickshire
WHO WOULD PLAY YOU IN A FILM OF YOUR LIFE? Tom Hardy
CAREER HIGHLIGHTS? Being a MCCC Young Cricketer and signing my first contract
SUPERSTITIONS? I put my pads on before my thigh guard
MOST MARKED CHARACTERISTIC? My off-drive
BEST PLAYER IN COUNTY CRICKET? Chris Woakes
TIPS FOR THE TOP? Pete McKay, Aaron Thomson, Sam Hain
IF YOU WEREN'T A CRICKETER? I'd be studying at university
DESERT ISLAND DISC? Drake – Take Care
FAVOURITE TV? Breaking Bad, Prison Break, Entourage
CRICKETING HEROES? Andrew Flintoff, Graham Thorpe, Marcus Trescothick
NON-CRICKETING HEROES? Paul Scholes
TWITTER FEED: @tom_lewis

CHRIS LIDDLE

RHB LMF

FULL NAME: Christopher John Liddle
BORN: February 1, 1984, Middlesbrough, Yorkshire
SQUAD NO: 11
HEIGHT: 6ft 4in
NICKNAME: Lids, Chuck
EDUCATION: Nunthorpe Comprehensive, Middlesborough; Teeside Tertiary College
TEAMS: Dhaka Gladiators, Leicestershire, Leicestershire 2nd XI, Sussex
CAREER: First-class: 2005; List A: 2006; T20: 2008

BEST BATTING: 53 Sussex vs Worcestershire, Hove, 2007
BEST BOWLING: 3-42 Leicestershire vs Somerset, Leicester, 2006

FAMILY TIES? My brother Andrew plays in the NYSD cricket league
CAREER HIGHLIGHTS? My T20 debut and the 2011 season, having previously missed the 2009 and 2010 seasons with injury
CRICKETING HEROES? Darren Gough, AB de Villiers, Marc Rosenberg
NON-CRICKETING HEROES? Jamie Redknapp
BEST PLAYER IN COUNTY CRICKET? Chris Nash
TIP FOR THE TOP? Luke Wells
IF YOU WEREN'T A CRICKETER? I'd be an electrician
WHEN RAIN STOPS PLAY? I'm on my iPad or messing around with some teammates
FAVOURITE FILM? Snatch
FAVOURITE TV? An Idiot Abroad, Emmerdale
DREAM HOLIDAY? A seaside apartment in the Maldives
SURPRISING SKILL? I'm an occcasional DJ for my friends
GUILTY PLEASURES? Chocolate biscuits
FANTASY SLIP CORDON? Keeper: Karl Pilkington, 1st: Cheryl Cole, 2nd: Jamie Redknapp, 3rd: Mila Kunis, 4th: Me, Gully: Jessica Biel
TWITTER FEED: @chrisliddle11

Batting	Mat	Inns	NO	Runs	HS	Ave	SR	100	50	Ct	St
First-class	19	17	8	125	53	13.88	55.30	0	1	6	0
List A	50	16	3	74	15	5.69	69.81	0	0	15	0
Twenty20	54	12	7	45	16	9.00	67.16	0	0	15	0

Bowling	Mat	Balls	Runs	Wkts	BBI	BBM	Ave	Econ	SR	5w	10
First-class	19	2230	1222	24	3/42	4/82	50.91	3.28	92.9	0	0
List A	50	1807	1758	69	5/18	5/18	25.47	5.83	26.1	1	0
Twenty20	54	1019	1303	68	5/17	5/17	19.16	7.67	14.9	1	0

ARRON LILLEY

RHB OB

FULL NAME: Arron Mark Lilley
BORN: April 1, 1991, Tameside, Lancashire
SQUAD NO: 19
HEIGHT: 6ft 1in
NICKNAME: The Big Show, Silly, Lils
EDUCATION: Mossley Hollins High School; Ashton Sixth Form
TEAMS: Lancashire, Lancashire 2nd XI, Lancashire Under-13s, Lancashire Under-15s, Lancashire Under-17s, Lancashire Under-19s
CAREER: First-class: 2013; List A: 2012; T20: 2013

BEST BATTING: 35* Lancashire vs Glamorgan, Manchester, 2013
BEST BOWLING: 1-41 Lancashire vs Worcestershire, Worcester, 2013

FAMILY TIES? My father and both grandads played cricket so I was brought up with the game from birth
WHO WOULD PLAY YOU IN A FILM OF YOUR LIFE? David Beckham or Bruce Willis
CAREER HIGHLIGHTS? Making my debut in front of more than 10,000 fans in the Roses T20 derby (shown live on Sky Sports). Making my full first-class debut against Glamorgan at Emirates Old Trafford
SUPERSTITIONS? I put my left pad on first
BEST PLAYER IN COUNTY CRICKET? Moeen Ali
TIPS FOR THE TOP? Alex Davies, Haseeb Hameed
IF YOU WEREN'T A CRICKETER? I'd be doing Biomechanical Science or Accounting
DESERT ISLAND DISC? Storm Queen – Look Right Through
FAVOURITE TV? TOWIE, Prison Break
CRICKETING HEROES? Ian Botham, Shane Warne
NON-CRICKETING HEROES? Mark Wright
WHEN YOU RETIRE? I'd like to become a physiotherapist for Manchester United
SURPRISING FACT? I'm the best footballer in the Lancashire squad!
TWITTER FEED: @Arronlilley20

Batting	Mat	Inns	NO	Runs	HS	Ave	SR	100	50	Ct	St
First-class	2	2	2	39	35*	-	108.33	0	0	0	0
List A	6	2	0	10	10	5.00	125.00	0	0	3	0
Twenty20	8	3	1	24	18	12.00	150.00	0	0	3	0

Bowling	Mat	Balls	Runs	Wkts	BBI	BBM	Ave	Econ	SR	5w	10
First-class	2	414	212	2	1/41	2/83	106.00	3.07	207.0	0	0
List A	6	228	172	10	4/30	4/30	17.20	4.52	22.8	0	0
Twenty20	8	162	187	5	1/21	1/21	37.40	6.92	32.4	0	0

TIM LINLEY

RHB RFM W1

SURREY

FULL NAME: Timothy Edward Linley
BORN: March 23, 1982, Horsforth, Leeds
SQUAD NO: 12
HEIGHT: 6ft 2in
NICKNAME: Sheephead, Bambi
EDUCATION: St Mary's RC Comprehensive;
Notre Dame Sixth Form College; Oxford
Brookes University
TEAMS: Middlesex 2nd XI, Nottinghamshire
2nd XI, Oxford UCCE, Surrey, Surrey 2nd XI,
Sussex, Sussex 2nd XI
CAREER: First-class: 2003; List A: 2009; T20:
2009

BEST BATTING: 42 Oxford UCCE vs Derbyshire, Oxford, 2005
BEST BOWLING: 6-57 Surrey vs Leicestershire, Leicester, 2011

WHO WOULD PLAY YOU IN A FILM OF YOUR LIFE? Anyone. If I've had a film made about me
I have obviously achieved something with my life
CAREER HIGHLIGHTS? Gaining promotion to Division One with Surrey and taking my first
five-wicket haul at The Oval in the County Championship vs Notts in 2012
SUPERSTITIONS? I always put my left pad on first. I never mess with Mother Cricket
MOST MARKED CHARACTERISTIC? Most people say I'm nice. I have no control over the tone
and volume of my voice or laugh
BEST PLAYER IN COUNTY CRICKET? Nick Compton, Peter Trego
TIP FOR THE TOP? Stuart Meaker will play Test cricket
FAVOURITE BOOK? The Alchemist by Paulo Coelho
SURPRISING FACT? I'm dyspraxic (look it up – it might explain a few things)
TWITTER FEED: @ViscountLinley

Batting	Mat	Inns	NO	Runs	HS	Ave	SR	100	50	Ct	St
First-class	54	73	15	477	42	8.22	34.54	0	0	20	0
List A	22	10	7	73	20*	24.33	86.90	0	0	2	0
Twenty20	7	2	0	9	8	4.50	112.50	0	0	2	0

Bowling	Mat	Balls	Runs	Wkts	BBI	BBM	Ave	Econ	SR	5w	10
First-class	54	9333	4638	170	6/57		27.28	2.98	54.9	5	1
List A	22	759	741	17	3/50	3/50	43.58	5.85	44.6	0	0
Twenty20	7	122	148	6	2/28	2/28	24.66	7.27	20.3	0	0

LIAM LIVINGSTONE

RHB LB

FULL NAME: Liam Stephen Livingstone
BORN: August 4, 1993, Barrow-in-Furness, Cumberland
SQUAD NO: 7
HEIGHT: 6ft 1in
NICKNAME: Livi
EDUCATION: Dane Ghyll Primary School; Chetwynde
TEAMS: Cumberland, Lancashire 2nd XI
CAREER: Yet to make first-team debut

WHO WOULD PLAY YOU IN A FILM OF YOUR LIFE? Adam Sandler. I think he can make any film funny
CAREER HIGHLIGHTS? Touring India with the England EPD U16 squad. Signing my first professional contract with Lancashire CCC. Scoring a 2nd XI T20 hundred vs Yorkshire
SUPERSTITIONS? I put my left pad on first and my right foot on to the pitch first
MOST MARKED CHARACTERISTIC? I'm competitive
BEST PLAYER IN COUNTY CRICKET? Glen Chapple – to be doing what he does at 40 years of age is phenomenal
IF YOU WEREN'T A CRICKETER? I'd be a fitness trainer of some sort
DESERT ISLAND DISC? Akon's first album
FAVOURITE TV? Prison Break
CRICKETING HEROES? Shane Warne
NON-CRICKETING HEROES? David Beckham
WHEN YOU RETIRE? I'd like to win the lottery and live on a beach somewhere
SURPRISING FACT? I broke both wrists at once trying to take a catch in India when I was 15
CRICKET RULE YOU'D CHANGE? No balls should be a free hit in any form of cricket
FANTASY SLIP CORDON? Keeper: James Corden, 1st: Adam Sandler, 2nd: Me, 3rd: David Beckham, Gully: Will Smith
TWITTER FEED: @liaml4893

GLAMORGAN

FULL NAME: David Liam Lloyd
BORN: June 15, 1992, St Asaph, Flintshire, Wales
SQUAD NO: 14
HEIGHT: 5ft 9in
NICKNAME: Ram, Lloydy
EDUCATION: Shrewsbury School
TEAMS: Glamorgan, Glamorgan 2nd XI, Wales Minor Counties
CAREER: First-class: 2012

BEST BATTING: 16 Glamorgan vs Gloucestershire, Cardiff, 2013

FAMILY TIES? My father played for the local club and county as a batsman
WHO WOULD PLAY YOU IN A FILM OF YOUR LIFE? Aaron Paul
CAREER HIGHLIGHTS? Making my debut, even though it didn't go too well!
SUPERSTITIONS? I put my equipment on in a certain order
MOST MARKED CHARACTERISTIC? Running like a ram
BEST PLAYER IN COUNTY CRICKET? Jim Allenby
TIP FOR THE TOP? Andrew Salter
IF YOU WEREN'T A CRICKETER? I'd work as a brewer
DESERT ISLAND DISC? Flo Rida – Good Feeling
FAVOURITE TV? Breaking Bad
CRICKETING HEROES? Jacques Kallis, Simon Jones
NON-CRICKETING HEROES? Eminem and Andy Morrell
ACCOMPLISHMENTS? Representing English Schools at football
WHEN YOU RETIRE? I'd like to become a coach
SURPRISING FACT? I'm a massive Wrexham FC fan
TWITTER FEED: @lloyddl2010

Batting	Mat	Inns	NO	Runs	HS	Ave	SR	100	50	Ct	St
First-class	3	5	1	27	16	6.75	34.61	0	0	0	0

Bowling	Mat	Balls	Runs	Wkts	BBI	BBM	Ave	Econ	SR	5w	10
First-class	3	-	-	-	-	-	-	-	-	-	-

MICHAEL LUMB

LHB RM R3 MVP23

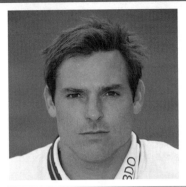

FULL NAME: Michael John Lumb
BORN: February 12, 1980, Johannesburg, Transvaal, South Africa
SQUAD NO: 45
HEIGHT: 6ft
NICKNAME: Joe, Lumby, China, Slumdog
EDUCATION: St Stithians College
TEAMS: England, Deccan Chargers, England Lions, Hampshire, Nottinghamshire, Queensland, Rajasthan Royals, Sydney Sixers, Yorkshire
CAREER: ODI: 2014; T20I: 2010; First-class: 2000; List A: 2001; T20: 2003

BEST BATTING: 221* Nottinghamshire vs Derbyshire, Nottingham, 2013
BEST BOWLING: 2-10 Yorkshire vs Kent, Canterbury, 2001
COUNTY CAPS: 2003 (Yorkshire); 2008 (Hampshire); 2012 (Nottinghamshire)

FAMILY TIES? My father Richard played for Yorkshire and my uncle Tich played for Natal and South Africa
CAREER HIGHLIGHTS? It would have to be playing for England and winning the World T20, beating the Aussies in the final! Winning the C&G Trophy with Hampshire at Lord's
SUPERSTITIONS? Too many to mention, they call me Rain Man!
CRICKETING HEROES? Graham Thorpe, Darren Lehmann, Stephen Fleming, Craig White, Shane Warne, Jacques Kallis
TIPS FOR THE TOP? Danny Briggs, James Vince
IF YOU WEREN'T A CRICKETER? I'd be a game ranger
WHEN RAIN STOPS PLAY? Probably read the papers with a coffee or play some form of stupid game in the changing room
FAVOURITE FILM? Man On Fire
GUILTY PLEASURES? Chocolate and biltong

Batting	Mat	Inns	NO	Runs	HS	Ave	SR	100	50	Ct	St
ODIs	3	3	0	165	106	55.00	81.28	1	0	1	0
T20Is	21	21	1	428	53*	21.40	134.59	0	2	8	0
First-class	166	277	18	9374	221*	36.19		19	51	103	0
List A	191	185	11	5502	110	31.62	85.95	4	41	66	0
Twenty20	163	162	11	3741	124*	24.77	141.11	1	21	53	0

Bowling	Mat	Balls	Runs	Wkts	BBI	BBM	Ave	Econ	SR	5w	10
ODIs	3	-	-	-	-	-	-	-	-	-	-
T20Is	21	-	-	-	-	-	-	-	-	-	-
First-class	166	330	255	6	2/10		42.50	4.63	55.0	0	0
List A	191	12	28	0	-	-	-	14.00	-	0	0
Twenty20	163	36	65	3	3/32	3/32	21.66	10.83	12.0	0	0

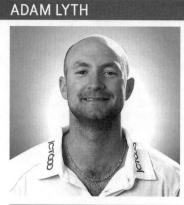

FULL NAME: Adam Lyth
BORN: September 25, 1987, Whitby, Yorkshire
SQUAD NO: 9
HEIGHT: 5ft 9in
NICKNAME: Lythy, Peanut
EDUCATION: Caedmon School; Whitby Community College
TEAMS: England Lions, England Under-19s, Yorkshire, Yorkshire 2nd XI
CAREER: First-class: 2007; List A: 2006; T20: 2008

BEST BATTING: 248* Yorkshire vs Leicestershire, Leicester, 2012
BEST BOWLING: 2-15 Yorkshire vs Somerset, Taunton, 2013
COUNTY CAP: 2010

FAMILY TIES? My father and brother played cricket for Scarborough
WHO WOULD PLAY YOU IN A FILM OF YOUR LIFE? Bruce Willis
CAREER HIGHLIGHTS? Being the first to a 1,000 runs in Division One in 2010 and subsequently receiving my county cap. Later that year I was selected on the Lions tour to Australia and the West Indies
MOST MARKED CHARACTERISTIC? My bald head
BEST PLAYER IN COUNTY CRICKET? Ben Stokes
TIPS FOR THE TOP? Ben Stokes, Gary Ballance
IF YOU WEREN'T A CRICKETER? I'd be a footballer
DESERT ISLAND DISC? Power Ballads
FAVOURITE TV? Only Fools And Horses
CRICKETING HEROES? Graham Thorpe
NON-CRICKETING HEROES? David Beckham
WHEN YOU RETIRE? I'd like to be an umpire
SURPRISING FACT? I played football for Manchester City
TWITTER FEED: @lythy09

Batting	Mat	Inns	NO	Runs	HS	Ave	SR	100	50	Ct	St
First-class	82	133	6	4777	248*	37.61		7	33	84	0
List A	74	68	6	1899	109*	30.62	87.67	1	9	25	0
Twenty20	51	45	1	873	78	19.84	123.47	0	2	19	0

Bowling	Mat	Balls	Runs	Wkts	BBI	BBM	Ave	Econ	SR	5w	10
First-class	82	613	452	7	2/15	2/15	64.57	4.42	87.5	0	0
List A	74	96	100	1	1/6	1/6	100.00	6.25	96.0	0	0
Twenty20	51	21	30	1	1/16	1/16	30.00	8.57	21.0	0	0

MATT MACHAN

LHB OB

FULL NAME: Matthew William Machan
BORN: February 15, 1991, Brighton, Sussex
SQUAD NO: 15
HEIGHT: 5ft 9in
NICKNAME: Mach, Meatball
EDUCATION: Hurstpierpoint College; Brighton College
TEAMS: Scotland, Sussex, Sussex 2nd XI
CAREER: ODI: 2013; T20I: 2013; First-class: 2010; List A: 2010; T20: 2012

BEST BATTING: 103 Sussex vs Somerset, Taunton, 2013
BEST BOWLING: 1-36 Scotland vs Australia A, Edinburgh, 2013

WHO WOULD PLAY YOU IN A FILM OF YOUR LIFE? Danny Dyer
CAREER HIGHLIGHTS? Scoring my maiden first-class hundred. Qualifying for the 2015 World Cup with Scotland
MOST MARKED CHARACTERISTIC? My good sense of humour
BEST PLAYER IN COUNTY CRICKET? David Murphy
TIP FOR THE TOP? Harry Finch
IF YOU WEREN'T A CRICKETER? I'd be living the dream abroad somewhere
DESERT ISLAND DISC? Ministry Of Sound
FAVOURITE TV? Breaking Bad, The Mentalist
CRICKETING HEROES? Marcus Trescothick, David Warner
NON-CRICKETING HEROES? My family
WHEN YOU RETIRE? I'd like to get into property and coaching
CRICKET RULE YOU'D CHANGE? I'd change 50-over games to 40 overs
TWITTER FEED: @mattmachan

Batting	Mat	Inns	NO	Runs	HS	Ave	SR	100	50	Ct	St
ODIs	11	11	0	392	114	35.63	80.65	1	1	3	0
T20Is	6	6	2	276	67*	69.00	131.42	0	3	2	0
First-class	12	16	1	442	103	29.46	60.38	1	2	6	0
List A	29	29	3	1041	126*	40.03	95.06	2	6	8	0
Twenty20	28	28	4	725	90*	30.20	127.64	0	6	12	0

Bowling	Mat	Balls	Runs	Wkts	BBI	BBM	Ave	Econ	SR	5w	10
ODIs	11	306	270	8	3/31	3/31	33.75	5.29	38.2	0	0
T20Is	6	99	108	3	3/23	3/23	36.00	6.54	33.0	0	0
First-class	12	90	72	1	1/36	1/59	72.00	4.80	90.0	0	0
List A	29	456	397	11	3/31	3/31	36.09	5.22	41.4	0	0
Twenty20	28	177	209	5	3/23	3/23	41.80	7.08	35.4	0	0

CALUM MACLEOD   RHB RMF

DURHAM

FULL NAME: Calum Scott MacLeod
BORN: November 15, 1988, Glasgow, Lanarkshire, Scotland
SQUAD NO: TBC
HEIGHT: 6ft 2in
NICKNAME: Cloudy, Highlander, Scot
EDUCATION: Hillpark School
TEAMS: Scotland, Durham, Scotland Under-19s, Warwickshire, Warwickshire 2nd XI
CAREER: ODI: 2008; T20I: 2009; First-class: 2007; List A: 2008; T20: 2009

BEST BATTING: 67 Scotland vs Kenya, Aberdeen, 2013
BEST BOWLING: 4-66 Scotland vs Canada, Aberdeen, 2009

WHO WOULD PLAY YOU IN A FILM OF YOUR LIFE? Liam Neeson
CAREER HIGHLIGHTS? My first Scotland cap, opening the bowling in the World T20 and my first century for Scotland
SUPERSTITIONS? I keep them to myself!
BEST PLAYER IN COUNTY CRICKET? Graham Onions
TIP FOR THE TOP? Young Scottish pace bowler Gavin Main
IF YOU WEREN'T A CRICKETER? I'd be a sports psychologist
DESERT ISLAND DISC? Dire Straits – Brothers In Arms
FAVOURITE TV? Sherlock
CRICKETING HEROES? Glenn McGrath and Sachin Tendulkar
NON-CRICKETING HEROES? Tiger Woods
WHEN YOU RETIRE? I'll move somewhere warmer with a golf course on my doorstep
SURPRISING FACT? I once presented a Scottish Gaelic TV show called De A Nis
TWITTER FEED: @calummacleod640

Batting	Mat	Inns	NO	Runs	HS	Ave	SR	100	50	Ct	St
ODIs	19	18	2	477	175	29.81	74.64	1	1	6	0
T20Is	15	14	1	289	57	22.23	106.64	0	3	5	0
First-class	11	15	3	277	67	23.08	48.51	0	2	5	0
List A	63	58	5	1261	175	23.79	80.06	2	4	28	0
Twenty20	31	30	3	864	104*	32.00	123.95	1	7	12	0

Bowling	Mat	Balls	Runs	Wkts	BBI	BBM	Ave	Econ	SR	5w	10
ODIs	19	342	289	8	2/26	2/26	36.12	5.07	42.7	0	0
T20Is	15	66	83	2	2/17	2/17	41.50	7.54	33.0	0	0
First-class	11	611	343	15	4/66	6/102	22.86	3.36	40.7	0	0
List A	63	827	745	20	3/37	3/37	37.25	5.40	41.3	0	0
Twenty20	31	84	93	2	2/17	2/17	46.50	6.64	42.0	0	0

WAYNE MADSEN

RHB OB R1 MVP24

FULL NAME: Wayne Lee Madsen
BORN: January 2, 1984, Durban, South Africa
SQUAD NO: 77
HEIGHT: 5ft 11in
NICKNAME: Madders, Mads
EDUCATION: Highbury Preparatory School; Kearsney College; University of South Africa
TEAMS: Derbyshire, Derbyshire 2nd XI, KwaZulu-Natal
CAREER: First-class: 2004; List A: 2004; T20: 2010

DERBYSHIRE

BEST BATTING: 231* Derbyshire vs Northamptonshire, Northampton, 2012
BEST BOWLING: 3-45 KwaZulu-Natal vs Eastern Province, Port Elizabeth, 2008
COUNTY CAP: 2011

FAMILY TIES? My uncles Mike Madsen, Trevor Madsen, Henry Fotheringham and my cousin Greg Fotheringham all played first-class cricket in South Africa. Trevor and Henry also represented South Africa
CAREER HIGHLIGHTS? Captaining Derbyshire to the Division Two Championship title in 2012, winning the Cricket Writers' Club County Championship Player Of The Year in 2013, winning the inaugural Christopher Martin-Jenkins Spirit Of Cricket Elite Award in 2013, scoring 231* and putting on the world's second-highest ninth-wicket partnership of 261 with Tom Poynton and winning the Provincial One-Day Cup with Kwa-Zulu Natal in 2007
MOST MARKED CHARACTERISTIC? Integrity
BEST PLAYER IN COUNTY CRICKET? Graham Onions
TIPS FOR THE TOP? Tom Knight, Greg Cork, Ben Cotton, Ben Stokes
CRICKETING HEROES? Trevor Madsen, Jonty Rhodes, Hansie Cronje, Dale Benkenstein
ACCOMPLISHMENTS? Representing South Africa at the 2006 Hockey World Cup in Germany and the Melbourne Commonwealth Games. My degree in Financial Management
SURPRISING FACT? Gunn & Moore were my hockey kit sponsors when I was 15, before they became my cricket kit sponsors at 17

Batting	Mat	Inns	NO	Runs	HS	Ave	SR	100	50	Ct	St
First-class	97	172	11	5951	231*	36.96	48.43	16	29	79	0
List A	57	52	10	1516	78	36.09	83.11	0	11	41	0
Twenty20	37	36	5	674	61*	21.74	116.00	0	3	8	0

Bowling	Mat	Balls	Runs	Wkts	BBI	BBM	Ave	Econ	SR	5w	10
First-class	97	950	494	10	3/45		49.40	3.12	95.0	0	0
List A	57	186	137	9	3/27	3/27	15.22	4.41	20.6	0	0
Twenty20	37	12	12	0	-	-	-	6.00	-	0	0

STEVE MAGOFFIN

LHB RFM W2 MVP55

FULL NAME: Steven James Magoffin
BORN: December 17, 1979, Corinda, Queensland, Australia
SQUAD NO: 64
HEIGHT: 6ft 4in
NICKNAME: Mal, Mags, Magsy, Emu
EDUCATION: Indooroopilly High School; Curtin University, Perth
TEAMS: Leicestershire 2nd XI, Queensland, Surrey, Surrey 2nd XI, Sussex, Western Australia, Worcestershire
CAREER: First-class: 2004; List A: 2004; T20: 2006

BEST BATTING: 79 Western Australia vs Tasmania, Perth, 2008
BEST BOWLING: 8-20 Sussex vs Somerset, Horsham, 2013

FAMILY TIES? My older brother Chris played grade cricket in Brisbane
WHO WOULD PLAY YOU IN A FILM OF YOUR LIFE? George Clooney!
CAREER HIGHLIGHTS? Hitting the winning runs in the 2011/12 Sheffield Shield final for Queensland Bulls. Touring South Africa for the second Test of Australia's tour in 2009 – I didn't play but it was a great experience
MOST MARKED CHARACTERISTIC? Being particularly lanky!
BEST PLAYER IN COUNTY CRICKET? Chris Rogers
TIP FOR THE TOP? Luke Wells
IF YOU WEREN'T A CRICKETER? Not too sure – it's all I've done! But I'd love to be a chef
DESERT ISLAND DISC? Coldplay Live Tour 2012 or The 12th Man Box Set (very popular in Oz!)
FAVOURITE TV? Seinfeld
CRICKETING HEROES? Curtly Ambrose, Glenn McGrath, Mike Hussey
NON-CRICKETING HEROES? Tiger Woods, Nathan Buckley (AFL player), Scott Pendlebury (AFL player)
FANTASY SLIP CORDON? Keeper: Kramer (from Seinfeld), 1st: Myself, 2nd: John Bishop, 3rd: Michael McIntyre, Gully: James Corden
TWITTER FEED: @magsy64

Batting	Mat	Inns	NO	Runs	HS	Ave	SR	100	50	Ct	St
First-class	104	144	35	2012	79	18.45	48.16	0	4	29	0
List A	51	29	19	225	24*	22.50	77.05	0	0	12	0
Twenty20	8	2	1	12	11*	12.00	171.42	0	0	1	0

Bowling	Mat	Balls	Runs	Wkts	BBI	BBM	Ave	Econ	SR	5w	10
First-class	104	20448	9098	369	8/20		24.65	2.66	55.4	13	2
List A	51	2556	2010	65	4/58	4/58	30.92	4.71	39.3	0	0
Twenty20	8	156	228	5	2/15	2/15	45.60	8.76	31.2	0	0

AZHAR MAHMOOD   RHB RMF

FULL NAME: Azhar Mahmood Sagar
BORN: Feburary 28, 1975, Rawalpindi, Pakistan
SQUAD NO: TBC
HEIGHT: 6ft
NICKNAME: Aju
EDUCATION: FG No.1 High School, Islamabad
TEAMS: Pakistan, Auckland, Barbados Tridents, Barisal Burners, Dhaka Gladiators, Islamabad, Kent, Kings XI Punjab, Lahore Badshahs, Rawalpindi, Surrey, United Bank
CAREER: Test: 1997; ODI: 1996; First-class: 1994; List A: 1994; T20: 2003

BEST BATTING: 204* Surrey vs Middlesex, The Oval, 2005
BEST BOWLING: 8-61 Surrey vs Lancashire, The Oval, 2002
COUNTY CAPS: 2004 (Surrey); 2008 (Kent)

CAREER HIGHLIGHTS? My first Test match, against South Africa in 1997. I scored 128* in the first innings, 50* in the second innings and also took two wickets to be named as Man of the Match
CRICKET MOMENTS TO FORGET? The 1999 World Cup final defeat to Australia
OTHER SPORTS FOLLOWED? Football (Manchester United)
OTHER SPORTS PLAYED? Snooker, football, kite-flying
RELAXATIONS? Listening to music, training and spending time with my family
TWITTER FEED: @AzharMahmood11

Batting	Mat	Inns	NO	Runs	HS	Ave	SR	100	50	Ct	St
Tests	21	34	4	900	136	30.00	50.79	3	1	14	0
ODIs	143	110	26	1521	67	18.10	76.50	0	3	37	0
First-class	176	274	32	7703	204*	31.83		9	42	142	0
List A	312	249	49	4326	101*	21.63		2	17	93	0
Twenty20	197	182	38	3714	106*	25.79	135.54	2	18	37	0

Bowling	Mat	Balls	Runs	Wkts	BBI	BBM	Ave	Econ	SR	5w	10
Tests	21	3015	1402	39	4/50	5/95	35.94	2.79	77.3	0	0
ODIs	143	6242	4813	123	6/18	6/18	39.13	4.62	50.7	3	0
First-class	176	29798	15337	611	8/61		25.10	3.08	48.7	27	3
List A	312	13634	10644	339	6/18	6/18	31.39	4.68	40.2	5	0
Twenty20	197	4115	5203	224	5/24	5/24	23.22	7.58	18.3	1	0

SAJ MAHMOOD   RHB RFM

ESSEX

FULL NAME: Sajid Iqbal Mahmood
BORN: December 21, 1981, Bolton, Lancashire
SQUAD NO: 19
HEIGHT: 6ft 4in
NICKNAME: Saj, King
EDUCATION: Smithills School
TEAMS: England, England A, England Lions, Essex, Lancashire, Lancashire Cricket Board, Marylebone Cricket Club, Western Australia
CAREER: Test: 2006; ODI: 2004; T20I: 2006; First-class: 2002; List A: 2002; T20: 2003

BEST BATTING: 94 Lancashire vs Sussex, Manchester, 2004
BEST BOWLING: 6-30 Lancashire vs Durham, Chester-le-Street, 2009
COUNTY CAP: 2007 (Lancashire)

CAREER HIGHLIGHTS? Playing for England and winning the County Championship
CRICKETING HEROES? Wasim Akram, Imran Khan
NON-CRICKETING HEROES? Muhammad Ali
IF YOU WEREN'T A CRICKETER? I'd have my own astrology business
WHEN RAIN STOPS PLAY? I drink cups of tea and play one hand-one bounce
FAVOURITE TV? Wildlife documentaries
DREAM HOLIDAY? Mauritius
ACCOMPLISHMENTS? Doing Level 11 on the bleep test
SURPRISING FACTS? I'm a qualified sailor, I play the banjo and I'm a very good listener

Batting	Mat	Inns	NO	Runs	HS	Ave	SR	100	50	Ct	St
Tests	8	11	1	81	34	8.10	50.31	0	0	0	0
ODIs	26	15	4	85	22*	7.72	84.15	0	0	1	0
T20Is	4	2	2	1	1*	-	50.00	0	0	1	0
First-class	119	154	19	2148	94	15.91	69.24	0	10	29	0
List A	153	82	23	541	29	9.16		0	0	23	0
Twenty20	69	31	8	183	34	7.95	146.40	0	0	18	0

Bowling	Mat	Balls	Runs	Wkts	BBI	BBM	Ave	Econ	SR	5w	10
Tests	8	1130	762	20	4/22	6/130	38.10	4.04	56.5	0	0
ODIs	26	1197	1169	30	4/50	4/50	38.96	5.85	39.9	0	0
T20Is	4	84	155	3	1/31	1/31	51.66	11.07	28.0	0	0
First-class	119	17103	10725	326	6/30		32.89	3.76	52.4	9	2
List A	153	6683	5985	210	5/16	5/16	28.50	5.37	31.8	1	0
Twenty20	69	1450	1920	77	4/21	4/21	24.93	7.94	18.8	0	0

DAWID MALAN

LHB LB R1 MVP57

FULL NAME: Dawid Johannes Malan
BORN: September 3, 1987, Roehampton, London
SQUAD NO: 29
HEIGHT: 6ft 1in
NICKNAME: AC
EDUCATION: Paarl Boys' High School; UNISA
TEAMS: Boland, Marylebone Cricket Club, Middlesex, Middlesex 2nd XI, Prime Doleshwar Sporting Club
CAREER: First-class: 2006; List A: 2006; T20: 2006

BEST BATTING: 156* Middlesex vs Cambridge MCCU, Cambridge, 2013
BEST BOWLING: 5-61 Middlesex vs Lancashire, Liverpool, 2012
COUNTY CAP: 2010

FAMILY TIES? My father [Dawid] played for Western Province B and Northern Transvaal B and my brother [Charl] played for MCC Young Cricketers and Loughborough University
WHO WOULD PLAY YOU IN A FILM OF YOUR LIFE? Brad Pitt
CAREER HIGHLIGHTS? Scoring a century in the T20 Cup quarter-final in 2008 and going on to win the final. Winning Division Two of the County Championship in 2011
SUPERSTITIONS? I have way too many to mention
MOST MARKED CHARACTERISTIC? Determination
BEST PLAYER IN COUNTY CRICKET? Chris Rogers
TIP FOR THE TOP? Sam Robson
IF YOU WEREN'T A CRICKETER? I'd be studying or would have qualified as a sports psychologist
DESERT ISLAND DISC? Train
CRICKETING HEROES? Gary Kirsten, Matthew Hayden
NON-CRICKETING HEROES? Tiger Woods
WHEN YOU RETIRE? I'd like to go into sports psychology
TWITTER FEED: @dmalan29

Batting	Mat	Inns	NO	Runs	HS	Ave	SR	100	50	Ct	St
First-class	95	161	12	5185	156*	34.79	52.31	10	27	117	0
List A	85	84	11	2676	134	36.65	84.57	4	14	27	0
Twenty20	69	66	17	1568	103	32.00	117.89	1	5	18	0

Bowling	Mat	Balls	Runs	Wkts	BBI	BBM	Ave	Econ	SR	5w	10
First-class	95	2596	1697	38	5/61	5/61	44.65	3.92	68.3	1	0
List A	85	551	572	15	2/4	2/4	38.13	6.22	36.7	0	0
Twenty20	69	270	321	14	2/10	2/10	22.92	7.13	19.2	0	0

SHOAIB MALIK

RHB OB

WARWICKSHIRE

FULL NAME: Shoaib Malik
BORN: February 1, 1982, Sialkot, Pakistan
SQUAD NO: TBC
HEIGHT: 6ft
TEAMS: Pakistan, Asia XI, Barbados Tridents, Delhi Daredevils, Gloucestershire, Gujranwala Cricket Association, Pakistan International Airlines, Pakistan Reserves, Sialkot Cricket Association, Sialkot Stallions, Warwickshire
CAREER: Test: 2001; ODI: 1999; T20I: 2006; First-class: 1997; List A: 1997; T20: 2005

BEST BATTING: 200 Pakistan International Airlines vs Faisalabad, Faisalabad, 2010
BEST BOWLING: 7-81 Pakistan International Airlines vs Water and Power Development Authority, Faisalabad, 2001

NOTES: Shoaib Malik has signed a six-match contract for the Birmingham Bears, Warwickshire's new one-day guise, for this summer's NatWest T20 Blast. His final game will be against the Nottinghamshire Outlaws on July 8. The allrounder was Pakistan captain from 2007-2009 and he made his Test-best score of 148* against Sri Lanka at Colombo in 2006. His best ODI bowling figures are 4-19, recorded in an ODI against Hong Kong. A capable off-spinner and combative batsman, he has a glittering record in Pakistani first-class cricket and appeared for Gloucestershire in 2003 and 2004, playing eight first-class and 12 List A matches. He was top scorer in the inaugural Caribbean Premier League last year, playing for Barbados Tridents, and he has also played for Hobart Hurricanes in the Big Bash League

Batting	Mat	Inns	NO	Runs	HS	Ave	SR	100	50	Ct	St
Tests	32	54	6	1606	148*	33.45	44.40	2	8	16	0
ODIs	216	193	25	5490	143	32.67	78.28	7	31	75	0
T20Is	55	51	12	907	57*	23.25	106.83	0	3	25	0
First-class	113	175	20	5626	200	36.29		15	25	58	0
List A	307	265	42	8348	143	37.43		14	49	120	0
Twenty20	156	145	43	3826	88*	37.50	120.69	0	25	70	0

Bowling	Mat	Balls	Runs	Wkts	BBI	BBM	Ave	Econ	SR	5w	10
Tests	32	2245	1291	21	4/42	4/94	61.47	3.45	106.9	0	0
ODIs	216	6768	5128	141	4/19	4/19	36.36	4.54	48.0	0	0
T20Is	55	308	355	16	2/7	2/7	22.18	6.91	19.2	0	0
First-class	113	13461	6603	226	7/81		29.21	2.94	59.5	8	1
List A	307	11516	8587	276	5/35	5/35	31.11	4.47	41.7	1	0
Twenty20	156	1684	1930	84	5/13	5/13	22.97	6.87	20.0	2	0

JOHNY MARSDEN RHB RFM

FULL NAME: Jonathan Marsden
BORN: April 7, 1993, Pembury, Kent
SQUAD NO: 29
HEIGHT: 6ft 3in
NICKNAME: Marso
EDUCATION: The King's School, Macclesfield; Oxford University
TEAMS: Derbyshire, Derbyshire 2nd XI, Derbyshire Under-15s, Derbyshire Under-17s, Oxford University
CAREER: First-class: 2013

BEST BOWLING: 3-32 Oxford University vs Cambridge University, Cambridge, 2013

FAMILY TIES? My dad played a lot at university and still plays club cricket. I spent many hours as a youngster down at our local club watching my dad play on a Saturday and my interest grew from those early days
WHO WOULD PLAY YOU IN A FILM OF YOUR LIFE? Paul Bettany
CAREER HIGHLIGHTS? My first five-fer for Derbyshire 2nd XI
SUPERSTITIONS? I don't believe in superstitions
MOST MARKED CHARACTERISTIC? Clear thinking
BEST PLAYER IN COUNTY CRICKET? Moeen Ali
TIP FOR THE TOP? Harvey Hosein at Derbyshire
IF YOU WEREN'T A CRICKETER? I'm still at university but I would probably end up working in the City somewhere if I didn't work in cricket
DESERT ISLAND DISC? Toto – Africa
FAVOURITE TV? Top Gear
CRICKETING HEROES? Glenn McGrath, Ian Botham, Shane Warne
NON-CRICKETING HEROES? Jonny Wilkinson and Nelson Mandela
ACCOMPLISHMENTS? Getting accepted to Oxford University
SURPRISING FACT? I once got a 'black out' on a charity version of the popular TV show Take Me Out
CRICKET RULE YOU'D CHANGE? The over restrictions for U17 players – I believe they should be allowed to bowl longer spells
TWITTER FEED: @JohnyMarsden

Batting	Mat	Inns	NO	Runs	HS	Ave	SR	100	50	Ct	St
First-class	1	-	-	-	-	-	-	-	-	0	0

Bowling	Mat	Balls	Runs	Wkts	BBI	BBM	Ave	Econ	SR	5w	10
First-class	1	152	64	3	3/32	3/64	21.33	2.52	50.6	0	0

HAMISH MARSHALL RHB RM R2

FULL NAME: Hamish John Hamilton Marshall
BORN: February 15, 1979, Warkworth, Auckland, New Zealand
SQUAD NO: 9
HEIGHT: 5ft 8in
NICKNAME: Marshy
EDUCATION: King's College, Auckland; Mahurangi College
TEAMS: New Zealand, Buckinghamshire, Gloucestershire, Northern Districts, Royal Bengal Tigers
CAREER: Test: 2000; ODI: 2003; T20I: 2005; First-class: 1999; List A: 1998; T20: 2005

BEST BATTING: 170 Northern Districts vs Canterbury, Rangiora, 2010
BEST BOWLING: 4-24 Gloucestershire vs Leicestershire, Leicester, 2009

FAMILY TIES? My twin brother James also played Test cricket for New Zealand
CAREER HIGHLIGHTS? My Test debut for New Zealand at The Wanderers and my first Test hundred vs Australia in Christchurch
SUPERSTITIONS? I always stand in the same spot at the non-striker's end
BEST PLAYER IN COUNTY CRICKET? Moeen Ali
TIPS FOR THE TOP? Chris Dent and Craig Miles
IF YOU WEREN'T A CRICKETER? I'd be working in property
DESERT ISLAND DISC? U2 – The Best Of
FAVOURITE TV? Friends
CRICKETING HEROES? Mark Waugh and Michael Bevan
FANTASY SLIP CORDON? Keeper: Drew Marshall, 1st: Keith Lemon, 2nd: Me, 3rd: Mick Jagger, Gully: Rory McIlroy

Batting	Mat	Inns	NO	Runs	HS	Ave	SR	100	50	Ct	St
Tests	13	19	2	652	160	38.35	47.31	2	2	1	0
ODIs	66	62	9	1454	101*	27.43	73.06	1	12	18	0
T20Is	3	3	0	12	8	4.00	85.71	0	0	1	0
First-class	208	346	23	11831	170	36.62			24	58	109	0
List A	278	264	24	6749	122	28.12			6	45	104	0
Twenty20	91	87	6	2044	102	25.23	135.18	2	7	44	0

Bowling	Mat	Balls	Runs	Wkts	BBI	BBM	Ave	Econ	SR	5w	10
Tests	13	6	4	0	-	-	-	4.00	-	0	0
ODIs	66	-	-	-	-	-	-	-	-	-	-
T20Is	3	-	-	-	-	-	-	-	-	-	-
First-class	208	3499	1768	37	4/24		47.78	3.03	94.5	0	0
List A	278	284	295	4	2/21	2/21	73.75	6.23	71.0	0	0
Twenty20	91	6	14	0	-	-	-	14.00	-	0	0

DAVID MASTERS

RHB RMF W4 MVP47

FULL NAME: David Daniel Masters
BORN: April 22, 1978, Chatham, Kent
SQUAD NO: 9
HEIGHT: 6ft 4in
NICKNAME: Hod, Hoddy
EDUCATION: Fort Luton High
TEAMS: Essex, Kent, Leicestershire
CAREER: First-class: 2000; List A: 2000; T20: 2003

ESSEX

BEST BATTING: 119 Leicestershire vs Sussex, Hove, 2003
BEST BOWLING: 8-10 Essex vs Leicestershire, Southend, 2011
COUNTY CAPS: 2007 (Leicestershire); 2008 (Essex); **BENEFIT YEAR:** 2013 (Essex)

FAMILY TIES? My dad Kevin played for Kent and Surrey and my brother Daniel played for Leicestershire
WHO WOULD PLAY YOU IN A FILM OF YOUR LIFE? David Beckham
CAREER HIGHLIGHTS? Winning a Lord's final
SUPERSTITIONS? Too many to mention
BEST PLAYER IN COUNTY CRICKET? There are plenty. County cricket is in a good place
TIP FOR THE TOP? Reece Topley is going to be one to look out for
DESERT ISLAND DISC? Whitney Houston's Greatest Hits
FAVOURITE TV? Match Of The Day
CRICKETING HEROES? Ian Botham
NON-CRICKETING HEROES? David Beckham and Sir Alex Ferguson
ACCOMPLISHMENTS? Getting married and having two wonderful children, Alfie and Harrison
FANTASY SLIP CORDON? Keeper: Paul Nixon, 1st: Sir Alex Ferguson, 2nd: Matt Walker, 3rd: David Beckham
TWITTER FEED: @DavehodMasters

Batting	Mat	Inns	NO	Runs	HS	Ave	SR	100	50	Ct	St
First-class	176	213	32	2533	119	13.99		1	6	55	0
List A	153	74	31	532	39	12.37		0	0	19	0
Twenty20	99	33	15	100	14	5.55	68.96	0	0	21	0

Bowling	Mat	Balls	Runs	Wkts	BBI	BBM	Ave	Econ	SR	5w	10
First-class	176	32694	14729	573	8/10		25.70	2.70	57.0	28	0
List A	153	6356	4791	148	5/17	5/17	32.37	4.52	42.9	2	0
Twenty20	99	1907	2350	75	3/7	3/7	31.33	7.39	25.4	0	0

GLENN MAXWELL

RHB OB

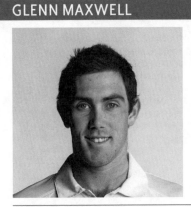

FULL NAME: Glenn James Maxwell
BORN: October 14, 1988, Kew, Melbourne, Victoria, Australia
SQUAD NO: TBC
HEIGHT: 5ft 11in
NICKNAME: The Big Show
TEAMS: Australia, Delhi Daredevils, Fitzroy-Doncaster, Hampshire, Hampshire 2nd XI, Melbourne Renegades, Mumbai Indians, Victoria, Victoria Second XI, Victoria Under-19s
CAREER: Test: 2013; ODI: 2012; T20I: 2012; First-class: 2011; List A: 2010; T20: 2010

BEST BATTING: 155* Australia A vs South Africa A, Pretoria, 2013
BEST BOWLING: 4-42 Victoria vs South Australia, Melbourne, 2012

TWITTER FEED: @Gmaxi_32
NOTES: Maxwell will play in this season's NatWest T20 Blast for Hampshire and could feature in other formats, depending on the availability of South African seamer Kyle Abbott. It will be the Australian allrounder's second spell at Hampshire, having previously represented the club in 2012. He fetched the highest bid at the 2013 IPL auction, with Mumbai Indians paying £637,000 for his services, and went on to play for Surrey in the 2013 FL t20. Made his Test debut during the 2013 series in India and is a regular for his country in limited-overs cricket. Holds the record for the fastest half-century in Australian domestic cricket, reaching the landmark in 19 balls against Tasmania in 2011

Batting	Mat	Inns	NO	Runs	HS	Ave	SR	100	50	Ct	St
Tests	2	4	0	39	13	9.75	52.70	0	0	2	0
ODIs	24	23	5	621	92	34.50	124.20	0	6	9	0
T20Is	15	11	2	138	27	15.33	140.81	0	0	5	0
First-class	27	46	3	1765	155*	41.04	74.72	4	11	22	0
List A	47	44	10	1235	145*	36.32	129.18	1	10	24	0
Twenty20	65	56	9	1030	82	21.91	149.92	0	4	29	0

Bowling	Mat	Balls	Runs	Wkts	BBI	BBM	Ave	Econ	SR	5w	10
Tests	2	246	193	7	4/127	4/127	27.57	4.70	35.1	0	0
ODIs	24	705	637	11	4/63	4/63	57.90	5.42	64.0	0	0
T20Is	15	180	221	8	2/15	2/15	27.62	7.36	22.5	0	0
First-class	27	2710	1562	40	4/42	5/66	39.05	3.45	67.7	0	0
List A	47	1349	1157	25	4/63	4/63	46.28	5.14	53.9	0	0
Twenty20	65	573	699	22	3/26	3/26	31.77	7.31	26.0	0	0

FULL NAME: Graeme John McCarter
BORN: October 10, 1992, Londonderry, Northern Ireland
SQUAD NO: 33
HEIGHT: 6ft 3in
NICKNAME: Macca, Melon
EDUCATION: Foyle College
TEAMS: Ireland, Gloucestershire, Gloucestershire 2nd XI, Ireland Under-13s, Ireland Under-15s, Ireland Under-19s
CAREER: First-class: 2011; List A: 2012

GLOUCESTERSHIRE

BEST BATTING: 29* Gloucestershire vs Yorkshire, Bristol, 2012
BEST BOWLING: 4-95 Gloucestershire vs Lancashire, Liverpool, 2013
COUNTY CAP: 2012

FAMILY TIES? My whole family have played cricket for the mighty Foxies back home
CAREER HIGHLIGHTS? Making my Gloucestershire debut at Lord's on TV and my international debut with Ireland
MOST MARKED CHARACTERISTIC? I have the best rig around
BEST PLAYER IN COUNTY CRICKET? Marcus Trescothick
TIP FOR THE TOP? Chris Dent
IF YOU WEREN'T A CRICKETER? I'd be struggling…
DESERT ISLAND DISC? Haim – The Wire
FAVOURITE TV? Family Guy
CRICKETING HEROES? Brett Lee and my first cricket captain, Jap
ACCOMPLISHMENTS? Doing a bungee jump
WHEN YOU RETIRE? I'd like to be a sports journalist
CRICKET RULE YOU'D CHANGE? The lbw rule – if the ball is going to hit the stumps the batter should be out, no matter where it hits or pitches
SURPRISING FACT? I've represented my country at badminton
FANTASY SLIP CORDON? Keeper: Jap, 1st: James Corden, 2nd: Hugh Hefner, 3rd: Liam Neeson, Gully: Brian Lara
TWITTER FEED: @GraemeMcCarter

Batting	Mat	Inns	NO	Runs	HS	Ave	SR	100	50	Ct	St
First-class	7	9	2	97	29*	13.85	32.65	0	0	1	0
List A	7	1	1	18	18*	-	100.00	0	0	1	0

Bowling	Mat	Balls	Runs	Wkts	BBI	BBM	Ave	Econ	SR	5w	10
First-class	7	996	618	15	4/95	6/170	41.20	3.72	66.4	0	0
List A	7	219	183	10	3/15	3/15	18.30	5.01	21.9	0	0

WARWICKSHIRE

FULL NAME: Peter John McKay
BORN: October 12, 1994, Staffordshire
SQUAD NO: 18
HEIGHT: 6ft 1in
NICKNAME: The Buff
EDUCATION: Polesworth International
Language College, Tamworth
TEAMS: Warwickshire, Warwickshire 2nd XI,
Warwickshire Under-19s
CAREER: First-class: 2013; List A: 2013; T20:
2013

BEST BATTING: 33 Warwickshire vs Nottinghamshire, Nottingham, 2013

WHO WOULD PLAY YOU IN A FILM OF YOUR LIFE? Adam Sandler
CAREER HIGHLIGHTS? Getting my first contract and representing the Bears
SUPERSTITIONS? Not changing my inners too regularly
MOST MARKED CHARACTERISTIC? Theatrical reactions
BEST PLAYER IN COUNTY CRICKET? Chris Woakes
TIP FOR THE TOP? Paul Best
IF YOU WEREN'T A CRICKETER? I'd like to work in sports media
DESERT ISLAND DISC? You Me At Six – Take Off Your Colours
FAVOURITE TV? Orange Is The New Black
CRICKETING HEROES? Adam Gilchrist
NON-CRICKETING HEROES? My auntie Shaz
ACCOMPLISHMENTS? I was head boy at school
WHEN YOU RETIRE? I'd like to live by the sea or be a groundsman

Batting	Mat	Inns	NO	Runs	HS	Ave	SR	100	50	Ct	St
First-class	2	4	1	45	33	15.00	23.80	0	0	0	0
List A	5	4	2	26	17*	13.00	104.00	0	0	4	1
Twenty20	10	4	3	3	2*	3.00	42.85	0	0	4	2

Bowling	Mat	Balls	Runs	Wkts	BBI	BBM	Ave	Econ	SR	5w	10
First-class	2	-	-	-	-	-	-	-	-	-	-
List A	5	-	-	-	-	-	-	-	-	-	-
Twenty20	10	-	-	-	-	-	-	-	-	-	-

LEWIS MCMANUS   RHB WK

FULL NAME: Lewis David McManus
BORN: October 9, 1994, Poole, Dorset
SQUAD NO: 18
HEIGHT: 5ft 10in
NICKNAME: Lewy
EDUCATION: Clayesmore School
TEAMS: Dorset, Dorset Under-13s, Dorset Under-15s, Dorset Under-17s, England Under-19s, Hampshire 2nd XI, Hampshire Cricket Academy
CAREER: Yet to make first-team debut

HAMPSHIRE

WHO WOULD PLAY YOU IN A FILM OF YOUR LIFE? Will Ferrell
CAREER HIGHLIGHTS? Scoring 105 for Hampshire 2nd XI vs Surrey 2nd XI, playing for England U19 and playing at Lord's aged 14 for MCC
SUPERSTITIONS? I put my kit on in the same order
BEST PLAYER IN COUNTY CRICKET? Michael Carberry
TIPS FOR THE TOP? James Vince, Matthew Fisher
FAVOURITE TV? Two And A Half Men, A League Of Their Own
CRICKETING HEROES? Adam Gilchrist, Andrew Flintoff
NON-CRICKETING HEROES? Floyd Mayweather, Usain Bolt, Rick Ross
WHEN YOU RETIRE? I want to live in the Caribbean
CRICKET RULE YOU'D CHANGE? You should get 12 runs for hitting the ball out of the ground
FANTASY SLIP CORDON? Keeper: Del Trotter, 1st: Karl Pilkington, 2nd: Usain Bolt, 3rd: Ronnie Corbett, Gully: Trigger
TWITTER FEED: @lewis_mcmanus

STUART MEAKER

RHB RF W1

SURREY

FULL NAME: Stuart Christopher Meaker
BORN: January 21, 1989, Pietermaritzburg, Natal, South Africa
SQUAD NO: 18
HEIGHT: 6ft
NICKNAME: Meaks, 10 Bears, 12 Bears and sometimes even 14 Bears
EDUCATION: Cranleigh School
TEAMS: England, England Lions, England Under-19s, Surrey, Surrey 2nd XI
CAREER: ODI: 2011; T20I: 2012; First-class: 2008; List A: 2008; T20: 2010

BEST BATTING: 94 Surrey vs Bangladeshis, The Oval, 2010
BEST BOWLING: 8-52 Surrey vs Somerset, The Oval, 2012
COUNTY CAP: 2012

CAREER HIGHLIGHTS? Making my debut for the England ODI side
MOST MARKED CHARACTERISTIC? Resilience
BEST PLAYER IN COUNTY CRICKET? Gareth Batty
TIP FOR THE TOP? Dom Sibley
DESERT ISLAND DISC? Kings Of Leon – Only By The Night
FAVOURITE TV? Family Guy
CRICKETING HEROES? Allan Donald, Dale Steyn
NON-CRICKETING HEROES? My grandfather
ACCOMPLISHMENTS? I was U10 regional high jump winner
WHEN YOU RETIRE? I'd like to live near a beach
SURPRISING FACT? I love a sci-fi film
TWITTER FEED: @SMeaker18

Batting	Mat	Inns	NO	Runs	HS	Ave	SR	100	50	Ct	St
ODIs	2	2	0	2	1	1.00	12.50	0	0	0	0
T20Is	2	-	-	-	-	-	-	-	-	1	0
First-class	51	66	11	857	94	15.58	37.57	0	4	6	0
List A	43	22	9	73	21*	5.61	52.14	0	0	9	0
Twenty20	22	5	3	27	17	13.50	150.00	0	0	9	0

Bowling	Mat	Balls	Runs	Wkts	BBI	BBM	Ave	Econ	SR	5w	10
ODIs	2	114	110	2	1/45	1/45	55.00	5.78	57.0	0	0
T20Is	2	47	70	2	1/28	1/28	35.00	8.93	23.5	0	0
First-class	51	7748	4865	169	8/52	11/167	28.78	3.76	45.8	9	1
List A	43	1517	1494	40	4/47	4/47	37.35	5.90	37.9	0	0
Twenty20	22	351	539	16	2/16	2/16	33.68	9.21	21.9	0	0

CRAIG MESCHEDE — RHB RMF MVP42

FULL NAME: Craig Anthony Joseph Meschede
BORN: November 21, 1991, Johannesburg, South Africa
SQUAD NO: 26
EDUCATION: King's College, Taunton
TEAMS: Somerset, Somerset 2nd XI
CAREER: First-class: 2011; List A: 2011; T20: 2011

SOMERSET

BEST BATTING: 62 Somerset vs Durham, Chester-le-Street, 2012
BEST BOWLING: 4-43 Somerset vs Surrey, Taunton, 2013

NOTES: South African-born with a German father, the Somerset allrounder was awarded a senior contract in June 2010. Impressed in the 2011 Caribbean T20, hitting 26 from just 11 balls against Combined Campuses and Colleges. Sachin Tendulkar was his maiden first-class wicket. Scored 53 from just 28 deliveries in a FL t20 victory against Glamorgan in 2011. Claimed nine wickets at 22 in the 2012 CB40, including 4-27 against Scotland, and finished as the joint second-highest wicket-taker in last year's YB40, with 22 wickets at 21.72. Took a career-best match haul of 7-80 in the penultimate County Championship game of 2013, against Surrey

Batting	Mat	Inns	NO	Runs	HS	Ave	SR	100	50	Ct	St
First-class	22	30	3	513	62	19.00	51.14	0	3	9	0
List A	28	16	3	256	40*	19.69	94.46	0	0	7	0
Twenty20	30	24	7	298	53	17.52	126.80	0	1	6	0

Bowling	Mat	Balls	Runs	Wkts	BBI	BBM	Ave	Econ	SR	5w	10
First-class	22	2144	1297	40	4/43	7/80	32.42	3.62	53.6	0	0
List A	28	890	836	36	4/5	4/5	23.22	5.63	24.7	0	0
Twenty20	30	253	372	16	3/9	3/9	23.25	8.82	15.8	0	0

ESSEX

FULL NAME: Jaik Charles Mickleburgh
BORN: March 30, 1990, Norwich, Norfolk
SQUAD NO: 32
HEIGHT: 5ft 10in
NICKNAME: Juddy
EDUCATION: Earsham Primary; Bungay Middle; Bungay High School
TEAMS: England Under-19s, Essex, Essex 2nd XI, Mid West Rhinos, Norfolk
CAREER: First-class: 2008; List A: 2010; T20: 2010

BEST BATTING: 243 Essex vs Leicestershire, Chelmsford, 2013
COUNTY CAP: 2013

CAREER HIGHLIGHTS? My record partnership with James Foster [339 vs Durham, 2010]
CRICKETING HEROES? Darren Gough
NON-CRICKETING HEROES? Rafa Nadal, David Beckham
TIPS FOR THE TOP? Adam Wheater, Reece Topley, Tymal Mills
BEST PLAYER IN COUNTY CRICKET? Marcus Trescothick
IF YOU WEREN'T A CRICKETER? I'd be a utility warehouse distributor
WHEN RAIN STOPS PLAY? Watching the clouds to see where the next batch is coming from
FAVOURITE TV? The Only Way Is Essex
FAVOURITE FILM? Saving Private Ryan
FAVOURITE BOOK? The Slight Edge
DREAM HOLIDAY? Mauritius
FANTASY SLIP CORDON? Keeper: James Foster, 1st: Wentworth Miller, 2nd: David Beckham, 3rd: Tori Wilson, Gully: Jamie T
TWITTER FEED: @JaikMickleburgh

Batting	Mat	Inns	NO	Runs	HS	Ave	SR	100	50	Ct	St
First-class	70	124	2	3523	243	28.87	44.71	6	17	47	0
List A	19	15	3	393	73	32.75	77.82	0	2	8	0
Twenty20	17	12	5	159	47*	22.71	100.63	0	0	8	0
Bowling	Mat	Balls	Runs	Wkts	BBI	BBM	Ave	Econ	SR	5w	10
First-class	70	78	50	0	-	-	-	3.84	-	0	0
List A	19	-	-	-	-	-	-	-	-	-	-
Twenty20	17	-	-	-	-	-	-	-	-	-	-

JAMES MIDDLEBROOK RHB OB W1 MVP100

FULL NAME: James Daniel Middlebrook
BORN: May 13, 1977, Leeds, Yorkshire
SQUAD NO: 7
HEIGHT: 6ft 1in
NICKNAME: Minders, Midhouse, Midi, Dog, Doggy, Brook
EDUCATION: Earsham Primary; Bungay Middle; Bungay High School
TEAMS: Essex, Marylebone Cricket Club, Northamptonshire, Yorkshire
CAREER: First-class: 1998; List A: 1998; T20: 2004

BEST BATTING: 127 Essex vs Middlesex, Lord's, 2007
BEST BOWLING: 6-78 Northamptonshire vs Kent, Northampton, 2013
COUNTY CAPS: 2003 (Essex); 2011 (Northamptonshire)

FAMILY TIES? My father played local Leeds and Bradford league cricket for Pudsey Congs CC and also managed the Yorkshire indoor cricket school for 11 years
WHO WOULD PLAY YOU IN A FILM OF YOUR LIFE? Daniel Craig
CAREER HIGHLIGHTS? Playing at Lord's, being part of a winning team at Essex in one-day cricket and getting to a final and winning the Pro40
SUPERSTITIONS? I always mark my run-up the same way and turn to my mark the same way. I put my pads and kit on the same way every time
BEST PLAYER IN COUNTY CRICKET? James Foster
TIPS FOR THE TOP? Joe Root, Jonathan Bairstow, Alex Wakely
IF YOU WEREN'T A CRICKETER? I'd be a fireman or policeman
DESERT ISLAND DISC? Michael Jackson – Man In The Mirror
BIGGEST DRESSING DOWN YOU'VE RECEIVED? Probably from Ronnie Irani
CRICKETING HEROES? John Emburey, Ian Botham, Shane Warne, Mark Waugh
FANTASY SLIP CORDON? Keeper: Ayrton Senna, 1st: Jeremy Clarkson, 2nd: James Bond, 3rd: Me, Gully: Eddie Murphy
TWITTER FEED: @midders07

Batting	Mat	Inns	NO	Runs	HS	Ave	SR	100	50	Ct	St
First-class	204	290	43	6999	127	28.33		10	30	97	0
List A	187	127	43	1686	57*	20.07		0	1	49	0
Twenty20	94	61	20	560	43	13.65	116.91	0	0	24	0

Bowling	Mat	Balls	Runs	Wkts	BBI	BBM	Ave	Econ	SR	5w	10
First-class	204	31625	16375	429	6/78		38.17	3.10	73.7	12	1
List A	187	6571	5159	142	4/27	4/27	36.33	4.71	46.2	0	0
Twenty20	94	1354	1715	46	3/13	3/13	37.28	7.59	29.4	0	0

GLOUCESTERSHIRE

FULL NAME: Craig Neil Miles
BORN: July 20, 1994, Swindon, Wiltshire
SQUAD NO: 34
HEIGHT: 6ft 4in
NICKNAME: Milo, Cheese String, Jedward
EDUCATION: Bradon Forest School, Swindon; Filton College, Bristol
TEAMS: Gloucestershire, Gloucestershire 2nd XI
CAREER: First-class: 2011; List A: 2011; T20: 2013

BEST BATTING: 50* Gloucestershire vs Essex, Bristol, 2013
BEST BOWLING: 6-88 Gloucestershire vs Lancashire, Liverpool, 2013
COUNTY CAP: 2011

FAMILY TIES? My brother [Adam] played for Cardiff MCCU
WHO WOULD PLAY YOU IN A FILM OF YOUR LIFE? Brad Pitt
CAREER HIGHLIGHTS? Being the fourth-youngest player to play for Gloucestershire and dismissing Ravi Bopara with my first ball in List A cricket
SUPERSTITIONS? I put my left pad on before my right if you call that a superstition!
MOST MARKED CHARACTERISTIC? My terrible lid
BEST PLAYER IN COUNTY CRICKET? Moeen Ali
TIPS FOR THE TOP? Matt Taylor, Gareth Roderick, Tom Helm
IF YOU WEREN'T A CRICKETER? I'd probably be at university
DESERT ISLAND DISC? Drake – Take Care
FAVOURITE TV? The Simpsons
CRICKETING HEROES? Andrew Flintoff, Will Gidman
NON-CRICKETING HEROES? Adam Miles
ACCOMPLISHMENTS? Not much apart from GCSEs!
WHEN YOU RETIRE? I'd like to have my own clothing company

Batting	Mat	Inns	NO	Runs	HS	Ave	SR	100	50	Ct	St
First-class	14	15	1	185	50*	13.21	46.01	0	1	1	0
List A	6	1	1	0	0*	-	0.00	0	0	1	0
Twenty20	2	1	0	2	2	2.00	50.00	0	0	1	0

Bowling	Mat	Balls	Runs	Wkts	BBI	BBM	Ave	Econ	SR	5w	10
First-class	14	2262	1395	45	6/88	7/135	31.00	3.70	50.2	3	0
List A	6	230	249	9	2/32	2/32	27.66	6.49	25.5	0	0
Twenty20	2	48	78	0	-	-	-	9.75	-	0	0

TYMAL MILLS

RHB LF

FULL NAME: Tymal Solomon Mills
BORN: August 12, 1992, Dewsbury, Yorkshire
SQUAD NO: 15
HEIGHT: 6ft 1in
NICKNAME: T, Tyrone, Tyson
EDUCATION: Mildenhall College of Technology; University of East London,
TEAMS: England Lions, England Performance Programme, England Under-19s, Essex, Essex 2nd XI, Suffolk
CAREER: First-class: 2011; List A: 2011; T20: 2012

ESSEX

BEST BATTING: 31* England Lions vs Sri Lanka Emerging Players, Colombo, 2014
BEST BOWLING: 4-25 Essex vs Glamorgan, Cardiff, 2012

WHO WOULD PLAY YOU IN A FILM OF YOUR LIFE? Denzel Washington
CAREER HIGHLIGHTS? Being selected for two England Lions tours and being asked to fly out to help England's Ashes preparation in Australia
MOST MARKED CHARACTERISTIC? My pace, I would say!
BEST PLAYER IN COUNTY CRICKET? Chris Woakes
TIPS FOR THE TOP? Kishen Velani, Nick Browne
IF YOU WEREN'T A CRICKETER? I'd be at university
DESERT ISLAND DISC? Drake – Take Care (album)
FAVOURITE TV? Suits
CRICKETING HEROES? I didn't have any really
NON-CRICKETING HEROES? My mum
WHEN YOU RETIRE? I'd like to go into journalism
SURPRISING FACT? I bowl left-arm but throw with my right
FANTASY SLIP CORDON? Keeper: Ari Gold, 1st: Meghan Markle, 2nd: Myself, 3rd: Michelle Keegan, Gully: Micky Flanagan
CRICKET RULE YOU'D CHANGE? There should only be one new ball in ODI cricket
TWITTER FEED: @tmills15

Batting	Mat	Inns	NO	Runs	HS	Ave	SR	100	50	Ct	St
First-class	22	26	10	153	31*	9.56	57.73	0	0	9	0
List A	20	6	4	4	2*	2.00	28.57	0	0	3	0
Twenty20	4	2	2	11	8*	-	100.00	0	0	0	0

Bowling	Mat	Balls	Runs	Wkts	BBI	BBM	Ave	Econ	SR	5w	10
First-class	22	2322	1367	38	4/25	5/79	35.97	3.53	61.1	0	0
List A	20	674	639	19	3/23	3/23	33.63	5.68	35.4	0	0
Twenty20	4	18	28	0	-	-	-	9.33	-	0	0

TOM MILNES
RHB RFM

FULL NAME: Thomas Patrick Milnes
BORN: October 6, 1992, Stourbridge, Worcestershire
SQUAD NO: 8
HEIGHT: 6ft 1in
NICKNAME: Milner
EDUCATION: Heart of England School
TEAMS: England Under-17s, England Under-19s, Warwickshire, Warwickshire 2nd XI, Warwickshire Under-14s, Warwickshire Under-15s, Warwickshire Under-17s
CAREER: First-class: 2011; List A: 2013

BEST BATTING: 52* Warwickshire vs Oxford MCCU, Oxford, 2013
BEST BOWLING: 7-39 Warwickshire vs Oxford MCCU, Oxford, 2013

CAREER HIGHLIGHTS? Being part of the 2012 Championship-winning side, making my Championship debut and signing my first professional contract
MOST MARKED CHARACTERISTIC? Being very keen! And ginger
IF YOU WEREN'T A CRICKETER? I'd probably be working in a shop
DESERT ISLAND DISC? Oasis – Definitely Maybe
FAVOURITE TV? Alan Partridge
CRICKETING HEROES? Andrew Flintoff, James Anderson, Dale Steyn
ACCOMPLISHMENTS? Passing my driving test and getting some grades at school
WHEN YOU RETIRE? I'd like to either coach or set up a business
SURPRISING FACT? I used to play football for Aston Villa and I love doing impressions
FANTASY SLIP CORDON? Keeper: Alan Partridge, 1st: Liam Gallagher, 2nd: Andrew Flintoff, 3rd: Myself, Gully: James Corden
TWITTER FEED: @TPMilnes8

Batting	Mat	Inns	NO	Runs	HS	Ave	SR	100	50	Ct	St
First-class	13	13	2	278	52*	25.27	45.57	0	1	3	0
List A	3	3	1	22	16	11.00	64.70	0	0	0	0

Bowling	Mat	Balls	Runs	Wkts	BBI	BBM	Ave	Econ	SR	5w	10
First-class	13	1135	717	22	7/39	9/94	32.59	3.79	51.5	1	0
List A	3	138	177	3	2/73	2/73	59.00	7.69	46.0	0	0

DARYL MITCHELL

RHB RM R3 MVP28

FULL NAME: Daryl Keith Henry Mitchell
BORN: November 25, 1983, Badsey, nr Evesham
SQUAD NO: 27
HEIGHT: 5ft 10in
NICKNAME: Mitch, Touc
EDUCATION: Prince Henry's, Evesham; University College, Worcester
TEAMS: Mountaineers, Worcestershire, Worcestershire 2nd XI
CAREER: First-class: 2005; List A: 2005; T20: 2005

BEST BATTING: 298 Worcestershire vs Somerset, Taunton, 2009
BEST BOWLING: 4-49 Worcestershire vs Yorkshire, Leeds, 2009

FAMILY TIES? My dad played club cricket and coaches Worcestershire Young Cricketers U13
CAREER HIGHLIGHTS? Winning the CB40 in 2011 and scoring 298 against Somerset
CRICKETING HEROES? Ian Botham, Graeme Hick
NON-CRICKETING HEROES? Paul McGrath
BEST PLAYER IN COUNTY CRICKET? Marcus Trescothick
TIP FOR THE TOP? Alexei Kervezee
IF YOU WEREN'T A CRICKETER? I'd be a PE teacher
WHEN RAIN STOPS PLAY? Playing Perudo or Football Manager
FAVOURITE TV? Shameless, Match Of The Day
FAVOURITE FILM? Dumb And Dumber
ACCOMPLISHMENTS? BSc Sports Studies. I won loads of football and darts trophies when I was younger and I played for Aston Villa's School of Excellence as a kid
FANTASY SLIP CORDON? Keeper: Tiger Woods (he'd have a few stories and maybe the odd golf tip), 1st: Paul McGrath (my favourite Villa player), 2nd: Me (I always stand at second slip), 3rd: Ian Botham (my cricketing hero), Gully: Rhod Gilbert (a bit of comedy for the long days in the dirt!)
TWITTER FEED: @mitchwccc

Batting	Mat	Inns	NO	Runs	HS	Ave	SR	100	50	Ct	St
First-class	115	211	25	6986	298	37.55	43.54	14	32	157	0
List A	92	79	14	2170	107	33.38	84.40	2	13	36	0
Twenty20	83	61	16	873	45	19.40	113.52	0	0	32	0

Bowling	Mat	Balls	Runs	Wkts	BBI	BBM	Ave	Econ	SR	5w	10
First-class	115	1589	814	19	4/49		42.84	3.07	83.6	0	0
List A	92	2068	1931	53	4/42	4/42	36.43	5.60	39.0	0	0
Twenty20	83	1073	1415	53	4/11	4/11	26.69	7.91	20.2	0	0

STEPHEN MOORE

RHB RM R4

FULL NAME: Stephen Colin Moore
BORN: November 4, 1980, Johannesburg, Transvaal, South Africa
SQUAD NO: 2
HEIGHT: 6ft
NICKNAME: Mandy
EDUCATION: St Stithians College, South Africa; Exeter University
TEAMS: Derbyshire, England Lions, Lancashire, Marylebone Cricket Club, Sussex 2nd XI, Worcestershire
CAREER: First-class: 2003; List A: 2003; T20: 2003

BEST BATTING: 246 Worcestershire vs Derbyshire, Worcester, 2005
BEST BOWLING: 1-13 Worcestershire vs Lancashire, Worcester, 2004
COUNTY CAP: 2011 (Lancashire)

WHO WOULD PLAY YOU IN A FILM OF YOUR LIFE? Leonardo DiCaprio
CAREER HIGHLIGHTS? Winning the County Championship title in 2011
SUPERSTITIONS? I put my left pad on before my right
MOST MARKED CHARACTERISTIC? Telling long stories
BEST PLAYER IN COUNTY CRICKET? Graham Onions
TIP FOR THE TOP? Moeen Ali
IF YOU WEREN'T A CRICKETER? I'd be an engineer
FAVOURITE TV? Friends
CRICKETING HEROES? Steve Waugh, Jacques Kallis
NON-CRICKETING HEROES? Roger Federer, Rafael Nadal
ACCOMPLISHMENTS? Starting a family and achieving my academic goals
WHEN YOU RETIRE? I'll go skiing
FANTASY SLIP CORDON? Keeper: Paul Romer, 1st: Michael McIntyre, 2nd: Professor Brian Cox, 3rd: Kate Beckinsale, Gully: Roger Federer
CRICKET RULE YOU'D CHANGE? I'd loosen bat, ball and equipment technology laws
TWITTER FEED: @stephen_moore6

Batting	Mat	Inns	NO	Runs	HS	Ave	SR	100	50	Ct	St
First-class	145	262	19	8843	246	36.39	57.15	17	41	72	0
List A	141	135	12	3774	118	30.68	77.13	5	25	38	0
Twenty20	99	93	11	2340	83*	28.53	132.42	0	16	28	0

Bowling	Mat	Balls	Runs	Wkts	BBI	BBM	Ave	Econ	SR	5w	10
First-class	145	342	321	5	1/13		64.20	5.63	68.4	0	0
List A	141	41	53	1	1/1	1/1	53.00	7.75	41.0	0	0
Twenty20	99	-	-	-	-	-	-	-	-	-	-

EOIN MORGAN

LHB RM R1

FULL NAME: Eoin Joseph Gerard Morgan
BORN: September 10, 1986, Dublin, Ireland
SQUAD NO: 7
HEIGHT: 5ft 9in
NICKNAME: Moggie, Morgs
EDUCATION: Catholic University School
TEAMS: England, Ireland, Bangalore Royal
Challengers, England A, Ireland A, Ireland
Under-19s, Kolkata Knight Riders, Middlesex,
Middlesex 2nd XI, Sydney Thunder
CAREER: Test: 2010; ODI: 2006; T20I: 2009;
First-class: 2004; List A: 2004; T20: 2006

BEST BATTING: 209* Ireland vs UAE, Abu Dhabi, 2007
BEST BOWLING: 2-24 Middlesex vs Nottinghamshire, Lord's, 2007
COUNTY CAP: 2008

TWITTER FEED: @Eoin16
NOTES: An Irishman by birth, Morgan switched his allegiance to England in April 2009 when he was named in England's 30-man provisional squad for the 2009 World T20. Made his ODI debut for his adopted nation against West Indies in May 2009 at Bristol and his international T20 debut a month later. His Test debut followed against Bangladesh in May 2010. Hit a maiden century in his third Test – 130 vs Pakistan at Trent Bridge. Dropped from England's Test side after the 2012 away series vs Pakistan and he has not played a Test match since. Awarded a central contract by England in September 2012 but his estrangement from the Test set-up saw him lose out the following year. After a lean 2013, Morgan rediscovered his form in the away ODI series against Australia in January 2014, averaging 56.4 and scoring a century in an improbable defeat at Brisbane. Has captained England in ODI and T20I cricket

Batting	Mat	Inns	NO	Runs	HS	Ave	SR	100	50	Ct	St
Tests	16	24	1	700	130	30.43	54.77	2	3	11	0
ODIs	113	107	21	3448	124*	40.09	87.13	6	21	46	0
T20Is	42	41	10	961	85*	31.00	132.00	0	4	20	0
First-class	78	127	15	3859	209*	34.45	51.13	9	18	63	1
List A	211	196	32	6296	161	38.39	87.98	11	37	79	0
Twenty20	128	118	19	2623	85*	26.49	130.36	0	10	57	0

Bowling	Mat	Balls	Runs	Wkts	BBI	BBM	Ave	Econ	SR	5w	10
Tests	16	-	-	-	-	-	-	-	-	-	-
ODIs	113	-	-	-	-	-	-	-	-	-	-
T20Is	42	-	-	-	-	-	-	-	-	-	-
First-class	78	97	83	2	2/24	2/24	41.50	5.13	48.5	0	0
List A	211	42	49	0	-	-	-	7.00	-	0	0
Twenty20	128	-	-	-	-	-	-	-	-	-	-

MAX MORLEY

LHB SLA

FULL NAME: Max Gary Morley
BORN: January 24, 1993, Huddersfield, Yorkshire
SQUAD NO: 77
EDUCATION: Holmfirth High School; New College, Huddersfield
TEAMS: Durham, Durham 2nd XI
CAREER: T20: 2013

TWITTER FEED: @maxmorley1
NOTES: Morley, a promising left-arm spinner, made his first-team debut for Durham in last season's FL t20, returning figures of 0-41 from his four overs against Lancashire at Chester-le-Street. He featured regularly for the club's 2nd XI in 2013, producing a match-winning spell of 4-25 from eight overs against Warwickshire in the 2nd XI Trophy. In 2011 he was awarded the Lawrence Bennett Trophy for the leading player at the St Peter's Festival for Yorkshire Schoolboys – an award previously won by Michael Vaughan back in 1991

Batting	Mat	Inns	NO	Runs	HS	Ave	SR	100	50	Ct	St
Twenty20	1	-	-	-	-	-	-	-	-	0	0

Bowling	Mat	Balls	Runs	Wkts	BBI	BBM	Ave	Econ	SR	5w	10
Twenty20	1	24	41	0	-	-	-	10.25	-	0	0

CHARLIE MORRIS　　　　　　　　　　RHB RMF

FULL NAME: Charles Andrew John Morris
BORN: July 6, 1992, Hereford
SQUAD NO: 31
HEIGHT: 6ft
NICKNAME: Moz, Duggy, GB
EDUCATION: Kingswood School; King's College, Taunton; Oxford Brookes University
TEAMS: Devon, Oxford MCCU, Worcestershire, Worcestershire 2nd XI
CAREER: First-class: 2012; List A; 2013; T20: 2013

BEST BATTING: 33* Oxford MCCU vs Warwickshire, Oxford, 2013
BEST BOWLING: 3-33 Oxford MCCU vs Warwickshire, Oxford, 2013

CAREER HIGHLIGHTS? Being offered a professional contract and representing Worcestershire
MOST MARKED CHARACTERISTIC? I'm enthusiastic
TIP FOR THE TOP? Freddie Coleman
IF YOU WEREN'T A CRICKETER? My aspiration if I didn't play cricket was to become a Royal Marines officer
DESERT ISLAND DISC? Empire Of The Sun – Walking On A Dream
FAVOURITE TV? Homeland
CRICKETING HEROES? Dale Steyn and Brett Lee
NON-CRICKETING HEROES? All my family, Phil Lewis, Graham Charlesworth, Mike Hutton and Dennis Breakwell
WHEN YOU RETIRE? I'd like to live in Devon, have a springer spaniel, travel, sail parts of the world and complete some outdoor challenges
TWITTER FEED: @morris_9

Batting	Mat	Inns	NO	Runs	HS	Ave	SR	100	50	Ct	St
First-class	5	8	3	79	33*	15.80	37.26	0	0	2	0
List A	5	2	2	7	6*	-	77.77	0	0	1	0
Twenty20	1	-	-	-	-	-	-	-	-	1	0

Bowling	Mat	Balls	Runs	Wkts	BBI	BBM	Ave	Econ	SR	5w	10
First-class	5	941	495	10	3/33	4/72	49.50	3.15	94.1	0	0
List A	5	194	210	6	2/25	2/25	35.00	6.49	32.3	0	0
Twenty20	1	12	14	0	-	-	-	7.00	-	0	0

GORDON MUCHALL

RHB RM

FULL NAME: Gordon James Muchall
BORN: November 2, 1982, Newcastle-upon-Tyne, Northumberland
SQUAD NO: 24
HEIGHT: 6ft
NICKNAME: Much
EDUCATION: Durham School
TEAMS: Durham, Durham 2nd XI
CAREER: First-class: 2002; List A: 2002; T20: 2003

BEST BATTING: 219 Durham vs Kent, Canterbury, 2006
BEST BOWLING: 3-26 Durham vs Yorkshire, Leeds, 2003
COUNTY CAP: 2005; BENEFIT YEAR: 2014

FAMILY TIES? My grandad played for Northumberland, my brother Paul played at Gloucestershire, my brother Matthew plays for Northumberland and my dad Arthur plays for Durham Over 50s
CAREER HIGHLIGHTS? Winning the Championship twice with Durham
CRICKETING HEROES? Mike Hussey, Robin Smith, Dale Benkenstein
NON-CRICKETING HEROES? Jonny Wilkinson
BEST PLAYER IN COUNTY CRICKET? Marcus Trescothick
TIPS FOR THE TOP? Hayden and Rory Mustard, Jack and Luke Benkenstein, Adam Muchall, Mitchell Killeen, Luca Di Venuto, Charlie Harmison
IF YOU WEREN'T A CRICKETER? I'd be a coach or personal trainer
FAVOURITE TV? None at the minute, but I loved 24 and Prison Break
FAVOURITE FILM? Forrest Gump, The Shawshank Redemption, Old School, Wedding Crashers
DREAM HOLIDAY? Caribbean
ACCOMPLISHMENTS? My son Adam
SURPRISING FACT? The last game of rugby I ever played was at Twickenham

Batting	Mat	Inns	NO	Runs	HS	Ave	SR	100	50	Ct	St
First-class	137	237	11	6537	219	28.92	53.84	11	33	93	0
List A	129	117	24	3195	101*	34.35		1	20	45	0
Twenty20	76	65	17	1345	66*	28.02	112.45	0	5	28	0

Bowling	Mat	Balls	Runs	Wkts	BBI	BBM	Ave	Econ	SR	5w	10
First-class	137	896	617	15	3/26		41.13	4.13	59.7	0	0
List A	129	168	144	1	1/15	1/15	144.00	5.14	168.0	0	0
Twenty20	76	12	8	1	1/8	1/8	8.00	4.00	12.0	0	0

STEVEN MULLANEY   RHB RM MVP70

FULL NAME: Steven John Mullaney
BORN: November 19, 1986, Warrington, Cheshire
SQUAD NO: 5
HEIGHT: 5ft 10in
NICKNAME: Mull, Cadet Mahoney
EDUCATION: St Mary's RC High School, Astley
TEAMS: England Under-19s, Khelaghar Samaj Kallyan Samity, Lancashire, Lancashire 2nd XI, Nottinghamshire
CAREER: First-class: 2006; List A: 2006; T20: 2006

BEST BATTING: 165* Lancashire vs Durham UCCE, Durham University, 2007
BEST BOWLING: 4-31 Nottinghamshire vs Essex, Nottingham, 2010

WHO WOULD PLAY YOU IN A FILM OF YOUR LIFE? Hugh Jackman
MOST MARKED CHARACTERISTIC? I have a blue moon tattooed on my inner thigh
BEST PLAYER IN COUNTY CRICKET? Harry Gurney
TIPS FOR THE TOP? George Bacon, Ben Kitt
IF YOU WEREN'T A CRICKETER? I'd be a PE teacher
DESERT ISLAND DISC? Westlife – Swear It Again
FAVOURITE TV? Coronation Street
CRICKETING HEROES? Andrew Flintoff, VVS Laxman
NON-CRICKETING HEROES? Gary Barlow, Dominic Healy
WHEN YOU RETIRE? I'd like to be involved in coaching
SURPRISING FACT? I toured France with the England U15 rugby league team
FANTASY SLIP CORDON? Keeper: Joe Hart, 1st: Kylie Minogue, 2nd: Johnny Vegas, 3rd: Luke Fletcher, Gully: Tess Daly
TWITTER FEED: @Mull05

Batting	Mat	Inns	NO	Runs	HS	Ave	SR	100	50	Ct	St
First-class	54	87	6	2774	165*	34.24	59.91	5	16	38	0
List A	60	41	7	664	61	19.52	90.71	0	2	35	0
Twenty20	55	34	11	368	53	16.00	128.22	0	1	26	0

Bowling	Mat	Balls	Runs	Wkts	BBI	BBM	Ave	Econ	SR	5w	10
First-class	54	2157	1146	22	4/31	4/48	52.09	3.18	98.0	0	0
List A	60	1820	1503	55	4/29	4/29	27.32	4.95	33.0	0	0
Twenty20	55	882	1127	36	4/19	4/19	31.30	7.66	24.5	0	0

DAVID MURPHY

RHB WK

FULL NAME: David Murphy
BORN: June 24, 1989, Welwyn Garden City, Hertfordshire
SQUAD NO: 19
HEIGHT: 6ft 1in
NICKNAME: Murph
EDUCATION: Richard Hale School; Loughborough University
TEAMS: Scotland, Loughborough MCCU, Loughborough UCCE, Northamptonshire, Northamptonshire 2nd XI
CAREER: ODI: 2013; T20I: 2013; First-class: 2009; List A: 2010; T20: 2010

BEST BATTING: 81 Northamptonshire vs Hampshire, Northampton, 2013

WHO WOULD PLAY YOU IN A FILM OF YOUR LIFE? Robert Downey Jr
CAREER HIGHLIGHTS? Scoring 69 not out on my first-class debut. Getting some good appreciation from David Lloyd in my first game on Sky Sports. Breaking the highest score for Northants Academy in the Northants Premiership
MOST MARKED CHARACTERISTIC? Ambition
BEST PLAYER IN COUNTY CRICKET? Marcus Trescothick
TIPS FOR THE TOP? Rob Newton, David Willey
DESERT ISLAND DISC? Jack Johnson – In Between Dreams
BIGGEST DRESSING DOWN YOU'VE RECEIVED? One of the many I received from the cricketing legend that was Graham Dilley which resulted in lots of laps of the Loughborough cricket pitch
CRICKETING HEROES? Steve Waugh, Jack Russell
ACCOMPLISHMENTS? Achieving a 2:1 in my Politics and Business Management degree from Loughborough, with a 1st in my dissertation
WHEN YOU RETIRE? I'll probably do something in line with my Politics degree

Batting	Mat	Inns	NO	Runs	HS	Ave	SR	100	50	Ct	St
ODIs	8	7	2	58	20*	11.60	49.15	0	0	8	3
T20Is	4	4	3	35	20	35.00	100.00	0	0	1	0
First-class	48	61	13	1351	81	28.14	43.70	0	10	139	9
List A	36	23	12	214	31*	19.45	71.81	0	0	21	11
Twenty20	39	19	7	129	20	10.75	103.20	0	0	18	5
Bowling	Mat	Balls	Runs	Wkts	BBI	BBM	Ave	Econ	SR	5w	10
ODIs	8	-	-	-	-	-	-	-	-	-	-
T20Is	4	-	-	-	-	-	-	-	-	-	-
First-class	48	6	3	0	-	-	-	3.00	-	0	0
List A	36	-	-	-	-	-	-	-	-	-	-
Twenty20	39	-	-	-	-	-	-	-	-	-	-

JACK MURPHY

LHB LFM

FULL NAME: Jack Roger Murphy
BORN: July 15, 1995, Haverfordwest, Pembrokeshire, Wales
SQUAD NO: 7
HEIGHT: 6ft 6in
NICKNAME: Smurf, Lanky
EDUCATION: Greenhill Secondary School
TEAMS: Wales Minor Counties
CAREER: Yet to make first-team debut

WHO WOULD PLAY YOU IN A FILM OF YOUR LIFE? Daniel Craig. He's a foot shorter than me and looks nothing like me, but he is awesome!

CAREER HIGHLIGHTS? Going to the West Indies on tour with the South and West of England and going to New Zealand, which was a great experience, playing with Simon Jones and seeing the pace he can bowl

SUPERSTITIONS? When I walk back to my mark before each ball I always turn the same way to run in to the crease. I don't know why, I always have – a bit like Morne Morkel

MOST MARKED CHARACTERISTIC? Being so tall and skinny. I also have some very skinny legs

BEST PLAYER IN COUNTY CRICKET? I'm only new on the scene so I have no real clue but surely Kevin Pietersen now that he's playing for Surrey

TIP FOR THE TOP? I think Will Rhodes from Yorkshire will be a very good player. He's already captain of England U19 and is a good allrounder

IF YOU WEREN'T A CRICKETER? I would have liked to join the forces, mainly the RAF. It has always appealed to me and looked like a good experience

CRICKETING HEROES? Simon Jones, as he was Welsh and a fast bowler. Especially watching him in the 2005 Ashes Tests. Also Andrew Flintoff for his attitude on and off the pitch

NON-CRICKETING HEROES? My mum and dad as I always look up to them for what they have done for me, my brother and my sister – always putting us first and wanting us to succeed

ACCOMPLISHMENTS? Not many really. Probably winning the U16 Welsh Schools Football Cup and the fact I'm punching above my weight with my girlfriend

SURPRISING FACT? I have never scored a hundred. I've scored 98, 97 twice and 96 twice. I just seem to bottle it every time I get close!

TWITTER FEED: @jmurf95

FULL NAME: Timothy James Murtagh
BORN: August 2, 1981, Lambeth, London
SQUAD NO: 34
HEIGHT: 6ft 1in
NICKNAME: Murts, Brows, Jack
EDUCATION: John Fisher, Purley
TEAMS: Ireland, British Universities, Middlesex, Middlesex 2nd XI, Surrey
CAREER: ODI: 2012; T20I: 2012; First-class: 2000; List A: 2000; T20: 2003

BEST BATTING: 74* Surrey vs Middlesex, The Oval, 2004
BEST BOWLING: 7-82 Middlesex vs Derbyshire, Derby, 2009
COUNTY CAP: 2008 (Middlesex)

FAMILY TIES? My uncle [Andy] played for Hampshire in the 70s and my brother [Chris] played for Surrey. My dad played for the Beckenham Merlins
CAREER HIGHLIGHTS? Gaining international honours with Ireland, getting capped at Middlesex, winning the T20 Cup in 2008 and bowling a ball above 80mph in a televised game
SUPERSTITIONS? I always shave on day one of a Championship game (my face, that is). Cash in on the lunches during Lord's games
BEST PLAYER IN COUNTY CRICKET? Graham Onions
TIPS FOR THE TOP? Toby Roland-Jones, Tom Helm, Ravi Patel, Ross Whiteley
BIGGEST DRESSING DOWN YOU'VE RECEIVED? I got called a "hairy-faced dingo" by Andrew Symonds many years ago
CRICKETING HEROES? Glenn McGrath, Martin Bicknell, Darren Gough
TWITTER FEED: @tjmurtagh

Batting	Mat	Inns	NO	Runs	HS	Ave	SR	100	50	Ct	St
ODIs	9	5	2	50	23*	16.66	75.75	0	0	1	0
T20Is	5	2	1	5	3	5.00	71.42	0	0	1	0
First-class	144	195	59	2940	74*	21.61		0	10	43	0
List A	145	92	34	675	35*	11.63		0	0	36	0
Twenty20	92	35	12	206	40*	8.95	105.64	0	0	20	0

Bowling	Mat	Balls	Runs	Wkts	BBI	BBM	Ave	Econ	SR	5w	10
ODIs	9	378	312	7	3/33	3/33	44.57	4.95	54.0	0	0
T20Is	5	101	112	5	2/24	2/24	22.40	6.65	20.2	0	0
First-class	144	24082	13122	487	7/82		26.94	3.26	49.4	21	3
List A	145	6308	5536	189	4/14	4/14	29.29	5.26	33.3	0	0
Twenty20	92	1805	2493	98	6/24	6/24	25.43	8.28	18.4	1	0

PHIL MUSTARD   LHB LB WK MVP18

FULL NAME: Philip Mustard
BORN: October 8, 1982, Sunderland, Co Durham
SQUAD NO: 19
HEIGHT: 5ft 11in
NICKNAME: Colonel
EDUCATION: Usworth Comprehensive
TEAMS: England, Barisal Burners, Durham, Durham Cricket Board, England Under-19s, Mountaineers
CAREER: ODI: 2007; T20I: 2008; First-class: 2002; List A: 2000; T20: 2003

BEST BATTING: 130 Durham vs Kent, Canterbury, 2006
BEST BOWLING: 1-9 Durham vs Sussex, Hove, 2013

CAREER HIGHLIGHTS? Making my England debut in Sri Lanka and New Zealand in 2007/08 and playing 10 ODIs. Winning our first trophy for Durham, the FP Trophy, in 2007, and then following up with two Championship victories in 2008 and 2009. Being asked to captain Durham in the middle of 2010
SUPERSTITIONS? A little one when I go out to bat: I always look high to my left. Not sure why, but it happens
BEST PLAYER IN COUNTY CRICKET? Marcus Trescothick
IF YOU WEREN'T A CRICKETER? I'd probably be selling things, which wouldn't be exciting, but it would be a job
WHEN RAIN STOPS PLAY? Playing cards, reading newspapers and every now and then going to the gym
ACCOMPLISHMENTS? Bringing up my two boys
GUILTY PLEASURES? Crisps
TWITTER FEED: @colonel19

Batting	Mat	Inns	NO	Runs	HS	Ave	SR	100	50	Ct	St
ODIs	10	10	0	233	83	23.30	92.46	0	1	9	2
T20Is	2	2	0	60	40	30.00	162.16	0	0	0	0
First-class	165	255	32	6953	130	31.17	62.88	6	42	553	18
List A	165	149	8	4366	143	30.96		7	27	163	41
Twenty20	139	132	7	3104	97*	24.83	125.87	0	17	63	32

Bowling	Mat	Balls	Runs	Wkts	BBI	BBM	Ave	Econ	SR	5w	10
ODIs	10	-	-	-	-	-	-	-	-	-	-
T20Is	2	-	-	-	-	-	-	-	-	-	-
First-class	165	7	9	1	1/9	1/9	9.00	7.71	7.0	0	0
List A	165	-	-	-	-	-	-	-	-	-	-
Twenty20	139	-	-	-	-	-	-	-	-	-	-

JOHANN MYBURGH RHB OB

FULL NAME: Johann Gerhardus Myburgh
BORN: October 22, 1980, Pretoria, Transvaal, South Africa
SQUAD NO: 6
TEAMS: Auckland, Canterbury, Durham, Durham 2nd XI, Hampshire, Hampshire 2nd XI, Northerns, Somerset, Titans
CAREER: First-class: 1997; List A: 1999; T20: 2005

BEST BATTING: 203 Northerns B vs Easterns, Pretoria, 1998
BEST BOWLING: 4-56 Canterbury vs Northern Districts, Hamilton, 2008

NOTES: Myburgh signed for Somerset ahead of the 2014 season after previous spells in county cricket with Hampshire and, more recently, Durham. The South African allrounder emigrated from his homeland to play cricket in New Zealand, where he represented Canterbury for whom he averages 51.71 in first-class cricket. He broke Graeme Pollock's long-standing record for the youngest scorer of a double-century in South African first-class cricket as a 17-year-old in 1998. He has been living in the UK for a number of years, playing for Sutton CC in the Surrey Championship. His younger brother, Stephan, plays international cricket for the Netherlands

Batting	Mat	Inns	NO	Runs	HS	Ave	SR	100	50	Ct	St
First-class	80	145	18	5509	203	43.37		13	32	52	0
List A	97	91	9	2344	112	28.58		1	14	20	0
Twenty20	45	41	7	969	88	28.50	113.33	0	4	13	0

Bowling	Mat	Balls	Runs	Wkts	BBI	BBM	Ave	Econ	SR	5w	10
First-class	80	2700	1392	31	4/56		44.90	3.09	87.0	0	0
List A	97	1682	1423	24	2/22	2/22	59.29	5.07	70.0	0	0
Twenty20	45	344	429	10	3/16	3/16	42.90	7.48	34.4	0	0

JIGAR NAIK — RHB OB

FULL NAME: Jigar Kumar Hakumatrai Naik
BORN: August 10, 1984, Leicester
SQUAD NO: 22
HEIGHT: 6ft 2in
NICKNAME: Jigs, Jiggles
EDUCATION: Nottingham Trent University; Loughborough University
TEAMS: Colombo Cricket Club, Leicestershire, Leicestershire 2nd XI, Leicestershire Cricket Board, Loughborough UCCE
CAREER: First-class: 2006; List A: 2003; T20: 2008

BEST BATTING: 109* Leicestershire vs Derbyshire, Leicester, 2009
BEST BOWLING: 7-96 Leicestershire vs Surrey, The Oval, 2010

WHO WOULD PLAY YOU IN A FILM OF YOUR LIFE? Maximus in Gladiator
CAREER HIGHLIGHTS? My maiden first-class five-wicket haul, my maiden first-class hundred, getting capped for Leicestershire, topping the national bowling averages in 2010 and being selected for the ECB's Potential Performance Programme in 2011
MOST MARKED CHARACTERISTIC? My long fingers
BEST PLAYER IN COUNTY CRICKET? James Taylor
TIPS FOR THE TOP? Moeen Ali, James Taylor, Mark Wood, Shiv Thakor
IF YOU WEREN'T A CRICKETER? I'd be a systems engineer
DESERT ISLAND DISC? Bollywood Greatest Hits
FAVOURITE TV? 24
CRICKETING HEROES? Claude Henderson, Erapalli Prasanna, Sachin Tendulkar
NON-CRICKETING HEROES? Roger Federer, Muhammad Ali
ACCOMPLISHMENTS? Getting married
CRICKET RULE YOU'D CHANGE? Revert back to four fielders inside the circle in one-day cricket after the powerplay
SURPRISING FACT? I play the tabla
TWITTER FEED: @jigarnaik

Batting	Mat	Inns	NO	Runs	HS	Ave	SR	100	50	Ct	St	
First-class	53	80	18	1332	109*	21.48	37.89	1	3	28	0	
List A	32	23	9	154	22*	11.00		0	0	4	0	
Twenty20	21	8	6	22	7*	11.00	110.00	0	0	4	0	

Bowling	Mat	Balls	Runs	Wkts	BBI	BBM	Ave	Econ	SR	5w	10	
First-class	53	7916	4285	130	7/96	8/133	32.96	3.24	60.8	5	0	
List A	32	1207	1083	26	3/21	3/21	41.65	5.38	46.4	0	0	
Twenty20	21	333	409	13	3/3	3/3	31.46	7.36	25.6	0	0	

ESSEX

FULL NAME: Graham Richard Napier
BORN: January 6, 1980, Colchester, Essex
SQUAD NO: 17
HEIGHT: 5ft 9in
NICKNAME: Plank, George, Napes
EDUCATION: Gilberd School, Colchester
TEAMS: Central Districts, England Lions, Essex, Essex 2nd XI, Essex Cricket Board, Mumbai Indians, Wellington
CAREER: First-class: 1997; List A: 1997; T20: 2003

BEST BATTING: 196 Essex vs Surrey, Croydon, 2011
BEST BOWLING: 7-90 Essex vs Leicestershire, Chelmsford, 2013
COUNTY CAP: 2003; BENEFIT YEAR: 2012

WHO WOULD PLAY YOU IN A FILM OF YOUR LIFE? Russell Crowe
CAREER HIGHLIGHTS? Testing myself against the world's best and scoring some runs. Winning the FP Trophy. Scoring 152*, including 16 sixes, in a T20 match. Being included in England's World T20 squad. Playing in the IPL for Mumbai Indians
SUPERSTITIONS? I always like to have lamb the evening before I bat
BEST PLAYER IN COUNTY CRICKET? Marcus Trescothick
TIPS FOR THE TOP? Reece Topley, Ben Foakes
IF YOU WEREN'T A CRICKETER? A photographer or a chef – potentially both
FAVOURITE TV? Africa by David Attenborough, Top Gear
CRICKETING HEROES? Graham Gooch, Viv Richards, Freddie Flintoff, Alastair Cook
NON-CRICKETING HEROES? Winston Churchill
WHEN YOU RETIRE? I'd like to play a lot of golf, not have to work too much and get plenty of sunshine!
FANTASY SLIP CORDON? Keeper: Russell Crowe, 1st: Winston Churchill, 2nd: Natalie Imbruglia, 3rd: Micky Flanagan, Gully: Elton John
TWITTER FEED: @Graham_Napier

Batting	Mat	Inns	NO	Runs	HS	Ave	SR	100	50	Ct	St
First-class	139	189	40	4864	196	32.64		6	28	51	0
List A	229	173	21	2861	79	18.82		0	14	54	0
Twenty20	102	79	14	1041	152*	16.01	145.59	1	0	29	0

Bowling	Mat	Balls	Runs	Wkts	BBI	BBM	Ave	Econ	SR	5w	10
First-class	139	19192	11429	334	7/90		34.21	3.57	57.4	10	0
List A	229	7895	6929	269	7/32	7/32	25.75	5.26	29.3	3	0
Twenty20	102	2143	2685	123	4/10	4/10	21.82	7.51	17.4	0	0

BRENDAN NASH

LHB LM R1 MVP82

FULL NAME: Brendan Paul Nash
BORN: December 14, 1977, Attadale, Western Australia, Australia
SQUAD NO: 40
HEIGHT: 5ft 8in
NICKNAME: Bubba
TEAMS: West Indies, Jamaica, Kent, Queensland, West Indies A
CAREER: Test: 2008; ODI: 2008; First-class: 2001; List A: 2001; T20: 2008

BEST BATTING: 207 Jamaica vs Trinidad and Tobago, St Augustine, 2011
BEST BOWLING: 2-7 Jamaica vs Combined Campuses and Colleges, Kingston, 2008
COUNTY CAP: 2013

WHO WOULD PLAY YOU IN A FILM OF YOUR LIFE? Denzel Washington
CAREER HIGHLIGHTS? Playing Test cricket and winning a series against England
SUPERSTITIONS? I put my right pad on first
IF YOU WEREN'T A CRICKETER? I'd be running a business or being a golf pro on a resort somewhere
FAVOURITE TV? Two And A Half Men (the old ones)
CRICKETING HEROES? Allan Border, Sir Garfield Sobers
NON-CRICKETING HEROES? Michael Jordan, Tiger Woods
FANTASY SLIP CORDON? Keeper: Master Yoda (because he would catch everything), 1st: Michael Jordan (I would ask him how he had the drive to succeed for himself and in a team environment), 2nd: Sir Garfield Sobers (to pick his brains about the game), 3rd: Tiger Woods (I'd ask how he handles the pressure he faces every day), Gully: Hugh Hefner (because he would have some great stories to tell)

Batting	Mat	Inns	NO	Runs	HS	Ave	SR	100	50	Ct	St
Tests	21	33	0	1103	114	33.42	43.28	2	8	6	0
ODIs	9	7	3	104	39*	26.00	73.75	0	0	1	0
First-class	119	195	28	6597	207	39.50		17	27	42	0
List A	83	62	16	1557	98*	33.84		0	8	25	0
Twenty20	8	6	1	84	26	16.80	87.50	0	0	1	0

Bowling	Mat	Balls	Runs	Wkts	BBI	BBM	Ave	Econ	SR	5w	10
Tests	21	492	247	2	1/21	1/21	123.50	3.01	246.0	0	0
ODIs	9	294	224	5	3/56	3/56	44.80	4.57	58.8	0	0
First-class	119	1495	695	22	2/7		31.59	2.78	67.9	0	0
List A	83	798	562	16	4/20	4/20	35.12	4.22	49.8	0	0
Twenty20	8	24	40	1	1/32	1/32	40.00	10.00	24.0	0	0

CHRIS NASH

RHB OB R3 MVP13

SUSSEX

FULL NAME: Christopher David Nash
BORN: May 19, 1983, Cuckfield, Sussex
SQUAD NO: 23
HEIGHT: 6ft
NICKNAME: Nashy, Nashdog, Spidey, Knocker, Hairpiece
EDUCATION: Collyers Sixth Form College; Loughborough University
TEAMS: Auckland, England Lions, Loughborough UCCE, Otago, Prime Doleshwar Sporting Club, Sussex
CAREER: First-class: 2002; List A: 2006; T20: 2006

BEST BATTING: 184 Sussex vs Leicestershire, Leicester, 2010
BEST BOWLING: 4-12 Sussex vs Glamorgan, Cardiff, 2010
COUNTY CAP: 2008

FAMILY TIES? My brother played 2nd XI cricket for Sussex before losing the ability to bowl
WHO WOULD PLAY YOU IN A FILM OF YOUR LIFE? Luke Wright
CAREER HIGHLIGHTS? Winning the County Championship in 2007 and T20 in 2009, my county cap in 2008, winning the Pro40 in 2009, playing for England Lions in 2011, being part of the EPP in 2010 and being named Sussex vice-captain from 2013
MOST MARKED CHARACTERISTIC? My biceps
BEST PLAYER IN COUNTY CRICKET? Luke Wright
TIPS FOR THE TOP? Philip Hudson, Ryan Leverton, Richard Hawkes, Ben Nash Jr and Luke Marshall
IF YOU WEREN'T A CRICKETER? I'd be sitting in a deckchair watching Sussex!
CRICKETING HEROES? Luke Wright, Mark Nash, John Barclay, Dr John Dew, Les Lenham
NON-CRICKETING HEROES? Les Lenham, Will Ferrell, Maverick and Goose
WHEN YOU RETIRE? I'll sit in a deckchair and watch Sussex!
SURPRISING FACT? I spent the holidays selling Christmas trees at my local garden centre when I was 19
TWITTER FEED: @chrisnash23

Batting	Mat	Inns	NO	Runs	HS	Ave	SR	100	50	Ct	St
First-class	129	220	17	7857	184	38.70	58.54	16	38	61	0
List A	89	82	3	2554	124*	32.32	90.98	2	16	22	0
Twenty20	102	96	14	1915	80*	23.35	118.20	0	8	32	0

Bowling	Mat	Balls	Runs	Wkts	BBI	BBM	Ave	Econ	SR	5w	10
First-class	129	4558	2517	70	4/12		35.95	3.31	65.1	0	0
List A	89	1249	1092	42	4/40	4/40	26.00	5.24	29.7	0	0
Twenty20	102	782	890	41	4/7	4/7	21.70	6.82	19.0	0	0

OLIVER NEWBY RHB RFM

FULL NAME: Oliver James Newby
BORN: August 26, 1984, Blackburn, Lancashire
SQUAD NO: 8
HEIGHT: 6ft 5in
NICKNAME: Newbz, News
EDUCATION: Ribblesdale High School; Myerscough College
TEAMS: Lancashire, Lancashire Cricket Board, Nottinghamshire
CAREER: First-class: 2003; List A: 2003; T20: 2003

BEST BATTING: 38* Nottinghamshire vs Kent, Nottingham, 2004
BEST BOWLING: 5-69 Gloucestershire vs Northamptonshire, Bristol, 2008

FAMILY TIES? My father played club cricket
WHY CRICKET? You get to travel the world playing sport
TIP FOR THE TOP? Jordan Clark
IF YOU WEREN'T A CRICKETER? I'd be looking for a rich widow
WHEN RAIN STOPS PLAY? Winding up Tom Smith for being bald and Glen Chapple for being old, ginger and rubbish at golf
FAVOURITE TV? Pointless
FAVOURITE FILM? Blades Of Glory
DREAM HOLIDAY? Thailand

Batting	Mat	Inns	NO	Runs	HS	Ave	SR	100	50	Ct	St
First-class	51	44	12	323	38*	10.09	40.37	0	0	8	0
List A	36	19	10	124	36*	13.77	85.51	0	0	4	0
Twenty20	13	5	2	15	6*	5.00	83.33	0	0	3	0

Bowling	Mat	Balls	Runs	Wkts	BBI	BBM	Ave	Econ	SR	5w	10
First-class	51	6465	4151	130	5/69		31.93	3.85	49.7	1	0
List A	36	1176	1207	35	5/35	5/35	34.48	6.15	33.6	1	0
Twenty20	13	178	238	7	2/34	2/34	34.00	8.02	25.4	0	0

ROB NEWTON

RHB LB

FULL NAME: Robert Irving Newton
BORN: January 18, 1990, Taunton, Somerset
SQUAD NO: 21
HEIGHT: 5ft 8in
NICKNAME: Ewok, KOTL
EDUCATION: Framlingham College
TEAMS: Northamptonshire, Northamptonshire 2nd XI
CAREER: First-class: 2010; List A: 2009; T20: 2010

BEST BATTING: 119* Northamptonshire vs Derbyshire, Northampton, 2012

WHO WOULD PLAY YOU IN A FILM OF YOUR LIFE? Warwick Davis
CAREER HIGHLIGHTS? Scoring a hundred in both innings of a first-class game [against Derbyshire]. Taking the new ball
BEST PLAYER IN COUNTY CRICKET? Darren Stevens
TIP FOR THE TOP? James Sales
IF YOU WEREN'T A CRICKETER? I'd be drinking the profits at my own bar
DESERT ISLAND DISC? Baha Men – Who Let The Dogs Out?
FAVOURITE TV? Entourage
CRICKETING HEROES? Ajaz Akhtar
NON-CRICKETING HEROES? Hank Moody, Vincent Chase
FANTASY SLIP CORDON? Keeper: Jack Brooks, 1st: Me, 2nd: Ben Howgego, 3rd: Gav Baker
TWITTER FEED: @robbienewts77

Batting	Mat	Inns	NO	Runs	HS	Ave	SR	100	50	Ct	St
First-class	33	53	6	1837	119*	39.08	65.04	5	7	8	0
List A	24	23	1	616	88*	28.00	92.21	0	2	3	0
Twenty20	14	13	1	178	38	14.83	108.53	0	0	0	0

Bowling	Mat	Balls	Runs	Wkts	BBI	BBM	Ave	Econ	SR	5w	10
First-class	33	13	19	0	-	-	-	8.76	-	0	0
List A	24	-	-	-	-	-	-	-	-	-	-
Twenty20	14	-	-	-	-	-	-	-	-	-	-

SAM NORTHEAST — RHB OB

FULL NAME: Sam Alexander Northeast
BORN: October 16, 1989, Ashford, Kent
SQUAD NO: 17
HEIGHT: 5ft 11in
NICKNAME: North, Bam, Nick Knight
EDUCATION: Harrow
TEAMS: England Under-15s, England Under-19s, Harrow School, Kent, Kent 2nd XI, Marylebone Cricket Club
CAREER: First-class: 2007; List A: 2007; T20: 2010

BEST BATTING: 176 Kent vs Loughborough MCCU, Canterbury, 2011
BEST BOWLING: 1-60 Kent vs Gloucestershire, Cheltenham, 2013
COUNTY CAP: 2012

CRICKET MOMENTS TO FORGET? Not scoring many runs in my first two appearances at Lord's in the Eton vs Harrow match
SUPERSTITIONS? I put my right pad on first
CRICKETERS PARTICULARLY ADMIRED? Graham Thorpe, Steve Waugh
TIP FOR THE TOP? Alex Blake
OTHER SPORTS PLAYED? Rackets, squash, cross-country running, football, rugby
OTHER SPORTS FOLLOWED? Football (Spurs), rugby (Bath)
FAVOURITE BAND? Starsailor, Snow Patrol, Florence And The Machine
RELAXATIONS? Fishing, gardening and playing rackets to release stress
TWITTER FEED: @sanortheast

Batting	Mat	Inns	NO	Runs	HS	Ave	SR	100	50	Ct	St
First-class	75	132	5	4000	176	31.49	51.34	6	24	42	0
List A	44	38	3	1047	115	29.91	78.01	1	6	12	0
Twenty20	34	27	7	476	61	23.80	114.69	0	2	9	0

Bowling	Mat	Balls	Runs	Wkts	BBI	BBM	Ave	Econ	SR	5w	10
First-class	75	162	141	1	1/60	1/60	141.00	5.22	162.0	0	0
List A	44	-	-	-	-	-	-	-	-	-	-
Twenty20	34	-	-	-	-	-	-	-	-	-	-

LIAM NORWELL

RHB RMF

FULL NAME: Liam Connor Norwell
BORN: December 27, 1991, Bournemouth, Dorset
SQUAD NO: 24
HEIGHT: 6ft 3in
NICKNAME: Pasty, Ivan Drago
EDUCATION: Redruth School
TEAMS: Gloucestershire, Gloucestershire 2nd XI
CAREER: First-class: 2011; List A: 2012; T20: 2012

BEST BATTING: 26 Gloucestershire vs Middlesex, Bristol, 2011
BEST BOWLING: 6-46 Gloucestershire vs Derbyshire, Bristol, 2011
COUNTY CAP: 2011

CAREER HIGHLIGHTS? Taking six-fer on my first-class debut in 2011 and a winning T20 debut against Somerset in front of a full house at Taunton
MOST MARKED CHARACTERISTIC? My ginger lid and slightly large feet
BEST PLAYER IN COUNTY CRICKET? Will Gidman. He's consistently outstanding across the past three seasons yet not given the credit he deserves
TIPS FOR THE TOP? Craig Miles and Miles Hammond
IF YOU WEREN'T A CRICKETER? I'd either have just finished university and be trying to find a job or I'd be in the Royal Marines
CRICKETING HEROES? Andrew Flintoff
ACCOMPLISHMENTS? I won the 100m sprint at Year 6 sports day, I once ate 12 pancakes on pancake day and I used to have the record on the basketball machine at Cribbs Causeway
SURPRISING FACT? At some point in my life I'd like to try and write a book
CRICKET RULE YOU'D CHANGE? Supersubs in T20: you should be able to make one change to your team at the midway point of the match but your sub has to be specified at the beginning
TWITTER FEED: @LCNorwell24

Batting	Mat	Inns	NO	Runs	HS	Ave	SR	100	50	Ct	St
First-class	18	25	12	121	26	9.30	23.00	0	0	4	0
List A	4	1	1	1	1*	-	33.33	0	0	0	0
Twenty20	4	1	1	1	1*	-	50.00	0	0	0	0

Bowling	Mat	Balls	Runs	Wkts	BBI	BBM	Ave	Econ	SR	5w	10
First-class	18	2520	1572	48	6/46	8/74	32.75	3.74	52.5	2	0
List A	4	162	177	9	6/52	6/52	19.66	6.55	18.0	1	0
Twenty20	4	78	123	4	2/41	2/41	30.75	9.46	19.5	0	0

FULL NAME: Niall John O'Brien
BORN: November 8, 1981, Dublin, Ireland
SQUAD NO: 81
HEIGHT: 5ft 8in
NICKNAME: Paddy, Nobi, Solano
EDUCATION: Marian College Dublin
TEAMS: Ireland, Ireland Under-19s, Kent, Leicestershire, Northamptonshire, Rangpur Riders
CAREER: ODI: 2006; T20I: 2008; First-class: 2004; List A: 2003; T20: 2004

BEST BATTING: 182 Northamptonshire vs Glamorgan, Cardiff, 2012
BEST BOWLING: 1-4 Kent v Cambridge UCCE, Cambridge, 2006
COUNTY CAP: 2011 (Northamptonshire)

FAMILY TIES? My dad captained Ireland and is an Irish Cricket Hall Of Fame inductee, my brother Kevin plays for Ireland alongside me and my brothers and sister all played cricket for Railway Union CC in Dublin
WHO WOULD PLAY YOU IN A FILM OF YOUR LIFE? Colin Farrell
CAREER HIGHLIGHTS? Playing first-class cricket in the UK, representing my country, travelling the world playing cricket and beating Pakistan, Bangladesh and England in World Cups
BEST PLAYER IN COUNTY CRICKET? Moeen Ali is an excellent player
TIP FOR THE TOP? Ben Duckett
CRICKET RULE YOU'D CHANGE? I don't like DRS
WHEN YOU RETIRE? I'd like to be a sports agent and continue to work in the media
SURPRISING FACT? I was in a Bollywood movie
TWITTER FEED: @niallnobiobrien

Batting	Mat	Inns	NO	Runs	HS	Ave	SR	100	50	Ct	St
ODIs	59	59	6	1481	72	27.94	67.07	0	11	39	7
T20Is	21	20	1	362	50	19.05	98.63	0	1	12	8
First-class	126	195	20	6232	182	35.61	55.15	12	30	329	36
List A	167	146	17	3834	121	29.72	76.02	2	24	135	32
Twenty20	109	93	12	1784	84	22.02	110.39	0	5	54	29

Bowling	Mat	Balls	Runs	Wkts	BBI	BBM	Ave	Econ	SR	5w	10
ODIs	59	-	-	-	-	-	-	-	-	-	-
T20Is	21	-	-	-	-	-	-	-	-	-	-
First-class	126	18	19	2	1/4	1/4	9.50	6.33	9.0	0	0
List A	167	-	-	-	-	-	-	-	-	-	-
Twenty20	109	-	-	-	-	-	-	-	-	-	-

GRAHAM ONIONS

RHB RFM W5 MVP14

DURHAM

FULL NAME: Graham Onions
BORN: September 9, 1982, Gateshead
SQUAD NO: 9
HEIGHT: 6ft 2in
NICKNAME: Bunny, Wills
EDUCATION: St Thomas More RC School, Blaydon
TEAMS: England, Dolphins, Durham, Durham Cricket Board, England Lions, Marylebone Cricket Club
CAREER: Test: 2009; ODI: 2009; First-class: 2004; List A: 2003; T20: 2004

BEST BATTING: 41 Durham vs Yorkshire, Headingley, 2007
BEST BOWLING: 9-67 Durham vs Nottinghamshire, Nottingham, 2012

FAMILY TIES? My uncle used to play
WHO WOULD PLAY YOU IN A FILM OF YOUR LIFE? Russell Crowe
CAREER HIGHLIGHTS? My Test debut, taking nine wickets against Notts and the Test match against West Indies in 2012 after my serious back injury
SUPERSTITIONS? I lick my fingers before I bowl
BEST PLAYER IN COUNTY CRICKET? Joe Root
TIP FOR THE TOP? Ben Stokes
IF YOU WEREN'T A CRICKETER? I'd be struggling! Maybe a PE teacher
CRICKETING HEROES? Darren Gough, Dale Steyn
ACCOMPLISHMENTS? Swimming badges as a teenager
WHEN YOU RETIRE? I want to be a coach
FANTASY SLIP CORDON? Keeper: Daniel Radcliffe, 1st: Russell Crowe, 2nd: Gazza, 3rd: David Beckham, Gully: George Best
TWITTER FEED: @BunnyOnions

Batting	Mat	Inns	NO	Runs	HS	Ave	SR	100	50	Ct	St
Tests	9	10	7	30	17*	10.00	30.92	0	0	0	0
ODIs	4	1	0	1	1	1.00	50.00	0	0	1	0
First-class	120	154	56	1304	41	13.30	52.39	0	0	27	0
List A	78	29	8	123	19	5.85	71.51	0	0	12	0
Twenty20	42	12	5	61	31	8.71	107.01	0	0	10	0

Bowling	Mat	Balls	Runs	Wkts	BBI	BBM	Ave	Econ	SR	5w	10
Tests	9	1606	957	32	5/38	7/102	29.90	3.57	50.1	1	0
ODIs	4	204	185	4	2/58	2/58	46.25	5.44	51.0	0	0
First-class	120	20342	11568	447	9/67		25.87	3.41	45.5	21	3
List A	78	3223	2726	87	4/45	4/45	31.33	5.07	37.0	0	0
Twenty20	42	888	993	31	3/25	3/25	32.03	6.70	28.6	0	0

FULL NAME: Craig Overton
BORN: April 10, 1994, Barnstaple, Devon
SQUAD NO: 12
HEIGHT: 6ft 6in
NICKNAME: Goober, Jeff
EDUCATION: West Buckland School
TEAMS: Devon, Devon Under-11s, Devon Under-13s, Devon Under-15s, Devon Under-17s, Devon Under-19s, Devon Under-21s, England Lions, England Under-19s, Somerset, Somerset 2nd XI
CAREER: First-class: 2012; List A: 2012

SOMERSET

BEST BATTING: 50 Somerset vs Durham, Taunton, 2012
BEST BOWLING: 4-38 Somerset vs Durham, Chester-le-Street, 2012

WHO WOULD PLAY YOU IN A FILM OF YOUR LIFE? Brad Pitt
CAREER HIGHLIGHTS? Taking 4-32 against Durham
SUPERSTITIONS? I put my left pad on first, then my right
MOST MARKED CHARACTERISTIC? My height
BEST PLAYER IN COUNTY CRICKET? Ben Stokes
TIPS FOR THE TOP? Tom Helm and Craig Miles
IF YOU WEREN'T A CRICKETER? I'd be studying at university
DESERT ISLAND DISC? Any Avicii Album
FAVOURITE TV? The Big Bang Theory
CRICKETING HEROES? Andrew Flintoff
NON-CRICKETING HEROES? David Beckham and Rory McIlroy
ACCOMPLISHMENTS? Passing my A-Levels, which I took in Bangladesh!
WHEN YOU RETIRE? I'd like to coach
SURPRISING FACT? My brother Jamie dropped me on my head when we were younger!
FANTASY SLIP CORDON? Keeper: Usain Bolt, 1st: Me, 2nd: David Beckham, 3rd: James Corden, Gully: Beyoncé
TWITTER FEED: @craigoverton12

Batting	Mat	Inns	NO	Runs	HS	Ave	SR	100	50	Ct	St
First-class	8	9	1	83	50	10.37	48.53	0	1	4	0
List A	7	7	1	69	20	11.50	82.14	0	0	3	0

Bowling	Mat	Balls	Runs	Wkts	BBI	BBM	Ave	Econ	SR	5w	10
First-class	8	817	430	13	4/38	6/87	33.07	3.15	62.8	0	0
List A	7	324	262	4	2/30	2/30	65.50	4.85	81.0	0	0

SOMERSET

FULL NAME: Jamie Overton
BORN: April 10, 1994, Barnstaple, Devon
SQUAD NO: 11
HEIGHT: 6ft 5in
NICKNAME: Goober, J
EDUCATION: West Buckland School
TEAMS: Devon, Devon Under-13s, Devon Under-14s, Devon Under-15s, Devon Under-17s, England Lions, England Under-19s, Somerset, Somerset 2nd XI
CAREER: First-class: 2012; List A: 2012

BEST BATTING: 34* Somerset vs Surrey, The Oval, 2012
BEST BOWLING: 6-95 Somerset vs Middlesex, Taunton, 2013

FAMILY TIES? My dad played for Devon and my twin brother [Craig] also plays for Somerset
WHO WOULD PLAY YOU IN A FILM OF YOUR LIFE? Daniel Craig
CAREER HIGHLIGHTS? Signing my contract with Somerset in 2012
SUPERSTITIONS? I always put my left pad on first and I always wear a jumper when batting
MOST MARKED CHARACTERISTIC? Being a twin
BEST PLAYER IN COUNTY CRICKET? Nick Compton
TIPS FOR THE TOP? Tom Helm, Tymal Mills, Matt Dunn
IF YOU WEREN'T A CRICKETER? I would be at university studying Sports Science
DESERT ISLAND DISC? Rihanna – Unapologetic
FAVOURITE TV? EastEnders
BIGGEST DRESSING DOWN YOU'VE RECEIVED? Getting a warning from the ICC in the U19 World Cup
CRICKETING HEROES? James Anderson, Andrew Flintoff
NON-CRICKETING HEROES? Rory McIlroy
WHEN YOU RETIRE? I would like to become a coach or a teacher
SURPRISING FACT? I play my club cricket at the same club as the late David Shepherd
FANTASY SLIP CORDON? Keeper: Me, 1st: Rory McIlroy, 2nd: Jack Whitehall, 3rd: Chris Ashton, Gully: Jamie Laing
TWITTER FEED: @JamieOverton

Batting	Mat	Inns	NO	Runs	HS	Ave	SR	100	50	Ct	St
First-class	16	24	8	186	34*	11.62	73.51	0	0	1	0
List A	14	7	4	47	14	15.66	95.91	0	0	6	0

Bowling	Mat	Balls	Runs	Wkts	BBI	BBM	Ave	Econ	SR	5w	10
First-class	16	2225	1450	41	6/95	7/134	35.36	3.91	54.2	1	0
List A	14	516	540	20	4/42	4/42	27.00	6.27	25.8	0	0

FULL NAME: William Thomas Owen
BORN: September 2, 1988, St Asaph, Flintshire, Wales
SQUAD NO: 34
HEIGHT: 6ft
NICKNAME: Swillo
EDUCATION: Prestatyn High School
TEAMS: Glamorgan, Glamorgan 2nd XI, Wales Minor Counties
CAREER: First-class: 2007; List A: 2010; T20: 2010

GLAMORGAN

BEST BATTING: 69 Glamorgan vs Derbyshire, Derby, 2011
BEST BOWLING: 5-124 Glamorgan vs Middlesex, Cardiff, 2011

CAREER HIGHLIGHTS? Claiming a five-wicket haul on my one-day debut against the Unicorns and scoring my maiden first-class fifty against Derby in 2011
CRICKETING HEROES? Simon Jones, being a Welsh lad growing up watching the 2005 Ashes series
BEST PLAYER IN COUNTY CRICKET? Marcus Trescothick is a prize scalp
TIP FOR THE TOP? Andrew Salter
IF YOU WEREN'T A CRICKETER? I'd be a policeman
WHEN RAIN STOPS PLAY? On the pool table in our dressing room – the time flies by!
FAVOURITE TV? Eastbound And Down
FAVOURITE FILM? Cool Runnings
FAVOURITE BOOK? Anything by Robert G Barrett
DREAM HOLIDAY? Barbados on a beach
GUILTY PLEASURES? Chocolate cookies
FANTASY SLIP CORDON? Keeper: Will Bragg, 1st: Ricky Gervais, 2nd: Michael McIntyre, 3rd: Darren Hughes
TWITTER FEED: @swillo88

Batting	Mat	Inns	NO	Runs	HS	Ave	SR	100	50	Ct	St
First-class	18	21	6	270	69	18.00	66.99	0	1	5	0
List A	25	13	7	78	13*	13.00	91.76	0	0	6	0
Twenty20	13	1	0	8	8	8.00	114.28	0	0	0	0

Bowling	Mat	Balls	Runs	Wkts	BBI	BBM	Ave	Econ	SR	5w	10
First-class	18	2368	1718	41	5/124	6/61	41.90	4.35	57.7	1	0
List A	25	771	782	37	5/49	5/49	21.13	6.08	20.8	1	0
Twenty20	13	189	291	8	3/21	3/21	36.37	9.23	23.6	0	0

TONY PALLADINO

RHB RMF W2

FULL NAME: Antonio Paul Palladino
BORN: June 29, 1983, Tower Hamlets, London
SQUAD NO: 28
HEIGHT: 5ft 11in
NICKNAME: Dino, Italian Stallion, Pallas
EDUCATION: Cardinal Pole Sixth Form College; Anglia Polytechnic University, Cambridge
TEAMS: Namibia, British Universities, Cambridge UCCE, Derbyshire, Essex, Essex 2nd XI, Essex Cricket Board
CAREER: First-class: 2003; List A: 2003; T20: 2005

BEST BATTING: 106 Derbyshire vs Australia A, Derby, 2012
BEST BOWLING: 7-53 Derbyshire vs Kent, Derby, 2012
COUNTY CAP: 2012 (Derbyshire)

FAMILY TIES? My dad played cricket in the Kent League
WHO WOULD PLAY YOU IN A FILM OF YOUR LIFE? Christian Bale
CAREER HIGHLIGHTS? Taking a hat-trick vs Leicestershire, my first-class hundred vs Australia A, taking 7-53 vs Kent and winning Division Two of the County Championship with Derbyshire
SUPERSTITIONS? I wear black socks, my watch on my right wrist and have a sweatband on the left
MOST MARKED CHARACTERISTIC? I'm a very bad loser
BEST PLAYER IN COUNTY CRICKET? Chris Woakes
TIPS FOR THE TOP? Ben Cotton and Tom Knight
DESERT ISLAND DISC? Edvard Grieg – In The Hall Of The Mountain King
CRICKETING HEROES? Ian Botham, Graeme Welch, Mark Turner and Tim Groenewald
WHEN YOU RETIRE? Sports writing, coaching and enjoying life
CRICKET RULE YOU'D CHANGE? I'd allow the use of sweets to shine the ball. It's been going on forever but now they've decided to get strict on it
SURPRISING FACT? I have English, Irish, Scottish and Italian heritage

Batting	Mat	Inns	NO	Runs	HS	Ave	SR	100	50	Ct	St
First-class	90	123	27	1438	106	14.97	47.78	1	5	26	0
List A	44	26	5	195	31	9.28	84.78	0	0	5	0
Twenty20	16	5	3	21	8*	10.50	87.50	0	0	2	0

Bowling	Mat	Balls	Runs	Wkts	BBI	BBM	Ave	Econ	SR	5w	10
First-class	90	14123	7448	248	7/53		30.03	3.16	56.9	10	0
List A	44	1650	1466	41	4/32	4/32	35.75	5.33	40.2	0	0
Twenty20	16	287	347	22	4/21	4/21	15.77	7.25	13.0	0	0

MONTY PANESAR
LHB SLA W6

FULL NAME: Mudhsuden Singh Panesar
BORN: April 25, 1982, Luton, Bedfordshire
SQUAD NO: 55
HEIGHT: 6ft 1in
EDUCATION: Bedford Modern School; Stopsley High School, Luton, Bedfordshire; Loughborough University
TEAMS: England, British Universities, England Lions, England Under-19s, Essex, Lions, Loughborough UCCE, Marylebone Cricket Club, Northamptonshire, Sussex
CAREER: Test: 2006; ODI: 2007; T20I: 2007; First-class: 2001; List A: 2002; T20: 2006

ESSEX

BEST BATTING: 46* Sussex vs Middlesex, Hove, 2010
BEST BOWLING: 7-60 Sussex vs Somerset, Taunton, 2012
COUNTY CAPS: 2006 (Northamptonshire); 2010 (Sussex)

TWITTER FEED: @MontyPanesar
NOTES: His first Test wicket was Sachin Tendulkar. Claimed a five-wicket haul (and eight wickets in all) in his first Ashes Test, at Perth in 2006. Helped secure an improbable draw in the first Ashes Test at Cardiff in 2009, batting with James Anderson for 37 minutes to deny Australia. Moved to Sussex after 10 years at Northamptonshire ahead of the 2010 season and took 200 first-class wickets at 27.37 in his four years with the club. At the end of 2012 he took 17 wickets in three Tests, including 11 at Mumbai, as England won in India for the first time in 28 years. A member of the Ashes touring party this winter, he featured in the defeats at Adelaide and Melbourne. Having spent time on loan at Essex in 2013, Panesar signed a two-year deal with the club in October last year

Batting	Mat	Inns	NO	Runs	HS	Ave	SR	100	50	Ct	St
Tests	50	68	23	220	26	4.88	29.37	0	0	10	0
ODIs	26	8	3	26	13	5.20	28.57	0	0	3	0
T20Is	1	1	0	1	1	1.00	50.00	0	0	0	0
First-class	197	243	80	1370	46*	8.40	34.14	0	0	38	0
List A	84	29	13	141	17*	8.81	56.17	0	0	14	0
Twenty20	31	7	2	7	3*	1.40	46.66	0	0	3	0

Bowling	Mat	Balls	Runs	Wkts	BBI	BBM	Ave	Econ	SR	5w	10
Tests	50	12475	5797	167	6/37	11/210	34.71	2.78	74.7	12	2
ODIs	26	1308	980	24	3/25	3/25	40.83	4.49	54.5	0	0
T20Is	1	24	40	2	2/40	2/40	20.00	10.00	12.0	0	0
First-class	197	44378	20167	644	7/60		31.31	2.72	68.9	34	5
List A	84	3701	2865	81	5/20	5/20	35.37	4.64	45.6	1	0
Twenty20	31	618	758	27	3/14	3/14	28.07	7.35	22.8	0	0

MATTHEW PARDOE

LHB LM

WORCESTERSHIRE

FULL NAME: Matthew Graham Pardoe
BORN: January 5, 1991, Stourbridge, Worcestershire
SQUAD NO: 19
HEIGHT: 6ft 1in
NICKNAME: Pards
EDUCATION: Haybridge High School and Sixth Form
TEAMS: Southern Rocks, Worcestershire, Worcestershire 2nd XI
CAREER: First-class: 2011; List A: 2011; T20: 2013

BEST BATTING: 102 Worcestershire vs Glamorgan, Worcester, 2013
BEST BOWLING: 2-34 Southern Rocks vs Mountaineers, Mutare, 2013

FAMILY TIES? All the family play or played for Belbroughton Cricket Club
WHO WOULD PLAY YOU IN A FILM OF YOUR LIFE? Matthew McConaughey or Channing Tatum
CAREER HIGHLIGHTS? My maiden first-class century vs Glamorgan and playing tour matches against Australia and South Africa
SUPERSTITIONS? I always put my front pad on first
MOST MARKED CHARACTERISTIC? Grit and determination
BEST PLAYER IN COUNTY CRICKET? Moeen Ali
IF YOU WEREN'T A CRICKETER? I'd be farming or teaching
DESERT ISLAND DISC? A cheese mixtape
FAVOURITE TV? Suits
CRICKETING HEROES? Matthew Hayden, Graeme Hick, AB de Villiers
NON-CRICKETING HEROES? Tiger Woods, Chris Hoy, Paul Scholes
ACCOMPLISHMENTS? Swimming for my county and dancing at the Nationals (ballroom and Latin)
SURPRISING FACT? I've never had a nose bleed
TWITTER FEED: @pardoe465

Batting	Mat	Inns	NO	Runs	HS	Ave	SR	100	50	Ct	St
First-class	47	86	5	2007	102	24.77	36.57	1	13	21	0
List A	5	5	0	118	42	23.60	55.14	0	0	3	0
Twenty20	1	1	0	1	1	1.00	100.00	0	0	-	-

Bowling	Mat	Balls	Runs	Wkts	BBI	BBM	Ave	Econ	SR	5w	10
First-class	47	239	119	3	2/34	2/34	39.66	2.98	79.6	0	0
List A	5	18	9	1	1/9	1/9	9.00	3.00	18.0	0	0
Twenty20	1	-	-	-	-	-	-	-	-	-	-

STEPHEN PARRY   RHB SLA

FULL NAME: Stephen David Parry
BORN: January 12, 1986, Manchester
SQUAD NO: 4
HEIGHT: 6ft
NICKNAME: Pazza
EDUCATION: Audenshaw High School,
Greater Manchester
TEAMS: England, Cumberland, England
Lions, Lancashire, Lancashire 2nd XI
CAREER: ODI: 2014; T20I: 2014; First-class:
2007; List A: 2009; T20: 2009

LANCASHIRE

BEST BATTING: 20 Lancashire vs Kent, Canterbury, 2013
BEST BOWLING: 5-23 Lancashire vs Durham UCCE, Durham University, 2007

CAREER HIGHLIGHTS? Playing for Lancashire and England
CRICKETING HEROES? Shane Warne
NON-CRICKETING HEROES? Muhammad Ali
BEST PLAYER IN COUNTY CRICKET? Marcus Trescothick
TIP FOR THE TOP? Jos Buttler
IF YOU WEREN'T A CRICKETER? I'd be fishing or travelling the world
WHEN RAIN STOPS PLAY? I spend my time relaxing or working on my game
FAVOURITE TV? Sky Sports News
FAVOURITE FILM? Hangover, Man On Fire
DREAM HOLIDAY? Barbados
ACCOMPLISHMENTS? Running a marathon
SURPRISING SKILL? I'm pretty much an elite table-tennis player
GUILTY PLEASURES? San Carlo for a meal and a bottle of Sancerre white wine
TWITTER FEED: @SDParry86

Batting	Mat	Inns	NO	Runs	HS	Ave	SR	100	50	Ct	St
ODIs	2	-	-	-	-	-	-	-	-	0	0
First-class	6	5	1	40	20	10.00	32.78	0	0	1	0
List A	56	24	9	222	31	14.80	79.85	0	0	15	0
Twenty20	56	14	8	53	11	8.83	103.92	0	0	7	0

Bowling	Mat	Balls	Runs	Wkts	BBI	BBM	Ave	Econ	SR	5w	10
ODIs	2	114	92	4	3/32	3/32	23.00	4.84	28.5	0	0
First-class	6	916	453	14	5/23	5/46	32.35	2.96	65.4	1	0
List A	56	2380	1973	69	5/17	5/17	28.59	4.97	34.4	1	0
Twenty20	56	1236	1414	63	4/23	4/23	22.44	6.86	19.6	0	0

JEETAN PATEL

RHB OB W2 MVP12

WARWICKSHIRE

FULL NAME: Jeetan Patel
BORN: May 7, 1980, Wellington, New Zealand
SQUAD NO: 5
HEIGHT: 5ft 11in
NICKNAME: Jeets
TEAMS: New Zealand, Warwickshire, Wellington
CAREER: Test: 2006; ODI: 2005; T20I: 2005; First-class: 2000; List A: 1999; T20: 2005

BEST BATTING: 120 Warwickshire vs Yorkshire, Birmingham, 2009
BEST BOWLING: 7-75 Warwickshire vs Somerset, Taunton, 2012
COUNTY CAP: 2012

NOTES: Took 5-145 on debut for Wellington against Auckland in 1999/00. Made his New Zealand Test debut at Cape Town against South Africa in April 2006 and took 3-117 in 42 overs, dismissing Graeme Smith, Boeta Dippenaar and AB de Villiers. Took Test-best figures of 5-110 against West Indies at Napier in 2008. Overseas player for Warwickshire in 2009, 2011, 2012 and 2013, taking 126 first-class wickets at 27.50 for the club, including eight five-wicket hauls. Took 52 wickets at 30.01 and scored 438 runs at 31.28 in the County Championship last season and returns as Warwickshire's overseas player for 2014

Batting	Mat	Inns	NO	Runs	HS	Ave	SR	100	50	Ct	St
Tests	19	30	7	276	27*	12.00	46.46	0	0	12	0
ODIs	39	13	7	88	34	14.66	58.66	0	0	12	0
T20Is	11	4	1	9	5	3.00	64.28	0	0	4	0
First-class	162	202	55	3260	120	22.17		1	17	77	0
List A	148	78	25	521	50	9.83		0	1	56	0
Twenty20	97	32	8	99	12	4.12	101.02	0	0	29	0

Bowling	Mat	Balls	Runs	Wkts	BBI	BBM	Ave	Econ	SR	5w	10
Tests	19	4723	2520	52	5/110	6/151	48.46	3.20	90.8	1	0
ODIs	39	1804	1513	42	3/11	3/11	36.02	5.03	42.9	0	0
T20Is	11	199	269	16	3/20	3/20	16.81	8.11	12.4	0	0
First-class	162	32205	15825	411	7/75		38.50	2.94	78.3	15	1
List A	148	6910	5371	159	4/16	4/16	33.77	4.66	43.4	0	0
Twenty20	97	1821	2215	90	4/27	4/27	24.61	7.29	20.2	0	0

RAVI PATEL

RHB SLA

FULL NAME: Ravi Hasmukh Patel
BORN: August 4, 1991, Harrow, Middlesex
SQUAD NO: 36
HEIGHT: 5ft 10in
NICKNAME: Rav
EDUCATION: Merchant Taylors' School;
Loughborough University
TEAMS: Loughborough MCCU, Middlesex,
Middlesex 2nd XI
CAREER: First-class: 2010; List A: 2010; T20:
2013

MIDDLESEX

BEST BATTING: 26* Middlesex vs Warwickshire, Uxbridge, 2013
BEST BOWLING: 5-69 Middlesex vs Cambridge MCCU, Cambridge, 2013

FAMILY TIES? My dad played university cricket in India
WHO WOULD PLAY YOU IN A FILM OF YOUR LIFE? Harry Podmore
CAREER HIGHLIGHTS? Making my T20 debut for Middlesex in front of a full house at Lord's
vs Essex in 2013. Making my County Championship debut for Middlesex vs Warwickshire at
Edgbaston in 2012. Getting Ricky Ponting out!
MOST MARKED CHARACTERISTIC? People say I'm quite funny
BEST PLAYER IN COUNTY CRICKET? Sam Robson
TIP FOR THE TOP? Ryan Higgins
DESERT ISLAND DISC? MMG – Self Made Volume 2
CRICKETING HEROES? Pragyan Ojha, Monty Panesar, Murali Kartik
NON-CRICKETING HEROES? Leonardo DiCaprio, Cristiano Ronaldo
ACCOMPLISHMENTS? Getting good A-Levels (ABB). Grade 5 on piano
SURPRISING FACT? I can speak decent German
CRICKET RULE YOU'D CHANGE? I'd make the minimum boundary length 90 yards on all
grounds to help spinners!
TWITTER FEED: @ravi36patel

Batting	Mat	Inns	NO	Runs	HS	Ave	SR	100	50	Ct	St
First-class	11	17	7	135	26*	13.50	40.17	0	0	3	0
List A	3	-	-	-	-	-	-	-	-	0	0
Twenty20	8	1	0	1	1	1.00	33.33	0	0	0	0

Bowling	Mat	Balls	Runs	Wkts	BBI	BBM	Ave	Econ	SR	5w	10
First-class	11	2121	1119	40	5/69	8/198	27.97	3.16	53.0	1	0
List A	3	114	128	4	2/41	2/41	32.00	6.73	28.5	0	0
Twenty20	8	168	186	10	4/18	4/18	18.60	6.64	16.8	0	0

SAMIT PATEL

RHB SLA R2 MVP2

FULL NAME: Samit Rohit Patel
BORN: November 30, 1984, Leicester
SQUAD NO: 21
HEIGHT: 5ft 8in
NICKNAME: Sarnie, Slippery
EDUCATION: Worksop College
TEAMS: England, England Lions, England Under-19s, Nottinghamshire
CAREER: Test: 2012; ODI: 2008; T20I: 2011; First-class: 2002; List A: 2002; T20: 2003

BEST BATTING: 256 Nottinghamshire vs Durham MCCU, Nottingham, 2013
BEST BOWLING: 7-68 Nottinghamshire vs Hampshire, Southampton, 2011
COUNTY CAP: 2008

FAMILY TIES? My dad played league cricket and my brother [Akhil] played for Notts for two years
CAREER HIGHLIGHTS? Making my ODI and Test debuts. Taking five wickets against South Africa at The Oval and scoring 70 off 40 balls at Chandigarh against India. Scoring 68 against Sri Lanka in the World T20
SUPERSTITIONS? I always put my right pad on first and always touch the floor before I cross the line as I am walking out to bat
BEST PLAYER IN COUNTY CRICKET? Chris Read
TIPS FOR THE TOP? Sam Billings and Joe Root
CRICKETING HEROES? Sachin Tendulkar, Stephen Fleming
SURPRISING FACT? I bowl left-handed but throw right-handed

Batting	Mat	Inns	NO	Runs	HS	Ave	SR	100	50	Ct	St
Tests	5	7	0	109	33	15.57	42.41	0	0	2	0
ODIs	36	22	7	482	70*	32.13	93.23	0	1	7	0
T20Is	18	14	2	189	67	15.75	109.24	0	1	3	0
First-class	129	201	13	7420	256	39.46	63.33	18	36	79	0
List A	185	159	25	4480	129*	33.43	83.69	3	24	53	0
Twenty20	129	114	20	2288	84*	24.34	123.54	0	14	39	0

Bowling	Mat	Balls	Runs	Wkts	BBI	BBM	Ave	Econ	SR	5w	10
Tests	5	606	257	4	2/27	2/36	64.25	2.54	151.5	0	0
ODIs	36	1187	1091	24	5/41	5/41	45.45	5.51	49.4	1	0
T20Is	18	252	321	7	2/6	2/6	45.85	7.64	36.0	0	0
First-class	129	14770	7491	185	7/68		40.49	3.04	79.8	3	1
List A	185	5884	5162	171	6/13	6/13	30.18	5.26	34.4	2	0
Twenty20	129	2244	2698	98	3/11	3/11	27.53	7.21	22.8	0	0

FULL NAME: Steven Andrew Patterson
BORN: October 3, 1983, Beverley, Yorkshire
SQUAD NO: 17
HEIGHT: 6ft 4in
NICKNAME: Dead Man, Patto
EDUCATION: Malet Lambert School; St Mary's Sixth Form College; Leeds University
TEAMS: Yorkshire, Yorkshire 2nd XI, Yorkshire Cricket Board
CAREER: First-class: 2005; List A: 2003; T20: 2009

YORKSHIRE

BEST BATTING: 53 Yorkshire vs Sussex, Hove, 2011
BEST BOWLING: 5-43 Yorkshire vs Nottinghamshire, Nottingham, 2010
COUNTY CAP: 2012

FAMILY TIES? My grandad played for Durham before World War II
CAREER HIGHLIGHTS? Making my Championship debut at Scarborough, receiving my 1st XI cap and playing in the Champions League T20
BEST PLAYER IN COUNTY CRICKET? Graham Onions
TIP FOR THE TOP? Gary Ballance
IF YOU WEREN'T A CRICKETER? I'd probably be working in finance
FAVOURITE TV? Gold Rush
CRICKETING HEROES? Glenn McGrath, Shaun Pollock
NON-CRICKETING HEROES? My grandad
ACCOMPLISHMENTS? Having my son
WHEN YOU RETIRE? I'll do lots of skiing
CRICKET RULE YOU'D CHANGE? There should be fewer overs in a day!
FANTASY SLIP CORDON? Keeper: Morgan Freeman, 1st: Tiger Woods, 2nd: Me, 3rd: Prince Harry, Gully: Alex Ferguson

Batting	Mat	Inns	NO	Runs	HS	Ave	SR	100	50	Ct	St
First-class	73	82	28	807	53	14.94	32.91	0	1	13	0
List A	52	21	15	128	25*	21.33		0	0	8	0
Twenty20	26	5	3	5	3*	2.50	50.00	0	0	4	0

Bowling	Mat	Balls	Runs	Wkts	BBI	BBM	Ave	Econ	SR	5w	10
First-class	73	11111	5469	192	5/43	8/94	28.48	2.95	57.8	3	0
List A	52	2235	1925	65	6/32	6/32	29.61	5.16	34.3	1	0
Twenty20	26	545	785	24	4/30	4/30	32.70	8.64	22.7	0	0

DAVID PAYNE

RHB LFM

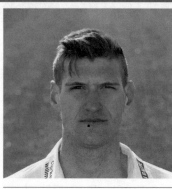

FULL NAME: David Alan Payne
BORN: February 15, 1991, Poole, Dorset
SQUAD NO: 14
HEIGHT: 6ft 2in
NICKNAME: Sid
EDUCATION: Lytchett Matravers Primary School; Lytchett Minster Secondary School and Sixth Form
TEAMS: Dorset, England Development XI, England Under-19s, Gloucestershire, Gloucestershire 2nd XI
CAREER: First-class: 2011; List A: 2009; T20: 2010

BEST BATTING: 62 Gloucestershire vs Glamorgan, Bristol, 2011
BEST BOWLING: 6-26 Gloucestershire vs Leicestershire, Bristol, 2011
COUNTY CAP: 2011

FAMILY TIES? My dad and brother played club cricket
WHO WOULD PLAY YOU IN A FILM OF YOUR LIFE? Ryan Gosling
CAREER HIGHLIGHTS? My professional debut for Gloucestershire, my first-class debut and six-wicket haul, going to the U19 World Cup and holding record one-day figures for Gloucestershire [7-29]
MOST MARKED CHARACTERISTIC? My quiff
BEST PLAYER IN COUNTY CRICKET? Ben Stokes
TIPS FOR THE TOP? Matt Dunn, Ned Eckersley
FAVOURITE TV? Friends, The Big Bang Theory, Take Me Out, Geordie Shore, Celebrity Juice
CRICKETING HEROES? Andrew Flintoff
NON-CRICKETING HEROES? David Beckham, Ryan Gosling, Justin Timberlake
ACCOMPLISHMENTS? Playing for AFC Bournemouth Academy
WHEN YOU RETIRE? I want to own my own clothing company
SURPRISING FACT? I probably go clothes shopping once every two weeks, minimum
CRICKET RULE YOU'D CHANGE? There should be 80 overs in a day for a four-day game
TWITTER FEED: @sidpayne7

Batting	Mat	Inns	NO	Runs	HS	Ave	SR	100	50	Ct	St
First-class	32	40	11	372	62	12.82	39.44	0	1	9	0
List A	36	14	11	56	18	18.66	74.66	0	0	10	0
Twenty20	23	11	5	29	10	4.83	96.66	0	0	2	0

Bowling	Mat	Balls	Runs	Wkts	BBI	BBM	Ave	Econ	SR	5w	10
First-class	32	4608	2719	82	6/26	9/96	33.15	3.54	56.1	2	0
List A	36	1409	1382	64	7/29	7/29	21.59	5.88	22.0	1	0
Twenty20	23	414	584	27	3/17	3/17	21.62	8.46	15.3	0	0

FULL NAME: Stephen David Peters
BORN: December 10, 1978, Harold Wood, Essex
SQUAD NO: 11
HEIGHT: 5ft 11in
NICKNAME: Pedro, Geezer
EDUCATION: Coopers' Company and Coborn School
TEAMS: Essex, Marylebone Cricket Club, Northamptonshire, Worcestershire
CAREER: First-class: 1996; List A: 1996; T20: 2003

NORTHAMPTONSHIRE

BEST BATTING: 222 Northamptonshire vs Glamorgan, Swansea, 2011
BEST BOWLING: 1-19 Essex vs Oxford UCCE, Chelmsford, 1999
COUNTY CAPS: 2002 (Worcestershire); 2007 (Northamptonshire); **BENEFIT YEAR:** 2013 (Northamptonshire)

WHO WOULD PLAY YOU IN A FILM OF YOUR LIFE? George Clooney
CAREER HIGHLIGHTS? Winning the U19 World Cup with England in 1998. Any hundred I score. Winning the Benson & Hedges Cup with Essex in 1998
SUPERSTITIONS? Habits more than superstitions. I did have loads but I binned them
MOST MARKED CHARACTERISTIC? I'm moody, stubborn and make terrible jokes
BEST PLAYER IN COUNTY CRICKET? Graham Onions
TIP FOR THE TOP? Rob Newton
DESERT ISLAND DISC? Nickelback
FAVOURITE TV? Gavin And Stacey
BIGGEST DRESSING DOWN YOU'VE RECEIVED? No dressing downs as such but plenty of disagreements! Matthew Hayden gave me an hour-long serve once when batting
SURPRISING FACT? I'm an international fly fisherman
FANTASY SLIP CORDON? Keeper: Kate Beckinsale, 1st: Natalie Imbruglia, 2nd: Halle Berry, 3rd: My wife
TWITTER FEED: @pedropeters222

Batting	Mat	Inns	NO	Runs	HS	Ave	SR	100	50	Ct	St
First-class	236	397	31	13168	222	35.97		31	64	184	0
List A	173	160	10	3386	107	22.57		2	20	47	0
Twenty20	24	20	3	300	61*	17.64	98.36	0	1	7	0

Bowling	Mat	Balls	Runs	Wkts	BBI	BBM	Ave	Econ	SR	5w	10
First-class	236	35	31	1	1/19		31.00	5.31	35.0	0	0
List A	173	-	-	-	-	-	-	-	-	-	-
Twenty20	24	-	-	-	-	-	-	-	-	-	-

ALVIRO PETERSEN   RHB OB R1

SOMERSET

FULL NAME: Alviro Nathan Petersen
BORN: November 25, 1980, Port Elizabeth,
Cape Province, South Africa
SQUAD NO: 73
HEIGHT: 5ft 10in
NICKNAME: Viro
TEAMS: South Africa, Essex, Glamorgan,
Lions, North West, Northerns, Somerset,
Titans
CAREER: Test: 2010; ODI: 2006; T20I: 2010;
First-class: 2000; List A: 2000; T20: 2004

BEST BATTING: 210 Glamorgan vs Surrey, The Oval, 2011
BEST BOWLING: 2-7 Northerns vs Easterns, Benoni, 2002
COUNTY CAP: 2011 (Glamorgan)

NOTES: Hit 80 against Zimbabwe in his second ODI. Made his Test debut in February 2010,
against India at Kolkata, scoring exactly 100 in his first innings and becoming only the third
South African to score a century on Test debut. Skippered Glamorgan in 2011. After a year
out of the South African side he was recalled in January 2012, scoring a hundred against
Sri Lanka in January, and was named as Graeme Smith's opening partner in the Test series
that took place in New Zealand in March of the same year. Made 235 runs at 21 in seven
Championship matches for Essex in 2012 before signing for Somerset ahead of the 2013
campaign. International commitments restricted him to just six first-class appearances last
year but he scored 562 first-class runs in that time, including two centuries. Expected to be
available for Somerset for the duration of the 2014 season

Batting	Mat	Inns	NO	Runs	HS	Ave	SR	100	50	Ct	St
Tests	30	54	3	1890	182	37.05	51.90	5	8	24	0
ODIs	21	19	1	504	80	28.00	82.62	0	4	5	0
T20Is	2	2	0	14	8	7.00	73.68	0	0	1	0
First-class	170	302	15	11368	210	39.60		34	46	131	0
List A	163	156	11	4859	145*	33.51		7	29	61	0
Twenty20	93	87	13	2091	84*	28.25	124.02	0	15	47	0

Bowling	Mat	Balls	Runs	Wkts	BBI	BBM	Ave	Econ	SR	5w	10
Tests	30	114	62	1	1/2	1/2	62.00	3.26	114.0	0	0
ODIs	21	6	7	0	-	-	-	7.00	-	0	0
T20Is	2	-	-	-	-	-	-	-	-	-	-
First-class	170	1256	668	12	2/7		55.66	3.19	104.6	0	0
List A	163	382	348	8	2/48	2/48	43.50	5.46	47.7	0	0
Twenty20	93	199	215	9	1/4	1/4	23.88	6.48	22.1	0	0

MARK PETTINI RHB RM R1

FULL NAME: Mark Lewis Pettini
BORN: August 7, 1983, Brighton, Sussex
SQUAD NO: 24
HEIGHT: 5ft 11in
NICKNAME: Swampy
EDUCATION: Comberton Village College;
Hills Road Sixth Form College; Cardiff
University
TEAMS: England Under-19s, Essex,
Mountaineers
CAREER: First-class: 2001; List A: 2001; T20:
2003

ESSEX

BEST BATTING: 209 Mountaineers vs Matabeleland Tuskers, Bulawayo, 2014
BEST BOWLING: 1-72 Essex vs Leicestershire, Leicester, 2012
COUNTY CAP: 2006

CRICKETING HEROES? Graham Gooch, Andy Flower, Ronnie Irani
TIPS FOR THE TOP? Adam Wheater, Tom Westley
OTHER SPORTS PLAYED? I play a bit of darts
OTHER SPORTS FOLLOWED? Football (Liverpool)
FAVOURITE BAND? The White Stripes, Foo Fighters, Editors
RELAXATIONS? Fishing, surfing, travelling, music
CAREER HIGHLIGHTS? Winning two Pro40 titles with Essex, being made Essex captain in
2007 and winning the FP Trophy in 2008

Batting	Mat	Inns	NO	Runs	HS	Ave	SR	100	50	Ct	St
First-class	139	233	36	6955	209	35.30	47.86	9	41	99	0
List A	152	141	10	3656	144	27.90	85.66	6	22	58	0
Twenty20	95	91	6	2221	87	26.12	127.20	0	13	32	0

Bowling	Mat	Balls	Runs	Wkts	BBI	BBM	Ave	Econ	SR	5w	10
First-class	139	132	263	1	1/72	1/72	263.00	11.95	132.0	0	0
List A	152	-	-	-	-	-	-	-	-	-	-
Twenty20	95	-	-	-	-	-	-	-	-	-	-

ESSEX

FULL NAME: Timothy James Phillips
BORN: March 13, 1981, Cambridge
SQUAD NO: 23
HEIGHT: 6ft 1in
NICKNAME: Pips
EDUCATION: Felsted School; Durham University
TEAMS: Durham UCCE, England Under-19s, Essex, Essex 2nd XI, Essex Cricket Board
CAREER: First-class: 1999; List A: 1999; T20: 2006

BEST BATTING: 89 Essex vs Worcestershire, Worcester, 2005
BEST BOWLING: 5-41 Essex vs Derbyshire, Chelmsford, 2006
COUNTY CAP: 2006

FAMILY TIES? My father played in the Manchester leagues and then some serious village cricket and and my brother Nick represented Essex at U16 level
CAREER HIGHLIGHTS? Representing England at the U19 World Cup in 2000, earning my 1st XI cap at Essex in 2006 and winning one-day trophies with Essex
CRICKETING HEROES? Brian Lara and Graham Thorpe for batting, Phil Tufnell and Daniel Vettori for bowling
NON-CRICKETING HEROES? Michael Johnson for his unique and amazing running technique. He also wrote a great book called Slaying The Dragon. And Jack White (The White Stripes) – serious guitar player!
TIPS FOR THE TOP? Adam Wheater and Reece Topley
IF YOU WEREN'T A CRICKETER? I'd be splitting my time between working and playing golf
WHEN RAIN STOPS PLAY? Normally playing some cards and consequently making Ryan ten Doeschate coffee all day long
FAVOURITE BOOK? Catcher In The Rye by JD Salinger
ACCOMPLISHMENTS? Completing a degree at Durham University
TWITTER FEED: @timphillips23

Batting	Mat	Inns	NO	Runs	HS	Ave	SR	100	50	Ct	St
First-class	76	106	17	1836	89	20.62		0	7	49	0
List A	81	47	22	489	58*	19.56		0	1	22	0
Twenty20	69	36	17	313	57*	16.47	119.92	0	1	33	0

Bowling	Mat	Balls	Runs	Wkts	BBI	BBM	Ave	Econ	SR	5w	10
First-class	76	9838	5896	128	5/41		46.06	3.59	76.8	1	0
List A	81	2556	2225	90	5/28	5/28	24.72	5.22	28.4	4	0
Twenty20	69	1076	1350	57	4/22	4/22	23.68	7.52	18.8	0	0

KEVIN PIETERSEN

RHB OB R3

FULL NAME: Kevin Peter Pietersen
BORN: June 27, 1980, Pietermaritzburg, Natal, South Africa
SQUAD NO: 24
HEIGHT: 6ft 4in
NICKNAME: KP, Kelves, Kapes, Kev
EDUCATION: Maritzburg College; UNISA
TEAMS: England, Deccan Chargers, Delhi Daredevils, Dolphins, Hampshire, Natal, Nottinghamshire, Royal Challengers Bangalore, Surrey
CAREER: Test: 2005; ODI: 2004; T20I: 2005; First-class: 1997; List A: 1999; T20: 2003

BEST BATTING: 254* Nottinghamshire vs Middlesex, Nottingham, 2002
BEST BOWLING: 4-31 Nottinghamshire vs Durham UCCE, Nottingham, 2003
COUNTY CAPS: 2002 (Nottinghamshire); 2005 (Hampshire)

TWITTER FEED: @KP24
NOTES: Born in South Africa, his first appearance in English cricket was as a bowling allrounder for Nottinghamshire in 2001. Qualifying for England via an English mother, he made his ODI debut in 2004 vs Zimbabwe at Harare and scored three centuries in his second ODI series, against South Africa in 2004. He became the fastest batsman ever to both 1,000 and 2,000 ODI runs. His Test debut came in the 2005 Ashes series, where his average of 52.55 was the highest of any England batsman. His Test-best score is 227, made against Australia at Adelaide in 2010. Had a brief spell as England captain in 2008/09. He was England's highest run-scorer in the 2013/14 Ashes in Australia but had his ECB contract terminated in February. He will play for Surrey in this year's NatWest T20 Blast and could be available to play for them in other competitions, depending on other commitments

Batting	Mat	Inns	NO	Runs	HS	Ave	SR	100	50	Ct	St
Tests	104	181	8	8181	227	47.28	61.72	23	35	62	0
ODIs	136	125	16	4440	130	40.73	86.58	9	25	40	0
T20Is	37	36	5	1176	79	37.93	141.51	0	7	14	0
First-class	213	352	23	16053	254*	48.79		49	70	151	0
List A	253	233	34	8112	147	40.76		15	46	85	0
Twenty20	85	82	12	2402	103*	34.31	137.10	1	13	35	0

Bowling	Mat	Balls	Runs	Wkts	BBI	BBM	Ave	Econ	SR	5w	10
Tests	104	1311	886	10	3/52	4/78	88.60	4.05	131.1	0	0
ODIs	136	400	370	7	2/22	2/22	52.85	5.55	57.1	0	0
T20Is	37	30	53	1	1/27	1/27	53.00	10.60	30.0	0	0
First-class	213	6431	3752	73	4/31		51.39	3.50	88.0	0	0
List A	253	2390	2122	41	3/14	3/14	51.75	5.32	58.2	0	0
Twenty20	85	384	514	17	3/33	3/33	30.23	8.03	22.5	0	0

STEFFAN PIOLET

RHB RM

SUSSEX

FULL NAME: Steffan Andreas Piolet
BORN: August 8, 1988, Redhill, Surrey
SQUAD NO: 21
HEIGHT: 6ft 1in
NICKNAME: Squiff, Geoff, Piles
EDUCATION: Warden Park School
TEAMS: Sussex, Sussex 2nd XI, Warwickshire, Worcestershire 2nd XI
CAREER: First-class: 2009; List A: 2009; T20: 2009

BEST BATTING: 30 Warwickshire vs Nottinghamshire, Nottingham, 2013
BEST BOWLING: 6-17 Warwickshire vs Durham UCCE, Durham, 2009

CAREER HIGHLIGHTS? Winning one-day trophies with Warwickshire and scoring hundreds in the 2nd XI
SUPERSTITIONS? They vary
CRICKETING HEROES? Jacques Kallis
NON-CRICKETING HEROES? Dave Grohl, Glenn Hoddle
BEST PLAYER IN COUNTY CRICKET? Marcus Trescothick
TIP FOR THE TOP? Ateeq Javid
IF YOU WEREN'T A CRICKETER? I'd be selling something
WHEN RAIN STOPS PLAY? I get on the iPhone, probably on Facebook or Twitter
FAVOURITE TV? Entourage
FAVOURITE FILM? Gran Torino, Old School
DREAM HOLIDAY? Vegas all the way!
SURPRISING SKILL? I can copy any accent in the world easily
GUILTY PLEASURES? Dancing, even though I'm terrible at it
SURPRISING FACTS? I'm half Norwegian, my birthday was 8/8/88, I was born at 8am and I weighed eight pounds. I can't stand chewing gum
TWITTER FEED: @Spiolet14

Batting	Mat	Inns	NO	Runs	HS	Ave	SR	100	50	Ct	St
First-class	4	7	1	78	30	13.00	38.80	0	0	4	0
List A	34	19	4	210	39	14.00	102.43	0	0	5	0
Twenty20	51	16	6	136	26*	13.60	107.93	0	0	12	0

Bowling	Mat	Balls	Runs	Wkts	BBI	BBM	Ave	Econ	SR	5w	10
First-class	4	414	241	14	6/17	10/43	17.21	3.49	29.5	1	1
List A	34	1127	1086	33	4/31	4/31	32.90	5.78	34.1	0	0
Twenty20	51	1011	1154	44	3/24	3/24	26.22	6.84	22.9	0	0

LIAM PLUNKETT   RHB RFM W3 MVP46

FULL NAME: Liam Edward Plunkett
BORN: April 6, 1985, Middlesbrough,
Yorkshire
SQUAD NO: 28
HEIGHT: 6ft 3in
NICKNAME: Pudsy
EDUCATION: Nunthorpe Comprehensive
TEAMS: England, Dolphins, Durham, Durham
2nd XI, Durham Cricket Board, England
Lions, England Under-19s, Yorkshire
CAREER: Test: 2005; ODI: 2005; T20I: 2006;
First-class: 2003; List A: 2003; T20: 2003

YORKSHIRE

BEST BATTING: 114 England Lions vs Sri Lanka A, Colombo, 2014
BEST BOWLING: 6-33 Yorkshire vs Leeds/Bradford MCCU, Leeds, 2013

CAREER HIGHLIGHTS? Making my England debut
CRICKETING HEROES? Glenn McGrath
OTHER SPORTS PLAYED? Swimming, golf
OTHER SPORTS FOLLOWED? Football (Middlesbrough, Arsenal)
TWITTER FEED: @Liam628
NOTES: After missing almost the entire 2012 season for Durham, Plunkett signed for
Yorkshire in October of that year. He claimed 42 first-class wickets in 2013 at 25.35,
including a career-best 6-33 against Leeds/Bradford University. He became only the
second player to record a five-wicket haul on his Championship debut for Durham, 5-53 vs
Yorkshire at Headingley in 2003. Made his England Test debut in November 2005 vs Pakistan
at Lahore and his home Test debut in 2006 against Sri Lanka at Lord's. His last Test was in
2007. He was selected for the England Lions tour of Sri Lanka in early 2014

Batting	Mat	Inns	NO	Runs	HS	Ave	SR	100	50	Ct	St
Tests	9	13	2	126	44*	11.45	39.62	0	0	3	0
ODIs	29	25	10	315	56	21.00	83.33	0	1	7	0
T20Is	1	-	-	-	-	-	-	-	-	0	0
First-class	124	169	31	3310	114	23.98		2	15	75	0
List A	124	84	30	1081	72	20.01	93.51	0	3	28	0
Twenty20	73	44	17	446	41	16.51	122.19	0	0	16	0

Bowling	Mat	Balls	Runs	Wkts	BBI	BBM	Ave	Econ	SR	5w	10
Tests	9	1538	916	23	3/17	6/60	39.82	3.57	66.8	0	0
ODIs	29	1363	1321	39	3/24	3/24	33.87	5.81	34.9	0	0
T20Is	1	24	37	1	1/37	1/37	37.00	9.25	24.0	0	0
First-class	124	19015	11526	370	6/33		31.15	3.63	51.3	10	1
List A	124	5173	4676	147	4/15	4/15	31.80	5.42	35.1	0	0
Twenty20	73	1278	1670	53	5/31	5/31	31.50	7.84	24.1	1	0

MIDDLESEX

FULL NAME: Harry William Podmore
BORN: July 23, 1994, Hammersmith, London
SQUAD NO: 23
HEIGHT: 6ft 3in
NICKNAME: Pods, Podders, Chav, Chadders
EDUCATION: Twyford High School
TEAMS: Middlesex 2nd XI, Middlesex Under-15s, Middlesex Under-17s
CAREER: Yet to make first-team debut

WHO WOULD PLAY YOU IN A FILM OF YOUR LIFE? Leonardo DiCaprio

CAREER HIGHLIGHTS? Signing my first professional contract

SUPERSTITIONS? Anything containing numbers has to be on 23! So radio volume, TV volume, car heaters, etc

BEST PLAYER IN COUNTY CRICKET? Eoin Morgan

TIP FOR THE TOP? Ryan Higgins is the stand-out for me

DESERT ISLAND DISC? 80s/90s Club Classics

FAVOURITE TV? The Only Way Is Essex, Come Dine With Me, Match Of The Day

CRICKETING HEROES? Freddie Flintoff, Ian Botham

NON-CRICKETING HEROES? David Beckham, Keith Lemon , Leonardo DiCaprio, my brother, my dad and my grandad

ACCOMPLISHMENTS? Two A-Levels. Not a lot else really

WHEN YOU RETIRE? I'd like to coach a professional team

SURPRISING FACT? I can't feel the top of my small finger on my left hand. It was chopped off in a door so I had plastic surgery on it

FANTASY SLIP CORDON? Keeper: Keith Lemon (he's a funny bloke), 1st: Me, 2nd: David Beckham (he's my hero), 3rd: Vinny Jones (top boy), Gully: Danny Dyer (I hope he misses the catch and wears one between the eyes!)

TWITTER FEED? @harrypod16

WILLIAM PORTERFIELD LHB OB

FULL NAME: William Thomas Stuart Porterfield
BORN: September 6, 1984, Londonderry, Northern Ireland
SQUAD NO: 10
HEIGHT: 5ft 11in
NICKNAME: Purdy, Porty
EDUCATION: Strabane Grammar School; Leeds Metropolitan University
TEAMS: Ireland, Gloucestershire, Marylebone Cricket Club, Warwickshire
CAREER: ODI: 2006; T20I: 2008; First-class: 2006; List A: 2006; T20: 2008

WARWICKSHIRE

BEST BATTING: 175 Gloucestershire vs Worcestershire, Cheltenham, 2010
BEST BOWLING: 1-29 Ireland vs Jamaica, Spanish Town, 2010

CAREER HIGHLIGHTS? Playing in the World Cup and captaining Ireland
BEST PLAYER IN COUNTY CRICKET? Marcus Trescothick
TIP FOR THE TOP? Paul Stirling
IF YOU WEREN'T A CRICKETER? I'd maybe be a farmer
WHEN RAIN STOPS PLAY? Anything that kills a bit of time
FAVOURITE TV? Two And A Half Men
FAVOURITE FILM? The Guard
FANTASY SLIP CORDON? Keeper: Frankie Boyle, 1st: Jimmy Carr, 2nd: John Bishop, 3rd: Kerry Katona
TWITTER FEED: @purdy34

Batting	Mat	Inns	NO	Runs	HS	Ave	SR	100	50	Ct	St
ODIs	68	68	3	2085	112*	32.07	67.93	6	10	35	0
T20Is	35	34	3	547	56*	17.64	113.48	0	1	13	0
First-class	93	153	6	4406	175	29.97	46.75	6	24	98	0
List A	163	162	6	5217	112*	33.44	73.21	7	32	77	0
Twenty20	101	100	5	2189	127*	23.04	124.87	1	10	43	0

Bowling	Mat	Balls	Runs	Wkts	BBI	BBM	Ave	Econ	SR	5w	10
ODIs	60	-	-	-	-	-	-	-	-	-	-
T20Is	30	-	-	-	-	-	-	-	-	-	-
First-class	77	108	138	2	1/29	1/29	69.00	7.66	54.0	0	0
List A	141	-	-	-	-	-	-	-	-	-	-
Twenty20	81	-	-	-	-	-	-	-	-	-	-

P

STUART POYNTER — RHB WK

DURHAM

FULL NAME: Stuart William Poynter
BORN: October 18, 1990, Hammersmith, London
SQUAD NO: 90
HEIGHT: 5ft 8in
NICKNAME: Poynts, Stuey
EDUCATION: Teddington School; Richmond College
TEAMS: Ireland, Durham 2nd XI, Ireland A, Ireland Under-19s, Marylebone Cricket Club Young Cricketers, Middlesex, Middlesex 2nd XI, Warwickshire
CAREER: First-class: 2010; List A: 2013

BEST BATTING: 63 Ireland vs Australia A, Stormont, 2013

FAMILY TIES? My brother [Andrew] plays for Ireland and my uncle used to
WHO WOULD PLAY YOU IN A FILM OF YOUR LIFE? Seth Rogen
CAREER HIGHLIGHTS? Making my debut for Ireland and playing in two U19 World Cups
MOST MARKED CHARACTERISTIC? My curly, ginger hair
IF YOU WEREN'T A CRICKETER? I'd be in coaching
DESERT ISLAND DISC? Anything by Route 94
FAVOURITE TV? Breaking Bad or The Only Way Is Essex
CRICKETING HEROES? Mark Boucher, David Nash, Jimmy Adams
NON-CRICKETING HEROES? Roger Federer, Ledley King
ACCOMPLISHMENTS? I played hockey for Middlesex
WHEN YOU RETIRE? I'd like to be a coach and help some young players out
SURPRISING FACT? I have two pet budgies called Boris and Beryl
FANTASY SLIP CORDON? Keeper: James Corden, 1st: Natalie Portman, 2nd: Pixie Lott, 3rd: Micky Flanagan, Gully: Me
TWITTER FEED: @spoynter_90

Batting	Mat	Inns	NO	Runs	HS	Ave	SR	100	50	Ct	St
First-class	8	9	0	201	63	22.33	63.20	0	1	23	2
List A	1	1	1	0	0*	-	-	0	0	4	0

Bowling	Mat	Balls	Runs	Wkts	BBI	BBM	Ave	Econ	SR	5w	10
First-class	8	-	-	-	-	-	-	-	-	-	-
List A	1	-	-	-	-	-	-	-	-	-	-

TOM POYNTON   RHB WK

FULL NAME: Thomas Poynton
BORN: November 25, 1989, Burton-on-Trent, Staffordshire
SQUAD NO: 23
HEIGHT: 5ft 10in
NICKNAME: Poynts, TP
EDUCATION: Repton School
TEAMS: Derbyshire, Derbyshire 2nd XI, England Under-19s
CAREER: First-class: 2007; List A: 2007; T20: 2007

BEST BATTING: 106 Derbyshire vs Northamptonshire, Northampton, 2012
BEST BOWLING: 2-96 Derbyshire vs Glamorgan, Cardiff, 2010

CAREER HIGHLIGHTS? Scoring my first first-class hundred for Derbyshire against Northamptonshire. Winning the County Championship Division Two title with Derbyshire in 2012
MOST MARKED CHARACTERISTIC? The Action Man scar on my left cheek
BEST PLAYER IN COUNTY CRICKET? Shivnarine Chanderpaul
TIPS FOR THE TOP? Tom Knight, Ben Cotton, Harvey Hosein
CRICKETING HEROES? Adam Gilchrist: such a destructive, game-changing player with the bat and a good gloveman. Bob Taylor: outstanding gloveman for Derbyshire and England
NON-CRICKETING HEROES? Lisa Lynch. Lisa was a close family friend who sadly lost her battle with cancer in 2013. She was an incredibly inspiring woman with the most amazing personality and fight. She wrote a book about her struggle with the disease called The C-Word and I urge anyone reading this to go and buy it or at least take the time to look her story up. She ran a blog which can be found at www.alrighttit.com. Her life and battle with cancer is going to be portrayed in a BBC drama this year with Sheridan Smith playing Lisa. Thinking about her gives me great perspective on what is important in life and reminds me that cricket is just a game
SURPRISING FACT? I used to sponsor the meerkats at Twycross Zoo

Batting	Mat	Inns	NO	Runs	HS	Ave	SR	100	50	Ct	St
First-class	33	50	6	941	106	21.38	40.84	1	5	81	6
List A	20	13	2	138	40	12.54	89.61	0	0	11	3
Twenty20	19	12	3	86	19	9.55	88.65	0	0	12	9

Bowling	Mat	Balls	Runs	Wkts	BBI	BBM	Ave	Econ	SR	5w	10
First-class	33	48	96	2	2/96	2/96	48.00	12.00	24.0	0	0
List A	20	-	-	-	-	-	-	-	-	-	-
Twenty20	19	-	-	-	-	-	-	-	-	-	-

LANCASHIRE

FULL NAME: Ashwell Gavin Prince
BORN: May 28, 1977, Port Elizabeth, Cape Province, South Africa
SQUAD NO: 5
HEIGHT: 5ft 9in
NICKNAME: Ash
TEAMS: South Africa, Africa XI, Eastern Province, Lancashire, Mumbai Indians, Nottinghamshire, Warriors, Western Province, Western Province Boland
CAREER: Test: 2002; ODI: 2002; T20I: 2005; First-class: 1995; List A: 1996; T20: 2004

BEST BATTING: 254 Warriors vs Titans, Centurion, 2009
BEST BOWLING: 2-11 South Africans vs Middlesex, Uxbridge, 2008
COUNTY CAPS: 2008 (Nottinghamshire); 2010 (Lancashire)

TWITTER FEED: @ashyp_5
NOTES: Prince is in his fourth spell with Lancashire and qualifies as a Kolpak player. The former South Africa batsman signed a two-year deal with the county ahead of the 2013 season after losing his central contract with South Africa and he scored three first-class centuries last year, amassing 1,169 runs at 48.70. In all he has scored 3,153 first-class runs for Lancashire at an average of 46.43, including 22 fifties and seven hundreds. In July 2006, he was appointed South Africa's first black captain in the absence of the injured Graeme Smith and he scored 11 centuries in his 66-match Test career, including a series-defining 149 against England at Headingley in 2008. Prince announced in March that he will be retiring from all forms of cricket at the end of the 2014 county season

Batting	Mat	Inns	NO	Runs	HS	Ave	SR	100	50	Ct	St
Tests	66	104	16	3665	162*	41.64	43.70	11	11	47	0
ODIs	52	41	12	1018	89*	35.10	67.77	0	3	26	0
T20Is	1	1	0	5	5	5.00	83.33	0	0	0	0
First-class	254	410	47	15760	254	43.41		37	82	194	0
List A	250	220	37	5911	128	32.30		3	31	113	0
Twenty20	79	77	6	1640	74	23.09	108.89	0	7	40	0

Bowling	Mat	Balls	Runs	Wkts	BBI	BBM	Ave	Econ	SR	5w	10
Tests	66	96	47	1	1/2	1/2	47.00	2.93	96.0	0	0
ODIs	52	12	3	0	-	-	-	1.50	-	0	0
T20Is	1	-	-	-	-	-	-	-	-	-	-
First-class	254	294	179	4	2/11		44.75	3.65	73.5	0	0
List A	250	91	86	0	-	-	-	5.67	-	0	0
Twenty20	79	4	5	0	-	-	-	7.50	-	0	0

RYAN PRINGLE RHB OB

FULL NAME: Ryan David Pringle
BORN: April 17, 1992, Sunderland, Co Durham
SQUAD NO: 17
HEIGHT: 6ft 1in
NICKNAME: Rhino
EDUCATION: Hetton School; Durham Sixth Form Centre; University of Sunderland
TEAMS: Durham, Durham 2nd XI, Northumberland
CAREER: List A: 2012; T20: 2013

FAMILY TIES? My dad and grandad both played club-level cricket

WHO WOULD PLAY YOU IN A FILM OF YOUR LIFE? Zac Efron

CAREER HIGHLIGHTS? It's always a highlight to play cricket in any format for Durham CCC. Specific highlight: taking 2-13 from four overs in a T20 vs Yorkshire

SUPERSTITIONS? I always put my left pad on before my right pad, my inner thigh guard before my outer thigh guard and I never ask for a drink in the 40s or 90s

MOST MARKED CHARACTERISTIC? I have an extremely large backside and a beard the majority of the time

BEST PLAYER IN COUNTY CRICKET? Ben Raine

TIPS FOR THE TOP? Graham Clark, Max Morley, Jack Burnham

IF YOU WEREN'T A CRICKETER? A Masters in Sports Psychology

FAVOURITE TV? Game Of Thrones, Sons Of Anarchy, Prison Break, Jeremy Kyle

CRICKETING HEROES? Ricky Ponting

NON-CRICKETING HEROES? My grandad, David Beckham

WHEN YOU RETIRE? I'd like to be a sports psychologist

SURPRISING FACT? I have a washing line tattooed around my ankle

CRICKET RULE YOU'D CHANGE? A no ball should result in a free hit across all formats of the game

FANTASY SLIP CORDON? Keeper: Jonah Hill, 1st: Me, 2nd: Andrew Flintoff, 3rd: Peter Griffin, Gully: Calisi (Game Of Thrones)

TWITTER FEED: @RyanPringle

Batting	Mat	Inns	NO	Runs	HS	Ave	SR	100	50	Ct	St
List A	11	5	0	48	26	9.60	82.75	0	0	2	0
Twenty20	11	6	1	22	14	4.40	104.76	0	0	2	0

Bowling	Mat	Balls	Runs	Wkts	BBI	BBM	Ave	Econ	SR	5w	10
List A	11	180	150	3	1/12	1/12	50.00	5.00	60.0	0	0
Twenty20	11	192	245	10	2/13	2/13	24.50	7.65	19.2	0	0

MATT PRIOR

RHB WK R3

FULL NAME: Matthew James Prior
BORN: February 26, 1982, Johannesburg, Transvaal, South Africa
SQUAD NO: 13
HEIGHT: 5ft 11in
EDUCATION: Brighton College, East Sussex
TEAMS: England, England A, England Lions, England Under-19s, Sussex, Sussex Cricket Board, Victoria
CAREER: Test: 2007; ODI: 2004; T20I: 2007; First-class: 2001; List A: 2000; T20: 2003

BEST BATTING: 201* Sussex vs Loughborough UCCE, Hove, 2004
COUNTY CAP: 2003; BENEFIT YEAR: 2012

WHO WOULD PLAY YOU IN A FILM OF YOUR LIFE? Jason Statham. Because he is part of the baldy, beardy group
MOST MARKED CHARACTERISTIC? The beard. Is that a characteristic?
DESERT ISLAND DISC? Album: Now That's What I Call Music 21. Song: Mr Bojangles. I love the Robbie Williams version
BIGGEST DRESSING DOWN YOU'VE RECEIVED? Peter Moores at Tunbridge Wells in 2001. We lost and hadn't played well and he went round the whole squad, one by one, and basically abused every single player. It was a thing of beauty
TWITTER FEED: @MattPrior13

Batting	Mat	Inns	NO	Runs	HS	Ave	SR	100	50	Ct	St
Tests	75	116	20	3920	131*	40.83	61.81	7	27	217	13
ODIs	68	62	9	1282	87	24.18	76.76	0	3	71	8
T20Is	10	8	2	127	32	21.16	127.00	0	0	6	3
First-class	242	369	42	12832	201*	39.24	66.85	27	74	611	41
List A	222	204	18	5072	144	27.26		4	28	187	31
Twenty20	83	77	5	1867	117	25.93	143.28	1	11	44	6

Bowling	Mat	Balls	Runs	Wkts	BBI	BBM	Ave	Econ	SR	5w	10
Tests	75	-	-	-	-	-	-	-	-	-	-
ODIs	68	-	-	-	-	-	-	-	-	-	-
T20Is	10	-	-	-	-	-	-	-	-	-	-
First-class	242	-	-	-	-	-	-	-	-	-	-
List A	222	-	-	-	-	-	-	-	-	-	-
Twenty20	83	-	-	-	-	-	-	-	-	-	-

LUKE PROCTER

LHB RMF

FULL NAME: Luke Anthony Procter
BORN: June 24, 1988, Oldham, Lancashire
SQUAD NO: 2
HEIGHT: 5ft 11in
EDUCATION: Counthill School, Oldham
TEAMS: Cumberland, Lancashire, Lancashire 2nd XI, Marylebone Cricket Club Young Cricketers
CAREER: First-class: 2010; List A: 2009; T20: 2011

LANCASHIRE

BEST BATTING: 106 Lancashire vs Gloucestershire, Bristol, 2013
BEST BOWLING: 7-71 Lancashire vs Surrey, Liverpool, 2012

CAREER HIGHLIGHTS? Winning the County Championship in 2011
SUPERSTITIONS? Putting my right pad on first
CRICKETING HEROES? Marcus Trescothick
TIP FOR THE TOP? Simon Kerrigan
IF YOU WEREN'T A CRICKETER? I'd not be doing a lot
WHEN RAIN STOPS PLAY? I listen to music and chat to the lads
FAVOURITE TV? Take Me Out
FAVOURITE FILM? Happy Gilmore
FAVOURITE BOOK? The Twilight series
DREAM HOLIDAY? Las Vegas
GUILTY PLEASURES? Chocolate
TWITTER FEED: @vvsprocter

Batting	Mat	Inns	NO	Runs	HS	Ave	SR	100	50	Ct	St
First-class	39	57	4	1704	106	32.15	42.57	1	10	7	0
List A	19	14	5	252	97	28.00	85.13	0	2	4	0
Twenty20	19	10	5	85	25*	17.00	91.39	0	0	5	0

Bowling	Mat	Balls	Runs	Wkts	BBI	BBM	Ave	Econ	SR	5w	10
First-class	39	2920	1678	53	7/71	8/79	31.66	3.44	55.0	2	0
List A	19	408	431	11	3/29	3/29	39.18	6.33	37.0	0	0
Twenty20	19	116	176	8	3/22	3/22	22.00	9.10	14.5	0	0

RICH PYRAH

RHB RM

YORKSHIRE

FULL NAME: Richard Michael Pyrah
BORN: November 1, 1982, Dewsbury, Yorkshire
SQUAD NO: 27
HEIGHT: 6ft
NICKNAME: RP, Pyro
EDUCATION: Ossett High School
TEAMS: Yorkshire, Yorkshire Cricket Board
CAREER: First-class: 2004; List A: 2001; T20: 2005

BEST BATTING: 134* Yorkshire vs Loughborough MCCU, Leeds, 2010
BEST BOWLING: 5-58 Yorkshire vs Nottinghamshire, Leeds, 2011
COUNTY CAP: 2010

CAREER HIGHLIGHTS? Receiving my 1st XI cap and scoring 117 vs Lancashire after we were 45-8
CRICKETING HEROES? Jacques Kallis, Sachin Tendulkar
NON-CRICKETING HEROES? My family
BEST PLAYER IN COUNTY CRICKET? Marcus Trescothick
TIPS FOR THE TOP? Joe Root, Jonny Bairstow
IF YOU WEREN'T A CRICKETER? I'd be some sort of businessman
FAVOURITE TV? EastEnders, One Born Every Minute
FAVOURITE FILM? Dumb And Dumber
FAVOURITE BOOK? The Beano comics!
DREAM HOLIDAY? Barbados
ACCOMPLISHMENTS? Having twins with my girlfriend
SURPRISING SKILL? I can down a bottle of VK in one second
SURPRISING FACT? I played for Sheffield Wednesday as a youngster
TWITTER FEED: @pyrah27

Batting	Mat	Inns	NO	Runs	HS	Ave	SR	100	50	Ct	St
First-class	42	51	6	1256	134*	27.91	56.22	3	6	20	0
List A	105	72	17	1020	69	18.54		0	2	35	0
Twenty20	84	59	17	510	42	12.14	112.83	0	0	31	0

Bowling	Mat	Balls	Runs	Wkts	BBI	BBM	Ave	Econ	SR	5w	10
First-class	42	3662	2145	49	5/58		43.77	3.51	74.7	1	0
List A	105	3388	3259	125	5/50	5/50	26.07	5.77	27.1	1	0
Twenty20	84	1476	1812	88	5/16	5/16	20.59	7.36	16.7	1	0

AZEEM RAFIQ

RHB OB

FULL NAME: Azeem Rafiq
BORN: February 27, 1991, Karachi, Pakistan
SQUAD NO: 30
HEIGHT: 5ft 10in
NICKNAME: Raffa
EDUCATION: Holgate School Sports College, Barnsley
TEAMS: Derbyshire, England Under-15s, England Under-17s, England Under-19s, Yorkshire, Yorkshire 2nd XI
CAREER: First-class: 2009; List A: 2009; T20: 2008

BEST BATTING: 100 Yorkshire vs Worcestershire, Worcester, 2009
BEST BOWLING: 5-50 Yorkshire vs Essex, Chelmsford, 2012

WHO WOULD PLAY YOU IN A FILM OF YOUR LIFE? Jackie Chan
CAREER HIGHLIGHTS? Playing in T20 Finals Day and the Champions League T20 and getting promoted to Division One of the County Championship
MOST MARKED CHARACTERISTIC? Confidence
BEST PLAYER IN COUNTY CRICKET? Graham Onions
TIPS FOR THE TOP? Ben Stokes, Adam Lyth
DESERT ISLAND DISC? PSY – Gangnam Style
FAVOURITE TV? Premier League Darts
BIGGEST DRESSING DOWN YOU'VE RECEIVED? I was banned for a month for a Twitter outburst
CRICKETING HEROES? Michael Vaughan, Anthony McGrath
NON-CRICKETING HEROES? Ryan Giggs
WHEN YOU RETIRE? I'd like to do something in business or in the media
FANTASY SLIP CORDON? Keeper: Megan Fox, 1st: Me, 2nd: Steven Patterson, 3rd: Ryan Giggs, Gully: Tiger Woods
TWITTER FEED? @AzeemRafiq30

Batting	Mat	Inns	NO	Runs	HS	Ave	SR	100	50	Ct	St
First-class	24	28	3	549	100	21.96	53.09	1	2	8	0
List A	20	14	6	146	34*	18.25	86.39	0	0	7	0
Twenty20	51	24	14	118	21*	11.80	95.93	0	0	19	0

Bowling	Mat	Balls	Runs	Wkts	BBI	BBM	Ave	Econ	SR	5w	10
First-class	24	3590	1900	54	5/50	8/115	35.18	3.17	66.4	1	0
List A	20	690	598	19	5/30	5/30	31.47	5.20	36.3	1	0
Twenty20	51	1044	1326	48	3/15	3/15	27.62	7.62	21.7	0	0

BEN RAINE

LHB RMF

FULL NAME: Benjamin Alexander Raine
BORN: September 14, 1991, Sunderland, Co Durham
SQUAD NO: 44
HEIGHT: 6ft
NICKNAME: Ranger, Chop King
EDUCATION: St. Aidan's Secondary School for Boys, Sunderland
TEAMS: Durham, Durham 2nd XI, Leicestershire, Leicestershire 2nd XI, Northumberland
CAREER: First-class: 2011; List A: 2011

BEST BATTING: 72 Leicestershire vs Lancashire, Manchester, 2013
BEST BOWLING: 4-98 Leicestershire vs Glamorgan, Swansea, 2013

CAREER HIGHLIGHTS? Recovering from a horrendous time at Durham to get a contract with Leicestershire, playing at Lord's for the first time, scoring my maiden County Championship fifty and taking four wickets on debut at Swansea

MOST MARKED CHARACTERISTIC? I'm a fighter and I enjoy a good battle

BEST PLAYER IN COUNTY CRICKET? There might be better, but the best I've played against is Will Gidman at Gloucestershire

TIPS FOR THE TOP? Mark Wood at Durham. He bowls quick and well. I've been thinking he should've been around the England Lions set-up for a few years now but he's finally getting the chance he deserves. Also, Ollie Freckingham at Leicestershire had a good maiden season last year and has worked really hard over the winter

CRICKETING HEROES? I always styled myself on Matthew Hayden. I loved how he batted. In modern cricket I really appreciate the work Brendon McCullum has done with New Zealand – a captain who has the full support of his boys and his country, plays with his heart and gives everything every time he plays

SURPRISING FACT? Founding member and, up till now, the only member of the North-East Leicestershire Black Pudding Appreciation Society

CRICKET RULE YOU'D CHANGE? The length of one-day games. The 50-over game is terrible compared to 40 overs – it's much slower and nowhere near as good to watch or play

TWITTER FEED: @BenRaine88

Batting	Mat	Inns	NO	Runs	HS	Ave	SR	100	50	Ct	St
First-class	6	10	1	201	72	22.33	38.06	0	1	1	0
List A	3	1	0	7	7	7.00	175.00	0	0	2	0

Bowling	Mat	Balls	Runs	Wkts	BBI	BBM	Ave	Econ	SR	5w	10
First-class	6	609	356	9	4/98	4/98	39.55	3.50	67.6	0	0
List A	3	90	101	2	2/59	2/59	50.50	6.73	45.0	0	0

BOYD RANKIN

LHB RFM W1

FULL NAME: William Boyd Rankin
BORN: July 5, 1984, Londonderry, Northern Ireland
SQUAD NO: 30
HEIGHT: 6ft 7in
NICKNAME: Boydo, Pierre
EDUCATION: Strabane Grammar School; Harper Adams University College
TEAMS: England, Ireland, Derbyshire, England Lions, Ireland Under-19s, Warwickshire, Warwickshire 2nd XI
CAREER: Test: 2014; ODI: 2007; T20I: 2009; First-class: 2007; List A: 2006; T20: 2009

WARWICKSHIRE

BEST BATTING: 43 ICC Combined XI vs England XI, Dubai, 2012
BEST BOWLING: 5-16 Warwickshire vs Essex, Birmingham, 2010

FAMILY TIES? My dad played club cricket and my brothers Robert and David have played for Ireland at U19 level, with David also playing for Ireland A. My sister plays club and Ireland development cricket
CRICKETING HEROES? I watched Curtly Ambrose and Glenn McGrath while I was growing up and have tried to emulate them
NON-CRICKETING HEROES? I'm a big fan of George Best
BEST PLAYER IN COUNTY CRICKET? Marcus Trescothick
TIPS FOR THE TOP? Paul Stirling of Middlesex is a real talent and the best striker of a cricket ball I've seen
IF YOU WEREN'T A CRICKETER? I would be back home in Ireland on the family farm
ACCOMPLISHMENTS? Getting my higher diploma in Agricultural Mechanisation
TWITTER FEED: @boydrankin

Batting	Mat	Inns	NO	Runs	HS	Ave	SR	100	50	Ct	St
Tests	1	2	0	13	13	6.50	54.16	0	0	0	0
ODIs	44	18	12	40	7*	6.66	36.36	0	0	6	0
T20Is	17	3	2	13	7*	13.00	81.25	0	0	6	0
First-class	66	77	33	361	43	8.20	40.88	0	0	18	0
List A	87	30	18	90	18*	7.50	48.64	0	0	11	0
Twenty20	29	7	4	19	7*	6.33	73.07	0	0	9	0

Bowling	Mat	Balls	Runs	Wkts	BBI	BBM	Ave	Econ	SR	5w	10
Tests	1	125	81	1	1/47	1/81	81.00	3.88	125.0	0	0
ODIs	44	2019	1632	53	4/46	4/46	30.79	4.84	38.0	0	0
T20Is	17	378	388	18	3/20	3/20	21.55	6.15	21.0	0	0
First-class	66	9736	5933	214	5/16	8/115	27.72	3.65	45.4	6	0
List A	87	3591	2943	103	4/34	4/34	28.57	4.91	34.8	0	0
Twenty20	29	606	566	33	4/9	4/9	17.15	5.60	18.3	0	0

ADIL RASHID   RHB LB W2 MVP45

YORKSHIRE

FULL NAME: Adil Usman Rashid
BORN: February 17, 1988, Bradford, Yorkshire
SQUAD NO: 3
HEIGHT: 5ft 9in
NICKNAME: Dilly, Dilo, Rash
EDUCATION: Heaton School, Bradford; Bellevue Sixth Form College, Bradford
TEAMS: England, England Lions, England Under-19s, Marylebone Cricket Club, South Australia, Yorkshire, Yorkshire 2nd XI
CAREER: ODI: 2009; T20I: 2009; First-class: 2006; List A: 2006; T20: 2008

BEST BATTING: 180 Yorkshire vs Somerset, Leeds, 2013
BEST BOWLING: 7-107 Yorkshire vs Hampshire, Southampton, 2008
COUNTY CAP: 2008

CAREER HIGHLIGHTS? Playing for England
CRICKETING HEROES? Sachin Tendulkar, Shane Warne
NON-CRICKETING HEROES? Muhammad Ali
BEST PLAYER IN COUNTY CRICKET? Marcus Trescothick
TIP FOR THE TOP? Moin Ashraf
IF YOU WEREN'T A CRICKETER? I'd be a taxi driver
FAVOURITE TV? Friends
FAVOURITE FILM? Scarface
DREAM HOLIDAY? Barbados
TWITTER FEED: @AdilRashid03

Batting	Mat	Inns	NO	Runs	HS	Ave	SR	100	50	Ct	5t
ODIs	5	4	1	60	31*	20.00	111.11	0	0	2	0
T20Is	5	2	1	10	9*	10.00	52.63	0	0	0	0
First-class	114	159	30	4534	180	35.14		7	26	54	0
List A	82	57	17	736	46*	18.40	84.98	0	0	27	0
Twenty20	77	47	12	422	36*	12.05	99.29	0	0	19	0

Bowling	Mat	Balls	Runs	Wkts	BBI	BBM	Ave	Econ	SR	5w	10
ODIs	5	204	191	3	1/16	1/16	63.66	5.61	68.0	0	0
T20Is	5	84	120	3	1/11	1/11	40.00	8.57	28.0	0	0
First-class	114	19713	11664	325	7/107	11/114	35.88	3.55	60.6	17	1
List A	82	3159	2741	81	4/38	4/38	33.83	5.20	39.0	0	0
Twenty20	77	1493	1904	81	4/20	4/20	23.50	7.65	18.4	0	0

OLLIE RAYNER

RHB OB MVP43

FULL NAME: Oliver Philip Rayner
BORN: November 1, 1985, Fallingbostel, Germany
SQUAD NO: 2
HEIGHT: 6ft 6in
NICKNAME: Mervin, Rocket, Morag, Kalvin, Donk
EDUCATION: St Bede's School, Eastbourne
TEAMS: England Lions, Middlesex, Sussex, Sussex 2nd XI, Sussex Cricket Board
CAREER: First-class: 2006; List A: 2006; T20: 2006

MIDDLESEX

BEST BATTING: 143* Middlesex vs Nottinghamshire, Nottingham, 2012
BEST BOWLING: 8-46 Middlesex vs Surrey, The Oval, 2013

CAREER HIGHLIGHTS? I was fortunate enough to be with Sussex through a very fruitful period regarding trophies. Also, scoring a ton on debut and and winning Division Two of the County Championship whilst on loan with Middlesex in 2011
SUPERSTITIONS? I put my left pad on first and my buckles in. I don't enjoy being on 13 at any stage whilst batting – it doesn't affect me badly enough to use it against me though!
CRICKETING HEROES? Freddie Flintoff, Chris Gayle, Adam Blackburn, Richard Smith
BEST PLAYER IN COUNTY CRICKET? Marcus Trescothick
TIPS FOR THE TOP? Sam Robson, Jonny Bairstow
FAVOURITE TV? Downton Abbey, Top Gear, The Simpsons, Family Guy
FAVOURITE FILM? Harry Potter, Dodgeball
FAVOURITE BOOK? Where's Wally?
DREAM HOLIDAY? Maldives. I would also like to visit the West Indies
GUILTY PLEASURES? I'm a Harry Potter nut
SURPRISING FACTS? I can actually spin the ball, I've lived in army barracks most of my life through my old man and I can only eat small sweets or chocolates in an even number – as an example Maltesers have to go in my mouth in multiples of two. Hence the weight!
TWITTER FEED: @Ollie2rayner

Batting	Mat	Inns	NO	Runs	HS	Ave	SR	100	50	Ct	St
First-class	79	101	20	2012	143*	24.83	53.45	2	10	93	0
List A	40	28	14	365	61	26.07	95.54	0	1	15	0
Twenty20	47	27	11	245	41*	15.31	109.37	0	0	11	0

Bowling	Mat	Balls	Runs	Wkts	BBI	BBM	Ave	Econ	SR	5w	10
First-class	79	11815	5698	173	8/46	15/118	32.93	2.89	68.2	7	1
List A	40	1290	1168	29	3/31	3/31	40.27	5.43	44.4	0	0
Twenty20	47	827	973	29	5/18	5/18	33.55	7.05	28.5	1	0

FULL NAME: Christopher Mark Wells Read
BORN: August 10, 1978, Paignton, Devon
SQUAD NO: 7
HEIGHT: 5ft 8in
NICKNAME: Reados, Readie
EDUCATION: Torquay Boys' Grammar School; University of Bath; Loughborough University
TEAMS: England, Devon, Gloucestershire, Nottinghamshire
CAREER: Test: 1999; ODI: 2000; T20I: 2006; First-class: 1998; List A: 1995; T20: 2004

BEST BATTING: 240 Nottinghamshire vs Essex, Chelmsford, 2007
COUNTY CAP: 1999 (Nottinghamshire); **BENEFIT YEAR:** 2009 (Nottinghamshire)

CAREER HIGHLIGHTS? Winning the County Championship twice
SUPERSTITIONS? Anything to keep the cricketing gods onside!
CRICKETING HEROES? Ian Botham, Ian Healy, Jack Russell
NON-CRICKETING HEROES? Sébastian Loeb
BEST PLAYER IN COUNTY CRICKET? Marcus Trescothick
TIP FOR THE TOP? Jos Buttler
IF YOU WEREN'T A CRICKETER? Racing and roadtesting cars or living the dream as a rock star
FAVOURITE FILM? Old School
FAVOURITE BOOK? Redwall by Brian Jacques – my son is named after a character in it
DREAM HOLIDAY? Barbados
ACCOMPLISHMENTS? Running the NYC marathon

Batting	Mat	Inns	NO	Runs	HS	Ave	SR	100	50	Ct	St
Tests	15	23	4	360	55	18.94	39.47	0	1	48	6
ODIs	36	24	7	300	30*	17.64	73.17	0	0	41	2
T20Is	1	1	0	13	13	13.00	118.18	0	0	1	0
First-class	290	435	71	13239	240	36.37		21	73	863	47
List A	299	240	66	5056	135	29.05		2	21	284	68
Twenty20	94	80	29	1249	58*	24.49	121.73	0	1	47	21

Bowling	Mat	Balls	Runs	Wkts	BBI	BBM	Ave	Econ	SR	5w	10
Tests	15	-	-	-	-	-	-	-	-	-	-
ODIs	36	-	-	-	-	-	-	-	-	-	-
T20Is	1	-	-	-	-	-	-	-	-	-	-
First-class	290	96	90	0	-	-	-	5.62	-	0	0
List A	299	-	-	-	-	-	-	-	-	-	-
Twenty20	94	-	-	-	-	-	-	-	-	-	-

DAN REDFERN   LHB OB

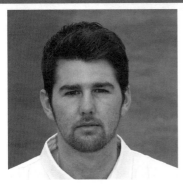

FULL NAME: Daniel James Redfern
BORN: April 18, 1990, Shrewsbury
SQUAD NO: 6
HEIGHT: 5ft 11in
NICKNAME: Redders, Reds
EDUCATION: Adams' Grammar School, Newport
TEAMS: Derbyshire, Derbyshire 2nd XI, England Under-19s, Leicestershire
CAREER: First-class: 2007; List A: 2006; T20: 2008

BEST BATTING: 133 Derbyshire vs Hampshire, Southampton, 2012
BEST BOWLING: 3-33 Derbyshire vs Durham, Chester-le-Street, 2013
COUNTY CAP: 2012 (Derbyshire)

FAMILY TIES? My grandfathers, father, brother, uncles and cousins all played for Leycett CC in Staffordshire
WHO WOULD PLAY YOU IN A FILM OF YOUR LIFE? Leonardo DiCaprio
CAREER HIGHLIGHTS? Scoring my maiden first-class hundred against Northamptonshire. Receiving my Derbyshire county cap in the year we were promoted to Division One
MOST MARKED CHARACTERISTIC? I'm unflappable and laid-back
BEST PLAYER IN COUNTY CRICKET? Moeen Ali
TIPS FOR THE TOP? Shiv Thakor, Harvey Hosein
IF YOU WEREN'T A CRICKETER? I'd be a coach or working in property development
DESERT ISLAND DISC? Anything from Stereophonics
FAVOURITE TV? QI or 8 Out Of 10 Cats
CRICKETING HEROES? Graham Thorpe, Brian Lara
NON-CRICKETING HEROES? Stephen Fry – incredible knowledge
WHEN YOU RETIRE? I'll relax, hopefully with a family, or start a building venture
SURPRISING FACT? I can turn my eyelids inside out and blow bubbles off my tongue
TWITTER FEED: @redfern_dan

Batting	Mat	Inns	NO	Runs	HS	Ave	SR	100	50	Ct	St
First-class	70	116	7	3213	133	29.47	53.92	2	23	37	0
List A	43	34	1	655	57*	19.84	74.77	0	3	10	0
Twenty20	14	11	0	103	43	9.36	99.03	0	0	5	0

Bowling	Mat	Balls	Runs	Wkts	BBI	BBM	Ave	Econ	SR	5w	10
First-class	70	757	460	10	3/33	3/43	46.00	3.64	75.7	0	0
List A	43	280	228	5	2/10	2/10	45.60	4.88	56.0	0	0
Twenty20	14	165	201	10	2/17	2/17	20.10	7.30	16.5	0	0

LANCASHIRE

FULL NAME: Luis Michael Reece
BORN: August 4, 1990, Taunton, Somerset
SQUAD NO: 21
EDUCATION: St Michael's School;
Myerscough College, Bilsborrow; Leeds
Metropolitan University
TEAMS: Lancashire, Lancashire 2nd XI,
Leeds/Bradford MCCU, Unicorns
CAREER: First-class: 2012; List A: 2011

BEST BATTING: 114* Leeds/Bradford MCCU vs Leicestershire, Leicester, 2013
BEST BOWLING: 4-28 Leeds/Bradford MCCU vs Leicestershire, Leicester, 2013

TWITTER FEED: @lreece17
NOTES: Connected to Lancashire since the age of 11, Reece was playing for Lancashire's
2nd XI from the age of 16 but was let go shortly after his 19th birthday. After a spell in
Australia he returned to go to Leeds Metropolitan University and worked his way back
into professional cricket, representing the Unicorns in the CB40 in 2011 and 2012. In May
2012 he scored 164 and took 7-21 – at one stage his figures read 5-0 – for Leeds/Bradford
MCCU in a three-day friendly against Sussex. Impressed enough to sign professional terms
with Lancashire in September 2012 and he signed off from university by captaining Leeds/
Bradford MCCU to a 102-run win over a full-strength Leicestershire side in April 2013,
scoring 114* and taking six wickets. Promoted to open the batting last year for Lancashire,
Reece scored one century and eight half-centuries, seven of which came consecutively, to
finish the campaign with an average of 54.81

Batting	Mat	Inns	NO	Runs	HS	Ave	SR	100	50	Ct	St
First-class	14	24	4	1011	114*	50.55	54.03	1	9	11	0
List A	20	18	4	348	59	24.85	84.26	0	1	5	0
Bowling	Mat	Balls	Runs	Wkts	BBI	BBM	Ave	Econ	SR	5w	10
First-class	14	684	378	14	4/28	6/67	27.00	3.31	48.8	0	0
List A	20	404	418	6	4/35	4/35	69.66	6.20	67.3	0	0

R

MIKE REED

RHB RFM

FULL NAME: Michael Thomas Reed
BORN: September 10, 1988, Leicester
SQUAD NO: 35
HEIGHT: 6ft 7in
NICKNAME: Frank, Denis Stracqualursi,
Trigger, Long, Marouane Fellani
EDUCATION: De Lisle Catholic Science
College; Cardiff University
TEAMS: Cardiff MCCU, Glamorgan,
Glamorgan 2nd XI, Wales Minor Counties
CAREER: First-class: 2012; List A: 2013

GLAMORGAN

BEST BATTING: 27 Glamorgan vs Kent, Canterbury, 2013
BEST BOWLING: 6-34 Glamorgan vs Cardiff MCCU, Cardiff, 2013

FAMILY TIES? My brother [Dominic] was part of the 2011 Unicorns squad
CAREER HIGHLIGHTS? Signing for Glamorgan and playing against first-class counties for Cardiff MCCU
CRICKETING HEROES? Brett Lee, Steve Harmison, Andrew Flintoff
NON-CRICKETING HEROES? Martin O'Neill
BEST PLAYER IN COUNTY CRICKET? Marcus Trescothick
TIPS FOR THE TOP? James Harris, Joe Root
IF YOU WEREN'T A CRICKETER? I'd be plugging numbers
FAVOURITE TV? Prison Break
FAVOURITE FILM? Blood Diamond
FAVOURITE BOOK? Any decent autobiography
DREAM HOLIDAY? Seychelles
ACCOMPLISHMENTS? Getting a Maths degree
GUILTY PLEASURES? Chocolate raisins
SURPRISING FACT? I have a large scar on my back from my time in Australia

Batting	Mat	Inns	NO	Runs	HS	Ave	SR	100	50	Ct	St
First-class	16	22	9	89	27	6.84	26.17	0	0	2	0
List A	3	-	-	-	-	-	-	-	-	1	0

Bowling	Mat	Balls	Runs	Wkts	BBI	BBM	Ave	Econ	SR	5w	10
First-class	16	2511	1430	46	6/34	7/46	31.08	3.41	54.5	2	0
List A	3	66	78	0	-	-	-	7.09	-	0	0

GARETH REES

LHB LM R2

FULL NAME: Gareth Peter Rees
BORN: April 8, 1985, Swansea, Wales
SQUAD NO: 28
HEIGHT: 6ft 2in
NICKNAME: Gums
EDUCATION: Coedcae Comprehensive;
Coleg Sir Gar; Bath University
TEAMS: Glamorgan, Glamorgan 2nd XI,
Wales Minor Counties
CAREER: First-class: 2006; List A: 2003; T20:
2009

BEST BATTING: 154 Glamorgan vs Surrey, The Oval, 2009
COUNTY CAP: 2009

WHO WOULD PLAY YOU IN A FILM OF YOUR LIFE? Vince Vaughn
CAREER HIGHLIGHTS? Being capped for Glamorgan
SUPERSTITIONS? There's no such thing as luck
MOST MARKED CHARACTERISTIC? Depends who you ask!
BEST PLAYER IN COUNTY CRICKET? Marcus Trescothick
TIPS FOR THE TOP? Andrew Salter, Aneurin Donald
IF YOU WEREN'T A CRICKETER? I'd be working in business
DESERT ISLAND DISC? Oasis – What's The Story Morning Glory?
FAVOURITE TV? Only Fools And Horses
CRICKETING HEROES? Brian Lara, Jason Gillespie, David Hemp, Steve James
ACCOMPLISHMENTS? Being able to complete my academic studies and work placements
alongside playing cricket
WHEN YOU RETIRE? Consulting
FANTASY SLIP CORDON? Keeper: Albert Einstein, 1st: Myself, 2nd: Will Ferrell, 3rd: Russell
Howard
TWITTER FEED: @garethprees28

Batting	Mat	Inns	NO	Runs	HS	Ave	SR	100	50	Ct	St
First-class	101	175	9	5514	154	33.21	48.09	13	30	79	0
List A	51	49	6	1535	123*	35.69		3	10	13	0
Twenty20	27	26	5	350	38	16.66	105.74	0	0	7	0
Bowling	Mat	Balls	Runs	Wkts	BBI	BBM	Ave	Econ	SR	5w	10
First-class	101	37	27	0	-	-	-	4.37	-	0	0
List A	51	3	2	0	-	-	-	4.00	-	0	0
Twenty20	27	12	25	0	-	-	-	12.50	-	0	0

JAMES REGAN

RHB WK

FULL NAME: James Alan Regan
BORN: May 30, 1994, Frimley, Surrey
SQUAD NO: 19
HEIGHT: 5ft 10in
NICKNAME: Reags
EDUCATION: King's College, Taunton; Oxford Brookes University
TEAMS: Hampshire Under-15s, Somerset, Somerset 2nd XI
CAREER: First-class: 2012

CAREER HIGHLIGHTS? Playing against South Africa in a tour match and making my first-class debut
SUPERSTITIONS? I scratch the pitch six times when taking guard
MOST MARKED CHARACTERISTIC? My kindness
BEST PLAYER IN COUNTY CRICKET? Marcus Trescothick
TIPS FOR THE TOP? Jos Buttler, Stuart Meaker, Joe Root
DESERT ISLAND DISC? Justin Bieber – As Long As You Love Me
FAVOURITE TV? Geordie Shore
CRICKETING HEROES? Adam Gilchrist, Kevin Pietersen
NON-CRICKETING HEROES? David Beckham
ACCOMPLISHMENTS? My GCSE results, living in Australia and playing semi-pro football
WHEN YOU RETIRE? I'd like to become a coach or trainer/physio
SURPRISING FACT? I listen to Justin Bieber to relax before batting
FANTASY SLIP CORDON? Keeper: Me, 1st: David Beckham, 2nd: Cristiano Ronaldo, 3rd: Megan Fox, Gully: Cheryl Cole
TWITTER FEED: @reganja23

Batting	Mat	Inns	NO	Runs	HS	Ave	SR	100	50	Ct	St
First-class	1	-	-	-	-	-	-	-	-	0	0

Bowling	Mat	Balls	Runs	Wkts	BBI	BBM	Ave	Econ	SR	5w	10
First-class	1	-	-	-	-	-	-	-	-	-	-

GEORGE RHODES   RHB RMF

WORCESTERSHIRE

FULL NAME: George Harry Rhodes
BORN: October 26, 1993, Worcester
SQUAD NO: 34
HEIGHT: 5ft 11in
NICKNAME: Rhodesy, Jnr Bump
EDUCATION: Chase Technology College; Worcester University
TEAMS: Worcestershire 2nd XI, Worcestershire Academy, Worcestershire Under-13s, Worcestershire Under-14s, Worcestershire Under-15s, Worcestershire Under-17s
CAREER: Yet to make first-team debut

FAMILY TIES? My father [Steve] played professional cricket for 22 years including international cricket and my grandfather [Billy] also played professional cricket
SUPERSTITIONS? No, I don't believe in all that rubbish!
CRICKETING HEROES? Alan Richardson – he's an absolute professional in every sense of the word
BEST PLAYER IN COUNTY CRICKET? Marcus Trescothick – easy question!
TIP FOR THE TOP? Alex Milton
IF YOU WEREN'T A CRICKETER? I'd have been a footballer or maybe a landscape gardener
FAVOURITE TV? The Inbetweeners – exactly my type of comedy
DESERT ISLAND DISC? Bobby McFerrin – Don't Worry Be Happy
WHEN YOU RETIRE? I'll finally go on a summer holiday – I'm thinking Barbados
ACCOMPLISHMENTS? I was conkers champion at Rushwick CofE Primary School between 2002 and 2004
SURPRISING FACTS? I always wanted to be a wicketkeeper but was never allowed
FANTASY SLIP CORDON? Keeper: Keith Lemon, 1st: Lee Evans, 2nd Karl Pilkington, 3rd: Megan Fox, Gully: Eddie Murphy
TWITTER FEED: @Ghrhodes

WILL RHODES

LHB RMF

FULL NAME: William Michael Harry Rhodes
BORN: March 2, 1995, Nottingham
SQUAD NO: 35
HEIGHT: 6ft 2in
NICKNAME: Codhead, Rhodesy
EDUCATION: Cottingham High School and Sixth Form College, Hull
TEAMS: England Under-17s, England Under-19s, Yorkshire, Yorkshire 2nd XI, Yorkshire Academy, Yorkshire Under-13s, Yorkshire Under-14s, Yorkshire Under-15s, Yorkshire Under-17s
CAREER: List A: 2013; T20: 2013

YORKSHIRE

FAMILY TIES? My brother Dom played for Yorkshire Schools and my father Rob is the best village cricketer East Yorkshire has ever seen!

WHO WOULD PLAY YOU IN A FILM OF YOUR LIFE? Matt Damon or Liam Neeson

CAREER HIGHLIGHTS? Making my debut for Yorkshire in May 2013, selection for England U19 in August 2013 and reaching the U19 World Cup semi-final in February 2014

SUPERSTITIONS? I mark/scratch my guard 10 times when I first come to the crease as a batsman

MOST MARKED CHARACTERISTIC? Apparently it's my terrible accent

BEST PLAYER IN COUNTY CRICKET? Gary Ballance

TIPS FOR THE TOP? Matthew Fisher, Ben Duckett, Joe Clarke

IF YOU WEREN'T A CRICKETER? I'd be a professional footballer

FAVOURITE TV? Made In Chelsea, I'm A Celebrity… Get Me Out Of Here!

CRICKETING HEROES? Michael Hussey, Marcus Trescothick

NON-CRICKETING HEROES? Nick Barmby

ACCOMPLISHMENTS? Gaining three A-Levels (I definitely thought I wouldn't!)

WHEN YOU RETIRE? I want to go travelling

SURPRISING FACT? I was once a schools cross-country champion aged 11

CRICKET RULE YOU'D CHANGE? You should get more runs depending on how big your six is

FANTASY SLIP CORDON? Keeper: Joe Clarke (very, very funny bloke) 1st: Myself, 2nd: Lucy Pinder (my favourite model), 3rd: Cheryl Cole (we may need a song if it's a long day in the field), Gully: Michael McIntyre (you need a comedian to keep everyone going!)

TWITTER FEED: @will_rhodes152

Batting	Mat	Inns	NO	Runs	HS	Ave	SR	100	50	Ct	St
List A	7	6	1	53	19*	10.60	80.30	0	0	2	0
Twenty20	2	2	0	13	13	6.50	65.00	0	0	0	0

Bowling	Mat	Balls	Runs	Wkts	BBI	BBM	Ave	Econ	SR	5w	10
List A	7	120	133	4	2/26	2/26	33.25	6.65	30.0	0	0
Twenty20	2	7	14	0	-	-	-	12.00	-	0	0

MICHAEL RICHARDSON

RHB WK

FULL NAME: Michael John Richardson
BORN: October 4, 1986, Port Elizabeth, Eastern Province, South Africa
SQUAD NO: 18
HEIGHT: 5ft 10in
NICKNAME: Chelsea, Rory, Richie
EDUCATION: Rondebosch Boys' High School; Stonyhurst College; Nottingham University
TEAMS: Badureliya Sports Club, Durham, Durham 2nd XI, Marylebone Cricket Club Young Cricketers
CAREER: First-class: 2010; List A: 2012; T20: 2013

BEST BATTING: 129 Durham vs Sussex, Hove, 2013

FAMILY TIES? My dad [Dave] played for South Africa and my cousin, uncle and grandad also played first-class cricket
WHO WOULD PLAY YOU IN A FILM OF YOUR LIFE? Leonardo DiCaprio
CAREER HIGHLIGHTS? My maiden first-class century and winning the County Championship in 2013
TIP FOR THE TOP? Ben Stokes
IF YOU WEREN'T A CRICKETER? I'd be an investment manager
DESERT ISLAND DISC? Damien Jurado – Ohio Remix
FAVOURITE TV? Sky Sports
CRICKETING HEROES? Neil McKenzie, Brian Lara
CRICKETING HEROES? Rafael Nadal
ACCOMPLISHMENTS? Getting my university degree
WHEN YOU RETIRE? I'd like to commentate
FANTASY SLIP CORDON? Keeper: José Mourinho, 1st: Jake White, 2nd: Rafa Nadal, 3rd: Myself, Gully: Schalk Burger
TWITTER FEED: @Richo18howu

Batting	Mat	Inns	NO	Runs	HS	Ave	SR	100	50	Ct	St
First-class	28	45	2	1285	129	29.88	56.50	2	7	61	1
List A	2	1	0	45	45	45.00	70.31	0	0	1	0
Twenty20	10	4	3	15	8*	15.00	107.14	0	0	4	0

Bowling	Mat	Balls	Runs	Wkts	BBI	BBM	Ave	Econ	SR	5w	10
First-class	28	24	13	0	-	-	-	3.25	-	0	0
List A	2	-	-	-	-	-	-	-	-	-	-
Twenty20	10	-	-	-	-	-	-	-	-	-	-

ADAM RILEY RHB OB

FULL NAME: Adam Edward Nicholas Riley
BORN: March 23, 1992, Sidcup, Kent
SQUAD NO: 33
HEIGHT: 6ft 2in
NICKNAME: Riles, Rilo, Sherman, Mad-Dog, Saggsy
EDUCATION: Beths Grammar School, Bexley; Loughborough University
TEAMS: Kent, Kent 2nd XI, Loughborough MCCU
CAREER: First-class: 2011; List A: 2011; T20: 2011

KENT

BEST BATTING: 21* Kent vs Hampshire, Canterbury, 2013
BEST BOWLING: 7-150 Kent vs Hampshire, Southampton, 2013

WHO WOULD PLAY YOU IN A FILM OF YOUR LIFE? Bradley Cooper
CAREER HIGHLIGHTS? Taking 7-150 vs Hampshire in 2013
SUPERSTITIONS? I wipe my hands on the crease before every over I bowl
MOST MARKED CHARACTERISTIC? My "strawberry blonde" hair!
BEST PLAYER IN COUNTY CRICKET? Darren Stevens
TIPS FOR THE TOP? Daniel Bell-Drummond and Adam Rossington
IF YOU WEREN'T A CRICKETER? I'd be a full-time Charlton Athletic supporter!
DESERT ISLAND DISC? Now 68
FAVOURITE TV? The Following
CRICKETING HEROES? Shane Warne
NON-CRICKETING HEROES? Alan Curbishley, Clive Mendonca and Dean Kiely
CRICKET RULE YOU'D CHANGE? I'd get five fielders back outside the circle in ODIs
TWITTER FEED: @AdamRiley92

Batting	Mat	Inns	NO	Runs	HS	Ave	SR	100	50	Ct	St
First-class	20	24	6	118	21*	6.55	20.73	0	0	8	0
List A	19	3	2	6	3*	6.00	50.00	0	0	6	0
Twenty20	15	5	4	8	5*	8.00	88.88	0	0	3	0

Bowling	Mat	Balls	Runs	Wkts	BBI	BBM	Ave	Econ	SR	5w	10
First-class	20	2212	1449	42	7/150	7/167	34.50	3.93	52.6	2	0
List A	19	624	593	15	2/32	2/32	39.53	5.70	41.6	0	0
Twenty20	15	298	351	10	2/15	2/15	35.10	7.06	29.8	0	0

OLIVER ROBINSON

RHB RMF

FULL NAME: Oliver Edward Robinson
BORN: December 1, 1993, Margate, Kent
SQUAD NO: 24
EDUCATION: King's School, Canterbury
TEAMS: Kent 2nd XI, Kent Under-13s, Kent
Under-15s, Kent Under-17s, Yorkshire,
Yorkshire 2nd XI
CAREER: List A: 2013

TWITTER FEED: @ollierob123
NOTES: Having been on the books at Kent, Robinson opted to leave the club in May last
year and joined Yorkshire after featuring for Leicestershire's 2nd XI. He made a strong
impression in a 2nd XI Championship fixture against Warwickshire last August, scoring 90*
and 30* from No.5 and taking 5-21 in the match. He finished the season first in the bowling
averages for Yorkshire's 2nd XI and third in the batting averages, scoring 1,282 runs and
taking 59 wickets. He played in three YB40 matches towards the end of last season and was
awarded his first professional contract in October

Batting	Mat	Inns	NO	Runs	HS	Ave	SR	100	50	Ct	St
List A	3	2	2	16	12*	-	100.00	0	0	4	0

Bowling	Mat	Balls	Runs	Wkts	BBI	BBM	Ave	Econ	SR	5w	10
List A	3	60	66	0	-	-	-	6.60	-	0	0

FULL NAME: Angus James Robson
BORN: February 19, 1992, Sydney, Australia
SQUAD NO: 8
HEIGHT: 5ft 8in
NICKNAME: Gus, Robbo
EDUCATION: Marcellin College, Randwick;
Australian College of Physical Education
TEAMS: Gloucestershire 2nd XI,
Leicestershire, Leicestershire 2nd XI, New
South Wales Under-19s
CAREER: First-class: 2013

LEICESTERSHIRE

BEST BATTING: 49 Leicestershire vs Gloucestershire, Bristol, 2013

FAMILY TIES? My brother Sam plays for Middlesex and my father Jim played for
Worcestershire 2nd XI
WHO WOULD PLAY YOU IN A FILM OF YOUR LIFE? Leonardo DiCaprio
CAREER HIGHLIGHTS? Scoring 49 on my first-class debut
SUPERSTITIONS? I check the wind each over using grass
MOST MARKED CHARACTERISTIC? Positivity
BEST PLAYER IN COUNTY CRICKET? Eoin Morgan
TIPS FOR THE TOP? Stephen Parry, Nick Nisbet
IF YOU WEREN'T A CRICKETER? I'd be playing another sport
DESERT ISLAND DISC? Taylor Swift – Red
FAVOURITE TV? One Tree Hill
CRICKETING HEROES? Ian Bell, Michael Atherton, Michael Clarke
NON-CRICKETING HEROES? Haile Gebrselassie
ACCOMPLISHMENTS? Progressing through a university course
WHEN YOU RETIRE? I'd like to be a PE teacher
SURPRISING FACT? I have a strong interest in sporting autobiographies
FANTASY SLIP CORDON? Keeper: Adam Sandler, 1st: Me, 2nd: Taylor Swift, 3rd: Tom DeLonge,
Gully: Harry Potter
TWITTER FEED: @gusrobson92

Batting	Mat	Inns	NO	Runs	HS	Ave	SR	100	50	Ct	St
First-class	3	4	0	59	49	14.75	39.33	0	0	0	0

Bowling	Mat	Balls	Runs	Wkts	BBI	BBM	Ave	Econ	SR	5w	10
First-class	3	6	11	0	-	-	-	11.00	-	0	0

SAM ROBSON

RHB LB R1

MIDDLESEX

FULL NAME: Sam David Robson
BORN: July 1, 1989, Sydney, Australia
SQUAD NO: 12
HEIGHT: 6ft
NICKNAME: Robbo, Leaguie
EDUCATION: Marcellin College, Randwick
TEAMS: Australia Under-19s, Eastern Suburbs, England Lions, England Performance Programme, Middlesex, Middlesex 2nd XI, New South Wales Under-19s
CAREER: First-class: 2009; List A: 2008; T20: 2011

BEST BATTING: 215* Middlesex vs Warwickshire, Birmingham, 2013
COUNTY CAP: 2013

FAMILY TIES? My father Jim played 2nd XI cricket for Worcestershire and my brother Angus is on the staff at Leicestershire
WHO WOULD PLAY YOU IN A FILM OF YOUR LIFE? Adam Sandler
CAREER HIGHLIGHTS? Getting capped by Middlesex and being selected for England Lions
SUPERSTITIONS? Watch the ball!
BEST PLAYER IN COUNTY CRICKET? Graham Onions or Ed Joyce
TIPS FOR THE TOP? Angus Robson, Tom Helm
IF YOU WEREN'T A CRICKETER? I don't know. Maybe a schoolteacher
DESERT ISLAND DISC? Britney Spears – Stronger
FAVOURITE TV? Seinfeld
CRICKETING HEROES? Shane Warne, Michael Vaughan, Steve Waugh, Andrew Flintoff
NON-CRICKETING HEROES? My father

Batting	Mat	Inns	NO	Runs	HS	Ave	SR	100	50	Ct	St
First-class	63	113	10	4307	215*	41.81	50.53	11	16	68	0
List A	8	6	0	169	65	28.16	74.44	0	1	3	0
Twenty20	4	4	2	53	28*	26.50	103.92	0	0	2	0

Bowling	Mat	Balls	Runs	Wkts	BBI	BBM	Ave	Econ	SR	5w	10
First-class	63	86	66	1	1/4	1/4	66.00	4.60	86.0	0	0
List A	8	-	-	-	-	-	-	-	-	-	-
Twenty20	4	-	-	-	-	-	-	-	-	-	-

GARETH RODERICK — RHB WK

FULL NAME: Gareth Hugh Roderick
BORN: August 28, 1991, Durban, Natal, South Africa
SQUAD NO: 27
HEIGHT: 6ft
NICKNAME: Roders
EDUCATION: Maritzburg College
TEAMS: Gloucestershire, Gloucestershire 2nd XI, KwaZulu-Natal, KwaZulu-Natal Inland Under-19s, Northamptonshire 2nd XI
CAREER: First-class: 2011; List A: 2011; T20: 2011

BEST BATTING: 152* Gloucestershire vs Kent, Canterbury, 2013

WHO WOULD PLAY YOU IN A FILM OF YOUR LIFE? Zac Efron
CAREER HIGHLIGHTS? My maiden first-class hundred against Kent in 2013
MOST MARKED CHARACTERISTIC? Being both skinny and fat at the same time – not impossible according to my teammates
BEST PLAYER IN COUNTY CRICKET? Jos Buttler
TIPS FOR THE TOP? Miles Hammond and Calvin Savage
IF YOU WEREN'T A CRICKETER? I'd still be studying some degree I had no interest in
DESERT ISLAND DISC? Green Day – American Idiot
FAVOURITE TV? How I Met Your Mother
CRICKETING HEROES? Steve Waugh and Mark Boucher
NON-CRICKETING HEROES? Nelson Mandela and my father
WHEN YOU RETIRE? I'll move somewhere exotic and live on the beach
SURPRISING FACT? I become extremely grumpy in cold weather
CRICKET RULE YOU'D CHANGE? There should be free hits for any type of no ball bowled
FANTASY SLIP CORDON? Keeper: Myself, 1st: Steve Waugh, 2nd: Jim Jeffries, 3rd: Cartman from South Park, Gully: My dad
TWITTER FEED: @Roders369

Batting	Mat	Inns	NO	Runs	HS	Ave	SR	100	50	Ct	St
First-class	25	36	9	1117	152*	41.37	47.05	2	5	53	1
List A	16	11	3	191	63	23.87	92.27	0	1	12	2
Twenty20	13	8	2	68	32	11.33	95.77	0	0	4	0

Bowling	Mat	Balls	Runs	Wkts	BBI	BBM	Ave	Econ	SR	5w	10
First-class	25	-	-	-	-	-	-	-	-	-	-
List A	16	-	-	-	-	-	-	-	-	-	-
Twenty20	13	-	-	-	-	-	-	-	-	-	-

CHRIS ROGERS

LHB LB R7

FULL NAME: Christopher John Llewellyn Rogers
BORN: August 31, 1977, Sydney, Australia
SQUAD NO: 1
HEIGHT: 5ft 11in
NICKNAME: Bucky
EDUCATION: Wesley College; Curtin University
TEAMS: Australia, Derbyshire, Leicestershire, Middlesex, Northamptonshire, Victoria, W Australia
CAREER: Test: 2008; First-class: 1998; List A: 1998; T20: 2005

BEST BATTING: 319 Northamptonshire vs Gloucestershire, Northampton, 2006
BEST BOWLING: 1-16 Northamptonshire vs Leicestershire, Northampton, 2006
COUNTY CAPS: 2008 (Derbyshire); 2011 (Middlesex)

FAMILY TIES? My father John played for New South Wales
CAREER HIGHLIGHTS? My Test debut in 2008 for Australia vs India, scoring 209 against Australia for Leicestershire in 2005 and scoring 319 against Gloucestershire in 2006
CRICKETING HEROES? Allan Border, Steve Waugh
NON-CRICKETING HEROES? Michael Jordan, Cadel Evans, Jack Reacher
BEST PLAYER IN COUNTY CRICKET? Marcus Trescothick
TIPS FOR THE TOP? Sam Robson, Alex Hales
WHEN RAIN STOPS PLAY? Coffee and crosswords
FAVOURITE TV? Entourage
FAVOURITE FILM? American Pie 2
FAVOURITE BOOK? Power Of One
DREAM HOLIDAY? South America
ACCOMPLISHMENTS? Journalism degree
GUILTY PLEASURES? Motorway service Burger Kings

Batting	Mat	Inns	NO	Runs	HS	Ave	SR	100	50	Ct	St
Tests	14	27	0	1030	119	38.14	47.44	4	5	9	0
First-class	260	464	32	21439	319	49.62		66	99	217	0
List A	159	153	14	5082	140	36.56		5	34	71	0
Twenty20	43	37	1	627	58	17.41	114.62	0	3	22	0

Bowling	Mat	Balls	Runs	Wkts	BBI	BBM	Ave	Econ	SR	5w	10
Tests	14	-	-	-	-	-	-	-	-	-	-
First-class	260	230	131	1	1/16	1/16	131.00	3.41	230.0	0	0
List A	159	24	26	2	2/22	2/22	13.00	6.50	12.0	0	0
Twenty20	43	-	-	-	-	-	-	-	-	-	-

TOBY ROLAND-JONES

RHB RMF W1

FULL NAME: Tobias Skelton Roland-Jones
BORN: January 29, 1988, Ashford, Middlesex
SQUAD NO: 21
HEIGHT: 6ft 4in
NICKNAME: Rojo, TRJ
EDUCATION: Hampton School; Leeds University
TEAMS: England Lions, Marylebone Cricket Club, Middlesex, Middlesex 2nd XI
CAREER: First-class: 2010; List A: 2010; T20: 2011

MIDDLESEX

BEST BATTING: 52 Middlesex vs Sussex, Lord's, 2012
BEST BOWLING: 6-63 Middlesex vs Nottinghamshire, Nottingham, 2013
COUNTY CAP: 2012

FAMILY TIES? My older brother Olly played for Middlesex 2nd XI and my dad used to coach age-group cricket
WHO WOULD PLAY YOU IN A FILM OF YOUR LIFE? Anyone with a sufficient-sized nose has my blessing
CAREER HIGHLIGHTS? My first five-wicket haul at Lord's vs Surrey, my hat-trick vs Derbyshire and representing England Lions in 2013
MOST MARKED CHARACTERISTIC? Anger when on the cricket pitch and off it, my nose. In our squad only Steven Finn has a bigger one
BEST PLAYER IN COUNTY CRICKET? From a bowling perspective, Graham Onions and Tim Murtagh stand out. I would say Ed Joyce as a batsman
TIPS FOR THE TOP? Ravi Patel, Tom Helm
DESERT ISLAND DISC? Michael Jackson – Thriller
FAVOURITE TV? The Sopranos, The Wire
CRICKETING HEROES? Ian Botham
WHEN YOU RETIRE? I like the idea of working in marketing
TWITTER FEED:? @tobyrj21

Batting	Mat	Inns	NO	Runs	HS	Ave	SR	100	50	Ct	St
First-class	40	55	12	692	52	16.09	47.82	0	1	13	0
List A	30	15	3	122	24	10.16	79.73	0	0	5	0
Twenty20	13	6	3	25	12	8.33	119.04	0	0	2	0

Bowling	Mat	Balls	Runs	Wkts	BBI	BBM	Ave	Econ	SR	5w	10
First-class	40	6494	3491	157	6/63	10/118	22.23	3.22	41.3	8	1
List A	30	1279	1219	52	4/44	4/44	23.44	5.71	24.5	0	0
Twenty20	13	264	364	16	4/25	4/25	22.75	8.27	16.5	0	0

YORKSHIRE

FULL NAME: Joseph Edward Root
BORN: December 30, 1990, Sheffield, Yorkshire
SQUAD NO: 5
HEIGHT: 6ft
NICKNAME: Rooty, Roota, Rootfish
EDUCATION: King Ecgbert School; Worksop College
TEAMS: England, England Lions, England Under-19s, Yorkshire, Yorkshire 2nd XI, Yorkshire Academy, Yorkshire Under-17s
CAREER: Test: 2012; ODI: 2013; T20I: 2012; First-class: 2010; List A: 2009; T20: 2011

BEST BATTING: 236 Yorkshire vs Derbyshire, Leeds, 2013
BEST BOWLING: 3-33 Yorkshire vs Warwickshire, Leeds, 2011
COUNTY CAP: 2012

FAMILY TIES? My dad played club cricket and represented Nottinghamshire 2nd XI. My brother [Billy] is currently playing 2nd XI on trial and is an ex-MCC Young Cricketer
CAREER HIGHLIGHTS? Winning the Ashes
MOST MARKED CHARACTERISTIC? Bowed legs and a baby face
BEST PLAYER IN COUNTY CRICKET? Marcus Trescothick
TIPS FOR THE TOP? Alex Lees, Matt Fisher, Eliot Callis, Billy Root
FAVOURITE TV? Sherlock
CRICKETING HEROES? Michael Vaughan
SURPRISING FACT? I'm learning to play the ukulele
CRICKET RULE YOU'D CHANGE? I'd get rid of umpire's call on DRS
TWITTER FEED: @joeroot05

Batting	Mat	Inns	NO	Runs	HS	Ave	SR	100	50	Ct	St
Tests	15	29	3	955	180	36.73	39.69	2	4	8	0
ODIs	26	25	3	853	107	38.77	78.11	1	5	10	0
T20Is	7	5	2	152	90*	50.66	139.44	0	1	4	0
First-class	58	99	12	3851	236	44.26	49.94	9	14	31	0
List A	54	52	6	1611	110*	35.02	78.12	2	9	20	0
Twenty20	34	28	6	562	90*	25.54	119.82	0	2	13	0

Bowling	Mat	Balls	Runs	Wkts	BBI	BBM	Ave	Econ	SR	5w	10
Tests	15	372	169	3	2/9	2/9	56.33	2.72	124.0	0	0
ODIs	26	474	471	10	2/15	2/15	47.10	5.96	47.4	0	0
T20Is	7	42	80	3	1/13	1/13	26.66	11.42	14.0	0	0
First-class	58	1539	818	14	3/33	3/33	58.42	3.18	109.9	0	0
List A	54	929	850	22	2/10	2/10	38.63	5.48	42.2	0	0
Twenty20	34	186	298	7	1/12	1/12	42.57	9.61	26.5	0	0

ADAM ROSSINGTON   RHB WK

FULL NAME: Adam Matthew Rossington
BORN: May 5, 1993, Edgware, Middlesex
SQUAD NO: 17
HEIGHT: 6ft
NICKNAME: Rosso, Tuggy
EDUCATION: Mill Hill School
TEAMS: England Under-19s, Middlesex, Middlesex 2nd XI
CAREER: First-class: 2010; List A: 2012; T20: 2011

BEST BATTING: 103* Middlesex vs Cambridge MCCU, Cambridge, 2013

WHO WOULD PLAY YOU IN A FILM OF YOUR LIFE? Jason Statham
CAREER HIGHLIGHTS? Scoring my first first-class hundred
SUPERSTITIONS? I always put my left pad on first
MOST MARKED CHARACTERISTIC? Determination
BEST PLAYER IN COUNTY CRICKET? Graham Onions
TIP FOR THE TOP? Daniel Bell-Drummond
IF YOU WEREN'T A CRICKETER? I would have tried to play golf
DESERT ISLAND DISC? Bastille – Bad Blood
FAVOURITE TV? Made In Chelsea
CRICKETING HEROES? Alec Stewart, Paul Weekes
ACCOMPLISHMENTS? Passing my A-Levels
WHEN YOU RETIRE? I want to start up my own coaching business
SURPRISING FACT? I can't ride a bicycle
CRICKET RULE YOU'D CHANGE? There should be free hits for front-foot no balls in four-day cricket
FANTASY SLIP CORDON? Keeper: Me, 1st: Lee Evans, 2nd: Ian Botham, 3rd: Kelly Brook, Gully: Arthur Guinness
TWITTER FEED: @Rossington17

Batting	Mat	Inns	NO	Runs	HS	Ave	SR	100	50	Ct	St
First-class	6	10	2	227	103*	28.37	64.12	1	1	16	1
List A	8	6	1	161	79*	32.20	95.83	0	1	8	2
Twenty20	20	19	2	266	74	15.64	131.68	0	1	12	3

Bowling	Mat	Balls	Runs	Wkts	BBI	BBM	Ave	Econ	SR	5w	10
First-class	6	-	-	-	-	-	-	-	-	-	-
List A	8	-	-	-	-	-	-	-	-	-	-
Twenty20	20	-	-	-	-	-	-	-	-	-	-

SURREY

FULL NAME: Jason Jonathan Roy
BORN: July 21, 1990, Durban, South Africa
SQUAD NO: 20
HEIGHT: 6ft
NICKNAME: JRoy
EDUCATION: Whitgift School
TEAMS: Chittagong Kings, England Lions, Surrey, Surrey 2nd XI
CAREER: First-class: 2010; List A: 2008; T20: 2008

BEST BATTING: 106* Surrey vs Glamorgan, The Oval, 2011
BEST BOWLING: 3-35 Surrey vs Warwickshire, Guildford, 2013

CAREER HIGHLIGHTS? Winning the CB40 with Surrey, getting promoted back to Division One of the County Championship with Surrey, my maiden first-class hundred against Glamorgan and being the first Surrey player to score a T20 hundred
CRICKETING HEROES? Jacques Kallis and Chris Gayle
BEST PLAYER IN COUNTY CRICKET? Marcus Trescothick
TIPS FOR THE TOP? All the Surrey youngsters
IF YOU WEREN'T A CRICKETER? I'd be a professional surfer
WHEN RAIN STOPS PLAY? Chatting in the dressing room
FAVOURITE TV? Two And A Half Men
FAVOURITE FILM? The Hangover
DREAM HOLIDAY? Mauritius or the Caribbean
GUILTY PLEASURES? Watching TV whilst eating a tub of ice cream
FANTASY SLIP CORDON? Keeper: Will Ferrell, 1st: Vince Vaughn, 2nd: Owen Wilson, 3rd: Jason Roy, Gully: Spider-Man
TWITTER FEED: @JasonRoy20

Batting	Mat	Inns	NO	Runs	HS	Ave	SR	100	50	Ct	St
First-class	32	57	4	1486	106*	28.03	80.28	1	6	25	0
List A	49	46	3	1251	131	29.09	106.10	4	6	15	0
Twenty20	67	64	2	1466	101*	23.64	134.86	1	7	33	0

Bowling	Mat	Balls	Runs	Wkts	BBI	BBM	Ave	Econ	SR	5w	10
First-class	32	96	97	5	3/35	3/35	19.40	6.06	19.2	0	0
List A	49	6	12	0	-	-	-	12.00	-	0	0
Twenty20	67	12	23	1	1/23	1/23	23.00	11.50	12.0	0	0

JACQUES RUDOLPH LHB LB R4

FULL NAME: Jacobus Andries Rudolph
BORN: May 4, 1981, Springs, Transvaal, South Africa
SQUAD NO: 4
HEIGHT: 5ft 10in
NICKNAME: Jakes
EDUCATION: Afrikaanse Hoer Seunskool
TEAMS: South Africa, Africa XI, Eagles, Glamorgan, Jamaica Tallawahs, Northerns, South Africa A, Surrey, Titans, Yorkshire
CAREER: Test: 2003; ODI: 2003; T20I: 2006; First-class: 1997; List A: 2000; T20: 2004

GLAMORGAN

BEST BATTING: 228* Yorkshire vs Durham, Leeds, 2010
BEST BOWLING: 5-80 Eagles vs Cape Cobras, Cape Town, 2007
COUNTY CAP: 2007 (Yorkshire)

CRICKETING HEROES? Justin Langer
CAREER HIGHLIGHTS? Making 222* on my Test debut
OTHER SPORTS FOLLOWED? Football (Manchester United)
FAVOURITE BAND? U2, Dire Straits, The Killers
RELAXATIONS? Fly-fishing and adventure motorbiking
NOTES: Scored 222* on his debut Test innings, against Bangladesh at Chittagong in 2003, as part of record-breaking unbeaten third-wicket stand of 429 with Boeta Dippenaar. Played for Yorkshire between 2007-2011, passing 1,000 runs in four consecutive seasons (2007-2010). Featured for Surrey in 2012 after losing his place in South Africa's Test side and signed a two-year deal with Glamorgan in September 2013, replacing Marcus North as the club's overseas player

Batting	Mat	Inns	NO	Runs	HS	Ave	SR	100	50	Ct	St
Tests	48	83	9	2622	222*	35.43	43.81	6	11	29	0
ODIs	45	39	6	1174	81	35.57	68.05	0	7	11	0
T20Is	1	1	1	6	6*	-	85.71	0	0	0	0
First-class	235	402	26	16645	228*	44.26		46	77	205	0
List A	224	212	31	8761	134*	48.40		13	61	83	0
Twenty20	102	92	13	2359	83*	29.86	114.18	0	14	31	0

Bowling	Mat	Balls	Runs	Wkts	BBI	BBM	Ave	Econ	SR	5w	10
Tests	48	664	432	4	1/1	1/1	108.00	3.90	166.0	0	0
ODIs	45	24	26	0	-	-	-	6.50	-	0	0
T20Is	1	-	-	-	-	-	-	-	-	-	-
First-class	235	4523	2572	58	5/80		44.34	3.41	77.9	3	0
List A	224	418	390	12	4/41	4/41	32.50	5.59	34.8	0	0
Twenty20	102	163	221	10	3/16	3/16	22.10	8.13	16.3	0	0

CHRIS RUSHWORTH   RHB RFM W1 MVP17

FULL NAME: Christopher Rushworth
BORN: July 11, 1986, Sunderland
SQUAD NO: 22
HEIGHT: 6ft 2in
NICKNAME: Rushy, Sponge, Pilko
EDUCATION: Castle View Comprehensive
TEAMS: Durham, Marylebone Cricket Club, Northumberland
CAREER: First-class: 2010; List A: 2004; T20: 2011

BEST BATTING: 28 Durham vs Yorkshire, Chester-le-Street, 2010
BEST BOWLING: 6-58 Durham vs Somerset, Taunton, 2013

FAMILY TIES? My dad played local league cricket, my brother played junior county and England stuff and now plays locally for Washington CC and my cousin Phil Mustard is current Durham wicketkeeper
WHO WOULD PLAY YOU IN A FILM OF YOUR LIFE? David Beckham – the bloke is a legend
CAREER HIGHLIGHTS? Winning the 2013 County Championship with Durham
BEST PLAYER IN COUNTY CRICKET? Graham Onions – a prolific wicket-taker over the last three seasons
TIPS FOR THE TOP? Paul Coughlin and James Thompson – both of Durham
IF YOU WEREN'T A CRICKETER? No idea!
DESERT ISLAND DISC? It would have to be a compilation of indie music – a bit of Oasis, Stereophonics and Courteeners, to name a few
FAVOURITE TV? Pretty much anything on Sky Sports 1
CRICKETING HEROES? Shaun Pollock was my favourite player to watch as a young boy
ACCOMPLISHMENTS? My little boy Henry
SURPRISING FACT? As a kid I reached brown belt in karate, only two marks away from black belt
TWITTER FEED: @rushworth22

Batting	Mat	Inns	NO	Runs	HS	Ave	SR	100	50	Ct	St
First-class	37	50	19	359	28	11.58	62.00	0	0	7	0
List A	33	14	7	49	12*	7.00	72.05	0	0	7	0
Twenty20	30	5	4	3	2	3.00	50.00	0	0	4	0

Bowling	Mat	Balls	Runs	Wkts	BBI	BBM	Ave	Econ	SR	5w	10
First-class	37	5591	2946	122	6/58	10/103	24.14	3.16	45.8	6	1
List A	33	1231	1089	57	5/31	5/31	19.10	5.30	21.5	2	0
Twenty20	30	557	749	30	3/19	3/19	24.96	8.06	18.5	0	0

RHB RMF

FULL NAME: Christopher James Russell
BORN: February 16, 1989, Newport, Isle of Wight
SQUAD NO: 18
HEIGHT: 6ft 1in
NICKNAME: Goober, Goobs, Spaniel
EDUCATION: Wroxall Primary School; Ventnor Middle School; Medina High School
TEAMS: Worcestershire, Worcestershire 2nd XI
CAREER: First-class: 2012; List A: 2010; T20: 2013

WORCESTERSHIRE

BEST BATTING: 22 Worcestershire vs Middlesex, Worcester, 2012
BEST BOWLING: 4-43 Worcestershire vs Warwickshire, Birmingham, 2012

WHO WOULD PLAY YOU IN A FILM OF YOUR LIFE? Johnny Depp
CAREER HIGHLIGHTS? Playing against South Africa in a two-day tour match and making my first-class debut against Warwickshire
SUPERSTITIONS? I always put my left pad on first
TIPS FOR THE TOP? Ben Stokes, James Taylor and Danny Briggs
IF YOU WEREN'T A CRICKETER? I'd like to work in animation and illustration
DESERT ISLAND DISC? Ed Sheeran – +
FAVOURITE TV? Celebrity Juice
WHEN YOU RETIRE? I'll chill on a beach in the Caribbean
FANTASY SLIP CORDON? Keeper: Keith Lemon, 1st: Nelson Mandela, 2nd: David Beckham, 3rd: Myself, Gully: Rhod Gilbert
TWITTER FEED: @Chris18Russell

Batting	Mat	Inns	NO	Runs	HS	Ave	SR	100	50	Ct	St
First-class	17	22	4	129	22	7.16	36.44	0	0	4	0
List A	6	1	1	1	1*	-	33.33	0	0	3	0
Twenty20	2	2	2	6	3*	-	66.66	0	0	0	0

Bowling	Mat	Balls	Runs	Wkts	BBI	BBM	Ave	Econ	SR	5w	10
First-class	17	2222	1493	36	4/43	6/117	41.47	4.03	61.7	0	0
List A	6	174	170	5	4/32	4/32	34.00	5.86	34.8	0	0
Twenty20	2	27	62	0	-	-	-	13.77	-	0	0

NORTHAMPTONSHIRE

FULL NAME: David John Grimwood Sales
BORN: December 3, 1977, Carshalton, Surrey
SQUAD NO: 5
HEIGHT: 6ft
NICKNAME: Jumble, Car-boot
EDUCATION: Caterham School
TEAMS: England A, Northamptonshire, Wellington
CAREER: First-class: 1996; List A: 1994; T20: 2003

BEST BATTING: 303* Northamptonshire vs Essex, Northampton, 1999
BEST BOWLING: 4-25 Northamptonshire vs Sri Lanka A, Northampton, 1999
COUNTY CAP: 1999; BENEFIT YEAR: 2007

NON-CRICKETING HEROES? Phil Taylor
BEST PLAYER IN COUNTY CRICKET? Stephen Peters
TIP FOR THE TOP? Alex Wakely
IF YOU WEREN'T A CRICKETER? I'd be a cricket coach or brick-layer
WHEN RAIN STOPS PLAY? I drink coffee and talk rubbish
FAVOURITE TV? I'm A Celebrity… Get Me Out Of Here!
FAVOURITE FILM? Any Given Sunday
FAVOURITE BOOK? Bravo Two Zero
DREAM HOLIDAY? Spain
ACCOMPLISHMENTS? My three boys
GUILTY PLEASURES? A cheeky Chinese and a few beers

Batting	Mat	Inns	NO	Runs	HS	Ave	SR	100	50	Ct	St
First-class	246	389	35	14037	303*	39.65		29	64	219	0
List A	267	254	35	7406	161	33.81		4	53	114	0
Twenty20	56	53	12	1209	78*	29.48	129.86	0	10	28	0

Bowling	Mat	Balls	Runs	Wkts	BBI	BBM	Ave	Econ	SR	5w	10
First-class	246	345	184	9	4/25		20.44	3.20	38.3	0	0
List A	267	84	67	0	-	-	-	4.78	-	0	0
Twenty20	56	12	23	1	1/10	1/10	23.00	11.50	12.0	0	0

MATT SALISBURY RHB RMF

FULL NAME: Matthew Edward Thomas Salisbury
BORN: April 18, 1993, Chelmsford, Essex
SQUAD NO: 18
HEIGHT: 6ft 1in
NICKNAME: Sals
EDUCATION: Shenfield High School; Anglia Ruskin University, Cambridge
TEAMS: Cambridge MCCU, Essex 2nd XI, Essex Under-15s, Essex Under-17s
CAREER: First-class: 2012

ESSEX

BEST BATTING: 5 Cambridge MCCU vs Essex, Cambridge, 2013
BEST BOWLING: 3-64 Cambridge MCCU vs Essex, Cambridge, 2013

WHO WOULD PLAY YOU IN A FILM OF YOUR LIFE? Will Ferrell
CAREER HIGHLIGHTS? Playing first-class cricket with Cambridge MCCU and earning my first contract with Essex
BEST PLAYER IN COUNTY CRICKET? Dave Masters
TIPS FOR THE TOP? Ben Foakes, Tymal Mills, Reece Topley, Kishen Velani
IF YOU WEREN'T A CRICKETER? I'd be getting more work done at university
DESERT ISLAND DISC? Kendrick Lamar – Section 80
FAVOURITE TV? Modern Family
NON-CRICKETING HEROES? Kevin Durant and LeBron James
ACCOMPLISHMENTS? Winning two national basketball titles at school
CRICKET RULE YOU'D CHANGE? Hitting the ball out of the ground should be worth 10 runs
FANTASY SLIP CORDON? Keeper: Ricky Gervais, 1st: Karl Pilkington, 2nd: Will Ferrell, 3rd: Stewart Francis, Gully: Shaquille O'Neal
TWITTER FEED? @mattsalisbury10

Batting	Mat	Inns	NO	Runs	HS	Ave	SR	100	50	Ct	St
First-class	4	5	2	10	5	3.33	24.39	0	0	1	0

Bowling	Mat	Balls	Runs	Wkts	BBI	BBM	Ave	Econ	SR	5w	10
First-class	4	696	443	10	3/64	4/117	44.30	3.81	69.6	0	0

ANDREW SALTER RHB OB

FULL NAME: Andrew Graham Salter
BORN: June 1, 1993, Haverfordwest, Pembrokeshire, Wales
SQUAD NO: 21
HEIGHT: 5ft 10in
NICKNAME: Salts
EDUCATION: Milford Haven School; Cardiff Metropolitan University
TEAMS: Cardiff MCCU, England Under-17s, England Under-19s, Glamorgan, Glamorgan 2nd XI, Wales Minor Counties
CAREER: First-class: 2012; List A: 2012

BEST BATTING: 21 Cardiff MCCU vs Warwickshire, Birmingham, 2012
BEST BOWLING: 3-66 Glamorgan vs Leicestershire, Swansea, 2013

FAMILY TIES? My dad played to university standard, inspiring both my brother and myself to play, and my brother represented West Wales at junior level

WHO WOULD PLAY YOU IN A FILM OF YOUR LIFE? It would have to be Christian Bale, as he was also born in Haverfordwest

CAREER HIGHLIGHTS? Reaching the YB40 final at Lord's last year is my biggest highlight so far. Taking a wicket with the first ball of my Championship career was also something that I'll never forget

MOST MARKED CHARACTERISTIC? I'd like to think the way I enjoy the game and show enthusiasm would be one of my marked characteristics. Either that or my nose – it gets a lot of attention

BEST PLAYER IN COUNTY CRICKET? Jim Allenby

TIP FOR THE TOP? Dave Lloyd has got awesome ability and it won't be long before he causes mayhem across the counties

IF YOU WEREN'T A CRICKETER? If sports teaching and coaching didn't work out then I would like to be a palaeontologist

CRICKETING HEROES? Robert Croft and Dean Cosker were my childhood cricketing role models. I also always enjoyed watching Graeme Swann ripping them and showing how you can be aggressive with off-spin bowling

TWITTER FEED: @AndySalts

Batting	Mat	Inns	NO	Runs	HS	Ave	SR	100	50	Ct	St
First-class	7	10	3	98	21	14.00	28.08	0	0	2	0
List A	6	3	1	6	3	3.00	60.00	0	0	1	0

Bowling	Mat	Balls	Runs	Wkts	BBI	BBM	Ave	Econ	SR	5w	10
First-class	7	860	512	13	3/66	5/100	39.38	3.57	66.1	0	0
List A	6	270	228	6	2/41	2/41	38.00	5.06	45.0	0	0

GURJIT SANDHU

RHB LMF

FULL NAME: Gurjit Singh Sandhu
BORN: March 24, 1992, Isleworth, Middlesex
SQUAD NO: 92
HEIGHT: 6ft 4in
NICKNAME: Gurj
EDUCATION: Isleworth and Syon School
TEAMS: Middlesex, Middlesex 2nd XI
CAREER: First-class: 2011; List A: 2012; T20: 2013

MIDDLESEX

BEST BATTING: 8 Middlesex vs Sri Lankans, Uxbridge, 2011
BEST BOWLING: 4-49 Middlesex vs Cambridge MCCU, Cambridge, 2013

CAREER HIGHLIGHTS? Making my first-class debut against Sri Lanka at Uxbridge
SUPERSTITIONS? My chain – I can't play without it. I feel naked when I don't have it around my neck
CRICKETING HEROES? Wasim Akram, Brian Lara
NON-CRICKETING HEROES? Dimitar Berbatov, Karl Pilkington, Batman
BEST PLAYER IN COUNTY CRICKET? Marcus Trescothick
TIP FOR THE TOP? James Taylor
FAVOURITE TV? The Fresh Prince Of Bel-Air
FAVOURITE FILM? Inception, Gladiator
DREAM HOLIDAY? Caribbean islands
ACCOMPLISHMENTS? Winning a Football Manger season with Brentford
GUILTY PLEASURES? Junk food
TWITTER FEED: @gurjitsandhu92

Batting	Mat	Inns	NO	Runs	HS	Ave	SR	100	50	Ct	St
First-class	4	2	1	15	8	15.00	51.72	0	0	0	0
List A	1	1	0	0	0	0.00	0.00	0	0	0	0
Twenty20	4	1	1	2	2*	-	25.00	0	0	0	0

Bowling	Mat	Balls	Runs	Wkts	BBI	BBM	Ave	Econ	SR	5w	10
First-class	4	378	239	6	4/49	4/55	39.83	3.79	63.0	0	0
List A	1	36	28	3	3/28	3/28	9.33	4.66	12.0	0	0
Twenty20	4	48	93	4	2/15	2/15	23.25	11.62	12.0	0	0

RAMNARESH SARWAN

RHB LB

FULL NAME: Ramnaresh Ronnie Sarwan
BORN: June 23, 1980, Wakenaam Island, Essequibo, Guyana
SQUAD NO: 53
HEIGHT: 5ft 9in
NICKNAME: Ronnie
TEAMS: West Indies, Gloucestershire, Guyana, Guyana Amazon Warriors, Kings XI Punjab, Leicestershire, Stanford Superstars
CAREER: Test: 2000; ODI: 2000; T20I: 2007; First-class: 1996; List A: 1996; T20: 2006

BEST BATTING: 291 West Indies vs England, Bridgetown, 2009
BEST BOWLING: 6-62 Guyana vs Leeward Islands, St John's, 2001
COUNTY CAP: 2005 (Gloucestershire)

NOTES: Sarwan was appointed as Leicestershire's new four-day captain in December 2012, replacing Matthew Hoggard. In 2012, his first season with Leicestershire, he scored 941 Championship runs, finishing just behind Hampshire's Jimmy Adams as Division Two's leading run-scorer. His international career saw him succeed Brian Lara as West Indies captain following the 2007 World Cup. He topped the batting averages in the 2008/09 Wisden Trophy against England, scoring 626 runs at an average of 104.33. He fell out of favour in 2011 but returned to the ODI side in February 2013, making 120* vs Zimbabwe in his second game back. His international recall and a subsequent injury limited his appearances for Leicestershire last year but the club are optimistic they will see much more of him in 2014

Batting	Mat	Inns	NO	Runs	HS	Ave	SR	100	50	Ct	St
Tests	87	154	8	5842	291	40.01	46.79	15	31	53	0
ODIs	181	169	33	5804	120*	42.67	75.74	5	38	45	0
T20Is	18	16	3	298	59	22.92	104.19	0	2	7	0
First-class	215	364	26	13221	291	39.11		33	70	152	0
List A	265	251	42	8488	120*	40.61		11	50	68	0
Twenty20	74	69	9	1151	70	19.18	104.54	0	5	24	0

Bowling	Mat	Balls	Runs	Wkts	BBI	BBM	Ave	Econ	SR	5w	10
Tests	87	2022	1163	23	4/37	7/96	50.56	3.45	87.9	0	0
ODIs	181	581	586	16	3/31	3/31	36.62	6.05	36.3	0	0
T20Is	18	12	10	2	2/10	2/10	5.00	5.00	6.0	0	0
First-class	215	4368	2351	56	6/62		41.98	3.22	78.0	1	0
List A	265	1130	1001	35	5/10	5/10	28.60	5.31	32.2	1	0
Twenty20	74	18	22	2	2/10	2/10	11.00	7.33	9.0	0	0

IAN SAXELBY

RHB RMF

FULL NAME: Ian David Saxelby
BORN: May 22, 1989, Nottingham
SQUAD NO: 21
HEIGHT: 6ft 2in
NICKNAME: Sax, Bugler, Piece
EDUCATION: Tuxford School; Oakham School
TEAMS: England Under-19s, Gloucestershire, Gloucestershire 2nd XI, Nottinghamshire 2nd XI
CAREER: First-class: 2008; List A: 2009; T20: 2009

BEST BATTING: 60* Gloucestershire vs Northamptonshire, Northampton, 2009
BEST BOWLING: 6-48 Gloucestershire vs Leicestershire, Cheltenham, 2012

FAMILY TIES? My two uncles [Kevin and Mark] played professionally and my father played England Schoolboys and 2nd XI cricket
WHO WOULD PLAY YOU IN A FILM OF YOUR LIFE? Rupert Grint
CAREER HIGHLIGHTS? Playing for England U19 and gaining my first professional contract
SUPERSTITIONS? I always put my pads on in the same way and I sit in the same place if someone is scoring runs
MOST MARKED CHARACTERISTIC? My excellent banter
IF YOU WEREN'T A CRICKETER? I'd be an engineer
FAVOURITE TV? Anything David Attenborough-based and Top Gear
CRICKETING HEROES? Richard Hadlee, Clive Rice, Curtly Ambrose, Courtney Walsh, Brain Lara
NON-CRICKETING HEROES? Martin Johnson
ACCOMPLISHMENTS? Playing for England U16 at rugby and my academic grades
WHEN YOU RETIRE? Banking or teaching
FANTASY SLIP CORDON? Keeper: Jeremy Clarkson, 1st Me, 2nd: David Attenborough, 3rd: James Bond
TWITTER FEED: @saxelby21

Batting	Mat	Inns	NO	Runs	HS	Ave	SR	100	50	Ct	St
First-class	38	55	17	626	60*	16.47	42.84	0	1	12	0
List A	17	8	3	30	7*	6.00	55.55	0	0	0	0
Twenty20	20	10	3	24	7*	3.42	60.00	0	0	3	0

Bowling	Mat	Balls	Runs	Wkts	BBI	BBM	Ave	Econ	SR	5w	10
First-class	38	5515	3264	106	6/48	10/142	30.79	3.55	52.0	3	1
List A	17	604	651	22	4/31	4/31	29.59	6.46	27.4	0	0
Twenty20	20	411	545	23	4/16	4/16	23.69	7.95	17.8	0	0

ROB SAYER

RHB OB

FULL NAME: Robert John Sayer
BORN: January 25, 1995, Huntingdon, Cambridgeshire
SQUAD NO: 18
TEAMS: Cambridgeshire, England Development Programme Under-19s, England Under-19s, Leicestershire 2nd XI
CAREER: Yet to make first-team debut

NOTES: Sayer is yet to make his first-team debut for Leicestershire but he played a key role in England's 2014 U19 World Cup campaign, which saw them finish in third place. He hit the winning runs in a shock quarter-final win over holders India and scored 18* and took 2-39 as England came up just short against Pakistan in the semi-final. During the 2013 season, Sayer took five-wicket hauls in both the 2nd XI Championship and in a 2nd XI friendly, and also posted his first half-century. He came through the youth system of the Huntingdonshire Cricket Board and has been awarded a summer contract by Leicestershire for 2014

AJMAL SHAHZAD

RHB RFM MVP98

FULL NAME: Ajmal Shahzad
BORN: July 27, 1985, Huddersfield, Yorkshire
SQUAD NO: 1
HEIGHT: 6ft
NICKNAME: Ajy, AJ
EDUCATION: Bradford Grammar School;
Woodhouse Grove School; Bradford
University; Leeds Metropolitan University
TEAMS: England, England Lions, Lancashire,
Nottinghamshire, Yorkshire
CAREER: Test: 2010; ODI: 2010; T20I: 2010;
First-class: 2006; List A: 2004; T20: 2006

BEST BATTING: 88 Yorkshire vs Sussex, Hove, 2009
BEST BOWLING: 5-51 Yorkshire vs Durham, Chester-le-Street, 2010
COUNTY CAP: 2010 (Yorkshire)

WHO WOULD PLAY YOU IN A FILM OF YOUR LIFE? Waj from Four Lions
CAREER HIGHLIGHTS? Playing and representing Yorkshire, Lancashire and
Nottinghamshire. Playing alongside some amazing professionals. Representing England.
Being part of a World T20-winning team and an Ashes-winning squad. Winning the YB40 in
2013 with Nottinghamshire
MOST MARKED CHARACTERISTIC? My strut
BEST PLAYER IN COUNTY CRICKET? Kevin Pietersen
TIPS FOR THE TOP? Gary Ballance, Ned Eckersley, Shiv Thakor, Ross Whiteley
CRICKETING HEROES? Darren Gough, Shoaib Akhtar, Wasim Akram, Sir Vivian Richards,
Kevin Pietersen
TWITTER FEED: @AJShahzad

Batting	Mat	Inns	NO	Runs	HS	Ave	SR	100	50	Ct	St
Tests	1	1	0	5	5	5.00	41.66	0	0	2	0
ODIs	11	8	2	39	9	6.50	65.00	0	0	4	0
T20Is	3	1	1	0	0*	-	0.00	0	0	1	0
First-class	71	95	23	1702	88	23.63	41.21	0	5	10	0
List A	68	39	10	368	59*	12.68	93.87	0	1	16	0
Twenty20	32	18	5	133	20	10.23	127.88	0	0	6	0

Bowling	Mat	Balls	Runs	Wkts	BBI	BBM	Ave	Econ	SR	5w	10
Tests	1	102	63	4	3/45	4/63	15.75	3.70	25.5	0	0
ODIs	11	588	490	17	3/41	3/41	28.82	5.00	34.5	0	0
T20Is	3	66	97	3	2/38	2/38	32.33	8.81	22.0	0	0
First-class	71	11284	6398	181	5/51	8/121	35.34	3.40	62.3	3	0
List A	68	3043	2698	101	5/51	5/51	26.71	5.31	30.1	1	0
Twenty20	32	630	850	24	3/30	3/30	35.41	8.09	26.2	0	0

JACK SHANTRY   LHB LMF MVP61

WORCESTERSHIRE

FULL NAME: Jack David Shantry
BORN: January 29, 1988, Shrewsbury, Shropshire
SQUAD NO: 11
HEIGHT: 6ft 4in
NICKNAME: Shants, Mincer, Length
EDUCATION: Priory School; Shrewsbury Sixth Form College; Manchester University
TEAMS: Minor Counties Under-25s, Shropshire, Worcestershire, Worcestershire 2nd XI
CAREER: First-class: 2009; List A: 2009; T20: 2010

BEST BATTING: 55* Worcestershire vs Northamptonshire, Worcester, 2013
BEST BOWLING: 7-60 Worcestershire vs Oxford MCCU, Oxford, 2013

FAMILY TIES? My brother [Adam] played for Northamptonshire, Warwickshire and Glamorgan before retiring due to injury in 2011. My dad played for Gloucestershire in the late 70s. My mum won 'most whites washed in a calendar year' in 1997
CAREER HIGHLIGHTS? Scoring 47* against Yorkshire in 2011 and watching Tim Bresnan fall to the ground in despair after Alan Richardson and myself skillfully dispatched the ball to all parts
CRICKETING HEROES? Sohail Tanvir, Alastair Cook, James Anderson, Dale Steyn
NON-CRICKETING HEROES? Sam Harris, Christopher Hitchens, Richard Dawkins, the owner of Bushwackers
ACCOMPLISHMENTS? My castles and moats report in Year 6. Thorough, in-depth and accurate. Not my words, the words of Mrs Pashley
SURPRISING SKILL? I can competently animate three sock puppets at once
SURPRISING FACT? I was once half-an-hour away from playing in the FA Cup (qualifying round) for Hyde United but the first-choice goalkeeper passed a late fitness test
TWITTER FEED: @JackShantry

Batting	Mat	Inns	NO	Runs	HS	Ave	SR	100	50	Ct	St
First-class	41	51	13	589	55*	15.50	47.69	0	2	12	0
List A	52	22	12	111	18	11.10	72.54	0	0	14	0
Twenty20	46	10	6	28	9*	7.00	80.00	0	0	9	0

Bowling	Mat	Balls	Runs	Wkts	BBI	BBM	Ave	Econ	SR	5w	10
First-class	41	7024	3567	109	7/60	8/101	32.72	3.04	64.4	4	0
List A	52	2052	2019	73	4/32	4/32	27.65	5.90	28.1	0	0
Twenty20	46	994	1243	55	4/33	4/33	22.60	7.50	18.0	0	0

CHARLIE SHRECK RHB RMF W7

FULL NAME: Charles Edward Shreck
BORN: January 6, 1978, Truro, Cornwall
SQUAD NO: 4
HEIGHT: 6ft 7in
NICKNAME: Shrecker, Ogre, Stoat, Chough
EDUCATION: Truro School
TEAMS: Cornwall, Kent, Leicestershire, Marylebone Cricket Club, Nottinghamshire, Wellington
CAREER: First-class: 2003; List A: 1999; T20: 2003

BEST BATTING: 19* Kent vs Glamorgan, Canterbury, 2013
BEST BOWLING: 8-31 Nottinghamshire vs Middlesex, Nottingham, 2006
COUNTY CAP: 2006 (Nottinghamshire)

CRICKETING HEROES? Viv Richards, Michael Holding, Ian Botham, Rob Key
CRICKET MOMENT TO FORGET? Being run out off the last ball of the game against Shropshire while walking off – we lost!
FAVOURITE BAND? Catcha Fire or Black Seeds
FAVOURITE FOOD? Anything I've cooked
FAVOURTIE FILM? The Lives Of Others
BEST CRICKETING MOMENT? Watching Andrew Parkin-Coates get Phil Mustard out after kicking the stumps down the wicket in his delivery stride
MOST ANNOYING HABIT? Not keeping the kitchen clean
MOST LIKELY TO BE? First home on a night out
LOOKALIKE? Anyone with an awesome afro
TWITTER FEED: @Shreck

Batting	Mat	Inns	NO	Runs	HS	Ave	SR	100	50	Ct	St
First-class	128	144	84	351	19*	5.85	25.77	0	0	34	0
List A	53	19	12	45	9*	6.42		0	0	13	0
Twenty20	22	6	5	10	6*	10.00	62.50	0	0	4	0

Bowling	Mat	Balls	Runs	Wkts	BBI	BBM	Ave	Econ	SR	5w	10
First-class	128	24977	13264	432	8/31		30.70	3.18	57.8	21	2
List A	53	2327	2037	63	5/19	5/19	32.33	5.25	36.9	2	0
Twenty20	22	457	597	23	4/22	4/22	25.95	7.83	19.8	0	0

GLOUCESTERSHIRE

FULL NAME: Thomas Weldon Shrewsbury
BORN: January 18, 1995, Southampton, Hampshire
SQUAD NO: 50
HEIGHT: 6ft 3in
NICKNAME: Shrew
EDUCATION: Wadebridge School; Wycliffe College
TEAMS: Cornwall Under-14s, Cornwall Under-15s, England Development Programme Under-19s, Gloucestershire, Gloucestershire 2nd XI
CAREER: First-class: 2013; T20: 2013

BEST BATTING: 2* Gloucestershire vs Northamptonshire, Northampton, 2013
BEST BOWLING: 1-94 Gloucestershire vs Glamorgan, Cardiff, 2013

FAMILY TIES? My father played as a young boy and introduced me to the game when we moved down to Cornwall. He became my coach and inspired me to persist with it at a very early age
WHO WOULD PLAY YOU IN A FILM OF YOUR LIFE? Channing Tatum, for his good looks and charm
CAREER HIGHLIGHTS? My biggest highlight was making my 1st XI debut for Gloucestershire in a T20 game against Glamorgan and being able to see how proud my parents were and give something back to them for all their hard work and support
MOST MARKED CHARACTERISTIC? My great hair
BEST PLAYER IN COUNTY CRICKET? Kevin Pietersen
TIP FOR THE TOP? Craig Miles
IF YOU WEREN'T A CRICKETER? I'd be at university or working on a building site
DESERT ISLAND DISC? Something by The Tallest Man On Earth
FAVOURITE TV? Made In Chelsea
CRICKETING HEROES? Chris Gayle, Freddie Flintoff
NON-CRICKETING HEROES? My grandad
WHEN YOU RETIRE? I'd like to go into teaching PE at a secondary or private school
TWITTER FEED: @tomshrewsbury1

Batting	Mat	Inns	NO	Runs	HS	Ave	SR	100	50	Ct	St
First-class	1	1	1	2	2*	-	10.00	0	0	0	0
Twenty20	1									0	0

Bowling	Mat	Balls	Runs	Wkts	BBI	BBM	Ave	Econ	SR	5w	10
First-class	1	138	94	1	1/94	1/94	94.00	4.08	138.0	0	0
Twenty20	1	6	3	0	-	-	-	3.00	-	0	0

DOMINIC SIBLEY

RHB OB

FULL NAME: Dominic Peter Sibley
BORN: September 5, 1995, Epsom, Surrey
SQUAD NO: 45
HEIGHT: 6ft 3in
NICKNAME: Sibo, Sibbers
EDUCATION: Whitgift School
TEAMS: England Under-19s, Surrey, Surrey 2nd XI, Surrey Under-13s, Surrey Under-14s, Surrey Under-15s, Surrey Under-17s
CAREER: First-class: 2013; List A: 2013

SURREY

BEST BATTING: 242 Surrey vs Yorkshire, The Oval, 2013

FAMILY TIES? My dad played a bit of Surrey age-group cricket
WHO WOULD PLAY YOU IN A FILM OF YOUR LIFE? Colin Farrell
CAREER HIGHLIGHTS? Scoring a hundred for England U19 against South Africa at the age of 17. Getting a summer contract for Surrey on my 17th birthday. Scoring three double-hundreds
SUPERSTITIONS? I always take my guard the first ball I face of every over
MOST MARKED CHARACTERISTIC? Being lanky, apparently
BEST PLAYER IN COUNTY CRICKET? Marcus Trescothick
TIPS FOR THE TOP? Ben Duckett, Josh Shaw, Jack Scriven and Jack Winslade
IF YOU WEREN'T A CRICKETER? I'd be working harder at school than I am at the moment
DESERT ISLAND DISC? Tyga – Well Done 3
FAVOURITE TV? Misfits
BIGGEST DRESSING DOWN YOU'VE RECEIVED? After a poor team performance in South Africa on a Surrey Academy tour
CRICKETING HEROES? Jacques Kallis, Sachin Tendulkar and Brian Lara
NON-CRICKETING HEROES? Muhammad Ali
ACCOMPLISHMENTS? I played a bit of rugby for Harlequins at age-group level and I was a National Independent School champion for football at Whitgift School
WHEN YOU RETIRE? I'd like to be a coach or a commentator
TWITTER FEED: @DomSibley

Batting	Mat	Inns	NO	Runs	HS	Ave	SR	100	50	Ct	St
First-class	3	4	0	264	242	66.00	42.71	1	0	1	0
List A	2	2	1	39	37	39.00	88.63	0	0	0	0

Bowling	Mat	Balls	Runs	Wkts	BBI	BBM	Ave	Econ	SR	5w	10
First-class	3	6	4	0	-	-	-	4.00	-	0	0
List A	2	-	-	-	-	-	-	-	-	-	-

PETER SIDDLE

RHB RFM

FULL NAME: Peter Matthew Siddle
BORN: November 25, 1984, Traralgon, Victoria, Australia
SQUAD NO: 12
HEIGHT: 6ft 2in
NICKNAME: Vicious, Dermie
TEAMS: Australia, Australia A, Melbourne Renegades, Nottinghamshire, Victoria
CAREER: Test: 2008; ODI: 2009; T20I: 2009; First-class: 2005; List A: 2005; T20: 2006

BEST BATTING: 103* Australia A vs Scotland, Edinburgh, 2013
BEST BOWLING: 6-43 Victoria vs South Australia, Melbourne, 2012

TWITTER FEED: @petersiddle403
NOTES: Nottinghamshire have signed Australian seamer Siddle as their overseas player for the 2014 season. He will be available for all the club's County Championship and 50-over matches. He was first called up to the Australian Test squad for the 2008 series against India and made his debut in the second match at Mohali, taking four wickets including that of Sachin Tendulkar. Made his home debut two months later against South Africa, claiming match figures of 8-113 in the third Test of the series at Sydney. He has taken 67 Ashes wickets in 20 Tests, including 16 at an average of 24.12 during the 2013/14 whitewash in Australia

Batting	Mat	Inns	NO	Runs	HS	Ave	SR	100	50	Ct	St
Tests	53	76	11	926	51	14.24	46.72	0	2	16	0
ODIs	17	4	2	21	9*	10.50	116.66	0	0	1	0
T20Is	2	1	1	1	1*	-	100.00	0	0	0	0
First-class	93	125	20	1713	103*	16.31	48.45	1	4	34	0
List A	42	21	8	96	25*	7.38	81.35	0	0	6	0
Twenty20	17	6	5	16	9*	16.00	100.00	0	0	2	0

Bowling	Mat	Balls	Runs	Wkts	BBI	BBM	Ave	Econ	SR	5w	10
Tests	53	11223	5522	188	6/54	9/104	29.37	2.95	59.6	8	0
ODIs	17	751	581	15	3/55	3/55	38.73	4.64	50.0	0	0
T20Is	2	48	58	3	2/24	2/24	19.33	7.25	16.0	0	0
First-class	93	18125	9053	326	6/43	9/77	27.76	2.99	55.5	15	0
List A	42	2026	1598	45	4/27	4/27	35.51	4.73	45.0	0	0
Twenty20	17	383	481	18	4/29	4/29	26.72	7.53	21.2	0	0

RYAN SIDEBOTTOM
LHB LFM W4 MVP77

FULL NAME: Ryan Jay Sidebottom
BORN: January 15, 1978, Huddersfield, Yorkshire
SQUAD NO: 11
HEIGHT: 6ft 4in
NICKNAME: Siddy
EDUCATION: King James' Grammar School, Almondbury
TEAMS: England, Nottinghamshire, Yorkshire
CAREER: Test: 2001; ODI: 2001; T20I: 2007; First-class: 1997; List A: 1997; T20: 2003

BEST BATTING: 61 Yorkshire vs Worcestershire, Worcester, 2011
BEST BOWLING: 7-37 Yorkshire vs Somerset, Leeds, 2011
COUNTY CAPS: 2000 (Yorkshire); 2004 (Nottinghamshire); **BENEFIT YEAR:** 2010 (Nottinghamshire)

FAMILY TIES? My father [Arnie] played for Yorkshire and England
CAREER HIGHLIGHTS? Taking a Test hat-trick against New Zealand and being a World T20 winner in 2010
SUPERSTITIONS? I always put my front foot over the boundary rope first
CRICKETING HEROES? Mark Ealham, Sir Ian Botham, my dad
FAVOURITE BOOK? Harry Potter
DREAM HOLIDAY? Thailand
GUILTY PLEASURES? Thai takeaway
SURPRISING FACTS? I love birdwatching and I collect Steiff bears
TWITTER FEED: @RyanSidebottom

Batting	Mat	Inns	NO	Runs	HS	Ave	SR	100	50	Ct	St
Tests	22	31	11	313	31	15.65	34.66	0	0	5	0
ODIs	25	18	8	133	24	13.30	68.55	0	0	6	0
T20Is	18	1	1	5	5*	-	125.00	0	0	5	0
First-class	189	236	67	2340	61	13.84		0	3	56	0
List A	186	89	39	552	32	11.04		0	0	39	0
Twenty20	77	24	17	138	17*	19.71	102.98	0	0	23	0

Bowling	Mat	Balls	Runs	Wkts	BBI	BBM	Ave	Econ	SR	5w	10
Tests	22	4812	2231	79	7/47	10/139	28.24	2.78	60.9	5	1
ODIs	25	1277	1039	29	3/19	3/19	35.82	4.88	44.0	0	0
T20Is	18	367	437	23	3/16	3/16	19.00	7.14	15.9	0	0
First-class	189	32803	15280	614	7/37		24.88	2.79	53.4	24	3
List A	186	8226	6134	198	6/40	6/40	30.97	4.47	41.5	2	0
Twenty20	77	1624	1902	82	4/25	4/25	23.19	7.02	19.8	0	0

JOHN SIMPSON LHB WK

FULL NAME: John Andrew Simpson
BORN: July 13, 1988, Bury, Lancashire
SQUAD NO: 20
HEIGHT: 5ft 11in
NICKNAME: Simmo
EDUCATION: St. Gabriel's RC High School
TEAMS: England Under-19s, Lancashire, Lancashire 2nd XI, Marylebone Cricket Club, Marylebone Cricket Club Young Cricketers, Middlesex, Middlesex 2nd XI
CAREER: First-class: 2009; List A: 2009; T20: 2009

BEST BATTING: 143 Middlesex vs Surrey, Lord's, 2011
COUNTY CAP: 2011

FAMILY TIES? My dad played Lancashire 2nd XI, England Amateurs and holds records in both Lancashire and Central Lancashire league cricket. My grandad and uncle played league cricket and my grandpa played in the Army. My cousin Ashley is on Lancashire's Academy and my other cousin Dominic is in Lancashire's age-group system
CAREER HIGHLIGHTS? Being capped by Middlesex in 2011, scoring my maiden first-class hundred for Middlesex and also winning Division Two of the Championship in 2011
MOST MARKED CHARACTERISTIC? I'm a hard worker and I'm very driven
BEST PLAYER IN COUNTY CRICKET? Chris Rogers, Sam Robson, Moeen Ali, Graham Onions
TIPS FOR THE TOP? Max Holden, Ryan Higgins
CRICKETING HEROES? Adam Gilchrist, Jack Russell, Ian Healy, Brian Lara
NON-CRICKETING HEROES? Tiger Woods, Roger Federer, LeBron James, Alan Shearer, Floyd Mayweather
ACCOMPLISHMENTS? Winning a few golf tournaments and the Middlesex golf longest drive
WHEN YOU RETIRE? I'd like to be living in a sunny climate playing golf all year round
SURPRISING FACT? My great-grandad and grandad both played rugby league for Great Britain and my dad played lacrosse for England
TWITTER FEED: @JohnSimpson_88

Batting	Mat	Inns	NO	Runs	HS	Ave	SR	100	50	Ct	St
First-class	67	105	14	2687	143	29.52	47.05	2	15	212	13
List A	42	28	6	567	82	25.77	87.36	0	3	26	5
Twenty20	27	21	1	302	60*	15.10	117.96	0	1	13	6

Bowling	Mat	Balls	Runs	Wkts	BBI	BBM	Ave	Econ	SR	5w	10
First-class	67	-	-	-	-	-	-	-	-	-	-
List A	42	-	-	-	-	-	-	-	-	-	-
Twenty20	27	-	-	-	-	-	-	-	-	-	-

RAMMY SINGH

RHB OB

FULL NAME: Ramanpreet Singh
BORN: February 19, 1993, Newcastle-upon-Tyne, Northumberland
SQUAD NO: 11
HEIGHT: 5ft 7in
NICKNAME: Loose Man
EDUCATION: Gosforth High School
TEAMS: Durham, Durham 2nd XI, England Under-19s, Northumberland
CAREER: First-class: 2012

BEST BATTING: 22 Durham vs Australia A, Chester-le-Street, 2012

WHY CRICKET? My dad's passion for the game inspired me to play
CAREER HIGHLIGHTS? Representing England U19 and scoring back-to-back hundreds for the Durham Academy in 2011
CRICKETING HEROES? Sachin Tendulkar, Viv Richards, MS Dhoni
NON-CRICKETING HEROES? Bhagat Singh, Mahatma Gandhi, Manny Pacquiao
BEST PLAYER IN COUNTY CRICKET? Marcus Trescothick
TIPS FOR THE TOP? Ben Stokes, Jonny Bairstow
IF YOU WEREN'T A CRICKETER? I'd be a lawyer
FAVOURITE FILM? The Shawshank Redemption
FAVOURITE BOOK? Wolf Brother
DREAM HOLIDAY? Marbella
ACCOMPLISHMENTS? Doing charity work in India
GUILTY PLEASURES? The casino
SURPRISING FACT? I have a deep hatred for tomatoes
TWITTER FEED: @rammy129

Batting	Mat	Inns	NO	Runs	HS	Ave	SR	100	50	Ct	St
First-class	1	2	0	34	22	17.00	73.91	0	0	1	0

Bowling	Mat	Balls	Runs	Wkts	BBI	BBM	Ave	Econ	SR	5w	10
First-class	1	-	-	-	-	-	-	-	-	-	-

BEN SLATER

LHB OB

FULL NAME: Benjamin Thomas Slater
BORN: August 26, 1991, Chesterfield, Derbyshire
SQUAD NO: 26
HEIGHT: 5ft 11in
NICKNAME: Slats, Slatsy, BennySlats
EDUCATION: Netherthorpe School; Leeds Metropolitan University
TEAMS: Bradford/Leeds UCCE, Derbyshire, Derbyshire 2nd XI, Southern Rocks
CAREER: First-class: 2012; List A: 2012; T20: 2012

BEST BATTING: 89 Southern Rocks vs Mashonaland Eagles, Harare, 2012

FAMILY TIES? Both my dad and grandad played local league cricket. My grandad was something of a league legend
WHO WOULD PLAY YOU IN A FILM OF YOUR LIFE? Ryan Gosling
CAREER HIGHLIGHTS? Making my Championship debut against Surrey – I fielded for a long time and watched Ricky Ponting score a big hundred. Scoring 66* to beat Sussex last year for Derbyshire's first victory in Division One in a long time. Scoring 89 on my debut for Southern Rocks in Zimbabwe, helping them to record their first ever first-class win
BEST PLAYER IN COUNTY CRICKET? Wayne Madsen and Graham Onions. Kevin Pietersen and Graeme Smith might be handy too
TIPS FOR THE TOP? Greg Cork, Dan Hodgson and Luis Reece
DESERT ISLAND DISC? All Saints – Pure Shores
CRICKETING HEROES? Brian Lara
NON-CRICKETING HEROES? David Beckham and Gary Roberts
ACCOMPLISHMENTS? Gaining a degree in Sports Business Management at Leeds Metropolitan University
CRICKET RULE YOU'D CHANGE? There should be a longer tea break in Championship games
TWITTER FEED: @BennySlats

Batting	Mat	Inns	NO	Runs	HS	Ave	SR	100	50	Ct	St
First-class	16	29	1	584	89	20.85	38.04	0	4	3	0
List A	7	6	0	109	46	18.16	52.65	0	0	1	0
Twenty20	4	4	0	161	57	40.25	105.22	0	1	0	0

Bowling	Mat	Balls	Runs	Wkts	BBI	BBM	Ave	Econ	SR	5w	10
First-class	16	9	28	0	-	-	-	18.66	-	0	0
List A	7	-	-	-	-	-	-	-	-	-	-
Twenty20	4	-	-	-	-	-	-	-	-	-	-

GRAEME SMITH

LHB OB

FULL NAME: Graeme Craig Smith
BORN: February 1, 1981, Johannesburg, Transvaal, South Africa
SQUAD NO: 15
HEIGHT: 6ft 3in
NICKNAME: Biff
TEAMS: South Africa, Africa XI, Cape Cobras, Gauteng, Hampshire Cricket Board, ICC World XI, Pune Warriors, Rajasthan Royals, Somerset, Surrey, Western Province
CAREER: Test: 2002; ODI: 2002; T20I: 2005; First-class: 2000; List A: 2000; T20: 2004

SURREY

BEST BATTING: 311 Somerset vs Leicestershire, Taunton, 2005
BEST BOWLING: 2-145 South Africa vs West Indies, St John's, 2005
COUNTY CAP: 2005 (Somerset)

NOTES: Smith became South Africa captain aged just 22 and made back-to-back double hundreds in his 11th and 12th Tests. Captained South Africa to their first series victory in Australia in 2009 and led the side to the No.1 Test ranking by beating England 2-0 in 2012. Reached 100 Tests as captain in February in 2014, against Pakistan at The Wanderers. Appointed as Surrey skipper on a three-year contract in November 2012 but missed the majority of the 2013 season with an ankle injury. Retired from international cricket in March after amassing more than 17,000 for South Africa across all formats and will be available for Surrey for the whole of the 2014 campaign

Batting	Mat	Inns	NO	Runs	HS	Ave	SR	100	50	Ct	St
Tests	117	205	13	9265	277	48.25	59.67	27	38	169	0
ODIs	197	194	10	6989	141	37.98	80.81	10	47	105	0
T20Is	33	33	2	982	89*	31.67	127.53	0	5	18	0
First-class	160	276	19	12653	311	49.23		36	50	231	0
List A	259	253	15	9331	141	39.20		14	67	137	0
Twenty20	84	84	6	2362	105	30.28	123.40	1	11	35	0

Bowling	Mat	Balls	Runs	Wkts	BBI	BBM	Ave	Econ	SR	5w	10
Tests	117	1418	885	8	2/145	2/145	110.62	3.74	177.2	0	0
ODIs	197	1026	951	18	3/30	3/30	52.83	5.56	57.0	0	0
T20Is	33	24	57	0	-	-	-	14.25	-	0	0
First-class	160	1786	1132	11	2/145		102.90	3.80	162.3	0	0
List A	259	1968	1796	47	3/30	3/30	38.21	5.47	41.8	0	0
Twenty20	84	96	148	4	3/23	3/23	37.00	9.25	24.0	0	0

GREG SMITH

RHB RMF/OB

ESSEX

FULL NAME: Gregory Marc Smith
BORN: April 20, 1983, Johannesburg, Transvaal, South Africa
SQUAD NO: 83
HEIGHT: 5ft 9in
NICKNAME: Smithy
EDUCATION: St Stithians College, South Africa; Future Fitness
TEAMS: Abahani Limited, Derbyshire, Essex, Griqualand West, Mountaineers, South Africa Academy, South Africa Under-19s
CAREER: First-class: 2003; List A: 2003; T20: 2007

BEST BATTING: 177 Essex vs Gloucestershire, Bristol, 2013
BEST BOWLING: 5-42 Derbyshire vs Northamptonshire, Chesterfield, 2010
COUNTY CAP: 2009 (Derbyshire)

FAMILY TIES? My dad used to be the financial advisor for the South African Cricket Board
WHO WOULD PLAY YOU IN A FILM OF YOUR LIFE? Ryan Gosling
CAREER HIGHLIGHTS? Getting my maiden first-class hundred and also getting to the final of the U19 World Cup in New Zealand
BEST PLAYER IN COUNTY CRICKET? Marcus Trescothick
TIPS FOR THE TOP? Reece Topley and Ben Foakes
IF YOU WEREN'T A CRICKETER? I would have hoped to make it in the tennis world
DESERT ISLAND DISC? The Killers
CRICKETING HEROES? Jacques Kallis, Sachin Tendulkar
NON-CRICKETING HEROES? Roger Federer, Nelson Mandela
ACCOMPLISHMENTS? I'm a qualified gym instructor and nutritional advisor
WHEN YOU RETIRE? I'd like to stay in cricket and either coach or be part of the fitness and training regime of a club
FANTASY SLIP CORDON? Keeper: Ricky Gervais, 1st: Roger Federer, 2nd: Simon Pilkington, 3rd: Ari Gold (Entourage), Gully: Bear Grylls
TWITTER FEED: @smithyg83

Batting	Mat	Inns	NO	Runs	HS	Ave	SR	100	50	Ct	St
First-class	108	178	16	5172	177	31.92	58.94	7	31	33	0
List A	100	99	9	2282	89	25.35	81.90	0	11	38	0
Twenty20	74	70	2	1351	100*	19.86	113.81	1	5	31	0

Bowling	Mat	Balls	Runs	Wkts	BBI	BBM	Ave	Econ	SR	5w	10
First-class	108	11143	6001	169	5/42		35.50	3.23	65.9	4	0
List A	100	2761	2591	69	4/53	4/53	37.55	5.63	40.0	0	0
Twenty20	74	736	963	41	5/17	5/17	23.48	7.85	17.9	2	0

GREG SMITH RHB LB

FULL NAME: Greg Phillip Smith
BORN: November 16, 1988, Leicester
SQUAD NO: 14
HEIGHT: 5ft 11in
EDUCATION: Oundle School; Durham University
TEAMS: Badureliya Sports Club, Durham MCCU, Durham UCCE, England Under-19s, Kibworth, Lankan Cricket Club, Leicestershire, Leicestershire 2nd XI
CAREER: First-class: 2008; List A: 2008; T20: 2012

BEST BATTING: 158* Leicestershire vs Gloucestershire, Leicester, 2010
BEST BOWLING: 1-64 Leicestershire vs Gloucestershire, Leicester, 2008

FAMILY TIES? My step-grandfather played for Sussex
CAREER HIGHLIGHTS? The 2010 T20 campaign
BEST PLAYER IN COUNTY CRICKET? Glen Chapple
TIP FOR THE TOP? Rammy Singh
IF YOU WEREN'T A CRICKETER? I'd be an Arctic explorer
DESERT ISLAND DISC? Damien Jurado – Ohio
FAVOURITE TV? Breaking Bad
CRICKETING HEROES? Will Jefferson, Justin Langer
NON-CRICKETING HEROES? Dr Peter Greenfield
ACCOMPLISHMENTS? Creating my own breed of apple
TWITTER FEED: @greg_smith14

Batting	Mat	Inns	NO	Runs	HS	Ave	SR	100	50	Ct	St
First-class	70	130	8	3441	158*	28.20	49.71	6	15	56	0
List A	32	32	3	639	135*	22.03	79.08	1	3	12	0
Twenty20	16	16	1	394	84	26.26	125.87	0	2	4	0

Bowling	Mat	Balls	Runs	Wkts	BBI	BBM	Ave	Econ	SR	5w	10
First-class	70	36	73	1	1/64	1/64	73.00	12.16	36.0	0	0
List A	32	-	-	-	-	-	-	-	-	-	-
Twenty20	16	-	-	-	-	-	-	-	-	-	-

GLAMORGAN

FULL NAME: Ruaidhri Alexander James Smith
BORN: August 5, 1994, Glasgow, Scotland
SQUAD NO: 20
HEIGHT: 6ft 2in
NICKNAME: Trigger
EDUCATION: The Cathedral School, Llandaff; Shrewsbury School; University of Bristol
TEAMS: Scotland, Glamorgan, Glamorgan 2nd XI, Scotland Under-19s, Wales Minor Counties
CAREER: First-class: 2013; List A: 2013

BEST BATTING: 39 Glamorgan vs Gloucestershire, Cardiff, 2013
BEST BOWLING: 3-50 Glamorgan vs Gloucestershire, Cardiff, 2013

FAMILY TIES? My dad used to play club cricket and he introduced me to the game
WHO WOULD PLAY YOU IN A FILM OF YOUR LIFE? Penn Badgley
CAREER HIGHLIGHTS? Taking a wicket with my first ball for Glamorgan
SUPERSTITIONS? I always put pads on in the same order and I never step on crease lines while the ball is dead
MOST MARKED CHARACTERISTIC? My competitiveness
BEST PLAYER IN COUNTY CRICKET? Graham Onions
TIP FOR THE TOP? Ed Barnard
IF YOU WEREN'T A CRICKETER? I'd try to be a rugby player
DESERT ISLAND DISC? I'd take the Harry Potter film series instead
FAVOURITE TV? Sherlock
CRICKETING HEROES? Andrew Flintoff and Jacques Kallis
NON-CRICKETING HEROES? Jonny Wilkinson
WHEN YOU RETIRE? I'd like to go into investment banking
SURPRISING FACT? I'm a Grade 5 pianist
CRICKET RULE YOU'D CHANGE? The number of fielders allowed out in a powerplay
FANTASY SLIP CORDON? Keeper: Jonny Wilkinson, 1st: Don Bradman, 2nd: Sherlock Holmes, 3rd: Me, Gully: Sir Viv Richards
TWITTER FEED: @RuaidhriSmith

Batting	Mat	Inns	NO	Runs	HS	Ave	SR	100	50	Ct	St
First-class	3	4	1	100	39	33.33	61.34	0	0	0	0
List A	5	3	1	9	7	4.50	56.25	0	0	2	0

Bowling	Mat	Balls	Runs	Wkts	BBI	BBM	Ave	Econ	SR	5w	10
First-class	3	366	274	10	3/50	5/87	27.40	4.49	36.6	0	0
List A	5	90	117	3	3/48	3/48	39.00	7.80	30.0	0	0

FULL NAME: Thomas Christopher Smith
BORN: December 26, 1985, Liverpool
SQUAD NO: 24
HEIGHT: 6ft 3in
NICKNAME: Smudger
EDUCATION: Parklands High School;
Runshaw College
TEAMS: England Under-19s, Lancashire,
Lancashire 2nd XI, Matabeleland Tuskers
CAREER: First-class: 2005; List A: 2005; T20:
2006

LANCASHIRE

BEST BATTING: 128 Lancashire vs Hampshire, Southampton, 2010
BEST BOWLING: 6-46 Lancashire vs Yorkshire, Manchester, 2009
COUNTY CAP: 2010

CAREER HIGHLIGHTS? Winning the County Championship in 2011
CRICKETING HEROES? Brian Lara, Andrew Flintoff
BEST PLAYER IN COUNTY CRICKET? Marcus Trescothick
TIP FOR THE TOP? Jordan Clark
WHEN RAIN STOPS PLAY? I listen to music
FAVOURITE TV? Entourage
FAVOURITE FILM? Wedding Crashers
DREAM HOLIDAY? Thailand
GUILTY PLEASURES? Curry
TWITTER FEED: @Tcp24

Batting	Mat	Inns	NO	Runs	HS	Ave	SR	100	50	Ct	St
First-class	83	118	21	2743	128	28.27	46.17	3	15	91	0
List A	62	52	10	1359	117	32.35	88.41	2	8	17	0
Twenty20	79	72	12	1750	92*	29.16	118.40	0	8	35	0

Bowling	Mat	Balls	Runs	Wkts	BBI	BBM	Ave	Econ	SR	5w	10
First-class	83	10338	5329	172	6/46		30.98	3.09	60.1	2	0
List A	62	2312	2011	73	4/48	4/48	27.54	5.21	31.6	0	0
Twenty20	79	1080	1417	44	3/12	3/12	32.20	7.87	24.5	0	0

TOM SMITH

RHB SLA

FULL NAME: Thomas Michael John Smith
BORN: August 29, 1987, Eastbourne, Sussex
SQUAD NO: 6
HEIGHT: 5ft 9in
NICKNAME: Smudge, Mooge
EDUCATION: Seaford Head Community College; Sussex Downs College
TEAMS: Gloucestershire, Middlesex, Middlesex 2nd XI, Surrey, Sussex, Sussex 2nd XI
CAREER: First-class: 2007; List A: 2006; T20: 2007

BEST BATTING: 50 Gloucestershire vs Leicestershire, Bristol, 2013
BEST BOWLING: 4-91 Gloucestershire vs Worcestershire, Cheltenham, 2013

WHO WOULD PLAY YOU IN A FILM OF YOUR LIFE? Josh Holloway (Sawyer from Lost)
CAREER HIGHLIGHTS? Taking 5-24 in a T20 game at Lord's vs Kent
SUPERSTITIONS? No real superstitions but I like to be clean-shaven on day one of a match
MOST MARKED CHARACTERISTIC? My monotone voice
BEST PLAYER IN COUNTY CRICKET? Andrew Hodd (Yorkshire)
TIPS FOR THE TOP? Sam Robson and Tom Helm
IF YOU WEREN'T A CRICKETER? I qualified as a plumber after school, so I guess I would be doing that – not that I was very good at it!
DESERT ISLAND DISC? The Kooks – Inside In/Inside Out
FAVOURITE TV? Modern Family, Homeland, Silent Witness, Waking The Dead
BIGGEST DRESSING DOWN YOU'VE RECEIVED? Chris Adams gave me one when he was captain of Sussex for giving away too many singles in the field
CRICKETING HEROES? Shane Warne, Saqlain Mushtaq and Dan Vettori
WHEN YOU RETIRE? I've completed my cricket coaching Level 3 so maybe a coaching job. I've also completed some work experience in the City for an investment management company, so that might be an avenue to explore after cricket

Batting	Mat	Inns	NO	Runs	HS	Ave	SR	100	50	Ct	St
First-class	22	31	5	430	50	16.53	32.25	0	1	6	0
List A	40	16	4	199	65	16.58	77.73	0	1	18	0
Twenty20	52	25	18	166	36*	23.71	111.40	0	0	19	0

Bowling	Mat	Balls	Runs	Wkts	BBI	BBM	Ave	Econ	SR	5w	10
First-class	22	2952	1691	29	4/91	5/124	58.31	3.43	101.7	0	0
List A	40	1371	1278	31	3/26	3/26	41.22	5.59	44.2	0	0
Twenty20	52	983	1193	49	5/24	5/24	24.34	7.28	20.0	1	0

WILL SMITH RHB OB MVP74

FULL NAME: William Rew Smith
BORN: September 28, 1982, Luton, Bedfordshire
SQUAD NO: 2
HEIGHT: 5ft 9in
NICKNAME: Smudger, Jiggy
EDUCATION: Bedford School; Durham University
TEAMS: Bedfordshire, British Universities, Durham, Durham UCCE, Hampshire, Nottinghamshire
CAREER: First-class: 2002; List A: 2002; T20: 2003

BEST BATTING: 201* Durham vs Surrey, Guildford, 2008
BEST BOWLING: 3-34 Durham UCCE vs Leicestershire, Leicester, 2005

FAMILY TIES? My brother played county age-group cricket
WHO WOULD PLAY YOU IN A FILM OF YOUR LIFE? Tom Cruise
CAREER HIGHLIGHTS? Winning four County Championships (one as captain of Durham)
MOST MARKED CHARACTERISTIC? My height
BEST PLAYER IN COUNTY CRICKET? Andre Adams
TIP FOR THE TOP? Liam Dawson
IF YOU WEREN'T A CRICKETER? I'd be a horse-racing pundit
DESERT ISLAND DISC? The Killers – Mr Brightside
FAVOURITE TV? Anything on Racing UK
CRICKETING HEROES? Graeme Fowler, Dale Benkenstein
NON-CRICKETING HEROES? My father Jim and my wife's father Paul
ACCOMPLISHMENTS? Being a loving husband and a devoted father
WHEN YOU RETIRE? I'll be a horse-racing pundit (see a theme here?!)
SURPRISING FACT? I have a tattoo…
FANTASY SLIP CORDON? Keeper: Myself, 1st: Stephen Fry, 2nd: AP McCoy, 3rd: Ross Noble, Gully: Jonty Rhodes
TWITTER FEED: @WillSmith_2

Batting	Mat	Inns	NO	Runs	HS	Ave	SR	100	50	Ct	St
First-class	122	204	12	6004	201*	31.27	42.93	14	19	67	0
List A	89	76	7	1865	120*	27.02	73.36	2	14	31	0
Twenty20	69	55	12	726	55	16.88	116.90	0	3	36	0

Bowling	Mat	Balls	Runs	Wkts	BBI	BBM	Ave	Econ	SR	5w	10
First-class	122	1137	768	15	3/34		51.20	4.05	75.8	0	0
List A	89	155	148	8	2/19	2/19	18.50	5.72	19.3	0	0
Twenty20	69	209	240	7	2/20	2/20	34.28	6.88	29.8	0	0

VIKRAM SOLANKI

RHB OB R6 MVP52

FULL NAME: Vikram Singh Solanki
BORN: April 1, 1976, Udaipur, Rajasthan, India
SQUAD NO: 42
HEIGHT: 6ft
NICKNAME: Vik
EDUCATION: Merridale Primary School; Regis School, Wolverhampton; The Open University
TEAMS: England, Rajasthan, Surrey, Worcestershire
CAREER: ODI: 2000; T20I: 2005; First-class: 1995; List A: 1993; T20: 2004

BEST BATTING: 270 Worcestershire vs Gloucestershire, Cheltenham, 2008
BEST BOWLING: 5-40 Worcestershire vs Middlesex, Lord's, 2004
COUNTY CAP: 1998 (Worcestershire); BENEFIT YEAR: 2007 (Worcestershire)

FAMILY TIES? My father played in India and my brother is a keen club cricketer
CAREER HIGHLIGHTS? Playing for England and captaining Worcestershire
SUPERSTITIONS? I have many habits but no superstitions
CRICKETING HEROES? Sachin Tendulkar, Graeme Hick, Wasim Akram
NON-CRICKETING HEROES? My father
BEST PLAYER IN COUNTY CRICKET? Marcus Trescothick
WHEN RAIN STOPS PLAY? You'll find me reading
FAVOURITE TV? House, Human Planet
FAVOURITE FILM? Gladiator
FAVOURITE BOOK? The Alchemist by Paulo Coelho
DREAM HOLIDAY? India, completing my Open University degree

Batting	Mat	Inns	NO	Runs	HS	Ave	SR	100	50	Ct	St
ODIs	51	46	5	1097	106	26.75	72.93	2	5	16	0
T20Is	3	3	0	76	43	25.33	124.59	0	0	3	0
First-class	313	526	32	17738	270	35.90		33	93	335	0
List A	394	364	31	10844	164*	32.56		16	62	158	0
Twenty20	76	74	1	1695	100	23.21	121.15	1	9	39	0

Bowling	Mat	Balls	Runs	Wkts	BBI	BBM	Ave	Econ	SR	5w	10
ODIs	51	111	105	1	1/17	1/17	105.00	5.67	111.0	0	0
T20Is	3	-	-	-	-	-	-	-	-	-	-
First-class	313	7195	4210	88	5/40		47.84	3.51	81.7	4	1
List A	394	1122	987	28	4/14	4/14	35.25	5.27	40.0	0	0
Twenty20	76	96	145	5	1/6	1/6	29.00	9.06	19.2	0	0

MATTHEW SPRIEGEL — LHB OB

FULL NAME: Matthew Neil William Spriegel
BORN: March 4, 1987, Epsom, Surrey
SQUAD NO: 28
HEIGHT: 6ft 3in
NICKNAME: Spriegs
EDUCATION: Whitgift School; Loughborough University
TEAMS: Loughborough UCCE, Northamptonshire, Surrey, Surrey 2nd XI
CAREER: First-class: 2007; List A: 2008; T20: 2008

BEST BATTING: 108* Surrey vs Bangladeshis, The Oval, 2010
BEST BOWLING: 3-75 Northamptonshire vs Worcestershire, Worcester, 2013

WHO WOULD PLAY YOU IN A FILM OF YOUR LIFE? Sacha Baron Cohen
CAREER HIGHLIGHTS? Winning the CB40 with Surrey in 2011. Making my County Championship debut at my old school. My maiden first-class hundred
MOST MARKED CHARACTERISTIC? My monotonous voice
BEST PLAYER IN COUNTY CRICKET? Marcus Trescothick
TIPS FOR THE TOP? Jason Roy, Stuart Meaker, Brian Williams
DESERT ISLAND DISC? Otto Knows – Million Voices
FAVOURITE TV? Entourage, The Office
BIGGEST DRESSING DOWN YOU'VE RECEIVED? From a 2nd XI coach when I pulled the seat from under him when he was sitting down in front of everyone at lunch. He was not amused
CRICKETING HEROES? Alec Stewart, Graham Thorpe, Mark Butcher
NON-CRICKETING HEROES? Jonny Wilkinson
SURPRISING FACT? I got an A* in Japanese at GCSE
TWITTER FEED: @Spriegs

Batting	Mat	Inns	NO	Runs	HS	Ave	SR	100	50	Ct	St
First-class	43	69	5	1444	108*	22.56	42.08	3	4	26	0
List A	71	63	19	1530	86	34.77	82.03	0	10	34	0
Twenty20	58	39	14	419	53*	16.76	91.88	0	1	23	0

Bowling	Mat	Balls	Runs	Wkts	BBI	BBM	Ave	Econ	SR	5w	10
First-class	43	1717	1042	24	3/75	3/75	43.41	3.64	71.5	0	0
List A	71	1985	1721	48	3/29	3/29	35.85	5.20	41.3	0	0
Twenty20	58	789	1003	31	4/33	4/33	32.35	7.62	25.4	0	0

CAMERON STEEL

RHB LB

FULL NAME: Cameron Tate Steel
BORN: September 13, 1995, San Francisco, United States
SQUAD NO: 22
HEIGHT: 5ft 10in
NICKNAME: Steely, Lex, Pup
EDUCATION: Millfield Preparatory School; Scotch College; Durham University
TEAMS: Middlesex 2nd XI, Somerset 2nd XI, Somerset Under-13s, Somerset Under-15s, Somerset Under-17s
CAREER: Yet to make first-team debut

FAMILY TIES? My sister has played state cricket for Western Australia
WHO WOULD PLAY YOU IN A FILM OF YOUR LIFE? Ryan Gosling
CAREER HIGHLIGHTS? Hitting a century on debut for Somerset 2nd XI and signing for Middlesex
SUPERSTITIONS? I always need to pad up in the same way
MOST MARKED CHARACTERISTIC? My terrible singing voice
BEST PLAYER IN COUNTY CRICKET? James Taylor
TIPS FOR THE TOP? Ryan Higgins, Tom Abell, Chris Jones
IF YOU WEREN'T A CRICKETER? I'd have a free weekend
DESERT ISLAND DISC? Ben Howard – Every Kingdom
FAVOURITE TV? Game Of Thrones or Friday Night Lights
CRICKETING HEROES? Mike Hussey and Freddie Flintoff
NON-CRICKETING HEROES? Andy Murray, Usain Bolt, Coach Taylor (Friday Night Lights)
ACCOMPLISHMENTS? I was West of England U9 chess champion
WHEN YOU RETIRE? I'd like to become an author
SURPRISING FACT? I was born in San Francisco, California and I have three passports: British, Australian and American
CRICKET RULE YOU'D CHANGE? It should be a free hit for any wide or no ball
FANTASY SLIP CORDON? Keeper: Frankie Boyle, 1st: Charlie Sheen, 2nd: Phil Dunphy (Modern Family), 3rd: Myself, Gully: Mila Kunis
TWITTER FEED: @CameronSteel2

DARREN STEVENS RHB RM R3 MVP3

FULL NAME: Darren Ian Stevens
BORN: April 30, 1976, Leicester
SQUAD NO: 3
HEIGHT: 5ft 11in
NICKNAME: Stevo, Daz, Hoover, Steve
EDUCATION: John Cleveland College; Charles Keene College
TEAMS: Dhaka Gladiators, England Lions, Kent, Leicestershire, Otago
CAREER: First-class: 1997; List A: 1997; T20: 2003

BEST BATTING: 208 Kent vs Middlesex, Canterbury, 2009
BEST BOWLING: 7-21 Kent vs Surrey, Canterbury, 2011
COUNTY CAPS: 2002 (Leicestershire); 2005 (Kent)

FAMILY TIES? My dad and grandad played local club cricket in Leicestershire
WHO WOULD PLAY YOU IN A FILM OF YOUR LIFE? Mark Wahlberg
CAREER HIGHLIGHTS? Winning the T20 for Leicestershire in 2004, winning the T20 for Kent in 2007 and winning the T20 for Dhaka Gladiators in 2012
SUPERSTITIONS? I put my left pad on first
BEST PLAYER IN COUNTY CRICKET? Marcus Trescothick
TIPS FOR THE TOP? Sam Northeast, Joshua Cobb, Sam Billings, Anamul Haque Bijoy
IF YOU WEREN'T A CRICKETER? I wouldn't like to think!
FAVOURITE TV? Homeland, CSI, 24
CRICKETING HEROES? Sir Isaac Vivian Alexander Richards
NON-CRICKETING HEROES? George Digweed
WHEN YOU RETIRE? I'd like to buy and sell houses, maybe coach, or the ultimate would be to play professional golf
FANTASY SLIP CORDON? Keeper: Cheryl Cole, 1st: Me, 2nd: Angelina Jolie, 3rd: Keith Lemon, 4th: George Digweed, Gully: Alan 'Lord' Sugar
TWITTER FEED? @Stevo208

Batting	Mat	Inns	NO	Runs	HS	Ave	SR	100	50	Ct	St
First-class	218	349	21	11578	208	35.29			28	55	161	0
List A	259	241	27	6532	133	30.52		5	42	104	0
Twenty20	149	139	37	3119	77	30.57	134.84	0	13	52	0

Bowling	Mat	Balls	Runs	Wkts	BBI	BBM	Ave	Econ	SR	5w	10
First-class	218	12765	6160	202	7/21		30.49	2.89	63.1	4	1
List A	259	3709	3078	97	5/32	5/32	31.73	4.97	38.2	2	0
Twenty20	149	1266	1603	64	4/14	4/14	25.04	7.59	19.7	0	0

PAUL STIRLING

RHB OB

FULL NAME: Paul Robert Stirling
BORN: September 3, 1990, Belfast, Northern Ireland
SQUAD NO: 39
HEIGHT: 5ft 10in
NICKNAME: The Hoover
EDUCATION: Belfast High School
TEAMS: Ireland, Ireland Under-13s, Ireland Under-15s, Ireland Under-17s, Ireland Under-19s, Ireland Under-23s, Middlesex, Sylhet Royals
CAREER: ODI: 2008; T20I: 2009; First-class: 2008; List A: 2008; T20: 2008

BEST BATTING: 115 Ireland vs Australia A, Belfast, 2013
BEST BOWLING: 2-43 Ireland vs Jamaica, Spanish Town, 2010

FAMILY TIES? My brother [Richard] played in the U19 World Cup in Sri Lanka with Eoin Morgan as the skipper
WHO WOULD PLAY YOU IN A FILM OF YOUR LIFE? James Corden
CAREER HIGHLIGHTS? Scoring a hundred at Lord's
SUPERSTITIONS? I put my left pad on before my right and drinking a Red Bull!
MOST MARKED CHARACTERISTIC? Terror accent
BEST PLAYER IN COUNTY CRICKET? Ed Joyce
TIP FOR THE TOP? Adam Rossington
CRICKETING HEROES? Ricky Ponting and Damien Martyn
NON-CRICKETING HEROES? George Best
SURPRISING FACT? I'm the only player to score three ODI centuries before turning 20
FANTASY SLIP CORDON? Keeper (standing up): Charles Colvile, 1st-5th: One Direction, Gully: Joey Barton, 2nd Gully: John Terry, Bowler: Dale Steyn
TWITTER FEED? @stirlo90

Batting	Mat	Inns	NO	Runs	HS	Ave	SR	100	50	Ct	St
ODIs	46	46	1	1658	177	36.84	94.15	5	6	21	0
T20Is	23	23	3	509	79	25.45	125.06	0	4	7	0
First-class	20	32	0	931	115	29.09	61.53	3	5	12	0
List A	101	99	4	3171	177	33.37	96.76	8	11	45	0
Twenty20	84	84	6	1957	82*	25.08	136.75	0	13	24	0

Bowling	Mat	Balls	Runs	Wkts	BBI	BBM	Ave	Econ	SR	5w	10
ODIs	46	1201	911	26	4/11	4/11	35.03	4.55	46.1	0	0
T20Is	23	246	286	10	3/21	3/21	28.60	6.97	24.6	0	0
First-class	20	669	345	6	2/43	3/92	57.50	3.09	111.5	0	0
List A	101	1853	1484	46	4/11	4/11	32.26	4.80	40.2	0	0
Twenty20	84	730	801	36	4/10	4/10	22.25	6.58	20.2	0	0

BEN STOKES

LHB RFM MVP6

FULL NAME: Benjamin Andrew Stokes
BORN: June 4, 1991, Christchurch, Canterbury, New Zealand
SQUAD NO: 38
HEIGHT: 6ft 2in
NICKNAME: Stokesy, Benji, Stoker
EDUCATION: Cockermouth School
TEAMS: England, Durham, Durham 2nd XI, England Lions, England Under-19s
CAREER: Test: 2013; ODI: 2011; T20I: 2011; First-class: 2010; List A: 2009; T20: 2010

DURHAM

BEST BATTING: 185 Durham vs Lancashire, Chester-le-Street, 2011
BEST BOWLING: 6-68 Durham vs Hampshire, Southampton, 2011

WHO WOULD PLAY YOU IN A FILM OF YOUR LIFE? Tom Hardy
CAREER HIGHLIGHTS? Making my Test debut
SUPERSTITIONS? Swiping my bat across the crease at the end of every over
BEST PLAYER IN COUNTY CRICKET? Marcus Trescothick
TIPS FOR THE TOP? Mark Wood, Paul Coughlin, Usman Arshad, Ben Whitehead
IF YOU WEREN'T A CRICKETER? I'd be on the dole
DESERT ISLAND DISC? Drake
FAVOURITE TV? The US Office
CRICKETING HEROES? Herschelle Gibbs
ACCOMPLISHMENTS? My son Layton
CRICKET RULE YOU'D CHANGE? You don't have to play if it's under 15 degrees celsius
TWITTER FEED: @benstokes38

Batting	Mat	Inns	NO	Runs	HS	Ave	SR	100	50	Ct	St
Tests	4	8	0	279	120	34.87	50.81	1	0	1	0
ODIs	18	14	0	202	70	14.42	72.14	0	1	7	0
T20Is	6	4	1	49	31	16.33	132.43	0	0	0	0
First-class	63	104	7	3451	185	35.57		9	14	37	0
List A	70	62	7	1370	150*	24.90	92.19	1	6	27	0
Twenty20	42	36	7	744	72*	25.65	129.39	0	3	12	0

Bowling	Mat	Balls	Runs	Wkts	BBI	BBM	Ave	Econ	SR	5w	10
Tests	4	701	492	15	6/99	8/161	32.80	4.21	46.7	1	0
ODIs	18	522	496	16	5/61	5/61	31.00	5.70	32.6	1	0
T20Is	6	48	92	0	-	-	-	11.50	-	0	0
First-class	63	5767	3599	125	6/68	8/161	28.79	3.74	46.1	2	0
List A	70	1504	1368	55	5/61	5/61	24.87	5.45	27.3	1	0
Twenty20	42	393	541	13	2/14	2/14	41.61	8.25	30.2	0	0

OLLY STONE

NORTHAMPTONSHIRE

FULL NAME: Oliver Peter Stone
BORN: October 9, 1993, Norwich, Norfolk
SQUAD NO: 9
HEIGHT: 6ft 2in
NICKNAME: Stoney
EDUCATION: Thorpe St Andrew High School;
Moulton College
TEAMS: England Under-19s, Norfolk,
Norfolk Under-17s, Northamptonshire,
Northamptonshire 2nd XI,
Northamptonshire Under-17s
CAREER: First-class: 2012; List A: 2012; T20:
2011

BEST BATTING: 26* Northamptonshire vs Yorkshire, Northampton, 2012
BEST BOWLING: 1-6 Northamptonshire vs Yorkshire, Northampton, 2012

WHO WOULD PLAY YOU IN A FILM OF YOUR LIFE? Owen Wilson
CAREER HIGHLIGHTS? Making my first-class debut and playing for England U19
MOST MARKED CHARACTERISTIC? My hair
TIPS FOR THE TOP? Gavin Griffiths, Dominic Sibley, Ben Duckett, Shiv Thakor
IF YOU WEREN'T A CRICKETER? I'd be at university
DESERT ISLAND DISC? Lighthouse Family
FAVOURITE TV? Soccer AM
CRICKETING HEROES? Paul Bradshaw
ACCOMPLISHMENTS? Passing my driving test
WHEN YOU RETIRE? I'd like to be a physio
SURPRISING FACT? David Willey is my third cousin
FANTASY SLIP CORDON? Keeper: Chris Gayle, 1st: Hulk Hogan, 2nd: James Corden, 3rd: Hugh
Hefner, Gully: Nicky Jayne
TWITTER FEED: @OllyStone2

Batting	Mat	Inns	NO	Runs	HS	Ave	SR	100	50	Ct	St
First-class	3	3	1	47	26*	23.50	65.27	0	0	3	0
List A	9	6	3	10	7*	3.33	30.30	0	0	3	0
Twenty20	5	1	0	0	0	0.00	0.00	0	0	2	0

Bowling	Mat	Balls	Runs	Wkts	BBI	BBM	Ave	Econ	SR	5w	10
First-class	3	384	202	5	1/6	2/41	40.40	3.15	76.8	0	0
List A	9	220	228	2	1/12	1/12	114.00	6.21	110.0	0	0
Twenty20	5	54	69	4	2/26	2/26	17.25	7.66	13.5	0	0

FULL NAME: Mark Daniel Stoneman
BORN: June 26, 1987, Newcastle-upon-Tyne, Northumberland
SQUAD NO: 26
HEIGHT: 5ft 10in
NICKNAME: Rocky
EDUCATION: Whickham Comprehensive School
TEAMS: Durham, Durham 2nd XI, England Under-19s
CAREER: First-class: 2007; List A: 2008; T20: 2010

DURHAM

BEST BATTING: 128 Durham vs Sussex, Hove, 2011

FAMILY TIES? My grandfather played and was later a local league umpire. My father played for many years as a local league professional
WHO WOULD PLAY YOU IN A FILM OF YOUR LIFE? Mark Wahlberg
CAREER HIGHLIGHTS? Being part of three County Championship-winning sides. Captaining Durham
MOST MARKED CHARACTERISTIC? My passion
BEST PLAYER IN COUNTY CRICKET? Graham Onions
TIP FOR THE TOP? Paul Coughlin
DESERT ISLAND DISC? ABBA's Greatest Hits
FAVOURITE TV? Game Of Thrones
CRICKETING HEROES? My dad, Brian Lara, Michael Di Venuto, Dale Benkenstein
NON-CRICKETING HEROES? Mark Wahlberg, Georges St-Pierre
WHEN YOU RETIRE? I'll go fishing and play golf
TWITTER FEED: @mark23stone

Batting	Mat	Inns	NO	Runs	HS	Ave	SR	100	50	Ct	St
First-class	83	144	5	4074	128	29.30	52.69	7	22	49	0
List A	32	30	3	1084	136*	40.14	95.00	3	5	11	0
Twenty20	14	14	0	270	51	19.28	107.14	0	1	8	0

Bowling	Mat	Balls	Runs	Wkts	BBI	BBM	Ave	Econ	SR	5w	10
First-class	83	-	-	-	-	-	-	-	-	-	-
List A	32	-	-	-	-	-	-	-	-	-	-
Twenty20	14	-	-	-	-	-	-	-	-	-	-

JAMES SYKES

LHB SLA

FULL NAME: James Stuart Sykes
BORN: April 26, 1992, Huntingdon
SQUAD NO: 80
HEIGHT: 6ft 2in
NICKNAME: Sykesy
EDUCATION: St Ivo School
TEAMS: Cambridgeshire, Leicestershire, Leicestershire 2nd XI
CAREER: First-class: 2013; List A: 2012; T20: 2012

BEST BATTING: 34 Leicestershire vs Worcestershire, Leicester, 2013
BEST BOWLING: 4-176 Leicestershire vs Essex, Chelmsford, 2013

FAMILY TIES? I don't have any apart from my father playing club cricket when he was younger
WHO WOULD PLAY YOU IN A FILM OF YOUR LIFE? Damien Lewis
CAREER HIGHLIGHTS? Signing a professional contract, making my debut in all formats of the game and playing at Lord's
MOST MARKED CHARACTERISTIC? Probably my hair
BEST PLAYER IN COUNTY CRICKET? Moeen Ali
TIPS FOR THE TOP? Shiv Thakor and Matt Dunn
IF YOU WEREN'T A CRICKETER? I'd be at university
DESERT ISLAND DISC? Kanye West – College Dropout
FAVOURITE TV? Friday Night Lights
CRICKETING HEROES? Shane Warne and Claude Henderson
NON-CRICKETING HEROES? David Beckham
ACCOMPLISHMENTS? Surviving five months in Adelaide with Ryan Buckley
WHEN YOU RETIRE? I'll open up a fashionable barbers establishment
SURPRISING FACT? I attended a ballet class when I was six years old
TWITTER FEED: @Sykesy20

Batting	Mat	Inns	NO	Runs	HS	Ave	SR	100	50	Ct	St
First-class	7	12	2	139	34	13.90	35.91	0	0	3	0
List A	15	7	3	30	15	7.50	76.92	0	0	2	0
Twenty20	2	1	1	2	2*	-	50.00	0	0	0	0

Bowling	Mat	Balls	Runs	Wkts	BBI	BBM	Ave	Econ	SR	5w	10
First-class	7	1197	733	12	4/176	4/176	61.08	3.67	99.7	0	0
List A	15	504	464	11	3/39	3/39	42.18	5.52	45.8	0	0
Twenty20	2	30	27	2	2/24	2/24	13.50	5.40	15.0	0	0

JONATHAN TATTERSALL

RHB LB

FULL NAME: Jonathan Andrew Tattersall
BORN: December 15, 1994, Harrogate, Yorkshire
SQUAD NO: 12
NICKNAME: Tatts
EDUCATION: King James' School, Knaresborough
TEAMS: England Development Programme Under-19s, England Under-19s, Yorkshire, Yorkshire 2nd XI, Yorkshire Under-13s, Yorkshire Under-14s, Yorkshire Under-15s
CAREER: List A: 2013

YORKSHIRE

TWITTER FEED: @JonnyTatts

NOTES: Tattersall was one of the key components of the England side that achieved third place in the 2014 U19 World Cup in UAE, scoring 95 from No.4 in the one-wicket defeat to Sri Lanka in the group stages. He started life as a leg-spinner and still considers himself an allrounder but it is his batting that helped him force his way into the Yorkshire first team last year, making his List A bow against Glamorgan in the YB40. He has played two U19 Tests and 22 U19 ODIs for his country, scoring five half-centuries

Batting	Mat	Inns	NO	Runs	HS	Ave	SR	100	50	Ct	St
List A	1	1	0	0	0	0.00	0.00	0	0	0	0

Bowling	Mat	Balls	Runs	Wkts	BBI	BBM	Ave	Econ	SR	5w	10
List A	1	-	-	-	-	-	-	-	-	-	-

WILLIAM TAVARÉ

RHB RMF

FULL NAME: William Andrew Tavaré
BORN: January 1, 1990, Bristol
SQUAD NO: 4
HEIGHT: 6ft 2in
NICKNAME: Tay, Tekkers, Zukkers
EDUCATION: Bristol Grammar School;
Loughborough University
TEAMS: Gloucestershire 2nd XI,
Loughborough MCCU, Marylebone Cricket
Club Universities
CAREER: First-class: 2010

BEST BATTING: 61 Loughborough MCCU vs Hampshire, Southampton, 2013

FAMILY TIES? My uncle Chris played for Kent, Somerset and England
WHO WOULD PLAY YOU IN A FILM OF YOUR LIFE? Jesse Eisenberg who played Mark
Zuckerberg in The Social Network – he's one of my lookalikes
CAREER HIGHLIGHTS? Scoring fifties in both innings against Kent for Loughborough at
Canterbury in front of my family
MOST MARKED CHARACTERISTIC? Quietness
BEST PLAYER IN COUNTY CRICKET? James Taylor
TIPS FOR THE TOP? Chris Dent, Luis Reece
IF YOU WEREN'T A CRICKETER? No idea, but something within sport
DESERT ISLAND DISC? Red Hot Chili Peppers – Greatest Hits
FAVOURITE TV? Entourage
CRICKETING HEROES? Graham Thorpe
NON-CRICKETING HEROES? Jonny Wilkinson
ACCOMPLISHMENTS? Getting a degree at Loughborough in Human Biology
WHEN YOU RETIRE? I'd like to travel the world
SURPRISING FACT? I was born in Bristol but moved to Dallas, Texas for a year when I was a
few weeks old
FANTASY SLIP CORDON? Keeper: Jonny Wilkinson, 1st: Shane Warne, 2nd: Me, 3rd: Billy
Connolly, Gully: Martin Johnson
TWITTER FEED: @wtav90

Batting	Mat	Inns	NO	Runs	HS	Ave	SR	100	50	Ct	St
First-class	5	9	1	262	61	32.75	46.20	0	3	0	0

Bowling	Mat	Balls	Runs	Wkts	BBI	BBM	Ave	Econ	SR	5w	10
First-class	5	-	-	-	-	-	-	-	-	-	-

BRAD TAYLOR

RHB OB

FULL NAME: Bradley Jacob Taylor
BORN: March 14, 1997, Winchester, Hampshire
SQUAD NO: TBC
TEAMS: Hampshire, Hampshire 2nd XI, Hampshire Under-15s, Hampshire Under-16s, Hampshire Under-17s
CAREER: First-class: 2013; List A: 2013

BEST BATTING: 20 Hampshire vs Lancashire, Southport, 2013
BEST BOWLING: 4-64 Hampshire vs Lancashire, Southport, 2013

NOTES: An emerging off-spinner, Taylor became the youngest Hampshire player to appear in the first team since 1867 when he played against Bangladesh A last August at the age of 16. Later that month he played against Lancashire in the YB40, returning figures of 2-50 including the wicket of former Australian Test opener Simon Katich. He made his County Championship debut against the same opposition a week later, taking 4-64 in the second-innings with South African batsman Ashwell Prince among his victims. He was subsequently picked for an England Development Programme squad to tour Sri Lanka in the Easter of 2014

Batting	Mat	Inns	NO	Runs	HS	Ave	SR	100	50	Ct	St
First-class	1	2	1	20	20	20.00	62.50	0	0	1	0
List A	2	1	1	2	2*	-	50.00	0	0	0	0

Bowling	Mat	Balls	Runs	Wkts	BBI	BBM	Ave	Econ	SR	5w	10
First-class	1	132	106	4	4/64	4/106	26.50	4.81	33.0	0	0
List A	2	90	73	4	2/23	2/23	18.25	4.86	22.5	0	0

GLOUCESTERSHIRE

FULL NAME: Jack Martin Robert Taylor
BORN: November 12, 1991, Banbury, Oxfordshire
SQUAD NO: 10
HEIGHT: 6ft
NICKNAME: Schlidd, J-Swag
EDUCATION: Chipping Norton School
TEAMS: Gloucestershire, Gloucestershire 2nd XI, Oxfordshire
CAREER: First-class: 2010; List A: 2011; T20: 2011

BEST BATTING: 63 Gloucestershire vs Glamorgan, Swansea, 2012
BEST BOWLING: 2-28 Gloucestershire vs Glamorgan, Swansea, 2012
COUNTY CAP: 2010

FAMILY TIES? My grandfather and father both played minor counties cricket for Oxfordshire. My brother Matt also plays for Gloucestershire
WHO WOULD PLAY YOU IN A FILM OF YOUR LIFE? Tom Cruise – I've been mistaken for him many times
CAREER HIGHLIGHTS? Taking 4-16 and scoring 38 on my T20 debut (a win versus rivals Somerset), my first-class debut for Gloucestershire and passing my ECB bowling test [in February 2014]
MOST MARKED CHARACTERISTIC? I'm loud, I have a steady beard and an average barnet
BEST PLAYER IN COUNTY CRICKET? Will Gidman. He continues to score runs and take wickets
TIPS FOR THE TOP? Matt Taylor, Craig Miles
CRICKETING HEROES? Jacques Kallis, the best allrounder of all-time
SURPRISING FACT? I have two tattoos: one is an inspirational quote and the other means 'lamb kebab'
CRICKET RULE YOU'D CHANGE? If you hit the ball out of the ground it should be worth 10
TWITTER FEED: @jacktaylor141

Batting	Mat	Inns	NO	Runs	HS	Ave	SR	100	50	Ct	St
First-class	12	19	2	451	63	26.52	72.27	0	2	8	0
List A	7	5	3	53	22*	26.50	165.62	0	0	1	0
Twenty20	10	10	1	53	38	5.88	84.12	0	0	2	0

Bowling	Mat	Balls	Runs	Wkts	BBI	BBM	Ave	Econ	SR	5w	10
First-class	12	1555	892	21	2/28	4/103	42.47	3.44	74.0	0	0
List A	7	250	207	9	3/37	3/37	23.00	4.96	27.7	0	0
Twenty20	10	139	178	8	4/16	4/16	22.25	7.68	17.3	0	0

JAMES TAYLOR

RHB LB R4 MVP34

FULL NAME: James William Arthur Taylor
BORN: January 6, 1990, Nottingham
SQUAD NO: 4
HEIGHT: 5ft 6in
NICKNAME: Jimmy, Titch
EDUCATION: Shrewsbury School
TEAMS: England, England Lions, England Under-19s, Leicestershire, Nottinghamshire, Shropshire, Worcestershire 2nd XI
CAREER: Test: 2012; ODI: 2011; First-class: 2008; List A: 2008; T20: 2008

NOTTINGHAMSHIRE

BEST BATTING: 242* England Lions vs Sri Lanka A, Dambulla, 2014
COUNTY CAPS: 2009 (Leicestershire); 2012 (Nottinghamshire)

CRICKETERS PARTICULARLY ADMIRED? Sachin Tendulkar
TIP FOR THE TOP? Shiv Thakor
RELAXATIONS? Fishing, shooting, hunting
FAVOURITE BAND? The Pussycat Dolls
TWITTER FEED: @jamestaylor20
NOTES: Taylor made his England Test debut against South Africa at Headingley in 2012. He captained the England Lions winter tour to Australia in 2012/13, having captained them several times before. Made his ODI debut against Ireland in 2011. Cricket Writers' Young Player of the Year in 2009. Joined Nottinghamshire ahead of the 2012 season after four successful seasons with Leicestershire and topped 1,000 first-class runs for the season in 2013, averaging 49.04. Enjoyed a successful tour of Sri Lanka with England Lions in early 2014, hitting 242* against Sri Lanka A in Dambulla. Graduated from minor counties cricket with Shropshire and the academy at Worcestershire to the playing staff at Leicestershire. Represented England in the 2008 U19 World Cup

Batting	Mat	Inns	NO	Runs	HS	Ave	SR	100	50	Ct	St
Tests	2	3	0	48	34	16.00	31.57	0	0	2	0
ODIs	2	2	0	26	25	13.00	52.00	0	0	0	0
First-class	104	168	24	6947	242*	48.24		17	31	71	0
List A	90	86	19	3401	115*	50.76	82.01	8	19	15	0
Twenty20	66	59	18	1447	62*	35.29	114.93	0	7	21	0

Bowling	Mat	Balls	Runs	Wkts	BBI	BBM	Ave	Econ	SR	5w	10
Tests	2	-	-	-	-	-	-	-	-	-	-
ODIs	2	-	-	-	-	-	-	-	-	-	-
First-class	104	228	176	0	-	-	-	4.63	-	0	0
List A	90	138	170	5	4/61	4/61	34.00	7.39	27.6	0	0
Twenty20	66	74	100	2	1/10	1/10	50.00	8.10	37.0	0	0

MATT TAYLOR

RHB LMF

GLOUCESTERSHIRE

FULL NAME: Matthew David Taylor
BORN: July 8, 1994, Banbury, Oxfordshire
SQUAD NO: 36
HEIGHT: 6ft 1in
NICKNAME: Melon, Swede, Balloon
EDUCATION: Chipping Norton School
TEAMS: Gloucestershire, Gloucestershire 2nd XI, Oxfordshire
CAREER: First-class: 2013; List A: 2011

BEST BATTING: 26* Gloucestershire vs Lancashire, Bristol, 2013
BEST BOWLING: 3-108 Gloucestershire vs Glamorgan, Cardiff, 2013

FAMILY TIES? My dad and grandad played minor counties cricket. My brother [Jack] also plays for Gloucestershire
WHO WOULD PLAY YOU IN A FILM OF YOUR LIFE? Leonardo DiCaprio. Gun actor!
CAREER HIGHLIGHTS? Opening the bowling on my Pro40 debut in 2011, my County Championship debut against Leicestershire and my first first-class wicket against Lancashire in 2013
SUPERSTITIONS? I put my left boot and left pad on first
MOST MARKED CHARACTERISTIC? My small head
BEST PLAYER IN COUNTY CRICKET? Will Gidman. Top role model!
TIPS FOR THE TOP? Miles Hammond, Craig Miles
IF YOU WEREN'T A CRICKETER? I'd be at university or hopefully living in the sun
DESERT ISLAND DISC? Bastille – Bad Blood
FAVOURITE TV? Sherlock
CRICKETING HEROES? Darren Gough, Allan Donald
NON-CRICKETING HEROES? Ronaldo, Leonardo DiCaprio
ACCOMPLISHMENTS? Getting my first 180 in darts and shooting 120 on Chipping Norton golf course
WHEN YOU RETIRE? I'd like to live on the beach and play golf
TWITTER FEED: @matt_taylor94

Batting	Mat	Inns	NO	Runs	HS	Ave	SR	100	50	Ct	St
First-class	3	3	2	31	26*	31.00	67.39	0	0	0	0
List A	2	1	1	7	7*	-	140.00	0	0	1	0

Bowling	Mat	Balls	Runs	Wkts	BBI	BBM	Ave	Econ	SR	5w	10
First-class	3	450	246	4	3/108	3/128	61.50	3.28	112.5	0	0
List A	2	83	89	4	2/43	2/43	22.25	6.43	20.7	0	0

ROB TAYLOR
LHB LM

FULL NAME: Robert Meadows Lombe Taylor
BORN: December 21, 1989, Northampton
SQUAD NO: 10
HEIGHT: 6ft 3in
NICKNAME: Tayls, Meadows
EDUCATION: Harrow School; Loughborough University
TEAMS: Scotland, Harrow School, Leicestershire, Leicestershire 2nd XI, Loughborough MCCU, Northamptonshire 2nd XI
CAREER: ODI: 2013; T20I: 2013; First-class: 2010; List A: 2012; T20: 2012

BEST BATTING: 101* Loughborough MCCU vs Leicestershire, Leicester, 2011
BEST BOWLING: 5-91 Leicestershire vs Kent, Leicester, 2012

FAMILY TIES? My dad played village cricket for Helmdon CC and my brother played for Stowe School
CAREER HIGHLIGHTS? Qualifying for the 2015 World Cup with Scotland
SUPERSTITIONS? I always put my right pad on first and always paint a smiley face at the top of my run-up
MOST MARKED CHARACTERISTIC? My bent nose
BEST PLAYER IN COUNTY CRICKET? James Taylor
TIP FOR THE TOP? Tom Wells
CRICKETING HEROES? Mitchell Johnson, Matthew Hayden
ACCOMPLISHMENTS? My university degree in Sports Management and cycling from Land's End to John O'Groats for the charity SOBS in 2012
WHEN YOU RETIRE? I'd like to be a property investor
SURPRISING FACT? Both of my little fingers are bent
TWITTER FEED: @robtaylor1989

Batting	Mat	Inns	NO	Runs	HS	Ave	SR	100	50	Ct	St
ODIs	8	7	2	109	46*	21.80	104.80	0	0	3	0
T20Is	4	4	2	71	41*	35.50	154.34	0	0	4	0
First-class	16	26	2	488	101*	20.33	56.74	1	1	8	0
List A	33	30	9	410	48*	19.52	104.59	0	0	13	0
Twenty20	27	20	7	250	41*	19.23	142.85	0	0	14	0

Bowling	Mat	Balls	Runs	Wkts	BBI	BBM	Ave	Econ	SR	5w	10
ODIs	8	455	366	13	3/39	3/39	28.15	4.82	35.0	0	0
T20Is	4	60	83	1	1/16	1/16	83.00	8.30	60.0	0	0
First-class	16	1943	1408	31	5/91	5/91	45.41	4.34	62.6	1	0
List A	33	1447	1317	45	3/39	3/39	29.26	5.46	32.1	0	0
Twenty20	27	426	508	26	4/11	4/11	19.53	7.15	16.3	0	0

TOM TAYLOR RHB RMF

FULL NAME: Thomas Alex Ian Taylor
BORN: December 21, 1994, Stoke-on-Trent, Staffordshire
SQUAD NO: 15
HEIGHT: 6ft 3in
NICKNAME: Audi, Hospital
EDUCATION: Trentham High School; Newcastle-under-Lyme College; Leeds Metropolitan University
TEAMS: Derbyshire 2nd XI
CAREER: Yet to make first-team debut

WHO WOULD PLAY YOU IN A FILM OF YOUR LIFE? Tom Cruise
CAREER HIGHLIGHTS? Making my debut for Derbyshire 2nd XI aged 16, getting my first hundred in a cup final and taking a five-wicket haul on my debut for Ticknall CC
SUPERSTITIONS? I walk right from the pavilion when walking around the boundary
MOST MARKED CHARACTERISTIC? My skinny legs
BEST PLAYER IN COUNTY CRICKET? Moeen Ali
IF YOU WEREN'T A CRICKETER? I'd be coaching cricket or I'd be a school teacher
DESERT ISLAND DISC? Arctic Monkeys – AM
FAVOURITE TV? Breaking Bad
CRICKETING HEROES? Viv Richards, Michael Holding
NON-CRICKETING HEROES? Tom Cruise
ACCOMPLISHMENTS? Making it to university. I'm currently studying Sports Science
WHEN YOU RETIRE? I want to become a teacher and a cricket coach at a high level
SURPRISING FACT? On an application form, in the place of birth section, I write 'hospital.' This is where my nickname originated from
TWITTER FEED: @TomTaylor43

RYAN TEN DOESCHATE

RHB RMF MVP65

FULL NAME: Ryan Neil ten Doeschate
BORN: June 30, 1980, Port Elizabeth, Cape Province, South Africa
SQUAD NO: 27
HEIGHT: 5ft 11in
NICKNAME: Tendo
TEAMS: Netherlands, All Stars, Canterbury, Chittagong Kings, Essex, Impi, Kolkata Knight Riders, Mashonaland Eagles, Otago, Tasmania, Western Province
CAREER: ODI: 2006; T20I: 2008; First-class: 2003; List A: 2003; T20: 2003

ESSEX

BEST BATTING: 259* Netherlands vs Canada, Pretoria, 2006
BEST BOWLING: 6-20 Netherlands vs Canada, Pretoria, 2006
COUNTY CAP: 2006

CRICKETING HEROES? Jacques Kallis, Kepler Wessels
OTHER SPORTS PLAYED? Rugby
OTHER SPORTS FOLLOWED? Football (Arsenal), rugby (Stormers)
FAVOURITE MUSICIAN? Phil Collins
RELAXATIONS? Golf, tennis, reading
NOTES: A Netherlands international who won the ICC Associate Player of the Year award in 2008, 2010 and 2011. Scored 686 runs at an average of 228.66 in the ICC Intercontinental Cup in 2006, recording four consecutive hundreds, including a competition record 259* vs Canada in Pretoria. Made a century (119) against England at Nagpur in the World Cup 2011, becoming the first batsman from the Netherlands to make a hundred in the World Cup finals. Went on to score a second century of the tournament against Ireland at Kolkata but has not represented his country since, instead focusing on county cricket and T20 franchises across the world

Batting	Mat	Inns	NO	Runs	HS	Ave	SR	100	50	Ct	St
ODIs	33	32	9	1541	119	67.00	87.70	5	9	13	0
T20Is	9	9	4	214	56	42.80	128.91	0	1	3	0
First-class	109	159	22	6426	259*	46.90		20	25	64	0
List A	164	136	41	4453	180	46.87		8	25	48	0
Twenty20	197	177	37	4119	121*	29.42	137.30	2	18	71	0

Bowling	Mat	Balls	Runs	Wkts	BBI	BBM	Ave	Econ	SR	5w	10
ODIs	33	1580	1327	55	4/31	4/31	24.12	5.03	28.7	0	0
T20Is	9	204	241	12	3/23	3/23	20.08	7.08	17.0	0	0
First-class	109	9383	6171	182	6/20		33.90	3.94	51.5	7	0
List A	164	4638	4377	147	5/50	5/50	29.77	5.66	31.5	1	0
Twenty20	197	1706	2289	90	4/24	4/24	25.43	8.05	18.9	0	0

SEAN TERRY

RHB OB

FULL NAME: Sean Paul Terry
BORN: August 1, 1991, Southampton, Hampshire
SQUAD NO: 10
HEIGHT: 5ft 11in
NICKNAME: Seany
EDUCATION: Aquinas College, Perth
TEAMS: Derbyshire 2nd XI, Hampshire, Hampshire 2nd XI, Marylebone Cricket Club Young Cricketers
CAREER: First-class: 2012; List A: 2012

BEST BATTING: 59* Hampshire vs Loughborough MCCU, Southampton, 2012

FAMILY TIES? My dad [Paul] played for Hampshire and England
WHO WOULD PLAY YOU IN A FILM OF YOUR LIFE? Jonah Hill
CAREER HIGHLIGHTS? My debut for Hampshire and my first first-class fifty
SUPERSTITIONS? I put my left pad on first
MOST MARKED CHARACTERISTIC? My massive calves
BEST PLAYER IN COUNTY CRICKET? James Vince
TIP FOR THE TOP? Michael Bates
DESERT ISLAND DISC? Jay-Z or Red Hot Chili Peppers' Greatest Hits
FAVOURITE TV? Geordie Shore
CRICKETING HEROES? My dad, AB de Villiers and Michael Clarke
NON-CRICKETING HEROES? My mum
ACCOMPLISHMENTS? Getting half-decent grades at school
WHEN YOU RETIRE? I would like to get into journalism
FANTASY SLIP CORDON? Keeper: Michael McIntyre, 1st: Jay-Z, 2nd: Jennifer Lawrence, 3rd: Myself, Gully: Denzel Washington
TWITTER FEED: @sterry91

Batting	Mat	Inns	NO	Runs	HS	Ave	SR	100	50	Ct	St
First-class	6	7	1	208	59*	34.66	46.95	0	3	5	0
List A	3	2	0	35	33	17.50	63.63	0	0	1	0

Bowling	Mat	Balls	Runs	Wkts	BBI	BBM	Ave	Econ	SR	5w	10
First-class	6	-	-	-	-	-	-	-	-	-	-
List A	3	-	-	-	-	-	-	-	-	-	-

SHIV THAKOR   RHB RMF

FULL NAME: Shivsinh Jaysinh Thakor
BORN: October 22, 1993, Leicester
SQUAD NO: 57
HEIGHT: 5ft 11in
NICKNAME: Shivy, Shiva, Shivametimbers
EDUCATION: Uppingham School
TEAMS: England Under-17s, England Under-19s, Leicestershire, Leicestershire 2nd XI
CAREER: First-class: 2011; List A: 2011; T20: 2013

BEST BATTING: 134 Leicestershire vs Loughborough MCCU, Leicester, 2011
BEST BOWLING: 3-57 Leicestershire vs Surrey, Leicester, 2011

FAMILY TIES? My father played cricket from a young age and his love of the game introduced me to it
WHO WOULD PLAY YOU IN A FILM OF YOUR LIFE? Ryan Gosling
CAREER HIGHLIGHTS? Scoring 134 on my first-class debut and becoming the youngest first-class centurion for Leicestershire CCC by doing so. Representing and captaining England U19
SUPERSTITIONS? Far too many to mention
MOST MARKED CHARACTERISTIC? Competitiveness
BEST PLAYER IN COUNTY CRICKET? Kevin Pietersen
TIPS FOR THE TOP? Ariyan Patel, Ben Duckett, Olly Stone
IF YOU WEREN'T A CRICKETER? I'd be studying PPE at university
FAVOURITE TV? The Mentalist
CRICKETING HEROES? Sachin Tendulkar, Jacques Kallis, Mark Rampakash
NON-CRICKETING HEROES? My mother and father
WHEN YOU RETIRE? I would like to stay in the game, either commentating or coaching
SURPRISING FACT? I still sleep with my teddy bear Baloo and I cannot swim
TWITTER FEED: @Thakor57

Batting	Mat	Inns	NO	Runs	HS	Ave	SR	100	50	Ct	St
First-class	24	39	6	1288	134	39.03	46.87	2	9	6	0
List A	18	18	3	342	83*	22.80	83.61	0	3	4	0
Twenty20	8	6	1	62	42	12.40	98.41	0	0	2	0

Bowling	Mat	Balls	Runs	Wkts	BBI	BBM	Ave	Econ	SR	5w	10
First-class	24	1141	796	16	3/57	3/57	49.75	4.18	71.3	0	0
List A	18	326	416	9	3/39	3/39	46.22	7.65	36.2	0	0
Twenty20	8	78	109	6	3/30	3/30	18.16	8.38	13.0	0	0

ALFONSO THOMAS
RHB RFM MVP35

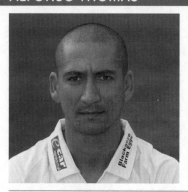

FULL NAME: Alfonso Clive Thomas
BORN: February 9, 1977, Cape Town, Cape Province, South Africa
SQUAD NO: 8
EDUCATION: Ravensmead Secondary School; Parrow High School, Cape Town
TEAMS: South Africa, Adelaide Strikers, Dhaka Gladiators, Dolphins, North West, Northerns, Pune Warriors, Somerset, Staffordshire, Titans, Warwickshire, Western Province
CAREER: T20I: 2007; First-class: 1998; List A: 2000; T20: 2004

BEST BATTING: 119* North West vs Northerns, Centurion, 2002
BEST BOWLING: 7-54 Titans vs Cape Cobras, Cape Town, 2005
COUNTY CAP: 2008 (Somerset)

TWITTER FEED: @alfonsothomas
NOTES: Came to the attention of the South African selectors in the 2003/04 season, claiming 36 wickets in eight SuperSport Series matches for Titans. He was drafted in to replace the injured Andre Nel in South Africa's Test squad that toured India in 2004 but didn't make his international debut until the age of 30, in a T20I against Pakistan in 2007. Signed with Somerset as a Kolpak player the following year and has not played for South Africa since. Leading wicket-taker in the 2010 FP t20 with 33 wickets, and took 109 wickets in all competitions that year. Claimed 42 first-class wickets at 25.64 last season. In all, he has taken 222 first-class wickets at 26.99 for Somerset

Batting	Mat	Inns	NO	Runs	HS	Ave	SR	100	50	Ct	St
T20Is	1	-	-	-	-	-	-	-	-	0	0
First-class	142	200	39	3826	119*	23.76		2	13	37	0
List A	156	76	35	586	28*	14.29		0	0	33	0
Twenty20	201	64	31	372	30*	11.27	104.49	0	0	60	0

Bowling	Mat	Balls	Runs	Wkts	BBI	BBM	Ave	Econ	SR	5w	10
T20Is	1	24	25	3	3/25	3/25	8.33	6.25	8.0	0	0
First-class	142	25445	12312	461	7/54		26.70	2.90	55.1	21	2
List A	156	6529	5572	206	4/18	4/18	27.04	5.12	31.6	0	0
Twenty20	201	4099	5025	235	5/24	5/24	21.38	7.35	17.4	1	0

IVAN THOMAS RHB RMF

FULL NAME: Ivan Alfred Astley Thomas
BORN: September 25, 1991, Greenwich, Kent
SQUAD NO: 5
HEIGHT: 6ft 4in
NICKNAME: Blade, Big Iv, Goober
EDUCATION: The John Roan School; University of Leeds
TEAMS: Kent, Kent 2nd XI, Kent Under-17s, Leeds/Bradford MCCU
CAREER: First-class: 2012

BEST BATTING: 11 Leeds/Bradford MCCU vs Yorkshire, Leeds, 2012
BEST BOWLING: 2-24 Leeds/Bradford MCCU vs Yorkshire, Leeds, 2012

WHO WOULD PLAY YOU IN A FILM OF YOUR LIFE? Will Smith
CAREER HIGHLIGHTS? Playing against South Africa
SUPERSTITIONS? Yes, too many
MOST MARKED CHARACTERISTIC? Big, ginger hair
BEST PLAYER IN COUNTY CRICKET? Graham Onions
TIP FOR THE TOP? Luis Reece
DESERT ISLAND DISC? Wu-Tang Clan – Enter The Wu-Tang: 36 Chambers
FAVOURITE TV? The Wire
CRICKETING HEROES? Andrew Flintoff
NON-CRICKETING HEROES? Shaka Zulu
ACCOMPLISHMENTS? Completing Tough Mudder
WHEN YOU RETIRE? I'd like to break into the hip-hop game
SURPRISING FACT? I'm a quarter Jamaican
FANTASY SLIP CORDON? Keeper: Method Man, 1st: Louis Theroux, 2nd: Kate Upton, 3rd: Phil from Modern Family, Gully: Kevin Bridges
TWITTER FEED: @ivanthomas_5

Batting	Mat	Inns	NO	Runs	HS	Ave	SR	100	50	Ct	St
First-class	6	10	5	49	11	9.80	29.87	0	0	1	0

Bowling	Mat	Balls	Runs	Wkts	BBI	BBM	Ave	Econ	SR	5w	10
First-class	6	861	365	12	2/24	3/45	30.41	2.54	71.7	0	0

MICHAEL THORNELY

RHB RM

LEICESTERSHIRE

FULL NAME: Michael Alistair Thornely
BORN: October 19, 1987, Camden, London
SQUAD NO: 7
HEIGHT: 6ft 1in
NICKNAME: Thorners, Major, Thor
EDUCATION: Brighton College
TEAMS: Kent 2nd XI, Leicestershire, Leicestershire 2nd XI, Mashonaland Eagles, Nottinghamshire 2nd XI, Somerset 2nd XI, Sussex, Sussex 2nd XI, Sussex Under-15s, Sussex Under-17s, Unicorns, Unicorns A
CAREER: First-class: 2007; List A: 2007; T20: 2012

BEST BATTING: 131 Leicestershire vs Glamorgan, Cardiff, 2012
BEST BOWLING: 2-14 Sussex vs Worcestershire, Hove, 2010

FAMILY TIES? My dad played when he was younger and my uncle played minor counties cricket
WHO WOULD PLAY YOU IN A FILM OF YOUR LIFE? Jason Statham, Bruce Willis or Vin Diesel
CAREER HIGHLIGHTS? Winning Division Two of the County Championship with Sussex in 2010
SUPERSTITIONS? My left pad goes on first
MOST MARKED CHARACTERISTIC? My large forehead
BEST PLAYER IN COUNTY CRICKET? Michael Carberry
TIP FOR THE TOP? Shiv Thakor
IF YOU WEREN'T A CRICKETER? I'd probably be sat behind a desk
DESERT ISLAND DISC? Shapeshifter – In Colour
FAVOURITE TV? Top Gear, Shark Week
CRICKETING HEROES? Mark Waugh
NON-CRICKETING HEROES? David Beckham
SURPRISING FACT? I was the U15 national long jump champion
CRICKET RULE YOU'D CHANGE? Free hit runs should be doubled
TWITTER FEED: @Thorners87

Batting	Mat	Inns	NO	Runs	HS	Ave	SR	100	50	Ct	St
First-class	39	67	2	1434	131	22.06	39.28	2	6	32	0
List A	46	42	2	1171	105*	29.27	85.34	1	6	13	0
Twenty20	10	8	2	51	20	8.50	83.60	0	0	3	0

Bowling	Mat	Balls	Runs	Wkts	BBI	BBM	Ave	Econ	SR	5w	10
First-class	39	794	527	10	2/14	2/14	52.70	3.98	79.4	0	0
List A	46	326	365	5	1/20	1/20	73.00	6.71	65.2	0	0
Twenty20	10	21	34	0	-	-	-	9.71	-	0	0

JAMES TOMLINSON   LHB LMF W2

FULL NAME: James Andrew Tomlinson
BORN: June 12, 1982, Winchester, Hampshire
SQUAD NO: 21
HEIGHT: 6ft 1in
NICKNAME: Tommo, Dangerous Dave, T-bird
EDUCATION: Cricklade College, Andover;
Cardiff University
TEAMS: British Universities, Cardiff MCCU,
Hampshire, Hampshire 2nd XI, Hampshire
Cricket Board, Wiltshire
CAREER: First-class: 2002; List A: 2000; T20:
2006

BEST BATTING: 42 Hampshire vs Somerset, Southampton, 2010
BEST BOWLING: 8-46 Hampshire vs Somerset, Taunton, 2008
COUNTY CAP: 2008

FAMILY TIES? My grandfathers played cricket in Carlisle and Hull respectively and one was a
member at Scarborough. My brothers Hugh and Ralph are passionate players and students
of the game
CAREER HIGHLIGHTS? Taking 8-46 and 7-85 at Taunton, taking 67 wickets in 2008 (the most
in the country), taking 53 wickets in 2013, winning at Canterbury in 2010 to stay up and any
wicket I take after June at the Ageas Bowl
BEST PLAYER IN COUNTY CRICKET? Chris Woakes
TIP FOR THE TOP? Tom Barber
DESERT ISLAND DISC? I would try to smuggle in as many songs/albums as possible,
probably get caught and consequently lose the privilege
FAVOURITE TV? The Thick Of It, Pointless
CRICKETING HEROES? Wasim Akram, Darren Gough, Bruce Reid, Tim Linley
NON-CRICKETING HEROES? Chris Packham
ACCOMPLISHMENTS? Definitely the arrival of my son Ernest last year

Batting	Mat	Inns	NO	Runs	HS	Ave	SR	100	50	Ct	St
First-class	98	124	56	683	42	10.04	28.73	0	0	22	0
List A	29	15	6	35	14	3.88		0	0	3	0
Twenty20	2	1	0	5	5	5.00	125.00	0	0	0	0

Bowling	Mat	Balls	Runs	Wkts	BBI	BBM	Ave	Econ	SR	5w	10
First-class	98	17399	9720	301	8/46		32.29	3.35	57.8	11	1
List A	29	1143	973	30	4/47	4/47	32.43	5.10	38.1	0	0
Twenty20	2	42	48	1	1/20	1/20	48.00	6.85	42.0	0	0

REECE TOPLEY

ESSEX

FULL NAME: Reece James William Topley
BORN: February 21, 1994, Ipswich, Suffolk
SQUAD NO: 6
HEIGHT: 6ft 6in
NICKNAME: Neil, Toppers
EDUCATION: Royal Hospital School
TEAMS: England Lions, England Under-19s, Essex, Essex 2nd XI
CAREER: First-class: 2011; List A: 2011; T20: 2012

BEST BATTING: 9 Essex vs Derbyshire, Chelmsford, 2011
BEST BOWLING: 6-29 Essex vs Worcestershire, Chelmsford, 2013
COUNTY CAP: 2013

FAMILY TIES? My father [Don] played for Essex and Surrey and my uncle [Peter] played for Kent
WHO WOULD PLAY YOU IN A FILM OF YOUR LIFE? Leonardo DiCaprio
BEST PLAYER IN COUNTY CRICKET? Moeen Ali
IF YOU WEREN'T A CRICKETER? Actor
DESERT ISLAND DISC? Jay-Z – Watch The Throne
FAVOURITE TV? TOWIE
CRICKETING HEROES? Wasim Akram
NON-CRICKETING HEROES? David Beckham
FANTASY SLIP CORDON? Keeper: David Beckham, 1st: Kelly Slater, 2nd: Amy Childs, 3rd: Megan Fox, Gully: Me
TWITTER FEED: @reece_topley

Batting	Mat	Inns	NO	Runs	HS	Ave	SR	100	50	Ct	St
First-class	25	29	13	34	9	2.12	15.74	0	0	7	0
List A	16	5	1	25	19	6.25	55.55	0	0	2	0
Twenty20	21	4	3	6	4*	6.00	46.15	0	0	5	0

Bowling	Mat	Balls	Runs	Wkts	BBI	BBM	Ave	Econ	SR	5w	10
First-class	25	4480	2515	93	6/29	11/85	27.04	3.36	48.1	5	1
List A	16	659	625	24	4/26	4/26	26.04	5.69	27.4	0	0
Twenty20	21	414	524	38	4/26	4/26	13.78	7.59	10.8	0	0

JAMES TREDWELL

LHB OB W1

FULL NAME: James Cullum Tredwell
BORN: February 27, 1982, Ashford, Kent
SQUAD NO: 15
HEIGHT: 5ft 11in
NICKNAME: Tredders, Pingu, Jimmy T
EDUCATION: Southlands Community Comprehensive
TEAMS: England, England A, England Lions, England Under-19s, Kent, Kent Cricket Board
CAREER: Test: 2010; ODI: 2010; T20I: 2012; First-class: 2001; List A: 2000; T20: 2003

BEST BATTING: 123* Kent vs New Zealanders, Canterbury, 2008
BEST BOWLING: 8-66 Kent vs Glamorgan, Canterbury, 2009
COUNTY CAP: 2007

FAMILY TIES? My father played a good level of club cricket for Ashford and Folkestone in the Kent League
CAREER HIGHLIGHTS? Being given the opportunity to play for England
MOST MARKED CHARACTERISTIC? My bald head
TIPS FOR THE TOP? Joe Root – he's already involved with England but there's plenty more to come from him. We have some good ones at Kent but I don't want to leave any out so I'm not going to name them all
CRICKETING HEROES? Shane Warne, David Gower
WHEN YOU RETIRE? Ideally I'd like to stay in cricket in some capacity but there are only so many positions to fill, so who knows!
SURPRISING FACT? I enjoy growing my own fruit and veg

Batting	Mat	Inns	NO	Runs	HS	Ave	SR	100	50	Ct	St
Tests	1	1	0	37	37	37.00	58.73	0	0	1	0
ODIs	30	15	8	59	16	8.42	47.20	0	0	9	0
T20Is	9	5	2	24	22	8.00	171.42	0	0	2	0
First-class	140	197	24	3837	123*	22.17	43.72	3	14	145	0
List A	214	139	50	1531	88	17.20		0	4	90	0
Twenty20	115	51	15	405	34*	11.25	109.16	0	0	34	0

Bowling	Mat	Balls	Runs	Wkts	BBI	BBM	Ave	Econ	SR	5w	10
Tests	1	390	181	6	4/82	6/181	30.16	2.78	65.0	0	0
ODIs	30	1378	1092	39	4/44	4/44	28.00	4.75	35.3	0	0
T20Is	9	155	218	5	1/16	1/16	43.60	8.43	31.0	0	0
First-class	140	24617	12586	352	8/66		35.75	3.06	69.9	12	3
List A	214	8828	6903	223	6/27	6/27	30.95	4.69	39.5	1	0
Twenty20	115	2171	2580	96	4/21	4/21	26.87	7.13	22.6	0	0

PETER TREGO

RHB RM W1 MVP7

SOMERSET

FULL NAME: Peter David Trego
BORN: June 12, 1981, Weston-super-Mare, Somerset
SQUAD NO: 7
HEIGHT: 6ft
NICKNAME: Tregs, Darcy, Pedro Tregos
EDUCATION: Wyvern Comprehensive
TEAMS: England, Central Districts, England Lions, Kent, Marylebone Cricket Club, Mashonaland Eagles, Middlesex, Middlesex 2nd XI, Somerset, Sylhet Royals
CAREER: First-class: 2000; List A: 1999; T20: 2003

BEST BATTING: 141 Central Districts vs Auckland, Auckland, 2013
BEST BOWLING: 6-59 Middlesex vs Nottinghamshire, Nottingham, 2005
COUNTY CAP: 2007 (Somerset)

WHO WOULD PLAY YOU IN A FILM OF YOUR LIFE? Johnny Depp
CAREER HIGHLIGHTS? My county cap, England Lions tours, playing in the Champions League T20 twice with Somerset, fighting early on to keep my career alive and winning the PCA MVP award in 2012
SUPERSTITIONS? Many, but mostly silly things like keeping the same sweatband for each different competition, same pants and batting socks – but washed regularly of course!
MOST MARKED CHARACTERISTIC? My tattoos
TIPS FOR THE TOP? Davis and Dexter Trego
DESERT ISLAND DISC? Green Day – Welcome To Paradise
BIGGEST DRESSING DOWN YOU'VE RECEIVED? All my memorable dressing downs happen at home!
CRICKETING HEROES? Graham Rose, Ian Botham, Justin Langer
NON-CRICKETING HEROES? George Best, David Beckham, Tiger Woods and still Lance Armstrong
SURPRISING FACT? My name is actually pronounced 'tree-go' not 'tray-go'
TWITTER FEED: @tregs140

Batting	Mat	Inns	NO	Runs	HS	Ave	SR	100	50	Ct	St
First-class	157	231	31	6580	141	32.90		10	39	68	0
List A	145	123	22	3015	147	29.85		4	15	45	0
Twenty20	132	120	15	2505	79	23.85	121.07		12	35	0

Bowling	Mat	Balls	Runs	Wkts	BBI	BBM	Ave	Econ	SR	5w	10
First-class	157	18172	10663	290	6/59		36.76	3.52	62.6	3	0
List A	145	4890	4602	142	5/40	5/40	32.40	5.64	34.4	2	0
Twenty20	132	1548	2180	69	4/27	4/27	31.59	8.44	22.4	0	0

CHRIS TREMLETT   RHB RFM

FULL NAME: Christopher Timothy Tremlett
BORN: September 2, 1981, Southampton, Hampshire
SQUAD NO: 33
HEIGHT: 6ft 8in
NICKNAME: Twiggy, Goober, Trem
EDUCATION: Taunton's College, Southampton
TEAMS: England, ECB National Academy, England Lions, Hampshire, Hampshire Cricket Board, Surrey
CAREER: Test: 2007; ODI: 2005; T20I: 2007; First-class: 2000; List A: 2000; T20: 2004

SURREY

BEST BATTING: 64 Hamphire vs Gloucestershire, Southampton, 2005
BEST BOWLING: 8-96 Surrey vs Durham, Chester-le-Street, 2013
COUNTY CAP: 2004 (Hampshire)

FAMILY TIES? My father [Tim] played for Hampshire and England A and my grandfather [Maurice] played for Somerset and England
WHO WOULD PLAY YOU IN A FILM OF YOUR LIFE? Jaws from the James Bond films
CAREER HIGHLIGHTS? Making my debuts for Hampshire, Surrey and England. Winning my first trophy in 2005 at Lord's. Winning the Ashes in 2010/11
MOST MARKED CHARACTERISTIC? Being very big and tall
BEST PLAYER IN COUNTY CRICKET? Michael Carberry
TIPS FOR THE TOP? Stuart Meaker and Joe Root
CRICKETING HEROES? Glenn McGrath, Curtly Ambrose, Robin Smith, Ian Botham
SURPRISING FACT? I can hide a tennis ball in my mouth
TWITTER FEED: @ChrisTremlett33

Batting	Mat	Inns	NO	Runs	HS	Ave	SR	100	50	Ct	St
Tests	12	15	4	113	25*	10.27	37.79	0	0	4	0
ODIs	15	11	4	50	19*	7.14	56.17	0	0	4	0
T20Is	1	-	-	-	-	-	-	-	-	0	0
First-class	133	167	42	2104	64	16.83		0	8	35	0
List A	131	81	27	550	38*	10.18		0	0	27	0
Twenty20	57	21	10	89	13	8.09	102.29	0	0	5	0

Bowling	Mat	Balls	Runs	Wkts	BBI	BBM	Ave	Econ	SR	5w	10
Tests	12	2902	1431	53	6/48	8/150	27.00	2.95	54.7	2	0
ODIs	15	784	705	15	4/32	4/32	47.00	5.39	52.2	0	0
T20Is	1	24	45	2	2/45	2/45	22.50	11.25	12.0	0	0
First-class	133	23185	12128	428	8/96		28.33	3.13	54.1	11	0
List A	131	6027	4919	175	4/25	4/25	28.10	4.89	34.4	0	0
Twenty20	57	1169	1434	73	4/16	4/16	19.64	7.36	16.0	0	0

SOMERSET

FULL NAME: Marcus Edward Trescothick
BORN: December 25, 1975, Keynsham, Somerset
SQUAD NO: 2
HEIGHT: 6ft 3in
NICKNAME: Banger, Tresco
EDUCATION: Sir Bernard Lovell School
TEAMS: England, Somerset
CAREER: Test: 2000; ODI: 2000; T20I: 2005; First-class: 1993; List A: 1993; T20: 2004

BEST BATTING: 284 Somerset vs Northamptonshire, Northampton, 2007
BEST BOWLING: 4-36 Somerset vs Young Australia, Taunton, 1995
COUNTY CAP: 1999; BENEFIT YEAR: 2008

TWITTER FEED: @Trescricket
NOTES: Trescothick's maiden Test appearance came against the West Indies at Old Trafford in 2000. His highest Test score was 219 against South Africa in a nine-wicket victory at The Oval in 2003. Played his last Test against Pakistan at the same ground in 2006. Wisden Cricketer of the Year in 2005 and PCA Player of the Year in 2000, 2009 and 2011. At the time of writing, he sits 15th on the all-time list of England run-scorers in Test cricket and he holds the English record for ODI hundreds. Passed 1,000 runs five years in a row between 2007 and 2011, with 1,673 runs in 2011 alone. He scored 843 Championship runs last season and will continue as Somerset club captain in 2014

Batting	Mat	Inns	NO	Runs	HS	Ave	SR	100	50	Ct	St
Tests	76	143	10	5825	219	43.79	54.51	14	29	95	0
ODIs	123	122	6	4335	137	37.37	85.21	12	21	49	0
T20Is	3	3	0	166	72	55.33	126.71	0	2	2	0
First-class	310	534	30	21064	284	41.79		51	104	426	0
List A	364	349	29	11985	184	37.45		28	61	143	0
Twenty20	74	73	5	2229	108*	32.77	155.22	2	17	24	0

Bowling	Mat	Balls	Runs	Wkts	BBI	BBM	Ave	Econ	SR	5w	10
Tests	76	300	155	1	1/34	1/34	155.00	3.10	300.0	0	0
ODIs	123	232	219	4	2/7	2/7	54.75	5.66	58.0	0	0
T20Is	3	-	-	-	-	-	-	-	-	-	-
First-class	310	2704	1551	36	4/36		43.08	3.44	75.1	0	0
List A	364	2010	1644	57	4/50	4/50	28.84	4.90	35.2	0	0
Twenty20	74	-	-	-	-	-	-	-	-	-	-

JONATHAN TROTT

RHB RM R6

FULL NAME: Ian Jonathan Leonard Trott
BORN: April 22, 1981, Cape Town, Cape Province, South Africa
SQUAD NO: 9
HEIGHT: 6ft
NICKNAME: Booger, Trotters
EDUCATION: Stellenbosch University
TEAMS: England, Boland, England Lions, Otago, South Africa Under-15s, South Africa Under-19s, Warwickshire, Western Province
CAREER: Test: 2009; ODI: 2009; T20I: 2007; First-class: 2000; List A: 2000; T20: 2003

BEST BATTING: 226 England vs Bangladesh, Lord's, 2010
BEST BOWLING: 7-39 Warwickshire vs Kent, Canterbury, 2003
COUNTY CAP: 2005; **BENEFIT YEAR:** 2014

TWITTER FEED: @Trotty
CRICKETING HEROES? Sachin Tendulkar, Adam Hollioake, Steve Waugh, Jacques Kallis
WHEN RAIN STOPS PLAY? Listening to music and watching sport
SURPRISING FACTS? I'm a San Francisco 49ers fan
NOTES: Represented South Africa A. Scored 245 on debut for Warwickshire 2nd XI. Hit 134 on County Championship debut for Warwickshire vs Sussex at Edgbaston in 2003. Made 119 on Test debut for England in the deciding match of the 2009 Ashes at The Oval. One of the four Wisden Cricketers of the Year for 2011. ICC Cricketer of the Year for 2011. Finished the 2013 ICC Champions Trophy as the tournament's second-highest run-scorer, with 229 runs at 57.25

Batting	Mat	Inns	NO	Runs	HS	Ave	SR	100	50	Ct	St
Tests	49	87	6	3763	226	46.45	47.39	9	18	29	0
ODIs	68	65	10	2819	137	51.25	77.06	4	22	14	0
T20Is	7	7	1	138	51	23.00	95.83	0	1	0	0
First-class	209	350	39	14053	226	45.18		33	70	184	0
List A	234	219	41	8346	137	46.88		15	57	69	0
Twenty20	77	72	16	2082	86*	37.17	114.90	0	13	18	0

Bowling	Mat	Balls	Runs	Wkts	BBI	BBM	Ave	Econ	SR	5w	10
Tests	49	702	398	5	1/5	1/5	79.60	3.40	140.4	0	0
ODIs	68	183	166	2	2/31	2/31	83.00	5.44	91.5	0	0
T20Is	7	-	-	-	-	-	-	-	-	-	-
First-class	209	5234	2953	61	7/39		48.40	3.38	85.8	1	0
List A	234	1552	1459	54	4/55	4/55	27.01	5.64	28.7	0	0
Twenty20	77	144	234	8	2/19	2/19	29.25	9.75	18.0	0	0

JIM TROUGHTON

LHB SLA R1

WARWICKSHIRE

FULL NAME: Jamie Oliver Troughton
BORN: March 2, 1979, Camden, London
SQUAD NO: 24
HEIGHT: 5ft 11in
NICKNAME: Troughts
EDUCATION: Trinity School, Leamington Spa; Birmingham University
TEAMS: England, Warwickshire, Warwickshire Cricket Board
CAREER: ODI: 2003; First-class: 2001; List A: 1999; T20: 2003

BEST BATTING: 223 Warwickshire vs Hampshire, Birmingham, 2009
BEST BOWLING: 3-1 Warwickshire vs Cambridge UCCE, Cambridge, 2004
COUNTY CAP: 2002; **BENEFIT YEAR:** 2013

FAMILY TIES? My great grandfather [Henry Crighton] played for Warwickshire and my younger brother [Wigsy Troughton] played for Warks youth and is a Stratford Panther
CAREER HIGHLIGHTS? My Warwickshire debut and first-team cap. Winning the B&H Cup final in 2002. Playing for England. Winning the Championship in 2004 and 2012. CB40 finalists in 2010 and 2012. Captaining Warwickshire
CRICKETING HEROES? Graham Thorpe, Brian Lara
NON-CRICKETING HEROES? Eric Cantona and Ian Brown (Stone Roses)
TIP FOR THE TOP? Chris Woakes
IF YOU WEREN'T A CRICKETER? I'd be an actor, teacher or graphic designer
WHEN RAIN STOPS PLAY? I draw caricatures, do some reading or hit the gym
SURPRISING FACTS? I suffered from a form of epilepsy as a child, I come from a family of actors and I played youth football for Stoke City
FANTASY SLIP CORDON? Keeper: Eric Cantona, 1st: Me, 2nd: Angelina Jolie, 3rd: Eddie Izzard, 4th: William Shakespeare, Gully: Bear Grylls

Batting	Mat	Inns	NO	Runs	HS	Ave	SR	100	50	Ct	St
ODIs	6	5	1	36	20	9.00	47.36	0	0	1	0
First-class	165	256	21	8390	223	35.70	48.50	19	43	86	0
List A	169	151	16	3654	115*	27.06		2	21	64	0
Twenty20	88	81	9	1740	68*	24.16	122.53	0	10	36	0

Bowling	Mat	Balls	Runs	Wkts	BBI	BBM	Ave	Econ	SR	5w	10
ODIs	6	-	-	-	-	-	-	-	-	-	-
First-class	165	2357	1416	22	3/1		64.36	3.60	107.1	0	0
List A	169	736	644	25	4/23	4/23	25.76	5.25	29.4	0	0
Twenty20	88	96	127	6	2/10	2/10	21.16	7.93	16.0	0	0

MARK TURNER — RHB RFM

FULL NAME: Mark Leif Turner
BORN: October 23, 1984, Sunderland
SQUAD NO: 6
HEIGHT: 6ft
NICKNAME: Tina, Beak
EDUCATION: Thornhill Comprehensive School
TEAMS: Derbyshire, Durham, England Under-19s, Somerset, Somerset 2nd XI
CAREER: First-class: 2005; List A: 2007; T20: 2005

BEST BATTING: 57 Somerset vs Derbyshire, Taunton, 2007
BEST BOWLING: 5-32 Derbyshire vs Northamptonshire, Northampton, 2011

FAMILY TIES? My brother Ian was a well-respected local league cricketer and my dad Ken used to bowl for hours at us in the backyard, so that counts
CAREER HIGHLIGHTS? Winning the Division Two title twice, once with Somerset and once with Derbyshire. Playing in a Lord's final – although we lost and I had a nightmare it was still an unbelievable experience
MOST MARKED CHARACTERISTIC? Probably my energy and being a bit of a 'mad-head.' I like to think I put 100 per cent into all I do
BEST PLAYER IN COUNTY CRICKET? James Anderson is a bowler who I could watch all day. Graham Onions' stats are just incredible, so he is right up there too
TIPS FOR THE TOP? Ben Stokes, Scott Borthwick and Mark Stoneman. Ben Cotton at Derbyshire also has real bowling potential
DESERT ISLAND DISC? Maxwell – Maxwell's Urban Hang Suite
NON-CRICKETING HEROES? David Beckham and Sven the doorman from Berghain in Berlin
ACCOMPLISHMENTS? Without doubt having the responsibility of raising my beautiful daughter Ivy
WHEN YOU RETIRE? I'd like to run my own business. A coffee shop would be ideal
TWITTER FEED: @Tina2310

Batting	Mat	Inns	NO	Runs	HS	Ave	SR	100	50	Ct	St
First-class	28	33	15	324	57	18.00	59.77	0	1	10	0
List A	41	15	7	67	15*	8.37	62.61	0	0	10	0
Twenty20	46	13	6	30	11*	4.28	63.82	0	0	10	0

Bowling	Mat	Balls	Runs	Wkts	BBI	BBM	Ave	Econ	SR	5w	10
First-class	28	3630	2526	59	5/32		42.81	4.17	61.5	1	0
List A	41	1487	1570	57	4/36	4/36	27.54	6.33	26.0	0	0
Twenty20	46	799	1177	44	4/35	4/35	26.75	8.83	18.1	0	0

FREDDIE VAN DEN BERGH

RHB SLA

FULL NAME: Freddie Oliver Edward van den Bergh
BORN: June 14, 1992, Bickley, Kent
SQUAD NO: 15
HEIGHT: 6ft 3in
NICKNAME: Vanders
EDUCATION: Whitgift School; Durham University
TEAMS: Durham MCCU, Surrey, Surrey 2nd XI
CAREER: First-class: 2011

BEST BATTING: 34 Surrey vs Nottinghamshire, Nottingham, 2013
BEST BOWLING: 4-84 Surrey vs Nottinghamshire, Nottingham, 2013

FAMILY TIES? My dad played when he was younger. He introduced me to the game and that's how I started playing cricket
WHO WOULD PLAY YOU IN A FILM OF YOUR LIFE? Leonardo DiCaprio
CAREER HIGHLIGHTS? Making my first-class debut for Surrey under Kevin Pietersen
MOST MARKED CHARACTERISTIC? Making the right decision under pressure
BEST PLAYER IN COUNTY CRICKET? Jonathan Trott
TIPS FOR THE TOP? Jason Roy and George Edwards
IF YOU WEREN'T A CRICKETER? I'd be studying at university
DESERT ISLAND DISC? Anything by Mumford And Sons
FAVOURITE TV? Suits, House Of Cards
CRICKETING HEROES? Shane Warne and Freddie Flintoff
NON-CRICKETING HEROES? Jonny Wilkinson and Tiger Woods
ACCOMPLISHMENTS? Getting a place at Durham University
WHEN YOU RETIRE? Something to do with sports and business
SURPRISING FACT? I used to play the oboe at school
CRICKET RULE YOU'D CHANGE? There should be longer tea breaks in four-day cricket
FANTASY SLIP CORDON? Keeper: James Corden, 1st: Harvey Specter (Suits), 2nd: Blake Lively, 3rd: Me, Gully: Jack Whitehall
TWITTER FEED: @freddievdb15

Batting	Mat	Inns	NO	Runs	HS	Ave	SR	100	50	Ct	St
First-class	4	5	1	53	34	13.25	58.24	0	0	0	0

Bowling	Mat	Balls	Runs	Wkts	BBI	BBM	Ave	Econ	SR	5w	10
First-class	4	679	399	10	4/84	5/145	39.90	3.52	67.9	0	0

KISHEN VELANI

RHB RM

FULL NAME: Kishen Shailesh Velani
BORN: September 2, 1994, Newham, London
SQUAD NO: 8
HEIGHT: 5ft 11in
NICKNAME: Joggy, Bruno
EDUCATION: Brentwood School
TEAMS: England Under-19s, Essex, Essex 2nd XI, Essex Under-13s, Essex Under-15s, Essex Under-17s
CAREER: First-class: 2013

ESSEX

BEST BATTING: 13 Essex vs Hampshire, Southampton, 2013

WHO WOULD PLAY YOU IN A FILM OF YOUR LIFE? Denzel Washington
CAREER HIGHLIGHTS? Playing for England U19 and making my first-class debut
MOST MARKED CHARACTERISTIC? Shyness
BEST PLAYER IN COUNTY CRICKET? Moeen Ali
TIPS FOR THE TOP? Tymal Mills, Reece Topley, Ben Foakes, Ben Duckett
IF YOU WEREN'T A CRICKETER? I'd be a golfer
DESERT ISLAND DISC? Drake – Take Care (Album)
FAVOURITE TV? Arrow
CRICKETING HEROES? Sachin Tendulkar
NON-CRICKETING HEROES? Kobe Bryant
ACCOMPLISHMENTS? Winning the Independent Schools final in football when I was 15
WHEN YOU RETIRE? I'll relax on a beach somewhere
CRICKET RULE YOU'D CHANGE? It should be a free hit every time a wide is bowled
FANTASY SLIP CORDON? Keeper: Sachin Tendulkar, 1st: Kobe Bryant, 2nd: James Corden, 3rd: Drake, Gully: Me
TWITTER FEED: @kishenvelani8

Batting	Mat	Inns	NO	Runs	HS	Ave	SR	100	50	Ct	St
First-class	1	2	0	22	13	11.00	44.00	0	0	0	0

Bowling	Mat	Balls	Runs	Wkts	BBI	BBM	Ave	Econ	SR	5w	10
First-class	1	12	8	0	-	-	-	4.00	-	0	0

JAMES VINCE

RHB RM R1 MVP19

FULL NAME: James Michael Vince
BORN: March 14, 1991, Cuckfield, Sussex
SQUAD NO: 14
HEIGHT: 6ft 2in
NICKNAME: Vincey
EDUCATION: Warminster School
TEAMS: England Lions, England Under-19s, Hampshire, Hampshire 2nd XI, Wiltshire
CAREER: First-class: 2009; List A: 2009; T20: 2010

BEST BATTING: 180 Hampshire vs Yorkshire, Scarborough, 2010
BEST BOWLING: 5-41 Hampshire vs Loughborough MCCU, Southampton, 2013
COUNTY CAP: 2013

FAMILY TIES? My old man couldn't have been any worse
CAREER HIGHLIGHTS? Winning the T20 and scoring my first hundred for Hampshire
SUPERSTITIONS? I put my kit on in the same order
CRICKETING HEROES? Stephen Parry, Jimmy Adams, Neil McKenzie
BEST PLAYER IN COUNTY CRICKET? Marcus Trescothick
TIP FOR THE TOP? Jos Buttler
WHEN RAIN STOPS PLAY? I chill out and abuse Batesy [Michael Bates]
FAVOURITE TV? TOWIE
FAVOURITE FILM? Taken
DREAM HOLIDAY? Maldives
TWITTER FEED: @vincey14

Batting	Mat	Inns	NO	Runs	HS	Ave	SR	100	50	Ct	St
First-class	71	113	12	3710	180	36.73	61.59	10	13	54	0
List A	67	66	6	2219	131	36.98	93.54	3	11	21	0
Twenty20	63	59	6	1457	85*	27.49	127.24	0	9	44	0

Bowling	Mat	Balls	Runs	Wkts	BBI	BBM	Ave	Econ	SR	5w	10
First-class	71	888	547	15	5/41	6/56	36.46	3.69	59.2	1	0
List A	67	66	56	1	1/18	1/18	56.00	5.09	66.0	0	0
Twenty20	63	36	30	1	1/5	1/5	30.00	5.00	36.0	0	0

GRAHAM WAGG

RHB LMF W2 MVP73

FULL NAME: Graham Grant Wagg
BORN: April 28, 1983, Rugby, Warwickshire
SQUAD NO: 8
HEIGHT: 6ft
NICKNAME: Waggy
EDUCATION: Ashlawn School, Rugby
TEAMS: Derbyshire, England A, England Under-19s, Glamorgan, Warwickshire, Warwickshire Cricket Board
CAREER: First-class: 2002; List A: 2000; T20: 2003

BEST BATTING: 108 Derbyshire vs Northamptonshire, Northampton, 2008
BEST BOWLING: 6-35 Derbyshire vs Surrey, Derby, 2009
COUNTY CAPS: 2007 (Derbyshire); 2013 (Glamorgan)

FAMILY TIES? My dad played 2nd XI cricket, minor counties and a good standard of Premier League – he could bowl a heavy ball and hit it a long way. My little man Brayden Wagg is just learning, so watch out for his name
CAREER HIGHLIGHTS? Getting my first contract at Warwickshire and playing for England Schools in all the age groups
CRICKETING HEROES? Ian Botham, Allan Donald, Viv Richards
BEST PLAYER IN COUNTY CRICKET? Marcus Trescothick, without a doubt
TIPS FOR THE TOP? James Taylor, James Harris, Brayden Wagg
IF YOU WEREN'T A CRICKETER? Full-time dad I suppose
WHEN RAIN STOPS PLAY? Feet up, maybe a bit of poker
FAVOURITE TV? Banged Up Abroad
FAVOURITE FILM? Green Mile
DREAM HOLIDAY? Vegas with a winning lottery ticket to go nuts over there
SURPRISING SKILL? I'm a dark horse on the snooker table
GUILTY PLEASURES? Eating too much in the winter

Batting	Mat	Inns	NO	Runs	HS	Ave	SR	100	50	Ct	St
First-class	101	142	13	3041	108	23.57	66.20	1	17	32	0
List A	105	87	13	1332	54	18.00		0	1	31	0
Twenty20	66	53	12	636	62	15.51	124.95	0	1	19	0

Bowling	Mat	Balls	Runs	Wkts	BBI	BBM	Ave	Econ	SR	5w	10
First-class	101	17268	10146	299	6/35		33.93	3.52	57.7	9	1
List A	105	3991	3934	121	4/35	4/35	32.51	5.91	32.9	0	0
Twenty20	66	1105	1430	59	5/14	5/14	24.23	7.76	18.7	1	0

YORKSHIRE

FULL NAME: James Charles Wainman
BORN: January 25, 1993, Harrogate, Yorkshire
SQUAD NO: 15
HEIGHT: 6ft 3in
NICKNAME: Wainers
EDUCATION: Leeds Grammar School
TEAMS: Yorkshire 2nd XI, Yorkshire Academy, Yorkshire Under-14s, Yorkshire Under-15s, Yorkshire Under-17s
CAREER: Yet to make first-team debut

WHO WOULD PLAY YOU IN A FILM OF YOUR LIFE? Leonardo DiCaprio
CAREER HIGHLIGHTS? Signing my professional contract with Yorkshire and winning the League Cup with Yorkshire Academy
SUPERSTITIONS? I always wear two pairs of socks
MOST MARKED CHARACTERISTIC? Teamwork
BEST PLAYER IN COUNTY CRICKET? Peter Trego
TIP FOR THE TOP? Alex Lees
IF YOU WEREN'T A CRICKETER? I'd be a student
FAVOURITE TV? Entourage
CRICKETING HEROES? Glenn McGrath, Dale Steyn, Morne Morkel
NON-CRICKETING HEROES? Nelson Mandela
WHEN YOU RETIRE? I'd like to do a ski season
TWITTER FEED: @JCWainman

DAVID WAINWRIGHT

LHB SLA W1

FULL NAME: David John Wainwright
BORN: March 21, 1985, Pontefract, Yorkshire
SQUAD NO: 21
HEIGHT: 5ft 9in
NICKNAME: Wainers
EDUCATION: Hemsworth High School; Loughborough University
TEAMS: Derbyshire, Loughborough UCCE, Police Sports Club, Yorkshire
CAREER: First-class: 2004; List A: 2005; T20: 2007

BEST BATTING: 104* Yorkshire vs Sussex, Hove, 2008
BEST BOWLING: 6-33 Derbyshire vs Northamptonshire, Derby, 2012
COUNTY CAPS: 2010 (Yorkshire); 2012 (Derbyshire)

FAMILY TIES? My father played league cricket and my grandfather bowled slow left-arm and played for Yorkshire Schoolboys
WHO WOULD PLAY YOU IN A FILM OF YOUR LIFE? Will Smith
CAREER HIGHLIGHTS? Winning the Division Two title in 2012 with Derbyshire
MOST MARKED CHARACTERISTIC? My little toes don't touch the floor
BEST PLAYER IN COUNTY CRICKET? Moeen Ali
TIP FOR THE TOP? Harvey Hosein
IF YOU WEREN'T A CRICKETER? I'd still be involved in sport in some capacity
DESERT ISLAND DISC? Will Smith – Big Willie Style
FAVOURITE TV? Family Guy
CRICKETING HEROES? Daniel Vettori, Brian Lara
NON-CRICKETING HEROES? Will Smith, Steven Gerrard
WHEN YOU RETIRE? I'm going to play crown green bowls
SURPRISING FACT? I've passed a plumbing course
CRICKET RULE YOU'D CHANGE? It shouldn't be a leg-side wide when a batsman reverse sweeps

Batting	Mat	Inns	NO	Runs	HS	Ave	SR	100	50	Ct	St
First-class	63	86	20	1706	104*	25.84	46.25	2	6	24	0
List A	70	34	19	294	40	19.60	76.96	0	0	21	0
Twenty20	37	12	8	60	15*	15.00	76.92	0	0	10	0

Bowling	Mat	Balls	Runs	Wkts	BBI	BBM	Ave	Econ	SR	5w	10
First-class	63	10766	5572	151	6/33		36.90	3.10	71.2	5	0
List A	70	2508	2063	57	4/11	4/11	36.19	4.93	44.0	0	0
Twenty20	37	683	794	33	3/6	3/6	24.06	6.97	20.6	0	0

ALEX WAKELY

RHB RM

FULL NAME: Alex George Wakely
BORN: November 3, 1988, London
SQUAD NO: 8
HEIGHT: 6ft 2in
NICKNAME: Wakers, Baby Seal
EDUCATION: Bedford School
TEAMS: Bedfordshire, England Under-19s, Northamptonshire, Northamptonshire 2nd XI
CAREER: First-class: 2007; List A: 2005; T20: 2009

BEST BATTING: 113* Northamptonshire vs Glamorgan, Cardiff, 2009
BEST BOWLING: 2-62 Northamptonshire vs Somerset, Taunton, 2007
COUNTY CAP: 2012

FAMILY TIES? My dad played minor counties cricket
WHO WOULD PLAY YOU IN A FILM OF YOUR LIFE? Matthew McConaughey
CAREER HIGHLIGHTS? Winning the T20 last year and scoring a hundred at Lord's
MOST MARKED CHARACTERISTIC? Being relaxed and smiley
BEST PLAYER IN COUNTY CRICKET? Gary Ballance
TIPS FOR THE TOP? James Kettleborough, Rob Keogh
IF YOU WEREN'T A CRICKETER? I would love to play golf but realistically I would work in the City or in marketing
DESERT ISLAND DISC? Fort Minor – Remember The Name
FAVOURITE TV? The Walking Dead, The Blacklist
CRICKETING HEROES? David Sales, Matthew Hayden, Mike Hussey, Ian Harvey
NON-CRICKETING HEROES? Michael Jordan, Bruce Wayne, Bill Gates, my grandad
ACCOMPLISHMENTS? Getting married and achieving 3 A-Levels
TWITTER FEED: @AlexWakely1
NOTES: Wakely ruptured his Achilles tendon during a pre-season tour of Barbados in March and is likely to miss the entire 2014 season while he undergoes rehabilitation

Batting	Mat	Inns	NO	Runs	HS	Ave	SR	100	50	Ct	St
First-class	79	122	5	3387	113*	28.94	45.93	2	21	43	0
List A	52	50	6	1364	102	31.00	85.62	1	9	16	0
Twenty20	59	58	9	1247	62	25.44	117.86	0	7	20	0

Bowling	Mat	Balls	Runs	Wkts	BBI	BBM	Ave	Econ	SR	5w	10
First-class	79	399	322	6	2/62	2/62	53.66	4.84	66.5	0	0
List A	52	132	107	5	2/14	2/14	21.40	4.86	26.4	0	0
Twenty20	59	12	29	0	-	-	-	14.50	-	0	0

MARK WALLACE — LHB WK R1 MVP48

FULL NAME: Mark Alexander Wallace
BORN: November 19, 1981, Abergavenny, Monmouthshire, Wales
SQUAD NO: 18
HEIGHT: 5ft 9in
NICKNAME: Gromit
EDUCATION: Crickhowell High School
TEAMS: Glamorgan, Wales Minor Counties
CAREER: First-class: 1999; List A: 1999; T20: 2003

GLAMORGAN

BEST BATTING: 139 Glamorgan vs Surrey, The Oval, 2009
COUNTY CAP: 2003; BENEFIT YEAR: 2013

FAMILY TIES? My father still plays club cricket for Abergavenny and turns out for Wales Over 50s and 60s
CAREER HIGHLIGHTS? Winning one-day trophies and captaining Glamorgan
CRICKETING HEROES? Ian Healy, Alec Stewart, Steve James, Brendon McCullum, Justin Langer
NON-CRICKETING HEROES? Rory McIlroy, Harry Potter
BEST PLAYER IN COUNTY CRICKET? Steve Davies
TIPS FOR THE TOP? James Taylor, James Harris, Andrew Salter
IF YOU WEREN'T A CRICKETER? I'd be a journalist or student
WHEN RAIN STOPS PLAY? Reading, playing pool, talking rubbish
FAVOURITE TV? Spooks, EastEnders
FAVOURITE FILM? The Harry Potter series, Blood Diamond, SWAT
ACCOMPLISHMENTS? My family: my wife and two kids (Harry and Ioan)
GUILTY PLEASURES? Lego
SURPRISING FACT? I work as a rugby writer in the winter for Media Wales and I'm a single handicap golfer
TWITTER FEED: @MarkWallace18

Batting	Mat	Inns	NO	Runs	HS	Ave	SR	100	50	Ct	St
First-class	216	342	26	9299	139	29.42		15	42	543	49
List A	189	154	29	2589	118*	20.71		2	7	166	44
Twenty20	99	78	22	1061	69*	18.94	126.46	0	1	38	24

Bowling	Mat	Balls	Runs	Wkts	BBI	BBM	Ave	Econ	SR	5w	10
First-class	216	6	3	0	-	-	-	3.00	-	0	0
List A	189	-	-	-	-	-	-	-	-	-	-
Twenty20	99	-	-	-	-	-	-	-	-	-	-

MAX WALLER

RHB LB

FULL NAME: Max Thomas Charles Waller
BORN: March 3, 1988, Salisbury, Wiltshire
SQUAD NO: 10
HEIGHT: 6ft
NICKNAME: Steam Kat
EDUCATION: Millfield School; Bournemouth University
TEAMS: Dorset, Gloucestershire 2nd XI, Somerset, Somerset 2nd XI
CAREER: First-class: 2009; List A: 2009; T20: 2009

BEST BATTING: 28 Somerset vs Hampshire, Southampton, 2009
BEST BOWLING: 3-33 Somerset vs Cambridge MCCU, Taunton, 2012

FAMILY TIES? My dad is an MCC playing member
CAREER HIGHLIGHTS? Playing in the Champions League T20. Getting the Man of the Match award in a Caribbean T20 match. Playing in Finals Day. My first-class debut
SUPERSTITIONS? I like to have the ball in my hand before handing my hat/jumper to the umpire
CRICKETING HEROES? Shane Warne, Jonty Rhodes
NON-CRICKETING HEROES? Ayrton Senna
BEST PLAYER IN COUNTY CRICKET? Marcus Trescothick
TIPS FOR THE TOP? Jamie Overton and Lewis Gregory
IF YOU WEREN'T A CRICKETER? Something business-related or a failed artist!
FAVOURITE TV? MOTD, Take Me Out, The OC, Prison Break, Hawaii Five-O
FAVOURITE FILM? Top Gun, Spread, Senna, Wedding Crashers, Cool Runnings
FAVOURITE BOOK? The Secret
DREAM HOLIDAY? Barbados
ACCOMPLISHMENTS? Having my paintings in an art shop (acrylics on canvas)
GUILTY PLEASURES? Chocolate
TWITTER FEED: @MaxTCWaller

Batting	Mat	Inns	NO	Runs	HS	Ave	SR	100	50	Ct	St
First-class	8	9	1	91	28	11.37	42.92	0	0	5	0
List A	39	14	10	71	25*	17.75	73.95	0	0	15	0
Twenty20	45	10	5	8	3	1.60	36.36	0	0	18	0

Bowling	Mat	Balls	Runs	Wkts	BBI	BBM	Ave	Econ	SR	5w	10
First-class	8	840	493	10	3/33	3/57	49.30	3.52	84.0	0	0
List A	39	1192	1126	28	3/39	3/39	40.21	5.66	42.5	0	0
Twenty20	45	798	958	48	4/16	4/16	19.95	7.20	16.6	0	0

STEWART WALTERS   RHB LB

FULL NAME: Stewart Jonathan Walters
BORN: June 25, 1983, Mornington, Victoria, Australia
SQUAD NO: 26
HEIGHT: 6ft 1in
NICKNAME: Forrest, Walts
EDUCATION: Guildford Grammar School, Perth
TEAMS: Glamorgan, Glamorgan 2nd XI, Surrey, Surrey 2nd XI
CAREER: First-class: 2006; List A: 2005; T20: 2006

BEST BATTING: 188 Surrey vs Leicestershire, The Oval, 2009
BEST BOWLING: 1-4 Surrey vs Durham, Chester-le-Street, 2007

FAMILY TIES? My father, grandfather and grandmother all played at a high level
WHO WOULD PLAY YOU IN A FILM OF YOUR LIFE? William Wallace from Braveheart
CAREER HIGHLIGHTS? The hundreds I've scored, captaining Surrey and signing a contract with Glamorgan
SUPERSTITIONS? It used to be to put my right pad on first but for some reason I put the left one on first for one game and scored some runs, so guess what my new superstition is!
MOST MARKED CHARACTERISTIC? Determination
BEST PLAYER IN COUNTY CRICKET? Kevin Pietersen
TIPS FOR THE TOP? Joe Root, James Harris, Jim Allenby, Robert Croft
IF YOU WEREN'T A CRICKETER? I'd be coaching cricket or doing fitness training
DESERT ISLAND DISC? Forever Young
FAVOURITE TV? The Mentalist
CRICKETING HEROES? Dean Jones, Steve Waugh, Simon Katich
WHEN YOU RETIRE? I'd like to be a batting coach or strength and conditioning coach
SURPRISING FACT? I'm the biggest bat badger in the dressing room. I'm always cleaning my bats and fixing little cracks – on my bats and others
TWITTER FEED: @stewiewalters

Batting	Mat	Inns	NO	Runs	HS	Ave	SR	100	50	Ct	St
First-class	65	108	7	3055	188	30.24	50.09	5	14	69	0
List A	67	61	10	1485	91	29.11	83.61	0	10	22	0
Twenty20	43	31	12	525	53*	27.63	111.94	0	1	28	0

Bowling	Mat	Balls	Runs	Wkts	BBI	BBM	Ave	Econ	SR	5w	10
First-class	65	432	245	3	1/4	1/9	81.66	3.40	144.0	0	0
List A	67	165	179	3	1/12	1/12	59.66	6.50	55.0	0	0
Twenty20	43	18	26	1	1/9	1/9	26.00	8.66	18.0	0	0

HUW WATERS

RHB RMF

FULL NAME: Huw Thomas Waters
BORN: September 26, 1986, Cardiff, Wales
SQUAD NO: 17
HEIGHT: 6ft 2in
NICKNAME: Muddy
EDUCATION: Llantarnam Comprehensive; Monmouth School; The Open University
TEAMS: Glamorgan, Wales Minor Counties
CAREER: First-class: 2005; List A: 2005; T20: 2010

BEST BATTING: 54 Glamorgan vs Surrey, Cardiff, 2011
BEST BOWLING: 7-53 Glamorgan vs Hampshire, Cardiff, 2012
COUNTY CAP: 2012

FAMILY TIES? Big Don played for Usk in the old Three Counties bowling left-arm seam – he swears if Hawk-Eye had been in use back then he would have bagged many more scalps!
CAREER HIGHLIGHTS? Making my debut for Glamorgan, taking my first five-wicket haul and receiving my county cap in 2012
DESERT ISLAND DISC? The Killers – Hot Fuss
FAVOURITE TV? Homes Under The Hammer
CRICKETING HEROES? My father and Glenn McGrath
NON-CRICKETING HEROES? Sir Alex Ferguson, Ryan Giggs
ACCOMPLISHMENTS? Renovating my flat – it took me the best part of a year but I got there in the end
WHEN YOU RETIRE? Hopefully I'll become a PE teacher or carry on coaching within the game
FANTASY SLIP CORDON? Keeper: Peter Kay, 1st: Sir Alex Ferguson, 2nd: Myself, 3rd: Glenn McGrath, Gully: Karl Pilkington

Batting	Mat	Inns	NO	Runs	HS	Ave	SR	100	50	Ct	St
First-class	51	69	36	411	54	12.45	21.03	0	1	12	0
List A	22	8	3	24	8	4.80	42.10	0	0	3	0
Twenty20	4	2	2	11	11*	-	84.61	0	0	0	0

Bowling	Mat	Balls	Runs	Wkts	BBI	BBM	Ave	Econ	SR	5w	10
First-class	51	6678	3425	110	7/53		31.13	3.07	60.7	3	0
List A	22	816	844	14	3/47	3/47	60.28	6.20	58.2	0	0
Twenty20	4	85	118	3	3/30	3/30	39.33	8.32	28.3	0	0

JON WEBB — RHB RM

FULL NAME: Jonathon Patrick Webb
BORN: January 12, 1992, Solihull, Warwickshire
SQUAD NO: 12
HEIGHT: 5ft 11in
NICKNAME: Webby
EDUCATION: Bromsgrove School; University of Leeds
TEAMS: Leeds/Bradford MCCU, Warwickshire 2nd XI
CAREER: First-class: 2012

BEST BATTING: 38 Leeds/Bradford MCCU vs Surrey, The Oval, 2012

FAMILY TIES? My dad played as a youngster and my brother Marc played through the Worcestershire age groups, also playing a game for the 2nd XI
WHO WOULD PLAY YOU IN A FILM OF YOUR LIFE? Stifler (Seann William Scott)
CAREER HIGHLIGHTS? Winning two out of three competitions with Leeds/Bradford MCCU and signing my first professional contract with Warwickshire
TIPS FOR THE TOP? Paul Best, Ben Cox
IF YOU WEREN'T A CRICKETER? I'd be a graphic designer
DESERT ISLAND DISC? John Mayer – Live In LA
FAVOURITE TV? Suits
CRICKETING HEROES? Ricky Ponting, AB de Villiers
NON-CRICKETING HEROES? John Mayer
ACCOMPLISHMENTS? Hopefully by the time this is published I will have a degree (a good one) from the University of Leeds
WHEN YOU RETIRE? I want to become a rock star
FANTASY SLIP CORDON? Keeper: Vince Vaughn, 1st: Me, 2nd: Sonny Bill Williams, 3rd: Johnny Cash, Gully: Winston Churchill

Batting	Mat	Inns	NO	Runs	HS	Ave	SR	100	50	Ct	St
First-class	4	8	0	77	38	9.62	39.28	0	0	3	0

Bowling	Mat	Balls	Runs	Wkts	BBI	BBM	Ave	Econ	SR	5w	10
First-class	4	-	-	-	-	-	-	-	-	-	-

LUKE WELLS

LHB OB

SUSSEX

FULL NAME: Luke William Peter Wells
BORN: December 29, 1990, Eastbourne, Sussex
SQUAD NO: 31
HEIGHT: 6ft 4in
NICKNAME: The Rinser, Dave
EDUCATION: St Bede's School, Upper Dicker
TEAMS: Colombo Cricket Club, England Lions, England Under-19s, Sussex, Sussex 2nd XI
CAREER: First-class: 2010; List A: 2010; T20: 2011

BEST BATTING: 208 Sussex vs Surrey, The Oval, 2013
BEST BOWLING: 2-28 Sussex vs Worcestershire, Horsham, 2011

FAMILY TIES? My father Alan played for Sussex, Kent and England and my uncle Colin played for Sussex, Derbyshire and England
CAREER HIGHLIGHTS? Definitely scoring my first double hundred at The Oval. Representing the England Lions vs Australia
SUPERSTITIONS? I only ever bat in the same pair of whites
MOST MARKED CHARACTERISTIC? Resilience
BEST PLAYER IN COUNTY CRICKET? Graham Onions
TIP FOR THE TOP? Matt Machan is improving year-on-year and is an exceptional talent
DESERT ISLAND DISC? Bastille – Bad Blood
FAVOURITE TV? Family Guy for comedy but I also love a bit of Criminal Minds now and then
CRICKETING HEROES? My father Alan, Sachin Tendulkar, Brian Lara and Matthew Hayden
WHEN YOU RETIRE? Preferably I'll coach. If not, then teaching
FANTASY SLIP CORDON? Keeper: Stewie Griffin, 1st: Ricky Gervais, 2nd: Sachin Tendulkar, 3rd: Myself, Gully: Gandalf
CRICKET RULE YOU'D CHANGE? The over-rate in four-day cricket should be one-over less per hour
TWITTER FEED: @luke_wells07

Batting	Mat	Inns	NO	Runs	HS	Ave	SR	100	50	Ct	St
First-class	51	86	7	2658	208	33.64	43.29	7	9	27	0
List A	11	7	0	35	17	5.00	61.40	0	0	1	0
Twenty20	1	1	0	3	3	3.00	50.00	0	0	0	0

Bowling	Mat	Balls	Runs	Wkts	BBI	BBM	Ave	Econ	SR	5w	10
First-class	51	804	496	7	2/28	2/33	70.85	3.70	114.8	0	0
List A	11	77	61	3	3/19	3/19	20.33	4.75	25.6	0	0
Twenty20	1	-	-	-	-	-	-	-	-	-	-

TOM WELLS
RHB RFM

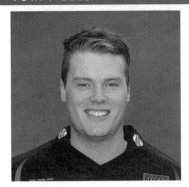

FULL NAME: Thomas Joshua Wells
BORN: March 15, 1993, Grantham, Lincolnshire
SQUAD NO: 9
HEIGHT: 6ft 2in
NICKNAME: Three Heads, Wellsy
EDUCATION: Gartree High School; Beauchamp College
TEAMS: Leicestershire, Leicestershire 2nd XI
CAREER: First-class: 2013; List A: 2012; T20: 2013

BEST BATTING: 82 Leicestershire vs Hampshire, Leicester, 2013
BEST BOWLING: 1-36 Leicestershire vs Lancashire, Leicester, 2013

WHO WOULD PLAY YOU IN A FILM OF YOUR LIFE? Robert Downey Jr – he's a pretty cool cat
CAREER HIGHLIGHTS? Making my first-class debut vs Lancashire and playing at Old Trafford and Lord's
MOST MARKED CHARACTERISTIC? The size of my head
BEST PLAYER IN COUNTY CRICKET? Moeen Ali
TIPS FOR THE TOP? Rob Sayers (Leicestershire), Adam Rossington (Middlesex)
IF YOU WEREN'T A CRICKETER? I'd be an ice road trucker
DESERT ISLAND DISC? Any Pitbull or Akon
FAVOURITE TV? Arrow
CRICKETING HEROES? Paul Nixon, Ian Botham
NON-CRICKETING HEROES? My old man
ACCOMPLISHMENTS? Getting through to the Daily Mail Rugby Cup quarter final with my college side
WHEN YOU RETIRE? I'll go and find somewhere hot and stay there for a very long time
SURPRISING FACT? Although everyone says I have the biggest head in the squad, I actually don't – that award goes to Greg Smith
TWITTER FEED: @t_wells15

Batting	Mat	Inns	NO	Runs	HS	Ave	SR	100	50	Ct	St
First-class	5	8	0	177	82	22.12	62.98	0	1	2	0
List A	4	4	3	92	32*	92.00	200.00	0	0	0	0
Twenty20	2	1	0	4	4	4.00	66.66	0	0	3	0

Bowling	Mat	Balls	Runs	Wkts	BBI	BBM	Ave	Econ	SR	5w	10
First-class	5	222	129	1	1/36	1/36	129.00	3.48	222.0	0	0
List A	4	-	-	-	-	-	-	-	-	-	-
Twenty20	2	-	-	-	-	-	-	-	-	-	-

RIKI WESSELS

RHB WK

FULL NAME: Matthew Hendrik Wessels
BORN: November 12, 1985, Marogudoore, Queensland, Australia
SQUAD NO: 9
HEIGHT: 5ft 11in
NICKNAME: Blood, Weasel, Riki Bobby
EDUCATION: Woodridge College, Port Elizabeth; University of Northampton
TEAMS: Abahani Limited, Khulna Royal Bengals, Mid West Rhinos, Nondescripts, Northamptonshire, Nottinghamshire
CAREER: First-class: 2004; List A: 2005; T20: 2005

BEST BATTING: 199 Nottinghamshire vs Sussex, Hove, 2012
BEST BOWLING: 1-10 Mid West Rhinos vs Matabeleland Tuskers, Bulawayo, 2009

CAREER HIGHLIGHTS? That has to be my first first-class hundred and also the finals I've taken part in
CRICKETING HEROES? Michael Slater, Justin Langer
NON-CRICKETING HEROES? All the soldiers currently fighting, having lost a few friends to the war myself
BEST PLAYER IN COUNTY CRICKET? Marcus Trescothick
TIPS FOR THE TOP? Chris Woakes, Alex Hales, Sam Wood
IF YOU WEREN'T A CRICKETER? I'd probably be in the Army on the front line
WHEN RAIN STOPS PLAY? I'm on the iPad with a Will Ferrell film or avoiding Paul Franks and his bad banter
FAVOURITE TV? Dr Who
DREAM HOLIDAY? Zanzibar – heat, beaches and beer
ACCOMPLISHMENTS? Helping Macmillan Cancer UK raise money and helping people who need it more than myself
SURPRISING FACTS? I've bungee jumped at Victoria Falls, I lived in Colombo for six months and I love hunting
TWITTER FEED: @RikiWessels

Batting	Mat	Inns	NO	Runs	HS	Ave	SR	100	50	Ct	St
First-class	123	201	16	6321	199	34.16	64.28	14	30	209	14
List A	124	116	13	2807	100	27.25	99.57	1	15	87	0
Twenty20	105	93	16	2020	86*	26.23	134.66	0	8	30	15

Bowling	Mat	Balls	Runs	Wkts	BBI	BBM	Ave	Econ	SR	5w	10
First-class	123	180	96	3	1/10	1/10	32.00	3.20	60.0	0	0
List A	124	49	48	1	1/0	1/0	48.00	5.87	49.0	0	0
Twenty20	105	-	-	-	-	-	-	-	-	-	-

FULL NAME: Thomas Westley
BORN: March 13, 1989, Cambridge
SQUAD NO: 21
HEIGHT: 6ft 2in
NICKNAME: Westie, Shellsy, Wezzo
EDUCATION: Linton Valley College; Hills Road Sixth Form College; University of Durham
TEAMS: Cambridgeshire, England Under-19s, Essex, Essex 2nd XI, Marylebone Cricket Club
CAREER: First-class: 2007; List A: 2006; T20: 2010

BEST BATTING: 185 Essex vs Glamorgan, Colchester, 2012
BEST BOWLING: 4-55 Durham MCCU vs Durham, Durham University, 2010
COUNTY CAP: 2013

FAMILY TIES? My dad, uncle and brother all play for Weston Colville Cricket Club. My dad also harbours ambitions to play for England Over 50s
WHO WOULD PLAY YOU IN A FILM OF YOUR LIFE? Matt Lucas
CAREER HIGHLIGHTS? Captaining England U19 and receiving my Essex county cap
SUPERSTITIONS? My left pad goes on first
BEST PLAYER IN COUNTY CRICKET? Jaik Mickleburgh
TIP FOR THE TOP? Kishen Velani
IF YOU WEREN'T A CRICKETER? I'd do something with my degree
DESERT ISLAND DISC? Swedish House Mafia – Don't You Worry Child
FAVOURITE TV? Sherlock
CRICKETING HEROES? Jacques Kallis, Ben Matthews, Max Nolan, Sachin Tendulkar, Dave Babbage, James Bunbury, Ben Lawrence
NON-CRICKETING HEROES? Giovanni Colussi
SURPRISING FACT? I was part of the first ever group of students to academically study Harry Potter
TWITTER FEED: @Westley21

Batting	Mat	Inns	NO	Runs	HS	Ave	SR	100	50	Ct	St
First-class	76	130	11	3777	185	31.73	49.98	7	18	43	0
List A	28	25	0	733	82	29.32	85.63	0	7	3	0
Twenty20	9	4	2	15	13	7.50	107.14	0	0	2	0

Bowling	Mat	Balls	Runs	Wkts	BBI	BBM	Ave	Econ	SR	5w	10
First-class	76	2693	1415	31	4/55	4/34	45.64	3.15	86.8	0	0
List A	28	216	201	4	1/9	1/9	50.25	5.58	54.0	0	0
Twenty20	9	12	13	1	1/7	1/7	13.00	6.50	12.0	0	0

IAN WESTWOOD
LHB OB

WARWICKSHIRE

FULL NAME: Ian James Westwood
BORN: July 13, 1982, Birmingham, Warwickshire
SQUAD NO: 22
HEIGHT: 5ft 7in
NICKNAME: Westy, Wezzo, Tot
EDUCATION: Solihull Sixth Form College
TEAMS: Warwickshire, Warwickshire Cricket Board
CAREER: First-class: 2003; List A: 2001; T20: 2005

BEST BATTING: 178 Warwickshire vs West Indies A, Birmingham, 2006
BEST BOWLING: 2-39 Warwickshire vs Hampshire, Southampton, 2009
COUNTY CAP: 2008

FAMILY TIES? My grandad was a member at Warwickshire and my brother played Warwickshire junior cricket
CAREER HIGHLIGHTS? Getting my county cap and being named club captain
CRICKETING HEROES? Stuart Eustace, Phil Stephenson, Vanraaj Padhaal
BEST PLAYER IN COUNTY CRICKET? Marcus Trescothick
TIPS FOR THE TOP? George and Isaac Maddy
IF YOU WEREN'T A CRICKETER? No idea!
WHEN RAIN STOPS PLAY? Playing iPhone games, eating and annoying the balding physio
FAVOURITE TV? House
FAVOURITE FILM? Old School
FAVOURITE BOOK? The Cricketers' Who's Who
DREAM HOLIDAY? Skegness
GUILTY PLEASURES? Sweets and Birmingham City FC

Batting	Mat	Inns	NO	Runs	HS	Ave	SR	100	50	Ct	St
First-class	122	206	20	6156	178	33.09	44.85	12	34	70	0
List A	60	50	9	940	65	22.92		0	3	7	0
Twenty20	38	27	12	342	49*	22.80	114.00	0	0	5	0

Bowling	Mat	Balls	Runs	Wkts	BBI	BBM	Ave	Econ	SR	5w	10
First-class	122	538	300	7	2/39		42.85	3.34	76.8	0	0
List A	60	264	227	3	1/28	1/28	75.66	5.15	88.0	0	0
Twenty20	38	54	91	5	3/29	3/29	18.20	10.11	10.8	0	0

ADAM WHEATER — RHB WK

FULL NAME: Adam Jack Wheater
BORN: February 13, 1990, Whipps Cross, Essex
SQUAD NO: 31
HEIGHT: 5ft 6in
NICKNAME: Wheats
EDUCATION: Millfield School
TEAMS: Badureliya Sports Club, Cambridge MCCU, England Under-19s, Essex, Essex 2nd XI, Essex Under-17s, Hampshire, Matabeleland Tuskers
CAREER: First-class: 2008; List A: 2010; T20: 2009

BEST BATTING: 164 Essex vs Northamptonshire, Chelmsford, 2011
BEST BOWLING: 1-86 Essex vs Leicestershire, Leicester, 2012

WHO WOULD PLAY YOU IN A FILM OF YOUR LIFE? Frodo Baggins
CAREER HIGHLIGHTS? My career-best score of 164 against Northants and having the opportunity to see the world through cricket
MOST MARKED CHARACTERISTIC? I'm argumentative
BEST PLAYER IN COUNTY CRICKET? Bowling: Dave Masters. Batting: Marcus Trescothick
TIPS FOR THE TOP? Reece Topley, Tymal Mills
IF YOU WEREN'T A CRICKETER? I'd find myself a very wealthy girlfriend I could sponge off
DESERT ISLAND DISC? At the moment it would be Snow Patrol's Greatest Hits
FAVOURITE TV? Jamie Oliver's cooking shows
CRICKETING HEROES? Alec Stewart, Nasser Hussain, Adam Gilchrist
ACCOMPLISHMENTS? I won a bottle of vodka at my local pub quiz
WHEN YOU RETIRE? I'll do a ski season in Canada
FANTASY SLIP CORDON? Keeper: Spider-Man (he's taking everyone's catches), 1st: Anthony Kiedis (he would have some stories to tell), 2nd: Micky Flanagan (just in case you had a long time in the field), 3rd: Shakira (to teach me Spanish)

Batting	Mat	Inns	NO	Runs	HS	Ave	SR	100	50	Ct	St
First-class	66	92	13	3150	164	39.87	70.12	6	18	95	3
List A	48	35	5	651	70	21.70	100.00	0	3	17	4
Twenty20	44	30	8	249	29	11.31	98.03	0	0	12	8

Bowling	Mat	Balls	Runs	Wkts	BBI	BBM	Ave	Econ	SR	5w	10
First-class	66	24	86	1	1/86	1/86	86.00	21.50	24.0	0	0
List A	48	-	-	-	-	-	-	-	-	-	-
Twenty20	44	-	-	-	-	-	-	-	-	-	-

GRAEME WHITE

RHB SLA

FULL NAME: Graeme Geoffrey White
BORN: April 18, 1987, Milton Keynes, Buckinghamshire
SQUAD NO: 87
HEIGHT: 5ft 11in
NICKNAME: Chalky
EDUCATION: Stowe School, Buckingham
TEAMS: England Under-19s, Northamptonshire, Northamptonshire 2nd XI, Nottinghamshire
CAREER: First-class: 2006; List A: 2007; T20: 2007

BEST BATTING: 65 Northamptonshire vs Glamorgan, Colwyn Bay, 2007
BEST BOWLING: 4-72 Nottinghamshire vs Durham, Nottingham, 2011

IF YOU WEREN'T A CRICKETER? I'd be a bus driver
DESERT ISLAND DISC? Kings Of Leon – Sex On Fire
BIGGEST DRESSING DOWN YOU'VE RECEIVED? For playing the reverse-sweep all the time
CRICKETING HEROES? Phil Tufnell, Bishen Bedi, Daniel Vettori
NON-CRICKETING HEROES? Olly Murs, Barack Obama
ACCOMPLISHMENTS? I won the Crazy Golf Championship in Skegness in 2010
WHEN YOU RETIRE? I'd like to be a social worker
FANTASY SLIP CORDON? Keeper: Paul Ince, 1st: Me, 2nd: Wayne Noon, 3rd: Beyoncé, Gully: David Capel

Batting	Mat	Inns	NO	Runs	HS	Ave	SR	100	50	Ct	St
First-class	24	36	5	441	65	14.22	44.14	0	2	8	0
List A	41	21	9	161	39*	13.41	84.73	0	0	13	0
Twenty20	41	13	6	71	26*	10.14	112.69	0	0	17	0

Bowling	Mat	Balls	Runs	Wkts	BBI	BBM	Ave	Econ	SR	5w	10
First-class	24	2870	1607	37	4/72	7/89	43.43	3.35	77.5	0	0
List A	41	1227	1107	40	5/35	5/35	27.67	5.41	30.6	1	0
Twenty20	41	587	725	38	5/22	5/22	19.07	7.41	15.4	1	0

WAYNE WHITE   RHB RMF

FULL NAME: Wayne Andrew White
BORN: April 22, 1985, Derby
SQUAD NO: 25
HEIGHT: 6ft 3in
NICKNAME: Chalky, Sticks, Waz
EDUCATION: John Port School, Derby;
Nottingham Trent University
TEAMS: Derbyshire, Derbyshire 2nd XI,
Lancashire, Leicestershire
CAREER: First-class: 2005; List A: 2006; T20:
2009

LANCASHIRE

BEST BATTING: 101* Leicestershire vs Derbyshire, Derby, 2010
BEST BOWLING: 5-54 Leicestershire vs Derbyshire, Derby, 2012
COUNTY CAP: 2012 (Leicestershire)

FAMILY TIES? My brother [Harry] is on the Derbyshire Academy
CAREER HIGHLIGHTS? Winning the T20 Cup and scoring my first hundred
CRICKETING HEROES? Mike Hendrick, Dominic Cork
BEST PLAYER IN COUNTY CRICKET? Marcus Trescothick
TIPS FOR THE TOP? Shiv Thakor, Liam Kinch
IF YOU WEREN'T A CRICKETER? I'd be trying to be a footballer
WHEN RAIN STOPS PLAY? iPod, Football Manager, annoying everyone
FAVOURITE TV? 90210
FAVOURITE FILM? Saving Private Ryan, Gladiator
FAVOURITE BOOK? The Cricketers' Who's Who
DREAM HOLIDAY? Grenada, Ibiza
ACCOMPLISHMENTS? Playing in the FA Cup and four years' no claims on my car insurance
SURPRISING SKILL? I can DJ
GUILTY PLEASURES? Dunking biscuits
TWITTER FEED? @wayneAwhite

Batting	Mat	Inns	NO	Runs	HS	Ave	SR	100	50	Ct	St
First-class	68	109	16	2418	101*	26.00	51.79	1	13	22	0
List A	62	50	14	702	46*	19.50	83.67	0	0	15	0
Twenty20	48	36	15	345	26	16.42	113.11	0	0	23	0

Bowling	Mat	Balls	Runs	Wkts	BBI	BBM	Ave	Econ	SR	5w	10
First-class	68	8386	5455	147	5/54		37.10	3.90	57.0	4	0
List A	62	1960	2108	56	6/29	6/29	37.64	6.45	35.0	1	0
Twenty20	48	573	927	21	3/27	3/27	44.14	9.70	27.2	0	0

ROSS WHITELEY   LHB LM

FULL NAME: Ross Andrew Whiteley
BORN: September 13, 1988, Sheffield, Yorkshire
SQUAD NO: 44
HEIGHT: 6ft 2in
NICKNAME: Rossco, Pico, Brick
EDUCATION: Repton School
TEAMS: Derbyshire, Derbyshire 2nd XI, Worcestershire
CAREER: First-class: 2008; List A: 2008; T20: 2011

BEST BATTING: 130* Derbyshire vs Kent, Derby, 2011
BEST BOWLING: 2-6 Derbyshire vs Hampshire, Derby, 2012

FAMILY TIES? My brother Adam played Derbyshire age groups and 2nd XI cricket
CAREER HIGHLIGHTS? My maiden century, at Northampton, and signing my first professional contract
SUPERSTITIONS? Every time I'm on strike I scrape my mark three times
CRICKETING HEROES? Martin Guptill, Shane Warne, Ben Hilfenhaus
NON-CRICKETING HEROES? Buddy Franklin
TIPS FOR THE TOP? Will Beer, Tom Poynton, Greg Smith
IF YOU WEREN'T A CRICKETER? Playing some other form of sport
FAVOURITE BOOK? Sniper One
TWITTER FEED: @RossWhiteley44

Batting	Mat	Inns	NO	Runs	HS	Ave	SR	100	50	Ct	St
First-class	35	57	7	1387	130*	27.74	44.54	2	6	19	0
List A	25	21	2	254	40	13.36	70.94	0	0	10	0
Twenty20	19	18	7	321	43	29.18	130.48	0	0	4	0

Bowling	Mat	Balls	Runs	Wkts	BBI	BBM	Ave	Econ	SR	5w	10
First-class	35	1921	1348	28	2/6	4/43	48.14	4.21	68.6	0	0
List A	25	210	223	5	1/17	1/17	44.60	6.37	42.0	0	0
Twenty20	19	36	46	2	1/12	1/12	23.00	7.66	18.0	0	0

OLLIE WILKIN — RHB RMF

FULL NAME: Oliver Wilkin
BORN: April 6, 1992, Ealing, Middlesex
SQUAD NO: 30
HEIGHT: 6ft 3in
NICKNAME: Oli, Wilks, Wilko
EDUCATION: Merchant Taylors' School; Loughborough University
TEAMS: Loughborough MCCU, Middlesex, Middlesex 2nd XI, Middlesex Under-15s, Middlesex Under-17s
CAREER: First-class: 2011; List A: 2013; T20: 2012

BEST BATTING: 38 Loughborough MCCU vs Northamptonshire, Loughborough, 2011
BEST BOWLING: 2-63 Loughborough MCCU vs Kent, Canterbury, 2011

WHO WOULD PLAY YOU IN A FILM OF YOUR LIFE? Matthew Perry
CAREER HIGHLIGHTS? Playing at Lord's in a Pro40 game and playing at a packed Chelmsford and Oval in the T20
MOST MARKED CHARACTERISTIC? My crooked nose
BEST PLAYER IN COUNTY CRICKET? Sam Robson
TIPS FOR THE TOP? Tymal Mills and his left-arm rockets
IF YOU WEREN'T A CRICKETER? Something in TV
DESERT ISLAND DISC? Something by Bastille
FAVOURITE TV? Arrow, Sherlock, 24
CRICKETING HEROES? Andrew Flintoff and Jacques Kallis
NON-CRICKETING HEROES? Sherlock Holmes
WHEN YOU RETIRE? I'd like to coach then live on a beach
SURPRISING FACT? I'm still a massive Disney fan
TWITTER FEED: @oliwilkin30

Batting	Mat	Inns	NO	Runs	HS	Ave	SR	100	50	Ct	St
First-class	3	6	0	138	38	23.00	57.26	0	0	1	0
List A	1	1	0	20	20	20.00	100.00	0	0	1	0
Twenty20	3	3	1	38	28	19.00	122.58	0	0	4	0

Bowling	Mat	Balls	Runs	Wkts	BBI	BBM	Ave	Econ	SR	5w	10
First-class	3	300	213	4	2/63	2/63	53.25	4.26	75.0	0	0
List A	1	48	44	2	2/44	2/44	22.00	5.50	24.0	0	0
Twenty20	3	24	20	4	3/12	3/12	5.00	5.00	6.0	0	0

DAVID WILLEY

LHB LFM MVP11

FULL NAME: David Jonathan Willey
BORN: February 28, 1990, Northampton
SQUAD NO: 15
HEIGHT: 6ft 1in
NICKNAME: Willow, Wildman, Will
EDUCATION: Northampton School for Boys
TEAMS: England Lions, England Under-19s, Northamptonshire, Northamptonshire 2nd XI
CAREER: First-class: 2009; List A: 2009; T20: 2009

BEST BATTING: 81 Northamptonshire vs Glamorgan, Northampton, 2013
BEST BOWLING: 5-29 Northamptonshire vs Gloucestershire, Northampton, 2011

FAMILY TIES? My dad [Peter] played a bit for Northants, Leicestershire and England
WHO WOULD PLAY YOU IN A FILM OF YOUR LIFE? Jack Bauer
CAREER HIGHLIGHTS? Playing in T20 Finals Day in 2009 and 2013 and taking 10 wickets in a match vs Gloucestershire
SUPERSTITIONS? I put my left pad on first and turn right at the end of my run-up
MOST MARKED CHARACTERISTIC? My massive chin
TIP FOR THE TOP? Ben Duckett
DESERT ISLAND DISC? Bob Marley – Legend
FAVOURITE TV? 24
CRICKETING HEROES? Peter Willey
ACCOMPLISHMENTS? Cycling from Land's End to John O'Groats for Cancer Research UK
WHEN YOU RETIRE? I'm going to sit on a beach in Australia
FANTASY SLIP CORDON? Keeper: Jason Statham, 1st: Sylvester Stallone, 2nd: Arnold Schwarzenegger, 3rd: Jean-Claude Van Damme, Gully: Jack Bauer
TWITTER FEED: @david_willey

Batting	Mat	Inns	NO	Runs	HS	Ave	SR	100	50	Ct	St
First-class	43	56	9	1325	81	28.19	58.31	0	10	10	0
List A	47	36	4	669	167	20.90	98.09	1	2	18	0
Twenty20	60	38	14	466	60	19.41	122.30	0	1	20	0

Bowling	Mat	Balls	Runs	Wkts	BBI	BBM	Ave	Econ	SR	5w	10
First-class	43	5919	3277	113	5/29	10/75	29.00	3.32	52.3	5	1
List A	47	1300	1197	33	3/28	3/28	36.27	5.52	39.3	0	0
Twenty20	60	770	917	53	4/9	4/9	17.30	7.14	14.5	0	0

KANE WILLIAMSON RHB OB

FULL NAME: Kane Stuart Williamson
BORN: August 8, 1990, Tauranga, New Zealand
SQUAD NO: 8
HEIGHT: 5ft 8in
NICKNAME: Nossy
EDUCATION: Tauranga Boys' College
TEAMS: New Zealand, Gloucestershire, Gloucestershire 2nd XI, New Zealand Under-19s, Northern Districts, Yorkshire
CAREER: Test: 2010; ODI: 2010; T20I: 2011; First-class: 2007; List A: 2007; T20: 2009

BEST BATTING: 284* Northern Districts vs Wellington, Lincoln, 2011
BEST BOWLING: 5-75 Nortern Districts vs Canterbury, Christchurch, 2008
COUNTY CAP: 2011 (Gloucestershire)

NOTES: Williamson will share Yorkshire's overseas player duties for 2014 with Australian batsman Aaron Finch, having had a short spell with the county towards the end of last year's campaign. The New Zealander, who previously played for Gloucestershire in 2011 and 2012, scored 403 first-class runs at 50.37 in his five appearances for the White Rose. He scored 131 on his maiden Test innings, against India at Ahmedabad in 2010, and he scored another century, his fifth in Tests, against the Indians during the Black Caps' series win in February 2014 – 113 at Auckland. In the preceding ODI series he scored 50+ in each of the five matches, becoming only the second player to achieve the feat in a five-match series

Batting	Mat	Inns	NO	Runs	HS	Ave	SR	100	50	Ct	St
Tests	31	56	2	1964	135	36.37	42.97	5	12	28	0
ODIs	54	49	6	1699	145*	39.51	79.06	3	11	18	0
T20Is	13	11	2	206	48	22.88	118.39	0	0	5	0
First-class	80	140	7	5628	284*	42.31	49.51	14	30	76	0
List A	102	95	14	3541	145*	43.71	80.05	7	22	38	0
Twenty20	54	47	5	834	79*	19.85	109.16	0	3	19	0

Bowling	Mat	Balls	Runs	Wkts	BBI	BBM	Ave	Econ	SR	5w	10
Tests	31	1615	905	22	4/44	4/44	41.13	3.36	73.4	0	0
ODIs	54	777	711	23	4/22	4/22	30.91	5.49	33.7	0	0
T20Is	13	40	70	2	1/6	1/6	35.00	10.50	20.0	0	0
First-class	80	5454	3107	71	5/75	5/59	43.76	3.41	76.8	1	0
List A	102	2054	1767	53	5/51	5/51	33.33	5.16	38.7	1	0
Twenty20	54	638	747	23	3/33	3/33	32.47	7.02	27.7	0	0

SURREY

FULL NAME: Gary Craig Wilson
BORN: February 5, 1986, Dundonald,
Northern Ireland
SQUAD NO: 14
HEIGHT: 5ft 9in
NICKNAME: Gaz, Wils, Suede
EDUCATION: Methodist College, Belfast
TEAMS: Ireland, Ireland Under-19s, Surrey,
Surrey 2nd XI
CAREER: ODI: 2007; T20I: 2008; First-class:
2005; List A: 2006; T20: 2008

BEST BATTING: 125 Surrey vs Leicestershire, Leicester, 2010

CAREER HIGHLIGHTS? Playing in the World Cup and beating England, plus my maiden
Championship and ODI hundreds
SUPERSTITIONS? I put my left pad on first
CRICKETING HEROES? Alec Stewart
NON-CRICKETING HEROES? David Beckham, Sir Alex Ferguson
BEST PLAYER IN COUNTY CRICKET? Marcus Trescothick
TIPS FOR THE TOP? Jason Roy, Paul Stirling
IF YOU WEREN'T A CRICKETER? I'd probably be a fireman or policeman
WHEN RAIN STOPS PLAY? On the internet, thinking about where I can next play golf
FAVOURITE TV? Spooks, The Apprentice, TOWIE
GUILTY PLEASURES? Haribo sweets, Sensations crisps
SURPRISING FACTS? I have the biggest head in the changing room in terms of volume and I
played Ulster Schools rugby
TWITTER FEED: @gwilson14

Batting	Mat	Inns	NO	Runs	HS	Ave	SR	100	50	Ct	St
ODIs	47	46	5	1076	113	26.24	73.14	1	7	31	9
T20Is	31	27	3	510	41*	21.25	91.39	0	0	18	2
First-class	43	64	8	1709	125	30.51		2	8	65	1
List A	121	107	11	2282	113	23.77	69.31	1	15	76	21
Twenty20	89	75	18	1472	54*	25.82	110.34	0	4	44	11
Bowling	Mat	Balls	Runs	Wkts	BBI	BBM	Ave	Econ	SR	5w	10
ODIs	47	-	-	-	-	-	-	-	-	-	-
T20Is	31	-	-	-	-	-	-	-	-	-	-
First-class	43	108	89	0	-	-	-	4.94	-	0	0
List A	121	-	-	-	-	-	-	-	-	-	-
Twenty20	89	-	-	-	-	-	-	-	-	-	-

JACK WINSLADE · RHB RMF

FULL NAME: Jack Robert Winslade
BORN: April 12, 1995, Epsom, Surrey
SQUAD NO: 77
HEIGHT: 5ft 10in
NICKNAME: Jacko, Winsey
EDUCATION: Whitgift School, Croydon
TEAMS: England Under-19s, Surrey 2nd XI, Surrey Under-13s, Surrey Under-14s, Surrey Under-15s, Surrey Under-17s
CAREER: Yet to make first-team debut

FAMILY TIES? My dad played when he was younger. He introduced my older brother to cricket which in turn inspired me to play

WHO WOULD PLAY YOU IN A FILM OF YOUR LIFE? Gerard Butler

CAREER HIGHLIGHTS? Playing in the ICC U19 World Cup for England [in 2014] and representing Surrey from the age of eight

MOST MARKED CHARACTERISTIC? My hair and teeth

BEST PLAYER IN COUNTY CRICKET? Kevin Pietersen

TIPS FOR THE TOP? Dom Sibley and Tom Curran

IF YOU WEREN'T A CRICKETER? I'd be a tattoo artist

DESERT ISLAND DISC? Drake – Nothing Was The Same

FAVOURITE TV? Made In Chelsea

CRICKETING HEROES? Alec Stewart, Andrew Flintoff

NON-CRICKETING HEROES? Thierry Henry

WHEN YOU RETIRE? I'll follow Arsenal home and away and hopefully see them win the Champions League

SURPRISING FACT? I'm a great singer

FANTASY SLIP CORDON? Keeper: Kevin Hart, 1st: Kim Kardashian, 2nd: Tom Curran, 3rd: Jack Winslade, Gully: Jay-Z

TWITTER FEED: @JackWinslade

CHRIS WOAKES

RHB RFM W2 MVP41

WARWICKSHIRE

FULL NAME: Christopher Roger Woakes
BORN: March 2, 1989, Birmingham, Warwickshire
SQUAD NO: 19
HEIGHT: 6ft 1in
NICKNAME: Woaksy, Woako, Wiz, GB
EDUCATION: Barr Beacon School
TEAMS: England, England Lions, England Under-19s, Marylebone Cricket Club, Sydney Thunder, Warwickshire, Wellington
CAREER: Test: 2013; ODI: 2011; T20I: 2011; First-class: 2006; List A: 2007; T20: 2008

BEST BATTING: 152* Warwickshire vs Derbyshire, Derby, 2013
BEST BOWLING: 7-20 Warwickshire vs Hampshire, Birmingham, 2011
COUNTY CAP: 2009

CAREER HIGHLIGHTS? Winning the CB40 in 2010 with Warwickshire and making my debut for England in Australia in January 2011
CRICKETING HEROES? Jacques Kallis
NON-CRICKETING HEROES? Paul 'God' McGrath
BEST PLAYER IN COUNTY CRICKET? Marcus Trescothick
TIP FOR THE TOP? Tom Milnes
IF YOU WEREN'T A CRICKETER? I'd be finishing university and struggling to find a job! I am very lucky to be doing something I love
FAVOURITE TV? An Idiot Abroad or A League Of Their Own
FAVOURITE FILM? Gladiator, The Hangover, Old School
TWITTER FEED: @crwoakes19

Batting	Mat	Inns	NO	Runs	HS	Ave	SR	100	50	Ct	St
Tests	1	2	1	42	25	42.00	50.60	0	0	0	0
ODIs	13	10	4	141	36	23.50	73.43	0	0	5	0
T20Is	4	3	2	37	19*	37.00	123.33	0	0	1	0
First-class	90	124	33	3665	152*	40.27		8	15	39	0
List A	80	51	17	630	49*	18.52	85.59	0	0	17	0
Twenty20	69	39	22	459	55*	27.00	134.21	0	1	30	0

Bowling	Mat	Balls	Runs	Wkts	BBI	BBM	Ave	Econ	SR	5w	10
Tests	1	144	96	1	1/96	1/96	96.00	4.00	144.0	0	0
ODIs	13	590	557	15	6/45	6/45	37.13	5.66	39.3	1	0
T20Is	4	66	113	2	1/29	1/29	56.50	10.27	33.0	0	0
First-class	90	15149	7704	301	7/20	11/97	25.59	3.05	50.3	13	3
List A	80	3094	2842	82	6/45	6/45	34.65	5.51	37.7	1	0
Twenty20	69	1284	1731	67	4/21	4/21	25.83	8.08	19.1	0	0

CHRIS WOOD   RHB LMF

FULL NAME: Christopher Philip Wood
BORN: June 27, 1990, Basingstoke, Hampshire
SQUAD NO: 25
HEIGHT: 6ft 3in
NICKNAME: Woody
EDUCATION: Amery Hill Secondary School; Alton College
TEAMS: England Under-19s, Hampshire, Hampshire 2nd XI
CAREER: First-class: 2010; List A: 2010; T20: 2010

BEST BATTING: 105* Hampshire vs Leicestershire, Leicester, 2012
BEST BOWLING: 5-41 Hampshire vs Loughborough MCCU, Southampton, 2012

CAREER HIGHLIGHTS? Winning the 2010 T20 competition
SUPERSTITIONS? I always put my right shoe on before my left
CRICKETING HEROES? Freddie Flintoff
NON-CRICKETING HEROES? David Beckham
BEST PLAYER IN COUNTY CRICKET? Marcus Trescothick
TIPS FOR THE TOP? James Vince, James Taylor, Ben Stokes
IF YOU WEREN'T A CRICKETER? I'd be a bin man
WHEN RAIN STOPS PLAY? Listening to music, playing on my phone or playing poker
FAVOURITE TV? A League Of Their Own
FAVOURITE FILM? Snatch
DREAM HOLIDAY? Las Vegas
ACCOMPLISHMENTS? I played in the FA Cup
SURPRISING FACT? I trialled for Chelsea FC
FANTASY SLIP CORDON? Keeper: Kelly Brook, 1st: Katy Perry, 2nd: Cheryl Cole, 3rd: Kim Kardashian
TWITTER FEED: @CWoody27

Batting	Mat	Inns	NO	Runs	HS	Ave	SR	100	50	Ct	St
First-class	30	42	3	907	105*	23.25	63.69	1	4	11	0
List A	47	24	8	169	41	10.56	94.41	0	0	17	0
Twenty20	56	14	6	72	18	9.00	107.46	0	0	19	0

Bowling	Mat	Balls	Runs	Wkts	BBI	BBM	Ave	Econ	SR	5w	10
First-class	30	4615	2302	78	5/41	7/49	29.51	2.99	59.1	2	0
List A	47	1920	1770	72	5/22	5/22	24.58	5.53	26.6	1	0
Twenty20	56	1109	1504	54	3/26	3/26	27.85	8.13	20.5	0	0

MARK WOOD

RHB RFM

DURHAM

FULL NAME: Mark Andrew Wood
BORN: January 11, 1990, Ashington, Northumberland
SQUAD NO: 33
HEIGHT: 6ft
NICKNAME: Woody
EDUCATION: Ashington High School
TEAMS: Durham, Durham 2nd XI, Durham Academy, England Lions, Northumberland
CAREER: First-class: 2011; List A 2011; T20: 2013

BEST BATTING: 58* Durham vs Nottinghamshire, Nottingham, 2013
BEST BOWLING: 5-32 England Lions vs Sri Lanka A Emerging Players, Colombo, 2014

FAMILY TIES? My dad and uncle [Derek and Neil Wood] played 1st XI cricket for Ashington CC and minor counties cricket for Northumberland
WHO WOULD PLAY YOU IN A FILM OF YOUR LIFE? Terry Crews
CAREER HIGHLIGHTS? Making my debut vs Durham University, my first first-class five-fer against Nottinghamshire at Trent Bridge, winning the County Championship, being selected for the England Lions and taking a five-fer against Sri Lanka A for England Lions in Colombo
MOST MARKED CHARACTERISTIC? I step back like a sprinter at the start of my run-up
BEST PLAYER IN COUNTY CRICKET? Graham Onions
TIPS FOR THE TOP? Tom Helm and Ben Raine
IF YOU WEREN'T A CRICKETER? Either living in Australia or studying to be a PE teacher. Or maybe both
FAVOURITE TV? Game Of Thrones
CRICKETING HEROES? Graham Onions, Stephen Harmison, Ben Harmison, Michael Holding
NON-CRICKETING HEROES? Lennox Lewis, David Beckham, Jonny Wilkinson
ACCOMPLISHMENTS? My degree in Sports Management and Development
SURPRISING FACT? I'm born on the same day as my dad
TWITTER FEED: @MAWood33

Batting	Mat	Inns	NO	Runs	HS	Ave	SR	100	50	Ct	St
First-class	14	21	4	373	58*	21.94	52.98	0	1	7	0
List A	14	7	3	28	15*	7.00	82.35	0	0	5	0
Twenty20	6	2	0	3	2	1.50	75.00	0	0	0	0

Bowling	Mat	Balls	Runs	Wkts	BBI	BBM	Ave	Econ	SR	5w	10
First-class	14	1976	1108	52	5/32	6/47	21.30	3.36	38.0	3	0
List A	14	498	439	17	3/23	3/23	25.82	5.28	29.2	0	0
Twenty20	6	96	167	1	1/20	1/20	167.00	10.43	96.0	0	0

SAM WOOD

LHB OB

FULL NAME: Samuel Kenneth William Wood
BORN: April 3, 1993, Nottingham
SQUAD NO: 23
HEIGHT: 6ft
NICKNAME: Woody
EDUCATION: Colonel Frank Seely School
TEAMS: England Under-19s, Nottinghamshire, Nottinghamshire 2nd XI, Nottinghamshire Under-14s, Nottinghamshire Under-15s, Nottinghamshire Under-17s
CAREER: First-class: 2011; List A: 2011

NOTTINGHAMSHIRE

BEST BATTING: 45 Nottinghamshire vs Surrey, The Oval, 2012
BEST BOWLING: 3-64 Nottinghamshire vs Surrey, The Oval, 2012

FAMILY TIES? My dad played league cricket
WHO WOULD PLAY YOU IN A FILM OF YOUR LIFE? Ryan Gosling, because he doesn't say much in his films
CAREER HIGHLIGHTS? Playing in the U19 World Cup in Australia and making my first-class debut
SUPERSTITIONS? I push my pads down before every ball
MOST MARKED CHARACTERISTIC? Not saying much
BEST PLAYER IN COUNTY CRICKET? Ben Stokes
DESERT ISLAND DISC? Time To Say Goodbye
FAVOURITE TV? Coronation Street
CRICKETING HEROES? Brian Lara
NON-CRICKETING HEROES? Muhammad Ali
WHEN YOU RETIRE? I'd like to get into coaching
SURPRISING FACT? I've got an obsession with Coronation Street
FANTASY SLIP CORDON? Keeper: Me, 1st: Lee Evans, 2nd: Peter Kay, 3rd: Ricky Gervais, Gully: Kevin Bridges
TWITTER FEED: @SamWood33

Batting	Mat	Inns	NO	Runs	HS	Ave	SR	100	50	Ct	St
First-class	2	2	0	47	45	23.50	39.83	0	0	0	0
List A	6	4	0	40	32	10.00	66.66	0	0	2	0

Bowling	Mat	Balls	Runs	Wkts	BBI	BBM	Ave	Econ	SR	5w	10
First-class	2	192	92	3	3/64	3/84	30.66	2.87	64.0	0	0
List A	6	144	128	5	2/24	2/24	25.60	5.33	28.8	0	0

BEN WRIGHT

RHB RM

FULL NAME: Ben James Wright
BORN: December 5, 1987, Preston, Lancashire
SQUAD NO: 29
HEIGHT: 5ft 11in
NICKNAME: Bej, Keller
EDUCATION: Cowbridge Comprehensive
TEAMS: England Under-19s, Glamorgan, Wales Minor Counties
CAREER: First-class: 2006; List A: 2006; T20: 2007

BEST BATTING: 172 Glamorgan vs Gloucestershire, Cardiff, 2007
BEST BOWLING: 1-14 Glamorgan vs Essex, Chelmsford, 2007
COUNTY CAP: 2011

CAREER HIGHLIGHTS? Scoring a hundred vs Middlesex at Lord's
CRICKETING HEROES? Andrew Flintoff, Matthew Maynard
NON-CRICKETING HEROES? Jonny Wilkinson
BEST PLAYER IN COUNTY CRICKET? Marcus Trescothick
TIP FOR THE TOP? Andrew Salter
IF YOU WEREN'T A CRICKETER? I'd be a fitness trainer
WHEN RAIN STOPS PLAY? I'm annoying people
FAVOURITE TV? Eastbound And Down
FAVOURITE FILM? Wedding Crashers
FAVOURITE BOOK? Jonny Wilkinson's autobiography
DREAM HOLIDAY? Hawaii
ACCOMPLISHMENTS? Playing rugby for Wales at U16 level
GUILTY PLEASURES? Pizza
TWITTER FEED: @bej29w

Batting	Mat	Inns	NO	Runs	HS	Ave	SR	100	50	Ct	St
First-class	77	128	10	3252	172	27.55	49.93	5	14	41	0
List A	71	65	12	1332	79	25.13	75.63	0	7	16	0
Twenty20	42	35	12	485	55*	21.08	103.85	0	1	12	0

Bowling	Mat	Balls	Runs	Wkts	BBI	BBM	Ave	Econ	SR	5w	10
First-class	77	276	174	2	1/14	1/14	87.00	3.78	138.0	0	0
List A	71	132	126	1	1/19	1/19	126.00	5.72	132.0	0	0
Twenty20	42	24	22	1	1/16	1/16	22.00	5.50	24.0	0	0

CHRIS WRIGHT
RHB RFM W1

FULL NAME: Christopher Julian Clement Wright
BORN: July 14, 1985, Chipping Norton, Oxfordshire
SQUAD NO: 31
HEIGHT: 6ft 3in
NICKNAME: Wrighty, The Baron, Almunia
EDUCATION: Eggars' Grammar School, Alton
TEAMS: British Universities, Cambridge MCCU, England Lions, Essex, Hampshire 2nd XI, Middlesex, Tamil Union, Warwickshire
CAREER: First-class: 2004; List A: 2004; T20: 2004

BEST BATTING: 77 Essex vs Cambridge MCCU, Cambridge, 2011
BEST BOWLING: 6-22 Essex vs Leicestershire, Leicester, 2008

CAREER HIGHLIGHTS? Winning the County Championship in 2012 and the FP Trophy in 2008
MOST MARKED CHARACTERISTIC? My awesome lid!
BEST PLAYER IN COUNTY CRICKET? Chris Woakes
DESERT ISLAND DISC? Linkin Park – Hybrid Theory
ACCOMPLISHMENTS? My two lovely children
FANTASY SLIP CORDON? Keeper: Me, 1st: Phil Edwards, 2nd: Tony Palladino, 3rd: Gareth James, Gully: Matt Hooper
TWITTER FEED: @ChrisWright1985

Batting	Mat	Inns	NO	Runs	HS	Ave	SR	100	50	Ct	St
First-class	89	107	26	1388	77	17.13	51.25	0	5	15	0
List A	90	38	17	219	42	10.42	78.49	0	0	16	0
Twenty20	46	11	7	23	6*	5.75	115.00	0	0	9	0

Bowling	Mat	Balls	Runs	Wkts	BBI	BBM	Ave	Econ	SR	5w	10
First-class	89	14382	8586	251	6/22		34.20	3.58	57.2	8	0
List A	90	3455	3217	91	4/20	4/20	35.35	5.58	37.9	0	0
Twenty20	46	915	1335	40	4/24	4/24	33.37	8.75	22.8	0	0

LUKE WRIGHT

RHB RMF MVP44

FULL NAME: Luke James Wright
BORN: March 7, 1985, Grantham
SQUAD NO: 10
HEIGHT: 6ft
NICKNAME: Wrighty
EDUCATION: Ratcliffe College;
Loughborough University
TEAMS: England, Abahani Limited,
Dhaka Gladiators, England Lions, Impi,
Leicestershire, Melbourne Stars, Pune
Warriors, Sussex, Wellington
CAREER: ODI: 2007; T20I: 2007; First-class:
2003; List A 2002; T20: 2004

BEST BATTING: 187 Sussex vs Middlesex, Lord's, 2013
BEST BOWLING: 5-65 Sussex vs Derbyshire, Derby, 2010
COUNTY CAP: 2007 (Sussex)

FAMILY TIES? My father is a very keen cricketer and a Level 2 coach. My brother [Ashley] played for Leicestershire
SUPERSTITIONS? Too many to mention
CRICKETING HEROES? Jacques Kallis, Andrew Flintoff
TWITTER FEED: @lukewright204
NOTES: Included in England's touring party for the 2009/10 Test series in South Africa, Wright narrowly missed out on a debut in the first match at Centurion. Since then he has featured regularly for his country in limited-overs cricket, playing a key role in the World T20 win in 2010 and finishing the 2012 edition as England's leading run-scorer, hitting 99* against Afghanistan to share the record for the highest score by an Englishman in T20 internationals with Alex Hales. Has represented T20 franchises across the world, hitting a 44-ball century for Melbourne Stars in the Big Bash League – at the time the fastest-ever ton in the tournament

Batting	Mat	Inns	NO	Runs	HS	Ave	SR	100	50	Ct	St
ODIs	50	39	4	707	52	20.20	86.21	0	2	18	0
T20Is	50	44	4	752	99*	18.80	136.97	0	4	14	0
First-class	86	126	16	4136	187	37.60	65.45	11	20	37	0
List A	172	138	21	3476	143*	29.70		8	9	52	0
Twenty20	183	164	15	3824	117	25.66	145.12	2	19	56	0

Bowling	Mat	Balls	Runs	Wkts	BBI	BBM	Ave	Econ	SR	5w	10
ODIs	50	1038	884	15	2/34	2/34	58.93	5.10	69.2	0	0
T20Is	50	318	445	17	2/24	2/24	26.17	8.39	18.7	0	0
First-class	86	7904	4653	117	5/65		39.76	3.53	67.5	3	0
List A	172	4752	4231	111	4/12	4/12	38.11	5.34	42.8	0	0
Twenty20	183	1787	2543	78	3/17	3/17	32.60	8.53	22.9	0	0

ALEX WYATT · RHB RFM

FULL NAME: Alexander Charles Frederick Wyatt
BORN: July 23, 1990, Roehampton
SQUAD NO: 16
HEIGHT: 6ft 7in
NICKNAME: Waz
EDUCATION: Oakham School; The Open University
TEAMS: Leicestershire, Leicestershire 2nd XI
CAREER: First-class: 2009; List A: 2009; T20: 2009

LEICESTERSHIRE

BEST BATTING: 28 Leicestershire vs Glamorgan, Swansea, 2013
BEST BOWLING: 3-35 Leicestershire vs Hampshire, Leicester, 2012

WHO WOULD PLAY YOU IN A FILM OF YOUR LIFE? Ryan Reynolds
CAREER HIGHLIGHTS? All of my debuts in all formats
MOST MARKED CHARACTERISTIC? My height
BEST PLAYER IN COUNTY CRICKET? Graham Onions
TIPS FOR THE TOP? Ned Eckersley, Josh Cobb, James Taylor
IF YOU WEREN'T A CRICKETER? I'd be a professional gamer
DESERT ISLAND DISC? Shania Twain – Come On Over
FAVOURITE TV? Sun, Sex And Suspicious Parents
CRICKETING HEROES? Glenn McGrath, Darren Gough, Anthony Ireland
NON-CRICKETING HEROES? Lloyd Tennant, Beyoncé, Rowan Atkinson, John Cleese
ACCOMPLISHMENTS? Four years' no claims on my car insurance until I hit a badger. Half-century on Flappy Birds. I once ate 38 fish fingers in one sitting when I was 10 years old
WHEN YOU RETIRE? I would love to travel the world and see as many cultures and countries as possible
TWITTER FEED: @acfwyatt

Batting	Mat	Inns	NO	Runs	HS	Ave	SR	100	50	Ct	St
First-class	23	30	12	145	28	8.05	45.45	0	0	3	0
List A	14	7	3	13	9*	3.25	68.42	0	0	2	0
Twenty20	4	1	1	0	0*	-	-	0	0	1	0

Bowling	Mat	Balls	Runs	Wkts	BBI	BBM	Ave	Econ	SR	5w	10
First-class	23	3505	1861	53	3/35	6/115	35.11	3.18	66.1	0	0
List A	14	452	478	11	2/36	2/36	43.45	6.34	41.0	0	0
Twenty20	4	78	92	3	3/14	3/14	30.66	7.07	26.0	0	0

MICHAEL YARDY

LHB SLA R2 MVP51

SUSSEX

FULL NAME: Michael Howard Yardy
BORN: November 27, 1980, Pembury, Kent
SQUAD NO: 20
HEIGHT: 6ft
NICKNAME: Yards, Paolo
EDUCATION: William Parker School, Hastings
TEAMS: England, Central Districts, Sussex, Sussex Cricket Board
CAREER: ODI: 2006; T20I: 2006; First-class: 2000; List A: 1999; T20: 2004

BEST BATTING: 257 Sussex vs Bangladeshis, Hove, 2005
BEST BOWLING: 5-83 Sussex vs Bangladeshis, Hove, 2005
COUNTY CAP: 2005; BENEFIT YEAR: 2014

CAREER HIGHLIGHTS? Success with Sussex and winning the World T20 in 2010
CRICKETING HEROES? Graham Gooch, Michael Atherton, Alec Stewart, Graham Thorpe
NON-CRICKETING HEROES? Paolo Di Canio, Paul Gascoigne
BEST PLAYER IN COUNTY CRICKET? Marcus Trescothick
IF YOU WEREN'T A CRICKETER? I'd be doing a proper job
WHEN RAIN STOPS PLAY? Reading, irritating people
FAVOURITE TV? Outnumbered
FAVOURITE FILM? Snatch
FAVOURITE BOOK? Tony Cascarino's autobiography
DREAM HOLIDAY? Maldives
SURPRISING SKILL? I've got a very sweet left foot
GUILTY PLEASURES? West Ham United

Batting	Mat	Inns	NO	Runs	HS	Ave	SR	100	50	Ct	St
ODIs	28	24	8	326	60*	20.37	69.06	0	2	10	0
T20Is	14	8	5	96	35*	32.00	133.33	0	0	8	0
First-class	173	287	27	9631	257	37.04		20	45	157	0
List A	205	175	31	3639	98*	25.27		0	23	75	0
Twenty20	108	84	29	1189	76*	21.61	103.93	0	2	38	0

Bowling	Mat	Balls	Runs	Wkts	BBI	BBM	Ave	Econ	SR	5w	10
ODIs	28	1332	1075	21	3/24	3/24	51.19	4.84	63.4	0	0
T20Is	14	276	299	11	2/19	2/19	27.18	6.50	25.0	0	0
First-class	173	3591	2119	28	5/83		75.67	3.54	128.2	1	0
List A	205	6287	5336	138	6/27	6/27	38.66	5.09	45.5	1	0
Twenty20	108	2059	2233	88	3/21	3/21	25.37	6.50	23.3	0	0

ASHAR ZAIDI

LHB SLA

FULL NAME: Syed Ashar Ahmed Zaidi
BORN: July 13, 1981, Karachi, Pakistan
SQUAD NO: 1
HEIGHT: 5ft 7in
NICKNAME: Ash, Ashi
TEAMS: Gazi Tank Cricketers, Islamabad, Islamabad Cricket Association, Islamabad Leopards, Sussex, Sussex 2nd XI
CAREER: First-class: 1999; List A: 1999; T20: 2006

SUSSEX

BEST BATTING: 202 Islamabad vs Sialkot, Sialkot, 2009
BEST BOWLING: 4-50 Islamabad vs Hyderabad, Hyderabad, 2009

WHO WOULD PLAY YOU IN A FILM OF YOUR LIFE? Myself. I would love to get my acting skills going
CAREER HIGHLIGHTS? Making 200 against Zimbabwe in 2005
BEST PLAYER IN COUNTY CRICKET? Too early to say for me, I haven't played much
TIPS FOR THE TOP? Callum Jackson, Harry Finch
IF YOU WEREN'T A CRICKETER? I'd be a hockey player
FAVOURITE TV? Friends
CRICKETING HEROES? Saeed Anwar, Wasim Akram
NON-CRICKETING HEROES? The Prophet Muhammad (pbuh)
ACCOMPLISHMENTS? Having a wonderful family
WHEN YOU RETIRE? Umpiring – I can't live without cricket
TWITTER FEED: @asharzaidi1981

Batting	Mat	Inns	NO	Runs	HS	Ave	SR	100	50	Ct	St
First-class	90	149	12	5238	202	38.23		11	26	76	0
List A	64	60	6	1863	109	34.50		3	10	25	0
Twenty20	9	9	1	166	42*	20.75	128.68	0	0	4	0

Bowling	Mat	Balls	Runs	Wkts	BBI	BBM	Ave	Econ	SR	5w	10
First-class	90	3357	1619	56	4/50		28.91	2.89	59.9	0	0
List A	64	1912	1347	51	4/39	4/39	26.41	4.22	37.4	0	0
Twenty20	9	150	203	4	2/16	2/16	50.75	8.12	37.5	0	0

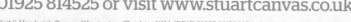

England
Women

CAPTAIN: Charlotte Edwards
HEAD OF PERFORMANCE: Paul Shaw

2014 SUMMER FIXTURES

August 13-16
England Women vs India Women
Test
Wormsley

August 21
England Women vs India Women
1st Royal London ODI
Scarborough

August 23
England Women vs India Women
2nd Royal London ODI
Scarborough

August 25
England Women vs India Women
3rd Royal London ODI
Lord's

September 1
England Women vs South Africa Women
1st NatWest International T20
Chelmsford

September 3
England Women vs South Africa Women
2nd NatWest International T20
Northampton

September 7
England Women vs South Africa Women
3rd NatWest International T20
Edgbaston

TAMMY BEAUMONT

RHB WK

FULL NAME: Tamsin Tilley Beaumont
BORN: March 11, 1991, Dover, Kent
SQUAD NO: 12
HEIGHT: 5ft 3in
NICKNAME: Tampy
EDUCATION: Sir Roger Manwood's School; Loughborough University
TEAMS: Diamonds, England Women, Kent Women
CAREER: Test: 2013; ODI: 2009; T20I: 2009

BEST BATTING: 1 England vs Australia, Wormsley, 2013

CAREER HIGHLIGHTS? Coming back from 2-0 down in an ODI series against India in 2012 to win 3-2 and showing a lot of character as a team in the process
MOST MARKED CHARACTERISTIC? I'm compassionate
IF YOU WEREN'T A CRICKETER? When I was younger I wanted to be a doctor but I'm not sure I could do that now as I get squeamish at hospital programmes these days!
CRICKETING HEROES? Charlotte Edwards, which is a bit cringe to admit now as she's my skipper. I always liked watching Brian Lara bat, apparently a couple of commentators have compared my bat-swing to him, although I'm not so sure about that!
ACCOMPLISHMENTS? Getting a 2:1 in Chemistry and Sports Science from Loughborough University. I surprised even myself because in my final year I was only in England for about half of the year and touring for the rest of it
WHEN YOU RETIRE? I'd probably like to give something back to the sport and do something that helps people
FANTASY SLIP CORDON? Keeper: Inspector Gadget (his go-go gadget arms would mean the rest of us wouldn't have to do much!), 1st: Miranda Hart (it would be funny to see her fall over while trying to catch one, plus her banter would be great), 2nd: Me, 3rd: Michael McIntyre (to keep us entertained all day), Gully: David Beckham
TWITTER FEED: @Tammy_Beaumont

Batting	Mat	Inns	NO	Runs	HS	Ave	SR	100	50	Ct	St
Tests	1	1	0	1	1	1.00	11.11	0	0	1	0
ODIs	21	15	4	207	44	18.81	42.33	0	0	6	4
T20Is	28	15	3	123	29*	10.25	71.09	0	0	6	4

Bowling	Mat	Balls	Runs	Wkts	BBI	BBM	Ave	Econ	SR	5w	10
Tests	1	-	-	-	-	-	-	-	-	-	-
ODIs	21	-	-	-	-	-	-	-	-	-	-
T20Is	28	-	-	-	-	-	-	-	-	-	-

KATHERINE BRUNT RHB RFM

FULL NAME: Katherine Helen Brunt
BORN: July 2, 1985, Barnsley
SQUAD NO: 26
HEIGHT: 5ft 5in
NICKNAME: Brunty, Nunny
EDUCATION: Penistone Grammar School
TEAMS: England Women, Yorkshire Women
CAREER: Test: 2004; ODI: 2005; T20I: 2005

BEST BATTING: 52 England vs Australia, Worcester, 2005
BEST BOWLING: 6-69 England vs Australia, Worcester, 2009

WHO WOULD PLAY YOU IN A FILM OF YOUR LIFE? Melissa McCarthy
CAREER HIGHLIGHTS? Being part of the Ashes Test series in 2005 and winning it for the first time in 42 years! Winning both World Cups in 2009 and winning back-to-back Ashes series in 2013/14
MOST MARKED CHARACTERISTIC? My aggression on the pitch
BEST PLAYER IN COUNTY CRICKET? Charlotte Edwards has dominated county cricket for 10 years
TIPS FOR THE TOP? Natalie Sciver, Jess Watson, Jodie Dibble, Amy Jones
IF YOU WEREN'T A CRICKETER? I'd be a UFC cage fighter
DESERT ISLAND DISC? Red Hot Chili Peppers – Greatest Hits
FAVOURITE TV? Educating Yorkshire, Grey's Anatomy
CRICKETING HEROES? Curtly Ambrose, Courtney Walsh, Darren Gough, Charlotte Edwards
NON-CRICKETING HEROES? Lionel Messi, Monica Seles, my dad
WHEN YOU RETIRE? I'll lie down, travel the world and then go into business with my brothers
CRICKET RULE YOU'D CHANGE? There should be unlimited bouncers!
TWITTER FEED: @KBrunt26

Batting	Mat	Inns	NO	Runs	HS	Ave	SR	100	50	Ct	St
Tests	9	11	4	110	52	15.71	26.50	0	1	2	0
ODIs	73	31	9	208	21*	9.45	80.30	0	0	17	0
T20Is	42	18	10	97	35	12.12	102.10	0	0	10	0

Bowling	Mat	Balls	Runs	Wkts	BBI	BBM	Ave	Econ	SR	5w	10
Tests	9	1722	707	34	6/69	9/111	20.79	2.46	50.6	2	0
ODIs	73	3598	1977	93	5/18	5/18	21.25	3.29	38.6	3	0
T20Is	42	918	737	41	3/6	3/6	17.97	4.81	22.3	0	0

FULL NAME: Kathryn Laura Cross
BORN: October 3, 1991, Manchester, Lancashire
SQUAD NO: 16
HEIGHT: 5ft 7in
NICKNAME: Crossy, Sunny
EDUCATION: Bury Grammar School; University of Leeds
TEAMS: England Academy Women, England Women, Lancashire Women, Sapphires
CAREER: Test: 2014; ODI: 2013; T20I: 2013

ENGLAND WOMEN

BEST BATTING: 3* England vs Australia, Perth, 2014
BEST BOWLING: 3-35 England vs Australia, Perth, 2014

WHO WOULD PLAY YOU IN A FILM OF YOUR LIFE? Ellen DeGeneres
CAREER HIGHLIGHTS? Retaining the Women's Ashes in Australia at the start of this year and winning the Test match at the WACA
SUPERSTITIONS? When walking to the start of my run-up I have to turn left at the top, I can't turn right
MOST MARKED CHARACTERISTIC? My sarcasm
BEST PLAYER IN COUNTY CRICKET? Jos Buttler – I'm excited to see him play at Lancashire
TIP FOR THE TOP? Our 16-year-old opening batter, Emma Lamb, who has just got into the Lancashire Academy
IF YOU WEREN'T A CRICKETER? I'd be a criminal or forensic psychologist
DESERT ISLAND DISC? Arctic Monkeys – Whatever People Say I Am, That's What I'm Not
CRICKETING HEROES? Andrew Flintoff and James Anderson
NON-CRICKETING HEROES? After recently reading his book, Nelson Mandela
WHEN YOU RETIRE? I'll live somewhere warm, travel the world and start a family
SURPRISING FACT? I was told at 15 years old that I would be blind by the time I was 18 due to a rare eye condition. Thankfully the doctors got it wrong!
TWITTER FEED: @katecross16

Batting	Mat	Inns	NO	Runs	HS	Ave	SR	100	50	Ct	St
Tests	1	2	1	3	3*	3.00	13.63	0	0	0	0
ODIs	6	2	1	1	1	1.00	12.50	0	0	0	0
T20Is	3	-	-	-	-	-	-	-	-	0	0

Bowling	Mat	Balls	Runs	Wkts	BBI	BBM	Ave	Econ	SR	5w	10
Tests	1	192	70	6	3/35	6/70	11.66	2.18	32.0	0	0
ODIs	6	234	194	5	4/51	4/51	38.80	4.97	46.8	0	0
T20Is	3	48	56	1	1/19	1/19	56.00	7.00	48.0	0	0

CHARLOTTE EDWARDS   RHB LB

FULL NAME: Charlotte Marie Edwards
BORN: December 17, 1979, Huntingdon
SQUAD NO: 23
HEIGHT: 5ft 9in
NICKNAME: Lottie
EDUCATION: Ramsey Abbey School
TEAMS: East Anglia Women, England Women, Kent Women, Northern Districts Women
CAREER: Test: 1996; ODI: 1997; T20I: 2004

BEST BATTING: 117 England vs New Zealand, Scarborough, 2004
BEST BOWLING: 2-28 England vs Australia, Harrogate, 1998

CAREER HIGHLIGHTS? Winning the World Cup in Sydney in 2009 and the World T20 in England in the same year
SUPERSTITIONS? I put my left pad on first
MOST MARKED CHARACTERISTIC? I'm passionate
BEST PLAYER IN COUNTY CRICKET? Sarah Taylor
TIPS FOR THE TOP? Amy Jones and Nat Sciver
IF YOU WEREN'T A CRICKETER? I'd be in the police
DESERT ISLAND DISC? Take That's Greatest Hits
FAVOURITE TV? Silent Witness
CRICKETING HEROES? Steve Waugh and Belinda Clark
NON-CRICKETING HEROES? Steffi Graf
ACCOMPLISHMENTS? Raising money for Macmillan nurses after sadly losing my dad to cancer
WHEN YOU RETIRE? I'd like to coach
FANTASY SLIP CORDON? Keeper: Miranda, 1st: David Beckham, 2nd: Steffi Graf, 3rd: Steve Waugh, Gully: Gary Barlow
TWITTER FEED? @Lottie2323

Batting	Mat	Inns	NO	Runs	HS	Ave	SR	100	50	Ct	St
Tests	21	39	5	1621	117	47.67		4	9	10	0
ODIs	178	167	21	5432	173*	37.20		8	42	48	0
T20Is	72	70	10	1921	92*	32.01	108.10	0	7	12	0

Bowling	Mat	Balls	Runs	Wkts	BBI	BBM	Ave	Econ	SR	5w	10
Tests	21	1118	577	12	2/28	2/54	48.08	3.09	93.1	0	0
ODIs	178	1627	1174	54	4/30	4/30	21.74	4.32	30.1	0	0
T20Is	72	297	321	9	3/21	3/21	35.66	6.48	33.0	0	0

GEORGIA ELWISS **RHB RMF**

FULL NAME: Georgia Amanda Elwiss
BORN: May 31, 1991, Wolverhampton, Staffordshire
SQUAD NO: 34
HEIGHT: 5ft 8in
NICKNAME: GG, Paddy
EDUCATION: Wolverhampton Girls' High School; Loughborough University
TEAMS: England Women, Sapphires, Staffordshire Women, Sussex Women
CAREER: ODI: 2011; T20I: 2011

WHO WOULD PLAY YOU IN A FILM OF YOUR LIFE? Miranda!
CAREER HIGHLIGHTS? Making my England debut in South Africa and winning the Player of the Series award against India in 2012
MOST MARKED CHARACTERISTIC? Maybe that I'm hardworking?
BEST PLAYER IN COUNTY CRICKET? Sarah Taylor, without a doubt!
TIPS FOR THE TOP? Nat Sciver and Amy Jones
IF YOU WEREN'T A CRICKETER? A singer on Broadway perhaps? I wish!
DESERT ISLAND DISC? Emeli Sandé – Our Version Of Events
FAVOURITE TV? Grey's Anatomy – it's an emotional rollercoaster!
CRICKETING HEROES? I used to love Allan Donald! I used to write him letters and everything. How lame! From the women's side Lucy Pearson was always the person I looked up to and I was very fortunate to be able to play alongside her a few times
ACCOMPLISHMENTS? Does nearly doing a skydive count?
WHEN YOU RETIRE? I'd like to be a nutritionist and set up my own practice
SURPRISING FACT? I had to have my tongue sewn back together after falling down the stairs and biting it off
FANTASY SLIP CORDON? Keeper: Sarah Taylor (I have to say that!), 1st: Me (it's either Sarah's or Swanny's), 2nd: Graeme Swann, 3rd: Alan Carr (for a bit of comedy value), Gully: Inspector Gadget (those arms would fly around to catch anything!)
TWITTER FEED: @Gelwiss

Batting	Mat	Inns	NO	Runs	HS	Ave	SR	100	50	Ct	St
ODIs	10	2	1	12	10	12.00	50.00	0	0	2	0
T20Is	5	-	-	-	-	-	-	-	-	0	0

Bowling	Mat	Balls	Runs	Wkts	BBI	BBM	Ave	Econ	SR	5w	10
ODIs	10	504	277	11	3/17	3/17	25.18	3.29	45.8	0	0
T20Is	5	85	81	4	2/30	2/30	20.25	5.71	21.2	0	0

TASH FARRANT

LHB LMF

FULL NAME: Natasha Eleni Farrant
BORN: May 29, 1996, Athens, Greece
SQUAD NO: 53
EDUCATION: Sevenoaks School
TEAMS: England Under-19s Women, England Women, Kent Women
CAREER: ODI: 2013; T20I: 2013

TWITTER FEED: @tashfarrant

NOTES: Left-arm seamer Farrant received her first England call up last June for the limited-overs series against Pakistan after she was initially picked out for the England Women's Talent Identification Programme. She impressed on her T20 debut, taking 2-15 as England secured a 70-run win, and was selected for the short-format leg of the 2014 Ashes tour. The Kent youngster featured in the first match of the T20 series at Hobart, bowling tidily as England claimed the win they needed to seal the Ashes. Made her ODI debut against West Indies at Port of Spain last November, taking 1-14 from seven overs in a comfortable victory

Batting	Mat	Inns	NO	Runs	HS	Ave	SR	100	50	Ct	St
ODIs	1	1	1	1	1*	-	12.50	0	0	0	0
T20Is	7	1	1	1	1*	-	100.00	0	0	0	0

Bowling	Mat	Balls	Runs	Wkts	BBI	BBM	Ave	Econ	SR	5w	10
ODIs	1	42	14	1	1/14	1/14	14.00	2.00	42.0	0	0
T20Is	7	161	138	4	2/15	2/15	34.50	5.14	40.2	0	0

LYDIA GREENWAY

LHB OB

FULL NAME: Lydia Sophie Greenway
BORN: August 6, 1985, Farnborough, Kent
SQUAD NO: 20
HEIGHT: 5ft 8in
NICKNAME: Lyd
EDUCATION: Hayes School; Loughborough College
TEAMS: England Women, Kent Women
CAREER: Test: 2003; ODI: 2003; T20I: 2004

BEST BATTING: 70 England vs South Africa, Shenley, 2003

FAMILY TIES? Our weekends were spent up at our local cricket club (Hayes CC, Kent) watching my dad play. My mum, brother and sister have all played too
WHO WOULD PLAY YOU IN A FILM OF YOUR LIFE? Sandra Bullock
CAREER HIGHLIGHTS? Winning two World Cups and being involved in Ashes victories
BEST PLAYER IN COUNTY CRICKET? Sarah Bartlett
TIPS FOR THE TOP? Nat Sciver has already made an impact at international level and Tash Farrant has taken her opportunities when they've been given to her
IF YOU WEREN'T A CRICKETER? Hopefully I'd still be playing some form of sport, probably hockey. Work-wise, I'd maybe be a personal trainer and still have some sort of involvement in cricket
DESERT ISLAND DISC? Hits Of The 80s
FAVOURITE TV? Friends – I could watch it all day!
CRICKETING HEROES? Adam Gilchrist and Marcus Trescothick
NON-CRICKETING HEROES? My family
ACCOMPLISHMENTS? Raising £10,000 for Breast Cancer Care by cycling from London to Paris with a friend
TWITTER FEED: @lydiagreenway

Batting	Mat	Inns	NO	Runs	HS	Ave	SR	100	50	Ct	St
Tests	12	20	1	315	70	16.57	30.37	0	2	14	0
ODIs	115	102	25	2354	125*	30.57	62.73	1	11	48	0
T20Is	65	58	17	1013	80*	24.70	98.73	0	2	36	0
Bowling	Mat	Balls	Runs	Wkts	BBI	BBM	Ave	Econ	SR	5w	10
Tests	12	-	-	-	-	-	-	-	-	-	-
ODIs	115	-	-	-	-	-	-	-	-	-	-
T20Is	65	-	-	-	-	-	-	-	-	-	-

JENNY GUNN

RHB RMF

FULL NAME: Jennifer Louise Gunn
BORN: May 9, 1986, Nottingham
SQUAD NO: 24
HEIGHT: 5ft 10in
NICKNAME: Trigger
EDUCATION: Rushcliffe Comprehensive
TEAMS: England Women, Nottinghamshire Women, South Australia Women
CAREER: Test: 2004; ODI: 2004; T20I: 2004

BEST BATTING: 44 England vs Australia, Perth, 2014
BEST BOWLING: 3-40 England vs Australia, Hove, 2005

WHO WOULD PLAY YOU IN A FILM OF YOUR LIFE? Sandra Bullock
CAREER HIGHLIGHTS? Winning five Ashes series and two World Cups
SUPERSTITIONS? I always jump sideways over the rope
MOST MARKED CHARACTERISTIC? It looks like I throw the ball when bowling
BEST PLAYER IN COUNTY CRICKET? Charlotte Edwards
IF YOU WEREN'T A CRICKETER? I'd be a chef, meteorologist or PE teacher
DESERT ISLAND DISC? Motown And Soul
FAVOURITE TV? Criminal Minds or any cooking show
CRICKETING HEROES? Glenn McGrath and Andrew Symonds
NON-CRICKETING HEROES? My dad
ACCOMPLISHMENTS? Gaining my 25m swimming badge and getting a distinction in ballet
CRICKET RULE YOU'D CHANGE? The toss should be held an hour before the game so you can warm up specifically for either batting or fielding
SURPRISING FACT? When I was younger I would make everyone be quiet so that I could sing Doris Day's Take Me Back To The Black Hills
TWITTER FEED: @gunnjenny

Batting	Mat	Inns	NO	Runs	HS	Ave	SR	100	50	Ct	St
Tests	10	17	0	322	44	18.94	30.06	0	0	5	0
ODIs	118	92	24	1422	73	20.91	56.42	0	5	36	0
T20Is	73	50	10	622	69	15.55	101.80	0	1	47	0

Bowling	Mat	Balls	Runs	Wkts	BBI	BBM	Ave	Econ	SR	5w	10
Tests	10	1967	586	24	3/40	4/67	24.41	1.78	81.9	0	0
ODIs	118	4874	3047	110	5/22	5/22	27.70	3.75	44.3	2	0
T20Is	73	767	828	41	5/18	5/18	20.19	6.47	18.7	1	0

DANIELLE HAZELL

FULL NAME: Danielle Hazell
BORN: May 13, 1988, Durham
SQUAD NO: 17
HEIGHT: 5ft 3in
NICKNAME: Pet
EDUCATION: Deerness Valley School
TEAMS: England Women, Sapphires, Yorkshire Women
CAREER: Test: 2011; ODI: 2009; T20I: 2009

ENGLAND WOMEN

BEST BATTING: 15 England vs Australia, Perth, 2014
BEST BOWLING: 2-32 England vs Australia, Sydney, 2011

WHO WOULD PLAY YOU IN A FILM OF YOUR LIFE? Rebel Wilson
CAREER HIGHLIGHTS? My England debut in 2009 in the West Indies
MOST MARKED CHARACTERISTIC? My northern accent
BEST PLAYER IN COUNTY CRICKET? Jenny Gunn
IF YOU WEREN'T A CRICKETER? I'd be a property tycoon
DESERT ISLAND DISC? Maria McKee – Show Me Heaven
FAVOURITE TV? Neighbours
CRICKETING HEROES? Ricky Ponting
NON-CRICKETING HEROES? Alan Shearer
FANTASY SLIP CORDON? Keeper: Me, 1st: Peter Andre, 2nd: Gavin Henson, 3rd: Alan Shearer, Gully: My mam
TWITTER FEED: @dani1788

Batting	Mat	Inns	NO	Runs	HS	Ave	SR	100	50	Ct	St
Tests	3	5	1	28	15	7.00	17.17	0	0	1	0
ODIs	33	16	3	177	24*	13.61	88.94	0	0	6	0
T20Is	48	22	7	145	18*	9.66	86.82	0	0	7	0

Bowling	Mat	Balls	Runs	Wkts	BBI	BBM	Ave	Econ	SR	5w	10
Tests	3	390	204	2	2/32	2/52	102.00	3.13	195.0	0	0
ODIs	33	1509	994	31	3/22	3/22	32.06	3.95	48.6	0	0
T20Is	48	1097	951	55	4/12	4/12	17.29	5.20	19.9	0	0

AMY JONES

RHB WK

FULL NAME: Amy Ellen Jones
BORN: June 13, 1993, Solihull, Warwickshire
SQUAD NO: 40
HEIGHT: 5ft 9in
NICKNAME: Jonesy
EDUCATION: John Willmott School; Loughborough College
TEAMS: Diamonds, England Academy Women, England Under-19s Women, England Women, Warwickshire Women
CAREER: ODI: 2013; T20I: 2013

FAMILY TIES? I was the first person in my family to play competitive cricket. My younger sister Emily played for Warwickshire age-group teams

WHO WOULD PLAY YOU IN A FILM OF YOUR LIFE? Fat Amy from Pitch Perfect!

CAREER HIGHLIGHTS? In terms of my own performances, my debut in India during the World Cup in 2013 was a definite highlight where I batted No.7 and made 41. The game was shown live on Sky Sports which definitely added to the pressure! As a team, the recent Ashes win in Australia was incredible and a tour I will never forget

SUPERSTITIONS? I put my left pad on before my right but that's it really

MOST MARKED CHARACTERISTIC? I've got a disproportionately long torso

BEST PLAYER IN COUNTY CRICKET? Charlotte Edwards

TIPS FOR THE TOP? Jess Watson from Yorkshire and Marie Kelly from Warwickshire

IF YOU WEREN'T A CRICKETER? I'd probably be playing football

DESERT ISLAND DISC? Anything by The Script

FAVOURITE TV? Grey's Anatomy

CRICKETING HEROES? Matt Prior

NON-CRICKETING HEROES? Sir Chris Hoy

ACCOMPLISHMENTS? Representing Aston Villa until U16

WHEN YOU RETIRE? I'd like to stay in the game, so probably coaching

SURPRISING FACT? I can sleep anywhere!

FANTASY SLIP CORDON? Keeper: Me, 1st: Miranda Hart, 2nd: Graeme Swann, 3rd: Ed Sheeran, Gully: Uncle Bryn from Gavin And Stacey

TWITTER FEED? @amyjones313

Batting	Mat	Inns	NO	Runs	HS	Ave	SR	100	50	Ct	St
ODIs	2	1	0	41	41	41.00	83.67	0	0	1	0
T20Is	5	4	0	21	14	5.25	61.76	0	0	0	0

Bowling	Mat	Balls	Runs	Wkts	BBI	BBM	Ave	Econ	SR	5w	10
ODIs	2	-	-	-	-	-	-	-	-	-	-
T20Is	5	-	-	-	-	-	-	-	-	-	-

HEATHER KNIGHT RHB RM

FULL NAME: Heather Clare Knight
BORN: December 26, 1990, Plymouth
SQUAD NO: 5
HEIGHT: 5ft 7in
NICKNAME: Trev
EDUCATION: Plymstock School; Cardiff University
TEAMS: Berkshire Women; Diamonds, England Academy Women, England Women, Rubies
CAREER: Test: 2011; ODI: 2010; T20I: 2010

BEST BATTING: 157 England vs Australia, Wormsley, 2013

FAMILY TIES? My brother played age-group county cricket for Devon and my dad was a seasoned bowler in the back garden
WHO WOULD PLAY YOU IN A FILM OF YOUR LIFE? Miranda Hart
CAREER HIGHLIGHTS? Winning the Ashes for the first time and being named Player of the Series in 2013
SUPERSTITIONS? I have to wear my lucky pants in every game I play for England
MOST MARKED CHARACTERISTIC? My large earlobes
TIP FOR THE TOP? Nat Sciver – talented allrounder who can also pull some serious shapes!
IF YOU WEREN'T A CRICKETER? I'd be moaning that I wasn't a cricketer
DESERT ISLAND DISC? The Verve – Urban Hymns
FAVOURITE TV? Dexter
CRICKETING HEROES? Mike Atherton, Marcus Trescothick
NON-CRICKETING HEROES? Steve Redgrave
ACCOMPLISHMENTS? Somehow getting a decent degree at Cardiff in Physiology whilst playing international cricket
WHEN YOU RETIRE? I'll go skiing – I love it but I haven't been able to do it whilst I'm playing
SURPRISING FACT? Two of my toes are slightly webbed!
TWITTER FEED: @Heatherknight55

Batting	Mat	Inns	NO	Runs	HS	Ave	SR	100	50	Ct	St
Tests	3	6	0	197	157	32.83	43.10	1	0	4	0
ODIs	42	38	9	846	72	29.17	62.25	0	5	10	0
T20Is	11	10	1	59	13	6.55	81.94	0	0	3	0

Bowling	Mat	Balls	Runs	Wkts	BBI	BBM	Ave	Econ	SR	5w	10
Tests	3	12	12	0	-	-	-	6.00	-	0	0
ODIs	42	72	48	3	2/15	2/15	16.00	4.00	24.0	0	0
T20Is	11	-	-	-	-	-	-	-	-	-	-

BETH LANGSTON

RHB RM

FULL NAME: Bethany Alicia Langston
BORN: September 6, 1992, Harold Wood, Essex
SQUAD NO: 42
HEIGHT: 5ft 7in
NICKNAME: Langers
EDUCATION: Hall Mead School; Coopers' Company and Coborn School Sixth Form; Loughborough University
TEAMS: England Cricket Board Development Women's XI, England Women, Essex Women
CAREER: T20I: 2013

FAMILY TIES? My dad and three older brothers all played cricket so I was always playing at the local cricket club

WHO WOULD PLAY YOU IN A FILM OF YOUR LIFE? Jennifer Lawrence

CAREER HIGHLIGHTS? Making my England debut in the West Indies in 2013

SUPERSTITIONS? When doing boundary laps I always have to walk to the right for runs when we are batting or to the left for wickets when we're fielding

MOST MARKED CHARACTERISTIC? Playing in glasses

BEST PLAYER IN COUNTY CRICKET? Charlotte Edwards

TIPS FOR THE TOP? Cordelia Griffith from Essex

IF YOU WEREN'T A CRICKETER? I would consider becoming a postwoman

DESERT ISLAND DISC? Kaiser Chiefs – Employment

FAVOURITE TV? Grey's Anatomy, Misfits

CRICKETING HEROES? Jimmy Anderson

NON-CRICKETING HEROES? Katherine Grainger

ACCOMPLISHMENTS? I was first violin in my secondary school orchestra

WHEN YOU RETIRE? I'd like to sit down with a hot chocolate and watch a box set

SURPRISING FACT? I am a distant relative of the inventor of the television John Logie Baird – so my dad tells me anyway!

FANTASY SLIP CORDON? Keeper: Nessa from Gavin And Stacey, 1st: Dr Sheldon Cooper, 2nd: Myself, 3rd: Rylan Clark, Gully: Maggie Smith

TWITTER FEED: @B_Langers92

Batting	Mat	Inns	NO	Runs	HS	Ave	SR	100	50	Ct	St
T20Is	2	-	-	-	-	-	-	-	-	1	0

Bowling	Mat	Balls	Runs	Wkts	BBI	BBM	Ave	Econ	SR	5w	10
T20Is	2	48	44	1	1/16	1/16	44.00	5.50	48.0	0	0

LAURA MARSH RHB OB

FULL NAME: Laura Alexandra Marsh
BORN: December 5, 1986, Pembury, Kent
SQUAD NO: 7
HEIGHT: 5ft 5in
NICKNAME: Marshy, Boggy
EDUCATION: Brighton College;
Loughborough University
TEAMS: England Development Squad
Women, England Women, Kent Women,
Rubies, Sussex Women
CAREER: Test: 2006; ODI: 2006; T20I: 2007

BEST BATTING: 55 England vs Australia, Wormsley, 2013
BEST BOWLING: 3-44 England vs India, Leicester, 2006

FAMILY TIES? Both my dad and brother played a bit but not at a representative level
CAREER HIGHLIGHTS? Winning ODI and T20 World Cups in 2009. Travelling to fantastic parts of the world and playing at amazing grounds. Playing with and meeting some great friends and teammates
MOST MARKED CHARACTERISTIC? My small head
BEST PLAYER IN COUNTY CRICKET? Nat Sciver
TIPS FOR THE TOP? Natasha Farrant – fast left-arm seamer who I play county cricket with at Kent. Nat Sciver – a hard-hitting allrounder and skillful bowler. Amy Jones – wicketkeeper-batsman and a natural talent
IF YOU WEREN'T A CRICKETER? I'd maybe be a golfer but definitely something in sport
FAVOURITE TV? Homeland or Dexter
WHEN YOU RETIRE? I want to have a family
SURPRISING FACT? I was a national javelin champion when I was 13
FANTASY SLIP CORDON? Keeper: AB de Villiers (great bum), 1st: Myself (good view!), 2nd: David Beckham (hero), 3rd: Mark Lane (great banter and his sledging would be priceless), Gully: Swanny (all-round comedy value)
TWITTER FEED: @lauramarsh7

Batting	Mat	Inns	NO	Runs	HS	Ave	SR	100	50	Ct	St
Tests	6	8	0	110	55	13.75	21.91	0	1	4	0
ODIs	69	41	7	479	67	14.08	66.34	0	1	14	0
T20Is	55	50	5	729	54	16.20	99.86	0	1	6	0

Bowling	Mat	Balls	Runs	Wkts	BBI	BBM	Ave	Econ	SR	5w	10
Tests	6	1289	475	14	3/44	4/83	33.92	2.21	92.0	0	0
ODIs	69	3540	2287	83	5/15	5/15	27.55	3.87	42.6	1	0
T20Is	55	1231	1073	51	3/17	3/17	21.03	5.22	24.1	0	0

NATALIE SCIVER

RHB RM

FULL NAME: Natalie Ruth Sciver
BORN: August 20, 1992, Tokyo, Japan
SQUAD NO: 39
HEIGHT: 5ft 10in
NICKNAME: Skiver
EDUCATION: Epsom College; Loughborough University
TEAMS: England Women, Rubies, Surrey Women
CAREER: Test: 2014; ODI: 2013; T20I: 2013

BEST BATTING: 49 England vs Australia, Perth, 2014
BEST BOWLING: 1-30 England vs Australia, Perth, 2014

WHO WOULD PLAY YOU IN A FILM OF YOUR LIFE? I'd love Sandra Bullock to play me, although I'm not sure she's even heard of cricket!
CAREER HIGHLIGHTS? Being back-to-back Ashes winners in 2013 and 2014
SUPERSTITIONS? Not yet, I'm sure as I play more I'll gain some though
MOST MARKED CHARACTERISTIC? Probably my two-tone encouragement on the pitch: either really high-pitched or really low-pitched depending on the situation
BEST PLAYER IN COUNTY CRICKET? Charlotte Edwards
TIPS FOR THE TOP? Jess Watson, Jodie Dibble
DESERT ISLAND DISC? Muse – Black Holes And Revelations
FAVOURITE TV? Desperate Housewives, Grey's Anatomy
CRICKETING HEROES? Andrew Flintoff, Ross Taylor
NON-CRICKETING HEROES? David Beckham
ACCOMPLISHMENTS? Holding David Beckham's hand at a football match!
WHEN YOU RETIRE? I would love to live on the beach and learn to surf
SURPRISING FACT? When I lived in Poland I came fourth out of all the girls in the country in a snowboarding slalom competition
TWITTER FEED: @natsciver

Batting	Mat	Inns	NO	Runs	HS	Ave	SR	100	50	Ct	St
Tests	1	2	0	72	49	36.00	33.33	0	0	1	0
ODIs	10	6	3	156	57	52.00	110.63	0	1	1	0
T20Is	13	12	3	184	37*	20.44	91.54	0	0	8	0

Bowling	Mat	Balls	Runs	Wkts	BBI	BBM	Ave	Econ	SR	5w	10
Tests	1	56	30	1	1/30	1/30	30.00	3.21	56.0	0	0
ODIs	10	256	182	10	3/19	3/19	18.20	4.26	25.6	0	0
T20Is	13	186	226	8	4/21	4/21	28.25	7.29	23.2	0	0

ANYA SHRUBSOLE — RHB RFM

FULL NAME: Anya Shrubsole
BORN: December 7, 1991, Bath, Somerset
SQUAD NO: 41
HEIGHT: 5ft 11in
NICKNAME: Hoof
EDUCATION: Hayesfield School;
Loughborough University
TEAMS: England Women, Rubies, Somerset
Women
CAREER: Test: 2013; ODI: 2008; T20I: 2008

ENGLAND WOMEN

BEST BATTING: 9 England vs Australia, Wormsley, 2013
BEST BOWLING: 4-51 England vs Australia, Perth, 2014

FAMILY TIES? My dad played minor counties cricket
WHO WOULD PLAY YOU IN A FILM OF YOUR LIFE? Jennifer Lawrence
CAREER HIGHLIGHTS? Winning the World Cup in 2009 and back-to-back Ashes wins
SUPERSTITIONS? Not moving when there is a good partnership
MOST MARKED CHARACTERISTIC? Knowledge of all things sport
BEST PLAYER IN COUNTY CRICKET? Sarah Taylor and Marcus Trescothick
TIPS FOR THE TOP? Nat Sciver and Sam Robson
IF YOU WEREN'T A CRICKETER? I'd be doing what I'm doing now, a degree
DESERT ISLAND DISC? Stevie Wonder – Songs In The Key Of Life
FAVOURITE TV? Grey's Anatomy
CRICKETING HEROES? Michael Holding and Malcolm Marshall
NON-CRICKETING HEROES? Nelson Mandela and Sir Steve Redgrave
ACCOMPLISHMENTS? Spending time working with autistic children
SURPRISING FACT? I'm very scared of dogs
FANTASY SLIP CORDON? Keeper: Micky Flanagan, 1st: Iron Man, 2nd: Myself, 3rd: Ryan
Gosling, Gully: Rebel Wilson
TWITTER FEED: @Anya_shrubsole

Batting	Mat	Inns	NO	Runs	HS	Ave	SR	100	50	Ct	St
Tests	2	3	0	16	9	5.33	44.44	0	0	1	0
ODIs	23	5	3	36	15*	18.00	72.00	0	0	9	0
T20Is	25	4	2	2	1*	1.00	40.00	0	0	8	0

Bowling	Mat	Balls	Runs	Wkts	BBI	BBM	Ave	Econ	SR	5w	10
Tests	2	480	204	10	4/51	7/99	20.40	2.55	48.0	0	0
ODIs	23	1021	708	24	5/17	5/17	29.50	4.16	42.5	1	0
T20Is	25	456	467	31	5/11	5/11	15.06	6.14	14.7	1	0

SARAH TAYLOR

RHB WK

FULL NAME: Sarah Jane Taylor
BORN: May 20, 1989, London Hospital, Whitechapel, London
SQUAD NO: 30
HEIGHT: 5ft 8in
NICKNAME: Squirt, Dave, Taylor
EDUCATION: Brighton College, East Sussex
TEAMS: England Development Squad Women, England Women, Rubies, Sussex Women
CAREER: Test: 2006; ODI: 2006; T20I: 2006

BEST BATTING: 38* England vs Australia, Wormsley, 2013

CAREER HIGHLIGHTS? The year 2009 as a whole: winning two World Cups and an ODI series against Australia, as well as retaining the Ashes. Scoring a hundred at Lord's
SUPERSTITIONS? I always have to put my left pad on first
MOST MARKED CHARACTERISTIC? My stupid voices!
TIP FOR THE TOP? Nat Sciver
DESERT ISLAND DISC? A Marianas Trench album. Or if it had to be one song then I would say Tidal Wave by Sub Focus
FAVOURITE TV? White Collar
CRICKETING HEROES? Graham Thorpe and Rebecca Rolls (New Zealand)
NON-CRICKETING HEROES? Steffi Graf – I used to play tennis and I just loved watching her play
ACCOMPLISHMENTS? Passing my driving test!
WHEN YOU RETIRE? I want to become an accountant, move to New Zealand, earn loads of money and live the dream
FANTASY SLIP CORDON? Keeper: Myself, 1st: Fat Amy (from Pitch Perfect), 2nd: Michael Clarke (a great pair of hands), 3rd: Lee Evans (he would make me laugh so much), Gully: David Attenborough (listening to his voice in person would be awesome!)
TWITTER FEED: @Sarah_Taylor30

Batting	Mat	Inns	NO	Runs	HS	Ave	SR	100	50	Ct	St
Tests	6	11	1	196	38*	19.60	49.87	0	0	11	2
ODIs	88	81	9	2856	129	39.66	79.42	5	14	68	35
T20Is	58	56	8	1505	77	31.35	111.23	0	11	16	32

Bowling	Mat	Balls	Runs	Wkts	BBI	BBM	Ave	Econ	SR	5w	10
Tests	6	-	-	-	-	-	-	-	-	-	-
ODIs	88	-	-	-	-	-	-	-	-	-	-
T20Is	58	-	-	-	-	-	-	-	-	-	-

FRAN WILSON

RHB OB

FULL NAME: Frances Claire Wilson
BORN: November 7, 1991, Farnham, Surrey
SQUAD NO: 35
HEIGHT: 5ft 4in
EDUCATION: Malmesbury Secondary School; University of Bath
TEAMS: England Academy Women, England Cricket Board Development Women's XI, England Women, Somerset Women
CAREER: ODI: 2010; T20I: 2010

ENGLAND WOMEN

WHO WOULD PLAY YOU IN A FILM OF YOUR LIFE? Sandra Bullock
CAREER HIGHLIGHTS? Making my England debut against Sri Lanka in 2010
SUPERSTITIONS? Nope, I'm not superstitious in the slightest
MOST MARKED CHARACTERISTIC? Others would say I'm gullible but I would say I'm trusting!
BEST PLAYER IN COUNTY CRICKET? Charlotte Edwards is obviously someone you would rather have on your team! Heather Knight is capable of consistently scoring big runs too
TIP FOR THE TOP? Tash Farrant
IF YOU WEREN'T A CRICKETER? I would be at university or travelling
DESERT ISLAND DISC? Anything by Maroon 5, The 1975 or Justin Timberlake
FAVOURITE TV? It's embarrassing but I love any kind of reality TV. Made In Chelsea is probably my favourite, followed by Geordie Shore
CRICKETING HEROES? I have always really admired the way Eoin Morgan bats
ACCOMPLISHMENTS? I used to play football and I was very proud to be made captain of the University of Bath first team. Also, working as a sport nutritionist intern for Gloucestershire CCC and the ECB during my work placement year at university was a great personal accomplishment
WHEN YOU RETIRE? I'm studying to become a sport nutritionist, so hopefully I'll go into this career path after cricket. I'd like to have my own business one day and I'd also love to travel the world
SURPRISING FACT? I went through a phase of sleep-eating fruit… could be worse!
TWITTER FEED: @fwilson07

Batting	Mat	Inns	NO	Runs	HS	Ave	SR	100	50	Ct	St
ODIs	2	1	0	0	0	0.00	0.00	0	0	2	0
T20Is	5	4	1	33	17	11.00	86.84	0	0	1	0
Bowling	Mat	Balls	Runs	Wkts	BBI	BBM	Ave	Econ	SR	5w	10
ODIs	2	-	-	-	-	-	-	-	-	-	-
T20Is	5	-	-	-	-	-	-	-	-	-	-

517

LAUREN WINFIELD RHB WK

FULL NAME: Lauren Winfield
BORN: August 16, 1990, York
SQUAD NO: 58
HEIGHT: 5ft 6in
NICKNAME: Moose
EDUCATION: Loughborough University
TEAMS: Diamonds, England Women, Yorkshire Women
CAREER: ODI: 2013; T20I: 2013

WHO WOULD PLAY YOU IN A FILM OF YOUR LIFE? Rebel Wilson, for no other reason than the fact that she is absolutely hilarious
CAREER HIGHLIGHTS? So far I would have to say making my England debut and winning back-to-back Ashes series
SUPERSTITIONS? Nothing as such. As long my boots are tied and my pads are strapped then I'm ready to go! I do like to chew gum when I bat though
MOST MARKED CHARACTERISTIC? My distinctive laugh
BEST PLAYER IN COUNTY CRICKET? Charlotte Edwards
TIPS FOR THE TOP? Jess Watson and Georgia Hennessy
IF YOU WEREN'T A CRICKETER? I'd probably further my studies and become a nutritionist, strength and conditioning coach or personal trainer
DESERT ISLAND DISC? Lighthouse Family – High and Ocean Drive
FAVOURITE TV? I'm not really a TV person but I do love Geordie Shore
CRICKETING HEROES? Graham Dilley, Alec Stewart and AB de Villiers
NON-CRICKETING HEROES? My mum and dad – they're great!
ACCOMPLISHMENTS? Playing football for Leeds United
SURPRISING FACT? I was the size of my mum's forearm when I was born
CRICKET RULE YOU'D CHANGE? That you can't be run out backing up. There is nothing more annoying as a batter
TWITTER FEED: @lozwinfield

Batting	Mat	Inns	NO	Runs	HS	Ave	SR	100	50	Ct	St
ODIs	5	5	2	67	31	22.33	55.83	0	0	1	0
T20Is	8	8	1	87	36	12.42	87.87	0	0	3	0

Bowling	Mat	Balls	Runs	Wkts	BBI	BBM	Ave	Econ	SR	5w	10
ODIs	5	-	-	-	-	-	-	-	-	-	-
T20Is	8	-	-	-	-	-	-	-	-	-	-

FULL NAME: Danielle Nicole Wyatt
BORN: April 22, 1991, Stoke-on-Trent, Staffordshire
SQUAD NO: 28
HEIGHT: 5ft 4in
NICKNAME: Dan, Danni, Waggy, Wag, Waggo
EDUCATION: St Peter's High School; Stoke-on-Trent Sixth Form College
TEAMS: Emeralds, England Women, Staffordshire Women
CAREER: ODI: 2010; T20I: 2010

ENGLAND WOMEN

FAMILY TIES? My dad plays cricket for my men's club Whitmore. My older brother Ryan used to play but quit when I started doing better than him and now my little brother Max plays for Whitmore and Staffordshire U14

CAREER HIGHLIGHTS? Beating Australia 4-1 in a T20 series in Australia with such an inexperienced team and beating Australia at Wormsley to retain our No.1 status in ODI cricket

SUPERSTITIONS? No, although if I do well in a game I'll wear the same socks the next game

MOST MARKED CHARACTERISTIC? I like to be known as a happy person who likes living life to the full! YOLO!

TIPS FOR THE TOP? There are a lot of good youngsters coming through, especially Nat Sciver and Amy Jones

IF YOU WEREN'T A CRICKETER? Maybe a window cleaner or I'd run my own car cleaning company. I love cleaning cars!

FAVOURITE TV? Coronation Street. I don't watch much TV but I love Corrie. I sit and watch it with my mum and a cuppa, without fail! It's a family tradition

CRICKETING HEROES? Andrew Flintoff and Graeme Swann

NON-CRICKETING HEROES? David Beckham. I can't believe I can say I've actually met him as well!

WHEN YOU RETIRE? I'll get married, have kids and have my own restaurant on the beach

SURPRISING FACT? I fell out of a tree when I was 10 after watching Tarzan with my brother and broke my wrist and foot. Awkward!

TWITTER FEED: @Danni_Wyatt

Batting	Mat	Inns	NO	Runs	HS	Ave	SR	100	50	Ct	St
ODIs	32	25	3	371	40	16.86	66.13	0	0	5	0
T20Is	50	35	6	395	41	13.62	102.33	0	0	7	0

Bowling	Mat	Balls	Runs	Wkts	BBI	BBM	Ave	Econ	SR	5w	10
ODIs	32	800	660	25	3/7	3/7	26.40	4.95	32.0	0	0
T20Is	50	705	666	46	4/11	4/11	14.47	5.66	15.3	0	0

The
Umpires

ROB BAILEY

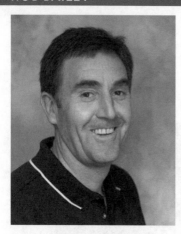

NAME: Robert John Bailey
BORN: October 28, 1963, Biddulph, Staffordshire
HEIGHT: 6ft 3in
NICKNAME: Bailers
APPOINTED TO FIRST-CLASS LIST: 2006
INTERNATIONAL PANEL: 2011-
ODIS UMPIRED: 8 (plus 3 as TV umpire)
T20IS UMPIRED: 10 (plus 3 as TV umpire)
COUNTIES AS PLAYER: Northamptonshire, Derbyshire
ROLE: Right-hand bat; off-spin bowler
COUNTY DEBUT: 1982 (Northamptonshire), 2000 (Derbyshire)
TEST DEBUT: 1988
ODI DEBUT: 1985

NOTES: Officiated at T20 Finals Day every year since 2008. Umpired five ODIs and five T20Is in 2013

Batting	Mat	Inns	NO	Runs	HS	Ave	SR	100	50	Ct	St
Tests	4	8	0	119	43	14.87	36.50	0	0	0	0
ODIs	4	4	2	137	43*	68.50	69.89	0	0	1	0
First-class	374	628	89	21844	224*	40.52	-	47	111	272	0
List A	396	376	65	12076	153*	38.82	-	10	79	111	0

Bowling	Mat	Balls	Runs	Wkts	BBI	BBM	Ave	Econ	SR	5w	10
Tests	4	-	-	-	-	-	-	-	-	-	-
ODIs	4	36	25	0	-	-	-	4.16	-	0	0
First-class	374	9713	5144	121	5/54	-	42.51	3.17	80.2	2	0
List A	396	3092	2564	72	5/45	5/45	35.61	4.97	42.9	1	0

NEIL BAINTON

NAME: Neil Laurence Bainton
BORN: October 2, 1970, Romford, Essex
HEIGHT: 5ft 8in
APPOINTED TO FIRST-CLASS LIST: 2006

UMPIRES

FAVOURITE GROUND? Colwyn Bay and Arundel. Most outgrounds are nice to go to
FIRST COUNTY PLAYER YOU GAVE OUT? I can't remember, but it was probably wrong!
CAREER HIGHLIGHT AS AN UMPIRE? Being appointed to the first-class list and my two
Tests as fourth umpire
NOTES: Has been reserve umpire in two Tests, two ODIs and two T20Is, as well as umpiring
in five women's ODIs and two women's T20Is

MARK BENSON

NAME: Mark Richard Benson
BORN: July 6, 1958, Shoreham, Sussex
HEIGHT: 5ft 9in
NICKNAME: Benny
APPOINTED TO FIRST-CLASS LIST: 2000
INTERNATIONAL PANEL: 2004-2006
ELITE PANEL: 2006-2010
TESTS UMPIRED: 28 (plus 9 as TV umpire)
ODIS UMPIRED: 72 (plus 25 as TV umpire)
T20IS UMPIRED: 19 (plus 6 as TV umpire)
COUNTY AS PLAYER: Kent
ROLE: Left-hand bat; off-spin bowler
COUNTY DEBUT: 1980
TEST DEBUT: 1986
ODI DEBUT: 1986

RITUALS OR QUIRKS? I like to change my hat and shoes every session
CAREER HIGHLIGHT AS AN UMPIRE? Officiating at the inaugural World T20 final in 2007 between India and Pakistan
MOST MEMORABLE DISMISSAL? I gave Mark Boucher out lbw in ODI when it pitched outside leg, was too high, going down leg and he also hit it. I was joking with him after (yes, we both saw the funny side) that it was probably a no ball as well!
FAVOURITE COUNTY GROUND? The old Southampton ground
SOMETHING WE DON'T KNOW ABOUT YOU? I'm ranked in the top 15 bridge players in Kent. I scored a century against every first-class county

Batting	Mat	Inns	NO	Runs	HS	Ave	SR	100	50	Ct	St
Tests	1	2	0	51	30	25.50	31.48	0	0	0	0
ODIs	1	1	0	24	24	24.00	41.37	0	0	0	0
First-class	292	491	34	18387	257	40.23	-	48	99	140	0
List A	269	257	11	7838	119	31.86	-	5	53	68	0

Bowling	Mat	Balls	Runs	Wkts	BBI	BBM	Ave	Econ	SR	5w	10
Tests	1	-	-	-	-	-	-	-	-	-	-
ODIs	1	-	-	-	-	-	-	-	-	-	-
First-class	292	467	493	5	2/55	-	98.60	6.33	93.4	0	0
List A	269	-	-	-	-	-	-	-	-	-	-

MARTIN BODENHAM

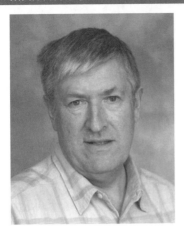

NAME: Martin John Dale Bodenham
BORN: April 23, 1950, Brighton
HEIGHT: 6ft 1in
APPOINTED TO FIRST-CLASS LIST: 2009
COUNTY AS PLAYER: Played for Sussex in a number of 2nd XI matches
ROLE: Right-hand bat; wicketkeeper

UMPIRES

NOTES: He is the first person to referee in football's Premier League and umpire first-class cricket. As a referee, he was in charge of three FA Cup semi-finals and the League Cup final in 1997, as well as being fourth official for the European Cup final between AC Milan and Barcelona in 1994. In his career he sent off Vinnie Jones for threatening to break an opponent's legs and gave Roy Keane a yellow card while he was going off on a stretcher. Umpired in five women's ODIs and five women's T20Is

NICK COOK

NAME: Nicholas Grant Billson Cook
BORN: June 17, 1956, Leicester
HEIGHT: 6ft
NICKNAME: Beast
APPOINTED TO FIRST-CLASS LIST: 2009
COUNTIES AS PLAYER: Leicestershire, Northamptonshire
ROLE: Right-hand bat; slow left-arm bowler
COUNTY DEBUT: 1978 (Leicestershire), 1986 (Northamptonshire)
TEST DEBUT: 1983
ODI DEBUT: 1984

RITUALS OR QUIRKS? I like to walk out to the left of my colleague
SOMETHING WE DON'T KNOW ABOUT YOU? I have two Siamese cats
NOTES: Officiated as TV umpire in the CB40 final at Lord's in 2011. Reserve umpire in two Tests, including last summer's Ashes Test at Old Trafford. Officiated in one women's Test, four women's ODIs and at 2012 T20 Finals Day

Batting	Mat	Inns	NO	Runs	HS	Ave	SR	100	50	Ct	St
Tests	15	25	4	179	31	8.52	23.58	0	0	5	0
ODIs	3	-	-	-	-	-	-	-	-	2	0
First-class	356	365	96	3137	75	11.66	-	0	4	197	0
List A	223	89	36	491	23	9.26	-	0	0	74	0

Bowling	Mat	Balls	Runs	Wkts	BBI	BBM	Ave	Econ	SR	5w	10
Tests	15	4174	1689	52	6/65	11/83	32.48	2.42	80.2	4	1
ODIs	3	144	95	5	2/18	2/18	19.00	3.95	28.8	0	0
First-class	356	64460	25507	879	7/34	-	29.01	2.37	73.3	31	4
List A	223	10077	6812	200	4/22	4/22	34.06	4.05	50.3	0	0

NIGEL COWLEY

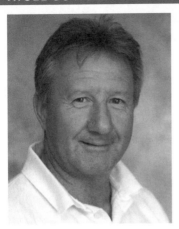

NAME: Nigel Geoffrey Charles Cowley
BORN: March 1, 1953, Shaftesbury, Dorset
HEIGHT: 5ft 7in
NICKNAME: Dougall
APPOINTED TO FIRST-CLASS LIST: 2000
COUNTIES AS PLAYER: Hampshire, Glamorgan
ROLE: Right-hand bat; off-spin bowler
COUNTY DEBUT: 1974 (Hampshire), 1990 (Glamorgan)

NOTES: Has stood as reserve umpire in four Tests and three ODIs and officiated in one women's ODI and one women's T20I

Batting	Mat	Inns	NO	Runs	HS	Ave	SR	100	50	Ct	St
First-class	271	375	62	7309	109*	23.35	-	2	36	105	0
List A	305	226	45	3022	74	16.69	-	0	5	69	0

Bowling	Mat	Balls	Runs	Wkts	BBI	BBM	Ave	Econ	SR	5w	10
First-class	271	32662	14879	437	6/48		34.04	2.73	74.7	5	0
List A	305	11704	8038	248	5/24	5/24	32.41	4.12	47.1	1	0

JEFF EVANS

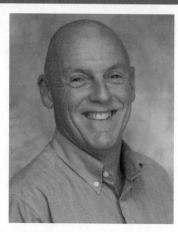

NAME: Jeffrey Howard Evans
BORN: August 7, 1954, Llanelli, Wales
HEIGHT: 5ft 8in
APPOINTED TO FIRST-CLASS LIST: 2001

CAREER HIGHLIGHT AS AN UMPIRE? Yet to come (hopefully)

FAVOURITE COUNTY GROUND? Worcester

MOST MEMORABLE DISMISSAL? I gave Brian Lara out lbw first ball of the Indian Cricket League

FUNNIEST MOMENT ON A CRICKET FIELD? Watching Vanburn Holder call "play" with the band of the Royal Gurkha Regiment playing the bagpipes at mid-off

BEST TEA ON THE COUNTY CIRCUIT? Lord's

FAVOURITE PASTIMES OUTSIDE OF CRICKET? Walking, rugby and skiing

SOMETHING WE DON'T KNOW ABOUT YOU? I spent the afternoon with Liam Neeson at a cousin's BBQ in London

NOTES: Played league cricket in South Wales as a right-hand bat. Has stood as reserve umpire in four Tests, two ODIs and two T20Is

STEVE GALE

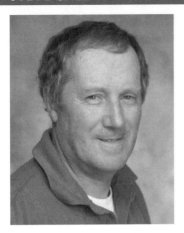

NAME: Stephen Clifford Gale
BORN: June 3, 1952, Shrewsbury, Shropshire
APPOINTED TO FIRST-CLASS LIST: 2011
ROLE: Right-hand bat; leg-spin bowler

UMPIRES

FAVOURITE COUNTY GROUND? I enjoy many county grounds. I did my first Championship game at Durham and Arundel is a great setting

FIRST COUNTY PLAYER YOU GAVE OUT? Jim Troughton

RITUALS OR QUIRKS? I always count the number of deliveries with six pound coins

CAREER HIGHLIGHT AS AN UMPIRE? England Lions vs Australia

FAVOURITE PASTIMES OUTSIDE OF CRICKET? I play a bit of golf and walk the Cornwall coast path

FUNNIEST MOMENT ON A CRICKET FIELD? During the Lions vs Australia match a bail flew about 50 yards and as a fielder went to collect it a large seagull picked it up and it sat on the pavilion for about five minutes with the bail in its beak

BEST TEA ON THE COUNTY CIRCUIT? The catering at most grounds is very good

SOMETHING WE DON'T KNOW ABOUT YOU? I umpired my first game at Lord's exactly 24 years to the date in August that I played there for Shrewsbury

NOTES: Gale spent three seasons on the reserve list following a playing career representing Shropshire in minor counties cricket between 1975 and 1987 before joining the full list in 2011

Batting	Mat	Inns	NO	Runs	HS	Ave	SR	100	50	Ct	St
List A	5	5	0	156	68	31.20	0	1	0	0	0

Bowling	Mat	Balls	Runs	Wkts	BBI	BBM	Ave	Econ	SR	5w	10
List A	5	-	-	-	-	-	-	-	-	-	-

STEVE GARRATT

NAME: Steven Arthur Garratt
BORN: July 5, 1953, Nottingham
HEIGHT: 6ft 2in
NICKNAME: Trigger
APPOINTED TO FIRST-CLASS LIST: 2008

RITUALS OR QUIRKS? I have no particular quirks or superstitions

CAREER HIGHLIGHT AS AN UMPIRE? My appointment to the first-class umpires panel in 2008

FAVOURITE GROUND? Lord's apart, probably Worcester or Canterbury

FUNNIEST MOMENT ON A CRICKET FIELD? At Canterbury in 2011, during the England Lions' match against Australia, an English batsman was bowled and one of the bails spiralled into the outfield. Before it could be retrieved a seagull flew down, picked it up in its beak and flew off with it!

BEST TEA ON THE COUNTY CIRCUIT? Lord's is the best ground for food, although Leicester is also very good

FAVOURITE PASTIMES OUTSIDE OF CRICKET? Watching sport and walking

SOMETHING WE DON'T KNOW ABOUT YOU? In 1980 I played rugby union at Murrayfield in the National Police Knockout Cup final

MICHAEL GOUGH

NAME: Michael Andrew Gough
BORN: December 18, 1979, Hartlepool
HEIGHT: 6ft 5in
NICKNAME: Goughy
APPOINTED TO FIRST-CLASS LIST: 2009
INTERNATIONAL PANEL: 2013-
ODIS UMPIRED: 2
T20IS UMPIRED: 3 (plus 3 as TV umpire)
COUNTIES AS PLAYER: Durham
ROLE: Right-hand bat; off-spin bowler
COUNTY DEBUT: 1998

SOMETHING WE DON'T KNOW ABOUT YOU? I'm a qualified football referee and a season-ticket holder at Hartlepool United
FAVOURITE GROUND? Worcester
RITUALS AND QUIRKS? I step onto the pitch with my left foot first and my left foot is also the first off the pitch
NOTES: Gough started umpiring in 2005 after retiring from the first-class game and was appointed to the ECB reserve list in 2006. He is believed to be the youngest first-class umpire in the history of the game. In 2011 he officiated at T20 Finals Day at Edgbaston and was named PCA Umpire of the Year. Has been reserve umpire in two Tests, including the Ashes Test at Durham last summer. Umpired the 2013/14 ICC World Cup Qualifier final between Scotland and UAE in February

Batting	Mat	Inns	NO	Runs	HS	Ave	SR	100	50	Ct	St
First-class	67	119	3	2952	123	25.44	-	2	15	57	0
List A	49	45	4	974	132	23.75	-	1	3	14	0

Bowling	Mat	Balls	Runs	Wkts	BBI	BBM	Ave	Econ	SR	5w	10
First-class	67	2486	1350	30	5/66	-	45.00	3.25	82.8	1	0
List A	49	1136	947	21	3/26	3/26	45.09	5.00	54.0	0	0

NAME: Ian James Gould
BORN: August 19, 1957, Taplow, Buckinghamshire
HEIGHT: 5ft 7in
NICKNAME: Gunner
APPOINTED TO FIRST-CLASS LIST: 2002
INTERNATIONAL PANEL: 2006-
ELITE PANEL: 2010-
TESTS UMPIRED: 37 (plus 13 as TV umpire)
ODIS UMPIRED: 87 (plus 24 as TV umpire)
T20IS UMPIRED: 20 (plus 12 as TV umpire)
COUNTIES AS PLAYER: Middlesex, Sussex
ROLE: Left-hand bat; wicketkeeper
COUNTY DEBUT: 1975 (Middlesex), 1981 (Sussex)
ODI DEBUT: 1983

NOTES: Officiated at T20 Finals Day at Edgbaston in 2004 and at The Oval in 2005 – including standing in both finals – and again at Edgbaston in 2009. PCA Umpire of the Year in 2005 and 2007. Umpired in the 2007 World Cup. Stood in the FP Trophy final at Lord's in 2007

Batting	Mat	Inns	NO	Runs	HS	Ave	SR	100	50	Ct	St
ODIs	18	14	2	155	42	12.91	63.78	0	0	15	3
First-class	298	399	63	8756	128	26.05	-	4	47	536	67
List A	315	270	41	4377	88	19.11	-	0	20	242	37

Bowling	Mat	Balls	Runs	Wkts	BBI	BBM	Ave	Econ	SR	5w	10
ODIs	18	-	-	-	-	-	-	-	-	-	-
First-class	298	478	365	7	3/10	-	52.14	4.58	68.2	0	0
List A	315	20	16	1	1/0	1/0	16.00	4.80	20.0	0	0

PETER HARTLEY

NAME: Peter John Hartley
BORN: April 18, 1960, Keighley, Yorkshire
HEIGHT: 6ft
NICKNAME: Jack
APPOINTED TO FIRST-CLASS LIST: 2003
INTERNATIONAL PANEL: 2006-2009
ODIS UMPIRED: 6 (plus 10 as TV umpire)
T20IS UMPIRED: 3 (plus 4 as TV umpire)
COUNTIES AS PLAYER: Warwickshire,
Yorkshire, Hampshire
ROLE: Right-hand bat; right-arm fast-
medium bowler
COUNTY DEBUT: 1982 (Warwickshire),
1985 (Yorkshire), 1998 (Hampshire)

NOTES: Officiated at T20 Finals Day in 2006 at Trent Bridge, including standing in the final. Umpired the FP Trophy final in 2007, the 2008 U19 World Cup final in Malaysia and the 2010 CB40 final. Has stood as TV umpire in nine Tests and reserve umpire in six Tests

Batting	Mat	Inns	NO	Runs	HS	Ave	SR	100	50	Ct	St
First-class	232	283	66	4321	127*	19.91	-	2	14	68	0
List A	269	170	62	1765	83	16.34	-	0	4	46	0

Bowling	Mat	Balls	Runs	Wkts	BBI	BBM	Ave	Econ	SR	5w	10
First-class	232	37108	20635	683	9/41	-	30.21	3.33	54.3	23	3
List A	269	12636	-	-	-	-	-	-	-	-	-

RICHARD ILLINGWORTH

NAME: Richard Keith Illingworth
BORN: August 23, 1963, Greengates
HEIGHT: 5ft 11in
NICKNAME: Harry, Lucy
APPOINTED TO FIRST-CLASS LIST: 2006
INTERNATIONAL PANEL: 2009-
ELITE PANEL: 2013-
TESTS UMPIRED: 7 (plus 2 as TV umpire)
ODIS UMPIRED: 28 (plus 17 as TV umpire)
T20IS UMPIRED: 9 (plus 2 as TV umpire)
COUNTIES AS PLAYER: Worcestershire, Derbyshire
ROLE: Right-hand bat; slow left-arm bowler
COUNTY DEBUT: 1982 (Worcestershire), 2001 (Derbyshire)
TEST DEBUT: 1991
ODI DEBUT: 1991

RITUALS OR QUIRKS? I always use six old penny coins to count the balls in an over
CAREER HIGHLIGHT AS AN UMPIRE? My debut Test match as an umpire between Bangladesh and West Indies. The recent Test series between South Africa and Australia was a real humdinger of a contest
FAVOURITE GROUND? Worcester
FUNNIEST MOMENT ON A CRICKET FIELD? In my playing days, a snake crossed the field during an A tour in Sri Lanka frightening to death all on the field. Fortunately we were batting at the time so we were able to see the funny side in the pavilion
BEST TEA ON THE COUNTY CIRCUIT? Most of the outgrounds as they make a huge effort and a great deal of pride goes into their teas
FAVOURITE PASTIMES OUTSIDE OF CRICKET? Watching sport and playing golf

Batting	Mat	Inns	NO	Runs	HS	Ave	SR	100	50	Ct	St
Tests	9	14	7	128	28	18.28	32.08	0	0	5	0
ODIs	25	11	5	68	14	11.33	57.14	0	0	8	0
First-class	376	435	122	7027	120*	22.45	-	4	21	161	0
List A	381	185	87	1458	53*	14.87	-	0	1	93	0

Bowling	Mat	Balls	Runs	Wkts	BBI	BBM	Ave	Econ	SR	5w	10
Tests	9	1485	615	19	4/96	6/150	32.36	2.48	78.1	0	0
ODIs	25	1501	1059	30	3/33	3/33	35.30	4.23	50.0	0	0
First-class	376	65868	26213	831	7/50	-	31.54	2.38	79.2	27	6
List A	381	16918	11157	412	5/24	5/24	27.08	3.95	41.0	2	0

RICHARD KETTLEBOROUGH

NAME: Richard Allan Kettleborough
BORN: March 15, 1973, Sheffield, Yorkshire
HEIGHT: 5ft 10in
NICKNAME: Ketts
APPOINTED TO FIRST-CLASS LIST: 2006
INTERNATIONAL PANEL: 2008-
ELITE PANEL: 2011-
TESTS UMPIRED: 20 (plus 10 as TV umpire)
ODIS UMPIRED: 40 (plus 22 as TV umpire)
T20IS UMPIRED: 9 (plus 6 as TV umpire)
COUNTIES AS PLAYER: Yorkshire, Middlesex
ROLE: Left-hand bat; right-arm medium
bowler
COUNTY DEBUT: 1994 (Yorkshire), 1998
(Middlesex)

RITUALS OR QUIRKS? I always take a picture of my children out to the middle with me
CAREER HIGHLIGHT AS AN UMPIRE? Officiating in my first Test match between Sri Lanka
and West Indies in Galle in 2010 and being appointed to the ICC Elite Panel in 2011
FAVOURITE GROUND? Trent Bridge and Scarborough

Batting	Mat	Inns	NO	Runs	HS	Ave	SR	100	50	Ct	St
First-class	33	56	6	1258	108	25.16	-	1	7	20	0
List A	21	16	4	290	58	24.16	-	0	1	6	0

Bowling	Mat	Balls	Runs	Wkts	BBI	BBM	Ave	Econ	SR	5w	10
First-class	33	378	243	3	2/26	-	81.00	3.85	126.0	0	0
List A	21	270	230	6	2/43	2/43	38.33	5.11	45.0	0	0

NIGEL LLONG

NAME: Nigel James Llong
BORN: February 11, 1969, Ashford, Kent
HEIGHT: 6ft
NICKNAME: Nidge
APPOINTED TO FIRST-CLASS LIST: 2002
INTERNATIONAL PANEL: 2004-2006 as TV umpire; 2006-present as full member
ELITE PANEL: 2012-
TESTS UMPIRED: 24 (plus 16 as TV umpire)
ODIS UMPIRED: 78 (plus 38 as TV umpire)
T20IS UMPIRED: 17 (plus 8 as TV umpire)
COUNTY AS PLAYER: Kent
ROLE: Left-hand bat; off-spin bowler
COUNTY DEBUT: 1990

NOTES: Officiated at T20 Finals Day at Edgbaston in 2004, including standing in the final, and again in 2007, 2009 and 2010. Umpired at the 2007, 2009 and 2012 ICC World T20 tournaments and the 2011 ICC World Cup

Batting	Mat	Inns	NO	Runs	HS	Ave	SR	100	50	Ct	St
First-class	68	108	11	3024	130	31.17	-	6	16	59	0
List A	136	115	24	2302	123	25.29	-	2	8	41	0

Bowling	Mat	Balls	Runs	Wkts	BBI	BBM	Ave	Econ	SR	5w	10
First-class	68	2273	1259	35	5/21	-	35.97	3.32	64.9	2	0
List A	136	1317	1210	40	4/24	4/24	30.25	5.51	32.9	0	0

GRAHAM LLOYD

NAME: Graham David Lloyd
BORN: July 1, 1969, Accrington, Lancashire
APPOINTED TO FIRST-CLASS LIST: 2014
COUNTY AS PLAYER: Lancashire
ROLE: Right-hand bat, right-arm medium bowler
COUNTY DEBUT: 1988
ODI DEBUT: 1996

RITUALS OR QUIRKS? I have no rituals or superstitions at all

CAREER HIGHLIGHT AS AN UMPIRE? Umpiring the Somerset vs India tour match a couple of years ago

FAVOURITE GROUND? Worcester

FUNNIEST MOMENT ON A CRICKET FIELD? Ian Austin doing his Bob Willis impression and losing his footing in his delivery stride, resulting in him rolling uncontrollably down the wicket

BEST TEA ON THE COUNTY CIRCUIT? Lord's

FAVOURITE PASTIMES OUTSIDE OF CRICKET? Horse-racing and football

SOMETHING WE DON'T KNOW ABOUT YOU? As a teenager I represented Lancashire and North of England at tennis

Batting	Mat	Inns	NO	Runs	HS	Ave	SR	100	50	Ct	St
ODIs	6	5	1	39	22	9.75	48.75	0	0	2	0
First-class	203	323	28	112279	241	38.23		24	64	140	0
List A	295	258	48	6117	134	29.12		4	29	67	0

Bowling	Mat	Balls	Runs	Wkts	BBI	BBM	Ave	Econ	SR	5w	10
ODIs	6	-	-	-	-	-	-	-	-	-	-
First-class	203	339	440	2	1/4		220.00	7.78		0	0
List A	295	72	103	1	1/23	1/23	103.00	8.58	72.0	0	0

JEREMY LLOYDS

NAME: Jeremy William Lloyds
BORN: November 17, 1954, Penang, Malaysia
HEIGHT: 5ft 11in
NICKNAME: Jerry
APPOINTED TO FIRST-CLASS LIST: 1998
INTERNATIONAL PANEL: 2002-2004 as TV
umpire; 2004-2006 as full member
TESTS UMPIRED: 5 (plus 10 as TV umpire)
ODIS UMPIRED: 18 (plus 22 as TV umpire)
T20IS UMPIRED: 1
COUNTIES AS PLAYER: Somerset,
Gloucestershire
ROLE: Left-hand bat; off-spin bowler
COUNTY DEBUT: 1979 (Somerset), 1985
(Gloucestershire)

NOTES: Stood in the C&G final in 2006. Officiated at T20 Finals Day in 2007, 2008 and 2012.
Umpired five Test matches between 2004 and 2005

Batting	Mat	Inns	NO	Runs	HS	Ave	SR	100	50	Ct	St
First-class	267	408	64	10679	132*	31.04	-	10	62	229	0
List A	177	150	26	1982	73*	15.98	-	0	5	58	0

Bowling	Mat	Balls	Runs	Wkts	BBI	BBM	Ave	Econ	SR	5w	10
First-class	267	24175	12943	333	7/88	-	38.86	3.21	72.5	13	1
List A	177	1522	1129	26	3/14	3/14	43.42	4.45	58.5	0	0

NEIL MALLENDER

NAME: Neil Alan Mallender
BORN: August 13, 1961, Kirk Sandall, Yorkshire
HEIGHT: 6ft
NICKNAME: Ghostie
APPOINTED TO FIRST-CLASS LIST: 1999
INTERNATIONAL PANEL: 2002-2004
TESTS UMPIRED: 3 (plus 5 as TV umpire)
ODIS UMPIRED: 22 (plus 10 as TV umpire)
COUNTIES AS PLAYER: Northamptonshire, Somerset
ROLE: Right-hand bat; right-arm fast-medium bowler
COUNTY DEBUT: 1980 (Northamptonshire), 1987 (Somerset)
TEST DEBUT: 1992

RITUALS OR QUIRKS? I will never choose an end to stand at. I think it's right to toss up for ends and you get whatever comes your way on the day
CAREER HIGHLIGHT AS AN UMPIRE? My debut as an international umpire, standing at Lord's with a full house
FAVOURITE GROUND? Taking Lord's out of the equation I have two favourites: Taunton and Chester-le-Street
MOST MEMORABLE DISMISSAL? Giving Sachin Tendulkar out lbw to Ronnie Irani at Lord's
SOMETHING WE DON'T KNOW ABOUT YOU? I love my rock/metal music. I'm a huge fan of Within Temptation and Rammstein and often listen to my music before going out to umpire as it seems to set me up for the day ahead

Batting	Mat	Inns	NO	Runs	HS	Ave	SR	100	50	Ct	St
Tests	2	3	0	8	4	2.66	36.36	0	0	0	0
First-class	345	396	122	4709	100*	17.18	-	1	10	111	0
List A	325	163	75	1146	38*	13.02	-	0	0	60	0

Bowling	Mat	Balls	Runs	Wkts	BBI	BBM	Ave	Econ	SR	5w	10
Tests	2	449	215	10	5/50	8/122	21.50	2.87	44.9	1	0
First-class	345	53215	24654	937	7/27	-	26.31	2.77	56.7	36	5
List A	325	15488	9849	387	7/37	7/37	25.44	3.81	40.0	3	0

DAVID MILLNS

NAME: David James Millns
BORN: February 27, 1965, Clipstone,
Nottinghamshire
HEIGHT: 6ft 3in
NICKNAME: Rocket Man
APPOINTED TO FIRST-CLASS LIST: 2009
COUNTIES AS PLAYER: Nottinghamshire,
Leicestershire
ROLE: Left-hand bat; right-arm fast bowler
COUNTY DEBUT: 1988 (Nottinghamshire),
1990 (Leicestershire)

RITUALS OR QUIRKS? I get into my umpiring gear as soon as I arrive at the ground. I like to take my time prior to the game to think about the day ahead

CAREER HIGHLIGHT AS AN UMPIRE? Middlesex vs Rajasthan Royals in 2009 in front of a full house at Lord's

FAVOURITE GROUND? Lord's – nothing in the world gets close to it

FUNNIEST MOMENT ON A CRICKET FIELD? Any time I had to watch from the non-striker's end when Alan Mullally tried to bat

BEST TEA ON THE COUNTY CIRCUIT? Somerset

FAVOURITE PASTIMES OUTSIDE OF CRICKET? Mountain biking, scuba diving, sailing, golf and gardening

SOMETHING WE DON'T KNOW ABOUT YOU? I have supported Manchester City since I was seven years old

Batting	Mat	Inns	NO	Runs	HS	Ave	SR	100	50	Ct	St
First-class	171	203	63	3082	121	22.01	-	3	8	76	0
List A	91	49	26	338	39*	14.69	-	0	0	18	0

Bowling	Mat	Balls	Runs	Wkts	BBI	BBM	Ave	Econ	SR	5w	10
First-class	171	26571	15129	553	9/37	-	27.35	3.41	48.0	23	4
List A	91	3931	3144	83	4/26	4/26	37.87	4.79	47.3	0	0

STEVE O'SHAUGHNESSY

NAME: Steven Joseph O'Shaughnessy
BORN: September 9, 1961, Bury, Lancashire
APPOINTED TO FIRST-CLASS LIST: 2011
COUNTIES AS PLAYER: Lancashire, Worcestershire
ROLE: Right-hand bat; right-arm medium bowler
COUNTY DEBUT: 1980 (Lancashire), 1988 (Worcestershire)

NOTES: O'Shaughnessy started umpiring in 2007 and was appointed to the full list for the 2011 season. He has officiated in three women's ODIs, including during last summer's Ashes series

Batting	Mat	Inns	NO	Runs	HS	Ave	SR	100	50	Ct	St
First-class	112	181	28	3720	159*	24.31	-		5	16	57	0

Bowling	Mat	Balls	Runs	Wkts	BBI	BBM	Ave	Econ	SR	5w	10
First-class	112	7179	4108	114	4/66	-	36.03	3.43	62.9	0	0
List A	176	5389	4184	115	4/17	4/17	36.38	4.65	46.8	0	0

TIM ROBINSON

NAME: Robert Timothy Robinson
BORN: November 21, 1958, Sutton-in-Ashfield, Nottinghamshire
HEIGHT: 6ft
NICKNAME: Robbo, Chop
APPOINTED TO FIRST-CLASS LIST: 2007
ODIS UMPIRED: 2
T20IS UMPIRED: 2 (plus 3 as TV umpire)
COUNTY AS PLAYER: Nottinghamshire
ROLE: Right-hand bat; right-arm medium bowler
COUNTY DEBUT: 1978
TEST DEBUT: 1984
ODI DEBUT: 1984

NOTES: TV umpire in the CB40 final in 2010 and stood in the CB40 final at Lord's in 2011. Umpired in six women's ODIs and three women's T20Is. Stood as reserve umpire in six Tests, including the Ashes Test at Lord's last summer. Umpired his first ODI last year, at Trent Bridge during England's series against New Zealand

Batting	Mat	Inns	NO	Runs	HS	Ave	SR	100	50	Ct	St
Tests	29	49	5	1601	175	36.38	41.62	4	6	8	0
ODIs	26	26	0	597	83	22.96	58.18	0	3	6	0
First-class	425	739	85	27571	220*	42.15	-	63	141	257	0
List A	397	386	40	11879	139	34.33	-	9	75	120	0

Bowling	Mat	Balls	Runs	Wkts	BBI	BBM	Ave	Econ	SR	5w	10
Tests	29	6	0	0	-	-	-	0.00	-	0	0
ODIs	26	-	-	-	-	-	-	-	-	-	-
First-class	425	259	289	4	1/22	-	72.25	6.69	64.7	0	0
List A	397	-	-	-	-	-	-	-	-	-	-

MARTIN SAGGERS

NAME: Martin John Saggers
BORN: May 23, 1972, King's Lynn, Norfolk
HEIGHT: 6ft 2in
NICKNAME: Saggs
APPOINTED TO FIRST-CLASS LIST: 2012
COUNTIES AS PLAYER: Durham, Kent
ROLE: Right-hand bat; right-arm fast-medium bowler
COUNTY DEBUT: 1996 (Durham), 1999 (Kent)
TEST DEBUT: 2003

NOTES: Retired from first-class cricket in 2009 and added to the reserve list of umpires in 2010. Umpired one women's ODI and two women's T20Is, including during last summer's Ashes at Chester-le-Street

Batting	Mat	Inns	NO	Runs	HS	Ave	SR	100	50	Ct	St
Tests	3	3	0	1	1	0.33	3.33	0	0	1	0
First-class	119	147	43	1165	64	11.20	-	0	2	27	0
List A	124	68	34	313	34*	9.20	-	0	0	23	0
Twenty20	10	1	0	5	5	5.00	62.50	0	0	2	0

Bowling	Mat	Balls	Runs	Wkts	BBI	BBM	Ave	Econ	SR	5w	10
Tests	3	493	247	7	2/29	3/62	35.28	3.00	70.4	0	0
First-class	119	20676	10513	415	7/79	-	25.33	3.05	49.8	18	0
List A	124	5622	4229	166	5/22	5/22	25.47	4.51	33.8	2	0
Twenty20	10	186	256	6	2/14	2/14	42.66	8.25	31.0	0	0

GEORGE SHARP

NAME: George Sharp
BORN: March 12, 1950, West Hartlepool
HEIGHT: 5ft 11in
NICKNAME: Sharpie, Blunt, Razor
APPOINTED TO FIRST-CLASS LIST: 1992
INTERNATIONAL PANEL: 1996-2002
TESTS UMPIRED: 15 (plus 1 as TV umpire)
ODIS UMPIRED: 31 (plus 13 as TV umpire)
COUNTY AS PLAYER: Northamptonshire
ROLE: Right-hand bat; left-arm medium
bowler; wicketkeeper
COUNTY DEBUT: 1968

NOTES: Stood in the 1997 and 2001 Ashes series and the 1999 ICC World Cup

Batting	Mat	Inns	NO	Runs	HS	Ave	SR	100	50	Ct	St
First-class	306	396	81	6254	98	19.85	-	0	21	565	90
List A	285	203	52	2377	51*	15.74	-	0	1	242	50

Bowling	Mat	Balls	Runs	Wkts	BBI	BBM	Ave	Econ	SR	5w	10
First-class	306	114	70	1	1/47	-	70.00	3.68	114.0	0	0
List A	285	-	-	-	-	-	-	-	-	-	-

ALEX WHARF

NAME: Alexander George Wharf
BORN: June 4, 1975, Bradford, Yorkshire
HEIGHT: 6ft 4in
NICKNAME: Gangster
APPOINTED TO FIRST-CLASS LIST: 2014
COUNTIES AS PLAYER: Yorkshire,
Nottinghamshire, Glamorgan
ROLE: Right-hand bat; right-arm medium-
fast bowler
COUNTY DEBUT: 1994 (Yorkshire), 1998
(Nottinghamshire), 2000 (Glamorgan)
ODI DEBUT: 2004

UMPIRES

NOTES: Wharf started umpiring after he retired as a player in 2009 and was added to the ECB's reserve list three years ago. He was reserve umpire in two ODIs between the Netherlands and Ireland in 2013

Batting	Mat	Inns	NO	Runs	HS	Ave	SR	100	50	Ct	St
ODIs	13	5	3	19	9	9.50	67.85	0	0	1	0
First-class	121	184	29	3570	128*	23.03		6	14	63	0
List A	155	109	22	1411	72	16.21		0	1	42	0
Twenty20	34	20	7	157	19	12.07	120.76	0	0	5	0

Bowling	Mat	Balls	Runs	Wkts	BBI	BBM	Ave	Econ	SR	5w	10
ODIs	13	584	428	18	4/24	4/24	23.77	4.39	32.4	0	0
First-class	121	16825	10941	293	6/59		37.34	3.90	57.4	5	1
List A	155	6497	5552	192	6/5	6/5	28.91	5.12	33.8	1	0
Twenty20	34	644	1028	39	4/39	4/39	26.35	9.57	16.5	2	0

PETER WILLEY

NAME: Peter Willey
BORN: December 6, 1949, Sedgefield
HEIGHT: 6ft 1in
NICKNAME: Will
APPOINTED TO FIRST-CLASS LIST: 1993
INTERNATIONAL PANEL: 1996-2003
TESTS UMPIRED: 25 (plus 7 as TV umpire)
ODIS UMPIRED: 34 (plus 16 as TV umpire)
COUNTIES AS PLAYER: Northamptonshire, Leicestershire
ROLE: Right-hand bat; off-spin bowler
COUNTY DEBUT: 1966 (Northamptonshire), 1984 (Leicestershire)
TEST DEBUT: 1976
ODI DEBUT: 1977

RITUALS OR QUIRKS? I put my counters and the bails in my hat each morning before going on to the field
CAREER HIGHLIGHT AS AN UMPIRE? Being selected as a Test umpire
FAVOURITE GROUND? Hove
SOMETHING WE DON'T KNOW ABOUT YOU? I'm not as miserable as people think
FAVOURITE PASTIME OUTSIDE OF CRICKET? Fishing

Batting	Mat	Inns	NO	Runs	HS	Ave	SR	100	50	Ct	St
Tests	26	50	6	1184	102*	26.90	42.37	2	5	3	0
ODIs	26	24	1	538	64	23.39	62.92	0	5	4	0
First-class	559	918	121	24361	227	30.56	-	44	101	235	0
List A	458	436	43	11105	154	28.25	-	10	67	124	0

Bowling	Mat	Balls	Runs	Wkts	BBI	BBM	Ave	Econ	SR	5w	10
Tests	26	1091	456	7	2/73	2/73	65.14	2.50	155.8	0	0
ODIs	26	1031	659	13	3/33	3/33	50.69	3.83	79.3	0	0
First-class	559	58635	23400	756	7/37	-	30.95	2.39	77.5	26	3
List A	458	18520	11143	347	4/17	4/17	32.11	3.61	53.3	0	0

WISDEN | 150 CLUB

THE WISDEN 150
LIMITED EDITION BAT

The Wisden 150 Limited Edition bat commemorates John Wisden's own sports equipment venture - individually numbered from 1 to 150 these bats are hand made in England by master bat maker Mike Hawk.

Fashioned from Grade 1 English willow, the bats are suitable for playing cricket at the highest level. However, we expect most owners will keep their bats under lock and key, well away from the field of play.

For more information or to order
this collector's item, visit

wisden150club.com/shop

Roll *of*
Honour

Division One

Team	Mat	Won	Lost	Draw	Tied	Pts
Durham	16	10	4	2	0	245.5
Yorkshire	16	7	2	7	0	221
Sussex	16	5	3	8	0	188
Warwickshire	16	5	2	9	0	186
Middlesex	16	6	5	5	0	182
Somerset	16	3	5	8	0	146
Nottinghamshire	16	2	5	9	0	146
Derbyshire	16	3	10	3	0	122
Surrey	16	1	6	9	0	116

Division Two

Team	Mat	Won	Lost	Draw	Tied	Pts
Lancashire	16	8	1	7	0	238
Northamptonshire	16	5	3	8	0	202
Essex	16	5	4	7	0	182
Hampshire	16	4	3	9	0	171
Worcestershire	16	5	6	5	0	167
Gloucestershire	16	4	4	8	0	167
Kent	16	3	2	11	0	151
Glamorgan	16	3	6	7	0	149
Leicestershire	16	0	8	8	0	79

ROLL OF HONOUR

Group A							
Team	Mat	Won	Lost	Tied	N/R	Pts	Net RR
Nottinghamshire	12	9	3	0	0	18	0.457
Northamptonshire	12	8	3	0	1	17	0.393
Sussex	12	6	4	0	2	14	0.464
Kent	12	6	6	0	0	12	0.229
Worcestershire	12	5	7	0	0	10	0.249
Netherlands	12	2	7	0	3	7	-1.157
Warwickshire	12	2	8	0	2	6	-0.929

Group B							
Team	Mat	Won	Lost	Tied	N/R	Pts	Net RR
Hampshire	12	9	3	0	0	18	0.734
Essex	12	8	4	0	0	16	0.972
Lancashire	12	7	4	0	1	15	-0.023
Durham	12	7	4	0	1	14.75	0.657
Surrey	12	4	6	0	2	10	-0.524
Derbyshire	12	3	6	0	3	9	-0.25
Scotland	12	0	11	0	1	1	-1.94

Group C							
Team	Mat	Won	Lost	Tied	N/R	Pts	Net RR
Somerset	12	8	3	0	1	17	1.006
Glamorgan	12	8	3	0	1	17	0.576
Middlesex	12	7	4	0	1	15	0.315
Gloucestershire	12	7	4	0	1	15	0.163
Leicestershire	12	5	7	0	0	10	-0.353
Yorkshire	12	3	9	0	0	6	-0.468
Unicorns	12	1	9	0	2	4	-1.196

SEMI-FINALS   Hampshire vs Glamorgan at Southampton – Sep 7, 2013: *Glamorgan won by 31 runs*
Glamorgan 234/4 (40/40 ov); Hampshire 203/8 (40/40 ov)
Nottinghamshire vs Somerset at Nottingham – Sep 9, 2013: *Notts won by 8 wickets*
Somerset 119 (25.4/35 ov); Nottinghamshire 122/2 (16.2/35 ov)

FINAL   Nottinghamshire vs Glamorgan at Lord's – Sep 21, 2013: *Notts won by 87 runs*
Nottinghamshire 244/8 (40/40 ov); Glamorgan 157 (33/40 ov)

ROLL OF HONOUR

North Division

Team	Mat	Won	Lost	Tied	N/R	Pts	Net RR
Nottinghamshire	10	7	3	0	0	14	1.009
Lancashire	10	5	3	2	0	12	0.177
Durham	10	6	4	0	0	11.75	0.317
Leicestershire	10	4	5	1	0	9	0.417
Derbyshire	10	4	6	0	0	8	-0.604
Yorkshire	10	2	7	1	0	5	-1.223

South Division

Team	Mat	Won	Lost	Tied	N/R	Pts	Net RR
Hampshire	10	8	1	0	1	17	0.81
Surrey	10	7	3	0	0	14	0.915
Essex	10	5	4	0	1	11	-0.04
Middlesex	10	5	5	0	0	10	-0.194
Kent	10	3	7	0	0	6	-0.941
Sussex	10	1	9	0	0	2	-0.52

Midlands/Wales/West Division

Team	Mat	Won	Lost	Tied	N/R	Pts	Net RR
Northamptonshire	10	7	3	0	0	14	0.329
Somerset	10	6	4	0	0	12	0.841
Glamorgan	10	5	5	0	0	10	-0.168
Warwickshire	10	5	5	0	0	10	-0.41
Worcestershire	10	4	6	0	0	8	-0.327
Gloucestershire	10	3	7	0	0	6	-0.245

QUARTER-FINALS Surrey vs Somerset at The Oval – Aug 6, 2013: *Surrey won by 3 wickets*
Somerset 148/6 (20/20 ov); Surrey 151/7 (19/20 ov)
Northamptonshire vs Durham at Northampton – Aug 6, 2013: *Northants won by 36 runs*
Northamptonshire 183/4 (20/20 ov); Durham 147/6 (20/20 ov)
Hampshire vs Lancashire at Southampton – Aug 7, 2013: *Hampshire won by 1 run*
Hampshire 202/3 (20/20 ov); Lancashire 201/4 (20/20 ov)
Nottinghamshire vs Essex at Nottingham – Aug 8, 2013: *Essex won by 47 runs*
Essex 187/6 (20/20 ov); Nottinghamshire 140 (17.2/20 ov)

SEMI-FINALS Essex vs Northamptonshire at Birmingham – Aug 17, 2013: *Northants won by 7 wickets*
Essex 168/5 (20/20 ov); Northamptonshire 171/3 (18.1/20 ov)
Hampshire vs Surrey at Birmingham – Aug 17, 2013: *Surrey won by 4 wickets*
Hampshire 142/9 (20/20 ov); Surrey 145/6 (19.2/20)

FINAL Northamptonshire vs Surrey at Birmingham – Aug 17, 2013: *Northants won by 102 runs (D/L method)* Northamptonshire 194/2 (18/18 ov); Surrey 92 (13.3/18 ov)

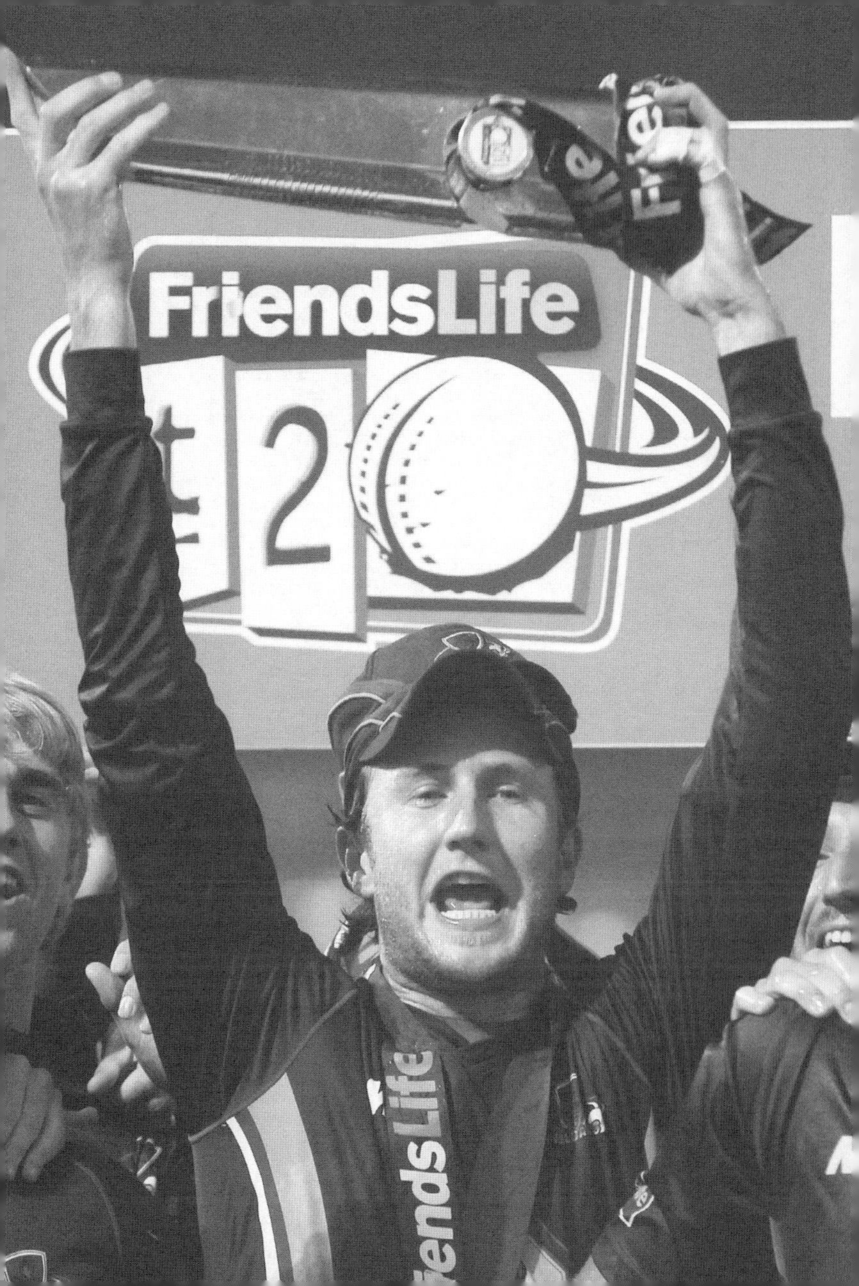

FriendsLife
t20
FriendsLife

Name	Mat	Inns	NO	Runs	HS	Ave	BF	SR	100	50	0	4s	6s
GS Ballance	15	22	1	1363	148	64.9	2515	54.19	6	6	0	167	11
EC Joyce	15	23	5	1152	204*	64	1949	59.1	2	6	0	145	5
JM Vince	16	23	4	1215	148	63.94	1849	65.71	5	6	0	178	8
DI Stevens	16	22	1	1304	205*	62.09	1620	80.49	4	7	0	166	22
J Allenby	16	25	5	1202	138*	60.1	1764	68.14	2	8	2	151	8
MM Ali	17	29	5	1420	250	59.16	2560	55.46	4	8	2	182	15
MW Goodwin	16	26	4	1263	194	57.4	2624	48.13	4	7	1	167	1
AJ Hall	16	21	4	936	130*	55.05	1888	49.57	3	5	1	120	1
LM Reece	12	20	4	877	114*	54.81	1617	54.23	1	8	1	125	5
AU Rashid	15	22	6	825	180	51.56	1353	60.97	3	3	2	110	3
CJL Rogers	18	33	3	1536	214	51.2	2681	57.29	4	9	1	202	4
APR Gidman	16	22	0	1125	211	51.13	1862	60.41	3	0	1	137	13
HJH Marshall	16	21	1	1007	149	50.35	1982	50.8	4	2	0	119	7
EJH Eckersley	17	29	3	1302	147	50.07	2429	53.6	4	4	0	183	3
LJ Evans	14	21	2	950	178	50	2014	47.16	3	4	2	131	4
GR Napier	17	23	7	796	102*	49.75	1091	72.96	1	7	2	95	18
M Klinger	16	26	3	1140	163	49.56	2189	52.07	4	4	0	135	11
JWA Taylor	18	25	3	1079	204*	49.04	2390	45.14	3	5	1	117	2
AG Prince	16	26	2	1169	134	48.7	2069	56.5	3	7	1	137	12
MJ Lumb	16	26	3	1120	221*	48.69	2213	50.61	4	3	4	142	5
BP Nash	17	27	4	1110	199*	48.26	1793	61.9	5	5	4	142	2
LA Dawson	17	26	4	1060	136*	48.18	2232	47.49	1	8	2	135	2
SD Robson	16	29	4	1180	215*	47.2	2112	55.87	4	3	4	148	2
RWT Key	17	28	3	1169	180	46.76	2242	52.14	5	3	0	139	4
CD Nash	18	30	4	1211	167*	46.57	2001	60.51	3	5	3	171	5
DJG Sales	16	23	3	919	255*	45.95	1597	57.54	3	1	0	128	6
V Chopra	17	28	4	1099	228*	45.79	2070	53.09	3	5	3	135	1
SM Davies	15	23	4	867	147	45.63	1489	58.22	2	3	1	112	1
CDJ Dent	16	27	2	1128	153	45.12	1963	57.46	2	7	1	167	6
NRD Compton	16	31	3	1260	166	45	2592	48.61	2	9	3	164	4
JHK Adams	17	26	4	990	219*	45	2222	44.55	3	3	7	140	2
EJM Cowan	11	21	3	776	81	43.11	1501	51.69	0	7	1	97	4
AW Gale	17	26	1	1076	272	43.04	2051	52.46	3	3	3	114	7
SR Patel	17	26	0	1104	256	42.46	1618	68.23	4	0	1	138	17
SJ Mullaney	15	23	0	965	125	41.95	1678	57.5	3	6	1	128	10
SG Borthwick	17	29	2	1121	135	41.51	1911	58.66	3	6	2	145	7
BC Brown	16	23	6	705	93	41.47	1263	55.81	0	6	1	82	1
JC Mickleburgh	13	21	1	829	243	41.45	1593	52.04	2	4	1	101	3
WL Madsen	17	32	2	1239	152	41.3	2546	48.66	3	8	1	164	1
VS Solanki	16	25	0	995	162	39.8	1761	56.5	2	5	2	141	9
TT Samaraweera	15	22	4	702	144*	39	1483	47.33	2	4	1	89	0
T Westley	11	20	0	774	163	38.7	1511	51.22	2	3	1	111	0
S Chanderpaul	15	27	4	884	129	38.43	1846	47.88	1	7	0	108	2
JS Foster	17	26	3	883	143	38.39	1573	56.13	1	6	2	107	2
JM Bairstow	16	26	1	955	186	38.2	1681	56.81	1	5	0	130	7
DKH Mitchell	18	32	4	1061	156	37.89	2332	45.49	2	6	1	132	0
TR Ambrose	14	22	2	747	105	37.35	1163	64.23	1	6	3	112	0
PA Jaques	14	21	0	770	152	36.66	1359	56.65	2	3	3	111	5
P Mustard	17	27	4	823	77	35.78	1507	54.61	0	7	3	113	6
JD Middlebrook	16	21	1	711	109	35.55	1358	52.35	1	6	1	101	3

Name	Mat	Overs	Mdns	Runs	Wkts	BBI	BBM	Ave	Econ	SR	5	10
TA Copeland	10	394.4	139	822	45	7/63	10/113	18.26	2.08	52.6	4	1
KW Hogg	15	436	105	1105	60	7/27	9/73	18.41	2.53	43.6	3	0
G Onions	14	452.1	94	1382	73	7/62	9/85	18.93	3.05	37.1	5	0
RJ Sidebottom	15	385.1	107	1012	53	4/27	7/73	19.09	2.62	43.6	0	0
A Richardson	16	541.4	157	1368	69	8/37	12/63	19.82	2.52	47.1	5	2
TJ Murtagh	13	444.1	113	1224	60	6/49	10/77	20.4	2.75	44.4	3	1
MG Hogan	14	512	133	1376	67	7/92	7/92	20.53	2.68	45.8	4	0
G Chapple	14	430.4	110	1099	53	9/14	8/56	20.73	2.55	48.7	2	0
SJ Magoffin	16	512	138	1379	65	8/20	12/31	21.21	2.69	47.2	3	1
WRS Gidman	14	407.2	88	1209	55	6/15	10/43	21.98	2.96	44.4	2	1
SC Kerrigan	15	474.2	108	1275	58	7/63	12/252	21.98	2.68	49	5	1
OP Rayner	14	376.3	78	1014	46	8/46	15/118	22.04	2.69	49.1	4	1
C Rushworth	15	423.2	105	1240	55	6/58	10/103	22.54	2.92	46.1	3	1
KHD Barker	11	345	83	1055	46	5/55	6/74	22.93	3.05	45	1	0
SA Patterson	17	435.5	130	1197	51	5/43	6/65	23.47	2.74	51.2	1	0
DD Masters	14	489.4	129	1209	51	6/41	9/70	23.7	2.46	57.6	4	0
JA Tomlinson	15	454.5	126	1281	53	5/44	6/72	24.16	2.81	51.4	1	0
DJ Willey	13	361.3	66	1122	45	5/67	8/110	24.93	3.1	48.2	2	0
AC Thomas	13	386.4	108	1077	42	5/69	7/147	25.64	2.78	55.2	1	0
JD Shantry	14	396.2	106	1183	45	7/60	8/101	26.28	2.98	52.8	2	0
GP Swann	8	339	61	1052	40	6/90	10/132	26.3	3.1	50.8	3	1
BA Stokes	14	351.4	59	1171	44	4/49	7/91	26.61	3.32	47.9	0	0
JE Anyon	14	399.4	77	1454	52	5/44	8/166	27.96	3.63	46.1	1	0
CJ Jordan	16	471.3	88	1719	61	6/48	9/155	28.18	3.64	46.3	4	0
RJW Topley	13	411.4	78	1364	48	6/29	11/85	28.41	3.31	51.4	3	1
HF Gurney	15	412.3	70	1376	48	5/81	7/148	28.66	3.33	51.5	1	0
LJ Fletcher	15	460.1	133	1288	43	5/52	9/108	29.95	2.79	64.2	2	0
JS Patel	16	576.1	139	1561	52	5/56	8/128	30.01	2.7	66.4	2	0
CN Miles	13	358	69	1315	43	6/88	7/135	30.58	3.67	49.9	3	0
GR Napier	17	479.1	86	1572	51	7/90	8/157	30.82	3.28	56.3	3	0
TD Groenewald	15	437.5	86	1404	45	5/30	8/114	31.2	3.2	58.3	3	0
J Allenby	16	391.5	109	951	30	4/16	7/47	31.7	2.42	78.3	0	0
MHA Footitt	13	380.5	57	1377	42	6/53	7/134	32.78	3.61	54.4	2	0
DI Stevens	16	403.4	111	1051	32	5/39	6/57	32.84	2.6	75.6	1	0
CT Tremlett	11	349.1	66	1057	32	8/96	8/96	33.03	3.02	65.4	2	0
TE Linley	12	438.1	106	1268	37	4/59	6/92	34.27	2.89	71	0	0
BAC Howell	17	355	85	1029	30	5/57	8/96	34.3	2.89	71	1	0
PD Trego	15	354.2	83	1071	31	4/69	6/83	34.54	3.02	68.5	0	0
DA Cosker	16	462.2	93	1318	37	5/120	6/121	35.62	2.85	74.9	1	0
MS Panesar	18	558	131	1543	40	5/95	9/95	38.57	2.76	83.7	2	0
CE Shreck	15	435.2	98	1316	33	4/65	4/91	39.87	3.02	79.1	0	0
GJ Batty	13	395.4	68	1141	27	5/71	6/104	42.25	2.88	87.9	2	0
A Shahzad	12	343.4	66	1125	26	3/21	6/128	43.26	3.27	79.3	0	0
OH Freckingham	15	399	61	1584	36	6/125	9/188	44	3.96	66.5	1	0
AU Rashid	15	359.5	39	1358	29	5/78	5/78	46.82	3.77	74.4	1	0
SR Patel	17	460.2	126	1316	28	3/40	5/169	47	2.85	98.6	0	0
DJ Balcombe	12	349	80	1101	22	5/104	6/165	50.04	3.15	95.1	1	0

FIRST-CLASS WICKETKEEPING *Minimum of 30 dismissals*

Name	Mat	Inns	Dis	Ct	St	Max Dis Mat	Dis/Inn
P Mustard	17	34	68	67	1	6 (6ct 0st)	2
BC Brown	16	27	64	61	3	5 (5ct 0st)	2.37
CMW Read	16	28	61	59	2	6 (6ct 0st)	2.178
JA Simpson	16	29	60	55	5	6 (6ct 0st)	2.068
D Murphy	14	24	55	51	4	5 (5ct 0st)	2.291
JS Foster	17	27	49	48	1	4 (4ct 0st)	1.814
MA Wallace	17	29	47	44	3	5 (5ct 0st)	1.62
C Kieswetter	12	18	44	41	3	5 (5ct 0st)	2.444
GH Roderick	13	20	43	43	0	4 (4ct 0st)	2.15
TR Ambrose	14	22	42	41	1	4 (4ct 0st)	1.909
GO Jones	15	24	41	40	1	5 (5ct 0st)	1.708
GD Cross	13	25	37	35	2	5 (5ct 0st)	1.48
BJ Haddin	7	14	34	33	1	5 (5ct 0st)	2.428
JM Bairstow	16	17	33	33	0	6 (6ct 0st)	1.941
MJ Prior	14	16	31	31	0	6 (6ct 0st)	1.937
T Poynton	12	20	30	27	3	3 (3ct 0st)	1.5

Name	Mat	Inns	Ct	Max	Ct/Inn
ME Trescothick	17	29	31	5	1.068
V Chopra	17	28	29	3	1.035
SG Borthwick	17	34	29	2	0.852
J Allenby	16	28	28	2	1
A Lyth	17	31	27	3	0.87
AP Agathangelou	11	20	24	3	1.2
LA Dawson	17	27	24	4	0.888
CJ Jordan	16	27	24	3	0.888
MM Ali	17	29	22	3	0.758
SD Robson	16	29	22	2	0.758
DKH Mitchell	18	31	21	2	0.677
SM Ervine	15	24	20	3	0.833
OP Rayner	14	25	20	2	0.8
CDJ Dent	16	29	20	4	0.689
PD Collingwood	15	30	20	3	0.666
R Clarke	13	22	19	2	0.863
DJ Malan	13	23	19	3	0.826
VS Solanki	16	28	18	3	0.642
JM Vince	16	25	17	3	0.68
JC Hildreth	17	29	17	3	0.586
SR Patel	17	30	17	3	0.566

#	Name	County	Batting	Bowling	Field	Capt.	Wins	Pld	Pts	Average
1	Ali, Moeen	Worcs	350.56	213.87	22	0	14	38	600	15.79
2	Patel, Samit	Notts	302.83	238.11	35	0	20	41	596	14.54
3	Stevens, Darren	Kent	330.75	199.1	24	0	12	37	566	15.3
4	Allenby, James	Glamorgan	323.25	171.5	28	0	16	37	538	14.55
5	Napier, Graham	Essex	182.52	295.19	17	0	19	40	514	12.84
6	Stokes, Ben	Durham	242.3	222.28	25	0	20	36	510	14.15
7	Trego, Peter	Somerset	291.18	177.92	15	0	15	37	499	13.49
8	Hogan, Michael	Glamorgan	47.45	404.7	18	0	17	36	487	13.54
9	Borthwick, Scott	Durham	277.88	148.17	38	0	23	39	487	12.49
10	Klinger, Michael	Gloucs	430.3	0	25	14	14	37	483	13.06
11	Willey, David	Northants	150.1	281.68	17	0	21	33	470	14.24
12	Patel, Jeetan	Warks	90.57	339.67	21	0	12	36	463	12.87
13	Nash, Chris	Sussex	317.22	112.7	16	4	12	37	462	12.48
14	Onions, Graham	Durham	23.9	403.47	7	0	15	23	449	19.54
15	Jordan, Chris	Sussex	72.63	317.26	33	0	10	27	433	16.03
16	Crook, Steven	Northants	148.59	256.11	7	0	19	33	431	13.05
17	Rushworth, Chris	Durham	16.35	378.6	10	0	23	37	428	11.57
18	Mustard, Phil	Durham	281.68	3.23	118	0	23	39	426	10.92
19	Vince, James	Hants	326.7	33.8	23	0	22	39	405	10.39
20	Davies, Steven	Surrey	309.01	0	82	0	13	36	404	11.22
21	Dawson, Liam	Hants	214.82	130.63	35	0	22	41	403	9.83
22	Kieswetter, Craig	Somerset	308.11	-0.87	82	0	13	29	402	13.87
23	Lumb, Michael	Notts	367.6	0	12	0	20	40	400	9.99
24	Madsen, Wayne	Derbyshire	307.28	46.18	23	10	10	36	396	11.01
25	Ballance, Gary	Yorks	364.03	-1.23	20	0	10	32	393	12.28
26	Chopra, Varun	Warks	329.82	-0.1	32	9	12	35	383	10.93
27	Carberry, Michael	Hants	328.08	12.42	8	0	21	34	370	10.88
28	Mitchell, Daryl	Worcs	248.4	60.35	28	14	14	38	365	9.59
29	Stoneman, Mark	Durham	309.17	0	19	12	23	39	363	9.31
30	Topley, Reece	Essex	3	315.96	11	0	17	36	347	9.65
31	Dexter, Neil	Middx	186.04	107.96	23	13	17	37	347	9.38
32	Groenewald, Tim	Derbyshire	53.08	269.07	15	0	8	29	345	11.9
33	Dent, Chris	Gloucs	282.53	23.64	24	0	14	37	344	9.31
34	Taylor, James	Notts	308.68	0	17	1	17	37	344	9.29
35	Thomas, Alfonso	Somerset	36.7	275.98	12	4	15	32	344	10.74
36	Howell, Benny	Gloucs	119.3	192.67	15	0	14	38	341	8.98
37	Clarke, Rikki	Warks	181.92	117.03	24	0	12	29	335	11.55
38	Prince, Ashwell	Lancs	286.79	0	28	0	20	37	335	9.04
39	Chapple, Glen	Lancs	41.12	250.77	13	14	14	26	333	12.8
40	Murtagh, Tim	Middx	19.74	295.74	4	0	10	22	329	14.98
41	Woakes, Chris	Warks	125.09	186.89	7	0	10	22	329	14.95
42	Meschede, Craig	Somerset	64.53	235.63	9	0	17	33	326	9.88
43	Rayner, Ollie	Middx	55.94	232.06	24	0	14	29	326	11.24
44	Wright, Luke	Sussex	290.1	19.89	8	0	8	21	326	15.52
45	Rashid, Adil	Yorks	185.97	118.02	11	0	11	31	326	10.52
46	Plunkett, Liam	Yorks	95.77	203.37	15	0	11	27	325	12.04
47	Masters, David	Essex	15.92	287.68	7	0	14	28	325	11.6
48	Wallace, Mark	Glamorgan	211.97	0	86	4	17	39	319	8.18
49	Hall, Andrew	Northants	140.52	152.39	13	0	11	25	317	12.69
50	Berg, Gareth	Middx	127.66	161.46	11	0	17	35	317	9.06

#	Name	County	Batting	Bowling	Field	Capt.	Wins	Pld	Pts	Average
51	Yardy, Michael	Sussex	219.03	74.89	12	0	11	35	317	9.05
52	Solanki, Vikram	Surrey	266.44	6.61	28	2	12	37	315	8.51
53	Gurney, Harry	Notts	8.45	280.13	8	0	18	36	315	8.74
54	Coles, Matt	Hants	63.51	218.81	22	0	10	32	314	9.81
55	Magoffin, Steve	Sussex	25.79	276.76	4	0	5	15	312	20.77
56	Eckersley, Ned	Leics	285.33	4.3	14	0	7	34	311	9.14
57	Malan, Dawid	Middx	263.01	1.47	29	0	17	34	310	9.13
58	Key, Rob	Kent	297.64	-1.79	4	0	9	32	309	9.66
59	Joyce, Ed	Sussex	277.07	0	15	8	9	27	309	11.45
60	Goodwin, Murray	Glamorgan	276.49	0	14	0	17	39	307	7.87
61	Shantry, Jack	Worcs	45.29	232.76	11	0	14	34	303	8.92
62	Cobb, Josh	Leics	212.75	60.08	12	9	9	33	303	9.19
63	Cosker, Dean	Glamorgan	47.89	222.12	16	0	17	38	303	7.96
64	Copeland, Trent	Northants	36.24	244	12	0	9	16	301	18.82
65	ten Doeschate, Ryan	Essex	210.67	62.93	12	0	15	30	301	10.03
66	Trescothick, Marcus	Somerset	235.45	0	39	13	13	34	300	8.84
67	de Bruyn, Zander	Surrey	135.61	132.68	21	0	11	35	300	8.58
68	Richardson, Alan	Worcs	13.24	276.29	4	0	6	18	300	16.64
69	Bopara, Ravi	Essex	195.37	73.97	15	0	14	26	298	11.47
70	Mullaney, Steven	Notts	155.98	92.93	30	0	19	38	298	7.84
71	Hogg, Kyle	Lancs	28.42	253.9	3	0	12	23	297	12.91
72	Denly, Joe	Middx	256.54	4.69	15	0	18	38	294	7.74
73	Wagg, Graham	Glamorgan	74.06	190.76	11	0	17	33	293	8.87
74	Smith, William	Durham	199.28	54.32	16	0	22	36	292	8.1
75	Adams, Jimmy	Hants	235.05	0	18	14	22	41	290	7.08
76	Ervine, Sean	Hants	156.64	87.21	25	0	21	39	290	7.43
77	Sidebottom, Ryan	Yorks	24.84	243.47	5	0	9	24	282	11.76
78	Chanderpaul, Shivnarine	Derbyshire	248.19	13.91	11	0	8	30	281	9.37
79	Foster, James	Essex	166.26	0	76	19	19	40	281	7.02
80	Hughes, Chesney	Derbyshire	248.62	4.72	17	0	9	33	279	8.46
81	Kerrigan, Simon	Lancs	19.25	235.17	12	0	12	24	279	11.62
82	Nash, Brendan	Kent	250.35	5.74	10	0	10	29	276	9.52
83	Batty, Gareth	Surrey	54.49	188.48	10	11	12	31	276	8.9
84	Lyth, Adam	Yorks	216.84	12.38	35	0	10	33	274	8.31
85	Katich, Simon	Lancs	244.54	0	12	0	17	31	273	8.81
86	Hildreth, James	Somerset	223.5	0	32	0	16	37	272	7.34
87	Fletcher, Luke	Notts	56.04	204.82	5	0	3	17	269	15.82
88	Gidman, Will	Gloucs	53.84	204.6	4	0	6	17	269	15.81
89	Dernbach, Jade	Surrey	9.95	242.44	5	0	11	28	268	9.59
90	Barker, Keith	Warks	52.94	203.44	6	0	6	14	268	19.17
91	Anyon, James	Sussex	20.68	233.83	4	0	7	19	266	13.97
92	Hales, Alex	Notts	232.2	0	13	0	20	35	265	7.58
93	Gidman, Alex	Gloucs	211.62	16.75	20	0	14	38	262	6.89
94	Gale, Andrew	Yorks	236.37	-1.04	6	10	10	30	261	8.71
95	Smith, Tom	Lancs	118.01	113.07	16	0	13	23	260	11.32
96	Coetzer, Kyle	Northants	224.08	8.55	7	0	20	32	260	8.13
97	Azharullah, Muhammad	Northants	1.49	236.89	4	0	17	28	260	9.28
98	Shahzad, Ajmal	Notts	50.54	192.23	4	0	13	27	260	9.62
99	Durston, Wes	Derbyshire	142.48	94.44	16	0	5	28	258	9.21
100	Middlebrook, James	Northants	113.77	112.5	11	0	20	36	257	7.15

Notes